Ius Comparatum – Global Studies in Comparative Law

For further volumes:
http://www.springer.com/series/11943

Wen-Yeu Wang
Editor

Codification in International Perspective

Selected Papers from the 2nd IACL Thematic Conference

🐴 Springer

Editor
Wen-Yeu Wang
College of Law
National Taiwan University
Taipei
Taiwan

ISSN 2214-6881   ISSN 2214-689X (electronic)
ISBN 978-3-319-03454-6   ISBN 978-3-319-03455-3 (eBook)
DOI 10.1007/978-3-319-03455-3
Springer Cham Heidelberg New York Dordrecht London

Library of Congress Control Number: 2014930430

Printed on acid-free paper

Springer is part of Springer Science+Business Media (www.springer.com)

Introduction to the Codification Books (two volumes)

Codification is the process of collecting and restating the law of a jurisdiction into a legal code. This process has often involved international dimensions and, as such, has long drawn the attention of comparative jurists. A historic example is the East Asian reception of Western laws, in particular the German Civil Code, in the 19th century. More recently, globalization has increased the relevance of this topic. Examples include the proposed Common European Sales Law and the codification efforts in the legal transition of former Soviet States. Consequently, comparative jurists are now challenged to apply the study of codification on an unprecedented scale. This published work, with its combination of comprehensiveness and depth, is a meaningful contribution to this endeavor.

As a matter of background, this work grew out of the IACL Thematic Conference on the subject of codification held at the National Taiwan University in May 2012. Scholars worldwide, including scholars from the common law and civil law systems, gathered in Taiwan to explore this important topic. Considering the theme of "codification" and its subtheme on East Asia, Taiwan offers a befitting setting for this historic event, for Taiwanese law represents a rare amalgamation of Continental civil law, common law, Confucianism and multicultural legacy.

This work is divided into two volumes. The first volume first provides an overview and explores codification from various theoretical perspectives and their attendant profound implications. It then addresses soft codification efforts, such as the Unidroit Principles of Commercial Contracts and the supranational codification of private law in Europe and its significance for third states.

Codification reform occurs as the ideology and rationales of the law evolve. A dramatic example is the codification of private law in former Soviet states in post-Soviet times, to which this volume next turns. In addition, different fields of law lend themselves differently to codification. This volume then focuses on different fields of law, including administrative procedure, criminal law and human rights law. These field-based studies are heavily informed by national perspectives and experiences, as codification differs in methods and results from across countries and must consider country-specific characteristics.

The second volume is devoted to East Asian Law. It first puts the codification in East Asia in context by exploring the defining characteristics of the East Asian legal family and by examining the codification and legal transplant of Western laws from an international perspective. It then discusses the codification experience from four fields of law, namely commercial law, administrative law, civil law and private international law by drawing upon national perspectives. The rich discourse and experience in East Asia serve to enrich the study of codification.

On behalf of the Taiwan Committee of the Academy, I would like to thank President Professor George Bermann and Secretary-General Professor Jürgen Basedow for their invaluable support and guidance along the way. I also appreciate the unwavering support of my colleagues at National Taiwan University College of Law. Lastly, I would like to thank our editors at the Springer, particularly Dr. Neil Olivier, for their professional editorial efforts.

Wen-Yeu Wang
College of Law, National Taiwan University
Taipei, Taiwan
Titular Member and Taiwan Chair
International Academy of Comparative Law

Preface

Jurists around the world know that the value of the law lies not only in its content, but also in its form. And no aspect of legal formalism has interested comparatists as much as the extent of legislative codification or non-codification across legal systems. It is well known that civil law systems have a tendency to favor the codification of law—or at least the codification of certain bodies of law—whereas codification, as it is typically understood, has not found special favor in the common law.

But the questions surrounding codification are far more complex than any simple dichotomy between civil law and common law systems can possibly capture. This is due in part to the complexity of codification itself. Thus, codification can itself take different forms and is, in any event, a matter of degree, since in no system is the law fully codified. Conversely, no modern system—no matter how unreceptive it may be to codification as a legislative method—is without codification altogether.

Even in a legal system that has long enjoyed codification, codification reform occurs, and not only because the content of the law has evolved. Codification cannot be, or should not be, static, so that even largely codified systems need to address the challenge of maintaining over time the coherence and systematization that codification promises, even as the law itself evolves. Thus any study of codification also entails processes of de-codification and recodification as well. We also know that, even limiting ourselves to largely codified systems, codification differs importantly in methods and results from country to country. Not least, different fields of law lend themselves differently to codification. This last observation caused the architects of this publication to build it very largely around fields of law, so that the distinctive experiences in codification across fields could be well understood and appreciated.

In short, the degree and manner of legal codification is not only an important aspect of law, but an exceedingly complex one. As a subject, it accordingly warrants an examination that is both in depth and wide-ranging. Up to now, no such enterprise had ever been undertaken.

The present two-volume work fills that gap. It grew out of a large international conference on the subject of codification held at the National Taiwan University in May 2012. The occasion was the second quadrennial thematic congress of the International Academy of Comparative Law. Historically, the Academy has held world congresses embracing a very wide range of topics—as many as thirty in any given congress. Several years ago, the Academy became highly conscious of the fact that there are limits in focus and depth to congresses of that magnitude. While those congresses have the important merit of attracting and assembling comparatists across a very wide range of interest, and will therefore continue to be held every four years (the next in Vienna in 2014), the Academy leadership thought it time to introduce an additional species of congress that would bear on a single theme, albeit a broadly conceived one. The first such thematic congress of the Academy was held in Mexico City in 2008 on the theme of unification of law. Codification turned out to be a similarly compelling subject for the next thematic congress to follow, which would be in Taiwan.

This publication itself is testimony to the importance and complexity of the subject of codification. Wisely, this volume is not entirely organized by jurisdiction. It begins with a general theoretical and historical view of codification, followed by a series of other "horizontal" inquiries. But a large portion of the work is organized around fields, and indeed an impressive range of them: from administrative procedure to sales law, from criminal law to commercial law, from human rights to private law generally. On the other hand, these field-based inquiries build upon specific national legal experiences, as evidenced by the large number of national reports out of which the synthetic general reports on each of the fields covered have grown. Only a methodology of that sort can achieve the combination of specificity and breadth of vision that the present work exemplifies.

It also seemed highly appropriate for the congress and the publication resulting from it to focus on Asia—not only because of the location of this congress in Taiwan, but also because codification is a subject of intense current interest in that part of the world. That perspective defined an important segment of the Taiwan congress and defines an important segment of the present publication, namely the second volume in this two-volume work. While focusing on Asia, this volume too is organized both around field and around country.

This study of codification, as well as de-codification and recodification, is therefore unprecedented in its richness—a richness that derives from its skillful combination of detail and breadth. The comparative law academy generally is indebted to all who contributed to this study and, above all, to Professor Wen Yeu Wang of National Taiwan University, who served as its principal inspiration and architect.

George A. Bermann
Columbia Law School, New York, N.Y.
President, International Academy of Comparative Law

Contents

Contributors

Jean-Bernard Auby Sciences Po Governance and Public Law Centre, Paris, France

Jürgen Basedow Max Planck Institute for Comparative and International Private Law, University of Hamburg, Hamburg, Germany

Tomer Broude Faculty of Law, Hebrew University of Jerusalem, Jerusalem, Israel

Lado Chanturia Tbilisi State University (Javakhishvili Tbilisi State University), Tbilisi, Georgia

Deborah A. DeMott Duke law school, Duke University, Durham, NC, USA

Akiko EJIMA Law School, Meiji University, Tokyo, Japan

Giuseppe Franco Ferrari Bocconi University, Milano, Italy

Whitmore Gray Michigan University, ANN ARBOR, America

Tatjana Josipović School of Law, University of Zagreb, Zagreb, Croatia

Uwe Kischel University of Greifswald, Faculty of Law and Economics, Greifswald, Germany

Hannu Kiuru Helsinki, Finland

Ida Lintel Former intern at the Netherlands Institute of Human Rights, HT, Utrecht, The Netherlands

Chang-fa Lo College of law, National Taiwan University, Taipei, Taiwan ROC

Irina Moroianu Zlătescu Romanian Institute for Human Rights, Bucharest, Romania

Luísa Neto Faculty of Law, University of Porto, Porto, Portugal

Leila Nadya Sadat School of Law, Washington University, St. Louis, Missouri, USA

Stephen C. Thaman School of Law, Saint Louis University, St. Louis, USA

Marthe Lot Vermeulen Former staff member of the Netherlands Institute of Human Rights, HT, Utrecht, The Netherlands

Yonatan Weisbrod Faculty of Law, Hebrew University of Jerusalem, Jerusalem, Israel

Reinhard Zimmermann Comparative and Private Law, Max Planck Institute, Hamburg, Germany

Fryderyk Zoll School of Law, University of Osnabrück, Osnabrück, Germany

Jagiellonian University, ul. Olszewskiego 2, Poland

About the Authors

Jean-Bernard Auby Professor of Law, Director of the Chair "Mutations of Public Action and Publi Right at Sciences Po.

Prof. Jürgen Basedow Director, Max Planck Institute for Comparative and International Private Law, and Professor of Law, University of Hamburg/Germany; 1986–1995 Professor at the University of Augsburg; 1995–1997 Free University of Berlin. Studies of Law and Sociology in Hamburg, Geneva/Switzerland, Pavía/Italy and at Harvard Law School, Cambridge/Mass./USA. Visiting professor at numerous foreign universities. 2000–2008 Member and Chairman, German Monopolies Commission. Since 2006 Secretary General, International Academy of Comparative Law. Associate Member, Institut de droit international.

Prof. Tomer Broude Sylvan M. Cohen Chair in Law Academic Director, Minerva Center for Human Rights Faculty of Law, Vice Dean at the Hebrew University of Jerusalem.

Prof. Lado Chanturia is a full professor of law at the Javakhishvili State University in Tbilisi, Georgia, and a visiting professor at the Christian-Albrechts-University of Kiel, Germany. Before, he was chairman of the Supreme Court of Georgia, Minister of Justice of Georgia, advisor to the President of Georgia, and senior advisor of the German International Cooperation (GIZ) for legal and judicial reforms in Central Asia. He was research fellow at the universities of Göttingen and Bremen, Germany, as well as at the Max Planck Institute for Comparative and International Private Law, Hamburg, Germany.

Prof. Deborah A. DeMott is the David F. Cavers Professor of Law, Duke University of School of Law. Professor DeMott served as the sole Reporter for the American Law Institute's Restatement (Third) of Agency; her other books and scholarly articles focus primarily on agency law, fiduciary obligation, and corporate governance. Professor DeMott received a B.A. from Swarthmore College and a J.D. from New York University School of Law.

Prof. Akiko EJIMA Meiji University Akiko Ejima is Professor of Constitutional Law, Meiji University, Tokyo, LLM in Law & Doctor of Law (Meiji University), Visiting Scholar at King's College, University of London, Visiting Fellow at Harvard

Law School and Visiting Scholar at Faculty of Law, University of Cambridge. Her research topics include the multi-layered human rights protection system (especially the European Convention on Human Rights), the symbiotic relationship between constitutional law and international human rights treaties (especially human rights situation in the United Kingdom), freedom and security and legal regulation of political finance.

Prof. Giuseppe F. Ferrari is Full professor of Public Comparative Law at Bocconi University, Milan where he teaches Public Comparative Law and Civil liberties and Human rights, and President of the Italian Association of Public Comparative and European Law. Prof. Ferrari is the author of more than 140 publications among books, articles and essays published in Italy and abroad. Apart from his scientific research activities, prof. Ferrari has been invited to give lectures all around the world, including at Hong Kong University and at Virginia Law School. Since 2002 he has been a member of the Committee of experts on Public Administration, established by the Economic and Social Council of the UN General Assembly.

Prof. Whitmore Gray Graduated from Michigan Law School 1957, Editor in Chief Michigan Law Review. Graduate study at University of Paris and Muenchen University. Visiting Professor Stanford University Law School, Tuebingen University, Muenster University, Kyoto University, Tokyo University, Fordham University 1988–2012 and Peking University School of Transnational Law Shenzhen 2008-Present. Lecturer and consultant re law reform in Thailand, Indonesia, Cambodia, Vietnam, Hong Kong and Philippines. Published English translations of Russian Republic Civil Code and Chinese General Principles of Civil Law and its Supreme Court Interpretation, and articles on civil law, commercial arbitration and legal education.

Prof. Dr. Sc. Tatjana Josipović is a professor of civil law of Faculty of Law, University of Zagreb. She teaches courses in Civil Law, European Private Law and Land Registry Law. She has written many scholarly and professional papers and several books on civil law and European private law and presented papers in numerous national and international conferences and seminars. Prof. Dr. Tatjana Josipović is a member of a number of scholarly and professional associations. She is a fellow of the Academy of Legal Sciences of Croatia; associate member of International Academy of Comparative Law, a member of the Croatian Society for Civil Law Science and Practice; the Society of European Contract Law (SECOLA); European Law Institute; Civil Law Forum for South East Europe. Prof. Dr. Tatjana Josipović was a head of the task-force preparing Croatia's accession negotiations in the chapter Right of Establishment and Freedom to Provide Services; member of the task-force preparing accession negotiations in the chapter Free Movement of Capital.

Prof. Uwe Kischel born 1964; assistant at the Max Planck Institute for Comparative and International Private Law, Hamburg 1991–1992; Dr. jur. Marburg 1992; LL.M. (Yale) 1992–1993; attorney-at-law (New York) 1994; clerkship at the German Constitutional Court 1995–1998; senior assistant, University of Mannheim 1998–2002; Habilitation, venia legendi (teaching qualification) for public law, public international law, European law, and comparative law, Mannheim 2002; substitute professor,

University of Heidelberg 2003; Mercator Professor of Public Law, European Law and Comparative Law, University of Greifswald, Germany, since 2003; chairman of the section for comparative public law of the German Society of Comparative Law, since 2008.

Prof. Hannu Kiuru Vice Chairiman of the Finnish National Committee, IACL, and legally trained substitute member of the Dscrimination Board engaged by the Finnish Supreme Court 1969–2005, Referendary Counsellor since 1984.

Former Chairman of the Prison Court, a special Court having the duty to isolate dangerous violent criminals and to order young criminals to a juvenile prison earlier attachments at Helsinki University, Justice and Interior Ministries and the Asylum Board, vice chairman.

Prof. Ida Lintel holds an LLM degree in Public International Law from the University of Utrecht (UU). Currently, she is studying Dutch Law at the UU. She works as a student-assistant at the Netherlands Institute of Human Rights (SIM).

Prof. Chang-fa Lo Justice, Constitutional Court, ROC (Taiwan); professor, National Taiwan University (NTU) College of Law; Former dean and chair/lifetime distinguished professor, NTU College of Law.

Prof. Luísa Neto (Lisboa, 1971) is a Professor at the Faculty of Law of the University of Porto (Portugal). Director of the Phd in Law at the same Faculty, and also working with other scientific and academic institutions in the teaching courses and post graduate studies. Member to the Senate of the University. Member of the Academic Board of the Center for Judicial Studies, elected by the Portuguese Parliament. Member of the Research Center for Forensic Sciences and of the Interdisciplinary Institute of the University of Porto. Key Scientific Areas of Interest/Research/Training—Constitutional Law, Fundamental Rights, Administrative Law, Media, Medical Law, Bioethics.

Prof. Leila Nadya Sadat is the Henry H. Oberschelp Professor at Washington University School of Law and Director of the Whitney R. Harris World Law Institute, where she teaches a variety of international and domestic courses. Prior to joining the faculty at Washington University, she practiced international business law and litigation in Paris, France for several years and was a stagiaire at the French Cour de Cassation and Conseil d'Etat. An award-winning and prolific scholar, Sadat is the author of more than 70 books, articles and essays published in the United States and abroad.

A graduate of Tulane, Columbia and the University of Paris Schools of Law, Sadat was recently elected to the U.S. Council on Foreign Relations and appointed Special Adviser on Crimes Against Humanity to the International Criminal Court. In 2011, she received the Alexis de Tocqueville Distinguished Fulbright Chair, and taught at the University of Cergy-Pontoise, in Paris, France.

Prof. Stephen C. Thaman J.D., University of California, Berkeley, 1975 Dr. iur., University of Freiburg, Germany, 1992 Faculty of Saint Louis University School of

Law Professor Stephen C. Thaman, a recognized expert on comparative criminal law and procedure, joined the SLU LAW faculty in 1995. He has consulted with Russia, Latvia, Georgia, Kyrgyzstan and Indonesia on the reform of their codes of criminal procedure.

His present scholarship focuses on a comparative analysis of exclusionary rules, jury systems in Asia, Latin America and Europe and a comparative perspective on the use of plea-bargaining and other alternative methods deciding criminal cases.

Prof. Marthe Lot Vermeulen holds an L.L.M. degree in International Human Rights Law from the Univeristy of Essex as well as a law degree in Dutch law from the University of Amsterdam. She has obtained her Dr.-title at the Utrecht University on the basis of her PhD research called 'Enforced Disappearance: Determining State Responsibility under the International Convention for the Protection of All Persons from Enforced Disappearance'. She is currently a trainee judge at the Amsterdam District Court.

Prof. Yonatan Weisbrod is an attorney in Israel and a graduate student at the Hebrew University of Jerusalem. Yonatan's areas of research include human rights, family law, and intellectual property.

Prof. Reinhard Zimmermann Director at the Max Planck Institute for Comparative and International Private Law, Hamburg. With the kind permission of the General Secretary of the International Academy of Comparative Law this lecture has previously been published in (2012) 8 European Review of Contract Law 367 et seq.

Prof. Irina Moroianu Zlătescu PhD jurist, professor at the National School of Political and Administrative Studies, professor at the Ecological University of Bucharest; Member of the International Academy of Comparative Law, Member of the Scientific Board of the International Encyclopaedia of Laws, Member of the Steering Committee of IDEF, Member of the Superior Council of Magistracy (2005–2011), Member of the UN WGPAD (2002–2010), Director of the Romanian Institute for Human Rights. Author of a large number of articles, studies, research works, and volumes; author of prefaces to scientific volumes, book reviews and reports; professional advisory opinion on bills.

Prof. Dr. hab. Fryderyk Zoll professor at the Jagiellonian University (Cracow, Poland) and the University Osnabrueck (Germany) doctor honoris causa of the University in Ternopil (Ukraine) Member of the Polish Codification Commission for the Private Law.

Part I
Codification: From a Broader Perspective

Chapter 1
Codification, Decodification and Recodification: History, Politics and Procedure

Whitmore Gray

First the author starts with his own US system, a common law system like those of many other countries around the world derived from that of England. In the US there is not a single system of private law, but rather 50 separate jurisdictions, and each one has created its own body of case law. There is little prospect for any uniform codification–and even the commonly cited Uniform Commercial Code is merely a model statute collecting several commercial sets of rules which was adopted by each state, and is subject to final interpretation by each state court.

In Europe the author studied first French, then German law, and he describes the basic dissimilarity of their civil codes–the older elegant French code with 150 years of case law at the time he was studying, and the precise and systematic German BGB, which even in its first 50 years had also given rise to a substantial body of case law. Both codes came to need some recodification to retain their dominant position in their legal system, but that has only been achieved in Germany.

He then studied and taught about first the Soviet, then the Chinese civil law, finding only slight European influence, and describes the effect of the historical cultural context and the economic systems on their codifications. Japan's civil code relied heavily on both French and German models, and is now under revision, inspired perhaps by the recent successful extensive German code revision. The author's subsequent work in law reform projects in Cambodia and Indonesia are described as models of the more complex situations in which new codes are being drafted and older codes being revised today. Indonesia in particular shows the need to account for the mixed influence of the older Dutch code and traditional adat law in an attempt to draft a satisfactory contemporary contract law.

This paper is based on informal remarks delivered at the opening session of the International Academy of Comparative Law Congress on Codification held in Taipei, May 24–26, 2012. The author would like to express his gratitude for the help of Bianca Lin in transcribing his original remarks and assisting in preparation of this final version.

Professor Emeritus, University of Michigan School of Law.

W. Gray (✉)
Michigan University, 150 S FIFTH AVE, ANN ARBOR, America
e-mail: whitgray@aol.com

W.-Y. Wang (ed.), *Codification in International Perspective,* Ius Comparatum – Global Studies in Comparative Law, DOI 10.1007/978-3-319-03455-3_1,
© Springer International Publishing Switzerland 2014

My congratulations to the organizers of this Congress of the International Academy of Comparative Law for having chosen a topic of real contemporary importance. Prof. Zimmerman and I have been asked to give introductory lectures on the history, politics and procedures of "Codification, Decodification and Recodification." My hope is that we can raise significant questions for discussion as we all proceed to more detailed discussions of codification in relation to a wide range of topics over the coming three days.

Prof. Zimmerman stands at the center of scholarship about the European birthplace of our modern ideas about codification. I come to the topic as somewhat of an outsider—someone whose primary legal education and practice has been in the United States. Fortunately for me my perspective was subsequently widened by study in France, Germany, and Japan, as well as interaction through teaching, research and interaction with the legal systems in other countries in Europe, Latin America and then finally extensive participation in law reform in Asia. I look forward to discussion in the coming sessions of some of the questions concerning codification that are raised in these opening remarks, and look forward to learning from all of you.

US Perspective True to our Common Law heritage, like the large family of the world's legal systems with roots in the English legal system, codification has not played a prominent role in our building of basic rules of law, done mainly through court decisions, nor is it prominent in our statutory law. Despite some movements toward codification over the years and some efforts at unification,[1] our private law, for example contract law, remains in large part state law—and different in each of the 50 states. Even our one well-known code—the Uniform Commercial Code—is not at the federal level, and was not intended to provide comprehensive coverage of its subject matter. In fact it was not really drafted as a comprehensive, unified "code" in the civilian sense, and covers only part of our "commercial" law—and in particular, only a rather limited part of our law of contract. Moreover, it only served as a model which was adopted state-by-state with statutory variations, each state version then of course subject to subsequent diverging judicial interpretations. We obviously have much to learn from our civilian cousins.

There seems to be little inclination in the US or in most other countries in the common law orbit at present to move from our case-law body of basic rules to true codification. Perhaps that will change as some common law countries feel a need to modernize their law. For example, I am told Uganda is moving in that direction, utilizing the comprehensive restatements of English common law of contract and tort created by the English for their modification and unification of law in colonial India. We in the US have been involved in a substantial effort of recodification of our Uniform Commercial Code, but even that modest effort became frustrated when the recodifiers reached the controversial substance of our sales law, and little more is expected to happen in the near future. Europeans often like to use our "Restatements" as though they were in fact almost codes, but this is far from the truth. The deep contradictions in our case law in 50 jurisdictions cannot be unified by academically

---

[1] For an overview of these developments, see W. Gray, "E Pluribus Unum? A Bicentennial Report on Unification of Law in the US" 50 Rabelszeitschrift 111–165 (1986).

choosing a uniform set of rules and ignoring the contradictory case law. The greatest success of sections of the Restatements has been those sections that have appealed to individual courts as a desirable way to resolve cases before them, and have therefore been adopted and become part of the case law of a particular jurisdiction.

Perspective from Study in Europe My introduction to serious codification came in France, so I first saw an example of a code on the way to decodification—an elegant code already embedded in 150 years of extensive decisional gloss—most of it interpretation but some of it definitely creative additions. That case law was referred to regularly by professors in classes dealing with the civil law, but the bigger question as to whether the system was ripe for recodification was not discussed. We all used a small one-volume edition of the Code Civil which contained extensive annotations of case law, and which also included where appropriate various ancillary statutes which were viewed as forming a part of the basic rules. In fact, by the period when I was studying—the 1950s—there had been extensive preparations made for a revised code—many volumes of travaux preparatoires—but it seemed already clear that that comprehensive recodification was not imminent.[2] Even with the substantial changes that have been made since, the basic structure of the Code civil is likely to remain intact.[3]

As I moved on to study in Germany, I found the structure of the hundred-year-younger BGB much more a dominant factor, though the volume of case law and its importance in deriving a positive rule of law in a given case again made a real impression on my common-law mind. Some of the individual code provisions had given rise to a mountain of case law—detailed rules had been developed in some areas of the law completely by judicial decisions. Behind all that creative and carefully argued case law the basic structure of the BGB remained intact, however, and I found a symmetry that I was unfamiliar with in US law—a major advantage of a careful codification. Prof. Mathias Reimann has given us four reasons for the success of the BGB, which we will do well to keep in mind as we consider below codification in other places and in other times and circumstances: (1) thorough drafting by skilled legal technicians; (2) a foundation in developed legal science—i.e. reflecting a historical sense for the raw materials; (3) creation of primarily elementary rules for long shelf life—leaving the details to subsequent interpretation in application; and (4) a code suitable for the political moment—in Germany the BGB was the child of German nationalism.[4]

When do even well and appropriately drafted codes become ripe for revision? Although this noble warrior had survived a tumultuous century of political change, late in its first century the BGB had reached a situation where the quantity and nature of the case law, the doctrinal writing and the volume of important ancillary statutes indicated a need for recodification. The desirability of taking into account other

---

[2] See R. Pascal, "Report on French Civil Code Revision Project" 11 La. L. Rev. Vol. 2, p. 23 (1951).

[3] For an overview of the continuing influence of the Code civil, see X. Blanc-Jouvan, "Worldwide Influence of the French Civil Code of 1804" in Cornell Law School Papers, Number 3 (2004).

[4] For an incisive review of the process in Germany, see M. Reimann, "The Good, the Bad, and the Ugly: The Reform of the German Law of Obligations" 83 Tul. L. Rev. 877 (2008–2009).

sources, such as the CISG, as well as European Community directives also indicated it might be the appropriate time for some substantial revision. By 1992, after a huge amount of effort by a broad-based commission, a proposal for a massive re-writing of the law of obligations had been achieved, but no action was taken to bring it to fruition. In 2000 the government surprised the legal community with its own substantial proposal for extensive revision—and a one-year timetable for adoption. How this led to the major revision of the BGB is a fascinating story that should be carefully considered as to method and substance, and we have Prof. Zimmerman with us as our expert informant on this topic.[5]

Because the French and German models came to be used in so many other countries with different traditions and different political needs, the subsequent mutations of these two systems have a broader significance as we look at codes in other countries. For example, in Japan in the initial stage of the codification process the French model was tried and found wanting in part, and the German model was found more suitable for building most of the new code. In other countries the Swiss model was used. As we talk later about Thailand, Cambodia, China and Indonesia we will see the importance of referring both to the original codification and its permutations over time—and of course the same could be said for looking at codes in Latin America, etc. Of course we should also keep in mind the models provided by important completely new codifications like those of the Netherlands and Quebec—not to overlook other similar examples of innovation in form and substance in the CISG and the Unidroit Principles of International Commercial Contracts.

Soviet Union and China My next focus after Europe was on the Soviet Union—another country where there had been codes in the past, but which really only had a collection-of-statues "code" at the time of the Bolshevik Revolution. The Russian Civil Code of the 1920s is an interesting study, and the Russian courts interpreted it to some extent in the light of European experience, but the interaction with the new economic system continued to be very important, and finally led to the enactment of new "fundamental principles" to be used as the basis for drafting new civil codes for all the republics.[6] Such a new Russian Republic Civil Code was enacted in 1964. As I prepared an English translation of that code, I felt some European influence, but when I asked about that in discussions with one of the drafters I was told that few of the drafters had any profound background in the French or German material.[7] The need to incorporate communist economic principles remained a principal concern, and there was at the time a strong ideological debate about whether there should be a separate "economic code" to implement the communist/socialist ideology, but in fact a unified format was chosen.

---

[5] For a thorough treatment of this revision, see R. Zimmerman, THE NEW GERMAN LAW OF OBLIGATIONS (Oxford U. Press 2005).

[6] See generally W. Gray, "Soviet Tort Law: The New Principles Annotated" 1964 U. Ill. L. F. 180–211 (1964).

[7] CIVIL CODE OF THE RUSSIAN FEDERATED SOCIALIST REPUBLIC, (English trans. By W. Gray and R. Stults) (Ann Arbor 1965).

At that time I wondered whether the other major communist country, the People's Republic of China, with only an amorphous legal system at the time, would move in that same direction and eventually produce its own "communist"—today "socialist" is their preferred term—Chinese Civil Code. To explore answers to that question, I began to teach a course on Communist Law jointly with a Chinese émigré former judge and scholar in 1961, and went to spend time in Hong Kong so as to follow legal developments in the turbulent period of the 1960s, getting information about developments on the Mainland through interviews with Chinese emigres and foreigners with first-hand experience there. By the time of my first visit to the Mainland in 1976 the legal system was still basically dormant—law schools were closed down and the judges we were allowed to interview said that they were doing political activism work among the masses rather than deciding cases.

It was not until 1986 that China finally produced a short civil code—"Basic Principles of Civil Law." Deng Xiaoping had been told by visiting Japanese businessmen that trade with China was hampered by the lack of civil legislation, so Deng ordered Chinese scholars to produce "civil law" as quickly as possible. In fact, in less than a year, committees of scholars and legislators produced a short, rather unevenly drafted code—ignoring a draft of a much more comprehensive civil code that had gone through successive drafts since the 1950s. When the project was first announced, I thought that China might have decided to follow the Soviet pattern—first enact a set of fundamental provisions that were to be used as guidelines for separate civil codes in each of the Soviet union republics. Instead what was produced in China was a short, simple comprehensive code, containing provisions covering civil status, obligations—i.e. basically contracts and torts—property, etc., sufficient to serve as a skeleton code regulating the whole area of traditional civil law—except for inheritance and family law, which, following the Soviet pattern, had already been the subject of earlier statutes. In the course of preparing an English translation of those "General Principles,"[8] it became clear that the only direct foreign input came from Soviet legislation, with which most of them were familiar—either through study in the Soviet Union or from Soviet textbooks and professors who had taught in China in the 1950s. Of course, in the back of the Chinese drafters' minds presumably was also a model for form and substance and terminology conveniently available in Chinese— the sophisticated civil code and related legal literature of the European-inspired civil code of the Republic of China here in Taiwan.

That first mini-codification and the subsequent comprehensive Chinese statutes enacted for contracts and property[9], now constitute a fertile field for comparative study of Chinese civil law, and a body of case law in the field is now also becoming available. Since China has not yet brought together its various comprehensive pieces of civil legislation into a Chinese Civil Code, that final chapter of codification remains

---

[8] "General Principles of Civil Law," (English trans. by W. Gray and R. Zheng) 34 Am. J. Comp. L. 715–743 (1986), and the later interpretive opinion of the Chinese Supreme Court in Law and Contemporary Problems, Spring 1989, p. 27 ff.

[9] The General Principles have not yet been superseded by the subsequent comprehensive statutues. In 2012 a professor at Peking University devoted the first part of his civil law course to full coverage of the General Principles.

to be written. Eventually some of China's long legal tradition—including codes that served as models for other countries in the region[10]—may find a place in China's legal system.

Other Asian Countries My next focus was on Japan, where during almost four years of teaching and study I came to appreciate the influences of the general culture and unique historical factors on the Japanese legal system in general, and on their codification in particular. The strong influence of German law on their code, and the extensive use of German doctrinal writing, particularly in the area of obligations law, was so apparent that it was easy to overlook the influence of the Japanese context. A distinguished Japanese professor of civil law visited my contracts class at the University of Michigan and spoke about the German influence on their law of obligations. He knew about Restatement Section 90 in modern American law, providing that a promise of gift became enforceable even without consideration once it had been relied on by the promisee, and said that the same idea had been adopted in Japan from German law. Thinking about a well-known American case, one of the students then asked this question: In Japan if an uncle promised to give his nephew $ 1000 so he could take a trip, and the nephew then took the trip, then if the uncle didn't pay, could the nephew sue to enforce the promise against the uncle? The professor was horrified, and said, "Of course not. In Japan a nephew would never sue his uncle!" Law on the books, or in the treatises—since that idea had been imported into Japanese doctrine from German legal doctrine—and what would happen in society were quite different.[11] The American contracts professor added that in fact the American cases that applied that idea had been in situations where the uncle had died and the nephew was only suing his estate!

In recent years the Japanese have also been engaged in a substantial revision of the contract provisions of the civil code, integrating into the code the very substantial case law regularly cited over the years.[12] Perhaps some of our Japanese colleagues here can bring us up to date on the progress and the scope of that revision, and in particular what attention has been paid to the revision of the German code. In fact, the Japanese experience will be of real interest to many other countries who are or probably should be trying to decide whether to incorporate into their German-inspired codes some of the recent German improvements—and in fact hopefully our colleagues here in Taiwan can tell us what is happening in that regard their German-inspired code.

Over a period of two years I was involved as an adviser in Indonesia in a proposed drafting of a new contract law. The Indonesian experience is quite unique, since Indonesia still today uses the Dutch Civil Code of 1847. That text was imposed in the colonial period, but was never officially translated into Indonesian. More surprising, independence was achieved more than 50 years ago and there is still no official Indonesian text! As part of a broad, foreign-funded program of modernization of the legal system a committee was established to draft a new contract law—not a new

---

[10] See generally J. Head, LAW CODES IN DYNASTIC CHINA, (Carolina Academic Press 2005).

[11] For examples see W. Gray, "Use and Non-Use of Contract Law in Japan," 17 Law in Japan 97–119 (1984).

[12] See "Working Group on Revision of Civil Code" (Japan Ministry of Justice 2012 ff.).

civil code—and a distinguished Dutch professor and I were named as advisers to that group. Our Western orientation and lack of in-depth knowledge of Indonesian law led us to initiate the process by giving them an Indonesian translation of the Unidroit Principles of International Commercial Contracts, thinking that that was a reasonable restatement of state-of-the-art thinking about satisfactory contract provisions. We suggested that they carefully review those substantive provisions and revise them or add to them to reflect what they thought was important in current Indonesian contract law and practice, and that we would then give our reactions and advice, giving them in effect a preview of the response they might expect to get to their revisions from lawyers in international practice who might have to use the new statute. Unfortunately the political situation imploded at that point, and that particular project was abandoned.

Assuming the process will continue, however, it will be of great interest to us as we look at the recodification process, because we now know that the majority of contract transactions in Indonesia were not in practice governed by the Dutch/Indonesian code provisions, but by the traditional *adat* customary law.[13] The drafters of a new contract law to replace the old code provisions will presumably be thinking in fact of a new statute which will take into account those *adat* provisions—a formidable task indeed, as well as considering the CISG and other foreign models. The committee pointed out to us that working with the present/old code provisions in practice had already become more complicated in recent years because after the enactment of the new civil code in the Netherlands, current Dutch legal literature no longer referred to provisions of the old code! Our idea of moving to a CISG/Unidroit base was in part to open up a substantial body of international literature that could be relied on in interpreting their new contract law. The task of drafting a comprehensive new code, building on the old French/Dutch code, the adat customary law—and possible accommodating Sharia influence in this largest Muslim country—will no doubt attract considerable scholarly attention in the near future, and possibly serve as a model for other post-colonial recodifications.

Cambodia presents a different set of conditions regarding questions concerning decodification and recodification. There was a long time lapse between the old French colonial code influence and modern legislation for Cambodia. When I arrived to consult about arbitration and contract law, the battle of foreign advisers was already under way. The American Bar Association opened an office with the help of the Asia Foundation and advisers from Australia to try to respond to immediate needs for law and lawyers. An effective program to train legal defenders was an early and successful project, even before legal education and lawyer training got under way. The French had come in with a program to aid in drafting new codes and to reestablish legal education, creating a close link with the faculty in Lyons. The French drafter of a new family code and a code of civil procedure said she needed little consultation with local people, and seemed to be basically replicating what she was familiar with in France. When I suggested meeting with the small group of local judges to discuss their ideas about civil procedure and the interface with arbitration law, she declined

---

[13] See C.F.G. Sunryati Hartono, "Indonesian Law on Contracts, (IDE JETRO) (Japan 2001).

and said she expected them to simply learn her new provisions. When I went ahead to meet with the local judges, I found the situation was more complicated than I had realized, because those I met with had only a Soviet legal education and Russian as their foreign language.

When I visited the law school, the dean asked me to lecture on contract law, but then was told by his French adviser/supervisor that he would only allow a Frenchmen to lecture there—and it didn't help that I offered to give the US contract law lecture in French! As for draft legislation, the ABA office for some reason had in hand a draft contract law done by a Singapore lawyer, which emphasized the role of consideration—an unacceptable focus for a contemporary American lawyer. Into this melee came the Japanese with a very commendable legal assistance program, re-using some of their statutory proposals from Vietnam. Obviously this confusion of assistance programs was a major problem for the local people trying to move as quickly as possible in very dicey political conditions. In fact, when I asked them if there was some positive, satisfactory assistance they could point me to as a model, they introduced me to their favorite adviser—a Canadian from Montreal with good legal credentials in both civil and common law, some administrative experience, and best of all, who was completely bilingual so that he could work with English input and produce drafts in French of what they wanted. Cambodia—and perhaps Vietnam and Laos, along with other post-colonial countries—pose for all of us the challenge as to what we as comparative law scholars/observers of the past have to contribute to the pressing questions of codification for their futures.

Finally, a question of general interest raised in Indonesia and Cambodia was how much attention should they pay to accommodating their future trade partners in creating contract laws that would be easy for foreigners to understand and deal with? Both countries have strong civil law colonial traditions, but after all they are also surrounded by potential trading partners with common law traditions—Australia, New Zealand, Hong Kong, Singapore, the Philippines, Malaysia, Myanmar and India. My suggestion in Indonesia and Cambodia was to use as much as possible the model of the Unidroit Principles of International Commercial Contracts—as state-of-the-art modern provisions designed to be as understandable as possible for both civil and common law users. Of course, an even more important general factor may be the legal education resources and scholarly commentators available in the near future in any developing country to deal with any new legislation, as well as the ability of those people to make use of foreign materials in foreign languages. In an ideal world the foreign legal advisers would be able to assist in creating local jurists familiar with not just grand civil law traditions and the common law, but able to follow the full variety of post-colonial experience in other countries.

We comparativists are being strongly challenged to put our historical and academic knowledge to work in building better statutes, whether in codification or recodification. Of course, as educators we are being challenged to turn out future lawyers, judges and arbitrators who will be able to negotiate the complex interactions between all of these new systems and the old systems which are still very much with us.

We should thank once again the organizers of this Congress for giving us a chance to expand our legal horizons and prepare us to contribute to the work of codification or recodification that lies ahead.

Chapter 2
Codification: The Civilian Experience Reconsidered on the Eve of a Common European Sales Law

Reinhard Zimmermann

1. Codification, in the words of Franz Wieacker, is 'a unique creation, hard-won and hard to be defended, of Central and Western Continental legal culture'.[1] For Max Weber, it constituted a culmination, in the field of law, of a specifically European quest for rationality.[2] At the same time, according to Pio Caroni, codification was a fundamental turning point, and thus ushered in a new era, in the history of European law.[3] The age of codification has in fact characteristically shaped our modern legal landscape and still, to a large extent, determines our legal mind.[4] A *codex*, originally, was a set of wooden tablets covered with material used for writing and

Director at the Max Planck Institute for Comparative and International Private Law, Hamburg. With the kind permission of the General Secretary of the International Academy of Comparative Law this lecture has previously been published in (2012) 8 *European Review of Contract Law* 367 *et seq.*

[1] F. Wieacker, 'Aufstieg, Blüte und Krisis der Kodifikationsidee', in *Festschrift für Gustav Boehmer* (Bonn: Roehrscheid 1954) 34 (translation from the German original here and throughout the article by R.Z., unless otherwise indicated).

[2] M. Weber, 'Die Entwicklungsbedingungen des Rechts' in: W. Gephart and S. Hermes (eds), *Wirtschaft und Gesellschaft*, Teilband 3: Recht (Tübingen: Mohr Siebeck 2010) 569 et seq.

[3] P. Caroni, *Gesetz und Gesetzbuch: Beiträge zu einer Kodifikationsgeschichte* (München: Helbing & Lichtenhahn 2003) viii.

[4] For earlier reflections on the same topic, see R. Zimmermann, 'Codification: History and Present Significance of an Idea' (1995) 3 *European Review of Private Law* 95 et seq. For recent overviews, see P. Caroni, 'Kodifikation', in *Handwörterbuch zur deutschen Rechtsgeschichte*, vol. II (Berlin: Schmidt 1978) 907 *et seq; P.* Caroni, 'Kodifikation', in *Enzyklopädie der Neuzeit* (Stuttgart: Metzler 2007) 855 *et seq* (referring to a 'revolutionary transformation'); B. Dölemeyer, 'Kodifizierung/Kodifikation', in *Der Neue Pauly: Enzyklopädie der Antike*, vol. 14 (*Rezeptions- und Wissenschaftsgeschichte*) (Stuttgart: Metzler 2000) 1003 *et seq*; J. P. Schmidt, 'Codification', in: J. Basedow, K. J. Hopt, R. Zimmermann (eds), *The Max Planck Encyclopedia of European Private Law* (MaxEuP) (Oxford: Oxford University Press 2012) 221 *et seq* (based upon a more extensive discussion in J. P. Schmidt, *Zivilrechtskodifikation in Brasilien* [Tübingen: Mohr Siebeck 2009] 133 *et seq*); N. Jansen and L. Rademacher, 'European Civil Code', in J. Smits (ed), *Elgar Encyclopedia of Comparative Law*, 2nd ed (Cheltenham: Elgar 2012).

R. Zimmermann (✉)
Comparative and Private Law, Max Planck Institute, mittelweg187,
20148 Hamburg, Germany
e-mail: r.zimmermann@mpipriv.de

W.-Y. Wang (ed.), *Codification in International Perspective,* Ius Comparatum – Global Studies in Comparative Law, DOI 10.1007/978-3-319-03455-3_2,
© Springer International Publishing Switzerland 2014

bound together in the form of a booklet.[5] *Codices*, in the sense of law books or collections of laws, have been produced since time immemorial: the Code of Hammurabi, the XII Tables, the *Codex Theodosianus*,[6] the so-called *leges barbarorum, Decretum Gratiani, Sachsenspiegel*,[7] *Siete Partidas*, and many more.[8] But the modern phenomenon of codification, referred to by Weber, Wieacker and Caroni, is a product of the age of Enlightenment,[9] and its principal manifestations were the Prussian code (*Preußisches Allgemeines Landrecht*) of 1794, the Austrian General Civil Code (*Allgemeines Bürgerliches Gesetzbuch* = ABGB) of 1811, and the French *Code civil* of 1804. The *Code civil* provided the model for the codifications of Dutch (1838), Italian (1865), Portuguese (1867) and Spanish private law (1888–1889). A second 'wave' of codifications caught Germany (1900), Switzerland (1881/1911/1937: Law of Obligations [*Obligationenrecht* = OR]; 1907/1912: Civil Code [*Zivilgesetzbuch* = ZGB]), and Greece (1946).[10] Italy (1942), Portugal (1967) and the Netherlands (from 1970 onwards) have recodified their private laws;[11] the Austrian (1914–1916) and German (particularly in 2002) codes have been the subject of major reforms; and similar reform processes are currently under way in France and Spain.[12] (The Prussian code, of course, was replaced by the German BGB.) From Central, Western, and Southern Europe the codification movement spread to other parts of the world,

---

[5] A. Berger, *Encyclopedic Dictionary of Roman Law* (Philadelphia: The American Philosophical Society 1953) 391; R. Cabrillac, *Les codifications* (Paris: Presses Universitaires de France 2002) 56 *et seq* (not only on the etymology but also on the history of the term *codex*).

[6] See, in the present context, I. Kroppenberg, 'Der gescheiterte Codex: Überlegungen zur Kodifikationsgeschichte des Codex Theodosianus' (2007) 10 *Rechtsgeschichte* 112. Kroppenberg, however, also uses the concept of codification to cover documents such as the *Codex Theodosianus*, and indeed the *XII Tables*: 'Mythos Kodifikation—Ein rechtshistorischer Streifzug' [2008] *Juristenzeitung* 910 (n 109). P. Caroni, '(De)Kodifikation: wenn historische Begriffe ins Schleudern geraten', in K. V. Maly and P. Caroni (eds), *Kodifikation und Dekodifikation des Privatrechts in der heutigen Rechtsentwicklung* (Prague: Karolinum 1998) 32 *et seq* criticizes this as an ahistorical projection of modern concepts into the past ('... if the concepts start floundering'). Others use the concept of codification in a wide, and untechnical, sense; see Cabrillac, n 5 above, 63 who proposes to define 'le noyau dur du concept de code comme un ensemble de règles juridiques mises en forme' and the concept of codification as 'cette operation de mise en forme de règles juridiques en un ensemble' (this is based on J. Vanderlinden, *Le concept de code en Europe occidentale du XIIIe au XIXe siècle: Essay de définition* [Bruxelles: Editions de l'Institut de Sociologie, Université libre de Bruxelles, 1967]).

[7] On the two latter see, in the present context, N. Jansen, *The Making of Legal Authority: Non-legislative Codifications in Historical and Comparative Perspective* (Oxford: Oxford University Press 2010) 21 *et seq.*

[8] For an overview, see Cabrillac, n 5 above, 10 *et seq.*

[9] Cabrillac, n 5 above, 33, refers to the '[s]iècle d'or de la codification'.

[10] On the spread of codifications throughout large parts of the world see Cabrillac, n 5 above, 40 *et seq*; Schmidt, in MaxEuP, n 4 above, 222 *et seq.*

[11] On the problems relating to recodification, see Cabrillac, n 5 above, 107 *et seq.*

[12] J. Cartwright, S. Vogenauer and S. Whittaker (eds), *Reforming the French Law of Obligations* (Oxford: Hart 2009); C. J. Delgado and M. J. P. García, 'The General Codification Commission and the Modernisation of the Spanish Law of Obligations' (2011) 19 *Zeitschrift für Europäisches Privatrecht* 601 *et seq.*

most notably to Eastern and South-Eastern Europe, East Asia, Latin America, the francophone countries of Africa, and the mixed legal systems of Israel, Québec and Louisiana.

All of these modern codes differ in a number of respects.[13] Predominantly they deal with general private law but sometimes (e.g. in Italy) they also include commercial law[14] (or even public law: the Prussian code); usually they have been drafted and redrafted by (a sequence of) committees but sometimes (e.g. in Switzerland) they are the product of individual masterminds;[15] mostly they are enacted, in their entirety, at one specific moment, but sometimes (e.g. in the Netherlands) their various parts are drafted and enacted in stages; normally, they apply directly, but sometimes (e.g. in Spain)[16] they are applicable only *in subsidio*, at least for certain parts of the relevant country and for certain areas of the law.

2. What, then, are the common characteristics constituting a codification in the modern, or technical, sense of the word? In the first place, codification is an act of legislation, i.e. its validity is based on the intervention of the state. However, in the words of Jeremy Bentham, the person who coined the term, codification is '[q]uite different [from] *ordinary* legislation' in view of the fact that here 'of the entire field of law ... some very large portion ... is to receive an entire new covering all at once'.[17] A codification, therefore, does not concern itself with individual issues that need to be regulated but covers *an area* of the law: general private law, the law of obligations (including or excluding commercial obligations), contract law, family law, etc. In addition, a codification aims to be comprehensive (or 'complete'). This ideal of completeness has three dimensions:[18] a codification should not contain gaps; it should replace the general law prevailing before its enactment[19] and thus constitute the new 'epicentre'[20] of the system of sources of law (for this reason, the *Codex Maximilianeus Bavaricus Civilis* of 1756 was not a modern codification);[21] and it

---

[13] Cf. also J. Fr. Behrend, 'Die neueren Privatrechts-Codificationen', in F. von Holtzendorff (ed), *Encyclopädie der Rechtswissenschaft*, Part I (Leipzig: Duncker & Humblot 1870) 229 *et seq* (Codifications 'can be very different, as far as their validity, object, content and size are concerned').

[14] See Schmidt, in MaxEuP, n 4 above, 210 *et seq.*

[15] See Cabrillac, n 5 above, 214 *et seq*; B. Mertens, *Gesetzgebungskunst im Zeitalter der Kodifikationen* (Tübingen: Mohr Siebeck 2004) 88 *et seq*; cf. also the remarks by Wieacker, n 30 below, 474.

[16] See C. Eckl, 'Código Civil', in MaxEuP, n 4 above, 225 *et seq*; for Prussia, see Behrend, n 13 above, 236.

[17] J. Bentham, 'Papers relative to Codification and Public Instruction', in J. Bowring (ed), *The Works of Jeremy Bentham*, vol. IV (Edinburgh: Tait 1843) 518.

[18] Mertens, n 15 above, 325 *et seq.* Generally on 'l'effet de complétude' of codifications, cf. also Cabrillac, n 5 above, 105 *et seq.*

[19] In the words of Bentham, n 17 above, 519, it has to 'reduce the old matter, in its whole extent, to a non-entity'; Cabrillac, n 5 above, 90: 'Dès son entrée en vigueur, le code efface d'un trait de plume le monde juridique qui le précède'.

[20] Caroni, n 3 above, 38.

[21] Justinian's *Corpus Juris*, though no longer taken to be the 'infallible legal gospel', was still to be attributed subsidiary force: W. X. A. Freiherr von Kreittmayr, *Anmerkungen über den Codicem Maximilianeum Bavaricum Civilem*, Part I (Munich: Vötter 1759), Chap. 2, § 9, no. 20.

should gather all the relevant legal rules in one place, i.e. not coexist with specific statutes within one and the same area of the law. No codification, however, has ever fully complied with this ideal.[22] Moreover, a codification is not just the recording of the rules pertaining to a certain field of law. It is based on the belief that the legal rules can be reduced to a rational system.[23] A codification, therefore, aims at presenting its subject matter as a logically consistent entity of legal rules and institutions. It thus promotes the internal coherence of the law and makes it more easily comprehensible. And it supplies both the conceptual tools and the intellectual matrix for the further development of the law. The third characteristic of a codification, therefore, is its systematic nature; hence Justinian's Code and Digest, or the *Decretum Gratiani*, do not constitute codifications in the same, technical sense as the *Code civil* or the German Civil Code (*Bürgerliches Gesetzbuch* = BGB).

But what about Justinian's Institutes? They were designed to provide a comprehensive and systematic account of Roman private law, and they were invested with the force of law.[24] None the less, no one today would regard them as a codification. Thus, probably, a fourth element has to be added to the definition of a codification, and this has to do with the form of the texts contained in a codification.[25] The Institutes were a legal textbook; and as such they contained 'a mixture of statement of present law, historical description and discussion of legal theory'.[26] In particular, also, they presented legal arguments which their reader might regard as more or less convincing. Modern codifications, however, even if their style of legal drafting displays considerable differences, tend to make clear that they are not intended to be a contribution to an academic discourse but that they are to be observed and applied

---

[22] That there may be gaps was acknowledged even by the draftsmen of the Prussian code. Since the middle of the 19th century it was generally recognized that any codification was bound to contain gaps; indeed, the draftsmen of the BGB deliberately left many questions open for determination by courts and legal scholarship. However, in modern terminology, we are dealing here with 'internal' gaps that can be filled on the basis of the code and its underlying principles.—All modern codifications intended to end the (subsidiary) application of Roman law. But the Austrian code allows the judge to refer to the principles of Natural law (§ 7 ABGB), while the Swiss Civil Code, if no relevant provision can be found for a legal problem, refers the judge to customary law as well as 'to the rule which he would, were he the legislator, adopt' (Art. 1 [2] ZGB).—The third dimension inherent in the notion of 'completeness' was largely taken account of only by the Prussian code. In the Introductory Act to the BGB, for example, close to 100 articles dealt with subject matters to be left to special legislation by the individual states; cf also *infra* text to n 82 below. For details, see Mertens, n 15 above, 326 *et seq*, 336 *et seq*, 344 *et seq*; Schmidt (2009), n 4 above, 134 *et seq*.

[23] Mertens, n 15 above, 421 *et seq*; S. Vogenauer, *Die Auslegung von Gesetzen in England und auf dem Kontinent* (Tübingen: Mohr Siebeck 2001) 649; Jansen and Rademacher, n 4, *sub* 4.

[24] O. Behrends, 'Die Institutionen Justinians als Lehrbuch, Gesetz und Ausdruck klassischen Rechtsdenkens', in O. Behrends, R. Knütel, B. Kupisch and H. H. Seiler (eds and transl) *Corpus Juris Civilis: Text und Übersetzung*, vol. I, 2nd ed (Heidelberg: Müller 1997) 279 *et seq*.

[25] Generally on 'text-related factors' concerning 'the making of legal authority' (though of 'non-legislative codifications' rather than of legislation), see Jansen, n 7 above, 99 *et seq*.

[26] American Law Institute, 'Report of the Committee on the Establishment of a Permanent Organization for the Improvement of the Law Proposing the Establishment of an American Law Institute' (1923) 1 *Proceedings of the American Law Institute* 20.

in practice. They are thus, to a greater or lesser extent,[27] based on the precept of *lex iubeat non disputet*.[28] A related point is made when it is stated that a codification is 'a new text, specifically drafted for the occasion'[29] rather than the official collection of laws or cases, or the compilation of fragments, from earlier legal literature.

3. Codification was a historical phenomenon originating in the 18th century, and implemented from the end of that century onwards.[30] What were the historical conditions responsible for it? (i) The idea of codification was closely associated with the rise of the modern sovereign state, exercising exclusive control over the legislative process.[31] (ii) It was thus a potent symbol of the one and undivided nation and of political unity (this is particularly apparent in the cases of Italy and Germany).[32] In the words of the main draftsman of the *Code civil*, Jean-Étienne Marie Portalis, it was to ensure that there were no longer Bretons, Alsatians or Provençals, but only Frenchmen.[33] (iii) Codifications also contributed towards cultural homogeneity within the new, sovereign states.[34] This is one of the reasons why they were drafted in the vernacular. (iv) They provided a response to a pervasive sense of crisis, as far as the administration of the law was concerned. For, on the one hand, Roman law had constituted the foundation of the *ius commune* prevailing in medieval and early modern Europe.[35] But its authority had been undermined by influential authors

---

[27] The Austrian and Prussian codes mark a transitional stage within a development from an instructive to a prescriptive style of legal drafting. The early modern legislation prior to the Prussian code (including the *Codex Maximilianeus Bavaricus Civilis* of 1756) has been described as constituting 'textbooks invested with the force of law'. For details, see Mertens, n 15 above, 312 *et seq*.

[28] This is one reason why the 'European Civil Code' envisaged by H. Collins is not a codification in the technical sense of the word: it is conceived as a 'framework of normative standards . . . rather than a complex body of detailed rules', i.e. a set of 'common legal principles'. The other reason is that this 'code' is supposed to operate 'as directive'; it 'would not comprise the sole source of private law. On the contrary, national private law systems must continue': H. Collins, *The European Civil Code: The Way Forward* (Cambridge: Cambridge University Press 2008) x, 2, 189.

[29] R.C. van Caenegem, *Judges, Legislators and Professors* (Cambridge: Cambridge University Press 1987) 42.

[30] The classical general account is F. Wieacker, *A History of Private Law in Europe* (Oxford: Clarendon Press 1995, transl Tony Weir from the 2nd German edition, 1967) 199 *et seq*.

[31] See D. Willoweit, *Deutsche Verfassungsgeschichte* (Munich: C.H. Beck 2009) 152 *et seq*. The connection with the state (first the modern territorial, then the 'nation' state) is also apparent from the title of S. Meder, 'Die Krise des Nationalstaates und ihre Folgen für das Kodifikationsprinzip' [2006] *Juristenzeitung* 477 *et seq*.

[32] Cf also Cabrillac, n 5 above, 154 *et seq*. For the rise of the sense of national identity in 19th century Europe, in cultural-historical perspective, see J. Leerssen, *National Thought in Europe* (Amsterdam: Amsterdam University Press 2006).

[33] See J.G. Locré, *La législation civile, commerciale et criminelle de la France, ou commentaire et complément des codes Français*, vol. I (Paris: Treuttel & Würz 1827) 348.—Generally, see Mertens, n 15 above, 30 *et seq*.

[34] See, eg, Leerssen, n 32 above, 137 *et seq*.

[35] N. Jansen, 'Ius Commune', in MaxEuP, n 4 above, 1006 *et seq*; *idem*, Legal Authority, n 7 above, 13 *et seq*.

such as Franciscus Hotomannus, Hermann Conring and Christian Thomasius.[36] It no longer appeared to be self-evidently right to apply a law that was riddled with inconsistencies, that had given rise to intricate doctrinal disputes, that was wedded to outdated and impractical subtleties, and that had been enacted by despotic rulers of another age and country.

(v) On the other hand, Roman law had never been on its own. The dualism of Empire and Church had been reflected in the dualism of Roman law and Canon law. Moreover, there was an enormous variety of territorial, regional and local laws, of statutes, customs and privileges that, in theory, enjoyed precedence before the courts. There were, of course, certain meta-rules that were supposed to govern the application of the law;[37] but what actually happened in the courtrooms across Europe was subject to considerable change, and it could vary from place to place and from subject area to subject area. Thus, potential litigants and lawyers were faced with 'a legal pluralism hardly imaginable today', entailing very considerable legal uncertainty.[38] Even a preliminary issue such as whether a secular or ecclesiastical court was competent to decide a dispute could give rise to lengthy and complex controversies.[39] (vi) The rulers of the age of Enlightenment were bound to be repelled by this state of affairs and regarded it as their duty to promote the public welfare by not only centralizing but also rationalizing and clarifying the law. The legal rules according to which justice was to be dispensed had to be made known so that everybody could be expected to adjust his behaviour accordingly.[40] This was the other reason why the codifications were no longer drafted in the traditional language of the learned lawyers, but in the vernacular.[41] (vii) At the same time, the mud holes of the glossators,[42] and their successors, had to be drained by laying down the law in an easily comprehensible form rather than in an overabundant and arcane legal literature. To this end, the monarchs and their officials could avail themselves of the systems and theories of the new, secularized brand of Natural law that had emerged in the course of the 17th century. Roman law was no longer *ratio scripta*; it was acceptable only in so far as it was in conformity with the principles of natural reason. A variety of writers (Hugo

---

[36] Cf. further R. Zimmermann, 'Christian Thomasius, the Reception of Roman Law and the History of the lex Aquilia', in *C. Thomasius, Larva Legis Aquiliae: The mask of the lex Aquilia torn off the action for damage done* (ed and transl Margaret Hewett) (Oxford: Hart 2000) 56 *et seq.*

[37] *Lex posterior derogat legi anteriori; lex specialis derogat legi generali; statuta sunt stricte interpretanda; ubi cessat statutum habet locum ius civile; qui habet regulam juris communi pro se, habet fundatam intentionem; see* J. Schröder, *Recht als Wissenschaft,* 2nd ed (Munich: Beck 2012) 19 *et seq,* 113 *et seq.*

[38] See P. Oestmann, *Rechtsvielfalt vor Gericht* (Frankfurt: Klostermann 2002) 681.

[39] For details, see now P. Oestmann, *Geistliche und weltliche Gerichte im Alten Reich: Zuständigkeitsstreitigkeiten und Instanzenzüge* (Köln: Böhlau 2012).

[40] This view presupposes that codifications are addressed (also) to the general population. During the age of Enlightenment, promotion of the general knowledge of the law was conceived as one of the state's tasks: for details, see Mertens, n 15 above, 251 *et seq*; Cabrillac, n 5 above, 218 *et seq.*

[41] For details, see Mertens, n 15 above, 386 *et seq*; cf also Cabrillac, n 5 above, 226 *et seq.*

[42] The expression, law derived 'ex lacunis glossatorum' (as opposed to 'ex genuinis fontibus'), was used by Christian Thomasius; see Zimmermann, n 36 above, 58.

Grotius, Samuel Pufendorf, Christian Wolff, Jean Domat) had set out to demonstrate how the solutions to individual cases could be derived from general propositions and how all the rules regulating human behaviour could be fitted into a system that was both internally consistent and consonant with human reason and the nature of man. That culminated in a jurisprudence constructed *more geometrico*; and it is obvious that this type of jurisprudence appealed to authorities eager to rationalize the administration of justice. (viii) Inherent in the idea of codification, however, was also an emancipatory element: for by making the legal rules both public and certain, it promoted the rule of law. Thus, it suited not only the interests of those who ruled but also those of the reformers; and it appeared to be in line with contemporary Enlightenment philosophers such as John Locke who saw the origin of state and law in a kind of contract concluded in order to ensure liberty, equality and the protection of property.

4. It was in this spirit that the Prussian, Austrian and French codes were drafted,[43] and it is interesting to see that the triumphal advance of the codification movement was only temporarily slowed down, but not stopped, when the intellectual climate changed: when the Romantic reaction led lawyers to lose faith in discovering a law of reason and to gain confidence, once again, in the traditions of the *ius commune* which could be moulded into a system of 'contemporary' Roman law. The great codification dispute in 1814[44] was to inspire the creation of the Historical School[45] and resulted in Germany not acquiring a code modelled on the *Code civil*.[46] None the less it was widely accepted, from about the middle of the 19th century onwards, that a German civil code was about to come. Among the German lawyers, as Bernhard Windscheid, one of Savigny's most faithful disciples, wrote in 1878, 'there are probably relatively few who have not, with all the strength of soul available to them, yearned for the great work of a German code of private law'.[47] Obviously, these sentiments were intimately related to the fulfilment of the national aspirations of

---

[43] Wieacker, n 30 above, 257 *et seq.*

[44] The relevant texts by A. F. J. Thibaut ('Über die Notwendigkeit eines allgemeinen bürgerlichen Rechts für Deutschland' [1814]) and F. C. von Savigny ('Vom Beruf unserer Zeit für Gesetzgebung und Rechtswissenschaft' [1814]) are easily accessible in H. Hattenhauer (ed), *Thibaut und Savigny: Ihre programmatischen Schriften*, 2nd ed (Munich: Vahlen 2002). For a recent discussion (the codification dispute as a 'mythical narrative'), see Kroppenberg [2008] *Juristenzeitung* 905 *et seq.*

[45] On which, see Wieacker, n. 30 above, 279 *et seq*; T. Rüfner, 'Historical School', in MaxEuP, n 4 above, 830 *et seq.* On Roman law in 19th century Germany, see Reinhard Zimmermann, *Roman Law, Contemporary Law, European Law: The Civilian Tradition Today* (Oxford: Oxford University Press 2001) 6 *et seq.*

[46] If Friedrich Carl von Savigny argued, famously and influentially, that the time was not yet 'ripe' for enacting a codification for the German states, he was inspired by the ideal of 'completeness' of a codification: it would have to contain a system of principles and rules that would make recourse to legal sources outside of the code unnecessary; such system, however, first had to be developed by contemporary legal scholarship; and his own most important work of a doctrinal nature, 'System des heutigen Römischen Rechts' (8 vols., 1840 *et seq*), attempted to do just that. Cf also Mertens, n 15 above, 342.

[47] B. Windscheid, 'Die geschichtliche Schule in der Rechtswissenschaft' (1878), in P. Oertmann (ed), *Gesammelte Reden und Abhandlungen* (Leipzig: Duncker & Humblot 1904) 70.

the German peoples, culminating in the creation of the (second) *Reich* in 1871. The
BGB of 1900, of course, was different, in many respects, from the codifications
of the era of the law of reason: it incorporated 19th century pandectist learning, it
was based on a systematic design that differed from its predecessors,[48] and it was
drafted in more abstract conceptual language.[49] But, then, the earlier codifications
also displayed considerable differences from each other; one need only compare the
'sprung diction of the Code civil, instinct with the ideal of equality and freedom
among citizens'[50] with the caring and fatherly tone of the Austrian code (or, indeed,
with the prolix casuistry of the Prussian code).[51] In spite of the fact that it was created
under different auspices, the BGB was a true codification in the sense sketched above.

5. If the story of the codification movement is a success story (as indeed it is),
this is in spite of the fact that some of the high hopes and expectations associated
with codifications have never been fulfilled; and that a number of myths and misconceptions have occasionally surrounded their nature and effects.[52] (i) According to
Montesquieu, '[l]es lois ne doivent point être subtiles: elles sont faites pour des gens
de médiocre entendement; elles ne sont point un art de logique, mais la raison simple
d'un père de famille'.[53] Other enlightenment lawyers, some of them involved in the
drafting of the Prussian and Austrian codes, harboured similar ideals.[54] And while
the codifications significantly reduced the complexity of legal sources, and thus also
of the application of the law, they never rendered the learned lawyer redundant. Even
a comprehensive and systematic body of written law cannot be fully understood and
safely applied by a layman. This is unavoidable, given the sophistication of our legal
culture and the complexity of the modern world. (ii) The codifications are acts of legislation and thus derive their authority from the state. Unlike most individual statutes
on taxation, trade or agriculture, however, they have not been written by members of
Parliament, nor even usually by government officials, but by distinguished experts
from legal practice or legal scholarship: Portalis and his three colleagues on the editorial committee, Karl Anton Freiherr von Martini and Franz Anton Felix von Zeiller,
Gottlieb Planck and Bernhard Windscheid, Walther Munzinger and Eugen Huber,

---

[48] See J. P. Schmidt, 'Pandektensystem', in MaxEuP, n 4 above, 1238 *et seq*; R. Zimmermann, *The
Law of Obligations: Roman Foundations of the Civilian Tradition* (Oxford: Clarendon Press 1996)
29 *et seq*.

[49] On the BGB, its origin and its characteristics, see H. Haferkamp, 'Bürgerliches Gesetzbuch',
in MaxEuP, n 4 above, 120 *et seq*; R. Zimmermann, 'The German Civil Code and the Development of Private Law in Germany', in *idem, The New German Law of Obligations: Historical and
Comparative Perspectives* (Oxford: Oxford University Press 2005) 5 *et seq*.

[50] K. Zweigert and H. Kötz, *An Introduction to Comparative Law,* 3rd ed (Oxford: Clarendon Press
1998, transl Tony Weir), 144; cf also M. Weber, n 2 above, 592.

[51] Zweigert and Kötz, n 50 above, 162, 137 *et seq*.

[52] See also H. Kötz, 'Taking Civil Codes Less Seriously' (1987) 50 *Modern Law Review* 1 *et seq*
(specifically addressing misconceptions prevailing in England).

[53] Ch.-L. de Secondat Montesquieu, *De l'Espit des Lois* 1748, Liv XXXIX, Chap. 16.

[54] Mertens, n 15 above, 380 *et seq*. Some lawyers, among them Carl Gottlieb Svarez (the principal
intellectual father of the Prussian code), argued that two codifications were necessary, one of them
for judges and legal scholars, the other for the general population ('Volkskodex').

Eduard Maurits Meijers. This still holds true today, as can be seen in the preparation of the reform of the French and German law of obligations (or of Austrian liability law).[55] And just as the codes have been drafted by experts, so they need to be applied by experts.

(iii) Of course, in a number of instances, the draftsmen of the codifications managed to settle, with a stroke of their pen, deeply-rooted doctrinal disputes, and sometimes they reversed the legal position prevailing under the *ius commune* because they regarded it as unsatisfactory. Very widely, however, the codifications did not contain 'new' law, as far as the substance of the rules contained in them is concerned. They rather bore certain characteristics of a restatement, for they were supposed to incorporate, and consolidate, 'the legal achievements of centuries'.[56] As a result, they were heavily impregnated by Roman law.[57] (iv) The codifications neither (as was sometimes feared)[58] ossified the law, nor did they constitute a 'prison cell'[59] for legal scholarship. They were the products of a legal tradition largely shaped by courts and legal scholarship, and they thus provided a statutory framework for the further development of the law by courts and legal writers.[60] Often those courts and legal writers perpetuated old thinking patterns, thus establishing lines of continuity linking the old law to the new.[61] With prudent, and characteristic, modesty Bernhard Windscheid, therefore, quite rightly described a code as 'no more than a moment in the development, . . . merely a ripple in the stream'.[62]

---

[55] See Cartwright, Vogenauer and Whittaker, n 12 above; Zimmermann, n 49 above, 30 *et seq*; H. Koziol, 'Gedanken zur österreichischen Schadenersatzreform', in Bundesministerium der Justiz (ed), *200 Jahre ABGB* (2012) 307 *et seq.*

[56] Windscheid, n 47 above, 75. Cf also Behrend, n 13, 230; Mertens, n 15 above, 33 *et seq*, 51 *et seq*; Cabrillac, n 5 above, 93 *et seq*; Jansen, n 7 above, 17.

[57] For the Code civil, see J. Gordley, 'Myths of the French Civil Code' (1994) 42 *American Journal of Comparative Law* 459 *et seq*; for the ABGB, see G. E. Kodek, '200 Jahre Allgemeines Bürgerliches Gesetzbuch—das ABGB im Wandel der Zeit' [2011] *Österreichische Juristenzeitung* 491 *et seq*; for the BGB, see R. Zimmermann, 'Römisches Recht und europäische Rechtskultur' [2007] *Juristenzeitung* 3 *et seq.*

[58] See Cabrillac, n 5, 96 *et seq* ('l'effet de cristallisation').

[59] H. Wüstendörfer, 'Die deutsche Rechtswissenschaft am Wendepunkt' (1913) 110 *Archiv für die civilistische Praxis* 224.

[60] Thus, the BGB was regarded by its draftsmen as 'an organic fabric of coherent rules. The seeds for its development are inherent in the principles on which they are based': Motive, in: B. Mugdan, *Die gesammten Materialien zum Bürgerlichen Gesetzbuch für das Deutsche Reich*, vol. I (Berlin: v. Decker 1899), 365. For France, see the famous, and often quoted statement by Portalis about the 'prinçipes féconds en conséquences' which it is the task of legislation to determine: Zweigert and Kötz, n 50 above, 90. In France and Austria, it took some time before this was realized by legal scholarship; see Vogenauer n 23 above, 650; Zweigert and Kötz, n 50 above, 96 *et seq*, 161 *et seq*. In Germany, Savigny's Historical School had established a strong and fertile tradition of doctrinal legal scholarship (which also significantly influenced France, Austria and many other jurisdictions from the second half of the 19th century onwards).

[61] See Zimmermann, n 49 above, 17 *et seq.*

[62] Windscheid, n 47 above, 75 *et seq.*

(v) It is occasionally thought that the codifications of the 19th and 20th centuries are manifestations of a specifically national legal culture of the country within which they apply; and that they therefore need to be preserved as part of Europe's rich tradition of cultural diversity (rather than be sacrificed on the altar of legal unification).[63] But this is correct only to a limited extent. It is true that the civil codes prevailing today differ in a number of respects, both as far as their content and 'style'[64] are concerned. But the awareness and appreciation of these characteristics in comparative perspective does not tend to be wide-spread among the general population, and often not even among lawyers; and their contribution towards a sense of national identity tends to be limited, at best. Resistance against legal unification on a European level is due, very largely, to the conservative impulse not to see a legal instrument that has been well-tried, and that is enveloped by thick and reasonably reliable layers of case law and legal doctrine, by something unfamiliar; and, of course, to well-founded scepticism about the quality of European legislation. Also, the differences originating in the fragmentation of the civilian tradition appear to be, much more often than not, historically contingent rather than determined by cultural conditions. They are indeed, 'diversités accidentelles entre législations régissant des peuples de même civilisation'.[65] This is, perhaps, most obvious for contract law (i.e. the field of law that usually tops any legal harmonization agenda),[66] but it is true much more widely, e.g. also in the law of succession. Specific legal rules and institutions tend to be transferred, mentally, to the shrine of national cultural heritage once they have been received, and used for some time, no matter whether they originated in another nation's law.[67] The history of the holograph will can, for example, be told along these lines.[68] Finally, the *Code civil* could hardly have served as a model for the codes of so many other countries if it had been wedded to a specifically French legal culture. And indeed, quite in line with their rationalist origins, neither the *Code civil* nor the ABGB had been conceived by its draftsmen as specifically French or Austrian.[69]

---

[63] On the issue of cultural diversity, and the relationship between code and culture, see Collins, n 28 above, 124 *et seq.*

[64] Zweigert and Kötz, n 50 above, 63 *et seq.*

[65] Edouard Lambert, *Congrès international de droit comparé, Procès-verbaux des séances et documents,* vol. I (1905), 38; cf also Jansen, n 7 above, 63.

[66] Cf O. Lando, Optional or Mandatory Europeanisation of Contract Law, (2000) 8 *European Review of Private Law* 61: 'Contract Law is not folklore'.

[67] For a similar argument, see R. Michaels, n 87 below, 153.

[68] R. Zimmermann, 'Testamentsformen: "Willkür" oder Ausdruck einer Rechtskultur?' (2012) 76 *RabelsZ* 471; this is based upon the research carried out in K. Reid, M. J. de Waal and R. Zimmermann (eds), *Testamentary Formalities* (Oxford: Oxford University Press 2011). Cf also, as far as the law relating to undeserving beneficiaries is concerned, R. Zimmermann, 'Erbunwürdigkeit: Die Entwicklung eines Rechtsinstituts im Spiegel europäischer Kodifikationen', in P. Apathy et al (ed), *Festschrift für Helmut Koziol* (Wien: Sramek 2010) 463 *et seq.*

[69] W. Brauneder, 'Vernünftiges Recht als überregionales Recht: Die Rechtsvereinheitlichung der österreichischen Zivilrechtskodifikationen 1786–1797–1811', in R Schulze (ed), *Europäische Rechts- und Verfassungsgeschichte* (Berlin: Duncker & Humblot 1991) 137.

(vi) None the less, once the codifications had entered into force, they came to be regarded as comprehensive and closed systems of legal rules,[70] constituting autonomous interpretational spaces.[71] After all, they were a piece of legislation, enacted by the legislature of a specific state and applicable only within the limited territory for which that legislature was competent to lay down the law. At the same time, the codifications moved to the centre stage in legal training and legal literature and became autonomous subjects of research and teaching,[72] giving rise to an inward-looking scholarship of an almost exclusively exegetical nature. That was to lead, eventually, to the *horizontal* isolation of the national legal doctrines developing around the national legal codifications, and thus to the national fragmentation also on the level of legal scholarship, that was characteristic for large parts of the 20th century. That, in turn, stimulated the rise of comparative law.[73] However, comparative law was seen to constitute a legal sub-discipline in its own right, entirely independent of the various national legal doctrines, and it consisted of, essentially, a comparison of *legal systems*.[74] Equally, codification marked the beginning of a great age of discovery for Roman law and legal history, for legal historians could now, unaffected by any consideration of how historical sources might be applied in contemporary legal practice, devote their attention to understanding those historical sources in the context of their bygone age.[75] The downside of this was a *vertical* isolation of the national legal doctrines:[76] in spite of all the continuities mentioned earlier—they were increasingly lost sight of and faded from the general consciousness[77]—legal scholarship was no longer conceived of as a 'historical science'.

(vii) But is a 'historical legal science' still possible today? Not if one regards contemporary law as 'something new, created by the need of the present day and

---

[70] See H. Hübner, *Kodifikation und Entscheidungsfreiheit des Richters in der Geschichte des Privatrechts* (Hanstein: Königstein 1980) 67.

[71] Cf also Cabrillac, n 5, 105 ('. . . comme un univers autonome qui se suffit à lui-même').

[72] This was different with regard to the Prussian code throughout the 19th century, and to the Austrian code for the second half of the 19th century as a result of the reforms inspired by Leo Graf Thun-Hohenstein and Joseph Unger when Roman law, in its contemporary, pandectist version, was attributed the status of a general theory of private law; see, for Prussia, P. Hellwege, 'Allgemeines Landrecht für die Preußischen Staaten', in MaxEuP, n 4 above, 58 *et seq*; for Austria, W. Doralt, 'Allgemeines Bürgerliches Gesetzbuch', in MaxEuP, n 4 above, 48.

[73] See the contributions in Part I of M. Reimann and R. Zimmermann (eds), *The Oxford Handbook of Comparative Law* (Oxford: Oxford University Press 2008); R. Michaels, 'Rechtsvergleichung', in MaxEuP, n 4 above, 297 *et seq*.

[74] J. Gordley, 'Comparative Law and Legal History', in Reimann and Zimmermann, n 73 above, 761.

[75] Zimmermann, n 45 above, 22 *et seq*.

[76] Cf. also Cabrillac, n 5 above, 90 *et seq* ('l'effet de rupture').

[77] The paradox is also noted by Cabrillac, n 5 above, 93 *et seq*, who refers to '[une] perte de mémoire' and to Portalis who stated: 'Si l'on peut dire qu'il n'y a rien de nouveau parce que le présent tient toujours plus ou moins au passé, on pourra dire aussi qu'il n'y a rien d'ancien, parce que les institutions ou les coutumes les plus anciennes sont dès leur origine constamment et plus ou moins modifiées par les institutions ou par les mœurs présentes'.

the sovereign will of the modern legislature'.[78] Applying the law would then be
fundamentally different from the pre-codification era when 'a legal source expressly
anchored in history'[79] was at the centre of the *ius commune*. However, even apart from
the fact that a codification is 'but a moment in the development',[80] that moment also
lies in the past. Two of the 'modern' codifications are now more than two centuries
old, others more than one century. They are still sources of law but they are also
historical documents, created at a specific time and reflecting specific conditions and
intellectual influences. They can, therefore, only properly be understood by way of
historical analysis, taking account not only of the *travaux préparatoires* but also of
the legal position prevailing before their enactment, no matter whether they were
intended to perpetuate that position or to change it. Moreover, they have become the
basis for doctrinal developments, spanning considerable periods of time, that have
to be understood and assessed in historical perspective as well. These are the reasons
why it has been thought necessary to publish a historical commentary to the BGB.[81]
Similar endeavours concerning the other codes would be most welcome.

(viii) No modern codification satisfies the ideal of 'completeness'.[82] Of course,
there are the layers of case law and legal doctrine which anybody who wishes to apply
the law has to be thoroughly familiar with. But there are also a number of areas of the
law the development of which has taken place largely outside of the framework of the
codifications.[83] The most prominent modern example is consumer contract law. In
Germany, this tradition of excluding from the general private law codification matters
which were considered to be of a special nature dates back to the 19th century, and
neither the statute concerning instalment sales (1894) nor the one imposing strict
liability for personal injuries sustained in the operation of a railway (1871) was,
therefore, included in the code.[84] The apparently uninhibited growth of ever new
specialized sub-disciplines, and the flood of legislation dealing with specific issues,

---

[78] K. Cosack, in H. Planitz (ed), *Die Rechtswissenschaft der Gegenwart in Selbstdarstellungen,* vol.
I (Leipzig: Meiner 1924) 16.

[79] Caroni, n 3 above, 39.

[80] *Supra* n 62.

[81] M. Schmoeckel, J. Rückert and R. Zimmermann (eds), *Historisch-kritischer Kommentar zum
BGB*, vol. I (Tübingen: Mohr Siebeck 2003); vol. II (Tübingen: Mohr Siebeck, 2007); vol. III
(Tübingen: Mohr Siebeck, 2013). For the programme of that endeavour, see the foreword of the ed-
itors as well as 31 *et seq*. See further Sonja Meier, 'Historisch-kritisches Kommentieren am Beispiel
des HKK', (2011) 19 *Zeitschrift für Europäisches Privatrecht* 537 *et seq*; M. Vec, 'Flagschiffe und
Stiefkinder: Rechtsgeschichte als historische Kommentierung des geltenden Rechts', (2011) 19
Zeitschrift für Europäisches Privatrecht 547 *et seq*; cf also, in this context, F. Ranieri, 'Europäische
Rechtsgeschichte zwischen Rechtsvergleichung und Rechtsdogmatik, zugleich eine Reflexion über
den Weg zu einem Europäischen Zivilrecht', (2011) 19 *Zeitschrift für Europäisches Privatrecht* 564
et seq.

[82] *Supra* n 22.

[83] For France, see Cabrillac, n 5 above, 74 *et seq*; for Germany, see R. Stürner, 'Der hundertste
Geburtstag des BGB—eine nationale Kodifikation im Greisenalter?', [1996] *Juristenzeitung* 742.

[84] For details, see R. Zimmermann, 'Consumer Contract Law and General Contract Law', in: *idem,
The New German Law of Obligations: Historical and Comparative Perspectives* (2005), 163 *et seq*;
Mertens, n 15 above, 348.

have led some authors in the second half of the 20th century to refer to a crisis of the idea of codification,[85] or even to an age of decodification.[86] Others have attempted to explain the situation by referring to two rationalities: the 'juridical' private law that has always existed as either common law or codification, and the 'instrumentalist' private law that has almost always taken the form of specific statutes.[87] But it is anything but easy to disentangle these rationalities. Is the protection of a typically disadvantaged party an extra-legal end which is pursued by 'instrumentalist' private law? That might explain the statutes on consumer protection. But what about the rules on 'usury' or undue influence which form part of the general private law? Or what about the rules on product liability and unfair standard terms of business? In spite of having been laid down (or still being laid down) in specific statutes, they reflect concerns and policies pursued more broadly within the general civil codes. The perception of two different rationalities also appears to inspire the call for the drafting of a separate code of consumer contract law.[88] But wherever such codes have been enacted on the national level they have turned out to be mere compilations.[89] They constitute neither a comprehensive nor a systematic set of rules. The most ambitious attempt to present the existing European consumer contract law 'in a systematic and coherent fashion', the so-called *Acquis* Principles,[90] has demonstrated that the *acquis communautaire* cannot possibly be understood without reference to the traditional European private law, as we find it in the existing national legal systems (*acquis commun*).[91] An assessment of the *Acquis* Principles should thus have put an end to the oil-and-water approach that wants to perpetuate the separation between two distinctive bodies of law. What is required is a renewed effort to integrate consumer contract law into a general code of contract law: for after having been properly revised in terms of intellectual coherence as well as consistency of concepts, policies and values,[92] it could easily be subjected to a juridical rationality under the

---

[85] Wieacker, n 1 above; cf also, eg, Meder, [2006] *Juristenzeitung* 483.

[86] N. Irti, *L'età della decodificazione*, 4th ed (Milan: Giuffrè 1999); cf also F. Kübler, 'Kodifikation und Demokratie', [1969] *Juristenzeitung* 645 *et seq*; Caroni, n 3 above, 87 *et seq*; Cabrillac, n 5, 114 *et seq*; Schmidt (2009), n 4 above, 146 *et seq*. But see H. Kötz, 'Schuldrechtsüberarbeitung und Kodifikationsprinzip', in A. Dieckmann et al (ed), *Festschrift für Wolfram Müller-Freienfels* (Zurich: Schulthess 1986) 395 *et seq*; Zimmermann, n 4 above, 105 *et seq*.

[87] R. Michaels, 'Of Islands and the Ocean: The Two Rationalities of European Private Law', in R. Brownsword, H. W. Micklitz, L. Niglia and S. Weatherill (eds), *The Foundations of European Private Law* (Oxford: Hart 2011) 139 *et seq*.

[88] See, e.g., C. Wendehorst, '1811 and all that—das ABGB im Prozess europäischer Rechtsentwicklung, in *Vienna Law Inauguration Lectures*, vol. 2 (Wien: Manz 2010) 36 *et seq*.

[89] This applies to the *Code de la Consommation* in France as much as to the *Codice del Consumo* in Italy and the *Konsumentenschutzgesetz* in Austria; see H. Rösler, 'Consumer and Consumer Protection Law', in MaxEuP, n 4 above, 372.

[90] Research Group on the Existing EC Private Law (Acquis Group), Principles of the Existing EC Contract Law (Acquis Principles), Contract II (Munich, Sellier, 2009), xxiii.

[91] N. Jansen and R. Zimmermann, 'Restating the Acquis Communautaire? A Critical Examination of the "Principles of the Existing EC Contract Law"', (2008) 71 *Modern Law Review* 516 *et seq*.

[92] For a proposal, see H. Eidenmüller, F. Faust, H. C. Grigoleit, N. Jansen, G. Wagner and R. Zimmermann, *Revision des Verbraucher-acquis* (Tübingen: Mohr Siebeck 2011); for a summary in

auspices of a material notion of freedom of contract. The rules on consumer protection can thus be seen as legitimate attempts to sustain private autonomy by providing mechanisms which aim at preventing contracts from coming into existence, or from being enforced, which cannot be regarded as the result of acts of self-determination of *both* parties concerned. All the mechanisms used in this context are perfectly familiar to general private law.[93]

6. Four of the five oldest private law codifications still in existence today have recently celebrated their 200th and 100th anniversaries respectively: the *Code civil* in 2004[94] and the ABGB in 2011[95] with considerable aplomb, the Swiss ZGB (2007)[96]

English, see H. Eidenmüller, F. Faust, H. C. Grigoleit, N. Jansen, G. Wagner and R. Zimmermann, 'Towards a Revision of the Consumer Acquis', (2011) 48 *Common Market Law Review* 1077 *et seq*; cf also, eg., S. Augenhofer, 'Die Zukunft des Europäischen Verbraucherrechts und seine Bedeutung für die Weiterentwicklung des Vertrags- und Wettbewerbsrechts', in S. Grundmann (ed), *Festschrift 200 Jahre Juristische Fakultät der Humboldt-Universität zu Berlin* (Berlin: De Gruyter 2010) 1062 *et seq.*

[93] For a detailed discussion along these lines, see C.-W. Canaris, 'Wandlungen des Schuldvertragsrechts—Tendenzen zu seiner "Materialisierung"', (2000) 200 *Archiv für die civilistische Praxis* 274 *et seq*; Zimmermann, n 84 above, 205 *et seq* (for further references cf, in particular, n 461).

[94] Cf *Le Code civil 1804–2004: Livre du Bicentenaire* (Paris: Dalloz 2004); Université Pantéon-Assas (Paris II) (ed), *1804–2004, Le Code civil: Un passé, un présent, un avenir* (Paris: Dalloz 2004); D. Heirbaut and G. Martyn (eds), *Napoleons nalatenschap: Tweehonderd jaar Burgerlijk Wetboek in België* (Mechelen: Kluwer 2005); J. Dunand and B. Winiger (eds), *Le Code civil Français dans le droit européen* (Bruxelles: Brulant 2005); Alain Wijffels (ed), *Le Code civil entre ius commune et droit privé européen* (Bruxelles: Brulant 2005); W. Schubert and M. Schmoeckel (eds), *200 Jahre Code civil: Die napoleonische Kodifikation in Deutschland und Europa* (Köln: Böhlau 2005); cf also the overview by L. Pfister, 'Zweihundertjähriges Jubiläum des Code civil', (2011) 33 *Zeitschrift für Neuere Rechtsgeschichte* 241 *et seq.*

[95] Österreichischer Juristentag (ed), *Festveranstaltung Österreichischer Juristentag und Bundesministerium für Justiz 200 Jahre ABGB vom 10. November 2011* (Vienna: Manz 2012); C. Fischer-Czermak, G. Hopf, G. Kathrein and M. Schauer (eds), *Festschrift 200 Jahre ABGB* (Vienna: Manz 2011); E. Berger (ed), *Österreichs Allgemeines Bürgerliches Gesetzbuch (ABGB): Eine europäische Privatrechtskodifikation*, vol. III (Berlin: Duncker & Humblot 2010); C. Fischer-Czermak, G. Hopf, G. Kathrein and M. Schauer (eds), *ABGB 2011: Chancen und Möglichkeiten einer Zivilrechtsreform* (Vienna: Manz 2008); B. Dölemeyer and H. Mohnhaupt (eds), *200 Jahre ABGB: Die österreichische Kodifikation im internationalen Kontext* (Frankfurt: Klostermann 2012); Kodek, [2011] *Österreichische Juristenzeitung* 490 *et seq*; R. Welser, 'Verdienste und Stärken des ABGB', [2012] *Juristische Blätter* 205 *et seq*; A. Thier, '200 Jahre Allgemeines Bürgerliches Gesetzbuch', (2011) 19 *Zeitschrift für Europäisches Privatrecht* 805 *et seq.*

[96] 'Hundert Jahre schweizerisches Zivilgesetzbuch', (2008) 72 *RabelsZ* 661 *et seq*; '100 Jahre ZGB', (2007) 126 II *Zeitschrift für Schweizerisches Recht*; '100 Jahre ZGB—Der Mut zur Lücke', (2008) 26 *recht* 41 *et seq*; P. Breitschmid and T. Ansay (ed), *100 Jahre Schweizerisches ZGB, 80 Jahre Türkisches ZGB* (Berlin: Berliner Wissenschafts-Verlag 2008); J. Dunand (ed), *Le centenaire du code civil suisse* (Paris: Société de Législation Comparée 2008); Association Franco-Suisse de Paris II, *Le centenaire du Code civil suisse* (Paris: Société de Législation Comparée 2008).

and OR (2011)[97] and the German BGB (2000)[98] in a more low key manner. It was widely agreed that by and large, and in spite of the desirability of certain reforms, the national codifications have stood the test of time and have served their respective national communities well. They have turned out to be sufficiently adaptable to constitute a satisfactory basis for the contemporary administration of justice in the field of private law.[99]

The national private laws of the member states of the European Union have, however, for the past 30 years, increasingly been subjected to the legislative activities of the European Union. European private law has emerged as a distinctive discipline.[100] But the approach adopted by the European legislature has been fragmentary and incoherent. That has been criticized again and again.[101] The question of a codification was thus bound to arise also on a European level. The first protagonist of this idea was the European Parliament when it issued, in 1989, a resolution 'on action to bring into line the private law of the Member States'.[102] It is, however, generally agreed that the European Union does not have the competence to introduce a comprehensive civil code along the lines of the national codifications. Under Article 114 TFEU measures for the approximation of the national laws may be adopted, as far as they have as their object the establishment and the functioning of the internal market.

---

[97] H. Honsell, '100 Jahre Schweizerisches Obligationenrecht' (2011) 130 *Zeitschrift für Schweizerisches Recht* 5 *et seq*; P. Pichonnaz, 'Le Centenaire du Code des obligations', (2011) 130 *Zeitschrift für Schweizerisches Recht* 117 *et seq*; previously, see H. Peter, E. W. Stark and P. Tercier (eds), *Hundert Jahre Schweizerisches Obligationenrecht* (Fribourg: Universitätsverlag 1982), (i.e. celebrating the centenary of the original version of the OR).

[98] See the references in Zimmermann, n 49 above, 28. Characteristic, as far as the BGB is concerned, also the passage by Haferkamp, n 49 above, 123, entitled 'an unloved codification'. This may be contrasted with what Cabrillac, n 5 above, 102 *et seq*, writes about the 'passions amoureuses' evoked by the *Code civil*.

[99] This also comes across in the relevant entries in MaxEuP, n 4 above; cf G. Rehm, 'Code civil', in MaxEuP, n 4 above, 200 *et seq*; Doralt, n 72 above, 45 *et seq*; H.P. Haferkamp, 'Bürgerliches Gesetzbuch (BGB)' in MaxEuP, n 4 above, 120 *et seq*; K. Siehr, 'Swiss Civil Code', in MaxEuP, n 4 above, 1644 *et seq*; *idem*, 'Swiss Code of Obligations', in MaxEuP, n 4 above, 1646 *et seq*.

[100] N. Jansen, 'European Private Law', in MaxEuP, n 4 above, 637 *et seq*; R. Zimmermann, 'Comparative Law and the Europeanization of Private Law', in Reimann and Zimmermann, n 73 above, 539 *et seq*.—This paper, in line with its historical character, focuses on codifications in the field of private law (and, under 7., on the question of a European Civil Code). For an insightful analysis of codification as a proposition for private international law on a European level, see A. M. E. Firrini, 'Qu'y a-t-il en un nom?: Un vrai code pour le droit international privé européen', in M. Fallon, P. Lagarde and S. Poillot-Peruzzetto (eds), *Quelle architecture pour un code européen de droit international privé?* (Bruxelles: Lang 2011) 27 *et seq*.

[101] *Inter alia* by the European Commission itself: 'Communication from the Commission to the European Parliament and Council, A More Coherent European Contract Law: An Action Plan', COM (2003) 68 final. For comprehensive criticism of the *acquis communautaire* in private law, see also Collins, n 28 above, 28 *et seq*.

[102] 'Resolution of the European Parliament of May 26, 1989 on action to bring into line the private laws of the Member States', OJ 1989 C 158, 400; cf also the contributions to A. Hartkamp, M. Hesselink, E. Hondius, C. Mak and E. du Perron (eds), *Towards a European Civil Code*, 4th ed (Alphen aan den Rijn: Wolters Kluwer 2011); M. Schmidt-Kessel, 'European Civil Code', in MaxEuP, n 4 above, 553 *et seq*; Jansen and Rademacher, n 4 above.

Such measures, arguably, include a codification of contract law.[103] It is not surprising, therefore, that this is the field on which the European Commission has focused its attention. A sequence of Communications was issued, first floating the idea of a codification of European contract law and then rejecting it, vacillating between a revision of the consumer *acquis* and the preparation of a document encompassing general contract law, sales contracts and insurance contracts, and introducing the notions of a Common Frame of Reference, an Optional Instrument, and a 'toolbox' for future action in the field of European contract law.[104] Ultimately, a two-pronged approach was adopted. On the one hand, a Consumer Rights Directive was issued on 25 October 2011.[105] It does not, of course, constitute a European consumer code, nor even a comprehensive compilation, but a fairly unambitious consolidation of two of the previously existing directives.[106] On the other hand, a Proposal for a Regulation on a Common European Sales Law was published on 11 October 2011.[107] This is a much more significant step which has already unleashed a barrage of publications.[108]

---

[103] J. Basedow, 'A common contract law for the common market', (1996) 33 *Common Market Law Review* 1187. It does not, incidentally, include the enactment of the optional instrument in the field of contract law that is presently contemplated by the European Commission; see Max Planck Institute for Comparative and International Private Law (MPI): 'Policy Options for Progress Towards a European Contract Law', (2011) 75 *RabelsZ* 386 *et seq.*

[104] See the contributions by S. Weatherill, M. J. Bonell, T. Wilhelmsson, B. Lurger and R. Zimmermann, in *4th European Jurists' Forum, Proceedings* (Vienna: Manz 2008), 3 *et seq*, 85 *et seq*, 111 *et seq*, 175 *et seq*, 185 *et seq.*

[105] Directive 2011/83/EU OJ 2011 L 304/64. For comment, see C. Wendehorst, 'Die neue Richtlinie über die Rechte der Verbraucher', in B. Schenk et al (ed), *Festschrift für Irmgard Griss* (Vienna: Sramek 2011) 717 *et seq*; E. Hall, G. Howells and J. Watson, 'The Consumer Rights Directive: An Assessment of its Contribution to the Development of European Consumer Contract Law', (2012) 8 *European Review of Contract Law* 139 *et seq*; O. Unger, 'Die Richtlinie über die Rechte der Verbraucher—Eine systematische Einführung', (2012) 20 *Zeitschrift für Europäisches Privatrecht* 270 *et seq.*

[106] For criticism and discussion of the previously intended, more comprehensive approach, based on the strategy of maximum harmonization, see B. Jud and C. Wendehorst (eds), *Neuordnung des Verbraucherprivatrechts in Europa* (Vienna: Manz 2009); G. Howells and R. Schulze (eds), *Modernising and Harmonising Consumer Contract Law* (Munich: Sellier 2009); B. Gsell and C. Herresthal (eds), *Vollharmonisierung im Privatrecht* (Tübingen: Mohr Siebeck 2009); M. Stürner (ed), *Vollharmonisierung im europäischen Verbraucherrecht?* (Munich: Sellier 2010).

[107] COM(2011) 635 final. The Common European Sales Law will be abbreviated CESL, the Draft submitted by the Commission DCESL. The DCESL has been published as Annex I to the Proposal for a Regulation on a Common European Sales Law (PR CESL).

[108] R. Zimmermann, 'Perspektiven des künftigen österreichischen und europäischen Zivilrechts: Zum Verordnungsvorschlag über ein Gemeinsames Europäisches Kaufrecht', [2012] *Juristische Blätter* 2 *et seq*; H. Eidenmüller, N. Jansen, E.-M. Kieninger, G. Wagner and R. Zimmermann, 'Der Vorschlag für eine Verordnung über ein Gemeinsames Europäisches Kaufrecht', [2012] *Juristenzeitung* 269 *et seq*; H. Schulte-Nölke, F. Zoll, N. Jansen and R. Schulze (eds), *Der Entwurf für ein optionales europäisches Kaufrecht* (Munich: Sellier 2012); O. Remien, S. Herrler and P. Limmer (eds), *Gemeinsames Europäisches Kaufrecht für die EU?* (Munich: Beck 2012); M. Schmidt-Kessel, *Ein einheitliches europäisches Kaufrecht?* (Munich: Sellier 2012); C. Wendehorst and B. Zöchling-Jud, *Am Vorabend eines Gemeinsamen Europäischen Kaufrechts* (Vienna: Manz 2012); B. Fauvarque-Cosson, 'Vers un droit commun européen de la vente', (2012) 188 *Recueil Dalloz* 34

This is not the right place to provide a critical assessment of the proposed Regulation and of the DCESL appended to it, save perhaps to state that the latter is not a codification in the sense described above.[109] For it is not intended to replace the previous law, i.e. the national legal rules on contract law, but to take its place next to them, as a second set of rules within the legal system of each of the EU's member states that may be chosen by the parties to a contract.[110] Moreover, it is not comprehensive, for the Regulation itself mentions a number of matters to which the national law designated by the relevant rules on private international law remains applicable. These matters include illegality and immorality, representation, plurality of debtors and creditors, assignment, and set-off.[111] None the less, the DCESL may be the nucleus of a European code of contract law properly so called, and perhaps even of a European Civil Code,[112] and thus it may be appropriate to assess its chances of success against the background of the historical experiences gathered with respect to the idea of codification on a national level. We will first consider the arguments that have, in the past, been advanced in favour of codifications of private law[113] and then look at other factors that have contributed to their success.

7. (i) A forceful argument in favour of codification has usually been the reduction of the complexity of legal sources. The European legal landscape today, however, looks neat and tidy when compared to that prevailing under the *ius commune*. There are, admittedly, close to 30 legal systems that may be applicable to a transnational

---

et seq; the contributions in [2012] *Revue des contrats* 191 *et seq*; 'Trenta giuristi europei sull'idea di codice europeo dei contratti', [2012] 1 *Contratto e Impresa/Europa (numero speciale)*; and see the contributions by A. Stadler, S. Grundmann, B. Zöchling-Jud, D. Looschelders and S. Lorenz to the conference of the *Zivilrechtslehrervereinigung* in (2012) 212 *Archiv für die civilistische Praxis* 467 *et seq*.

[109] Generally on the phenomenon of 'transjurisdictional codifications', see J. Basedow, 'Transjurisdictional Codification', (2009) 83 *Tulane Law Review* 974 *et seq* (pointing out that there is no such thing, so far, and stating, in particular, that the Convention on Contracts for the International Sale of Goods [CISG] is no codification in the sense outlined above). Cf also Jansen and Rademacher, n 4 above, *sub* 2 ('None of [the standard features of a civil code] may be taken for granted in respect of a European Civil Code').

[110] See Recital 10 to the PR CESL; for comment, see MPI, n 103 above, 400 *et seq*; Matteo Fornasier, '"28." versus "2. Regime"—Kollisionsrechtliche Aspekte eines optionalen europäischen Vertragsrechts', (2012) 76 *RabelsZ* 401 *et seq*; Eidenmüller, Jansen, Kieninger, Wagner and Zimmermann, [2012] *Juristenzeitung* 273 *et seq*; A. Stadler, 'Anwendungsvoraussetzungen und Anwendungsbereich des Common European Sales Law' (CESL), (2012) 212 *Archiv für die civilistische Praxis* 473 *et seq*.

[111] Recital 27 to the PR CESL. But there are even more gaps; see Zimmermann, [2012] *Juristische Blätter* 9. On the problem of gap-filling, see MPI, n 10 above, 409 *et seq*.

[112] This is the ambition of the draftsmen of the 'Draft Common Frame of Reference'; see N. Jansen and R. Zimmermann, '"A European Civil Code in All But Name": Discussing the Nature and Purposes of the Draft Common Frame of Reference', (2010) 69 *Cambridge Law Journal* 98 *et seq*.

[113] For a detailed analysis concerning the first wave of codifications, see P. A. J. van den Berg, *The Politics of European Codification: A History of the Unification of Law in France, Prussia, the Austrian Monarchy and the Netherlands* (Gronigen: Europa Law Publishers 2007). This analysis provides the basis for the first four of the following points. Cf. also Jansen and Rademacher, n 4 above, *sub* 1.

legal dispute. But the conflict rules have, in important areas, been unified[114] and, as a result, the same substantive law will prevail wherever a dispute is litigated. Determination of the rules of a foreign legal system will not be easy,[115] and a unification also of the substantive law will, therefore, entail practical advantages. But unlike under the *ius commune* it is not unclear which legal rules have to be applied.[116] This also takes care of the closely related argument of legal certainty to be established, or at least advanced, by way of codification.[117] The contrary may be true here, for the promulgation of a European codification would, for the foreseeable future and until the European Court of Justice has established Union-wide interpretative standards, have a distinctly unsettling effect.[118] Also, legal proceedings would neither become fewer in number, nor be shortened.

(ii) Some of the older codifications served what may be termed a 'constitutional' function: they were supposed to provide citizens with certainty about their rights and duties within, and vis-à-vis, the State. At the same time, they established the civil freedoms as well as many other essential principles characterizing our private laws until today: the freedom of contract and of testation, the recognition of private property, equality before the law, etc. This was done particularly emphatically in the *Code civil*,[119] but was noticeable also to a greater or lesser extent in the other codes. Today, the national constitutions largely discharge this function; after all, they no longer merely deal with the organization of the state, as they did in the 19th century, but usually contain a catalogue of basic rights. On a supranational level in Europe we have the European Convention on Human Rights as well as the Charter of Fundamental Rights that is referred to in Article 6 (1) of the Treaty of the European Union; we therefore no longer need a civil code for this specific purpose.[120]

---

[114] See the Rome I (contractual obligations), Rome II (non-contractual obligations), Rome III (divorce and legal separation) Regulations and the Proposal for a Regulation concerning the law of succession: R. Schulze and R. Zimmermann (eds), *Europäisches Privatrecht: Basistexte*, 4th ed (Baden-Baden: Nomos 2012) I.90-I.105. (The proposal has, in the meantime, become the EU Succession Regulation of 2012).

[115] Cf, eg, Ole Lando, 'Principles of European Contract Law and UNIDROIT Principles: Moving from Harmonisation to Unification?', (2003) 8 *Uniform Law Review* 124 *et seq.*

[116] Cf also Jansen, n 7 above, 66.

[117] Cabrillac, n 5 above, 68 *et seq*, 136 *et seq.*

[118] Eidenmüller, Jansen, Kieninger, Wagner and Zimmermann, [2012] *Juristenzeitung* 286; J. Cartwright, "'Choice is good." Really?', (2011) 7 *European Review of Contract Law* 347.

[119] Van den Berg, n 113 above, 28 *et seq* subsumes this under the heading of the 'political-theoretical' argument in favour of codification; cf also P. Malaurie, Les dix premières années de notre siècle et le droit civil, [2010] *La Semaine Juridique* 781; Cabrillac, n 5 above, 104; Basedow, (2009) 83 Tulane Law Review 985.—For a modern constitutionalist argument in favour of a civil code, see Collins, n 28 above, 91 *et seq.*

[120] At least not a civil code in the sense in which the term is normally—and also presently—understood. A 'civil code' in the sense of an 'economic constitution' along the lines envisaged by Collins, n 28 above, 91 *et seq* is quite a different matter and may, indeed, be a useful device to contribute towards 'an integrated transnational civil society out of which a common European identity could be constructed', 2.

(iii) The enactment of private law codifications often either followed closely on the heels of the creation of a modern state and thus constituted an expression of its sovereignty and a symbol of its national unity, or was intended to contribute towards cultural homogeneity and a national consciousness. The European Union is not a nation state, nor even a state; it is an international organization *sui generis*.[121] A codification of European private law can be seen as part of a process of state formation, just as a Union citizenship or symbols such as an anthem or a flag.[122] This, in fact, is what many observers fear: a European code will have a highly symbolic significance and thus, in a way, substitute for the failure of the project of a Constitutional Treaty.[123] Given the prevailing mood among the citizens and governments of the EU member states, any argument in favour of a codification of European law based on such practical-political consideration—historically the 'practical-political' considerations were the most influential ones[124]—is likely to be counterproductive: statehood on the European level is not as fervently desired as it was in 19th century Germany or Italy; nor does it arouse the kind of patriotism characteristic of revolutionary or post-revolutionary France. It should also be noted that a CESL will have to be published in the 23 official languages of the European Union, all of them possessing the same binding force. While this will give rise to considerable difficulties in the application of a uniform European codification,[125] it is also a poignant reminder that—unlike with the national codifications[126]—language cannot, on a European level, serve the function of a cultural glue. There is no European vernacular.[127]

(iv) It has usually been argued that a codification of private law, and in particular contract law, will facilitate trade and thus be beneficial to the economy. This is, in fact, the main reason advanced by the European Commission in favour of a CESL: it is to improve the functioning of the internal market by facilitating cross-border trade. By subjecting contracts to a uniform legal regime, it should be possible for

---

[121] N. Colneric, 'European Union', in MaxEuP, n 4 above, 641 *et seq.*

[122] Van den Berg (n. 113), 277 who concludes his book with the following statement: 'Is the project of a European codification part of a process of state formation after all? This Study makes clear that this is at least a possibility', 278; cf. also Jansen, n 7 above, 14.

[123] N. Colneric, 'European Constitution', MaxEuP, n 4 above, 572 *et seq.*—For the ideological link between the Constitutional Treaty and a European civil code (though one conceived as an 'Economic Constitution'), see Collins, n 28 above, *15 et seq. 91 et seq.*

[124] Van den Berg, n 113 above, 23 *et seq,* 273.

[125] MPI, (2011) 75 RabelsZ 431 *et seq.*

[126] The Swiss codification constitutes an exception in view of the four official languages recognized in Switzerland. The Austrian code also had to be translated into a number of different languages in order to take account of the different nationalities united under the Habsburg crown; see W. Brauneder, 'Gesetzgebungslehre und Kodifikationspraxis am Beispiel des ABGB', in Dölemeyer and Mohnhaupt, n 95 above, 38.

[127] T. Weir, 'Die Sprachen des europäischen Rechts: Eine skeptische Betrachtung', (1995) 3 *Zeitschrift für Europäisches Privatrecht* 368 *et seq.* Cf also Collins, n 28 above, 142 *et seq,* urging to resist '[the] temptation to devise a European Civil Code in one language'.—The English that is in the process of informally acquiring the status of a modern *lingua Franca* will never have the same culturally homogenizing effect as, eg, French for France. On the use of English cf also, in the present context, the remarks in [2007] *Neue Juristische Wochenschrift* 3332 *et seq.*

businesses to lower their transaction costs.[128] This is a plausible argument, though it is not as strong as is often made out.[129] Tax laws, language problems, licensing and registration requirements and, particularly, the difficulties involved in litigating cases and enforcing judgments in other jurisdictions are at least as significant as the transaction costs caused by differing contract laws.[130] Also, a number of examples can be given of countries where differing contract laws hardly appear to be perceived as a trade barrier; English and Scots law provide an instructive example.[131] Finally, the DCESL seems to be intended mainly for electronic trading,[132] where special goodwill practices and reputational mechanisms considerably reduce the practical relevance of the legal regime.[133]

(v) If we now turn our attention to other factors that have contributed to the success of the national codifications we must note, in the first place, that their preparation usually took a long time and/or was facilitated by the existence of a well-established and well-documented legal doctrine. Pandectist legal scholarship, as expounded by Bernhard Windscheid and other writers, provided the basis for the BGB; none the less, it took 22 years to prepare the code.[134] The history of the Austrian codification reaches back to 1753 and thus extends over 58 years;[135] the process was decisively advanced by Freiherr von Martini, who could draw upon generations of learning on Roman law, more recently neatly dressed up in Natural law's clothing.[136] Walther Munzinger's[137] Swiss Code of Obligations was only 13 years in the making, but could be based upon Johann Caspar Bluntschli's[138] Code of Private Law of Zurich as well as upon the so-called Dresden Draft for a law of obligations. The preparation

---

[128] 'Explanatory Memorandum PR CESL' sect. 1; 'Communication from the Commission to the European Parliament, the Council, the European Economic and Social Committee and the Committee of the Regions: A Common European Sales Law to facilitate cross-border transactions in the single market', COM(2011) 636 final, section 1. For critical comment, see Collins, n 28, 63 *et seq.*

[129] According to two 'eurobarometer' surveys, the differing legal regimes do not, in the opinion of a large majority of businesses, constitute significant obstacles to crossborder trade: eurobarometers 320 and 321 (both from 2011), as referred to by Eidenmüller, Jansen, Kieninger, Wagner and Zimmermann, [2012] *Juristenzeitung* 286.

[130] Eidenmüller, Jansen, Kieninger, Wagner and Zimmermann, [2012] *Juristenzeitung* 286.

[131] T. Weir, 'Divergent Legal Systems in a Single Member State', (1998) 6 *Zeitschrift für Europäisches Privatrecht* 564 *et seq.*

[132] See, e.g., Recital 26 PR CESL.

[133] Walter Doralt, 'Rote Karte oder grünes Licht für den Blue Button? Zur Frage eines optionalen europäischen Vertragsrechts', (2011) 211 *Archiv für die civilistische Praxis* 24 *et seq.*

[134] Overview in Haferkamp n 99 above, 120 *et seq*; Zimmermann, n 49 above, 12 *et seq.*

[135] Overview in Doralt, n 72 above, 46.

[136] Including, of course, the textbooks he had written himself. Martini was Professor of Natural Law, Institutions (of Roman Law) and Roman Legal History at the University of Vienna. For details, particularly also on his activities as a legal author, see M. Hebeis, *Karl Anton von Martini (1726–1800): Leben und Werk* (Lang 1996).

[137] On Munzinger, see U. Fasel, 'Walther Munzinger—Vorbereiter der Schweizer Rechtseinheit', (2003) 11 *Zeitschrift für Europäisches Privatrecht* 345 *et seq.*

[138] On Bluntschli, see T. Bühler, 'J. C. Bluntschli', (2009) 17 *Zeitschrift für Europäisches Privatrecht* 91 *et seq.*

of the *Code civil* took hardly more than ten years, but its true fathers were authors whose works date from much earlier, particularly Jean Domat and Robert-Joseph Pothier.[139] The DCESL, by contrast, has been prepared in great haste (within a mere 1 ½ years)[140] and is based, apart from the international Sales Convention, upon sets of model rules (Principles of European Contract Law, UNIDROIT Principles of International Commercial Contracts, *Acquis* Principles, Principles of European Law on Sales and Service Contracts, and Draft Common Frame of Reference)[141] that had been published only relatively recently and have not, so far, been subjected to rigorous scrutiny from an academic or practical point of view.

(vi) The national codes were thus manifestations of a tradition of legal scholarship; with reference to the BGB, it has even been said that 'the code does not contain the source of law in itself but in the legal scholarship from which it was created'.[142] As a consequence, the codifications were also designed in a way that left room for further scholarly development of the law.[143] The DCESL, on the other hand, is hardly embedded in a similarly strong tradition of a genuinely European

---

[139] See Rehm, n 99 above, 201 *et seq*; on the *Ordonnances* as precursors of French legal unity, see G. Rehm, 'Ordonnances' in MaxEuP, n 4 above, 1226 *et seq*.

[140] The 'Expert Group' charged with the drafting of the DCESL was set up at the end of April 2010 (Commission Decision 2010/233/EU of 26th April 2010, OJEC 2010 L 105/109) and produced a 'Feasibility Study for a future instrument in European Contract Law' at the beginning of May 2011; that Feasibility Study served as the basis for the DCESL, published in October 2011.

[141] Part III of the *Principles of European Contract Law* (= PECL; eds Ole Lando, Eric Clive, André Prüm, Reinhard Zimmermann) was published in 2003, the second edition of the *Acquis Principles* (n 90 above) appeared in 2009 (first edition 2007), the *Principles of European Law* of the Study Group on a European Civil Code on *Sales* (= PELS; eds Ewoud Hondius, Viola Heutger, Christoph Jeloschek, Hanna Sivesand and Aneta Wiewiorowska) in 2008 and on *Service Contracts* (eds Maurits Barendrecht, Chris Jansen, Marco Loos, Andrea Pinna, Rui Cascão and Stéphanie van Gulijk) in 2007, the *Draft Common Frame of Reference* (eds Christian von Bar and Eric Clive) in 2008 (Interim Outline Edition) and 2009 (Full Edition), the new and extended version of the *UNIDROIT Principles of International Commercial Contracts* (ed UNIDROIT) in 2011 (the previous, second version in 2004). For the details, see Reinhard Zimmermann, 'The Present State of European Private Law', (2009) 57 *American Journal of Comparative Law* 479 *et seq*; idem, 'Europäisches Privatrecht—Irrungen, Wirrungen', in *Begegnungen im Recht—Ringvorlesung zu Ehren von Karsten Schmidt* (Tübingen: Mohr Siebeck 2011) 322 *et seq*.—On the nature of these instruments as 'non-legislative codifications', see Jansen, n 7 above, 59 *et seq*.

[142] H. H. Jakobs, *Wissenschaft und Gesetzgebung im bürgerlichen Recht nach der Rechtsquellenlehre des 19. Jahrhunderts* (Paderborn: Schöningh 1983) 160.

[143] This had not always been the approach adopted by the draftsmen of the age of Enlightenment. The Prussian code is notorious for its 'passion for completeness and comprehensiveness' (Zweigert and Kötz, n 50 above, 137; Zweigert and Kötz also quote Wolfgang Kunkel's *dictum* that the Code was a 'monstrous anti-intellectual undertaking'; but this may be a modern exaggeration that does not do justice to the intentions of the code's draftsmen: see Mertens, n 15 above, 287 *et seq*; Hellwege, n 72 above, 58) and for its prohibition against taking account of legal doctrine so as not to 'corrupt' the law by means of 'independent' interpretation (on the tradition of such provisions, see H.-J. Becker, 'Kommentier- und Auslegungsverbot', in Erler [ed], *Handwörterbuch zur deutschen Rechtsgeschichte*, n 4 above, 963 *et seq*). Similar sentiments prevailed, initially, in Austria, the distrust against judicial interpretation, let alone development, of the law also in France; see Hübner, n 70 above, 27 *et seq*; M. Miersch, *Der sogenannte référé législatif* (Baden: Nomos 2000); Cabrillac, n 5 above, 107 *et seq*. For Italy, see A. Braun, 'Professors and Judges in Italy: It Takes Two to Tango', (2006) 26 *Oxford Journal of Legal Studies* 671 *et seq*.

legal scholarship. Hein Kötz's pionieering book on European Contract Law only dates from 1996;[144] and while much has been achieved since then,[145] the national legal systems still constitute the primary objects of legal scholarship today. Contract law is probably the field with the most far-reaching pre-existing common ground, but even here there are issues with unresolved conceptual divergences, such as assignment, representation, or plurality of debtors,[146] which have been regarded as unfit for inclusion in the DCESL. The tensions between *acquis communautaire* and *acquis commun* continue to persist,[147] and there have also been repeated shifts in the systematic design of European rules on contract law.[148] In most other fields of private law a codificatory consolidation appears to be unimaginable, given the scarcity of scholarly groundwork.[149]

(vii) Apart from legal scholarship and the legislature, the courts have always been protagonists of legal development in Europe. The *ius commune* was a 'learned', i.e. scholarly, law but it was also a *jurisprudentia forensis*.[150] Part of the success of the traditional codes is due to the fact that strong and centralized Supreme Courts were in place to ensure the uniform application, on the national level, of the uniform law. The French *Cour de cassation* dates back to the legislation of the French Revolution,[151]

---

[144] H. Kötz, *Europäisches Vertragsrecht*, vol. I (1996) (dealing, however, only with formation, validity, and content of contracts, as well as with contract and third parties); vol. II (on non-performance and remedies for non-performance, and to be written by another author) has not, to date, appeared.

[145] For an overview, see Zimmermann, n 100 above, 548 *et seq.*

[146] On representation, see D. Moser, *Die Offenkundigkeit der Stellvertretung im deutschen und englischen Recht sowie in den internationalen Regelungsmodellen* (Tübingen: Mohr Siebeck 2010), J. Kleinschmidt, 'Representation', in MaxEuP, n 4 above, 1455 *et seq*; on assignment, see E.-M. Kieninger, 'Das Abtretungsrecht des DCFR', (2010) 18 *Zeitschrift für Europäisches Privatrecht* 724 *et seq*, H. Kötz, 'Assignment', in MaxEuP, n 4 above, 75 *et seq*; on plurality of debtors, see S. Meier, 'Schuldnermehrheiten im europäischen Vertragsrecht', (2011) 211 *Archiv für die civilistische Praxis* 435 *et seq*; eadem, 'Solidary Obligations', in MaxEuP, n 4 above, 1573 *et seq.*

[147] Jansen and Zimmermann, (2008) 71 *Modern Law Review* 505 *et seq.*

[148] Thus, the DCFR saw contract law as an integral part of a law of obligations; this decision has, in the meantime, been reversed (Feasibility Study and DCESL). The most surprising structural peculiarity of the DCESL consists in its part IV, entitled 'Obligations and remedies of the parties to a sales contract . . .'; for details and criticism, see Eidenmüller, Jansen, Kieninger, Wagner and Zimmermann, [2012] Juristenzeitung 272; cf also M. Storme, (2011) 19 *European Review of Private Law* 343 ('. . . the main step backwards').

[149] See N. Jansen, *Binnenmarkt, Privatrecht und europäische Identität* (Tübingen: Mohr Siebeck 2004); Zimmermann, (2009) 57 *American Journal of Comparative Law* 494 *et seq.*

[150] H. Coing, *Europäisches Privatrecht*, vol. I (Munich: Beck 1985), 124 *et seq*; for further references, see R. Zimmermann, 'Roman-Dutch Jurisprudence and its Contribution to European Private Law', (1992) 66 *Tulane Law Review* 1712.

[151] The *Cour de cassation* is special insofar as its task was originally to see to it that the courts did not deviate from the text of the *Code civil*; even interpreting a provision of the code was regarded as such deviation. But, in view of the fact that the text of the *Code civil* itself eventually recognized the need for, and legitimacy of, judicial interpretation, the *Cour de cassation* gradually took over the task of interpreting the code and of reversing judgments of the lower courts not because they had interpreted the code but because they had interpreted it wrongly: Zweigert and Kötz, n 50 above, 120.

the Austrian *Oberster Gerichtshof* was the successor of Maria Theresia's *Oberste Justizstelle*, created in 1749 as part and parcel of the formation of the Austrian state,[152] the modern Federal Court (*Bundesgericht*) for Switzerland was established in 1875, the German *Reichsgericht* in 1879. Within the European Union, of course, we have the European Court of Justice. It has to ensure that the law is observed in the interpretation and application of the European treaties and of the Union's secondary laws. It is no longer merely the Constitutional Court of the European Union,[153] for, with the increase of secondary legislation, it has had to answer more and more questions in all kinds of legal fields, including contract law. But it would not, in its present structure, be able to cope with the flood of requests for preliminary rulings that would result from the enactment of a CESL. A fundamental reform of the European court structure would thus appear to be necessary for a comprehensive act of legislation in the field of private law to stand any chance of success.[154]

(viii) 'It is difficult to deny', writes Nils Jansen,[155] 'that private law is in fact largely autonomous [vis-à-vis] political decision-making'. This is one of the reasons why codifications of private law have been written 'by commissions of scholars and other legal experts'. That is also true of the DCESL which has been prepared by an 'Expert Group'.[156] But that group has operated, from the outset, under unfortunate auspices.[157] The selection of its members was subject to considerable criticism;[158] it was given much too little time to accomplish its task and was, moreover, for a long time left in the dark about what task exactly it was supposed to accomplish; it was chaired by an official of the European Commission; and it was not really independent but had to follow, at crucial junctures, directions by the Commission. These factors will not enhance the inclination of the legal community (or rather: the

---

[152] E. Bruckmüller, 'Über die Lage der Habsburgermonarchie in den Jahrzehnten zwischen Maria Theresia und Metternich in Hinblick auf die Kodifikation des ABGB', in Dölemeyer and Mohnhaupt, n 95 above, 11.

[153] But see J. Pirrung, 'European Court of Justice', in MaxEuP, n 4 above, 583 *et seq.*

[154] MPI, (2011) 75 *RabelsZ* 434; J Basedow, 'The Court of Justice and Private Law: Vacillations, General Principles and the Architecture of the European Judiciary', (2010) 18 *European Review of Private Law* 443 *et seq.*

[155] Jansen, n 7 above, 4.

[156] For a list of its members, see 'Einsetzung einer Expertengruppe für einen gemeinsamen Referenzrahmen im Bereich des europäischen Vertragsrechts', (2010) 18 *Zeitschrift für Europäisches Privatrecht* 955.

[157] For details, see Zimmermann, 'Irrungen and Wirrungen', n 141 above, 338 *et seq.* The insider's story is presented by H. Schulte-Nölke, 'Vor- und Entstehungsgeschichte des Vorschlags für ein Gemeinsames Europäisches Kaufrecht', in Schulte-Nölke, Zoll, Jansen and Schulze, n 108 above, 1 *et seq.*

[158] J. Basedow, H. Eidenmüller, C. Grigoleit, S. Grundmann, N. Jansen, E.-M. Kieninger, H.-P. Mansel, W.-H. Roth, G. Wagner and R. Zimmermann, 'Ein europäisches Privatrecht kommt—aber zu welchem Preis?', *Frankfurter Allgemeine Zeitung* of 1 July 2010, 8; K. Riesenhuber, 'A Competitive Approach to EU Contract Law', (2011) 7 *European Review of Contract Law* 123 *et seq*; W. Doralt, 'Strukturelle Schwächen in der Europäisierung des Privatrechts', (2011) 75 *RabelsZ* 270 *et seq*; S. Grundmann, 'Kosten und Nutzen eines Europäischen Optionalen Kaufrechts,' (2012) 212 *Archiv für die civilistische Praxis* 530 *et seq.*

various national legal communities) to accept the DCESL as a text emulating the existing national codifications in respectability.

8. All in all, therefore, the auspices for a European Code of Contract Law, let alone a Civil Code, are far from ideal. There is no common language in which it could be drafted. There is no Supreme Court in private law matters which could effectively ensure its uniform application. There is not yet a sufficiently strong European legal scholarship that could sustain it. Some arguments can be advanced in favour of a European code but they are fairly weak, and they lack any emotional appeal. In particular, there is not yet a strong feeling of European identity (comparable to the feeling of national identity in the 19th century) that would give wings to such endeavour. And there is no sense of crisis that would make a codification appear indispensable.

At the same time the task to be accomplished is much more difficult than it was with any of the codifications in the past. A European code will have to encompass about thirty so far largely autonomous legal systems. Among them will be, for the first time, the English common law that is widely perceived to be very different from the continental tradition[159] and that has, so far, been hostile to the idea of codification.[160] Draftsmen of a European codification cannot resort to a well-established European legal doctrine but only to untested model rules of an academic nature. A codification of the law of torts/delict, unjustified enrichment,[161] or property law appears to be inconceivable today. There is not enough common ground on a structural and conceptual level, and no agreement as to which of the various solutions found in the member states of the European Union is superior. The only fields in which a codification is at least imaginable are general contract law and the law of sales. But even here there are considerable difficulties. The *acquis communautaire* is in poor shape. There is no masterplan as to how to integrate the *acquis communautaire* with the *acquis commun*. As to the latter, a comparison of the various sets of model rules reveals that in spite of much common ground there are also many differences in detail. There has been no concerted effort to assess these differences in comparative perspective.[162] Instead, one revision has followed the other with no explanation as to

---

[159] I do not share that perception; see, e.g., R. Zimmermann, 'Der europäische Charakter des englischen Rechts: Historische Verbindungen zwischen civil law und common law,' (1993) 1 *Zeitschrift für Europäisches Privatrecht* 4 *et seq*; idem, 'Roman Law and the Harmonization of Private Law in Europe', in: Towards a European Civil Code', n 102 above, 42 *et seq*. But *perceptions* also matter!

[160] For an attempt to correct misconceptions prevailing in England about codifications, see Kötz, n 52 above, 1 *et seq*; cf also Cabrillac, n 5 above, 45 *et seq* (codification not 'foncièrement incompatible' with the common law); Collins, n 28 above, 170 *et seq*. M. Bussani, on the other hand, calls on the civilian lawyers to rally around the project of a European Civil Code: 'A Streetcar Named Desire: The European Civil Code in the Global Legal Order', (2009) 83 *Tulane Law Review* 1083 *et seq*.

[161] For the law relating to *negotiorum gestio*, see N. Jansen, 'Negotiorum Gestio and Benevolent Intervention in Another's Affairs: Principles of European Law?', (2007) 15 *Zeitschrift für Europäisches Privatrecht* 958 *et seq*.

[162] For three specific areas, see N. Jansen and R. Zimmermann, 'Contract Formation and Mistake in European Contract Law: A Genetic Comparison of Transnational Model Rules', (2011) 31 *Oxford Journal of Legal Studies* 625 *et seq*; R. Zimmermann, 'Die Auslegung von Verträgen: Textstufen transnationaler Modellregelungen', in R. Richardi et al (eds), *Festschrift für Eduard Picker* (Tübingen: Mohr Siebeck 2010), 1353 *et seq*.

why certain choices have been made or certain changes have been implemented. It now appears to be widely acknowledged that the DCFR project was an overambitious aberration,[163] and thus the wheel has been pulled round again. Whether, in view of the complex interactions between contract law, torts/delict, and unjustified enrichment, a codification confined to contract law is practicable, is another unresolved issue.[164]

The European Commission is now proposing what it regards as the least intrusive solution: the enactment of an optional instrument that will have to prove its mettle in legal practice. But even this proposal entails dangers,[165] at least if the optional instrument is as full of gaps and difficulties of application, and as immature in its substance, as the DCESL is.[166] And it raises the question whether European legal harmonization has to be brought about by way of legislation. Implicit in this is an inquiry as to whether private law can be conceived without, or beyond, the state.[167] This is all the more pertinent in view of the fact that before the age of codification, for obvious reasons, private law and its validity were not connected with the idea of the sovereign state's control over the law.[168] The *ius commune* was a kind of common law developed by courts and legal writers on the basis of a body of legal rules that had come to be *usu receptum*. It had an inherent flexibility and potential for adaptation and development.[169] And since its validity was not confined by political borders, it was constitutive of, and sustained by, a European legal scholarship. The English common law, developed within a state that had been centralized at an early stage, has also not been 'enacted' by any ruler, but was developed predominantly by the courts (and also, from time to time and, since the 19th century increasingly, by legal writers). In the United States we have the 'Restatements' which have rendered a significant contribution to the emergence of the notion of a national private law.[170] The Restatements have inspired the work of the Lando Commission which resulted in the publication of the Principles of European Contract Law,[171] and they may also inspire the agenda of the European Law Institute[172] (the creation of which has, in turn,

---

[163] See Zimmermann, 'Irrungen and Wirrungen', n 141 above, 336.

[164] This was the consideration that led Christian von Bar to extend the DCFR-project beyond contract law; see C. von Bar, 'Die Mitteilung der Europäischen Kommission zum Europäischen Vertragsrecht', (2001) 9 *Zeitschrift für Europäisches Privatrecht* 799 *et seq.*

[165] They are analyzed in Eidenmüller, Jansen, Kieninger, Wagner and Zimmermann, [2012] *Juristenzeitung* 285 *et seq.*

[166] See the summary of a special meeting of private law professors from Germany, Austria and Switzerland in Bonn on 20/21 April 2012, (2012) 212 *Archiv für die civilistische Praxis* 471.

[167] For a detailed investigation, see N. Jansen and R. Michaels (eds), *Beyond the State: Rethinking Private Law* (Tübingen: Mohr Siebeck 2008); Fabrizio Cafaggi, 'Private Regulation in European Private Law', in: Hartkamp, Hesselink, Hondius, Mak and du Perron n 102 above, 91 *et seq.*

[168] 'It is general historical knowledge that the connection between the law and the state is of rather recent origin': Jansen, n 7 above, 13.

[169] H. J. Berman, *Law and Revolution: The Formation of the Western Legal Tradition* (Cambridge, Massachusetts: Harvard University Press 1983) 9.

[170] R. Michaels, 'Restatements', in MaxEuP, n 4 above, 1464 *et seq*; Jansen, n 7 above, 50 *et seq.*

[171] *Supra*, n 140.

[172] R. Zimmermann, 'Challenges for the European Law Institute', (2012) 16 *Edinburgh Law Review* 5 *et seq.*

been suggested by the success of the American Law Institute, a private institution that has been founded 'to promote the clarification and simplification of the law . . . [and] to serve the better administration of justice').[173]

These are just some of the alternatives to legislative unification of the law. A number of other strategies for strengthening convergence are imaginable,[174] among them legal education.[175] Ultimately everything depends on whether one wants to see a European legal culture grow before a reference text is cast in legislation, or whether one shares the belief that the growth of a European legal culture can be decisively advanced by an act of legislation.[176] In this sense, it is the dispute between Savigny and Thibaut revived, after 200 years, on a European level.[177] We no longer believe in the exemplary character of a historical source of law as *ratio scripta*, and we have lost the confidence to figure out a 'law of reason'. Nor do we have much trust in the rationality of the political process, particularly at the European level. As legal scholars we rely on the strength of rational arguments exchanged in an open discourse. Codification is not, of course, a 'prison cell'[178] but it has a tendency to limit the parameters of such discourse. At the present stage of the development, such limitation would appear to me to be distinctly unwelcome.[179]

---

[173] J Zekoll, 'Das American Law Institute—ein Vorbild für Europa?', in R. Zimmermann (ed), *Nichtstaatliches Privatrecht: Geltung und Genese* (Tübingen: Mohr Siebeck 2008) 101 *et seq.*

[174] See, e.g., the contributions to the symposium 'Alternativen zur legislatorischen Rechtsverein-heitlichung', (1992) 56 *RabelsZ* 215 *et seq*; Collins, n 28 above, 210 *et seq.*

[175] A. Flessner, 'Rechtsvereinheitlichung durch Rechtswissenschaft und Juristenausbildung', (1992) 56 *RabelsZ* 243 *et seq*; H. Kötz, 'Europäische Juristenausbildung', (1993) 1 *ZEuP* 268 *et seq*; F. Ranieri, *Juristen für Europa* (Münster: LIT-Verlag 2006) (with comprehensive references); cf also A. Voßkuhle, 'Das Leitbild des "europäischen Juristen"—Gedanken zur Juristenausbildung und zur Rechtskultur in Deutschland', (2010) 1 *Rechtswissenschaft* 326 *et seq.*

[176] The latter view is taken, e.g., by O. Lando, 'Culture and Contract Law', (2007) 3 *European Review of Contract Law* 17 *et seq*; idem, (2003) 8 Uniform Law Review 123 *et seq*; J. Basedow, 'A common contract law for the common market', (1996) 33 *Common Market Law Review* 1192 *et seq*; idem, 'Codification of Private Law in the European Union: The Making of a Hybrid', (2001) 9 *European Review of Private Law* 35 *et seq*. The idea of a code, on the model of the national codes, at the European level is rejected by, *inter alia*, J. Smits, 'The Draft Common Frame of Reference, Methodological Nationalism and the Way Forward', (2008) 4 *European Review of Contract Law* 270 *et seq*; S. Grundmann, 'On the Unity of Private Law from a Formal to a Substance-Based Concept of Private Law', (2010) 18 *European Review of Private Law* 1055 *et seq*; *idem*, 'The Future of Contract Law', (2011) 7 *European Review of Contract Law* 509 *et seq* (codification is without alternatives for the development of a coherent supranational contract law, but 'the classical form of codes cannot be reconciled with the complexity of the modern, globalized world').

[177] The parallel is also explicitly drawn by Lando, (2003) 8 *Uniform Law Review* 127 *et seq.*—For lessons that can be learnt for the emergence of a European private law from the history of unification of regionally defined private laws in 19th century Germany, see A. J. Kanning, 'The Emergence of a European Private Law: Lessons from 19th Century Germany', (2007) 27 *Oxford Journal of Legal Studies* 193 *et seq.*

[178] *Supra*, n. 59.

[179] See also, along very similar lines, Doralt, (2011) 75 *RabelsZ* 268 *et seq*; Grundmann, (2012) 212 *Archiv für die civilistische Praxis* 502 *et seq.*

References

Articles in Law Reviews

American Law Institute: Report of the Committee on the Establishment of a Permanent Organization for the Improvement of the Law Proposing the Establishment of an American Law Institute, (1923) 1 Proceedings of the American Law Institute 20

Bar, C. von: Die Mitteilung der Europäischen Kommission zum Europäischen Vertragsrecht, (2001) 9 Zeitschrift für Europäisches Privatrecht 799

Basedow, J.: A common contract law for the common market, (1996) 33 Common Market Law Review 1169

Basedow, J.: Codification of Private Law in the European Union: The Making of a Hybrid, (2001) 9 European Review of Private Law 35

Basedow, J.: Transjurisdictional Codification, (2009) 83 Tulane Law Review 973

Basedow, J.: The Court of Justice and Private Law: Vacillations, General Principles and the Architecture of the European Judiciary, (2010) 18 European Review of Private Law 443

Basedow, J., H. Eidenmüller, H.-C. Grigoleit, S. Grundmann, N. Jansen, E.-M. Kieninger, H.-P. Mansel, W.-H. Roth, G. Wagner and R. Zimmermann: Ein europäisches Privatrecht kommt— aber zu welchem Preis?, Frankfurter Allgemeine Zeitung of 1 July 2010, 8

Braun, A.: Professors and Judges in Italy: It Takes Two to Tango, (2006) 26 Oxford Journal of Legal Studies 665

Bühler, T.: Johann Caspar Bluntschli (1808–1881), (2009) 17 Zeitschrift für Europäisches Privatrecht 91

Bussani, M.: The European Civil Code in the Global Legal Order, (2009) 83 Tulane Law Review 1083

Canaris, C.-W.: Wandlungen des Schuldvertragsrechts—Tendenzen zu seiner "Materialisierung", (2000) 200 Archiv für die civilistische Praxis 273

Cartwright, J.: "Choice is good." Really?, (2011) 7 European Review of Contract Law 335

Delgado, C. J. and M. J. P. García: The General Codification Commission and the Modernisation of the Spanish Law of Obligations, (2011) 19 Zeitschrift für Europäisches Privatrecht 601

Doralt, W.: Strukturelle Schwächen in der Europäisierung des Privatrechts, (2011) 75 RabelsZ 260

Doralt, W.: Rote Karte oder grünes Licht für den Blue Button? Zur Frage eines optionalen europäischen Vertragsrechts, (2011) 211 Archiv für die civilistische Praxis 1

Eidenmüller, H., F. Faust, N. Jansen, G. Wagner and R. Zimmermann: Towards a Revision of the Consumer Acquis, (2011) 48 Common Market Law Review 1077

Eidenmüller, H., N. Jansen, E. Kieninger, G. Wagner and R. Zimmermann: Der Vorschlag für eine Verordnung über ein Gemeinsames Europäisches Kaufrecht, [2012] Juristenzeitung 269

Fasel, U.: Walther Munzinger—Vorbereiter der Schweizer Rechtseinheit, (2003) 11 Zeitschrift für Europäisches Privatrecht 345

Fauvarque-Cosson, B.: Vers un droit commun européen de la vente, (2012) 188 Recueil Dalloz 34

Flessner, A.: Rechtsvereinheitlichung durch Rechtswissenschaft und Juristenausbildung, (1992) 56 RabelsZ 243

Fornasier, M.: "28." versus "2. Regime"—Kollisionsrechtliche Aspekte eines optionalen europäischen Vertragsrechts, (2012) 76 RabelsZ 401

Gordley, J.: Myths of the French Civil Code, (1994) 42 American Journal of Comparative Law 459

Grundmann, S.: On the Unity of Private Law from a Formal to a Substance-Based Concept of Private Law, (2010) 18 European Review of Private Law 1055

Grundmann, S.: The Future of Contract Law, (2011) 7 European Review of Contract Law 490

Grundmann, S.: Kosten und Nutzen eines Europäischen Optionalen Kaufrechts, (2012) 212 Archiv für die civilistische Praxis 502

Hall, E., G. Howells and J. Watson: The Consumer Rights Directive: An Assessment of its Contribution to the Development of European Consumer Contract Law, (2012) 8 European Review of Contract Law 139

Honsell, H.: 100 Jahre Schweizerisches Obligationenrecht, (2011) 130 Zeitschrift für Schweizerisches Recht 5

Jansen, N.: Negotiorum Gestio and Benevolent Intervention in Another's Affairs: Principles of European Law?, (2007) 15 Zeitschrift für Europäisches Privatrecht 958

Jansen, N. and R. Zimmermann: Restating the Acquis Communautaire? A Critical Examination of the "Principles of the Existing EC Contract Law", (2008) 71 Modern Law Review 505

Jansen, N. and R. Zimmermann: "A European Civil Code in All But Name": Discussing the Nature and Purposes of the Draft Common Frame of Reference, (2010) 69 Cambridge Law Journal 98

Jansen, N. and R. Zimmermann: Contract Formation and Mistake in European Contract Law: A Genetic Comparison of Transnational Model Rules, (2011) 31 Oxford Journal of Legal Studies 625

Kanning, A. J.: The Emergence of a European Private Law: Lessons from 19th Century Germany, (2007) 27 Oxford Journal of Legal Studies 193

Kieninger, E.-M.: Das Abtretungsrecht des DCFR, (2010) 18 Zeitschrift für Europäisches Privatrecht 724

Kodek, G. E.: 200 Jahre Allgemeines Bürgerliches Gesetzbuch—das ABGB im Wandel der Zeit, (2011) Österreichische Juristenzeitung 490

Kötz, H.: Taking Civil Codes Less Seriously, (1987) 50 Modern Law Review 1

Kötz, H.: Alternativen zur legislatorischen Rechtsvereinheitlichung, (1992) 56 RabelsZ 215

Kötz, H.: Europäische Juristenausbildung, (1993) 1 Zeitschrift für Europäisches Privatrecht 268

Kroppenberg, I.: Der gescheiterte Codex: Überlegungen zur Kodifikationsgeschichte des Codex Theodosianus, (2007) 10 Rechtsgeschichte 112

Kroppenberg, I.: Mythos Kodifikation—. Ein rechtshistorischer Streifzug, [2008] Juristenzeitung 905

Kübler, F.: 'Kodifikation und Demokratie', [1969] Juristenzeitung 645

Lando, O.: Principles of European Contract Law and UNIDROIT Principles: Moving from Harmonisation to Unification?, (2003) 8 Uniform Law Review 123

Lando, O.: Culture and Contract Law, (2007) 3 European Review of Contract Law 1

Malaurie, P.: Les dix premières années de notre siècle et le droit civil, [2010] La Semaine Juridique 781

Max Planck Institute for Comparative and International Private Law (MPI): Policy Options for Progress Towards a European Contract Law, (2011) 75 RabelsZ 371

Meder, S.: Die Krise des Nationalstaates und ihre Folgen für das Kodifikationsprinzip, [2006] Juristenzeitung 477

Meier, S.: Schuldnermehrheiten im europäischen Vertragsrecht, (2011) 211 Archiv für die civilistische Praxis 435

Meier, S.: Historisch-kritisches Kommentieren am Beispiel des HKK, (2011) 19 Zeitschrift für Europäisches Privatrecht 537

Pfister, L.: Zweihundertjähriges Jubiläum des Code civil, (2011) 33 Zeitschrift für Neuere Rechtsgeschichte 241

Pichonnaz, P.: Le Centenaire du Code des obligations, (2011) 130 Zeitschrift für Schweizerisches Recht 117

Ranieri, F.: Europäische Rechtsgeschichte zwischen Rechtsvergleichung und Rechtsdogmatik, zugleich eine Reflexion über den Weg zu einem Europäischen Zivilrecht, (2011) 19 Zeitschrift für Europäisches Privatrecht 564

Riesenhuber, K.: A Competitive Approach to EU Contract Law, (2011) 7 European Review of Contract Law 115

Smits, J.: The Draft Common Frame of Reference, Methodological Nationalism and the Way Forward, (2008) 4 European Review of Contract Law 270

Stadler, A.: Anwendungsvoraussetzungen und Anwendungsbereich des Common European Sales Law (CESL), (2012) 212 Archiv für die civilistische Praxis 473

Storme, M.: Editorial, (2011) 19 European Review of Private Law 343
Stürner, R.: Der hundertste Geburtstag des BGB—eine nationale Kodifikation im Greisenalter?, [1996] Juristenzeitung 741
Symposium: Hundert Jahre schweizerisches Zivilgesetzbuch, (2008) 72 RabelsZ 661
Thier, A.: 200 Jahre Allgemeines Bürgerliches Gesetzbuch, (2011) 19 Zeitschrift für Europäisches Privatrecht 805
Unger, O.: Die Richtlinie über die Rechte der Verbraucher—Eine systematische Einführung, (2012) 20 Zeitschrift für Europäisches Privatrecht 270
Vec, M.: Flaggschiffe und Stiefkinder: Rechtsgeschichte als historische Kommentierung des geltenden Rechts, (2011) 19 Zeitschrift für Europäisches Privatrecht 547
Voßkuhle, A.: Das Leitbild des "europäischen Juristen"—Gedanken zur Juristenausbildung und zur Rechtskultur in Deutschland, (2010) 1 Rechtswissenschaft 326
Wagner, G. and R. Zimmermann: Sondertagung der Zivilrechtslehrervereinigung zum Vorschlag für ein Common European Sales Law, (2012) 212 Archiv für die civilistische Praxis 467
Weir, T.: Die Sprachen des europäischen Rechts: Eine skeptische Betrachtung, (1995) 3 Zeitschrift für Europäisches Privatrecht 368
Weir, T.: Divergent Legal Systems in a Single Member State, (1998) 6 Zeitschrift für Europäisches Privatrecht 564
Welser, R.: Verdienste und Stärken des ABGB, [2012] Juristische Blätter 205
Wüstendörfer, H.: Die deutsche Rechtswissenschaft am Wendepunkt, (1913) 110 Archiv für die civilistische Praxis 219
Zimmermann, R.: Roman-Dutch Jurisprudence and its Contribution to European Private Law, (1992) 66 Tulane Law Review 1685
Zimmermann, R.: Der europäische Charakter des englischen Rechts: Historische Verbindungen zwischen civil law und common law, (1993) 1 Zeitschrift für Europäisches Privatrecht 4
Zimmermann, R.: Codification: History and Present Significance of an Idea, (1995) 3 European Review of Private Law 95
Zimmermann, R.: Römisches Recht und europäische Rechtskultur, [2007] Juristenzeitung 1
Zimmermann, R.: The Present State of European Private Law, (2009) 57 American Journal of Comparative Law 479
Zimmermann, R.: Challenges for the European Law Institute, (2012) 16 Edinburgh Law Review 5
Zimmermann, R.: Perspektiven des künftigen österreichischen und europäischen Zivilrechts: Zum Verordnungsvorschlag über ein Gemeinsames Europäisches Kaufrecht [2012] Juristische Blätter 2
Zimmermann, R.: Testamentsformen: "Willkür" oder Ausdruck einer Rechtskultur? (2012) 76 RabelsZ 471
100 Jahre ZGB—Der Mut zur Lücke, (2008) 26 recht 41
100 Jahre ZGB (2007) 126 II Zeitschrift für Schweizerisches Recht

Books and contributions to books

Association Franco-Suisse de Paris II: Le centenaire du code civil suisse. (Paris: Société de Législation Comparée, 2008)
Augenhofer, S.: Die Zukunft des Europäischen Verbraucherrechts und seine Bedeutung für die Weiterentwicklung des Vertrags- und Wettbewerbsrechts. In: S. Grundmann (ed): Festschrift 200 Jahre Juristische Fakultät der Humboldt-Universität zu Berlin. (Berlin: De Gruyter, 2010)
Behrend, J. F.: Die neueren Privatrechts-Codificationen. In: F. von Holtzendorff (ed): Encyclopädie der Rechtswissenschaft, Part I. (Leipzig: Duncker & Humblot, 1870)
Behrends, O.: Die Institutionen Justinians als Lehrbuch, Gesetz und Ausdruck klassischen Rechtsdenkens. In: O. Behrends, R. Knütel, B. Kupisch, H. H. Seiler (eds and transl.): Corpus Juris Civilis: Text und Übersetzung, vol. I, 2nd ed. (Heidelberg: Müller, 1997)

Bentham, J.: Papers relative to Codification and Public Instruction. In: J. Bowring (ed): The Works of Jeremy Bentham, vol. IV. (Edinburgh: Tait, 1843)

Berger, A.: Encyclopedic Dictionary of Roman Law. (Philadelphia: The American Philosophical Society, 1953)

Berger, E. (ed): Österreichs Allgemeines Bürgerliches Gesetzbuch (ABGB): Eine europäische Privatrechtskodifikation, vol III. (Berlin: Duncker & Humblot, 2010)

Berman, H. J.: Law and Revolution: The Formation of the Western Legal Tradition. (Cambridge, Massachusetts: Harvard University Press, 1983)

Brauneder, W.: Vernünftiges Recht als überregionales Recht: Die Rechtsvereinheitlichung der österreichischen Zivilrechtskodifikationen 1786–1797–1811. In: R Schulze (ed): Europäische Rechts- und Verfassungsgeschichte. (Berlin: Duncker & Humblot, 1991)

Breitschmid, P. and T. Ansay (ed): 100 Jahre Schweizerisches ZGB, 80 Jahre Türkisches ZGB. (Berlin: Berliner Wissenschafts-Verlag, 2008)

Cabrillac, R.: Les codifications. (Paris: Presses Universitaires de France, 2002)

Caroni, P.: Kodifikation. In: Handwörterbuch zur deutschen Rechtsgeschichte, vol. II. (Berlin: Schmidt 1978)

Caroni, P.: (De)Kodifikation: wenn historische Begriffe ins Schleudern greaten. In: K. V. Maly and P. Caroni (eds): Kodifikation und Dekodifikation des Privatrechts in der heutigen Rechtsentwicklung. (Prague: Karolinum, 1998)

Caroni, P.: Gesetz und Gesetzbuch: Beiträge zu einer Kodifikationsgeschichte. (München: Helbing & Lichtenhahn, 2003)

Caroni, P.: Kodifikation. In: Enzyklopädie der Neuzeit. (Stuttgart: Metzler, 2007)

Cartwright, J., S. Vogenauer and S. Whittaker (eds): Reforming the French Law of Obligations. (Oxford: Hart, 2009)

Coing, H.: Europäisches Privatrecht, vol. I. (Munich: Beck, 1985)

Collins, H.: The European Civil Code: The Way Forward. (Cambridge: Cambridge University Press, 2008)

Dölemeyer, B.: Kodifizierung/Kodifikation. In: Der Neue Pauly: Enzyklopädie der Antike, vol. 14 (Rezeptions- und Wissenschaftsgeschichte). (Stuttgart: Metzler, 2000)

Dölemeyer, B. and H. Mohnhaupt (eds): 200 Jahre ABGB: Die österreichische Kodifikation im nternationalen Kontext. (Frankfurt: Klostermann, 2012)

Dunand, J. (ed): Le centenaire du code civil Suisse. (Paris: Société de Législation Comparée 2008)

Dunand, J. and B. Winiger (eds): Le Code civil Français dans le droit européen. (Bruxelles: Brulant 2005)

Eidenmüller, H., F. Faust, H. C. Grigoleit, N. Jansen, G. Wagner and R. Zimmermann: Revision des Verbraucher-acquis. (Tübingen: Mohr Siebeck, 2011)

Fallon, M., P. Legarde and S. Poillot-Peruzzetto (eds): Quelle architecture pour un code européen de droit international privé?. (Bruxelles: Lang, 2011)

Fischer-Czermak, C., G. Hopf, G. Kathrein and M. Schauer (eds): ABGB 2011: Chancen und Möglichkeiten einer Zivilrechtsreform. (Vienna: Manz, 2008)

Fischer-Czermak, C., G. Hopf, G. Kathrein and M. Schauer (eds): Festschrift 200 Jahre ABGB. (Vienna: Manz, 2011)

Gsell, B. and C. Herresthal (eds): Vollharmonisierung im Privatrecht. (Tübingen: Mohr Siebeck, 2009)

Hartkamp, A., M. Hesselink, E. Hondius, C. Mak and E. du Perron (eds): Towards a European Civil Code, 4th ed. (Alphen aan den Rijn: Wolters Kluwer, 2011)

Hattenhauer, H. (ed): Thibaut und Savigny: Ihre programmatischen Schriften, 2nd ed. (Munich: Vahlen, 2002)

Hebeis, M.: Karl Anton von Martini (1726–1800): Leben und Werk. (Bruxelles: Lang, 1996)

Heirbaut, D. & G. Martyn (eds): Napoleons nalatenschap: Tweehonderd jaar Burgerlijk Wetboek in België. (Mechelen: Kluwer, 2005)

Howells, G. and R. Schulze (eds): Modernising and Harmonising Consumer Contract Law. (Munich: Sellier, 2009)

Hübner, H.: Kodifikation und Entscheidungsfreiheit des Richters in der Geschichte des Privatrechts. (Hanstein: Königstein, 1980)

Irti, N.: Létà della decodificazione 4th ed. (Milan: Giuffrè, 1999)

Jakobs, H. H.: Wissenschaft und Gesetzgebung im bürgerlichen Recht nach der Rechtsquellenlehre des 19. Jahrhunderts. (Paderborn: Schöningh, 1983)

Jansen, N.: Binnenmarkt, Privatrecht und europäische Identität. (Tübingen: Mohr Siebeck, 2004)

Jansen, N.: The Making of Legal Authority: Non-legislative Codifications in Historical and Comparative Perspective. (Oxford: Oxford University Press, 2010)

Jansen, N. and R. Michaels (eds): Beyond the State: Rethinking Private Law. (Tübingen: Mohr Siebeck, 2008)

Jansen, N. and L. Rademacher: European Civil Code. In: J. Smits (ed): Elgar Encyclopedia of Comparative Law, 2nd ed. (Cheltenham: Elgar, 2012)

Jud, B. and C. Wendehorst (eds): Neuordnung des Verbraucherprivatrechts in Europa. (Vienna: Manz, 2009)

Kötz, H.: Schuldrechtsüberarbeitung und Kodifikationsprinzip. In: A. Dieckmann, R. Frank, H. Hanisch and S. Simitis (ed): Festschrift für Wolfram Müller-Freienfels. (Zurich: Schulthess, 1986)

Kötz, H.: Europäisches Vertragsrecht, vol I & vol II. (Tübingen: Mohr Siebeck, 1996)

Koziol, H.: Gedanken zur österreichischen Schadenersatzreform. In: Bundesministerium der Justiz (ed): 200 Jahre ABGB. (2012)

Kreittmayer, W. X. A. Freiherr von: Anmerkungen über den Codicem Maximilianeum Bavaricum Civilem, Part I. (Munich: Vötter, 1759)

Lambert, E.: [Discours]. In: Congrès international de droit comparé, Procès-verbaux des séances et documents, vol. I. (1905)

Leerssen, J.: National Thought in Europe. (Amsterdam: Amsterdam University Press, 2006)

Locré, J. G.: La législation civile, commerciale et criminelle de la France, ou commentaire et complément des codes Français, vol. I. (Paris: Treuttel & Würz, 1827)

Mertens, B.: Gesetzgebungskunst im Zeitalter der Kodifikationen. (Tübingen: Mohr Siebeck, 2004)

Michaels, M.: Of Islands and the Ocean: The Two Rationalities of European Private Law. In: R. Brownsword, H. W. Micklitz, L. Niglia, S. Weatherill (eds): The Foundations of European Private Law. (Oxford: Hart, 2011)

Miersch, M.: Der sogenannte référé legislative. (Baden: Nomos, 2000)

Montesquieu, Ch.-L. de Secondat: De l'Espit des Lois. (1748)

Moser, D.: Die Offenkundigkeit der Stellvertretung im deutschen und englischen Recht sowie in den internationalen Regelungsmodellen. (Tübingen: Mohr Siebeck, 2010)

Mugdan, B.: Die gesammten Materialien zum Bürgerlichen Gesetzbuch für das Deutsche Reich, vol I. (Berlin: v. Decker, 1899)

Oestmann, P.: Rechtsvielfalt vor Gericht. (Frankfurt: Klostermann, 2002)

Oestmann, P.: Geistliche und weltliche Gerichte im Alten Reich: Zuständigkeitsstreitigkeiten und Instanzenzüge. (Köln: Böhlau, 2012)

Österreichischer J. (ed): Festveranstaltung Österreichischer Juristentag und Bundesministerium für Justiz 200 Jahre ABGB vom 10. November 2011. (Vienna: Manz, 2012)

Peter, H., E. W. Stark and P. Tercier (eds): Hundert Jahre Schweizerisches Obligationenrecht. (Fribourg: Universitätsverlag, 1982)

Planitz, H. (ed): Die Rechtswissenschaft der Gegenwart in Selbstdarstellungen, vol. I. (Leipzig: Meiner, 1924)

Ranieri, F.: Juristen für Europa. (Münster: LIT-Verlag, 2006)

Reid, K., M. J. de Waal and R. Zimmermann (eds): Testamentary Formalities. (Oxford: Oxford University Press, 2011)

Reimann, M. and R. Zimmermann (eds): The Oxford Handbook of Comparative Law. (Oxford: Oxford University Press, 2008)

Remien, O., S. Herrler and P. Limmer (eds): Gemeinsames Europäisches Kaufrecht für die EU?. (Munich: Beck, 2012)

Schmidt, J. P.: Codification. In: J. Basedow, K. J. Hopt, R. Zimmermann (eds): The Max Planck Encyclopedia of European Private Law (MaxEuP). (Oxford: Oxford University Press, 2012)

Schmidt-Kessel, M.: Ein einheitliches europäisches Kaufrecht?. (Munich: Sellier, 2012)

Schmoeckel, M., J. Rückert and R. Zimmermann (eds): Historisch-kritischer Kommentar zum BGB, vol. I. (Tübingen: Mohr Siebeck, 2003); vol. II. (Tübingen: Mohr Siebeck, 2007); vol. III. (due to appear in 2013)

Schröder, J.: Recht als Wissenschaft, 2nd ed. (Munich: Beck, 2012)

Schubert, W. and M. Schmoeckel (eds): 200 Jahre Code civil: Die napoleonische Kodifikation in Deutschland und Europa. (Köln: Böhlau, 2005)

Schulte-Nölke, H., F. Zoll, N. Jansen and R. Schulze (eds): Der Entwurf für ein optionales europäisches Kaufrecht. (Munich: Sellier, 2012)

Schulze, R. and R. Zimmermann (eds): Europäisches Privatrecht: Basistexte, 4th ed. (Baden-Baden: Nomos, 2012)

Stürner, M. (ed): Vollharmonisierung im europäischen Verbraucherrecht?. (Munich: Sellier, 2010)

Université Panthéon-Assas (Paris II) (ed): (2004) 1804–2004, Le Code civil: Un passé, un présent, un avenir. (Paris: Dalloz, 2004)

van Caenegem, R. C.: Judges, Legislators and Professors. (Cambridge: Cambridge University Press, 1987)

van den Berg, P. A. J.: The Politics of European Codification: A History of the Unification of Law in France, Prussia, the Austrian Monarchy and the Netherlands. (Gronigen: Europa Law Publishers, 2007)

Vogenauer, S.: Die Auslegung von Gesetzen in England und auf dem Kontinent. (Tübingen: Mohr Siebeck, 2001)

Weatherill, S., M. J. Bonell, T. Wilhelmsson, B. Lurger and R. Zimmermann: 4th European Jurists' Forum, Proceedings. (Vienna: Manz, 2008)

Weber, M.: Die Entwicklungsbedingungen des Rechts. In: W. Gephart and S. Hermes (eds) Max Weber, Wirtschaft und Gesellschaft, Teilband 3: Recht. (Tübingen: Mohr Siebeck, 2010)

Wendehorst, C.: 1811 and all that—das ABGB im Prozess europäischer Rechtsentwicklung. In: Vienna Law Inauguration Lectures vol 2. (Wien: Manz, 2010)

Wendehorst, C.: Die neue Richtlinie über die Rechte der Verbraucher. In: B. Schenk, E. Lovrek, G. Musger and M. Neumayr (ed) Festschrift für Irmgard Griss. (Vienna: Sramek, 2011)

Wendehorst, C. and B. Zöchling-Jud: Am Vorabend eines Gemeinsamen Europäischen Kaufrechts. (Vienna: Manz, 2012)

Wieacker, F.: Aufstieg, Blüte und Krisis der Kodifikationsidee. In: Festschrift für Gustav Boehmer. (Bonn: Roehrscheid, 1954)

Wieacker, F.: A History of Private Law in Europe. (Oxford: Clarendon Press, 1995, transl. Tony Weir from the 2nd German edition, 1967)

Wijffels, A. (ed): Le Code civil entre ius commune et droit privé européen. (Bruxelles: Brulant, 2005)

Willoweit, D.: Deutsche Verfassungsgeschichte. (Munich: C.H. Beck, 2009)

Windscheid, B.: Die geschichtliche Schule in der Rechtswissenschaft. In: Paul Oertmann (ed) Gesammelte Reden und Abhandlungen. (Leipzig: Duncker & Humblot, 1904)

Zekoll, J.: Das American Law Institute—ein Vorbild für Europa?'. In: R. Zimmermann (ed) Nichtstaatliches Privatrecht: Geltung und Genese. (Tübingen: Mohr Siebeck, 2008)

Zimmermann, R.: The Law of Obligations: Roman Foundations of the Civilian Tradition. (Oxford: Clarendon Press, 1996)

Zimmermann, R.: Christian Thomasius, the Reception of Roman Law and the History of the lex Aquilia. In: C. Thomasius (ed and transl Margaret Hewett) Larva Legis Aquiliae: The mask of the lex Aquilia torn off the action for damage done. (Oxford: Hart, 2000)

Zimmermann, R.: Roman Law, Contemporary Law, European Law: The Civilian Tradition Today. (Oxford: Oxford University Press, 2001)

Zimmermann, R.: The New German Law of Obligations: Historical and Comparative Perspectives. (Oxford: Oxford University Press, 2005)

Zimmermann, R.: Erbunwürdigkeit: Die Entwicklung eines Rechtsinstituts im Spiegel europäischer Kodifikationen. In: P. Apathy, R. Bollenberger, P. Bydlinski, G. Iro, E. Karner, M. Karollus (ed) Festschrift für Helmut Koziol. (Wien: Sramek, 2010)

Zimmermann, R.: Die Auslegung von Verträgen: Textstufen transnationaler Modellregelungen. In: T. Lobinger, R. Richardi, J. Wilhelm (eds) Festschrift für Eduard Picker. (Tübingen: Mohr Siebeck, 2010)

Zimmermann, R.: Europäisches Privatrecht—Irrungen, Wirrungen. In: Begegnungen im Recht—Ringvorlesung zu Ehren von Karsten Schmidt. (Tübingen: Mohr Siebeck, 2011)

Zweigert, K. and H. Kötz (transl. Tony Wier): An Introduction to Comparative Law, 3rd ed. (Oxford: Clarendon Press, 1998)

Part II
Soft Codification of Private Law

Chapter 3
Supranational Codification of Private Law in Europe and Its Significance for Third States

Jürgen Basedow

3.1 Bases and Types of EU Private Law Legislation

The initial objective of the European Economic Community was not the harmonization or unification of laws, but the integration of markets. This goal is to be achieved by the implementation of so-called basic freedoms, i.e. the free movement of goods and of workers, of services and capital, and the freedom of establishment. Single provisions of the Treaty instruct and empower the Union to enact legislation designed to remove barriers imposed by national law. The competences of the Union resulting therefrom are specific; unlike a sovereign State, the Union neither has an all-embracing legislative competence nor a competence for whole areas of the law such as commercial law or private law.[1] Instead the European Commission which has the exclusive right to make legislative proposals, has to find the right basis for each legislative initiative.

Many of the specific treaty provisions also determine the type of possible legislation, i.e. regulation or directive. While regulations are directly applicable within each Member State and produce rights and obligations for the single citizens and companies, directives put the Member States under a duty to adjust their internal law. Thus directives, the main vehicles of private law legislation, so far, need to be implemented, leaving the choice of form and method of implementation to the Member States. National courts do not apply the directive, but the implementing legislation.

---

[1] The former member of the European Commission Martin Bangemann wrote in 1994: "The European treaties draw narrow limits to the possibility to create a consistent and comprehensive European private law. There is no provision in the Treaty that would empower the European Union to the unification of private law which would however be indispensible for an initiative of the European Union in accordance with the principle of conferral.", see Bangemann, Martin. 1994. Privatrechtsangleichung in der Europäischen Union. *Zeitschrift für Europäisches Privatrecht* 377, 378 (my translation, J.B.).

J. Basedow (✉)
Max Planck Institute for Comparative and International Private Law,
University of Hamburg, Mittelweg187, D-20148, Hamburg, Germany
e-mail: basedow@mpipriv.de

W.-Y. Wang (ed.), *Codification in International Perspective,* Ius Comparatum – Global
Studies in Comparative Law, DOI 10.1007/978-3-319-03455-3_3,
© Springer International Publishing Switzerland 2014

Since Member States enjoy a certain latitude of transposition, distortions as between the Member States' laws are inevitable. They are only slightly diminished by the duty of the courts to interpret the national law in conformity with the directive.[2]

Take the example of the directive on unfair terms in consumer contracts.[3] This directive has been implemented in various different forms and at different places of the respective national legal order:[4] in the national civil codes, in a special consumer code, in a general contract act; in special statutes on commercial practices, on consumer contracts, and on general conditions of contract, and finally in statutory instruments which almost literally copy the directive. Some of these instruments are, just like the directive, limited in scope to consumer transactions (e.g. France, Italy), others are equally applicable to commercial contracts (Germany, The Netherlands). The annex of the Directive which contains "an indicative and non-exhaustive list of the terms which may be regarded as unfair" (Article 3 para. 3) has been transformed into a binding blacklist in Member States such as Germany or Austria, while Scandinavian countries have not implemented that annex at all. As compared with the legal situation before 1993, the divergences between national laws have not visibly been reduced.

As a legislative instrument, the regulation provides for greater uniformity, since it is directly applicable. But it is not available everywhere. There are two types of regulations. Next to the binding and mandatory ones which have to be applied by every judge in a Member State, the Union has, in more recent years, developed a second type of regulation that creates so-called optional instruments, e.g. the Community trade mark[5] or the European company (Societas Europaea).[6] The latter type of regulation does not supersede national law, but supplements it. It creates additional possibilities to what Member State law already offers. For example, a company, whether from inside or outside of Europe, may choose to register a trademark in the single Member States or in one go at the Union level; it may even do both at the same time. There is currently a certain political tendency towards this type of optional legislation[7] which is less encroaching upon national law.

---

[2] ECJ 10 April 1984, case 14/83 (Sabine von Colson and Elisabeth Kamann v. Land Nordrhein-Westfalen), [1984] E.C.R. 1891 cons. 26.

[3] Council Directive (93/13/EEC) of 5 April 1993 on unfair terms in consumer contracts, OJ 1993 L 95/29.

[4] As to a comparative survey in respect of the current state of implementation of Directive 93/13 see Basedow, Jürgen. 2007. Vorbemerkung zu § 305 BGB. In *Münchener Kommentar zum Bürgerlichen Gesetzbuch, 5th ed.*, eds. Kurt Rebmann, Roland Rixecker and Franz Jürgen Säcker, par. 22–49. Munich: Beck.

[5] Regulation (EC) No. 40/94 of 20 December 1993 on the Community trade mark, OJ 1994 L 11/1; the regulation has been replaced by Regulation (EC) No. 207/2009 of 26 February 2009, OJ 2009 L 78/1.

[6] Regulation (EC) No. 2157/2001 of 8 October 2001 on the Statute for a European company (SE), OJ 2001 L 294/1.

[7] See the strategy paper drafted by the former Commissioner Mario Monti, A new strategy for the single market—At the service of Europe's economy and society. Report to the President of the European Commission José Manuel Barroso, 9.5.2010, p. 93 (availabe at http://ec.europa.eu/bepa/pdf/monti_report_final_10_05_2010_en.pdf); see also the opinion issued by the Economic and Social Committee, The 28th Modell—an alternative allowing less lawmaking at Community level, Doc. INT/499—CESE 758/2010 of 27 May 2010.

The Community's powers to legislate in the field of contract law essentially flow from Articles 114 and 115 Treaty on the Functioning of the European Union (TFEU) which provide the basis for the establishment of the internal market. But in some particular areas the Union makes use of special competences to issue regulations, e.g. on the carriage of goods or passengers.[8] Another example are the so-called block exemption regulations that immunize certain categories of agreements against the prohibition of cartels.[9] Directives issued under what are now Articles 19 and 153 TFEU combat discrimination in employment contracts[10], in activities of a self-employed nature,[11] and even more generally with respect to the supply of goods and services.[12] For company law, Article 50(2)(g) TFEU has served as a basis for a considerable number of directives.[13] The regulations providing for optional instruments like the Community Trade Mark mentioned above have so far been issued under the subsidiary powers conferred upon the Union by what is now Article 352 TFEU.[14] The present Article 81 TFEU has already served as a legal basis for a whole series of regulations on the conflict of laws, inter alia the Rome I Regulation on the law applicable to contractual obligations.[15]

The number of legislative acts of a purely private law nature is quite impressive, probably beyond eighty, and many other mixed acts contain single provisions on private law aspects.[16] These acts are fragmentary in nature, dealing with very specific situations such as the conclusion of consumer contracts outside business

---

[8] See e.g. Regulation (EC) No 261/2004 of the European Parliament and of the Council of 11 February 2004 establishing common rules on compensation and assistance to passengers in the event of denied boarding and of cancellation or long delay of flights, and repealing Regulation (EEC) No 295/91, OJ 2004 L 46/1, based upon Articles 91 and 100 TFEU.

[9] See e.g. Commission Regulation (EC) No 2790/1999 of 22 December 1999 on the application of Article 81(3) of the Treaty to categories of vertical agreements and concerted practices, OJ 1999 L 336/21, based on Article 103 TFEU.

[10] See e.g. Council Directive (2000/78/EC) of 27 November 2000 establishing a general framework for equal treatment in employment and occupation, OJ 2000 L 303/16.

[11] Directive 2010/41/EU of the European Parliament and of the Council of 7 July 2010 on the application of the principle of equal treatment between men and women engaged in an activity in a self-employed capacity and repealing Council Directive 86/613/EEC, OJ 2010 L 180/1.

[12] See e.g. Council Directive (2004/113/EC) of 13 December 2004 implementing the principle of equal treatment between men and women in the access to and supply of goods and services, OJ 2004 L 373/37.

[13] See e.g. Second Council Directive (77/91/EEC) of 13 December 1976 on coordination of safeguards which, for the protection of the interests of members and others, are required by Member States of companies within the meaning of the second paragraph of Article 58 of the Treaty, in respect of the formation of public limited liability companies and the maintenance and alteration of their capital, with a view to making such safeguards equivalent, OJ 1977 L 26/1.

[14] See above at fn. 8 and 9.

[15] Regulation (EC) No. 593/2008 of the European Parliament and of the Council of 17 June 2008 on the law applicable to contractual obligations (Rome I), OJ 2008 L 177/6.

[16] Almost 10 years ago, I edited a collection of the existing private law acts in four languages, see Basedow, Jürgen (ed.). 1999–2002. *European Private Law—Sources*, vol. 1–3. The Hague: Kluwer Law International. In more recent years, many further acts have been adopted.

premises, cross-border money transfers or the compensation of passengers who are denied boarding on overbooked flights. While there is no comprehensive approach, the legislation of the Union may be grouped into certain thematic clusters, in particular company law, labour law, consumer contract law, civil liability, commercial communication, copyright and intellectual property, private international law and international civil litigation.

The acts differ widely in form and nature. They often provide for diverse rules on similar issues, and they are definitely not the results of an overarching legislative plan. Irrespective of their legal form as directive or regulation, they are always embedded in the context of divergent national laws which determine their significance to a certain extent. These deficits explain that a call for more consistency has been made as early as 30 years ago.

3.2   The Quest for a General Framework of Contract Law

The need for more consistency has triggered scholarly activities since the 1980s. In those years, an expert group composed of law professors from various European countries and chaired by the Danish professor Ole Lando set out for drafting the Principles of European Contract Law (PECL).[17] The method employed by this group was that of the American restatements of law adopted since the 1920s by the American Law Institute.[18] The primary purpose was to restate the common rules and principles of the law. As far as the positive legal rules of the various legal systems differ—and this occurs more often in Europe than in the US—the restatements do not necessarily follow the majority of the legal systems compared, but try to improve the law by selecting what is thought to be the best solution.[19]

The rules and principles resulting from this work have been formulated and arranged in the rather succinct and systematic style of continental codes. Like their American counterparts, the rules are supplemented by comments that explain their content, purpose and possible application. In addition, the Principles of European Contract Law contain notes on the comparative background of the rule or principle in question. Translations into various languages other than English have been

---

[17] Lando, Ole and Hugh Beale (eds.). 2000. *Principles of European Contract Law—Parts I and II*. The Hague: Kluwer Law International; Lando, Ole, Eric Clive, André Prüm and Reinhard Zimmermann (eds.). 2003. *Principles of European Contract Law—Part III*, The Hague: Kluwer Law International.

[18] See Clark, David S. 1992. The Sources of Law. In *Introduction to the law of the United States*, eds. Tuğrul Ansay and David S. Clark, 33 and 45. Deventer/Boston: Kluwer Law and Taxation Publ.; as to a more comprehensive review see Schwartz, Alan and Robert E. Scott. 1995. The Political Economy of Private Legislatures. *U. Pa. L. Rev.* 143:595–654.

[19] Goode, Roy. 1997. International Restatements of Contract and English Contract Law. *Uniform L. Rev.* 231 at 234.

published. The example of the Commission on European Contract Law has been followed by other groups, dealing with tort law,[20] with insurance contract law,[21] with the law of trusts[22] and with private international law[23]. The most recent offspring of this movement is a group on European family law.[24]

The various groups have transcended the traditional methods of research: their work is not confined to a comparative analysis of the existing legal rules of the various Member States. They are openly promoting harmonization by drafting and discussing common rules. This shift towards scholarly activism has become even clearer in the successor project of the PECL, the so-called Study Group on a European Civil Code.[25] It was a kind of superstructure to various working teams dealing with sales, services and long-term contracts, extra-contractual obligations, trusts, credit securities, the transfer and rental of moveable property, loan agreements and gratuities contracts.

The European Commission had declared itself incompetent in the area of general private law over many years.[26] But in 2001, the Commission published a communication on European contract law, which for the first time openly raised the question whether and how the Union should deal with contract law in Europe.[27] After a lively discussion the Commission presented, as a next step, an action plan on a more coherent European contract law in 2003.[28] That document outlined three types of possible action: The improvement of the *acquis communautaire* in the field of contract law, e.g. by the adoption of a kind of European consumer code; the elaboration of EU-wide

---

[20] Koziol, Helmut. 2004. Die "Principles of European Tort Law" der "European Group on Tort Law". *Zeitschrift für Europäisches Privatrecht* 234–259.

[21] Heiss, Helmut. 2005. Europäischer Versicherungsvertrag—Initiativstellungnahme des Europäischen Wirtschafts- und Sozialausschusses verabschiedet. *Versicherungsrecht* 1–4.

[22] Hayton, David J., Sebastianus C. J. J. Kortmann and Hendrik L. E. Verhagen. 1999. *Principles of European Trust Law*. The Hague: Kluwer Law International; see also "Principles of European Trust Law". 1999. *Zeitschrift für Europäisches Privatrecht* 748 with an introduction by Hayton, David J., Sebastianus C. J. J. Kortmann and Hendrik L. E. Verhagen.

[23] Visit the homepage of the European Group for Private International Law at http://www.gedip-egpil.eu .

[24] See "Gründung der Kommission für Europäisches Familienrecht". 2002. *Zeitschrift für Europäisches Privatrecht* 194 and visit the homepage of the Commission on European Family Law at http://www.law.uu.nl/priv/cefl .

[25] See Wurmnest, Wolfgang. 2003. Common Core, Grundregeln, Kodifikationsentwürfe, Acquis-Grundsätze—Ansätze internationaler Wissenschaftlergruppen zur Privatrechtsvereinheitlichung in Europa. *Zeitschrift für Europäisches Privatrecht* 714 et sEq. and visit the homepage of the Study Group on a European Civil Code at http://www.sgecc.net/ .

[26] See above at fn. 5.

[27] Communication from the Commission to the Council and the European Parliament on European contract law, COM(2001) 398 final of 11 July 2001; as to the possibilities thereby provided for see the anthologies of Schulte-Nölke, Hans and Reiner Schulze (eds.). 2002. *Europäisches Vertragsrecht im Gemeinschaftsrecht*. Köln: Bundesanzeiger and of Grundmann, Stefan and Jules H. V. Stuyck (eds.). 2002. *An Academic Green Paper on European Contract Law*. The Hague: Kluwer Law International.

[28] Communication from the Commission to the European Parliament and the Council—A more coherent European contract law—An action plan, COM(2003) 68 final of 12 February 2003.

standard contract terms, a proposal which is no longer pursued; and the adoption of a horizontal European contract act as an optional instrument applicable only if chosen by the parties.

The idea of an optional contract act was soon watered down to a so-called Common Frame of Reference.[29] Its outline contained nine sections, seven of which deal with general contract law and the general law of obligations, following closely the structure of the PECL. For the remaining two sections, rules on the sale of goods and insurance contracts were envisaged. By contrast to its content, the legal nature and significance of a Common Frame of Reference remained unclear. It was said to be a toolbox for the internal work of the European Commission, but the use by other European institutions, e.g. by the Court of Justice, was explicitly reserved.

For the preparation of the Common Frame of Reference, the Commission created and sponsored a joint network on European private law in 2005.[30] The network published its proposal for the said Draft Common Frame of Reference (DCFR) in 2009.[31] The scope and methodological approach of the various parts of the DCFR differ widely. While the insurance group has confined itself to mandatory provisions which are indisputably needed for the establishment of the single insurance market in Europe, the other parts of the DCFR deal with some issues of contract law such as donation which are not only void of any practical need at the European level, but for whose implementation a legislative basis in the Treaty would be lacking. The examples make clear that the various groups have been inspired by divergent considerations: While some have tried to go a step forward in the gradual development of the law of the Union, always in the shadow of the empowering provisions of the Treaty, others have simply taken a national civil code as a blue-print.

A new European Commission took office in 2010. One of the vice-presidents of the Commission, Ms. Viviane Reding who has served on the European Commission since 1999 and before gathered much experience in the European Parliament, has taken over the responsibility for the newly created Directorate General (DG) Justice. The political experience and determination of Vice-President Reding heading a new DG account for the most recent Commission initiative in the field of contract law.

---

[29] Communication from the Commission to the European Parliament and the Council—European Contract Law and the revision of the *acquis*: the way forward, COM(2004) 651 final of 11 October 2004.

[30] See Bar, Christian von, Hans Schulte-Nölke. 2005. Gemeinsamer Referenzrahmen für europäisches Schuld- und Sachenrecht. *Zeitschrift für Rechtspolitik* 165 and visit the homepage of the Joint Network on European Private Law at http://www.copecl.org.

[31] Bar, Christian von, Eric Clive. 2009. *Principles, Definitions and Model Rules of European Private Law—Draft Common Frame of Reference (DCFR)*, vol. 1–6. Munich: Sellier; the Principles of European Insurance Contract Law which form part of the Draft Common Frame of Reference were published separately, see Basedow, Jürgen, John Birds, Malcolm Clarke, Herman Cousy and Helmut Heiss (eds.). 2009. *Principles of European Insurance Contract Law (PEICL)*. Munich: Sellier.

In April 2010, the Commission established an Expert Group on a Common Frame of Reference in the area of European contract law.[32] The names of the experts were soon made public;[33] a majority of them had already been involved in the work of either the *Aquis* Group or the Study Group on a European Civil Code. They could hardly be expected to subject the academic DCFR, i.e. their own work product, to a critical scholarly assessment. This fact again shows the determination of the European Commission to go ahead with the contract law project. Soon after, a Green Paper on policy options in the field of contract law was published.[34] It initiated a further consultation of the European public concerning conceptual aspects such as the relation of the prospective legal rules on consumer contracts to those on commercial contracts, the substantive and geographical scope of application and the choice between seven options for a future European contract law outlined in the document. At a careful reading it turned out that the Commission was no longer heading for the white elephant of a common frame of reference, but for an optional instrument on European contract law.

The work product of the Expert Group was published in May 2011 as a so-called Feasibility Study which was confined to sales law and several aspects of general contract law.[35] In October 2011 the Commission finally adopted the Proposal for a Regulation on a Common European Sales Law (CESL).[36] It provides for an optional instrument which will only apply where the parties so agree. Its coverage is analogous to the one of the Feasibility Study, dealing with the sale of goods, the supply of digital content and the provision of some related services. The future CESL is meant to apply only to cross-border sales and only to contracts between either businesses and consumers, or between businesses provided that one of them is a small or medium enterprise (SME). One of the parties must be habitually resident in an EU Member State. The so-called "chapeau rules" contain a number of further complicated details of the scope of the instrument.

The framing of the Proposal as an optional instrument will create a number of problems. The insurance group has in fact conceived its own Principles of European Insurance Contract Law (PEICL) as a draft for an optional instrument.[37] The text of the PEICL gives evidence of various problems raised by this concept, e.g. with regard to third parties, in respect of the precontractual phase, or in private international law. The general part of the DCFR does not take account of these difficulties,

---

[32] Commission Decision of 26 April 2010, setting up the Expert Group on a Common Frame of Reference in the area of European contract law, OJ 2010 L 105/109.

[33] European Commission convenes legal expert group to seek solutions on contract law, Press Release of the European Commission No. IP/10/595 of 21 May 2010.

[34] Green Paper from the Commission on policy options for progress towards a European Contract Law for consumers and businesses, COM(2010) 348 final of 1 July 2010.

[35] See the Press Release IP/11/523 of the European Commission of 3 May 2011; see the link to the feasibility study containing almost 200 draft rules as an annex.

[36] Proposal for a Regulation of the European Parliament and of the Council on a Common European Sales Law, COM (2011) 635 of 11 October 2011.

[37] See Article 1:102 PEICL, above at fn. 34.

and the Expert Group does not appear to have studied the matter carefully. In the further course of the legislative proceedings hard decisions will have to be taken. In all reasonable likelihood, it would however appear that the model of the optional instrument is least intrusive with regard to national law and has a fair chance of being chosen.

3.3 Perspectives for Asia

The Proposal for CESL is a hotspot of current scholarly and political debates in EU countries. But what could be the significance of this project for third countries, in particular in Asia? If CESL will be nothing but a non-binding Common Frame of Reference (CFR) adopted for the internal use of the European institutions, it will have little effect outside Europe. People would probably argue: "If the Europeans do not have sufficient trust in their own product to make it binding, why should we take account of it?"

CESL will receive more attention if adopted as an optional instrument. The optional instrument triggers a kind of referendum in business life. The more often it will be agreed upon by contracting parties to govern their transaction, the greater will be its persuasive authority both inside and outside the European Union. Given the focus of CESL on consumer contracts it might very well be accepted as a kind of model in non-EU countries which aim at consumer protection. For example, the People's Republic of China (PRC) drafted its own contract law in 1999,[38] drawing from the model of the UNIDROIT Principles of International Commercial Contracts[39] which are void of the dimension of consumer protection.[40] Assuming that growing prosperity in the PRC arouses claims for more consumer protection CESL might serve as a crystallization of European experience and a benchmark for Chinese legislation.

The significance of CESL might be even greater in commercial practice. Would CESL be an option to be chosen as the law governing for example transactions between Asian and European companies? Could they agree on such a European text

---

[38] Contract Law of the People's Republic of China, adopted at the Second Session of the 9th National People's Congress on March 15, 1999, Zhonghua Renmin Gongheguo Guowuyuan Gongbao, April 19, 1999, Issue No. 11, p. 388; the help of Dr. Benjamin Pissler of the Max Planck Institute for Comparative and International Private Law at Hamburg in finding this reference is gratefully acknowledged. An English translation is available on the website "Judicial protection of IPR in China", organized by Judge Jiang Zhipei of the Supreme People's Court of the People's Republic of China: http://www.chinaiprlaw.com/English/laws/laws2.htm .

[39] UNIDROIT, Principles of International Commercial Contracts, 2004.

[40] On the role of the UNIDROIT Principles of International Commercial Contracts of 1994 as a model for the Chinese contract law, see Yuqing, Zhang and Huang Danhan. 2000. The new Contract Law in the People's Republic of China and the UNIDROIT Principles of International Commercial Contracts: A brief comparison. *Uniform Law Review* 429–440 at 430: "In drafting the new Contact Law, the Chinese legislators referred extensively to the UNIDROIT Principles of international commercial contracts. Many articles of the new contract law, in particular those in the chapter on general provisions, are similar in spirit to the UNIDROIT Principles."

instead of any national law? The convenience of that solution cannot be assessed before the final text of such an instrument is known. Already now, one source of uncertainty emerges from the Proposal however: since one of the parties to a business-to-business transaction must be a SME, agreement on CESL would be excluded for many contracts made between big traders.

The application of CESL would moreover depend on choice-of-law rules. According to the Proposal the agreement on CESL is valid in European courts if the law applicable to the contract is the law of a Member State under the so-called Rome I Regulation.[41] This approach which makes the application of CESL dependent on the prior recourse to choice-of-law rules is usually designated as the 2nd model. It is meant to create, alongside the autonomous national sales law, a second sales law that is available where the law of a Member State applies in accordance with the rules of the Rome I Regulation.[42]

But would courts outside the EU accept such a choice? This will depend on the private international law of the respective forum state. What about courts in Asia? The basic principle governing international contracts is nowadays party autonomy. Whether in Korea,[43] the PRC,[44] Taiwan,[45] Hong Kong[46] or Japan[47]—it is primarily up to the parties to choose the applicable law. But this is usually meant to refer to the law of a State. Does it include the law the EU which is not a State? A Japanese author, Professor Nishitani, has argued that a European contract law promulgated by

---

[41] See above at fn. 18.

[42] See recital 10 of the proposed CESL Regulation, above at fn. 49: "The agreement to use the Common European Sales Law should be a choice exercised within the scope of the respective national law which is applicable pursuant to Regulation (EC) No 593/2007 [Rome I] . . .".

[43] See § 25 of Law no. 6465 of 7 April 2001 on Private International Law, German translation in RabelsZ 2006 70:342.

[44] See Article 41 of the Statute on the application of laws to civil relationships involving foreign elements of the People's Republic of China, adopted by the 17th Session of the Standing Committee of the Eleventh National People's Congress on 28 October 2010, English translation in YB PIL 2010 12:669; for the previous law laid down by the Supreme People's Court see Pissler, Benjamin. 2007. Neue Regeln des Obersten Volksgerichts zum Internationalen Vertragsrecht der Volksrepublik China. *Zeitschrift für Chinesisches Recht* 337–346; Wolff, Lutz-Christian. 2008. VR China: Neue IPR-Regeln für Verträge. *IPRax* 55–61; Barth, Marcel and Gary Lock. 2007. Die aktuelle Auslegung des Obersten Volksgerichts zum Internationalen Vertragsrecht in China. *Recht der Internationalen Wirtschaft* 820–825, with an English translation of the provisions on 823–825.

[45] See Article 20 of the Act Governing the Application of Laws in Civil Matters Involving Foreign Elements of 26 May 2010, English translation by Chen, Rong-Chwan. Taiwan. In *Codification in East Asia*, ed. Wen-Yeu Wang, Springer International Publishing Switzerland, forthcoming in 2014.

[46] See Johnston, Graeme. 2005. *The Conflict of Laws in Hong Kong*, 190. Hong Kong: Sweet & Maxwell Asia; Wolff, Lutz-Christian. 2010. Hong Kong's Conflict of Contract Laws: *Quo Vadis?*. *Journal of Private International Law* 6:465–498 at 468.

[47] Act no. 78 of 2006, English translation in Basedow, Jürgen, Harald Baum and Yuko Nishitani (eds.). 2008. *Japanese and European Private International Law in Comparative Perspective*. 405 et sEq. Tuebingen: Mohr Siebeck.

the European legislature could be chosen under existing choice-of-law rules.[48] It is submitted that this is the correct approach. If the European Union adopts CESL, that regulation, being directly applicable and effective, forms part of the law of each EU Member State.[49] Private international law which includes the possibility of applying foreign law, pursues the objective of a so-called harmony of decisions: the outcome of a dispute should not depend on the competent court. Therefore, the reference of choice-of-law rules to a foreign law implies the expectation that the foreign law will be applied, by the domestic court, in the same way it is applied in its country of origin. If that is true, a court outside the European Union that has to apply, under its own private international law, the law of any Member State of the European Union, would have to apply that law in accordance with the framework of EU law which is respected in that Member State. This would include the application of CESL where chosen by the parties. Thus an optional instrument of European contract law might create an opportunity for business in Asia to focus, in their relations with European companies from various countries, on a single set of contract law rules, thereby avoiding the intransparency and costs generated by 28 or 29 (Scotland) contract law systems at the national level.

3.4   Conclusion

In the European legal history of the last 200 years, private law has moved from an essentially all-European body of principles and scholarship to a concomitant of the nation state, although the national roots of private law are rather fragile. For the last 30 years or so, the pendulum appears to be swinging back. The progressive integration of European markets heightens our consciousness of various impediments including the divergences of contract law. The institutional framework of the European Union favours the harmonization of laws as compared with the traditional instrument of the international treaty. Moreover, the European Union is endowed with a Supreme Court which allows maintaining uniformity once it has been achieved in the statute book and which may even develop that uniformity further. But the most recent political initiative directed towards the adoption of a Common European Sales Law is above all attributable to the persistent efforts of European legal scholarship. Scholars have not confined themselves to the interpretation of legislative acts and judgments handed down by the institutions of the Union. Rather, a series of comparative research projects and repeated analyses of the deficits of the internal market have confirmed

---

[48] Nishitani, Yuko. 2008. Party Autonomy and its Restrictions by Mandatory Rules in Japanese Private International Law: Contractual Conflicts Rules. In *Japanese and European Private International Law in Comparative Perspective*, eds. Basedow, Baum, Nishitani, 77 at 87–89.

[49] See Lenaerts, Koen and Piet van Nuffel. 1999. *Europees Recht in Hoofdlijnen*, no. 711, 689. Antwerpen: Maklu: "A regulation automatically belongs to the highest norms of the internal legal order of the Member States without any implementation into national law being necessary for that purpose." (My translation from the Dutch original, J.B.; Koen Lenaerts is a judge at the European Court of Justice and a professor of law at the University of Leuven, Belgium).

the significant role an independent legal scholarship plays for the development of the legal system.

References

Books

Bar, Christian von, Eric Clive (2009). *Principles, Definitions and Model Rules of European Private Law—Draft Common Frame of Reference (DCFR)*, vol. 1–6.

Basedow, Jürgen (ed.). (1999–2002) *European Private Law—Sources*, vol. 1–3.

Basedow, Jürgen, Harald Baum and Yuko Nishitani (eds.). (2008) *Japanese and European Private International Law in Comparative Perspective*.

Basedow, Jürgen, John Birds, Malcolm Clarke, Herman Cousy and Helmut Heiss (eds.). (2009) *Principles of European Insurance Contract Law (PEICL)*.

Clark, David S.(1992). Introduction to the law of the United States.

Franco Ferrari (2000) The Unification of International Commercial Law.

Gerhard Köbler and Hermann Nehlsen (eds.) (1997) Festschrift für Karl Kroeschell zum 70. Geburtstag.

Grundmann, Stefan and Jules H. V. Stuyck (eds.). (2002) *An Academic Green Paper on European Contract Law*.

Hayton, David J., Sebastianus C. J. J. Kortmann and Hendrik L. E. Verhagen. (1999) *Principles of European Trust Law*.

Johnston, Graeme. (2005). *The Conflict of Laws in Hong Kong*.

Kurt Rebmann, Roland Rixecker and Franz Jürgen Säcker, (*2007*) *Münchener Kommentar zum Bürgerlichen Gesetzbuch, 5th ed.*

Lando, Ole and Hugh Beale (eds.). (2000) *Principles of European Contract Law—Parts I and II*.

Lando, Ole, Eric Clive, André Prüm and Reinhard Zimmermann (eds.). (2003) *Principles of European Contract Law—Part III*.

Legrand, Pierre (1999) *Fragments on Law-as-Culture*.

Lenaerts, Koen and Piet van Nuffel. (1999) *Europees Recht in Hoofdlijnen*.

Marc van Hoecke and François Ost (2000) *The Harmonisation of European Private Law*.

Mauro Cappelletti (1978) *New Perspectives for a Common Law of Europe*.

Schulte-Nölke, Hans and Reiner Schulze (eds.). (2002) *Europäisches Vertragsrecht im Gemeinschaftsrecht*.

Articles

Bar, Christian von, Hans Schulte-Nölke. (2005) Gemeinsamer Referenzrahmen für europäisches Schuld- und Sachenrecht. *Zeitschrift für Rechtspolitik 165*.

Barth, Marcel and Gary Lock. (2007) Die aktuelle Auslegung des Obersten Volksgerichts zum Internationalen Vertragsrecht in China. *Recht der Internationalen Wirtschaft 820–825*.

Goode, Roy (1997) International Restatements of Contract and English Contract Law. Uniform L. *Rev. 231 at 234*.

"Gründung der Kommission für Europäisches Familienrecht" (2002) *Zeitschrift für Europäisches Privatrecht 194*.

Hayton, David J., Sebastianus C. J. J. Kortmann and Hendrik L. E. Verhagen.(1999). Principles of European Trust Law, *Zeitschrift für Europäisches Privatrecht 748*.

Heiss, Helmut. (2005). Europäischer Versicherungsvertrag—Initiativstellungnahme des Europäischen Wirtschafts- und Sozialausschusses verabschiedet. *Versicherungsrecht 1–4*.

Koziol, Helmut. (2004). *Zeitschrift für Europäisches Privatrecht 234–259.*

Nishitani, Yuko (2008) Party Autonomy and its Restrictions by Mandatory Rules in Japanese Private International Law: Contractual Conflicts Rules. *In Japanese and European Private International Law in Comparative Perspective*, eds. Basedow, Baum, Nishitani, 77 at 87–89.

Pissler, Benjamin (2007) Neue Regeln des Obersten Volksgerichts zum Internationalen Vertragsrecht der Volksrepublik China, *Zeitschrift für Chinesisches Recht 337–346.*

Schwartz, Alan and Robert E. Scott. (1995) The Political Economy of Private Legislatures. *U. Pa. L. Rev.* 143:595–654.

Wolff, Lutz-Christian (2008) VR China: Neue IPR-Regeln für Verträge. *IPRax* 55–61.

Wolff, Lutz-Christian. (2010) Hong Kong's Conflict of Contract Laws: Quo Vadis?. *Journal of Private International Law 6:465–498 at 468.*

Wurmnest, Wolfgang. 2003. Common Core, Grundregeln, Kodifikationsentwürfe, Acquis-Grundsätze—Ansätze internationaler Wissenschaftlergruppen zur Privatrechtsvereinheitlichung in Europa. *Zeitschrift für Europäisches Privatrecht 714 et seq.*

Yuqing, Zhang and Huang Danhan. (2000) The new Contract Law in the People's Republic of China and the UNIDROIT Principles of International Commercial Contracts: A brief comparison. *Uniform Law Review 429–440 at 430.*

Cases

ECJ 10 April 1984, case 14/83 (Sabine von Colson and Elisabeth Kamann v. Land Nordrhein-Westfalen), [1984] E.C.R. 1891 cons. 26.

Internet and Other Sources

Judicial protection of IPR in China, organized by Judge Jiang Zhipei of the Supreme People's Court of the People's Republic of China:,http://www.chinaiprlaw.com/English/laws/laws2.htm.

Mario Monti, Report to the President of the European Commission José Manuel Barroso, 9.5.2010, p. 93, availabe at http://ec.europa.eu/bepa/pdf/monti_report_final_10_05_2010_en.pdf.

The homepage of the European Group for Private International Law at, http://www.gedip-egpil.eu.

The homepage of the Commission on European Family Law at, http://www.law.uu.nl/priv/cefl.

The homepage of the Study Group on a European Civil Code at, http://www.sgecc.net/.

The homepage of the Joint Network on European Private Law at, http://www.copecl.org.

Statute

Contract Law of the People's Republic of China, adopted at the Second Session of the 9th National People's Congress on March 15, 1999, Zhonghua Renmin Gongheguo Guowuyuan Gongbao, April 19, 1999, Issue No. 11, p. 388.

Council Directive (93/13/EEC) of 5 April 1993 on unfair terms in consumer contracts, OJ 1993 L 95/29.

Council Directive (2000/78/EC) of 27 November 2000 establishing a general framework for equal treatment in employment and occupation, OJ 2000L 303/16.

Council Directive (2004/113/EC) of 13 December 2004 implementing the principle of equal treatment between men and women in the access to and supply of goods and services, OJ 2004L 373/37.

Directive 2010/41/EU of the European Parliament and of the Council of 7 July 2010 on the application of the principle of equal treatment between men and women engaged in an activity in a self-employed capacity and repealing Council Directive 86/613/EEC, OJ 2010L 180/1.

Regulation (EC) No. 40/94 of 20 December 1993 on the Community trade mark, OJ 1994L 11/1.
Regulation (EC) No. 2157/2001 of 8 October 2001 on the Statute for a European company (SE), OJ 2001L 294/1.
Regulation (EC) No. 261/2004 of the European Parliament and of the Council of 11 February 2004 establishing common rules on compensation and assistance to passengers in the event of denied boarding and of cancellation or long delay of flights, and repealing Regulation (EEC) No 295/91, OJ 2004L 46/1.
Regulation (EC) No. 593/2008 of the European Parliament and of the Council of 17 June 2008 on the law apploicable to contractual obligations (Rome I), OJ 2008L 177/6.
Second Council Directive (77/91/EEC) of 13 December 1976 on coordination of safeguards which, for the protection of the interests of members and others, are required by Member States of companies wihtin the meaning of the second paragraph of Article 58 of the Treaty, in srespect of the formation of public limited liability companies and the maintenance and alteration of their capital, with a view to making such safeguards equivalent, OJ 1977L 26/1.

Others

Communication from the Commission to the Council and the European Parliament on European contract law, COM (2001) 398 final of 11 July 2001.
Communication from the Commission to the European Parliament and the Council—A more coherent European contract law—An action plan, COM (2003) 68 final of 12 February 2003.
Communication from the Commission to the European Parliament and the Council—European Contract Law and the revision of the acquis: the way forward, COM (2004) 651 final of 11 October 2004.
Commission Decision of 26 April 2010, setting up the Expert Group on a Common Frame of Reference in the area of European contract law, OJ 2010L 105/109.
Green Paper from the Commission on policy options for progress towards a European Contract Law for consumers and businesses, COM (2010) 348 final of 1 July 2010.
Law no. 6465 of 7 April 2001 on Private International Law, German translation in RabelsZ 2006 70:342.
Press Release of the European Commission No. IP/10/595 of 21 May 2010.
Press Release IP/11/523 of the European Commission of 3 May 2011.
Proposal for a Regulation of the European Parliament and of the Council on a Common European Sales Law, COM (2011) 635 of 11 October 2011.
The Economic and Social Committee, The 28th Modell—an alternative allowing less lawmaking at Community level, Doc. INT/499—CESE 758/2010 of 27 May 2010.
UNIDROIT, Principles of International Commercial Contracts, 2004.

Chapter 4
The Soft Codification of the UNIDROIT Principles of International Commercial

Contracts: Process and Outcome

Chang-fa Lo

4.1 Introduction

There are different types of process for codifying a legal text. Most commonly found codification exists in the forming of a statute being conducted under the direct auspices of the State's authority and being eventually passed through the legislative process in a specific jurisdiction. Such type of codification is also commonly used to establish international norms, such as treaties and other international agreements.

Another important codification is "soft codification" or "non-State codification". It can be understood as the legal rules being elaborated in writing in a systemic way, not with any automatic binding force, but for the purpose of being incorporated by the transacting parties or being used by the courts or arbitral tribunals as applicable rules with the nature of *lex mercatoria* or the principles of law, or as the supplementary basis for law interpretation. Such soft codification is used both at national and international levels.

An Italian Professor Vittorio Scialoja once Stated: ". . . the community of commercial relations existing between civilized nations should lead to the reconstruction, at least partially, of a 'common' law which was for centuries a powerful force for civilization in Europe, and which was destroyed . . . in the great movement of renovation which began in the eighteenth century."[1] Non-State codification of international private law can be seen as a process of reconstructing some kind of "international common law" to be directly or indirectly used by traders from different nations and applied by courts and arbitral tribunals in different jurisdictions.

Comparing with State codification, which is the process of codifying legal principles by individual States, non-State codification of law normally involves many States or experts from many States. Thus although non-State codification is not supported

---

[1] The Statement was quoted from Michael Joachim Bonell, The UNIDROIT Initiative for the Progressive Codification of International Trade Law, 27(2) Int'l and Comp. L. Q, 413 (1978).

C.-fa Lo (✉)
College of law, National Taiwan University, Fl.12, No.223,
Kun-Ming Street, Taipei, Taiwan ROC
e-mail: lohuang@ntu.edu.tw

W.-Y. Wang (ed.), *Codification in International Perspective,* Ius Comparatum – Global
Studies in Comparative Law, DOI 10.1007/978-3-319-03455-3_4,
© Springer International Publishing Switzerland 2014

by States' legislative powers to make them enforceable in different jurisdictions, the results of such non-State codification could have wider implications concerning the possible applications by traders at international level.

Due to the difference between the soft-codification and the State codification and due to the importance of such soft codification, it is of high practical and theoretical significance to look more into the process of such codification. The paper uses the UNIDROIT Principles of International Commercial Contracts (hereinafter "UNIDROIT Principles"; it is also called by some authors as the "PICC") as an example to review the codification process and to examine whether there are positive experiences for other fields of law to learn.

The UNIDROIT Principles is a comprehensive and widely covering rules to deal with almost all substantive aspects of international commercial contracts, including the general provisions to cover freedom of contract, biding character, mandatory rules, good faith principle, usages and practice, among other things; formation of contract and authority of agents; validity of contract; interpretation of contract terms; content and third party rights; performance; non-performance; set-off; assignment of rights; transfer of obligations and assignment of contracts; and limitation periods.[2] The contents of the UNIDROIT Principles are "sufficiently flexible to take account of the constantly changing circumstances brought about by the technological and economic developments affecting cross-border trade practice and attempt to ensure fairness in international commercial relations."[3]

The paper is not to examine the substantive contents of the UNIDROIT Principles, but to focus on the codification aspects of the Principles, including their initiation, criteria, stages, sources being based, function, reception and application, authority and legitimacy, and State's participation. It is hoped that the review will provide useful basis for other fields of law to consider the value of soft codification.

4.2 Initiators and Drafters of the UNIDROIT Principles

4.2.1 The Institutional Initiator of the UNIDROIT Principles

Although, as in most international initiatives, actually many key persons were behind the initiation of the UNIDROIT Principles, institutionally, it was the International Institute for the Unification of Private Law (UNIDROIT) responsible for the initiation and realization of the codification for the international commercial contracts principles. The UNIDROIT Principles were drafted and first published in 1994 and then revised in 2004 and 2010 by UNIDROIT. UNIDROIT is an independent intergovernmental organization, first established as an auxiliary organ of the League

---

[2] See the text of the UNDROIT Principles at http://www.unidroit.org/english/principles/contracts/principles2004/integralversionprinciples2004-e.pdf.

[3] See the Introduction to the 1994 Edition, attached to the text of the UNIDROIT Principle. Available at http://www.unidroit.org/english/principles/contracts/principles2004/integralversionprinciples2004-e.pdf.

of Nations and reestablished in 1940 based on the Statute of UNIDROIT,[4] with the purpose of "studying needs and methods for modernizing, harmonizing and coordinating and in particular commercial law as between States and groups of States and to formulate uniform law instruments, principles and rules to achieve those objectives."[5] The independent status of UNIDROIT "has enabled it to pursue working methods which have made it a particularly suitable forum for tackling more technical and correspondingly less political issues."[6]

UNIDROIT has the General Assembly as the ultimate decision-making organ of UNIDROIT, composed of one representative from each member Government. The General Assembly elects 25 members to the Governing Council to supervise all policy aspects, which in turn appoints the Secretary-General to carry out work programs.[7] In short, the Institute and its operation have very close connection with its member countries.

The purpose for the initiation of the UNIDROIT Principle was to comprehensively elaborate principles of international commercial contracts so as to "establish a balanced set of rules designed for use throughout the world irrespective of the legal traditions and the economic and political conditions of the countries in which they are to be applied."[8] In 1971, the Governing Council decided to include the subject of such elaboration in the Work Programme of UNIDROIT. In the beginning, the Council set up a small Steering Committee, composed of three professors representing the civil law, the common law and the socialist systems, for the purpose of conducting preliminary inquiries about the feasibility of the project. It was until 1980, a Working Group being established under the Governing Council for preparing the draft of the Principles.[9] And thus the drafting process was formally launched.[10] From the explanation, it is apparent that UNIDROIT played very unique and important institutional role in the codification of the UNIDROIT Principles.

4.2.2   Individual Initiators and Drafters of the UNIDROIT Principles

The idea of creating a non-binding set of rules "reflecting the common principles that can be extracted from the case law of the various countries" was suggested by the

---

[4] The Statute can be found at http://www.unidroit.org/mm/statute-e.pdf.

[5] See the official website of UNIDROIT at http://www.unidroit.org/dynasite.cfm?dsmid=103284.

[6] *Id.*

[7] http://www.unidroit.org/dynasite.cfm?dsmid=103284.

[8] See the Introduction to the 1994 Edition, attached to the text of the UNIDROIT Principle. Available at http://www.unidroit.org/english/principles/contracts/principles2004/integralversionprinciples2004-e.pdf.

[9] See the Introduction to the 1994 Edition, attached to the text of the UNIDROIT Principle. Available at http://www.unidroit.org/english/principles/contracts/principles2004/integralversionprinciples-2004-e.pdf.

[10] *Id.*

then Secretary-General of UNIDROIT, Mario Matteucci in 1968.[11] This was before the Steering Committee mentioned above was established.

The original duty of the Working Group was for "Progressive Codification of International Trade Law" when it was established in 1980. The initiative was revised to "preparation of Principles for International Commercial Contracts" in 1985.[12] The Working Group included academics and lawyers who were experts of major legal systems throughout the world. They were participating in the discussions in their personal capacity, not representing the views of their governments.[13] These members of the Working Group were the real drafters of the UNIDRIOT Principles. In addition, the Group also circulated its drafts to a wide range of expert to invite comments.[14] Thus, experts not formally within the system also indirectly participated in the drafting process.

4.3 Criteria of Codification under UNIDRIOT

UNIDROIT has its own comprehensive "legislative policy"[15] to serve as the criteria of codifying legal rules. Concerning the selection of subjects and scope of rules to be codified, it is stated that: "UNIDROIT's basic statutory objective is to prepare modern and where appropriate harmonized uniform rules of private law understood in a broad sense."[16] But it also indicates that "experience has demonstrated a need for occasional incursion into public law especially in areas where hard and fast lines of demarcation are difficult to draw or where transactional law and regulatory law are intertwined. Uniform rules prepared by UNIDROIT are concerned with the unification of substantive law rules; they will only include uniform conflict of law rules incidentally."[17]

According to UNIDROIT, there are a number of factors being used to determine the eligibility of subjects for uniform law treatment. "Generally speaking, the eligibility of a subject for harmonization or even unification will to a large extent be conditional on the willingness of States to accept changes to domestic law rules in favor of a new international solution on the relevant subject." "Similar considerations will also tend to determine the most appropriate sphere of application to be given to uniform rules, that is to say, whether they should be restricted to truly cross-border transactions or extended to cover internal situations as well. While commercial law topics tend

---

[11] Stefan Vogenauer and Jan Kleinheisterkamp, *Commentary on the UNIDROIT principles of international commercial contracts (PICC)*, at 7 (Oxford University Press, 2009).

[12] *Id.*

[13] *Id.*

[14] See the "Introduction to the 1994 Edition" attached to the PICC.

[15] Since the rules drafted and adopted by UNIDROIT are not legislations in strict sense, the term "legislative policy" used by UNIDROIT is actually referring to the "soft-codifying policy".

[16] http://www.unidroit.org/dynasite.cfm?dsmid=103284.

[17] *Id.*

to make for most of the international harmonization initiatives, the broad mandate given to UNIDROIT allows the organization to deal with non-commercial matters as well."[18]

In addition to the factors to decide whether to codify certain legal rules or principles, UNIDROIT also lays down factors to determine the kinds of instrument to be prepared. It is stated that: "The uniform rules drawn up by UNIDROIT have, in keeping with its intergovernmental structure, generally taken the form of international Conventions, designed to apply automatically in preference to a State's municipal law once all the formal requirements of that State's domestic law for their entry into force have been completed. However, alternative forms of unification have become increasingly popular in areas where a binding instrument is not felt to be essential. Such alternatives may include model laws which States may take into consideration when drafting domestic legislation or general principles which the judges, arbitrators and contracting parties they address are free to decide whether to use or not. Where a subject is not judged ripe for uniform rules, another alternative consists in the legal guides, typically on new business techniques or types of transaction or on the framework for the organization of markets both at the domestic and the international level. Generally speaking, 'hard law' solutions (i.e. Conventions) are needed where the scope of the proposed rules transcends the purely contractual relationships and where third parties' or public interests are at stake as is the case in property law."[19] Apparently, UNIDROIT considered that a subject of principles of international commercial contracts is ripe for uniform rules and thus it decided to resort to soft law approach in codifying principles.

4.4   Stated Stages of Codification under UNIDROIT and the Actual Process for the Principles

4.4.1   The Standard Methods of Codification Under UNIDROIT

According to UNIDROIT, there are the standard methods to formulate rules.[20] The initiation of the UNIDROIT Principles was based on certain objectively stated criteria. The reasons are basically not political in nature. It is not for the purpose of transcending States or keeping States out of the process. As a matter of fact, States play key role in supporting the drafting the adopting the codified documents.

Basically, a number of stages will have to be gone through to ultimately realize or finalize the codification process. Soft codification might involve different stages of such process when comparing with State codifications of domestic laws. For instance, codification of the Taiwan's Civil Code involved the drafting process by some eminent

---

[18] *Id.*

[19] *Id.*

[20] http://www.unidroit.org/dynasite.cfm?dsmid=103284.

scholars from foreign countries, the discussion and amendment process among the experts and with different parts of government agencies, and the ultimate passage of the draft by the legislative body. However, the soft codifications generally do not involve the last stage, i.e., the legislative stage.

Nevertheless, it must also be noted that different kinds of soft codification might also involve different stages of codification. Most other soft codification processes do not involve some kind of inter-governmental negotiations, nor formal adoption or approval process. However, the codification process by UNIDROIT will, in principle, go through inter-governmental negotiation stage and the "passing" stage.

According to UNIDROIT, there are the following stages to be gone through for the purpose of codifying some legal rules. These are more formal and far more complicated than many other soft codification processes:

Preliminary Stage (Drafting Stage)

Once a subject of codification has been entered on UNIDROIT's Work Programme, the Secretariat of the Institute "will draw up a feasibility study and/or a preliminary comparative law report designed to ascertain the desirability and feasibility of law reform. Where appropriate and funding permitting, an economic impact assessment study is also carried out. The report, which may include a first rough draft of the relevant principles or uniform rules, will then be laid before the Governing Council which, if satisfied that a case has been made out for taking action, will typically ask the Secretariat to convene a study group, traditionally chaired by a member of the Council, to prepare a preliminary draft Convention or one of the alternatives mentioned above. The membership of such study groups, made up of experts sitting in their personal capacity, is a matter for the Secretariat to decide. In doing so, the Secretariat will seek to ensure as balanced a representation as possible of the world's different legal and economic systems and geographic regions."[21]

Intergovernmental Negotiation Stage

After the preliminary stage, "[a] preliminary draft instrument prepared by the study group will be laid before the Governing Council for approval and advice as to the most appropriate further steps to be taken. In the case of a preliminary draft Convention, the Council will usually ask the Secretariat to convene a committee of governmental experts whose task will be to finalize a draft Convention capable of submission for adoption to a diplomatic Conference. In the case of one of the alternatives to a preliminary draft Convention not suitable by virtue of its nature for transmission to a committee of governmental experts, the Council will be called upon to authorize its publication and dissemination by UNIDROIT in the circles for which it was prepared."[22]

---

[21] http://www.unidroit.org/dynasite.cfm?dsmid=103284.
[22] *Id.*

States' participation in this stage is more active and constant. "Full participation in UNIDROIT committees of governmental experts is open to representatives of all UNIDROIT member States. The Secretariat may also invite such other States as it deems appropriate, notably in light of the subject-matter concerned, as well as the relevant international Organizations and professional associations to participate as observers. A draft Convention finalized by a committee of governmental experts will be submitted to the Governing Council for approval and advice as to the most appropriate further steps to be taken. Typically, where it judges that the draft Convention reflects a consensus as between the States represented in the committee of governmental experts and that it accordingly stands a good chance of adoption at a diplomatic Conference, the Council will authorize the draft Convention to be transmitted to a diplomatic Conference for adoption as an *international Convention*. Such a Conference will be convened by one of UNIDROIT's member States."[23]

Publication of UNIDROIT Working Materials

UNIDROIT has its Proceedings and Papers to publish the Annual Reports on the activity of the Institute, summaries of the conclusions reached by the Governing Council, the reports on the annual sessions of the General Assembly, the final texts of instruments prepared, documents adopted and the preparatory work.

Cooperation with Other International Organizations

UNIDROIT maintains close ties of cooperation with other intergovernmental and non- governmental organizations. UNIDROIT is sometimes commissioned by other international organizations to prepare comparative law studies and/or draft conventions designed to serve as the basis for the preparation and finalization of international instruments by those organizations.[24]

4.4.2   Actual Process for the Codification of the UNIDROIT Principles

According to the above procedures, normally a preliminary draft instrument prepared by the study group should be submitted to the Governing Council for approval and advice as to the most appropriate further steps to be taken. However, the real situation for the process of the first edition (1994 edition) of the UNIDROIT Principles was quite different.

In the Working Group stage, the participants were not able to resolve some issues so as to form their consensus. They decided to submit them to the Governing Council for decision. The Governing Council decided that it would not formally approve

---

[23] *Id.*

[24] *Id.*

the Principles but only to authorize their publication. Apparently, this is not the procedure usually applied, and even not a procedure applied for the codification process of any other instrument under UNIDROIT.[25] However, this does not mean that the Governing Council failed to take any step in the realization of codification of the UNIDROIT Principles. As a matter of fact, the Governing Council did offer its advices on the policy to be followed, "especially in those cases where the Group had found it difficult to reach consensus."[26]

Different from the situation of 1994 edition, later editions (the 2004 and 2010 editions) of the UNIDROIT Principles were formally adopted by the Governing Council of UNIDROIT.[27]

4.5 Sources and Materials Being Based upon by the Codification of the UNIDROIT Principles

Although the UNIDROIT Principles are only a set of non-binding rules, the sources were actually from the existing legislations and case laws of different countries. As described by some authors, the drafters "almost exclusively relied on the legislations and the case law of Western legal systems, without necessarily giving priority to the civil law or the common law tradition. Regard was usually had to the contract laws of the USA (with frequent references to the UCC and the Restatement 2d Contracts), England, France, Germany, and Italy. But the contract laws of smaller jurisdictions were influential we well, particularly those that were in the process of being codified, such as the Netherlands (1992) and Quebec (1994)."[28]

As mentioned earlier, the purpose for the initiation of the UNIDROIT Principles was to comprehensively elaborate principles of international commercial contracts so as to "establish a balanced set of rules designed for use throughout the world irrespective of the legal traditions and the economic and political conditions of the countries in which they are to be applied."[29] Therefore, the drafters were not merely copying provisions from these sources and materials. The materials served only as references for the drafters to conduct their deliberations. The results have been that most provisions in the UNIDROIT Principles represented the general rules embodied in the majority of jurisdictions; whereas some others were created by the drafters. As indicated in the "Introduction to the 1994 Edition" published by UNIDROIT, the most part of the UNIDROIT Principles "reflect concepts to be found in many, if not all, legal systems. Since however the UNIDROIT Principles are intended to

---

[25] Stefan Vogenauer and Jan Kleinheisterkamp, *supra* note 11, at 9.

[26] See the "Introduction to the 1994 Edition" published by UNIDROIT.

[27] http://www.unidroit.org/english/principles/contracts/main.htm.

[28] Stefan Vogenauer and Jan Kleinheisterkamp, *supra* note 11, at 9.

[29] See the Introduction to the 1994 Edition, attached to the text of the UNIDROIT Principle. Available at http://www.unidroit.org/english/principles/contracts/principles2004/integralversionprinciples2-004-e.pdf.

provide a system of rules especially tailored to the needs of international commercial transactions, they also embody what are perceived to be the best solutions, even if still not yet generally adopted."

4.6 Function of the Codification of UNIDROIT Principles

Broadly speaking, there are three fundamental functions from the codification of the UNIDROIT Principles, namely the restatement function, the law function, and the model function.[30]

The UNIDROIT Principles themselves are in the form of a "restatement". The restatement function is shown by the fact that the most part of the UNIDROIT Principles "reflect concepts to be found in many, if not all, legal systems" and they are "intended to provide a system of rules especially tailored to the needs of international commercial transactions, they also embody what are perceived to be the best solutions, even if still not yet generally adopted", as mentioned above. So the Principles are partly the restatement of existing laws and partly the best practice of law to be applied by the parties of international transactions.

The law function is reflected in the following aspects: First, the parties can agree that their contract be governed by the UNIDROIT Principles. Actually, parties in the international commercial transactions are encouraged to expressly choose the Principles as the rules of law governing their contract. Second, even if the parties fail to include the UNIDROIT Principles as the applicable law of their contract, the Principles can still be applied "as a manifestation of 'general principles of law', the 'lex mercatoria' or the like referred to in the contract."[31] Third, if it is in an arbitration proceeding and if the arbitrators are permitted to apply "the rules of law which they determine to be appropriate" under the rules of arbitration (such as ICC Rules), the arbitral tribunal might still be able to apply the UNIDROIT Principles as the appropriate rules of law to decide the dispute.[32] Fourth, the UNIDROIT Principles can also serve as a means to interpret and to supplement international uniform law instruments (such as the UN Convention on Contracts for the International Sale of Goods, (CISG)), or as a means of interpreting and supplementing domestic law.[33] But certainly, these interpreting and supplementing functions would depend largely on the nature of the issues.

The model function is also indicated in the Preamble of the UNIDROIT Principles. It states that the UNIDROIT Principles "may serve as a model for national and international legislators." In addition to serving as a model to States, they also serve

---

[30] See Ralf Michaels, *Preamble*, in COMMENTARY (supra n. 2) nos. 1–8.

[31] See the preamble of UNIDROIT Principles.

[32] *Id.*

[33] *Id.* See also Anukarshan Chandrasenan, *UNIDROIT Principles to Interpret and Supplement the CISG: An Analysis of the Gap-filling Role of the UNIDROIT Principles*, 11 *Vindobona J. Int'l Comm. L. and Arb.* 65 (2007).

as a model for private parties when they draft their contract. The Preamble of the UNIDROIT Principles states in this regard that "the Principles may also serve as a guide for drafting contracts. In particular the Principles facilitate the identification of the issues to be addressed in the contract and provide a neutral legal terminology equally understandable by all the parties involved."

4.7 Reception and Legitimacy of and States' Participation in the Codification of the UNIDROIT Principles

4.7.1 Reception and Application

The result of soft codification is a set of certain rules recommended by the institution.

After codification, the codified principles are still "soft law", i.e., the law not to be enforced through public force.[34] Thus the reception of the UNDROIT Principles does not depend on the States' action based on their sovereign powers, but on the private parties and courts or arbitral tribunals making use of them.

Although in academic circles, the UNIDROIT Principles do arouse considerable interest, their opinions concerning the practical use of the Principles are divided.[35]

However, according to a statistical analysis, the outcome of the Principles being used is quite positive. It states: "First, the number of arbitral tribunals and domestic courts which have used the UNIDROIT Principles is considerable, as is their location, spread all over the world. Second, also the fact that the parties involved in the respective disputes were situated in so many different countries may be seen as confirmation that the UNIDROIT Principles are increasingly known worldwide. Finally, the substantive scope of application of the UNIDROIT Principles, though centering mainly on sales contracts, also covers a great variety of other important international commercial contracts, especially service contracts, distribution contracts and licensing contracts."[36]

4.7.2 Authority and Legitimacy

The suggestion by Nils Jansen that non-State codifications gain an important part of their reputation not from their substantive qualities but from their coherent and

---

[34] Gabrielle Kaufmann-Kohler, *Soft Law in International Arbitration: Codification and Normativity*, J. Int'l Dispute Settlement, 1 at 2 (2010).

[35] Gabrielle Kaufmann-Kohler, *Soft Law in International Arbitration: Codification and Normativity*, J. Int'l Dispute Settlement, 1 at 2 (2010).

[36] *Id.* at 721.

orderly form of the text and that the existence as a written and accessible text[37] do apply to the building of the authoritative position of the UNIDROIT Principles. But, still, the quality of the codification and the reputation of the drafters and the drafting institution together also contribute to the wide recognition of the authority of the UNIDROIT Principles.

Also the process of codification involves the participation by experts nominated by the contracting members of the Institute. Outside experts were also invited to make comments during the process. There is also the approving process by the Governing Council, the members of which were representatives from contracting countries. In other words, the Principles are formulated in a semi-democratic manner (i.e., quite wide participations), widely endorsed by a large number of countries, which are basically the main regions where traders are coming from. These all contribute to the establishment of the authority and legitimacy of the Principles.

4.7.3   States' Participation

As mentioned above, although the UNIDROIT Principles were only the result of a soft codification, actually States have certain high degree of involvement in the codification process. The whole process, including the establishment of the Working Group and the secretariat and financial supporting as well as the final endorsement of the Principles, was conducted and made under UNIDROIT, an intergovernmental organization. Thus, although States do not directly engage in the "State-to-State negotiation" and the "ratification" of the text of the UNIDOIT Principles, their involvements are so apparent and crucial.

Concerning the codified UNIDROIT Principles relating to States' law, if the parties agree to use them as the governing law for their contract or if the parties agree to use general principles of law, the Principles can be applied as the applicable law or as a manifestation of "general principles of law". It is also possible that the UNIDROIT Principles can be used for interpreting and supplementing domestic law.[38] It is also contemplated to have the UNIDROIT Principles serving as a model for national legislations. Thus the relations between States' law and the Principles are obvious, although they might not be so direct and intimate.

---

[37] NILS JANSEN, THE MAKING OF LEGAL AUTHORITY chap. 4 (Oxford University Press 2010).

[38] *Id*. See also Anukarshan Chandrasenan, *UNIDROIT Principles to Interpret and Supplement the CISG: An Analysis of the Gap-filling Role of the UNIDROIT Principles*, 11 *Vindobona J. Int'l Comm. L. and Arb*. 65 (2007).

4.8   Some Concluding Remarks

This chapter examines the soft codification process of the UNIDROIT Principles, including their initiation, criteria, stages, sources being based, function, reception and application, authority and legitimacy, and State's participation. It finds the codification is not that "soft".

The non-State codification of the Principles is actually the collaborative efforts by experts in international contract law from wide range of countries, under an intergovernmental organization, with States' systemic supports and endorsement. If we look at the States' involvement and participation in the process, it is apparent that such non- State codification process is not done in genuinely and purely private setting. States' involvement is quite substantial. They actually participated in the process in an indirect way. But individual drafters were still given very high degree of autonomy in formulating their drafts. Such public-private cooperation is an excellent model for providing a solid foundation for the Principles to be widely welcome and accepted. The codification of the UNDROIT Principles is definitely a positive experience to be shared for possible soft codification of law in other fields.

References

Books and Chapters

NILS JANSEN, THE MAKING OF LEGAL AUTHORITY chap. 4 (Oxford University Press 2010)
Stefan Vogenauer and Jan Kleinheisterkamp, *Commentary on the UNIDROIT principles of international commercial contracts (PICC)*, at 7 (Oxford University Press, 2009)

Journals and Articles

Anukarshan Chandrasenan, *UNIDROIT Principles to Interpret and Supplement the CISG: An Analysis of the Gap-filling Role of the UNIDROIT Principles*, 11 *Vindobona J. Int'l Comm. L. and Arb.* 65 (2007)
Eleonora Finazzi Agrò, *The Impact of the UNIDROIT Principles in International Dispute Resolution in Figures*, Rev. dr. unif. 2011, 719, at 719
Gabrielle Kaufmann-Kohler, *Soft Law in International Arbitration: Codification and Normativity*, J. Int'l Dispute Settlement, 1 at 2 (2010)
Michael Joachim Bonell, *The UNIDROIT Initiative for the Progressive Codification of International Trade Law*, 27(2) Int'l and Comp. L. Q, 413 (1978)

Deborah A. DeMott is the David F. Cavers Professor of Law, Duke University of School of Law. Professor DeMott served as the sole Reporter for the American Law Institute's Restatement (Third) of Agency; her other books and scholarly articles focus primarily on agency law, fiduciary obligation, and corporate governance. Professor DeMott received a B.A. from Swarthmore College and a J.D. from New York University School of Law.

Online Publications

Ralf Michaels, *Preamble*, in COMMENTARY, UNDROIT Principles, at: http://www.unidroit.org/english/principles/contracts/principles2004/integralversionprinciples2004-e.pdf

UNDROIT Principles:

http://www.unidroit.org/english/principles/contracts/principles2004/integralversionprinciples2004 e.pdf

http://www.unidroit.org/english/principles/contracts/principles2004/integralversionprinciples2004 e.pdf

http://www.unidroit.org/dynasite.cfm?dsmid=103284.

Chapter 5
Restatements and Non-State Codifications of Private Law

Deborah A. DeMott

5.1 Introduction

This paper offers a vantage point through which to assess the phenomenon of projects codifying private law that are undertaken by private persons or institutions, distinct from legislatures and state-sponsored codification and law-revision projects. My institutional focus is the American Law Institute (ALI), which since its founding in 1923 has promulgated Restatements in many areas of the law, plus work in statutory form—most notably the Uniform Commercial Code and the Model Penal Code—and projects that generate "Principles" to guide legal development within their specific fields. A private tax-exempt organization,[1] the ALI chooses its own members and has developed elaborate procedures and internal practices, some of which are discussed below. Although the ALI's early history is significant to understanding its ongoing work,[2] my temporal focus is contemporary and is shaped by my experience as the Reporter for the ALI's Restatement (Third) of Agency, adopted and promulgated by the ALI in 2005.[3] Agency (Third) succeeds Agency (Second), which in 1958 succeeded the original Restatement of Agency, completed in 1933. Although the

---

[1] Although the ALI is not an instrumentality of the United States or of any state, its federal tax-exempt status means its property and net income are not subject to taxation, and its public-regarding purposes make it eligible to receive tax-deductible contributions from donors.

[2] On the early history, see the numerous sources cited in, e.g., Adams, Kristin David. 2004. The Folly of Uniformity: Lessons from the Restatement Movement. Hofstra Law Review 33:423, 432n.41. (hereinafter cited as Adams, Lessons).

[3] Publication in final form followed in 2006. The ALI publishes Restatements pursuant to a long-lived joint venture with the West Publishing Company. The ALI (not the individual Restatement Reporter) owns the copyright interest in the work.

D. A. DeMott (✉)
Duke law school, Duke University, 210 Science Drive,
Box 90360, Durham NC 27708-0360, USA
e-mail: DeMott@law.duke.edu

W.-Y. Wang (ed.), *Codification in International Perspective,* Ius Comparatum – Global Studies in Comparative Law, DOI 10.1007/978-3-319-03455-3_5,
© Springer International Publishing Switzerland 2014

successive Restatements of Agency are my primary concern, I refer to the history of other Restatements, in particular those covering Torts.

It is incontestable that the ALI's work—and in particular the project of restating private-law subjects like agency—is not static. That is, change external to the ALI itself and the texts it promulgates tends to prompt other changes, including shifts in the functions that a Restatement serves, the structure of Restatements as texts, and the succession of one Restatement by another, as well as the nature of the work that the ALI undertakes. For reasons I discuss later, more of the ALI's work following the first generation of Restatements consisted of statutory projects. To be sure, the ALI's relatively long life among contemporary sponsors of non-state codifications highlights the phenomenon of change with more immediacy than is so for younger institutions and the texts they sponsor. Nonetheless, responses to change warrant thought in connection with other non-state projects that promulgate texts intended to be authoritative or influential. The goals and purposes for which the ALI was founded imply that its work may be dynamic over time. Its ALI's Certificate of Incorporation states that

> The particular business and objects of the society are educational, and are to promote the clarification and simplification of the law and its better adaptation to social needs, to secure the better administration of justice, and to encourage and carry on scholarly and scientific work.[4]

These organizational purposes, as applied to an ongoing organization that endures over time, may require new texts that supplant old ones.[5]

The ALI's history also invites reflection on the nature of its influence and the status of its authority in the development of law in the United States, plus shifts in these over time. I suspect that one's prototype of the law and of legal change shapes how these questions might be framed and answered. Some prototypes may be a better descriptive fit for some jurisdictions than others. Two opposing prototypes come to mind. First, an author or sponsor of a legal text intended to be authoritative could be characterized as an architect making design choices that are articulated through rules that, stated ex ante, are determinative of subsequent outcomes to which the rules apply. The end result, like a structurally-sound building constructed on the basis of an architect's plans, is static. Change within this prototype requires either outflanking the rule system or amending it. Although an author or sponsor of legal change within this prototype might be a state instrumentality—such as a civil code commission or other official drafting body—non-state actors may sponsor legal change through wide-sweeping work with an architectural or ex-ante quality, comparable to the ALI's initial and ongoing projects concerning the Uniform Commercial Code.

---

[4] American Law Institute. 1923. Certificate of Incorporation. www.ali.org/doc/charter.pdf. Accessed 27 Feb 2013.

[5] For recognition that "it was natural for the restatements to get out of date," see Jansen, Nils and Ralf Michaels. 2007. Private Law and the State: Comparative Perceptions and Historical Observations 15, 57. 2008. Beyond the State: Rethinking Private Law. (Nils Jansen & Ralf Michaels eds. 2008).

In contrast, consider the relationships implied by Jan Fabre's sculpture, *Searching for Utopia*, a cast I saw on display in south Amsterdam at the intersection of Apollolaan and Beethovenstraat.[6] *Searching for Utopia* is a monumental work in bronze that depicts a large and finely-detailed tortoise, mounted by a small human figure (the sculptor himself) who holds reins through which the tortoise might be directed. The label accompanying the sculpture proposed that it be understood as a visualization of the wisdom of making incremental and slow progress towards Thomas More's *Utopia* or its non-fictional counterparts. However, the sculpture invites multiple understandings. For our immediate purposes, the relationship between the rider and the giant tortoise may capture some of the relationship between the ALI as promulgator of Restatements and the onward development of law in the United States on subjects that the Restatements cover. Like Jan Fabre's giant tortoise, the law may be guided in its development when judges apply rules as clarified or simplified by a Restatement. And like the human rider atop the tortoise, the two remain separate actors because the ALI is an autonomous institution separate from courts and the state more generally.

Alternatively, courts may ignore a Restatement's suggestive reins, as a giant tortoise may proceed on a course otherwise determined by it. The influence or authority of a non-state legal text within this prototype may occur incrementally, necessarily awaiting the long view for assessment and incorporating the prospect of significant variation, both from the text and among courts. Depending on their subject, the force of a Restatement's reins will vary and, within subjects, vary from issue to issue. This variation may be a function of issues and subjects: some are more controversial than others and individual Restatements vary in other ways, including their continuing vitality over time. Moreover, Restatements for some subjects—torts in particular—necessarily reflect the inseparable impact of institutions of civil procedure on substantive legal rules. This is because the significance of the lay jury in shaping tort doctrine in the United States, as reflected in the Restatements. Although this effect might be characterized as a distortion of tort doctrine,[7] more neutrally it constitutes just another circumstance shaping tort law,[8] comparable perhaps to a tortoise's instinct to amble toward water or food. In any event, and as discussed below, qualities inescapably present in the ALI's work—its mutability over time and its variability in influence—help explain the emphasis with which the organization has defined itself as the author of work it promulgates.

---

[6] For an image of Searching for Utopia, see Fabre, Jan. 2011. Searching for Utopia. www.panoramio.com//photo/55203509. Accessed 27 Feb 2013.

[7] See Green, Michael. 2011. The Impact of the Civil Jury on American Tort Law. Pepperdine Law Review. 38: 337.

[8] One documented example of another circumstance is the influence of lobbying by pro-defendant organizations to champion the enactment of statutes that cap recoveries or, one way or another, reduce the prospect of recovery. See Cross, Frank. 2011. Tort Law and the American Economy. Minnesota Law Review 96:28. Professor Cross's data show no negative effects associated with more pro-plaintiff tort law; indeed pro-plaintiff tort law appears to be associated with economic growth. Id. at 86–89.

5.2 Authors and Procedures

It is no mere matter of legal form or commercial expediency that the ALI itself holds the copyright interest in Restatements. Reporters, who are responsible for drafting and researching, are not the ALI's employees (and thus Restatements are not so obviously characterized as works made for hire) but, according to the Institute's *Handbook*, a Reporter "reports *to* the Institute by means of a series of drafts, which are then reviewed according to the deliberative processes established by the Institute and revised as a result of these processes."[9] Most Reporters are full-time professors of law; all are appointed by the ALI's Council on the recommendation of its Director. Under the ALI's bylaws, publication of any work as that of the ALI requires "approval by both the membership and the Council,"[10] which is the Institute's governing body. An impasse between a Reporter and the Council may lead to the Reporter's resignation. This occurred most recently to my knowledge in the Restatement project on economic torts. As the Reporter's 2007 letter of resignation characterized the dispute,

> At the meeting I presented Council Draft No. 2 covering much of the field of economic negligence. There was strong disagreement voiced at the meeting with the direction taken in the draft. The draft states the law of economic negligence (and in particular negligent misstatement) in terms that emphasize its relation to contract law and that distinguish the law of economic negligence from accident law involving physical harm. The criticism was that the law of economic negligence should be situated within a general tort of negligence . . . .[11]

In 2010, the project resumed with a new Reporter. Although the 2012 Tentative Draft submitted by the ALI's Council to the ALI Annual Meeting explained that courts "impose tort liability for economic loss more selectively than liability for other types of harm,"[12] liability for negligent misrepresentations "depends on the same standard of care familiar from other cases of negligence," with the defendant's duty limited in a number of respects.[13]

As this example illustrates, the ALI's organizational structure is complex and is geared to enhance the institutional character of authorship of the ALI's end-products. Many components of this structure and its processes tend to distance the Restatements themselves from the individual Reporters associated with them, enveloping the final product in a carapace of institutional authorship. To be sure, individual Reporters

---

[9] American Law Institute. 2005. Capturing the Voice of the American Law Institute: A Handbook for ALI Reporters and Those Who Review Their Work 1. www.ali.org/doc/stylemanual.pdf. Accessed 27 Feb 2013. (hereinafter cited as ALI, Handbook).

[10] American Law Institute. Bylaw 6. www.ali.org/doc/Bylaws07/pdf. Accessed 27 Feb 2013.

[11] Feldthusen, Bruce. 2011. What the United States Taught the Commonwealth About Pure Economic Loss: Time to Repay the Favor. Pepperdine Law Review. 38:309, 319–320. (quoting Letter from Mark P. Gergen, Fondren Chair of Faculty Excellence, University of Texas School of Law, to Advisers, Consultants, and Council Members, American Law Institute (Dec. 2007)).

[12] Restatement (Third) of Torts: Liability for Economic Harm § 1,cmt.c. 2012. (Tentative Draft No. 1, Apr. 4, 2012).

[13] Id. § 5, cmt. b.

remain the first movers for each text, and retain what may be considerable powers of persuasion to champion their work, but collapsing authorship of a Restatement into an individual Reporter's persona misunderstands both the ALI and Restatements.

The ALI's deliberative processes include, for each Restatement project, a group of Advisers appointed by the Institute's Council and a separate group (the Members Consultative Group) composed of members who choose to receive working drafts from the project and who have the opportunity to meet as a group with the Reporter. Unlike the ALI's Council and its membership, the Advisers and Members Consultative Group associated with a Restatement do not hold veto powers. Depending on the subject, interim drafts of Restatement projects may attract wider audiences among practicing lawyers, academics, and organized interest groups. As in its earliest days, the ALI's work continues to proceed, project-by-project, through in-person meetings at which successive drafts produced by the Reporter are reviewed. Thus, delineated procedures, iterative consultations and revisions, and sequential approvals all shape the outcome of any Restatement's text.[14]

From its early days, the ALI's leadership worked to assure some measure of consistency across Restatement projects. During the sequence of meetings that led to the first Restatement of Agency, the ALI's first Director, William Draper Lewis, often instructed the Reporter for Agency to consult with the Reporter for another subject to co-ordinate their terminology or treatment of overlapping questions, occasionally directing the Agency Reporter to obtain an answer to a specific question from another project's Reporter.[15] Reporters for other projects occasionally attended meetings of the Advisers for Agency and were credited with solving problems in drafting the Restatement's text.[16] The ALI's practices in its early days are consistent with an organization that took its work and itself seriously. A stenographer made a transcript of the exchanges at Advisers' meetings, followed by transmission of a transcription via carbon paper on onion-skin copies to the Reporter and each Adviser.[17]

More recently, the ALI formalized its general expectations of Reporters in a 2005 *Handbook*, which was "conceived as a means of both articulating and preserving an

---

[14] Schwartz, Alan and Robert E. Scott. 1995. The Political Economy of Private Legislatures. University of Pennsylvania Law Review 143:595, 650. Their primary focus in this article, revisions to the UCC, may limit the force of the article's conclusions as applied to Restatements. The general conclusions are that a "private legislature" (like the ALI) "will have a strong status quo bias and sometimes will be captured by private interests." Id. But apart from a brief treatment of an early round of work on the Restatement Third of Torts applicable to one issue in products liability, *see id.* at 648–649, the article does not address Restatement projects.

[15] DeMott, Deborah A. 2007. The First Restatement of Agency: What Was the Agenda?. Southern Illinois Law Journal 32: 17, 24.

[16] Id. at 24–25.

[17] This practice has been discontinued. The records it created are, unsurprisingly, full of insight into the intellectual and institutional development of the ALI's work in its early era. The ALI continues to publish transcripts of its Annual Meetings, but the earlier practice of publishing minutes from Council meetings has also been discontinued. The Institute's Archives (which are not complete) are maintained by and accessible through the University of Pennsylvania. The Biddle Law Library. www.law.upenn.edu/bll/archives/ali/. Accessed 27 Feb 2013.

appropriately uniform style for the various products of the Institute . . . ."[18] The *Hand-book* recognizes that "the prospects for achieving and maintaining a comprehensive "Restatement of the Law appear increasingly remote" because "today's Restatements tend to be separate articulations of increasingly discrete areas of the law," and the ALI has many projects that do not aim to produce Restatements.[19] Nonetheless, a characteristic style is, in the *Handbook*'s estimation, worth attempting to articulate and preserve.[20] The ALI itself, in other words, has an authorial voice that character-izes and identifies its work and distinguishes it from the published work of individual legal scholars.

The ALI's self-developed and actively-enforced "voice" could be characterized as a formal element intended to enhance the authority of its work. As stated in the *Handbook*, the ALI's objective "is to speak with an authority that transcends that of any individual, no matter how expert, and any segment of the profession, standing alone."[21] The ALI's style, as "the manner in which its voice is presented, must transcend the styles and idiosyncracies of individual Reporters to make that asserted authority credible."[22]

The ALI's concern that its authorial persona be manifested in a recognizable voice is consistent with Nils Jansen's emphasis on the form in which Restatements are written as crucial to their authority, distinct from the persuasiveness of their content.[23] Early on, the ALI's founders disdained treatise- or textbook-like discursive treatments of the law that mixed statements of present law with history and legal theory. Instead, the Restatements were to consist of "normative 'statement[s] of the principles of the law'" drafted "'with the care and precision of a well-drawn statute', and with 'the mental attitude . . . of those who desire to express the law in statutory form.'"[24] Single and decisive rules of law should be articulated even in the face of uncertainty about the present state of the law.[25] And assuring that such articulations occur in a consistent voice is integral to their form.

To be sure, it is important not to overstate form's significance. As discussed below, some jurisdictions never followed or adopted the law on some issues as articulated in the Restatements. Moreover, later generations of Restatements include components in addition to decisively-articulated rules in statutory-like form, in particular further commentary and the Reporter's research notes. On the other hand, form matters greatly in legal discourse. As Marta Madero explains, "legal language partly functions

---

[18] American Law Institute. Handbook at 3. www.ali.org/doc/stylemanual.pdf. Accessed 28 Feb 2013.

[19] *Id*. at 2–3.

[20] *Id*. at 3.

[21] *Id*. at 2.

[22] Id.

[23] See Jansen, Nils. 2010. The Making of Legal Authority: Non-legislative Codifications in Historical and Comparative Perspective 107–108.

[24] Id. at 105, quoting American Law Institute, Report of the Committee Proposing the Establishment of an American Law Institute 20.

[25] *Id*.

like the neoclassical Latin of the humanists" because it was not intended as 'breathless statement of fresh perceptions of the world.'"[26] Legal language constitutes, like any language, "'a collective attempt to simplify and arrange experience in manageable parcels.'"[27] Perhaps form matters, not more that it does in legal discourse generally, but for distinctive reasons in the realm of Restatements. In particular, their core functions seem inexorably linked to the style in which they are written.

5.3   Material

The essential material on which a Restatement draws is the decisional law of courts in the United States with the objective of stating underlying principles that give coherence to a subject. This is unsurprising in light of the concern of the ALI's founders that "the underlying principles of the common law had become obscured by the ever-growing mass of decisions in the many different jurisdictions, state and federal, within the United States."[28] In Benjamin Cardozo's assessment, the "fecundity of our case law"[29] had become problematic; and, beneath sheer numbers of cases, many courts obscured the legal principles on which decisions turned, leading to considerable uncertainty in some jurisdictions. The ALI's founders also understood that courts and judicial decisions are not "fungible."[30] In some jurisdictions, many issues remained unresolved by any case. And some courts were viewed as more authoritative than others. As Herbert Wechsler (the ALI's third Director) wrote in 1969 of the first Restatement of Torts, "[e]ven as a law student 40 years ago, I knew that germinal opinions like those of Judge Cardozo in the *Palsgraf* case . . . had been embraced in the drafts of the first Restatement long before they had much following in other courts in the view that they were right and should be followed . . . .."[31]

Complicating the question of sources, contemporary Restatements may draw upon other materials, most importantly statutes. The ALI's *Handbook* (2005) embraces statutes as legal sources much more broadly that did the ALI's founding document (1923), in which "the existing law" was said to be found "in the decisions and

---

[26] Madero, Marta. 2010. Tabula Picta: Painting and Writing in Medieval Law 3, quoting Baxandall, Michael, Giotto and the Orators. 1971. Humanist Observers of Painting in Italy and the Discovery of Pictorial Composition. 1350–1450, 47. Many thanks to Emily Kadens for alerting me to Madero's book.

[27] Id. at 3, quoting Baxandall, supra note 26, at 44.

[28] American Law Institute. Handbook at 4–5. www.ali.org/doc/stylemanual.pdf. Accessed 28 Feb 2013.

[29] Cardozo, Benjamin N. 1924. The Growth of the Law 4, quoted in King, Joseph H. 2011. The Torts Restatement's Inchoate Definition of Intent for Battery, and Reflections on the Province of Restatements. Pepperdine Law Review 38: 623, 651.

[30] King, supra note 29, at 662.

[31] Wechsler, Herbert. 1969. The Course of the Restatements. American Bar Association Journal 55:147, 149. Quoted in King, supra note 29, at 663.

scattered statutes."[32] A major interim development, acknowledged by the *Handbook*, is "the growing prevalence of statutes in the traditional fields of the common law" with some statutes "essentially codifications of the common law."[33] Separately, the ALI might determine that a statute that alters and supersedes a common-law rule is preferable and so state in a Restatement.[34]

According normative force to statutes represents a sharp departure from the ALI's earlier days. The Agency Restatements are illustrative. Restatement (Third) of Agency relies on widely-adopted statutes that supersede common-law rules. For example, it states that an individual principal's loss of capacity does not automatically terminate an agent's actual authority; the agent's authority terminates only when the agent has notice that the principal's loss of capacity is permanent or that the principal has been adjudicated to lack capacity.[35] This is contrary to the position taken in Restatement (Second) of Agency but is consistent with the widespread adoption of statutes that do not automatically void an agent's actual authority upon the principal's loss of capacity. These include a Uniform Commercial Code (UCC) provision protecting a bank (acting as agent) when a customer loses capacity, contemporary partnership legislation, as well as statutes in many states that permit the creation of durable powers of attorney.

In contrast, consider an episode at the 1927 Annual Meeting when discussion turned to a provision in the first Restatement of Agency that preserved the common-law rule that a woman's marriage, by destroying her capacity to consent, also eliminated her ability to be bound by transactions entered into by an agent on her behalf, even an agent appointed before the marriage. Many states by that time had by statute abolished the common-law rule. An ALI member rose from the floor, characterized the common-law rule as "barbarous," and urged the Reporter to omit it from the draft unless he could determine that some states still followed it. This recommendation was not adopted.[36] Restatement (Second) of Agency, promulgated in 1957, demoted the issue to a Comment, which states that "[i]t is not within the scope of the Restatement of this Subject to state in detail the rules by which it is determined whether a person has capacity. The common grounds for incapacity are minority, marriage by a woman . . . ."[37].

---

[32] American Law Institute. Handbook at 7. www.ali.org/doc/stylemanual.pdf. Accessed 28 Feb 2013. ("and scattered statutes" is italicized in the Handbook, but not in the founding document).

[33] Id.

[34] Id. at 8.

[35] Restatement (Third) of Agency § 3.08 (1).

[36] DeMott, supra note 15, at 36.

[37] Restatement (Second) of Agency § 122.cmt.a. A further comment seems to reflect the assumption that the common-law rule retained vitality as applied to married women, observing that "[w]here incapacity is created by marriage, by becoming an enemy alien, by losing citizenship or by conviction of a crime, the incapacity operates from the moment it is created until the condition ends." *Id.* cmt. d. Likewise, a comment to an earlier sections states that "[t]o the extent that a married woman can contract or appoint others as agent, she has capacity to appoint her husband to contract or do other acts on her account, aside from statute." Id. § 22, cmt. a.

Contemporary Restatements may also refer to foreign law "for application by analogy," in the *Handbook*'s formulation.[38] Perhaps more strongly, the *Handbook* urges "[r]eporters to be alert to the possibility that a comparative-law perspective may enrich a particular explication and analysis of U.S. law."[39] On this score, both the second and third Agency Restatements included, among the advisers, members of law faculties in the United Kingdom.[40] When reliable English-language sources were available, Restatement Third of Agency discusses relevant rules from jurisdictions other than the United States, England and Wales, and Commonwealth jurisdictions. As it happens, in many business activities to which agency law is especially relevant— in particular those activities reliant on non-employee intermediaries such as brokers in shipping, reinsurance, and investment securities—the contemporary common law appears to share more similarities across common-law jurisdictions than in other private-law subjects. And the underlying business activity often takes place in multiple jurisdictions. Thus, the Third Restatement of Agency may make more use of comparative-law references than do other contemporary Restatements.

5.4 Functions

The ALI's *Handbook* acknowledges that, from the beginning, "two impulses at the heart of the Restatement process" underlie a central tension: "the impulse to recapitulate the law as it presently exists and the impulse to reformulate it, thereby rendering it clearer and more coherent while subtly transforming it in the process."[41] It is also possible, as Joseph King recently wrote, that in retrospect the founders' vision for the functions to be served by Restatements may appear more "crystallized or manifest" than the reality during the ALI's early work.[42] After all, the Restatement enterprise was novel, and how the founders' initial intentions are now understood is difficult to detach from an assessment of the end-products. Moreover, these end-product Restatements differed, as did their Reporters, in their relative caution or boldness.[43] For example, a member speaking at the ALI's 1932 Annual Meeting

---

[38] American Law Institute. Handbook at 10. www.ali.org/doc/stylemanual.pdf. Accessed 28 Feb 2013.

[39] *Id.*

[40] For the Second Restatement, L.C.B. Gower served as an adviser through the third tentative draft. Professor Gower was at the time a visiting professor at Harvard Law School. See Restatement (Second) of Agency viii. For the Third Restatement, Professors Francis M.B. Reynolds (Worcester College, Oxford) and Gareth Jones (Trinity College, Cambridge) served as advisers, Professor Jones throughout the project's duration and Professor Reynolds from 1999 onward. Restatement (Third) of Agency v.

[41] ALI, Handbook at 4.

[42] See King, supra note 29, at 659.

[43] Kelley, Patrick J. 2007. Introduction: Did the First Restatement Adopt a Reform Agenda?. Southern Illinois Law Journal 32:3.

noted the relative intellectual modesty of the Reporters[44] for Agency in contrast with some of their colleagues. He urged the Reporter, Warren A. Seavey, and his advisers "to 'lay down the rule which he thinks the courts should adopt rather than try to derive a rule from the decisions which is not fully developed.'"[45] But Seavey replied that, when confronted by a rule that seemed unsound, "he had two options: 'To recite what the courts have decided or to say nothing.'"[46]

Cautious though it may have been, the first Restatement of Agency legitimated the subject by giving a coherent account of it. Agency's intellectual merit—or its status as a distinctive subject—had previously been questioned by Roscoe Pound[47] and challenged by Oliver Wendell Holmes with Holmes claiming that agency doctrine consisted of no more than a fiction identifying agent with principal, plus common sense.[48] Seavey responded aggressively to Holmes in a 1920 law review article, arguing that scholarship could, through careful examination of judicial opinions, identify the operative elements and consequences of agency relationships, thereby "finding the rhyme and reason of the law which has grown on the fertile soil of a three party relationship."[49] One measure of the first Restatement's success and influence and that of the successive two Restatements is that no competing account has emerged—no comprehensive treatise challenges the Restatement's treatment of agency law in the United States. Indeed, the last comprehensive scholarly treatise on the law of agency in the United States was published in 1914.[50] Its author, Floyd R. Mechem, served until his death in 1928 as the Reporter for the first Restatement. The Agency Restatements thus became central to how lawyers and judges understood the subject and to the conceptual structure for teaching agency-law topics in law school curricula. In this respect, the Agency Restatements serve a function comparable to the celebrated English-law treatise, Bowstead and Reynolds on Agency, now in its nineteenth edition,[51] because, like *Bowstead and Reynolds*, the Agency Restatements occupy uncontested intellectual terrain as comprehensive accounts of the subject.

---

[44] Floyd R. Mechem served as the initial Reporter from 1923 until his death in 1928. He was succeeded by Warren A. Seavey, who completed the first Restatement and served as the sole Reporter for the second Agency Restatement. See DeMott, supra note 15, at 18–23.

[45] Id. at 31, quoting Warren A. Seavey, Discussion of the Restatement of Agency Tentative Draft No. 7, 10 A.L.I. Proc. 318 (1931–1932).

[46] Id.

[47] DeMott, supra note 15, at 28–30.

[48] Holmes, Oliver Wendell. 1923. The Common Law: 180–183. 1891. Agency I. Harvard Law Review 4: 345–350–351. 1891. Agency II. Harvard Law Review 5:1, 14.

[49] Seavy, Warren A. 1920. The Rationale of Agency. Yale Law Journal 29:859. Seavey reported in his memoirs that this article was the basis on which he was invited to join the Restatement project as an adviser to the first Reporter, Floyd Mechem. As it happens, the Harvard Law Review (Holmes's publisher) rejected Seavey's article, according to Seavey. He joined Harvard's faculty in 1929. DeMott, supra note 15, at 22 n. 74.

[50] Mechem, Floyd R. A Treatise on the Law of Agency: Including not only a Discussion of the General Subject but also Special Chapters on Attorneys, Auctioneers, Brokers and Factors. (1st ed. 1889, 2nd ed. 1914).

[51] Bowstead and Reynolds. 2010. Agency. P.G. Watts ed. 20th ed.

In contrast, the first Restatement of Contracts (1932), with Samuel Williston as Reporter, differs in many ways from Arthur L. Corbin's later (1950) magisterial treatise.[52] Characterized as "something of a realist *eminence grise*," Corbin wrote a comprehensive account of contract law that challenged the Restatement position's on doctrinal points and, more broadly, reflected Corbin's emphasis on the importance of facts in judicial decision-making.[53] Readers who sought one had an alternative to the Restatement, and Corbin's treatise was a work of wide scope and manifest scholarly depth. Similarly, in Torts, the first Restatement (1939) was followed by extensive writing by Leon Green[54] and by William L. Prosser's treatise.[55] Green and Prosser provided accounts of tort doctrine that were far from identical, but both challenged the Restatement. Indeed, Prosser in turn served as the initial Reporter for the second Torts Restatement.

The ALI's *Handbook*, published in 2005, recognizes that Restatements may have a predictive (or leading-edge) function, in addition to clarifying and simplifying the law as it stands at the time of drafting. That is, "a significant contribution of the Restatements has also been anticipation of the direction in which the law is tending and expression of that development in a manner consistent with previously established principles."[56] As discussed above, as research resources the Agency Restatements serve a function comparable to well-regarded continuing treatises in the English tradition. But scholarly work in that tradition does not (or at least not necessarily) serve the leading-edge function embraced by the *Handbook* for Restatements.

As discussed above, the Reporters for the first Restatement of Agency did not aspire to anticipate or guide legal development. It may be that, for Restatements as a whole as an ongoing institutional project, endorsing and embracing this further goal became possible only after the relatively cautious precedents set by the first Restatements.[57] They established the ALI's institutional credibility. But perhaps each generation of Restatements is or was feasible or credible only in its own times. The first Restatements were the product of a simpler era's law in the United States. A larger audience believed in the existence of a general common law, a belief reinforced by the ability of federal courts to develop general federal common law in cases involving disputes between parties of diverse citizenship. This landscape changed dramatically with the Supreme Court's 1938 decision in *Erie R.R. v. Tompkins*, which required federal district courts, in cases involving state-law claims, to apply the same common law as would a state court sitting in the same state.[58] By the early 1960's, one leading federal appellate judge, Henry Friendly, characterized his function in

---

[52] Corbin, Arthur L. 1950. Corbin on Contracts.

[53] Duxbury, Neil. 1995. Patterns of American Jurisprudence 140.

[54] E.g., Green, Leon A. 1927. The Rationale of Proximate Cause. 1930. Judge and Jury.

[55] Prosser, William L. 1952. Handbook of the Law of Torts.

[56] American Law Institute. Handbook at 5. www.ali.org/doc/stylemanual.pdf. Accessed 28 Feb 2013.

[57] Adams, Kristin David. 2007. The American Law Institute: Justice Cardozo's Ministry of Justice?. Southern Illinois Law Journal 32:173, 182.

[58] 1938. United States 304:64.

interpreting state law as "akin to that of Charlie McCarthy, the famous ventriloquist's dummy . . . ." and an intellectually unsatisfying task.[59] Relatedly, to aspire to guide legal development or anticipate it, as opposed to continuing in the cautious vein of the first generation of Restatements, makes a distinctive contribution.

After the first generation of Restatements the province of the common law itself, as a matter of positive law, became part of a legal landscape that included more statutes, more administrative regulation, as well as more legitimation of diffusion in common-law rules across jurisdictions. That's not to say that empirically such diffusion occurred, but *Erie* blessed its legitimacy. Thus, it plausible that a more explicitly normative orientation for Restatements would follow in a more complex era, the common-law basics having already been addressed by the first generation of Restatements. To continue on exclusively in their vein would be, in Suzanne Lepsius's assessment, to indulge in an exercise in an "artificial common law," a construct unlikely to help a lawyer win a case and, after *Erie*, implausible as a portrait of "the actual law in force . . . ."[60]

5.5   Reception and Application

In two jurisdictions, the Restatements are treated by statute as the de facto common law. In the Northern Mariana Islands, which became a United States Commonwealth in 1986, the 1984 Code provides that "the rules of the common law as expressed in the Restatements of the law approved by the American Law Institute . . . shall be the rules of decision in the courts of the Commonwealth in the absence of written or customary law to the contrary . . . ."[61] Comparable language was added to the Code of the Virgin Islands in 1957.[62] Kristin David Adams suggests that the history of the Virgin Islands, a Danish colony before they became a dependency of the United States in 1917, suggests an absence of "any immediate intention to permit the Islands to

---

[59] Dorsen, David M. 2012. Henry Friendly: Greatest Judge of His Era. 314. Judge Friendly, a member of the ALI's Council from 1961 until his death in 1986, was an influential participant in several ALI projects. Id. at 132. These involved the jurisdiction of federal and state courts, administrative law, corporate governance, conflicts of laws, codification of the federal securities laws, international jurisdiction, and a pre-arraignment code for prisoners. Id. Only one of these—conflict of laws—was a Restatement project. Overall Friendly's legal world was not the simpler common-law era reflected in the first generation of Restatements. His pre-judicial career involved complex business transactions and service as the general counsel of Pan American Airways. Although he wrote influential opinions applying common-law doctrines, his biographer emphasizes Friendly's distinctive contributions to business law in judicial opinions and, in extra-judicial writings, to public-law questions and court reform. Id. at 346.

[60] Lepsius, Suzanne. Taking the Institutional Context Seriously: A Comment on James Gordley. 232, 242, in Nils Jansen and Ralf Michaels, supra note 5.

[61] Northern Mariana Code. 7:§ 3401.

[62] Virgin Island Code. § 4.

create their own laws."[63] The 1957 Code provision followed a 1921 Code provision comparable to prior colonial codes but focused on the common law of the United States, not Danish law.[64] Thus, writes Professor Adams, "[a]fter so many years of colonial rule, it may have felt more natural to the Islands at that time [1921] to look to the United States, an external source, for their laws."[65]

Of course, in general Restatement provisions are not the object of wholesale incorporation by statute. Assessing their success often requires a retrospective look at their influence on courts and on scholarly discourse. For many years, the ALI itself published an annual table of cumulative case citations to each individual Restatement, broken down state-by-state. Torts topped the last cumulative list by a large margin, followed by Contracts, then Agency.[66] These citation counts, however, do not reveal whether the cited point was part of the case's holding, or an obiter dictum, or even in a dissenting opinion from a divided court. Thus, proceeding with a finer-grained methodology may better assess relative success. A well-known example is judicial reception of the provision in Restatement Second, Torts on strict liability for harm caused by a defective product. Many state courts treated the provision—Section 402A—as tantamount to a statute, in one scholar's assessment elevating the section and its comments to the status of "holy writ."[67] But this does not mean that courts uniformly adopted the principle stated in Section 402A; Delaware, North Carolina, and Massachusetts did not.[68] Nor did the status of Section 402A signal an end to evolution in the law. Over time, many courts confined the strict liability principle to instances of manufacturing defect, as opposed to claims of defective design or inadequate warning. The ALI followed suit; Section 402A was succeeded by a separate component of the third Torts Restatement focused solely on Products Liability that confines strict liability to manufacturing defects.[69]

---

[63] Adams, Kristin David. 2004. The Folly of Uniformity: Lessons from the Restatement Movement. Hofstra Law Review 33: 423, 429.

[64] *Id.* at 428–429.

[65] *Id.* at 429.

[66] See American Law Institute. 2004 Annual Report Published Case Citations to Restatements of the Law. www.ali.org/annualreports/2004/AM04_07-RestatementCitations04.pdf In particular, as of March 1, 2004, state and federal courts in the United States had cited the Restatements in published opinions 161,486 times. Of that total, Torts accounted for 67,336 citations, Contracts for 28,739, and Agency for 15,830. Conflict of Laws trailed Agency with 13,496 citations followed by Judgments with 10,773 and Trusts at 10,704. The table also breaks down citations to each Restatement on a state-by-state basis. These numbers are not adjusted for the overall number of published opinions from courts in particular states. Cumulatively across Restatements, California accounted for the largest number of citations (8264) followed by Pennsylvania (7874) and New York (6628). The 2004 data are the latest available, at least publicly.

[67] Henderson, James A., Jr. and Aaron D. Twerski. 1995. A Proposed Revision of Section 402A of the Restatement (Second) of Torts. Cornell Law Review 77:1512. Quoted in, inter alia, Vandall, Frank J. 1995. The Restatement (Third) of Torts, Products Liability, Section 2(B): Design Defect. Temple Law Review 68:167.

[68] Christie, George C. 2012. The Law of Torts. 5th edition. In those states, product-defect cases are within the ambit of general negligence or warranty law.

[69] 1997. Restatement (Third) of Torts: Product Liability § 2.

5.6 Authority, Legitimacy, and Influence

The history of the Restatements sketched in this essay fits within the prototype of
Searching for Utopia with which the paper began. Like the reins held by the rider
astride the giant tortoise, the Restatements do not control their subsequent reception
by courts. At times, as discussed above, Restatements may succeed in anticipating
legal development; whether this constitutes guidance—as when the tortoise responds
to a rein—or simply percipience—as when the rider casts his rein in the direction
he predicts the tortoise will take—may depend on the observer's methodology and
perspective. The ALI, as the Restatements' institutional author, constructed its voice
and other elements of its authorial persona, such as the elaborate deliberative and
iterative procedures that precede the final promulgation of a text as a Restatement,
to enhance their usefulness, credibility, and persuasiveness.

The paper also demonstrates that some ambiguity accompanies the underlying
terminology of authority and, for that matter, private law. To Nils Jansen, to say
that a legal text is authoritative means that "the legal profession accept[s] it as an
ultimate source of the law, without requiring further legal reason to do so."[70] The
relative authoritativeness of legal texts, when authorities conflict, is a function of
"how they are applied and interpreted by professional lawyers and in the course
of legal argument."[71] As a consequence, a text's authority may not be stable over
time and any asserted hierarchy among texts is always contestable.[72] It is implicit,
though, that legal "authority" stemming otherwise than from the state cannot be
entirely self-constructed by its promulgator, depending as it does on its reception
by legal audiences. Thus, as the ALI summarizes the character of its authority in
the Handbook, "[a]n unelected body like the American Law Institute has limited
competence and no special authority to make major innovations in matters of public
policy. Its authority derives rather from its competence in drafting precise and internally consistent articulations of the law."[73] One might add, however, that within
the law of agency, "authority" itself is a term that connotes the right or power of
legally-consequential representation of another person. Perhaps confusion with this
meaning of "authority" underlies claims that Restatements stem from an unrepresen-
tative institution, one not chosen through politically-accountable processes or even
the legal profession as a whole. But this critique confines the meaning of "authority"
to its agency sense, as opposed to credibility and reception by an intended audience.

To some legal practitioners and scholars in the United States, the term "private
law" would not be common usage. Once again one's prototype may be significant,
and for some that prototype is contract law. However, as discussed above, the Restatements were significant in articulating and furthering the development of tort law
in the United States. Involving as it does the direct imposition by the law of duties,

---

[70] Jansen, supra note 23, at 43.

[71] Id. at 43–44.

[72] Id. at 44.

[73] ALI, Handbook at 5.

tort law is often controversial and can be the object of political disputes. Does it lie outside the province of private law, as Leon Green long argued?[74] Regardless of its characterization, tort law's presence within the Restatements is important to understanding their history, accomplishments, and limitations.

Finally, and for many reasons, contemporary Restatements speak to an audience of disbelief in the existence of one common law that exists autonomously of invading influences, including statutes.[75] Such a belief is inconsistent with the institutional circumstances of law and its development in the United States, which include the fact of federalism that underlies the *Erie* doctrine and procedural institutions such as lay juries. How to assess authority, influence, and success for a Restatement are more interesting questions once their contemporary audience comes into view.

References

Articles

Adams, Kristin David. 2004. The Folly of Uniformity: Lessons from the Restatement Movement. Hofstra Law Review 33.

Adams, Kristin David. 2004. The Folly of Uniformity: Lessons from the Restatement Movement. Hofstra Law Review 33.

Adams, Kristin David. 2007. The American Law Institute: Justice Cardozo's Ministry of Justice? Southern Illinois Law Journal 32.

Bradford, Anu & Eric Posner (2011), *Universal Exceptionalism in International Law*, 52 Harvard International Law Journal 1.

Cardozo, Benjamin N. 1924. The Growth of the Law 4, quoted in King, Joseph H. 2011. The Torts Restatement's Inchoate Definition of Intent for Battery, and Reflections on the Province of Restatements. Pepperdine Law Review 38.

Cross, Frank. 2011. Tort Law and the American Economy. Minnesota Law Review 96.

DeMott, Deborah A. 2003. Statutory Ingredients of Common Law Change: Issues in the Development of Agency Doctrine. Commercial Law and Practice 56.

DeMott, Deborah A. 2007. The First Restatement of Agency: What Was the Agenda?. Southern Illinois Law Journal 32.

E.g., Leon A. Green, Tort Law Public Law in Disguise, 38 Tex. L. Rev. 1 (1959)

Feldthusen, Bruce. 2011. What the United States Taught the Commonwealth About Pure Economic Loss: Time to Repay the Favor. Pepperdine Law Review. 38.

Green, Michael. 2011. The Impact of the Civil Jury on American Tort Law. Pepperdine Law Review. 38.

Holmes, Oliver Wendell. 1923. The Common Law:180–183. 1891. Agency I. Harvard Law Review 4: 345–350-351. 1891. Agency II. Harvard Law Review 5:1, 14.

Jansen, Nils and Ralf Michaels. 2007. Private Law and the State: Comparative Perceptions and Historical Observations 15, 57. 2008. Beyond the State: Rethinking Private Law. (Nils Jansen & Ralf Michaels eds. 2008).

---

[74] E.g., Leon A. Green, Tort Law Public Law in Disguise, 38 Tex. L. Rev. 1 (1959).

[75] For further discussion, see DeMott, Deborah A. 2003. Statutory Ingredients of Common Law Change: Issues in the Development of Agency Doctrine. Commercial Law and Practice 56, 68–73. Sarah Worthington ed.

Kelley, Patrick J. 2007. Introduction: Did the First Restatement Adopt a Reform Agenda?. Southern Illinois Law Journal 32.

Schwartz, Alan and Robert E. Scott. 1995. The Political Economy of Private Legislatures. University of Pennsylvania Law Review 143.

Seavy, Warren A. 1920. The Rationale of Agency. Yale Law Journal 29.

Vandall, Fank J. 1995. The Restatement (Third) of Torts, Products Liability, Section 2(B): Design Defect. Temple Law Review 68.

Books

Bowstead and Reynolds. 2010. Agency. P.G. Watts ed.20th ed.

Christie, George C. 2012. The Law of Torts. 5th edition.

Corbin, Arthur L. 1950. Corbin on Contracts.

Dorsen, David M. 2012. Henry Friendly: Greatest Judge of His Era. 314.

Duxbury, Neil. 1995. Patterns of American Jurisprudence 140.

E.g., Green, Leon A. 1927. The Rationale of Proximate Cause. 1930. Judge and Jury.

Jansen, Nils. 2010. The Making of Legal Authority: Non-legislative Codifications in Historical and Comparative Perspective.

Madero, Marta. 2010. Tabula Picta: Painting and Writing in Medieval Law.

Mechem, Floyd R. A Treatise on the Law of Agency: Including not only a Discussion of the General Subject but also Special Chapters on Attorneys, Auctioneers, Brokers and Factors. (1st ed. 1889, 2nd ed. 1914).

Prosser, William L. 1952. Handbook of the Law of Torts.

Restatement (Third) of Torts: Liability for Economic Harm § 1, cmt.c. 2012. (Tentative Draft No. 1, Apr. 4, 2012).

Internet and Other Sources

American Law Institute. 2005. Capturing the Voice of the American Law Institute: A Handbook for ALI Reporters and Those Who Review Their Work 1. www.ali.org/doc/stylemanual.pdf. Accessed 27 Feb 2013.

American Law Institute. Bylaw 6. www.ali.org/doc/Bylaws07/pdf. Accessed 27 Feb 2013.

American Law Institute. Handbook at 10. www.ali.org/doc/stylemanual.pdf. Accessed 28 Feb 2013.

American Law Institute. Handbook at 3. www.ali.org/doc/stylemanual.pdf. Accessed 28 Feb 2013.

American Law Institute. Handbook at 4–5. www.ali.org/doc/stylemanual.pdf. Accessed 28 Feb 2013.

American Law Institute. Handbook at 5. www.ali.org/doc/stylemanual.pdf. Accessed 28 Feb 2013.

American Law Institute. Handbook at 7. www.ali.org/doc/stylemanual.pdf. Accessed 28 Feb 2013.

American Law Institute. 1923. Certificate of Incorporation. www.ali.org/doc/charter.pdf. Accessed 27 Feb 2013.

American Law Institute. 2004 Annual Report Published Case Citations to Restatements of the Law. www.ali.org/annualreports/2004/AM04_07-RestatementCitations04.pdf.

Fabre, Jan. 2011. Searching for Utopia. www.panoramio.com//photo/55203509.

The Biddle Law Library. www.law.upenn.edu/bll/archives/ali/. Accessed 27 Feb 2013.

Part III
Codification of Private Law
in Post-Soviet Times

Chapter 6
Codification of Private Law in Post-Soviet States of the CIS and Georgia

Lado Chanturia

6.1 Introduction

The collapse of the Soviet Union and the emergence of new independent States triggered a new wave of codification of private law. As a natural and logical response to the defeat and the collapse of the planned economy there followed the reform of the socialist civil law and the adoption of new civil codes in all states of the former Soviet Union,[1] for which the Western European codifications of civil law served as models.[2]

Although the codification of civil law was not alien even for the Soviet Union,[3] in fact it was for precisely this reason that Soviet civil law was considered as part of the continental European legal family, the existence of the ideologically motivated legal concepts of Soviet civil law caused great concern regarding this affiliation.[4]

---

[1] The following states gained their national independence after the collapse of the Soviet Union: Armenia, Azerbaijan, Belarus, Estonia, Georgia, Kazakhstan, Kyrgyzstan, Latvia, Lithuania, Moldova, Russia, Tajikistan, Turkmenistan, the Ukraine, and Uzbekistan. Estonia, Latvia and Lithuania are members of the European Union. All other states except Georgia are members of the Commonwealth of Independent States (CIS), which was founded after the collapse of the Soviet Union. On the reform of private law in post-Soviet countries of the Caucasus and Central Asia, see: *Knieper Rolf, Chanturia Lado, Schramm Hans-Joachim*, The Private Law in the Caucasus and Central Asia, BWV 2010, pp. 36 ff. (In German).

[2] *Boguslawskij Mark, Knieper Rolf*, (Ed.), Wege zu neuem Recht. Materialien internationaler Konferenzen in Sank Petersburg und Bremen. GTZ, Berlin Verlag Arno Spitz, 1998; *Knieper Rolf*, Rechtsreformen entlang der Seidenstraße, Nomos, 2007.

[3] See *Reich Norbert*, Sozialismus und Zivilrecht, Frankfurt/M., Athenäum Verlag 1972.

[4] *Neumeyer* in *David/Grasmann*, Einführung in die großen Rechtssysteme der Gegenwart, C. H. Beck Verlag, 1988, S. 50 ff., *Zweigert/Kötz*, Einführung in die Rechtsvergleichung, 3. Aufl. Mohr Siebeck, 1996, p. V.

L. Chanturia (✉)
Tbilisi State University (Javakhishvili Tbilisi State University), 1,
Chavchavdze Ave., 0179 Tbilisi, Georgia
e-mail: chanturialado@yahoo.com

Olshausenstr. 75, D-24118 Kiel, Germany

W.-Y. Wang (ed.), *Codification in International Perspective,* Ius Comparatum – Global Studies in Comparative Law, DOI 10.1007/978-3-319-03455-3_6,
© Springer International Publishing Switzerland 2014

The doctrinal principles of Soviet civil law confirmed this doubt, because the civil law of the Western States was considered as hostile and alien for a socialist society.[5] Accordingly, the new codification is significantly different from the old Soviet one, from both a content and legal drafting standpoint.[6]

The plan or command economy was also reflected in civil law and led to the invention of special legal constructions for socialist economic relations, such as the *plan and the contract, the operational management, Kontraktatsia* etc. The civil law doctrine provided numerous arguments and explanations of the features and advantages of socialist civil law.[7] During the 70-year reign of Communism, private autonomy or freedom of contract and private property or freedom of association were strictly forbidden phenomena that were used exclusively for the critique of capitalist legal systems.[8] For these reasons, the reforms in the field of civil law put into effect after the collapse of the Soviet Union were considered in the legal literature of post-Soviet states as a rebirth of private law.[9]

6.2 Models for the Codification of Civil Law

There are two models of codification of civil law. The first one aims to achieve the reform on the basis of its own knowledge and experience collected during the soviet time. The second one targets the reception of developed legal systems.

6.2.1 Model Civil Code (MCC) for CIS Countries

The first model is based on the Model Civil Code for CIS countries, the first part of which (General Provisions and Law on Things) was adopted on 29 October 1994. With the adoption of the second part (Special Law of Obligations) on 13 May 1995

---

[5] As an example: *Raicher V.K.*, Graschdansko-pravovie sistemi antagonisticheskich formatsij, Problemi graschdanskogo i administrativnogo prava, Leningrad, 1962 (In Russian).

[6] *Osakwe Christopher*, Sravnitelnyi Analiz Grazhdanskikh Kodeksov Rossii I Kazakhstana 1994 G.: Biopsiia ekonomicheskikh Konstitutsii Dvukh Postsovetskikh Respublik Uchebnoe Posobie, Almaty, 1998.

[7] For example, the monograph by Professor *Venediktov A. V.*, Gosudarstvennaja socialistićeskaja sobstvennost 'Izd-vo AN SSSR, Moscow, Leningrad, 1948 (*Venediktov*, National Socialist property (in Russian)), in which the construction of operational management was introduced. In addition, each textbook contained a chapter on the civil law of the capitalist countries, which dealt mainly with the criticism of civil law in those countries.

[8] *Raicher V.K.*, Graschdansko-pravovie sistemi antagonisticheskich formatsij. Problemi graschdanskogo i administrativnogo prava, Leningrad, 1962 (In Russian).

[9] For example: *Alekseev S. S.* Graschdanskij kodeks. Sametki is istorii podgotovki proekta ... in Graschdanskij kodeks Rossii. Problemi. Teorija. Praktika. Moskva. 1998, pp. 25 ff.

and the third part (intellectual property) on 16 June 2003 came the creation of a model law for the codification of civil law for the CIS countries.[10]

This model civil code is largely identical with the almost simultaneously adopted Civil Code of Russia and is the foundation of the civil codes of following countries: Armenia, Azerbaijan (in part), Kazakhstan, Kyrgyzstan, Tajikistan and Uzbekistan.

The MCC is, in essence, a product of joint efforts by the lawyers from the CIS countries, under the auspices of the Moscow Research Center for Private Law, which was established in the early 1990s in order to carry out the civil law reform.

6.2.2   Civil Code of Georgia (CCG)

While the MCC tries to create a civil code for a market economy through its own knowledge and experience, the Civil Code of Georgia is mostly an adoption of the civil codes of the developed western legal systems. This was carried out with the strong support of German lawyers, which explains why relicts of old Soviet law are largely absent.[11]

A choice should have been made between the participation of the group elaborating the CIS model code, composed mainly of Soviet specialists in civil law, and cooperation with Germans educated in the traditions of the country of classic civil law. The opinion of chairman of the Georgian working group professor *Sergo Jorbenadze* proved to be decisive in making the choice.[12]

Separate parts of the Civil Code prepared by members of the commission and written in Georgian were translated into German. On the basis of their expertise, German colleagues were able to elaborate a new version of the code, every single sentence and article of which was continuously revised during the course of 4 years. It was a very intricate work which was further complicated by the fact that Georgian law was completely different from that of many institutes. Georgian legal language was also unequipped for such institutes.

Work on the text of the draft Code was continued in Parliament. Every sentence and clause of the Code constituted once again the basis for discussion during 1 year.[13] Unanimity existing between the governing political power and representatives of opposition during the process of working on the code deserve special acknowledgement. It is probably the most unprecedented occasion in the history of

---

[10] *Trunk Alexander*, Harmonization of International Commercial Law within the Commonwealth of Independent States, in Unification and Harmonization of International Commercial Law. Interaction or Deharmonization? Fogt Morten M., (ed), Wolters Kluwer, 2012, p. 225.

[11] *Chanturia Lado*, The Development of Civil Law in Georgia in Georgia in Transition *King/Khubua* (eds.), Frankfurt am Main, 2009, p. 1-17. *Chanturia Lado*, Das neue Zivilgesetzbuch Georgiens: Verhältnis zum deutschen Bürgerlichen Gesetzbuch in: Aufbruch nach Europa. 75 Jahre Max-Planck-Institut für Privatrecht, *Jürgen Basedow, Ulrich Drobnig, Reinhard Ellger, Klaus J. Hopt, Hein Kötz, Rainer Kulms, Ernst-Joachim Mestmäcker* (Hrsg.), Mohr Siebeck, 2001, p. 893–904.

[12] About history and specifics of the Georgian Civil Law see: *Chanturia Lado* (2006), Introduction to the General Part of the Civil Law, Moscow, Statut (in Russian).

[13] As a result, differences exist between the text of draft code submitted to Parliament and the final text of the Code.

the Georgian Parliament where the Members of Parliament so diligently worked on the text of the law, on every clause of it.[14]

The CCG was adopted on 26 June 1997.

The CCG was not drafted as a law of transitional time. It was created as a law intended to survive for many decades. So called conjecture norms usually adopted with the aim of the achievement of particular purposes and expressing interests of particular groups are alien to the Civil Code.

The Civil Code of Turkmenistan (1999) and partly also the Civil Code of Azerbaijan followed the Georgian model.

6.2.3   Features of the MCC for CIS

The MCC takes the role of a so-called super law and includes virtually all areas of private law, including corporate law, bankruptcy law, etcetera, but only in general provisions without detailed legal regulations. Therefore, the MCC contains general provisions for almost all areas of private law with simultaneous references to specific legislative acts.

To fulfil the task of a super law, the MCC grants itself the rank of a second constitution and defines that all the laws of private law have to comply with the civil code (paragraph 2 of Article 2 of the MCC). This principle is often overridden because the special laws ignore the provisions of the civil code.

The concept of the super law shows another special feature: the MCC contains a number of institutions of public law, such as operational management, full commercial use, procurement law, and privatization etcetera.

Another feature of the MCC distinguishes it from traditional civil codes: it contains no family law.

The MCC contains International Private Law and Law on Intellectual Property.

6.2.4   Features of the CCG

In contrast to the MCC is the CCG is a pure act of private law. It contains only the relevant provisions for private law and does not interfere in the field of public law.

Since the CCG does not contain any legal matters of other areas of law, parallel legal rules and regulations are largely unknown and the law practice does not face any practical difficulties in this regard.

The CCG contains the family law.

The CCG does not contain International Private Law and Intellectual Property which are subject of separate laws.

---

[14] It had an impact on the voting results: the Civil Code was passed unanimously. In addition to the text of the draft code, all amendments made as a result of consideration, as well as voting results, are kept in my personal files.

6.3   The Problems with the Implementation of the MCC

Despite the comprehensive codification and transformations of private law carried out, some dogmatic versions recall the old Soviet past and present a few questions: How prepared is the civil law for the new challenges of the development of private law? Are the new civil codes sufficient for a new system of private law, or must they be subjected to a new reform, and if so, of what kind? That the civil codes are in need of reform was confirmed by the draft of reform of the Civil Code of the Russian Federation.[15]

Some experiences from the legal systems of the region suggest that the newly formed private legal systems are not free of the old Soviet burdens, some of which shall be expanded upon here.

6.3.1   Impacts of Soviet Civil Law Doctrine

Application of a Doctrine of Soviet Civil Law

The classics of Soviet civil law and their opinions have quite often been referred to in discussions about the current problems facing modern private law, such as regarding legal entities or the freedom of contract.[16]

Similarly still present is the Soviet doctrine on the special legal status of the state in civil law, which continues to prevail in the civil law of many post-Soviet states. This doctrine tries to justify the legislative powers of the state within civil law. The fact that the state is considered in private law as a private person has been seen in the legal literature, as during Soviet times, as a characteristic of the *bourgeoisie state* (burjuasnogo Gosudarstva),[17] although the civil codes of equality between state and private individuals is laid down in civil law.[18]

It seems to be very doubtful whether this and similar theories are able to explain the current problems of civil law and a market economy. Therefore, the elaboration of a new theory of civil law, taking into account the particularities of the transitional

---

[15] The concept of reform of the Civil Code of the Russian Federation, together with the official explanation: http://www.mpipriv.de/de/data/pdf/2010_01_13_01.pdf; http://privlaw.ru.

[16] Unlike many: *Sukhanov E.A.* O juriditscheskich litsach publitschnogo prava, Vestnik Arbitraschnogo Suda Possijskoi Federatsij, No. 4/2011 p. 11 ff. So calls a prominent Russian professor for the rejection of the notion of legal persons under public law. He draws upon the opinion of Prof. *Venediktov*, considered in Soviet civil law as the inventor of the construction of operational management or state property, for support for the assertion that legal entities of public law are only characteristic for the civil codes of the bourgeoisie (*burjuasnje kodexi*): *EA Sukhanov* O juriditscheskich litsach publitschnogo prava, p. 11.

[17] *Bratus S.N.,* subjectivity graschdanskogo prava. Moskva, 1950, pp. 238–242. To justify the refusal of construction of the legal person of public law Prof. Suchanov has drawn attention to this opinion: E.A. *Sukhanov*, O juriditscheskich litsach publitschnogo prava, pp. 16–17.

[18] For example, article 124 of the Civil Code of Russia.

societies, is a necessary prerequisite for the development of private law in the post-Soviet states; similar to how the Russian legal scholars of the nineteenth Century did so for Russia.[19]

The Continuation of Discussions Regarding Soviet Law

Discussions guided within Soviet law about the *socialist economic law* survive and cause considerable difficulties for both the economy and for the application of the Law.[20] With the adoption and entry into force of its Civil Code and Economic Code on the same day, the Ukraine has created a classic example of legal uncertainty.[21] The two laws contain identical legal matters, but they regulate them differently. The destructive impact of this legal and political decision-making is particularly evident in court cases where a litigant argues its basis for a claim under the Economic code, and the other under the Civil Code. The courts decide at the discretion of the judge whether to apply the Economic Code or the Civil Code.[22]

This contradictory legislation will now be transferred to Kazakhstan, where the legal department of the Presidential Administration initiated the concept of Economic Code. It aims at the adoption of an economic code which is similar to the Ukrainian law, and contains provisions relevant for economic activities in parallel with the provisions in the Civil Code of Kazakhstan. The plan has met with fierce resistance from the lawyers in Kazakhstan, and justifiably so.[23]

The idea of economic code can be used as an expression, and the result, of decades-long, long overdue, but till now ongoing discussions about the system of law and the position of commercial law within this system.[24] A scientific debate can never do any harm, but it is unnecessarily burdensome to legal transformation in post-Soviet states today, and creates significant legal uncertainty, especially since this concept also enjoys political recognition and support.[25]

---

[19] Among the well-known and respected Russian scientists of this time are: *Meyer*, Scherschenevich, Pokrovskji etc.

[20] Details about the origins and development of the theory of socialist economic law: *Yoffe* O., O chosiaystvennom Právě (teorija i praktika) in Graschdanskoe sakonodatelstvo, Isbrannoe, Tom II, *A.G. Didenko* (Ed.), Almaty, 2008, pp. 100–132. (In Russian).

[21] The Civil Code and the Economic Code of Ukraine was adopted on 01.16.2003 and entered into force as from 01.01.2004.

[22] http://civilista.ru/news.php?id=29: Presentation by Prof. Dr. *Kusnetsova N.S.* in Almaty on 29/09/2011.

[23] The Open Letter to the numerous Kazakh lawyers at the Justice Department in the country about the inappropriateness of the adoption of the Economic Code: Journal jurist, 7/2011, pp. 12–14.

[24] Detail on this debate in Soviet and post-Soviet law: *Suleimenov M.K.*, paper presented at the international civil law conference in Almaty on 29/09/2011: http://civilista.ru/news.php?id=29.

[25] *Mamutov* V.K., The concept of an Economic Code of Ukraine, WGO, 1994, pp. 373–379.

The Methods of Commentary

A further problem is related to the use of methods of commenting on civil codes. Although all the legal systems of the region allow for comments on civil codes, they do not meet the standards of the commentary according to German law.[26] They include on the one hand, no reliable literature sources from which one could see an inventory of the state of research in this area. On the other hand, they do not reflect case law and, therefore, they do not provide information about the judicial interpretation and application of various legal provisions in practice.

Due to the current methods of commentary is it almost impossible to credibly document the development of private law in the countries of the region, and for this reason they are not appropriate for impact assessment or the courts. The commentary on civil code is, in this context, perhaps the most important, most valuable, and most responsible service of civil law and practice.[27]

6.3.2 Lack of a Pragmatic Approach

Legal Form of Legal Entities

The close reading of some institutions and provisions in the civil codes increases the concern that a number of regulations are often not well thought out, especially regarding their pragmatism. For example, the wide definition of the forms of legal entities may be seen as evidence for the lack of a pragmatic approach.[28]

Characteristic of the law of many post-Soviet countries is a very broad (often too wide) application of the construction of a legal entities (legal persons), which is expressed in the recognition of almost all associations of persons as legal entities, such as peasant farms or cooperatives of apartment owners. In spite of this fact, the literature attempts to conclusively depict the several types of legal entities, although this presentation is not always in line with the legislation.[29]

Legal persons are, according to the prevailing opinion in post-Soviet law, merely a construction of private law. Only private law provides the State and its organizations with specific forms of legal persons. The power of the State to establish legal entities beyond the borders of civil law is also ignored, although the State has established and practiced numerous such entities.[30]

---

[26] *Galliamova*, N. S. (ed.) Kommentarij k Graždanskomu kodeksu Respubliki Kyrgyzstan. Chasti pervoi. Tom I Akademija, Biškek, 2005 (*Galliamova* (ed.), Commentary on the Civil Code of the Republic of Kyrgyzstan. Part I, Volume I (Russian)), k Kommentarij Graschdanskomu kodeksu Respubliki tschasti pervoi Tajikistan, Dushanbe, 2004, etc.

[27] *Knieper/Chanturia*, introduction to the commentary of Kazakhstan's Civil Code, Volume I (in Russian), Almaty, 2007, pp. 4 ff.

[28] As evidence, there are nearly 40 types of legal entities in Russian law.

[29] *Knieper/Chanturia/Schramm*, Private law in the Caucasus and Central Asia.

[30] As an example: *V.E. Chirkin*, Legal Person of Public Law, Moscow, Norma, 2007 (in Russian).

Types of Real Rights

The lack of pragmatic approach is also conspicuous in the regulation of real rights in the civil codes that follow the MCC, which are insufficiently regulated. There is no systemized catalogue of these rights[31] and also the practical significance of the final settlement of these rights, so called *nummerus clauses*, is not recognized.[32] This provides for legal uncertainty. In the existing system of rights in rem, in which every right to use has its own content and special features, uncertainty in the formation and fixation of the real rights is inevitable.[33]

For these reasons, unification of real rights in the civil codes is necessary. The features of special rights, widely discussed in the literature, should be reflected in the law. Otherwise, the dogmatic interpretations of existing rights on things are misleading because they do not correspond to the actual legal situation. Evidence for this inconsistency may be the assertion of the existence of a *numerus clausus* of real rights, although a *numerus clausus* of real rights in the civil codes that follow the MCC is not anchored.[34]

Another criticism aimed at the systematization of limited real rights, which is made in the laws of the region, is that it necessitates the construction of special rights for each type of object. This could lead to overproduction of limited real rights. Water use or forest use rights as limited rights are demonstrative examples. In German law, rights, such as the land use right or the right of abode, could be allocated to the usufruct or easements (easements), without inventing a special right on land use. The fragmentation of the real rights for objects can lead to significant legal uncertainty. The limited real rights are absolute rights, such as property, and to design them according to individual objects would weaken the main function of the protection against everyone.[35]

Duplicate Statutory Provisions

The lack of a pragmatic approach is also reflected in the dubious legal technique of civil codes, according to which civil code must contain the basic provisions on other special statutory law subjects, whose detailed legal regulation is left to special laws. This usually results in a pre-programmed conflict between the Civil Code and the various individual laws, the solution for which presents the courts with a difficult task.

---

[31] As an example: *Galliamova* (ed.), Commentary on the Civil Code of the Kyrgyz Republic, Vol II, 2005, Article 228, p. 32.

[32] An overview of the classification of real rights and method of research: *Babaev, A.B.*, Sistema veščnych Prav, Wolters Kluwer, Moscow, 2006 (Babaev, system of real rights (in Russian)).

[33] *Knieper/Chanturia/Schramm*, Das Privatrecht im Kaukasus und Zentralasiens, pp. 247 ff.

[34] *Knieper/Chanturia/Schramm*, Das Privatrecht im Kaukasus und Zentralasiens, pp. 247 ff.

[35] *Knieper/Chanturia/Schramm*, Das Privatrecht im Kaukasus und Zentralasiens, pp. 288 ff.

In addition, the civil codes often limit the right of naming the object, without sufficiently detailed regulation, and with reference to other abstract legislation, such as the Uzbek Civil Code concerning legal persons. In approximately 50 articles can be found over 60 references to other laws, most of which have not yet been adopted.

The issue of dual regulation has been known since the adoption of the MCC in the 1990s,[36] but the criticism has become loud and clear in recent times.[37] The Judiciary considers this so-called war of laws as very serious and unsustainable.

6.3.3   Overestimation of the Role of Civil Law

Definition of Extraneous Conditions for the State

The overestimation of the role of the civil codes, which expresses itself often in the imposition of specific duties upon the state, such as the foundation of all legal entities of the State under the civil code or the definition of sale rules of state-owned property under the provisions of the civil code, makes the civil code the subject of frequent changes and amendments. Every time the State makes economic policy decisions, such as the provision of strategic objects or the privatization of state-owned assets, the civil code has to be changed and this leads to the instability of private law.

Participation in private legal relations is not the main task of the State and, therefore, the civil code cannot be the main economic law for the State. The economic policy decisions of the State are beyond private law and the State cannot balance its decisions like a private person under the civil code. The State may also make contracts outside of the civil code, and this cannot be denied on the ground that the contract is a civil law term.

For these reasons, it can be stated that the overestimation of the role of civil law is unrealistic and does not lead to legal certainty.

The Unjustified Extension of the Subject Matter of Civil Law

A further expression of the overestimation of civil law is, on the one hand, the unjustified expansion of the subject matter of civil law, and on the other hand, the exclusion of purely civil matters, such as family law. Both lead to the erosion of civil law by the fact that the actual legal regulation of the legal matter is shifting into other special laws. For example, the civil codes contain provisions on commercial corporations, but these corporations are regulated in separate laws. The provisions of the civil code are therefore devoid of purpose, since they are not applicable in corporate law.

---

[36] *Boguslavskji/Knieper*, Wege zu neuem Recht, Berlin Verlag, 1996, pp. 38 ff.

[37] For example, the presentation by *Prof. Rusanova* at the conference in Almaty on 30.09.2011: *Рузанова* В.Д. "Система гражданского права и система гражданского законодательства: грани взаимодействия". http://civilista.ru/news.php?id=29.

6.3.4   Reform Areas of Civil Law

The need for deleting unrelated provisions from civil codes has become a constant topic of civil law discussions. I would like to remark upon some areas of reform.

Legal Persons

According to the concept of the MCC, the legal entity is an exclusive term of civil law, and therefore, all legal persons must be enshrined in the civil code, including those that will be established by the State. Accordingly, the government entities that are known in German law as legal persons of public law are contained in the civil code, although the civil code contains no specific provisions regarding these persons. The specific regulation is left to individual laws.

The idea that civil law is entitled only to legal persons who could be founded by private persons is alien to the MCC. The supposed range of civil law, therefore, covers all entities, which goes beyond the boundaries of private law and makes the rules of the civil codes on legal persons inapplicable. It is therefore recommended that private law should be confined exclusively to the legal persons of private law.

The controversial concept of the MCC on legal entities generates misunderstandings and confusions in the discussions of legal persons of public law, the latter of which are considered as a new legal form of legal persons and not as unrelated phenomena of private law.[38] Legal persons governed by public law must not be created under the civil law, but in public law. Therefore, it is not a new legal form of legal entities, but rather a concept of public law.

The need to reduce the number of legal forms used in some countries has full support.[39] For regulatory reasons, it is also necessary and appropriate that the law has a clear, transparent, and plausible set of legal forms for legal entities.[40]

Possession

Possession is one of the institutes of law whose legal nature and practical importance understood and interpreted very differently in the legal systems of the Caucasus and Central Asia. The determination of the legal nature of possession is further complicated by the fact that civil codes do not contain clear rules about possession.

---

[38] As an example: Vestnik visschego arbitraschnogo Rossijskoi Federatsii Suda, 4/2011, p. 6.

[39] For example, in Russia: *Suchanov Evgenij* A., Die Körperschaften im modernen russischen Zivilrecht in VDRW-Mitteilungen 49-50/ 2011, S. 5 ff., Turbanov Alexander, Probleme der Klassifizierung der juristischen Personen: Fortsetzung der Diskussion, Vestnik visschego arbitraschnogo Suda Rossijskoi Federatsii, 7/2011, p. 9.

[40] See a comparison of legal forms of entities in different jurisdictions: *Chanturia Lado*, Legal forms of companies (A Comparative Analysis) (Организационно-правовые формы корпораций (сравнительно-правовой анализ), in:Law, Economic, Prosperity: Current issues of legal reform in Turkmenistan, *Nuryev Yagmir, Chanturia Lado* (ed) Ashgabat, 2010, pp. 180-194 (in Russian).

There are two models of regulation of possession: the first one is the MCC and the second one is the Civil Codes of Georgia and Turkmenistan, but also of Azerbaijan. The latter lean more towards the German Civil Code in matters of possession.[41]

A significant factor in the regulation of possession is the fact that the legal system grants protection to the factual possession of objects, without having knowledge of the legal basis of this possession. The concept of possession is used to provide the numerous possessors with legal certainty and protection which occurs in everyday business and is not required to show any visible evidence of the legality of their possession. The legal nature of possession in the countries of the MCC is extensively debated. This is essentially due to discrepancy between the literature and the laws governing possession. This problem is remarkable in the legal systems that follow the MCC. Common to them is the fact that possession has no independent meaning, and it is considered an element of property and other rights in rem.[42] In addition, the literature of these countries defines a totally different concept, as is clear from the civil codes. The influence of Pandectists is very evident, although the actual legal situation is not consistent.[43]

It should also be noted that case law hardly uses the legal concept of possession. Possession is more suitable for the treatment of the claim of the owner into account (so-called *rei vindicatio*). The causes of the lack of use of possession are, in my opinion, both incomplete legal regulations and the lack of research into this institute. Possession has, so far, not earned its rightful role.

The reason for the unclear legal status of possession may be the fact that it is simultaneously considered as a right, but also as an actual rule. Hence the difficulty in determining who is actually the possessor. I consider the criticism expressed towards this regulation to be justified.[44]

The Public Law Institutes Concerning the State

The civil codes that follow the Model Civil Code contain some legal institutions constructed for the state, which systematically belong to public law, namely administrative law. These include, above all, operational management and the right of economic management.

Although the differences between the right of economic management and operational management are expressed in the literature, is it also recognized that this distinction is very difficult.[45] Fundamentally, they are identical institutions with identical tasks. These tasks can be defined as functions of the internal organization of state property, which is of course a legitimate duty of every State. It is more concerned with rules and relationships of administrative law that continue to burden the

---

[41] *Knieper/Chanturia/Schramm*, Das Privatrecht im Kaukasus und Zentralasiens, pp. 251 ff.

[42] *Knieper/Chanturia/Schramm*, Das Privatrecht im Kaukasus und Zentralasiens, p. 253.

[43] *Knieper/Chanturia/Schramm*, Das Privatrecht im Kaukasus und Zentralasiens, p. 251.

[44] *Solotych Stefanie,* Das Zivilgesetzbuch der Russischen Föderation, Nomos, 2001, Bd. I., p. 50.

[45] *Knieper/Chanturia/Schramm*, Das Privatrecht im Kaukasus und Zentralasiens, p. 299.

private law relationships of the participants, because they create special rights for certain subjects who represent the state.

Although the institute of operational management is applied widely in the countries of the region even 20 years after the collapse of the Soviet Union, there are increasing opinions that this construction causes some problems for the development of the market and private initiative. This assessment must be upheld. The State should regulate the management of state property and the responsibilities of individual government units in the context of administrative law. Direct impact on the participants of private legal relations should not have these regulations.

Delivery of Goods for State Needs

The Civil Code of Russia contains a chapter on the delivery of goods for state needs. The content of Article 525 of the civil code indicates that there are basically norms of administrative law concerning public contracts by the State and includes only rudimentary private law regulations.

Although in the Russian literature, the presence of this institute is considered to be characteristic of Russian law,[46] it is actually an internationally-known instrument of public procurement. From the perspective of civil law, it is therefore irrelevant and misplaced.

References

Books

Babaev, A.B. (2006) Sistema veščnych Prav. Wolters Kluwer, Moscow (in Russian).
Boguslavskji, Mark/Knieper, Rolf (ed.) (1996) Wege zu neuem Recht, Materialien internationaler Konferenzen in Sank Petersburg und Bremen. GTZ, Berlin Verlag Arno Spitz (in German).
Bratus S.N. (1950) subjectivity graschdanskogo prava. Moscow (in Russian).
Chanturia Lado (2006), Introduction to the General Part of the Civil Law, Moscow, Statut (in Russian).
Chirkin, V.E. (2007) Legal Person of Public Law, Moscow, Norma, (in Russian).
David/Grasmann (1988) Einführung in die großen Rechtssysteme der Gegenwart, C. H. Beck Verlag (in German).
Galliamova, N. S. (2005) (ed.) Kommentarij Graždanskomu kodeksu Respubliki Kyrgyzstan. Chasti pervoi. Tom I-II Akademija, Biškek (Galliamova (ed.), Commentary on the Civil Code of the Republic of Kyrgyzstan. Part I, Volume I (in Russian).
Graschdanskij kodeks Rossii. (1998) Problemi. Teorija. Praktika. Moskva. (in Russian).
Knieper Rolf (2007) Rechtsreformen entlang der Seidenstraße, Nomos.
Knieper Rolf, Chanturia Lado, (2007), introduction to the commentary of Kazakhstan's Civil Code, Volume I, Almaty (in Russian).
Knieper Rolf, Chanturia Lado, Schramm Hans-Joachim (2010) The Private Law in the Caucasus and Central Asia (Das Privatrecht im Kaukasus und Zentralasiens), BWV 2010 (in German).

---

[46] Graschdanskoe Pravo, pod red. E.A. *Suchanov*, 3. Aufl. Bd. II, Moskau, 2007, pp. 57–59.

Mamutov, V.K. (1994) The concept of an Economic Code of Ukraine, WGO (in Russian).

Nuryev Yagmir, Chanturia Lado (ed) (2010), Law, Economic, Prosperity: Current issues of legal reform in Turkmenistan, Ashgabat (in German, Russian and Turkmen).

Osakwe Christopher (1998) Sravnitelnyi Analiz Grazhdanskikh Kodeksov Rossii I Kazakhstana 1994 G. Biopsiia ekonomicheskikh Konstitutsii Dvukh Postsovetskikh Respublik Uchebnoe Posobie, Almaty (in Russian).

Raicher V.K. (1962) Graschdansko-pravovie sistemi antagonisticheskich formatsij, Problemi graschdanskogo i administrativnogo prava, Leningrad (in Russian).

Reich Norbert (1972) Sozialismus und Zivilrecht, Frankfurt/M., Athenäum Verlag (in German).

Solotych Stefanie (2001) Das Zivilgesetzbuch der Russischen Föderation, Nomos, Bd. I. (in German).

Sukhanov E.A. (ed) (2007) Graschdanskoe Pravo, 3. ed Vol. II, Moscow.

Venediktov A. V., (1948) Gosudarstvennaja socialističeskaja sobstvennost 'Izd-vo AN SSSR, Moscow, Leningrad, (Venediktov, National Socialist property (in Russian).

Yoffe, O. (2008), O chosiaystvennom Právě (teorija i praktika). In: Graschdanskoe sakonodatelstvo, Isbrannoe, Tom II, Didenko A.G. (ed.), Almaty (in Russian).

Zweigert Konrad, Kötz Hein (1996) Einführung in die Rechtsvergleichung, 3. Aufl. Mohr Siebeck (in German).

Statues

Civil Code of Georgia.
Civil Code of Russia.
Model Civil Code for CIS.

Other Sources

Alekseev S. S. (1998) Graschdanskij kodeks. Sametki is istorii podgotovki proekta ... in Graschdanskij kodeks Rossii. Problemi. Teorija. Praktika. Moskva. 1998, pp. 25 ff. (in Russian).

Basedow Jürgen, Drobnig Ulrich, Ellger Reinhard, Hopt Klaus J., Kötz Hein, Kulms Rainer, Mestmäcker Ernst-Joachim (Hrsg.), (2001), Aufbruch nach Europa. 75 Jahre Max-Planck-Institut für Privatrecht, Mohr Siebeck.

Chanturia Lado (2001) Das neue Zivilgesetzbuch Georgiens: Verhältnis zum deutschen Bürgerlichen Gesetzbuch. In: Jürgen Basedow, Ulrich Drobnig, Reinhard Ellger, Klaus J. Hopt, Hein Kötz, Rainer Kulms, Ernst-Joachim Mestmäcker (Hrsg.) Aufbruch nach Europa. 75 Jahre Max-Planck-Institut für Privatrecht, Mohr Siebeck (in German).

Chanturia Lado (2009) The Development of Civil Law in Georgia. In: Transition *King/Khubua* (eds.), Frankfurt am Main.

Chanturia Lado (2010) Legal forms of companies (A Comparative Analysis) (Организационно-правовые формы корпораций (сравнительно-правовой анализ). In: Right economic prosperity Current issues of legal reform in Turkmenistan, Ashgabat (in Russian).

Kuznetsova, N.S., (2011), Presentation in Almaty on 29/09/2011: http://civilista.ru/news.php?id=29. (in Russian).

Rusanova V.D. (2011) Systema grashdanskogo prava i systema grashdanskogo zakonodatelstva: grani vzaimodeistvija *at the conference in Almaty on 30.09.2011: http://civilista.ru/news.php?id=29* (In Russian).

Sukhanov, E.A. (2011) O juriditscheskich litsach publitschnogo prava, Vestnik Arbitraschnogo Suda Possijskoi Federatsij, No. 4/2011(in Russian).

Sukhanov, Evgenij A. (2011) Die Körperschaften im modernen russischen Zivilrecht in VDRW-Mitteilungen 49-50/ 2011(In German).

Suleimenov M.K., paper presented at the international civil law conference in Almaty on *29/09/2011: http://civilista.ru/news.php?id=29* (in Russian).

The concept of reform of the Civil Code of the Russian Federation, together with the official explanation: http://www.mpipriv.de/de/data/pdf/2010_01_13_01.pdf; http://privlaw.ru (in Russian).

The Open Letter to the numerous Kazakh lawyers at the Justice Department in the country about the inappropriateness of the adoption of the Economic Code: Journal jurist, 7/2011(in Russian).

Trunk Alexander, Harmonization of International Commercial Law within the Commonwealth of Independent States, in Unification and Harmonization of International Commercial Law. Interaction or Deharmonization? Fogt Morten M., (ed), Wolters Kluwer, 2012, p. 223–235.

Turbanov, Alexander (2011) Probleme der Klassifizierung der juristischen Personen: Fortsetzung der Diskussion, Vestnik visschego arbitraschnogo Suda Rossijskoi Federatsii, 7/2011(in Russian).

Chapter 7
Private Law Codification in The Republic of Croatia

An Example of Legal Reform in Post-Socialist Countries in South-East Europe

Tatjana Josipović

7.1 Introduction

The codification of private law in the Republic of Croatia started very intensively immediately after the country gained independence in 1991. Prior to that, Croatia had been one of the socialist republics of the former Socialist Federative Republic of Yugoslavia (SFRY) which had developed a form of the socialist legal system that partly differed from that of all other former socialist countries. The socialist legal order of the former Yugoslavia was aimed at the development of a socialist society based on workers' self-management. The main features of the legal system at the time were collective social ownership, a planned economy and so-called associated labour in socially owned enterprises. A special form of ownership was developed in the former SFRY—social ownership. This was based on completely different principles from ownership relations in continental Europe based on individualistic concepts of the right of ownership and the autonomy of individuals. The socialist concept of ownership corresponded to the collectivistic goals of the socialist order, workers' self-management and associated labour in enterprises. Social ownership was completely contrary to private ownership. The definition of social ownership was of a very unusual dogmatic nature (even illogical): things that were socially owned were described as "everybody's and nobody's" and used by "associated labour" as the means of production and the satisfaction of other needs.[1] Such a concept of social ownership had a negative impact on the subsequent development of private law in all republics of the former Yugoslavia. Many classical legal institutions and private law principles were deformed, and many traditional private law rules were repressed or modified. As opposed to public law, which had a dominant role in the socialist

---

[1] See Gavella, N. et al: Stvarno pravo, sv.I, Zagreb, 2007. p. 814; Vedriš-Klarić: Osnove imovinskog prava, Zagreb, 1983, p. 248–284.

T. Josipović (✉)
School of Law, University of Zagreb, Trg marsala Tita 3, 10000 Zagreb, Croatia
e-mail: tatjana.josipovic@zg.t-com.hr

W.-Y. Wang (ed.), *Codification in International Perspective,* Ius Comparatum – Global Studies in Comparative Law, DOI 10.1007/978-3-319-03455-3_7,
© Springer International Publishing Switzerland 2014

legal order, private law became extremely marginalised. Private law legislation thus developed at a very slow pace. Still, some traditional private law areas such as family law and labour law developed quite independently from all other private law areas. They had their own development within socialist law, partly because these particular branches of law were marked by the strong influence of public law (e.g. labour law) and partly because some private law areas had to be harmonised with the principles of socialist society (e.g. family law).

A radical change in the position and role of private law took place in all the countries that emerged after the breakup of the former Yugoslavia and accompanied independence and the transition to market economies. This is when the intensive re-codification of private law began. Private law reform started, aimed at two key largely overlapping goals: the creation of a new and modern private law order, based on a market economy, and the harmonisation of private law with the law of the European Union. The reform was shaped by several factors. First, in the reform of the so-called "classical" private law areas, a crucial impact was that of the continental European systems under whose influence private law had developed before World War II. An exception was only related to some new legal areas that were developing in individual countries, either independently or under the influence of Anglo-Saxon law (such as registered liens on chattels and rights).[2] Second, private law reform was and still is under the significant influence of the process of harmonisation with EU law, particularly in the area of the law of contract and indemnification. In addition, priority in the reform was given to private law areas which were important for a market economy (e.g. real property law, labour law, company law). As far as the method of re-codification is concerned, so far a segmented approach has been applied to the organisation of individual private law areas, similar to the situation that existed in the former SFRY.[3] Some private law areas are regulated by some new, or amended, separate acts such as the Ownership Act, the Obligations Act, the Inheritance Act, the Family Act, etc.[4] In most states emerging from the breakup of the former Yugoslavia, there is still no discussion on the adoption of civil codes[5] and there is still a tendency to regulate individual private law areas by separate laws. These characteristics of private law reforms can be detected to a greater or

---

[2] For non possessory/registered security rights over movables see national reports (Formar Yugoslav Republic of Macedonia, Croatia, Bosnina and Herzegovina, Serbia, Montenegro) and comparative analyses (published in english) in Civil Law Forum for South East Europe—Collection of studies and analyses First Rergional Conference Cavtat, Beograd, 2010, Vol. II, p. 11–142, 275–300, http://www.gtz.de/de/dokumente/gtz2010-en-civil-law-forum-vol-2.pdf.

[3] The former SFRY did not have a civil code because there were no basic conditions in terms of the constitutional competence for the adoption of a civil code. At that time, it was not possible to introduce a civil code because of the complicated division of jurisdiction of individual private law segments between the Federation and the socialist republics. The jurisdiction changed with time and the republics progressively assumed jurisdiction for the regulation of individual private law segments (family law, succession law, condominium ownership and housing law, etc.) but not the entire civil law system.

[4] Such an approach to re-codification is the result of a segmented organisation of private law from the socialist period (see note 3).

[5] At present, only in the Republic of Serbia and the Republic of Macedonia are there ongoing and long-term projects aimed at the development of civil codes.

lesser extent in all the newly emerged states in the territory of what used to be Yugoslavia.[6][7] We shall analyse below the impact of all these factors on the re-codification of private law in the Republic of Croatia. As we have already stated, private law reform started immediately after the gaining of independence (1991) and it intensified after the signing of the Stabilisation and Association Agreement between the Republic of Croatia and the European Communities and their Member States.[8]

7.2   The Impact of the Austrian Civil Code on the Development of Croatian Private Law

7.2.1   In General

The Austrian Civil Code (ACC) (*Allgemeines Bürgerliches Gesetzbuch* (ABGB)) had a decisive impact on the development of Croatian private law. Many years of its application in the territory of today's Croatia were of utmost significance in the

---

[6] For example, the impact of EU law on private law reform is not the same in all these countries and this is the result of their different status in the European integration. The Republic of Slovenia became a member of the EU in 2004. The Republic of Croatia become a member on 1 July 2013. Some countries have the status of candidate country, and some of potential candidate. For more details on the statuses of countries from the territory of the former Yugoslavia in the process of European integrations, see http://europa.eu/about-eu/countries/index_en.htm.

[7] For more see Perović, J.: Contract Law in Serbia, p. 87–108; Trstenjak, V.: Private Law Reform in Slovenia—European Perspective, p. 123–148; Povlakić, M.: Property Law Reform in Bosnia and Herzegovina, p. 205–236, Nikolić, D.: Property Law Reform in Serbia: Both Autonomous Legal Development and Legal Transplant, p. 237–268, Vasiljević, M.: The Serbian Law on Commercial Companies, p. 269–294 (all articles published in Private Law in Eastern Europe, ed. Jessel-Holst, Ch, Kulms, R, Trunk, A., Tübingen, 2010); Rijavec, V.: Die Grundzüge des Erbrechts in Slowenien, p. 95–122; Povlakić, M.: Grundzüge des Erbrechts in Bosninen und Herzegovina, p. 141–162; Salma.J.: Die Entwicklung des Erbrechts in Serbien, p. 163–188. (all articles published in Erbrechtsentwicklung in Zentral-und Osteurpa, Hrsg:Welser, Wien, 2009); Povlakić, M.: Die Schuldrechtsreform und der Konsumentenschutz in Bosnien und Herzegowina unter besonderer Berücksichtigung der Umsetzung der Klauselrichtlinine, p. 137–166; Salma, J.: Verbraucherrecht in Serbine im Lichte gemeinschaftlicher Vorgaben, p. 167–196 (all articles published in Konsumentenschutz in Zentral-und Osteuropa, Hrsg: Welser, Wien, 2010); see national reports (Formar Yugoslav Republic of Macedonia, Croatia, Bosnina and Herzegovina, Serbia, Montenegro): Security Rights in Movables, Security right in Immovables and comparative analyses (published in english), Civil Law Forum for South East Europe—Collection of studies and analyses First Rergional Conference Cavtat, Beograd, 2010, Vol. II, p. 11–142, 275–300, http://www.gtz.de/de/dokumente/gtz2010-en-civil-law-forum-vol-2.pdf; see national reports (Slovenia, Croatia, Bosnina and Herzegovina, Serbia): Flexibilität der Grundpfandrechte in Europa, Red. Stöcker, O. M. Berlin, 2006, Band I, p. 33–86, 157–198, 371–403; Berlin, 2007, Band II, p. 131–190.

[8] The Association Agreement between the Republic of Croatia on the one part and the European Communities and their Member States on the other (Official Gazette—International Agreements, 14/01). See the English version at < http://narodne-novine.nn.hr/clanci/medunarodni/328068.html >. See the English version of the Accession Treaty at http://www.mvep.hr/custompages/static/hrv/files/111201-Ugovor%20o%20pristupanjuENG.pdf.

development of Croatian private law. The impact of the ACC was not only decisive in the past for the development of Croatian private law because it bridged the transition from feudal to modern civil society, but because it also had a significant impact on the development of Croatian private law itself at the time when it was developing under the strong influence of socialist law.[9] The ACC also played an important role in the development of the new private law system of the Republic of Croatia when, after gaining its independence, a legal system based on a market economy, free entrepreneurship and private ownership started developing. On the one hand, in all these phases of the development of Croatian private law, the ACC provisions were the basic source of organisation of individual civil law relations among private persons. On the other hand, it was the ACC that was the model for the organisation of individual private law areas in contemporary Croatian law. In any case, this did not interrupt the active existence of the ACC in Croatian law. Regardless of the fact that Croatia has passed a whole series of civil law acts originally stipulated by the ACC, its provisions are still very much alive in practice as a specific legal source for the organisation of private law relations which emerged prior to the adoption of the new and valid legislation.

7.2.2 Direct Application of the ACC as the Main Source of Private Law (1812–1945)

The ACC was gradually introduced in some Croatian territories in the period from 1812 to 1853.[10] With the entry into force of the ACC, the then Croatian-Hungarian law ceased to be applied as a separate law in the territory of Croatia. With its entry into force, the conditions were created for the development of a new Croatian legal and liberal society, a new judiciary and modern procedural law through which the ACC provisions were to be applied in practice. The ACC continued to exist as Croatian law, i.e. as the Croatian Civil Code even after the Croatian-Hungarian Agreement of 1868 by which, among other things, the legislative autonomy of Croatia was recognised. However, the ACC remained in force in the Croatian territories which were not connected to the Hungarian Crown but were parts of the Austrian portion of the Austro-Hungarian Empire. The ACC remained an important civil law source even after World War I (WWI) when Croatia became part of the Kingdom of Serbs, Croats and Slovenes (in 1929, it became the Kingdom of Yugoslavia). The application of the ACC provisions was considered as a temporary and transitional solution until the Croatian Parliament passed new civil law acts. They remained in force until the end of WWI. The Kingdom of Serbs, Croats and Slovenes and the Kingdom of Yugoslavia never passed their own civil codes with validity in the entire territory of

---

[9] Beside the ACC, other Austrian regulations also had a major influence on Croatian private law. The land register, civil proceedings, *ex parte* proceedings, the service of notaries public and a number of other services were also organised around the model of Austrian law.

[10] For more see Gavella, N et al: Das ABGB in Kroatien, Österreichs Allegemeines Bürgerliches Gesetzbuches ABGB, Hrsg. Berger, E., Band III, Berlin 2010, p. 163–180.

the State. The ACC had been and therefore remained the most important source of civil law regulation in all the territories in which it had existed as a civil law source before WWI.

7.2.3   Indirect Application of the ACC in Croatian Socialist Law—Application as "Legal Rules"

Even at the time when Croatia was a part of the socialist legal order, the ACC still played a very important role in the regulation of private law relations. After WWI, by the Act on the Invalidity of Regulations Adopted Prior to 6 April 1941 and During the Occupation (1946), all regulations adopted prior to 6 April 1941 and during the occupation were derogated. This was the beginning of a new phase in the history of Croatian private law characterised by the abandonment of the continental-European legal circle and inclusion into the socialist legal circle. This was when the application of the ACC, as a direct source of civil law, ceased to exist in all Croatian territories where its provisions had been directly applied as the basic source of the legal organisation of civil law relations.

Nevertheless, despite the fact that the ACC had "lost its legal force" as a result of the Act on Invalidity of Regulations Adopted Prior to 6 April 1941 and During the Occupation (1946), the provisions of the ACC in reality continued to be applied. Although the new socialist law was based on collectivistic principles, a planned economy and Marxist ideology, the need for civil law regulation of the legal relations between individuals continued to exist. There was still a need to provide for private law relations between individuals in terms of family relations, inheritance, ownership, contractual relations and the like. Taking all this into account, at the time of the application of the socialist law in Croatia, the ACC assumed a new and very specific role. Because of the lack of valid regulations in the area of family law, inheritance law, civil obligations and real property law, the ACC provisions became an indirect source for the regulation of these civil law segments. In the socialist Republic of Croatia, the ACC provisions became a bridge and a link between the continental European legal circle to which Croatia had belonged before World War II, and the new socialist law that was increasingly developing in the then Croatia.

However, the ACC provisions were no longer applied as positive law but only as "legal rules".[11] Their application was permitted in the case of legal relations not provided for in the positive regulations, namely where the existing gaps in the legislation had to be filled. Private law relations that were not provided for in the positive body of law were regulated in accordance with the content of the ACC provisions. With time, some ACC provisions lost their meaning when private law relations were concerned. Eventually, numerous ACC provisions could no longer be applied to the new legal relations arising from the dominant impact of the collectivistic socialist legal

---

[11] The ACC provisions were applied on the basis of the Act on Invalidity of Regulations Adopted Prior to 6 April 1941 and During the Occupation (1946). In their decisions, the courts referred to this Act and only indirectly to a particular ACC provision.

order (e.g. social ownership relations). A number of new regulations were adopted to provide for particular private law segments and they gradually eliminated the need for the application of the relevant ACC provisions (for example, the Basic Marriage Act (1946), the Inheritance Act (1955), the Obligations Act (1978), the Act on Basic Ownership Relations (1980)). However, some private law segments remained unregulated in positive law until the end of the socialist period, and the ACC provisions continued to be applied as legal rules. Thus, the ACC provisions carried on being applied to personal easements, neighbourhood law, contracts on donation.

7.2.4   The ACC as a Model for Private Law Regulations in Socialism

The role of the ACC at the time of the application of the socialist law was not limited to filling the gaps in some private law areas. The ACC had a significant impact on the concept of positive legal regulation of individual civil law areas during socialist times. The best example is the former Yugoslav Act on Basic Ownership Relations of 1980 which largely followed the tradition of the ACC in terms of real property relations. Under the influence of the ACC, various real property principles were stipulated, such as the principle of the causal tradition for the acquisition of real property rights on movables and immovables, the rule on the acquisition of movables from non-owners, and the principle of strict accessoriness of liens.[12] Interestingly enough, even at that time some rules of the German Civil Code were adopted in property law. For example, possession was regulated on the model of German law (so-called objective concept of possession).

7.3   The Impact of the ACC on Contemporary Croatian Private Law (1991 →)

7.3.1   Continuation of the Indirect Application of the ACC

Even after the independence of the Republic of Croatia in 1991, the ACC continued to be an important factor in the regulation and development of individual private law areas. On the one hand, some paragraphs of the ACC continued to apply as legal rules because after Croatia had become independent not all private law areas were provided for by valid regulations (e.g. contracts on donation, personal easements). On the other hand, the tradition of the ACC continued to have a strong impact on Croatian private law reform because of the need to re-join the continental European legal circle.

After its independence, Croatia started a very complex process of reforming its legal system in order to adjust it to that of a market economy. As part of the reform,

---

[12] Gavella, N et al: Das ABGB in Kroatien, p. 183–189.

special efforts were made to modernise some private law areas which had been neglected, marginalised or under-regulated in socialist Croatia (e.g. real property law, company law), or were developing under the major influence of public law (e.g. labour law).[13] The lack of corresponding legal regulations from various civil law areas whose stipulation had previously been under federal jurisdiction was bridged by the adoption in the Croatian legal system of numerous federal Yugoslav regulations from the area of civil substantive and procedural laws. By virtue of separate acts on adoption, the former federal acts, somewhat amended, became Croatian positive legislation.[14] However, despite the fact that Croatia, upon its independence, adopted a number of federal laws from the private law area in its legal system, gaps continued to exist in terms of some civil law institutions where no Croatian regulation existed. Therefore, the legal sources for the regulation of these gaps continued to be those that were valid in the territory of Croatia on 6 April 1941. Thus, the provisions of the ACC remained an important legal source to fill the gaps in the area of civil law. The ACC rules applied on the basis of a separate Act on the Application of Regulations Adopted Prior to 6 April 1941 (1991). By virtue of this Act, it was permitted to apply, as legal rules, the regulations that had been in force on 6 April 1941 (including the ACC) if, pursuant to separate regulations, they had already applied in the Republic of Croatia until the day of the entry into force of the mentioned Act. This application was possible to the relations that were not provided for by the valid regulations of the Republic of Croatia and if the rules were in accordance with the Constitution and the law of the Republic of Croatia.[15]

However, the importance of the ACC for the regulation of civil law relations gradually decreased because they started to be regulated by positive Croatian regulations. The need for the application of ACC rules on new real property relations (personal easements) ceased to exist when the Act on Ownership and Other Real Property Rights entered into force on 1 January 1997.[16] The application of the ACC provisions on contracts of donation terminated when the new Obligations Act (1 January

---

[13] For more details, see Josipović, T.: *Anpassung des kroatischen Zivilrechts and europäische Standards,* Welser *(HRSG): Privatrechtsentwicklung in Zentral- und Osteuropa,* Wien, 2008, pp. 141–159; Gavella, N., Borić, T.: *Sachenrecht in Kroatien,* Wien 2010, pp. 19–27; Borić, T.: *Eigentum und Privatisierung in Kroatien und Ungarn,* Wien, 1996; Borić, T., Petrović, S.: *Gesellschaftsrecht und Wirtschaftsprivatrecht in Kroatien,* Wien, 2000.

[14] Cf. *Zakon o preuzimanju Zakona o osnovnim vlasničkopravnim odnosima,* OG 53/1991 (The Act on the Adoption of the Act on the Basic Ownership Relations), *Zakon o preuzimanju Zakona o obveznim odnosima,* OG 73/1991 (The Act on the Adoption of the Obligations Act), *Zakon o preuzimanju Zakona o parničnom postupku,* OG 53/1991 (The Act on the Adoption of the Civil Procedure Act), *Zakon o preuzimanju Zakona o izvršnom postupku,* OG 73/1991 (The Act on the Adoption of the Enforcement Act), *Zakon o preuzimanju Zakona o rješavanju sukoba zakona s propisima drugih zemalja,* OG 53/1991 (The Act on the Adoption of the Law on the Resolution of Conflict of Laws with the Regulations of Other Countries), et al.

[15] About court practice see more Josipović, T.: 200 Jahre der ABGB-Anwendung in Kroatien—135 Jahre als Gesetz und 65 Jahre als "Rechtsregeln", Festschrift 200 Jahre ABGB, Band II, Hrsg. Fischer-Czermak, C., Hopf, G,Kathrein, G.,Schauer, M, Wien 2011 p. 157–174.

[16] Official Gazette 91/1996, 91/96, 68/98, 137/99, 22/00, 73/00, 129/00, 114/01, 79/06, 141/06, 146/08, 38/09, 153/09, 143/12.

2006) entered into force.[17] However, even then the need for the application of the ACC provisions as legal rules did not end. All the new positive regulations from the civil law area, completely filling the gaps that had previously required the application of the provisions of the ACC as legal rules, expressly stipulated that on the legal relations, emerging prior to their entry into force, the rules which had been valid at the time of their existence had to be applied.[18] Therefore, numerous provisions of the ACC are still very much present in practice and are applied as legal rules for the regulation of civil law relations that had emerged prior to the entry into force of the new civil law legislation.

7.4 The Impact of the ACC on New Legislation

7.4.1 In General

The existence of some provisions of the ACC continued to exist to some extent even when their content was incorporated in the new civil law regulations. The long-standing tradition of the application of the ACC and other Austrian regulations ensuing from the ACC in the territory of Croatia has had a decisive impact on the legal regulation of many Croatian private law institutions. The regulation of individual private law institutions based on the model of Austrian law was aimed at ensuring legal continuity and security in legal transactions. Thus, the new Obligations Act of 2005 provided for partnership, contracts of donation and contracts of loan for use based on the model of the ACC.[19] [20] The concept of some of these contracts, the rights and duties of the parties to the contract, the form of contract, the subcategories of some of these contracts (e.g. donation with a charge, donation *mortis causa*, donation without transfer to possession), termination of contract, etc. were regulated on the model of Austrian law provisions. However, the most extensive impact of the ACC and Austrian law is reflected in the provisions of the new Croatian real property law.

7.4.2 Particular Impact on the New Real Property Law

The new Croatian real property law is largely regulated on the model of the Austrian real property law provided for in the ACC and other regulations such as the

---

[17] Official Gazette 35/05, 41/08. 125/11.

[18] Cf., for example, Art 1163/1 of the Obligations Act (2005), Art. 388/2 of the Act on Ownership and Other Real Property Rights (1996).

[19] See Arts 479–498 (donation), Arts 509–518 (loan for use), Arts 637–660 (partnership).

[20] See more Gavella, N et al: Das ABGB in Kroatien, p. 192–195; Josipović, T.: Das ABGB in Kroatien -historische Geltung und Bedeutung für die kroatische Zivilgesetzgebung von Heute, 200 Jahre Allgemeines Bürgerliches Gesetzbuch (ABGB) und Europäische Vertragsrecht, 23. Europäische Notarentage 2011, Hrsg. Kodek, G.E, Wien, 2012, 65–70; Josipović, T.: Property Law Reform in Croatia Between Legal Transplants and ASutonomous Development, Private Law in Eastern Europe, ed. Jessel-Holst, Ch, Kulms, R, Trunk, A., Tübingen, 2010), p. 191–194.

Condominium Act (*öWohnungseigentumsgesetz*), the Right to Build Act (*öBaurecht-gesetz*), and the Land Register Act (*öGrundbuchsgesetz*).[21] The Act on Ownership and other Real Rights/OA (in force since 1 January 1997), developed on the model of Austrian property law, provides for the traditional principles of property law (the principle of a closed number of property rights, the principle of absoluteness, the principle of publicity), some types of real rights (ownership/co-ownership/joint ownership/condominium, personal and real easements, real encumbrances, liens, the right to build), acquisition, termination and protection of individual real rights, restriction of real rights, and the concept of things and their division into movables and immovables. In this sense, there are similarities not only with respect to the regulation of particular property law institutions but also in the approach to drafting legislation which provides for real property relations. The Ownership Act (OA), just like the ACC, does not make any distinction between the regulation of movables and immovables (only when this is necessary for some particular types of things where it provides for some specific characteristics (e.g. conditions for the acquisition of ownership on the basis of a legal transaction). However, unlike the ACC, the OA has more detailed provisions for some real rights, particularly when it comes to conditions for acquisition, protection of trust and the legal foundations for the termination of real rights.[22] In addition, the OA also contains very detailed rules on the legal position of foreigners in legal transactions concerning property[23] and very complex rules on the transition to the new real property regulation after the transformation of social ownership and the establishment of a legal unity of an immovable (the principle of *superficie solo cedit*).[24]

If compared to individual provisions of the ACC, we can say that there are some deviations from Austrian real property law that result from a different approach in the regulation of individual real property institutions. The Croatian OA has adopted an objective concept of possession: the rules of the German Civil Code on the acquisition of movables from non-owners. Unlike the Austrian law, the OA has adopted the principle of exemption of actions for the protection of real rights from the application of the statute of limitations.

7.4.3 Graduality of the Private Law Reform—A Reform Without a Civil Code

Re-codification of Croatian private law was not done in the same way, and its scope differed in various areas. In some areas, the changes were very systematic and

---

[21] For more on Croatian real property law, see Gavella, N., Borić, T.: *Sachenrecht in Kroatien*, Wien, 2000, pp. 19–115. In this publication, there is also a German translation of the *EDRG* (pp. 16–298).

[22] See more Gavella, N et al: Das ABGB in Kroatien, p. 189–192

[23] See Josipović, T.: Harmonisation of Croatian Real Property Law with EU Law, Private Law Reform in South-East Europe—Liber Amicorum Christa Jessel-Holst, Belgrade, 2010, pp. 280–305.

[24] See *supra* under note 4.

complete, and in others only minimal changes were introduced. The reform of the Croatian private law system was carried out without the adoption of a comprehensive civil code. It was introduced gradually with the adoption of separate laws for particular private law areas. At the legislative level, the reform has now been substantially completed. A large amount of new private law legislation has been adopted, covering the most important segments such as property law, land registration law, the law of obligations, family law, succession law, commercial law and labour law. These areas are mostly regulated on the model of Austrian law but the influence of German law can also be traced (e.g. bankruptcy law, company law). However, in some areas of private law, autonomous development, free of any foreign influence, can still be found. This is particularly obvious in those areas in which a transition had to be made from an old (socialist) legal regulation to a new legal regulation,[25] as well as in areas in which the modernisation of private law relationships was conditioned by the development of social and family relationships rather than directly by a transition to a market economy. During the reform, the obligation of the Republic of Croatia to harmonise its legislation with that of the EU was also taken into account. All private law areas which belonged to the area of the application of EU law were harmonised with the *acquis communautaire*.

Substantial changes were necessary in the areas of private law which constituted the biggest obstacles to the new economic regulation. Economic reform called for new real property law, company law and labour law. The previous "socialist" laws governing these areas were no longer suitable for the regulation of these relations. They were fully abolished. Social ownership, socially owned enterprises and administrative management of the economy were also abolished. They have been replaced with new legal institutions based on liberal and individualistic concepts and private autonomy and initiative. An overall **real property reform** was carried out with the adoption of the Act on Ownership and Other Real Rights (effective as of 1 January 1997). The OA abolished social ownership, which was transformed into private ownership. The regulation of real property rights is again founded on the classical and traditional principles of property law (e.g. the principle of *superficies solo cedit*). Some new real property rights have been introduced (the right to build) and the legal regulation of individual rights has been brought into line with the principle of *superficies solo cedit* (condominium). A new system of secured transactions has been introduced. The protection of trust in legal transactions involving movables and immovables has increased. At the same time, new regulations on the land register and its digitisation, and the digitisation of the cadastre have been adopted. The Enforcement Act of 1996 introduced a special type of security—the fiduciary transfer of ownership. The reform of the system of secured transactions continued and registered liens on movables were introduced by the Act on the Register of Security Rights in Chattels and Rights before a Court or the Notaries Public/Register Act

---

[25] Thus, for example, separate laws were passed on the transformation of socially owned enterprises, as well as regulations on the restitution of property and regulations on the transformation of social ownership. For further details on transformation and privatisation, see Borić/Petrović, Gesselschaftsrecht und Wirtschaftsprivatrecht in Kroatien, Wien, 2000. p. 199–214.

(2005).[26] **Labour law reform** was carried out by the Labour Act of 1995. Labour law relations are again regulated as separate private law relations based on a labour contract. The general provisions of the law of contract apply subsidiarily to labour contracts. The **company law reform** started with the adoption of the Companies Act in 1993. The Companies Act provides for various types of companies which enhance the development of free entrepreneurship and a market economy (joint stock companies, limited liability companies, limited liability partnership, etc.). Companies are mostly regulated on the model of German law. Beside the Companies Act, separate regulations have been adopted on the commercial court register and on notaries public. New regulations exist on foreign exchange operations, securities, bills of exchange, cheques, as well as on banks, bankruptcies and in many other areas. All these reforms have resulted in a completely new legal framework for efficient market operations and free movement of capital and services. The new legal framework is constantly being developed and adjusted to EU requirements for the free movement of goods, services and capital. All regulations in the area of commercial and financial law have constantly been harmonised with European legislation.

In some legal areas, however, only minor and the most urgent changes have been introduced. These are mostly areas which did not have any crucial impact on the economic development of the country (e.g. succession law), or those whose regulation had already corresponded to that of a market economy (e.g. contract law). **The law of succession** was changed only with the adoption of the Inheritance Act of 2003. In the new Inheritance Act, the freedom of testamentary succession was extended, narrowing the circle of forced heirs and extending the circle of legal heirs to include extra-marital spouses, a register of wills was introduced, and notaries public were authorised to conduct inheritance proceedings.[27] **Family law** changed fundamentally with the Family Act of 2003 which replaced the Family Act of 1998. In the new Family Act of 2003, the previously adopted principles of equality of children born in wedlock and those born out of wedlock have been kept, as well as equality between marital and extra-marital spouses in real property relationships. In addition, the rights of children are regulated in accordance with international conventions on the rights of children. At the same time, a separate Act on Same-Sex Partnership was adopted[28] providing for relationships in same-sex unions (the obligation of maintenance, property relationships, etc.).[29] A new piece of legislation on **obligations (contract, law of torts)**, the Obligations Act (Obl.A), entered into force only on 1 January 2006. Prior to that, the Obligations Act of 1978 had been effective and was

---

[26] For more see Josipović, T.: Property Law Reform in Croatia Between Legal Transplants and ASutonomous Development, Private Law in Eastern Europe, ed. Jessel-Holst, Ch, Kulms, R, Trunk, A., Tübingen, 2010), p. 191–180-199.

[27] For further details on succession law, see International Encyclopedia of Laws, Family and Succession Law (Suppl. 27– Croatia), The Hague 2005, pp. 40–44, 191–268; JOsipović, T.: Erbrecht in der Republik Kroatien, Erbrechtsentwicklung in Zentral-und Osterupa, Hrsg:Welser, Wien, 2009 p. 189–202.

[28] Official Gazette 116/03.

[29] For further details, see International Encyclopedia of Laws, Family and Succession Law (Suppl. 27– Croatia), pp. 132–145, 170, 172.

considered modern ever since its entry into force because it offered a satisfactory
level of freedom of contracting and of protection of private parties to the contract.
The new Obligations Act has kept the so-called monistic regulation of contractual
relations: the same rules apply to all contractual relations regardless of whether the
parties are private persons or traders. The Obl.A only exceptionally lays down some
particularities when it comes to relations between traders. There is no commercial
code in Croatia. It is important to emphasise that the new Obl.A is adjusted to the
new European standards enshrined in the laws of contract and tort. In its general part,
the new Obl.A sets forth the principles of the law on obligations and describes the
existence, types and effects of obligations, and the legal and business capacities of
the parties. In a separate part, the Obl.A contains provisions dealing with contractual
relations (in general and in relation to 35 different types of contract), as well as extra-
contractual obligations. It has incorporated many European directives concerning all
kinds of obligations. However, the directives which deal with consumer contracts
have been incorporated in a separate Consumer Protection Act (CPA), because the
Obl.A does not provide for a law regulating **consumer contracts**. We can say that by
now all the guidelines concerning the legal protection of consumers have been incorporated into Croatian law. They have become parts of the same piece of legislation,
the Consumer Protection Act, which, besides general provisions on the protection of
consumers, also contains separate provisions on each type of consumer contract in
accordance with the European directives. The legislator has opted for a segmented
approach to the regulation of individual consumer contracts by having transposed almost verbatim the contents of the directives dealing with particular types of consumer
contracts. Therefore, we can say that at this point there is still no general system of
law of consumer contracts which would be valid for all contractual relations with a
consumer on the one side and a trader on the other. The Consumer Protection Act in
only one place brings together all the rules on individual consumer contracts which
are regulated on the basis of the European guidelines. In relations to the Obl.A, the
Consumer Protection Act is a *lex specialis*. The provisions of the Obl.A apply to
the obligations between consumers and trader only subsidiarily, that is, the Obl.A
applies only if the Consumer Protection Act does not stipulate differently.[30]

7.4.4 Transition to a New Private Regulation (A Property Law Example)

One of the biggest problems in private law reform has been the regulation of the
transition from the old to the new private law regulation. Major problems have arisen
in the area of real property law where the adoption of the Act on Ownership (OA) and
Other Real Rights resulted in a real seismic shift. The most important steps in real

---

[30] For more see Josipović, T.: Verbraucherschutz in der Republik Kroatien, Konsumentenschutz
in Zentral-und Osteuropa, Hrsg: Welser, Wien, 2010 p. 53–80; Josipović, T.: Europäisierung des
Schuldrechts in Kroatien, Die Reform des Privatrechts in Mittel-und Osteuropa, Hrsg., Lazar, J.
Trnava, 2009, p. 107–131.

property reform were the final abolition of social ownership and its transformation into private ownership, as well as the return to the principle of the legal unity of real property (the principle of *superficies solo cedit*).[31] Indeed, the transformation of social ownership over certain real property had partly been carried out even before the OA entered into force. It was carried out in such a way that the socially owned enterprises that were holders of the rights over socially owned property changed their status and became private enterprises (e.g. joint stock companies). With transformation to private enterprises, rights over socially owned property were *ex lege* transformed into ownership for those persons who, prior to the process of privatisation, had the right to use the same property.[32] In the case of some real property (e.g. agricultural land, forest land), social ownership ceased to exist on the basis of various separate laws making this property *ex lege* fall under the ownership of the Republic of Croatia. The process of transformation included restitution, whereby property that had been nationalised and confiscated was returned to its former owners.[33] The process of transformation of social into private ownership finally ended when the OA entered into force on 1 January 1997. Since its entry into force, social ownership has no longer existed.

The establishment of a real property system based on only one type of ownership (private ownership) and a return to the principle of legal unity of real estate required special regulation to provide for the transition of existing social ownership to the new system. It was necessary to establish a transitory system with maximum recognition of the principles of acquired subjective rights over socially owned property. These rights, despite the fact that they had existed over socially owned property, had proprietary and economic value that had to be preserved during the transition to a new real property regulation. On the other hand, the transition had to be structured in such a way as to ensure a speedy and simple, but legally secure, transition to the new regulation of ownership. The legal effects of the transition were established *ex lege*, i.e. with the entry into force of the transitional and final provisions of the OA (1 January 1997).

The establishment of a real property system based solely on private ownership required a cessation of subjective rights on socially owned property. Those rights could only be transformed into the right of ownership or some other right provided for in the OA. On the basis of the transitional and final provisions of the OA (Articles 354–365), rights over socially owned property were transformed into the right of ownership whereby their holder is known. The owners of property that used to be in

---

[31] The principle of the legal unity of real property for buildings built on socially owned plots was abandoned in the socialist era: the building was privately owned by the builder who had the right to use the socially owned plot. The principle of unity of real property was also abandoned in the regulation of freehold division (condominium ownership). The owner of a flat in a socially owned building had only the right to use the land. The owner of a flat in a privately owned building co-owned the land and jointly owned the common parts of the building.

[32] The Act on the Transformation of Publicly Owned Enterprises, Official Gazette 19/91, 45/92, 83/92, 16/93, 94/93, 2/94, 9/95.

[33] The Act on Compensation for Assets Seized During the Yugoslav Communist Rule (Official Gazette 92/96, 92/99, 80/02, 81/02.

social ownership (*ex lege*), or their heirs or other legal successors, now had ownership over the privatised socially owned property. New presumptions were also introduced to facilitate the proving of ownership acquired by transformation. A person is deemed to be the owner of a piece of real property if the right to use the former socially owned property was entered in his or her favour in the land register. In cases where it is not possible to establish from the land register who the holder of the right to use the socially owned property is, the State is considered to be the owner.

The establishment of the legal unity of real property also required special transition in all cases where the land and the building had previously been legally separated. The legal unity of real property was established in such a way that the land and the building erected on it became unified real property (Articles 366–373 OA). The owner of the building erected on socially owned land prior to the entry into force of the OA then became the owner of the land on which the building was erected. When the OA became effective, the owners of flats became the co-owners of the entire property (land + building) and their legal position was also governed by the provisions of the OA regulating condominium (Articles 66–99 OA).

7.5 Conclusion

A great deal has already been done in terms of the re-codification of Croatian private law, particularly at the legislative level. However, the road to modern private law regulation is not easy. Croatia is still faced with many problems in the process of developing its new private law system:

- Private law regulations are often passed without sufficient professional coordination and without systematic analyses of the problems. Regulations often remain incomplete and mutually conflicting. There are often many gaps and this is why regulations are often amended. This has a negative impact on legal security.
- Transitional regimes are a special problem. In the case of extensive systemic acts (e.g. the Act on Ownership and Other Real Rights), it was necessary to provide for a transition from the old to the new legal regulation. The transition had to be made by observing the principles of acquired rights. Problems arose because many of the rights were abolished (e.g. the right to use things in social ownership). Such rights had to be substituted by the corresponding rights within the new legal system (e.g. ownership, lease). This is where the Croatian legislator had to show extreme creativity because no examples could be found in the legislation of other countries. The transition from the old to the new legal regulation is one of the biggest problems in practice, calling for the efficient application of new regulations.
- A problem was also the establishment of an optimal relationship between private law and public law norms. Private law norms in many general regulations are often suppressed in favour of public law norms in numerous separate regulations (e.g. in the case of the separate legal regulation of immovables). This has a negative impact on private autonomy and on the realisation of private rights.

- Special problems have also arisen in the process of the harmonisation of Croatian private law with that of Europe. There is no systematic approach to an analysis of the goals and contents of the directives and the ways of their implementation in Member States. In most cases, implementation boils down to the transposition of the exact wording and the translation of directives. No systematic adjustments of other private law segments are made. However, this is much needed because European private law is very fragmented. Its implementation requires a systematic approach to the reform of the entire private law body. The task is very complex even for the very well-established private law systems of some Member States, let alone for those that are new, as is the case with the Croatian private law system.
- Problems also arise in the implementation of the new regulations because the necessary legal infrastructure is not sufficiently developed. There are problems connected with the insufficient education, particularly of older generations of lawyers. Corresponding computer technology support is also lacking.
- The new private law institutions provided for in the new regulations are often not even used in practice. The new legislation, modelled on contemporary foreign legislations, enables the use of various financial transactions, security of claims and financial arrangements. However, they have not taken hold in practice for various reasons. The most important one is the lack of the necessary economic and legal infrastructure to enable their application in practice. For example, the land register has not been updated. Various real property securities, priority mortgages and the like cannot be realised in practice.
- Case law in terms of the implementation of the new legislation is not yet well established.
- In practice, there are often problems connected with the efficiency of the legal system. The realisation and protection of rights are slow and insecure. This all leads to the public perception that the legal system is imperfect.
- Nowadays, very high standards are needed in the application of laws. Constant changes require the rapid development of the legal profession, permanent education and training. This also calls for greater dynamics in the process of changing programmes at law schools and faculties and the constant introduction of new teaching methods. Lawyers with a university degree who work in the judiciary or administration need to be constantly trained and equipped with new knowledge.

All these problems have a negative impact on the overall impression of the Croatian private law system. In terms of legislation, a very high level of modernisation and Europeanisation of Croatian private law has already been achieved. However, its re-codification has not yet been completed. Private law contents are still incomplete and they are not rounded off as a logical and functional whole. At the beginning, a segmented approach turned out to be an appropriate way of developing the new Croatian private law system. It enabled speedy, but only essential, interventions to be made to eliminate obstacles to the market economy. However, we must ask ourselves how such a gradual development of the Croatian private law order will reflect on the subsequent harmonisation of all its segments. In the Republic of Croatia, no plan has been worked out for the development of the entire private law system—a system with a reasonable number of regulations, a reasonable content, scope and quality which together can ensure private autonomy and develop economic relations. The principles on which such a system must be based have not yet been defined. An integral concept of codification of individual private law segments has not been adopted. As we have already said, the contents of individual pieces of legislation either overlap or are mutually conflicting. Different terminology is used. This all leads to the question about whether it would be better to synthesise various individual regulations into an integral civil code or keep this segmented approach to the development of the Croatian private law system.

References

Accession Treaty, http://www.mvep.hr/custompages/static/hrv/files/111201-Ugovor%20o%20 pristupanjuENG.pdf.
Borić, T.: *Eigentum und Privatisierung in Kroatien und Ungarn*, Wien, 1996.
Borić, T., Petrović, S.: *Gesellschaftsrecht und Wirtschaftsprivatrecht in Kroatien*, Wien, 2000.
Borić/Petrović: *Gesselschaftsrecht und Wirtschaftsprivatrecht in Kroatien*, Wien, 2000.
Flexibilität der Grundpfandrechte in Europa, Red. Stöcker, O. M., Band I, Berlin, 2006.
Gavella, N., Borić, T.: *Sachenrecht in Kroatien*, Wien 2010.
Gavella, N et al: *Das ABGB in Kroatien*, Österreichs Allgemeines Bürgerliches Gesetzbuches ABGB, Hrsg. Berger, E., Band III, Berlin 2010.
Gavella, N. et al: *Stvarno pravo, sv.I*, Zagreb, 2007.
International Encyclopedia of Laws, Family and Succession Law (Suppl. 27– Croatia), The Hague 2005.
Josipović, T.: *Anpassung des kroatischen Zivilrechts and europäische Standards,* Welser *(HRSG): Privatrechtsentwicklung in Zentral- und Osteuropa*, Wien, 2008.
Josipović, T.: *Harmonisation of Croatian Real Property Law with EU Law*, Private Law Reform in South-East Europe—Liber Amicorum Christa Jessel-Holst, Belgrade, 2010.
Josipović, T.: *200 Jahre der ABGB-Anwendung in Kroatien—135 Jahre als Gesetz und 65 Jahre als "Rechtsregeln"*, Festschrift 200 Jahre ABGB, Band II, Hrsg. Fischer-Czermak, C., Hopf, G, Kathrein, G., Schauer, M, Wien 2011.
Josipović, T.: Das *ABGB in Kroatien -historische Geltung und Bedeutung für die kroatische Zivilgesetzgebung von Heute*, 200 Jahre Allgemeines Bürgelisches Gesetzbuch (ABGB) und Europäische Vertragsrecht, 23. Europäische Notarentage 2011, Hrsg. Kodek, G.E, Wien, 2012.
Josipović, T.: *Erbrecht in der Republik Kroatien*, Erbrechtsentwicklung in Zentral-und Osteuropa, Hrsg: Welser, Wien, 2009.
Josipović, T.: *Europäisierung des Schuldrechts in Kroatien*, Die Reform des Privatrechts in Mittel- und Osteuropa, Hrsg., Lazar, J. Trnava, 2009.
Josipović, T.: *Property Law Reform in Croatia Between Legal Transplants and Autonomous Development*, Private Law in Eastern Europe, ed. Jessel-Holst, Ch, Kulms, R, Trunk, A., Tübingen, 2010.
Josipović, T.: *Verbrauchesschutz in der Republik Kroatien*, Konsumenteschutz in Zentral-und Osteuropa, Hrsg: Welser, Wien, 2010.
Nikolić, D: Property Law Reform in Serbia: Both Autonomous Legal Development and Legal Transplant, Private Law in Eastern Europe, ed. Jessel-Holst, Ch, Kulms, R, Trunk, A., Tübingen, 2010.
Perović, J.: *Contract Law in Serbia*, Private Law in Eastern Europe, ed. Jessel-Holst, Ch, Kulms, R, Trunk, A., Tübingen, 2010.
Povlakić, M.: *Die Schuldrechtsreform und der Konsumenteschutz in Bosnien und Herzegowina unter besonderer Berücksichtigung der Umsetzung der Klauselrichtlinine*, Konsumenteschutz in Zentral-und Osteuropa, Hrsg: Welser, Wien, 2010.

Povlakić, M.: *Grundzüge des Erbrechts in Bosninen und Herzegovina*, Erbrechtsentwicklung in Zentral-und Osteuropa, Hrsg: Welser, Wien, 2009.

Povlakić, M.: *PropertyLaw Reform in Bosnia and Herzegovina*, Private Law in Eastern Europe, ed. Jessel-Holst, Ch, Kulms, R, Trunk, A., Tübingen, 2010.

Rijavec, V.: Die Grundzüge des Erbrechts in Slowenien, Erbrechtsentwicklung in Zentral-und Osteuropa, Hrsg: Welser, Wien, 2009.

Salma, J.: *Verbraucherrecht in Serbine im Lichte gemeinschaftlicher Vorgaben*, Konsumentenschutz in Zentral-und Osteuropa, Hrsg: Welser, Wien, 2010.

Salma. J.: *Die Entwicklung des Erbrechts in Serbien*, Erbrechtsentwicklung in Zentral-und Osteuropa, Hrsg: Welser, Wien, 2009.

Security Rights in Movables, Security right in Immovables and comparative analyses (published in english), Civil Law Forum for South East Europe—Collection of studies and analyses First Rergional Conference Cavtat, Vol. II, Beograd, 2010, http://www.gtz.de/de/dokumente/gtz2010-en-civil-law-forum-vol-2.pdf.

The Association Agreement between the Republic of Croatia on the one part and the European Communities and their Member States on the other (Official Gazette—International Agreements, 14/01, http://narodne-novine.nn.hr/clanci/medunarodni/328068.html

Trstenjak, V.: *Private Law Reform in Slovenia—European Perspective*, Private Law in Eastern Europe, ed. Jessel-Holst, Ch, Kulms, R, Trunk, A., Tübingen, 2010.

Vasiljević, M.: *The Serbian Law on Commercial Companies*, Private Law in Eastern Europe, ed. Jessel-Holst, Ch, Kulms, R, Trunk, A., Tübingen, 2010.

Vedriš-Klarić: *Osnove imovinskog prava*, Zagreb, 1983.

Chapter 8
A Civil Code Outside of Reality—The Polish Codification of the Year 1964, Its Origin, Development and Future

Fryderyk Zoll

8.1 Introduction

The Polish civil code from the year 1964[1] is still in force. Almost 50 years for the private law codification is not an especially impressive result. It cannot be compared with the major European codification. The French[2] and Austrian[3] civil codes are more than 200 years in force, the Spanish[4] and German[5] codes have passed the line of 100 years, and the Italian[6] code reaches also an impressive age. It is however not fully justified comparison. The Polish civil code has been adopted in a quite specific time. The country was ruled by a communist regime, which claimed a complete reorganization of the society, including its economic structure.[7] The fact that the Polish code has been adopted in the non-democratic regime it is not unique in the history of the private law codifications. Rather the opposite is true. The majority of the codes, which are still the valid law in Europe, were not adopted in the full democratic environment. Principally however these systems did not interfere fundamentally in the market-oriented economy. The non-democratic regime of the communist state was going to reshape the whole economic system. This new economy should be based on the state-owned property deprived of the freedom of contract. The communist

---

[1] Law of April 23, 1964 (Dziennik Ustaw No. 16, Chap. 93).

[2] Law of March 21, 1804.

[3] Law of January 1, 1812 (JGS No. 946/1811).

[4] Law of July 24, 1889 (Gaceta de Madrid No 206 of July 25, 1889).

[5] Law of August 18, 1896 (RGBl. 1896, p. 195, No. 21), in force since January 1, 1900.

[6] Law of 1865; replaced by Law of March 16, 1942 (Gazzetta Ufficiale April 17, 1942, No 91), in force since April 21, 1942.

[7] W. Glatz, Die Novellierung des polnischen Zivilgesetzbuches, ROW 1993, p. 44; M. Pazdan, Zur Änderung des polnischen Zivilrechts, OsteuropaR 1991, p. 16; J.Poczobut, Die Reform des polnischen Zivilrechts, ZEuP 1999, pp. 75 (77, 79, 90).

F. Zoll (✉)
School of Law, University of Osnabrück, Süsterstr.28, 49074 Osnabrück, Germany
e-mail: fzoll@uos.de

Jagiellonian University, 31-007 Cracow, ul. Olszewskiego 2, Poland

W.-Y. Wang (ed.), *Codification in International Perspective,* Ius Comparatum – Global Studies in Comparative Law, DOI 10.1007/978-3-319-03455-3_8,
© Springer International Publishing Switzerland 2014

regime needed also the civil law which was reversing the basic principles of the classical private law. Therefore the civil codes of the communist countries were facing a fundamental challenge with the reintroduction of the free market economy. Could they be maintained at least through certain period or their replacement become immediately urgent?[8] The majority of the Central and Eastern European countries have already replaced the old communist civil codes[9] by the modern codifications.[10] The Polish civil code from the year 1964 is still in force and albeit the new codification is also envisaged, the replacement will still require a lot of time.[11] The old code does not want to become just a part of history.[12] More than 20 years after transition it fulfills still its function. In this paper I would like to answer the questions, how this is possible and where the limits of the innovation of this code are.

8.2 The "Surrealistic Codification"?

The codification of the year 1964 has been prepared in quite harsh and inconvenient times. It was the time, in which the short thaw[13] after the year 1956 was gone. Any, even limited democratization of the system was not in sight. It was however also any more the stalinistic time. Certain limited, but also important relaxation of the pressure has however happened. This political change was however also a very important factor in the final result, which the Codification Commission working on the draft has eventually produced. The Commission had evidently slightly more space and air in the process of drafting.

To understand the fate of the Polish codification from the year 1964 is not possible without knowing the history of the unification of the law in Poland. This story begins at the time of gaining the independence after the First World War. At the end of the eighteenth century Poland has lost his independence as a result of being divided by Prussia, Russia and Austria.[14] With the Polish partition and the loss of the independence also the original Polish legal system and tradition disappeared.[15]

---

[8] F. Zoll, Die Arbeiten am neuen polnischen Zivilgesetzbuch, OsteuropaR 2012, p. 29 (30).

[9] F. Zoll, Die Arbeiten am neuen polnischen Zivilgesetzbuch, OsteuropaR 2012, p. 29.

[10] It has happened in Lithuania, Estonia, Czech Republic, Romania, Ukraine and Russia. The new civil code has been prepared in Hungary. The Slovakian draft is advanced. In Latvia the pre-war civil code has replaced the civil law of the Soviet origin.

[11] See F. Zoll, Die Arbeiten am neuen polnischen Zivilgesetzbuch, OsteuropaR 2012, p. 29 (39).

[12] On the disunity over the requirement to a new codification of the Polish civil law, also see: N. Bulicz/F. Merli, Democracy, Rule of Law, Market Economy and EU-Membership: The Rebuilding of Polish Law, in: F. Merli/G. Wagner, New Poland in Europe, Innsbruck 2006, p. 165 (176 et sEq.).

[13] W. Glatz, Die Novellierung des polnischen Zivilgesetzbuches, ROW 1993, p. 44.

[14] F. Zoll, Future of European Contract Law from the Perspective of a Polish Scholar, in: Scripta Iuris Europaei, Special Issue: European Contract Law 2006, ERA-Forum; p. 90.

[15] W. Rozwadowski, Tradycje rzymskie w polskim prawie cywilnym, in: M. Safjan, System Prawa Prywatnego, Prawo cywilne—część ogólna, Warsaw 2007, p. 3.

It has been replaced by various legal systems.[16] On the Polish territory (within the borders which has been fixed in the period between the great wars) there were five legal systems in force: German, Austrian, French, Russian and Hungarian.[17] With the regaining of the independence in the year 1918 the unification of the law was one of the important agendas in order to unify the divided country.[18]

This agenda has been endorsed by the Codification Commission. The Commission has considered an option to take over one of the legal systems which was in force on the Polish territory.[19] They decided however that the new state needs a law which will be common for all parts of Poland.[20] They have decided to work on the new codification.[21] It is not my intention to present the process of the codification, due to the fact that I have presented it in various papers in English and German.[22] It must be only stressed that the works of the Codification Commission were one of the founding events of the contemporary Polish legal tradition.[23] The Commission was operating until 1939 (but some works continued in the underground under the German occupation). The Commission has consisted of the best Polish jurists of these times—professors and practitioners.[24] They have been educated and experienced in different

---

[16] J.Poczobut, Die Reform des polnischen Zivilrechts, ZEuP 1999, p. 75.

[17] See: A. Mączyński, Das ABGB in Polen, in: Festschrift 200 Jahre ABGB, Vienna 2011, vol. I, p. 188; L. Górnicki, Prawo cywilne w pracach Komisji Kodyfikacyjnej Rzeczypospolitej Polskiej w latach 1919–1939, Wroclaw 2000, p. 69; F. Zoll: Future of European Contract Law from the Perspective of a Polish Scholar, in: Scripta Iuris Europaei, Special Issue: European Contract Law 2006, ERA-Forum; p. 90.

[18] W. Dajczak, The Polish way to a unified law of contract—local curiosity or contribution to the European debate today?, in: C. von Bar/A. Wudarski, Deutschland und Polen in der europäischen Rechtsgemeinschaft, Munich 2012, p. 13 (15); K. Sójka-Zielińska, Wielkie kodyfikacje cywilne, Historia i współczesność, Warsaw 2009, p. 15; J.Poczobut, Die Reform des polnischen Zivilrechts, ZEuP 1999, p. 75 (76); F. Zoll: Future of European Contract Law from the Perspective of a Polish Scholar, in: Scripta Iuris Europaei, Special Issue: European Contract Law 2006, ERA-Forum; p. 90.

[19] L. Górnicki, Prawo cywilne w pracach Komisji Kodyfikacyjnej Rzeczypospolitej Polskiej w latach 1919–1939, Wroclaw 2000, pp. 72–74; F. Zoll, Future of European Contract Law from the Perspective of a Polish Scholar, in: Scripta Iuris Europaei, Special Issue: European Contract Law 2006, ERA-Forum; p. 90 (91).

[20] L. Górnicki, Prawo cywilne w pracach Komisji Kodyfikacyjnej Rzeczypospolitej Polskiej w latach 1919–1939, Wroclaw 2000, p. 18.

[21] L. Górnicki, Prawo cywilne w pracach Komisji Kodyfikacyjnej Rzeczypospolitej Polskiej w latach 1919–1939, Wroclaw 2000, p. 74; J.Poczobut, Die Reform des polnischen Zivilrechts, ZEuP 1999, p. 75 (76).

[22] F. Zoll, Contract Law in the draft of the New Polish Civil Code, in: R. Schulze/F. Zoll, The Law of Obligations in Europe, 2013; id., Die Arbeiten am neuen polnischen Zivilgesetzbuch, OsteuropaR 2012, pp. 29–39; id., Future of European Contract Law from the Perspective of a Polish Scholar, in: Scripta Iuris Europaei, Special Issue: European Contract Law 2006, ERA-Forum; pp. 90–95.

[23] T. Maciejewski, Leksykon historii prawa i ustroju, Warsaw 2010, p. 217.

[24] A. Lityński, Historia Prawa Polski Ludowej, Warsaw 2005, p. 184; T. Maciejewski, Leksykon historii prawa i ustroju, Warsaw 2010, p. 216; F. Zoll, Die Arbeiten am neuen polnischen Zivilgesetzbuch, OsteuropaR 2012, p. 29 (34); id., Future of European Contract Law from the Perspective of a Polish Scholar, in: Scripta Iuris Europaei, Special Issue: European Contract Law 2006, ERA-Forum; p. 90.

legal traditions and these experiences they have used in their codification work.[25] These jurists have brought into discussion the various legal concepts from different legal systems in Europe. The Commission was looking for the sources of inspiration not only in those systems which were in force on the Polish territory. Also the Swiss civil code and the French-Italian draft for the civil code were analyzed carefully. In the year 1933 the new Law of Obligations has been adopted.[26] This draft which has been prepared by the Commission was one of the most important achievements of the Polish legislation. Every rule was a result of the broad comparative analysis.[27] The code has merged different European traditions. The drafters were seeking to propose the "best rules".[28]

Other parts of the intended codification were not equally advanced. The progressive matrimonial law was not accepted; the succession law reached only the conceptual phase. For the property law the first drafts were presented. The Second World War interrupted abruptly the work of the official work of the Commission, although certain activities were continued in the underground.[29] The drafters have continued their work after the end of the war. The new regime of the country, dominated by the communists, has had still other things to do and did not interfere into the drafting process too excessively.[30] Therefore at the end of the 1946 the unification of the private law in Poland has been completed.[31] The system was not codified yet, the different domains of the private law like property, succession law etc., were put into various decrees. The content of these laws was a result of the achievements of the pre-war Codification Commission. The emerging new non-democratic, oppressive regime had not yet sufficient time to reshape the content of the law in books. The reality of the legal life was changing however with enormous velocity. The system of justice has been adjusted to the stalinistic world very quickly. Only the law in books remained the old world (which also could not be described as "democratic" because of the completely different concept of freedom, economic order and rules of law). The new regime has however not omitted taking to influence the statutory

---

[25] L. Górnicki, Prawo cywilne w pracach Komisji Kodyfikacyjnej Rzeczypospolitej Polskiej w latach 1919–1939, Wroclaw 2000, p. 5. See also A. Mączyński, Das ABGB in Polen, in: Festschrift 200 Jahre ABGB, Vienna 2011, vol. I, p. 187; F. Zoll, Future of European Contract Law from the Perspective of a Polish Scholar, in: Scripta Iuris Europaei, Special Issue: European Contract Law 2006, ERA-Forum; p. 90 (91).

[26] L. Górnicki, Prawo cywilne w pracach Komisji Kodyfikacyjnej Rzeczypospolitej Polskiej w latach 1919–1939, Wroclaw 2000, p. 403; J.Poczobut, Die Reform des polnischen Zivilrechts, ZEuP 1999, p. 75 (76).

[27] On this comparative tradition of the Polish law see: K. Sójka-Zielińska, Wielkie kodyfikacje cywilne, Historia i współczesność, Liber 2009, p. 15.

[28] L. Górnicki, Prawo cywilne w pracach Komisji Kodyfikacyjnej Rzeczypospolitej Polskiej w latach 1919–1939, Wroclaw 2000, pp. 438–455.

[29] L. Górnicki, Prawo cywilne w pracach Komisji Kodyfikacyjnej Rzeczypospolitej Polskiej w latach 1919–1939, Wroclaw 2000, p. 57.

[30] F. Zoll, Future of European Contract Law from the Perspective of a Polish Scholar, in: Scripta Iuris Europaei, Special Issue: European Contract Law 2006, ERA-Forum; p. 90 (91 et sEq.).

[31] A. Lityński, Historia Prawa Polski Ludowej, Warsaw 2005, p. 184.

laws. The most prominent example were the so called "general provisions of the civil law" which were substituting the general part of the civil law. The structure of the Polish civil law shows that the system was moving towards the pandectistic structure.[32] The general provisions of the civil law were strongly ideologically influenced[33] and seeking to formulate the directives of the interpretation, which objection was to deprive the free-market oriented rules of the civil code their liberal content. For the communist legislators however it was not enough. They started immediately with the drafting of the entirely new code—a "real" communist civil code, reflecting fully-fledged the new ideology. Although this draft of the code, containing reduced and compressed relicts of the civil law, had already been almost prepared, it fortunately has never been adopted. It was so strongly criticized by the legal doctrine, which despite of the lack of the academic freedom, limiting the possibility of running the necessary discussion, managed to present the flaws of this draft in such a very clear way, that even the communist government has not decided to adopt this draft.[34] The time was also changing. After the death of Stalin some limited political thaw has slowly come and also the political pressure to adopt the civil law which would destroy all achievements of the Codification Commission has been relaxed. The new Codification Commission has been appointed with the objective to prepare a new draft for the code.[35] The members of this commission were however linked quite closely to the old Commission from the pre-war time.[36] Some of them were members of this old commission or the members of that Commission were their academic masters. The new Commission did not intent to reverse the results achieved by the old Codification Commission. The opposite was the true.[37] They wanted to preserve the core of existing law,[38] but they were also ready to make the necessary concessions to regime. Generally they have decided to merge the decrees governing the different part of the civil law into one book—the Civil Code. They were going rather to compile the scattered matter of the civil law and not to adopt the entirely new civil code. Even against the Soviet sample the family law supposed form one of the books of the civil code. Finally this latter idea has been rejected and the family law has been put into one separated code, following the Soviet's example.[39] Practically

---

[32] F. Zoll, Die Arbeiten am neuen polnischen Zivilgesetzbuch, OsteuropaR 2012, p. 29 (31).

[33] W. Glatz, Die Novellierung des polnischen Zivilgesetzbuches, ROW 1993, p. 44 (47).

[34] L. Górnicki, System, zakres oraz koncepcja kodyfikacyjna prawa prywatnego in: M. Safjan, System Prawa Prywatnego, Prawo cywilne—część ogólna, Warsaw 2007, pp. 112–113.

[35] J.Poczobut, Die Reform des polnischen Zivilrechts, ZEuP 1999, p. 75 (77).

[36] F. Zoll, Die Arbeiten am neuen polnischen Zivilgesetzbuch, OsteuropaR 2012, p. 29.

[37] A. Lityński, Historia Prawa Polski Ludowej, Warsaw 2005, p. 185; J.Poczobut, Die Reform des polnischen Zivilrechts, ZEuP 1999, p. 75 (77).

[38] F. Zoll, Die Arbeiten am neuen polnischen Zivilgesetzbuch, OsteuropaR 2012, p. 29; id., Future of European Contract Law from the Perspective of a Polish Scholar, in: Scripta Iuris Europaei, Special Issue: European Contract Law 2006, ERA-Forum; p. 90 (91 et sEq.).

[39] L. Górnicki, System, zakres oraz koncepcja kodyfikacyjna prawa prywatnego, in: M. Safjan, System Prawa Prywatnego, Prawo cywilne—część ogólna, Warsaw 2007, p. 111; J.Poczobut, Die Reform des polnischen Zivilrechts, ZEuP 1999, p. 75 (78); F. Zoll, Die Arbeiten am neuen polnischen Zivilgesetzbuch, OsteuropaR 2012, p. 29 (31 et sEq.).

however it did not cause the essential difference. The family law code was and is still treated as the integrated part of the civil law—it is actually a "fifth book" of the civil code, despite of the formal separation.[40]

The result of the codification work was the code from the year 1964. This code could be regarded as the completion of the work of the pre-war Codification Commission.[41] Almost all essential legal concepts and institutions have been taken over from the Law of Obligations from the year 1933 and the post-war decrees.[42] The text of the civil code was however not identical with those old laws. Modifications have occurred on several levels. The language of the new code has become more abstract. The Law of Obligations from the year 1933 was formulated in the way quite close to the Swiss tradition of legislation.[43] The rules were formulated in the quite simple manner, without reaching a very high level of the abstraction. The new code from the year 1964 was much more technically and abstract formulated in this respect. It is in certain sense (from the point of view of the redaction of the rules) more German then Swiss. This more abstract technical approach was not ideologically neutral. It is easier to fill the rules by contents harvested from the intrusive political ideology, if they are more abstract and by this way more flexible and can be easier bended by the means of the interpretation.[44] The new code has got also a pandectistic structure.[45] At the time as the Law of Obligations from the year 1933 has been adopted, the structure of the prospective civil code has not been decided yet.[46] The Law of Obligations was developed in order to be capable to be fit in the very different structure[47] and the further discussion was postponed. The essential move

[40] L. Górnicki, System, zakres oraz koncepcja kodyfikacyjna prawa prywatnego, in: M. Safjan, System Prawa Prywatnego, Prawo cywilne—część ogólna, Warsaw 2007, p. 115; A. Lityński, Historia Historia prawa Polski Ludowej, Warsaw 2004, S. 242; F. Zoll, Die Arbeiten am neuen polnischen Zivilgesetzbuch, OsteuropaR 2012, p. 29 (31 et sEq.).

[41] A. Lityński, Historia Prawa Polski Ludowej, Warsaw 2005, p. 185; A. Mączyński, Das ABGB in Polen, in: Festschrift 200 Jahre ABGB, Vienna 2011, vol. I, p. 192; F. Zoll, Die Arbeiten am neuen polnischen Zivilgesetzbuch, OsteuropaR 2012, p. 29; id., Future of European Contract Law from the Perspective of a Polish Scholar, in: Scripta Iuris Europaei, Special Issue: European Contract Law 2006, ERA-Forum; p. 90 (91 et sEq.).

[42] A. Lityński, Historia Prawa Polski Ludowej, Warsaw 2005, p. 189; F. Zoll, Die Arbeiten am neuen polnischen Zivilgesetzbuch, OsteuropaR 2012, p. 29.

[43] F. Zoll, Die Arbeiten am neuen polnischen Zivilgesetzbuch, OsteuropaR 2012, p. 29 (32).

[44] F. Zoll, Die Arbeiten am neuen polnischen Zivilgesetzbuch, OsteuropaR 2012, p. 29 (32).

[45] J.Poczobut, Die Reform des polnischen Zivilrechts, ZEuP 1999, p. 75 (79); F. Zoll, Die Arbeiten am neuen polnischen Zivilgesetzbuch, OsteuropaR 2012, p. 29 (32).

[46] See: L. Górnicki, System, zakres oraz koncepcja kodyfikacyjna prawa prywatnego in: M. Safjan, System Prawa Prywatnego, Prawo cywilne—część ogólna, Warsaw 2007, p. 107; F. Zoll, Die Arbeiten am neuen polnischen Zivilgesetzbuch, OsteuropaR 2012, p. 29 (33); id., Future of European Contract Law from the Perspective of a Polish Scholar, in: Scripta Iuris Europaei, Special Issue: European Contract Law 2006, ERA-Forum; p. 90 (91 et sEq.).

[47] W. Dajczak, The Polish way to a unified law of contract—local curiosity or contribution to the European debate today?, in: C. von Bar/A. Wudarski, Deutschland und Polen in der europäischen Rechtsgemeinschaft, Munich 2012, p. 13 (15); J.Poczobut, Die Reform des polnischen Zivilrechts, ZEuP 1999, p. 75 (86).

towards the German like structure[48] of the code has been done by the adoption of the mentioned "general provisions of the civil law". The civil code from the year 1964 has finally perfected the structure with the integrated general part, succeeded by the law of property, law of obligations and the succession law.[49] The family law was put, as mentioned above, into the autonomous code.[50] It could be discussed, whether the pandectistic structure of the code has been selected just for the neutral, pure technical reason or because this abstract structure with the set of ideological rules on the beginning of the code was also more sensitive to the ideological influence.

The code has contained also several rules which were reflecting clearly the ideology of the country. Among them were the mentioned general rules determining the directive of the interpretation of the rules of the code in compliance with the dominating ideology.[51] In various places of the code the communist reality has left its traces.[52] The second book of the code was (and is) the property law. The positioning of the property law as the second book was also an effect of the considerations of this time. It was symbolic that the property law was put before the book on obligations. This should stress the special relevance of the patrimonial relationships for the organization of the society. In the second book however there were not so many rules which could be clearly identified with the political regime. Some typical communist concepts concerning the stratification of the different categories of ownership were clearly expressed, albeit these categories from the perspective of the private law did not produce too many special effects. The state property was stronger protected.[53] It was not possible to acquire the state property by the acquisitory prescription. In the third book concerning law of obligation there were several sets of the rules governing the contractual relationships between the state-owned enterprises. It was a particular contract law, deprived of the freedom of contract. The succession law, the last book of the civil code, reflected the reality of the communist system also in different ways.[54] The circle of the statutory heirs was quite limited and the state could become quite quickly a statutory successor. The protection of the next to the kin by the system of the mandatory portion was (and still is) quite strong. The succession of farms was subjected to numerous special exceptions limiting extensively the principle of the testamentary freedom.

It was also a succession law, which was adjusted to the needs of the relatively poor society. The inherited estates were predominantly of little value. For this reason the system was quite simple[55] (e.g. prohibition of conditional appointments, exclusion of the *fideicommissum*, simplified system of the liability of the successors for the debts

---

[48] J.Poczobut, Die Reform des polnischen Zivilrechts, ZEuP 1999, p. 75 (86).

[49] F. Zoll, Die Arbeiten am neuen polnischen Zivilgesetzbuch, OsteuropaR 2012, p. 29 (34–39).

[50] F. Zoll, Die Arbeiten am neuen polnischen Zivilgesetzbuch, OsteuropaR 2012, p. 29 (32).

[51] W. Glatz, Die Novellierung des polnischen Zivilgesetzbuches, ROW 1993, p. 44 (47).

[52] J.Poczobut, Die Reform des polnischen Zivilrechts, ZEuP 1999, pp. 75 (77, 79).

[53] W. Glatz, Die Novellierung des polnischen Zivilgesetzbuches, ROW 1993, p. 44 (50); J.Poczobut, Die Reform des polnischen Zivilrechts, ZEuP 1999, p. 75 (79).

[54] F. Zoll, Die Arbeiten am neuen polnischen Zivilgesetzbuch, OsteuropaR 2012, p. 29 (30 et sEq.).

[55] F. Zoll, Die Arbeiten am neuen polnischen Zivilgesetzbuch, OsteuropaR 2012, p. 29 (30 et sEq.).

of the estate)—in such society it was not needed to preview the more sophisticated institutions of the law of succession, Such sophistication would make sense, if the estates were large and also possibly charged by numerous debts.

The family law as seen from the perspective of the 1964 was quite progressive, taking into account the cultural conservatism of the Polish society. It has also roots in the projects prepared by the pre-war Codification Commission. The draft for the matrimonial law (so called Lutostański draft) from the year 1929 was a shock in Poland, due to the concept of quite liberal approach to the matter of the marriage.[56] Because of the general criticism of this draft (due to its liberal content, but not the quality, which was undisputed) the draft was rejected but not forgotten. Directly after the war the adopted decree on matrimonial law was based on this draft. The new family law was however prepared and adopted in the year 1952. The new Polish family law was the effect of the joined draft prepared by the Polish and Czechoslovakian commission. Because this law was an effect of the consent in this international working group, all issues on which the parties could not agree upon were left out and therefore the short code was full of gaps. The case law of both countries was quite different and the Polish-Czech family code was not treated as a successful example of transnational unification of the law. Therefore the new family law has been prepared only on the national level.

The core of the civil code was however not strongly affected by the time of its origin. The majority of the rules was deeply rooted in the ideas and concepts elaborated before the war. It could be mostly seen in the law of obligations. The principle of the freedom of contract was not explicitly named but its validity was widely accepted (outside of the contract law of the state enterprises). The rules on performance and non-performance were forming a modern system, which could efficiently work also in the free-market society. Even the law of property (at least on the level of the pure private law relationships) was in core not different from the law of the Western continental tradition. After the events of 1989 and the great political and economic transition the code could be maintained without too far reaching economic legislative intervention. The code was drafted by a way that the parts clearly affected by the communist ideology or the adjusted to the communist economic legal system were very easy to delete from the text without infringing the structure of the code. They have formed simply the alien component in the body of the code.

In the communist time the reality of the legal life was quite remote from the standards arising from the civil code. Big parts of the civil law legislation concerning the state-owned enterprises were adopted by the government in the form of the regulation. The civil code has contained a rule authorizing the government to adopt such rules deviating from the rules provided by the civil code. The government has used this authorization quite often, reducing the practical role of the code. And until the political and economic transition it was the fate of the code, so it was the law in books, but with quite little practical relevance.

---

[56] L. Górnicki, Prawo cywilne w pracach Komisji Kodyfikacyjnej Rzeczypospolitej Polskiej w latach 1919–1939, Wroclaw 2000, pp. 201–206.

The drafters of the Polish civil code did not want to destroy the results of this incredible legislative undertaking, which was the Polish Codification Commission acting between the years 1919–1939.[57] For some Western nations the civil codes are important monuments of their culture. For Poland the Codification Commission forms an equally important part of the legal culture and memory. It was also clear for the drafters of the civil code from the year 1964. They have created a code, which has preserved the quality of the Law of Obligations from the year 1933,[58] also as an important achievement of the application of the comparative methodology for the legislative work.[59]

There are not official motives to the code from the year 1964. It was never explained why such motives have not been prepared and published. I can only suspect that it was deliberately done in order not to be forced to disclose this vicinity to the pre-war liberally envisaged private law. It does not mean that all of the members of the Commission from the year 1964 were rebels against the communist regime. Some of them were quite closely associated with this political direction, but they were also excellent jurists and they perceived themselves as a part of the tradition of this deep comparative discussion between the wars. Therefore the Polish civil law tradition has not been broken. It has been continued by the high quality of the Polish civil code from the year 1964.

The codification of the year 1964 can be regarded as "surrealistic". In certain sense it was a codification which has not fulfilled the objective of such undertaking. The codification should be rather adjusted to the economic and political reality of the country. But it is quite fortunate, that the drafters have violated this principle. The high quality of the code was an important factor of the fact that the Polish doctrine of the private law in the time of the communism has kept also accordingly on the high level and that it has continued to maintain the permanent contact to the Western legal doctrines. It has facilitated the Polish transformation and the transformation of the Polish legal system immensely.

8.3 A Need for a New Codification?

It is a legitimate question whether if the code from the year 1964 was so good it is a need to replace it. From several years the new Polish Codification Commission of the Civil Law has been established with the objective to prepare the new Polish civil code. About the need of the new codification I have discussed in several papers.[60]

---

[57] F. Zoll, Die Arbeiten am neuen polnischen Zivilgesetzbuch, OsteuropaR 2012, p. 29.

[58] M. Pazdan, Zur Änderung des polnischen Zivilrechts, OsteuropaR 1991, p. 16 (22).

[59] A. Lityński, Historia prawa Polski Ludowej, Warsaw 2004, p. 242; F. Zoll, Die Arbeiten am neuen polnischen Zivilgesetzbuch, OsteuropaR 2012, p. 29 (32).

[60] F. Zoll, Contract Law in the draft of the New Polish Civil Code, in: R. Schulze/F. Zoll, The Law of Obligations in Europe, 2013; id., Die Arbeiten am neuen polnischen Zivilgesetzbuch, OsteuropaR 2012, pp. 29–39; id., Future of European Contract Law from the Perspective of a Polish Scholar, in: Scripta Iuris Europaei, Special Issue: European Contract Law 2006, ERA-Forum; pp. 90–95.

The largest disadvantage of the new code is its inflexible[61] pandectistic structure which makes difficult to adjust the Polish private law to the European directives. It is also true that there is a space for innovation. In the world dominated by the technology, in the world, where the services become more important than sales[62] and in the world where the function of property also has to be redefined, in the world of essential changes of the structure of family, the law rooted in the pre-war time loses its capability to solve the contemporary problems. Hence it is inevitable to start the work on the new codification,[63] which will be responsive to the challenges of the twenty-first century. It is not necessary however to replace the old code due to its communist origin, but because our time requires a new approach to the legislation.[64] Despite of the new concept for the codification the old code has not fully exhausted its potential of modernization. It is quite likely that it will remain in force through certain time, which does not need to be especially short.

References

Books and Articles

Bulicz, N./F. Merli, Democracy, Rule of Law, Market Economy and EU-Membership: The Rebuilding of Polish Law. In: F. Merli/G. Wagner (2006) New Poland in Europe, Innsbruck

Dajczak, W. The Polish way to a unified law of contract—local curiosity or contribution to the European debate today? In: C. von Bar/A. Wudarski (2012) Deutschland und Polen in der europäischen Rechtsgemeinschaft, Munich

Glatz, W. (1993) Die Novellierung des polnischen Zivilgesetzbuches, ROW

Górnicki, L. (2000) Prawo cywilne w pracach Komisji Kodyfikacyjnej Rzeczypospolitej Polskiej w latach 1919–1939, Wroclaw

Górnicki, L. (2007) System, zakres oraz koncepcja kodyfikacyjna prawa prywatnego. In: M. Safjan, System Prawa Prywatnego, Prawo cywilne—część ogólna, Warsaw

Lityński, A. (2004) Historia prawa Polski Ludowej, Warsaw

Lityński, A. (2005) Historia Prawa Polski Ludowej, Warsaw

Maciejewski, T. (2010) Leksykon historii prawa i ustroju, Warsaw

Mączyński, A. (2011) Das ABGB in Polen, in: Festschrift 200 Jahre ABGB, Vienna 2011, vol. I, pp. 187, 188, 192

Pazdan, M. (1991) Zur Änderung des polnischen Zivilrechts, OsteuropaR

Poczobut, J. (1999) Die Reform des polnischen Zivilrechts, ZEuP 1999

Rozwadowski, W. (2007) Tradycje rzymskie w polskim prawie cywilnym. In: M. Safjan, System Prawa Prywatnego (2007) Prawo cywilne—część ogólna, Warsaw

Schulze, R./F. Zoll, (2013) The Law of Obligations in Europe

Sójka-Zielińska, K (2009) Wielkie kodyfikacje cywilne, Historia i współczesność, Liber

Sójka-Zielińska, K. (2009) Wielkie kodyfikacje cywilne, Historia i współczesność, Warsaw

---

[61] F. Zoll, Die Arbeiten am neuen polnischen Zivilgesetzbuch, OsteuropaR 2012, p. 29 (32).

[62] F. Zoll, Die Arbeiten am neuen polnischen Zivilgesetzbuch, OsteuropaR 2012, p. 29 (31).

[63] W. Glatz, Die Novellierung des polnischen Zivilgesetzbuches, ROW 1993, p. 44 (54); F. Zoll, Die Arbeiten am neuen polnischen Zivilgesetzbuch, OsteuropaR 2012, p. 29.

[64] F. Zoll, Die Arbeiten am neuen polnischen Zivilgesetzbuch, OsteuropaR 2012, p. 29 (30).

Zoll, F. (2006) Future of European Contract Law from the Perspective of a Polish Scholar. In: Scripta Iuris Europaei, Special Issue: European Contract Law 2006, ERA-Forum
Zoll, F. (2012) Die Arbeiten am neuen polnischen Zivilgesetzbuch, OsteuropaR

Statues

Law of 1865; replaced by Law of March 16, 1942 (Gazzetta Ufficiale April 17, 1942, No 91), in force since April 21, 1942
Law of April 23, 1964 (Dziennik Ustaw No. 16, Chap. 93).
Law of August 18, 1896 (RGBl. 1896, p. 195, No. 21), in force since January 1, 1900.
Law of January 1, 1812 (JGS No. 946/1811)
Law of July 24, 1889 (Gaceta de Madrid No 206 of July 25, 1889)
Law of March 21, 1804 (French Civil Law)

Part IV
Codification of Administrative Procedure

Chapter 9
Codification of the Law of Administrative Procedure General Perspectives

Jean-Bernard Auby

9.1 Framing the Issue

9.1.1 Administrative Procedure?

The first delineating question to be considered is: what do GAPA refer to as "administrative procedure"? Some remarks deserve to be made here.

In most cases, GAPAs do not worry about defining administrative, nor procedure, but some do. Thus, article 2 of the Croatian GAPA states: "*An administrative matter is any matter in which an administrative body in an administrative procedure adjudicates the rights, obligations or legal interests of natural persons or legal entities or other parties (hereinafter: the parties) by directly applying laws, other regulations and general acts regulating a specific administrative field*". Let us mention also that some GAPAs restrict their field of application to cases where the administration is acting "under public law"—the German APA does so, for example": but what this means is not explained in the GAPA itself.

A crucial delimitation issue, here, is the one between administrative procedure and procedure before courts when they are adjudicating on administrative issues. It essentially depends on one divide, separating systems in which there is a clear-cut boundary between courts and administrative bodies from those in which there is an intermediary area of quasi-judicial administrative bodies, of "tribunals" as they are called in the tradition of many common law systems. Where the separation is clear, as it is the case in most European continental systems[1], also in Taïwan, then, the GAPA will normally apply only to administrative bodies and leave aside all judicial procedure: an exception is Sweden, whose GAPA covers –but in different

---

[1] Although the European convention on human rights, through its article 6 concerning the principle of fair trial, tends to blur to some extent the distinction because, under this article 6, some administrative bodies must be considered as having a judicial function.

J.-B. Auby (✉)
Sciences Po Governance and Public Law Centre, 13 rue de l'Université, 75007 Paris, France
e-mail: jeanbernard.auby@sciencespo.fr

W.-Y. Wang (ed.), *Codification in International Perspective,* Ius Comparatum – Global Studies in Comparative Law, DOI 10.1007/978-3-319-03455-3_9,
© Springer International Publishing Switzerland 2014

chapters- procedure before administrative authorities and procedure before courts in administrative litigation. What about systems in which there is a grey zone of "tribunals", as it is the case in many legal systems belonging to the common law tradition? Few of them have a GAPA, but at least the USA have one, and it does apply to mixed bodies, such as the "administrative law judges" which adjudicate in first instance on appeals exercised within agencies.

Some GAPAs concern themselves with defining what "procedure" means. It is the case of the Portuguese one, whose article 1 establishes that administrative procedure is the "*disciplined succession of acts and formalities leading to the formation of the will of the Public Administration or its implementation*", and of the German one, whose article 9 reads: "*For the purposes of this Act, administrative procedure shall be the activity of authorities having an external effect and directed to the examination of basic requirements, the preparation and adoption of an administrative act or to the conclusion of an administrative agreement under public law; it shall include the adoption of the administrative act or the conclusion of the agreement under public law*".

That said, as it will appear further on, some GAPAs do not strictly restrict themselves to dealing with procedural issues and encroach upon substantive ones, which they considered as strongly related to the former. Some of them, for example, will have provisions on –not only procedural- conditions of legality and illegality of administrative acts, others will lay rules concerning administrative liability, on administrative discretion, and so on. In fact, the most recent GAPAs would apparently tend to do what the Finnish report describes as "widening the scope. . . from merely procedural matters to matters concerning qualitative standards of administrative behavior in general".

9.1.2   *Codification or Not?*

One could think that codification of administrative procedure is rather recent practice –except for some marked historical references- and can only be found in a minority of systems. The reality seems to be quite different, and apparently, the number of systems in which there is a GAPA is impressive. They include, at least: Austria, Bulgaria, Chile, Croatia, the Czech Republic, Denmark, Estonia, Finland, Germany, Greece, Hungary, Italy, Japan, Luxembourg, the Netherlands, Norway, Peru, Poland, Portugal Serbia, South Korea, Spain, Sweden, Switzerland, Taiwan, the United States. Among countries which do not have a GAPA one counts several common law ones—the United Kingdom, but many others, with the important exception of the USA[2], also Israel-, and some non-common law systems like the French one, China, Paraguay, for example.

---

[2] Australia has, since 1975 and 1977, two acts concerning administrative adjudication which include some provisions on administrative procedure strictly speaking.

The underlying logics of the divide must not be too simply apprehended. One could think that the existence of a GAPA reflects a particular stress national administrative law puts on procedural issues, but this would be contradicted by the fact that some legal traditions in which procedure has always considered as essential do not have a GAPA—the British example is the best possible-, while there is one in some systems where procedure is traditionally not considered as central to administrative law like in Germany, or where administrative law is traditionally rather informal like in Denmark or in Finland.

Slightly more important in determining if one national system has or does not have a GAPA is the fact that, in this system, administrative law is mainly judge-made law or has been significantly built through written law. This factor explains why most of common law systems do not have a GAPA, but also, more strikingly, why the French system, which is normally rather fond of codes, does not have a GAPA: French administrative judges have always wanted to keep all vital aspects of administrative law, including the procedural ones, in command.

9.2 The Making of GAPAs

In the countries belonging to the–incomplete- inventory we have presented above, here are the dates when the GAPAs were adopted: Austria in 1925, Bulgaria in 1979 with a new version in 2006, Chile in 2008, Croatia in 1931 –when it was part of Yougoslavia-, with new versions in 1956 and 2009, the Czech Republic in 1928, with a new version in 2004, Denmark in 1987, Estonia in 1936 with a new one in 2001, Finland in 1982 with a new version in 2003, Germany in 1976, Greece in 1999, Hungary, Italy in 1990, Japan in 1996, Luxembourg in 1978, the Netherlands in 1994, Norway in 1967, Peru in 1967, Poland in 1928 with a new version in 1961, Portugal in 1991, Serbia in 1997, South Korea in 1996, Spain in 1889 with a new one in 1992, Sweden in 1986, Switzerland in 1968, Taiwan in 1999, the United States in 1946.

In the rather complex history which this constitutes, three phases emerge especially. The era of founding models is illustrated by the Spanish one, and, more significantly it seems, by the Austrian one, which inspired several other central European countries. The post-war period was characterized by the establishment of what would become the two most influential models: the US one and the German one. In the more recent period, from the 90s onwards, a large number of new GAPAs appeared, especially in post-communist countries, in which codification of administrative procedure was one the important reformatory tools used in order to combat the administrative abuses which were one of the pleas of the communist regimes.

The elaboration process of GAPAs took more or less time: in the USA, it unfolded between 1939 and 1946 and included the achievement of 27 separate monographs on 33 agencies, in Germany, it was preceded by twenty years of debate. It was sometimes the occasion of strong discussion, the projected GAPA stimulating opposition, in particular from various administrative authorities: the local authorities especially in Denmark, for example.

In general, the GAPAs were prepared by committees of experts, composed with administrators, judges, academics: in Finland, the GAPA was drafted by a working group made of civil servants, counseled by university professors and judges from the Supreme Administrative Court … In Greece, a first draft, elaborated by an academic-oriented committee, was rejected, and was followed by a second one, drafted by a committee consisting mainly of judges, and finally adopted. The presence of foreign experts in the elaboration committee is mentioned at least in the case of Estonia.

In various cases, external influences made themselves feel, even if no direct foreign contribution was included. Before the second world war, the Austrian model was, as it has been mentioned, quite influential in central Europe: in the post-communist era, countries of the latter had an eye on the German model, as it is noted in the Estonian report. The same central-European countries also drew intellectual input from the Council of Europe's Recommendations.

9.3 The Content of GAPAs: General Orientations

Let us try, now, to give an overview of what the general orientations of the various GAPAs are. We will first examine the scope they cover (1), then the way they combine with the other sources of administrative procedure rules in their legal system (2) and finally the basic concepts and principles they rely on (3).

Incidentally, one striking difference between the GAPAs is their size, their more or less detailed character. The spectrum, here, goes from slim models, in which just some rules deemed essential are formulated—one example is the Swedish GAPA, which has only 33 articles-, to stretching ones in which one finds a vast array of not only principles but also rules concerning various concrete issues –the Croatian one, for example, with its 292 articles-.

9.3.1 Scope

One can observe rather big differences in the scope of issues that is covered by the various GAPAs. The main ones are related to the bodies and the fields of administration which are covered, and to the kinds of administrative acts which are submitted to the APA. But many other variations can be observed.

In Terms of Bodies Regulated

The institutional perimeter of GAPAs is subject to variations on three main aspects.

The main target of GAPAs is constituted by national agencies. Nevertheless, in most cases, at least where the state is unitary, local administrative bodies are also concerned. This is the case even in a "regional" state like Spain—whose institutional architecture is in between unitarism and federalism-: its GAPA is expressly said to be applicable to administrative bodies of the autonomous communities and local governments[3]. Sometimes, procedural requirements commonly applicable to national and local administrative bodies are complemented for the latter by another piece, specific, of legislation: the Finnish report mentions such an arrangement.

In federal systems, there are in general two tiers of GAPAs: one federal applicable to federal agencies, and normally one in every state, applicable to statal authorities: this is the case in Brazil, in the United States, in Switzerland. Things are slightly more complex in those of federal systems in which federal policies are partly implemented by statal administrations: in Germany, which is a typical example of this, the federal Administrative Procedure Act is made applicable to *"official bodies . . . of the Länder and local authorities and other public law entities subject to the supervision of the Länder where these execute federal legislation on behalf of the federal authorities"*[4]. In general, the content of statal GAPAs is very much inspired by the federal one.

Whether the GAPA is, or not, applicable to independent agencies is subject to variations. In general, they are included in the GAPA's scope of application: this is the case in the United States, for example, where the Administrative Procedure Act is common law for all federal agencies. Then, in many cases, the GAPA just submit them to some basic rules, and, for the rest, refers to special regulations, made by legislation or elaborated by the agencies themselves.

One important issue –considering the contemporary development of "outsourcing", "contracting out" and the like- is whether the GAPA is deemed applicable to private entities entrusted with public functions or powers. Explicit provisions in that direction can be found in many GAPAs, among which: the Croatian one –whose article 1 refers to *"legal entities vested with public powers"*, the Finnish one, the Norwegian one—§ 1 of the Public Administration Act: *"A private legal person shall be considered an administrative agency in cases where such person makes individual decisions or issues regulations"*-, the Serbian one—article 2 of the Law on General Administrative Procedure: *"Companies and other organizations shall also act in compliance with the present Law in exercise of their legally granted public powers when making decisions or performing other activities* (defined as administrative by article 1)", the Taïwanese one. In other cases, the scope of GAPAs has not be extended to private entities: thus in Denmark, or in Estonia.

In Terms of Fields of Administration Covered

The question, here, is whether the GAPA is meant to apply to all administrative activities in all possible fields, or if some fields of administration are left aside because they are thought to require specific procedural rules.

Many GAPAs exclude from their scope some fields of administration: taxes in the Czech GAPA, taxes and planning in the Norwegian one, *"procedures of the federal*

---

[3] Article 2.

[4] Article 1.

or local tax authorities" in the German one[5], taxes, *"proceedings relating to the jurisdiction of Polish diplomatic representations and consular offices"* and *"cases arising from . . . organizational hierarchy in relations between State bodies and other State organizational units"* in the Polish one[6], *"the executive activity of the Swedish Enforcement Authority"* and *"the activities of police authorities, public prosecutors, the Swedish Tax Agency, the Swedish Customs Service or the Coast Guard relating to crime prevention"* in the Swedish one[7], *"acts in relation to matters concerning diplomacy, military and safeguard of national security"* in the Taïwanese one[8].

Quite often, the fields of administration which are put outside the ambit of the GAPA are so dealt with because their procedures are submitted to a separate and specific piece of legislation. There are variations on the way this kind of specific legislation combines with the GAPA: we will come back to this further on. In some systems, there are limitations to the possibility of specific legislation: in the Croatian system, for example, only certain issues of administrative procedure can be differently regulated than in the GAPA, in Denmark, a "Guide to good lawmaking" issued by the Ministry of Justice prescribes that no specific legislation on administrative procedure would be made unless it has been thoroughly examined that the general rules would not suffice, in Germany the existence of the GAPA compels the legislator at least to justify explicitly any deviation from its procedural model.

Of course, submitting some administrative activities to special rules can be done without rejecting them outside the GAPA: by including these special rules in the GAPA itself, in a separate chapter. It is, for example, what the Polish GAPA does with social insurance.

As to the Kinds of Administrative Acts Included

The administrative act, or decision or order, etc. . . . . plays in general an important role in GAPAs: one of the main function of the latter, if not their predominant function, is to determine under which procedural mechanisms administrative acts are elaborated, implemented, modified, and so on. The concept of administrative act is sometimes really the backbone of GAPAs, it is always a central ingredient: we will come back to that further on.

Then, differences appear. One, of major importance, is between GAPAs which apply both to administrative decisions of a regulatory character and administrative decisions aimed at one or several individuals, and those which apply only to the latter. The US Administrative Procedure Act belongs to the first category, being applicable to adjudication—deciding about particular situations- and rulemaking—decisions issuing rules-: so also do the Estonian one, the Portuguese one. On the contrary, the German Administrative Procedure Act is only applicable to individual decisions –in

---

[5] Article 2.

[6] Article 3.

[7] Sect. 32.

[8] Article 3.

fact, in German Law, regulatory decisions taken by administrative authorities do not have the nature of "administrative acts" -: so are, too, the Czech one, the Dutch one, the Polish one, the Swiss one.

When the GAPA applies both to administrative decisions and individual decisions, it often submit the two species to different rules: in the Norvegian Public Administration Act, there is one chapter on general rules, three on individual decisions, and one on regulations.

As everyone knows, the divide between "regulatory" or "general" decisions, and "individual" or "particular" ones is not so clear-cut. Some administrative decisions are on the edge between the two categories: those which apply to a given area—urban plans, typically-, or the decision to fund a project. Some GAPAs will assimilate them to regulations or individual decisions: thus, the Finnish Administrative Procedure Act applies to decisions that have general applicability in a given area and that are not to their nature regulatory, while it normally covers only individual decisions. Others will rather provide these "mixed" or "intermediate" acts with a group of special rules: it is what the German Administrative Procedure Act does with plans.

An issue which is in general not explicitly addressed in the GAPAs is whether it is applicable to the administrative "soft law", ie purely internal decisions, or non obligatory acts, and so on: it is accepted that the German Administrative Procedure Act does not apply to factual administrative actions like administrative warnings, recommendations or non-legally binding forms of consensual administrative action. Apparently, the regulation of their procedure—if there exists any- is often left to other sources of administrative law: exceptions exist, and for example the Czech Administrative Procedure Code is on some aspects applicable to informal acts like opinions, certifications, communications.

What about contracts made by public authorities? Apparently, half of the GAPAs consider that they are an issue which is foreign to them, and half include provisions concerning them. Among those which contain some provisions concerning contracts: the Czech one, the Croatian one, the Finnish one, the Estonian one, the German one, the Greek one, the Taiwanese one. Among those which do not regulate contractual procedures: the Polish one, the Portuguese one, the US one. It must be added that provisions found in GAPAs which include something about public contracts are in general a few. Furthermore, they tend to concentrate on jurisdictional issues- who is entitled to decide on contracts and sign them, and so on-: competitive procedures for the choice of the contractor are regulated elsewhere. In the Danish Administrative Procedure Act, the only provisions applicable to contracts are those on impartiality and confidentiality.

As to Issues Regulated

Within the variable limits they establish as to the bodies, the fields of administration, the kinds of acts they include, the spectrum of issues GAPAs address is also variable. Let us just give some examples of a few which are regulated only in some GAPAs (those which are frequently considered will appear in the successive developments).

Some GAPAs contain provisions about the enforcement of administrative decisions: this is the case of the Czech one –except when it comes to the execution of monetary decisions, another text being then applicable-, of the Croatian one, of the Dutch one, of the Serbian one[9], of the Spanish one[10].

Some GAPAs include provisions concerning the administrative acts legality—apart from the special issue of whether the infringement of procedural requirements of GAPAs affects the legality of administrative decisions, to which we will turn further on-: the German one, in articles 44 and sq., concerning the invalidity of an administrative act, and its consequences, the Spanish one, whose articles 62 and 63 deal with the different forms of nullity which can affect an administrative act, the Taiwanese one, whose article 112 addresses the situation where an administrative act is only partially illegal.

Organisational Issues

Beyond procedural issues strictly speaking, some GAPAs concern themselves with various organizational ones, which they deem connected with administrative procedure.

Thus, some GAPAs will specifically consider the situation where the administrative decision is taken by a collective body, and establish rules about notification, majority requirements and so on: so do the Croatian one[11], the Greek one[12] the Serbian one[13], the Spanish one[14], the Swedish one[15].

Various provisions concerning the relations between different administrative authorities can also be detected: about delegation of competences by an authority to another one in the Greek one[16] and the Spanish one[17], about "conferences of services" in which different administrative bodies commonly involved in one particular procedure will coordinate, in the Italian one[18] and the Spanish one[19], about agreements between different administrative authorities—in the line of "conferences of services" or not -in the Italian one[20].

---

[9] Articles 261 and sq.

[10] Articles 93 and sq.

[11] Article 25.

[12] Articles 13 and sq.

[13] Article 192.

[14] Article 22 and sq.

[15] Sect. 18.

[16] Article 8 and sq.

[17] Article 15 and sq.

[18] Article 14 and sq.

[19] Article 5.

[20] Article 15.

The Polish Code of Administrative Procedure declares itself applicable to disputes regarding jurisdiction between administrative bodies[21]. The German Administrative Procedure Act establishes a principle of *"authorities' duty to assist one another"*[22], the Spanish one a principle of *"institutional loyalty"* in relations between administrative authorities[23]: this is certainly related to the fact that both states are composite ones— one federal, one "regional"-, in which coordination between administrative entities raise sometimes specific problems.

The Spanish GAPA, in its article 11, lays down some rules concerning the creation of administrative bodies by the various administrations.

Conflicts of Interest

Some GAPAs do not include any rules concerning the situations of conflict of interest in which administrative authorities could be placed –which does not mean, of course, that the matter is not regulated elsewhere, by written law or case law: for example, the Danish one. Others address the issue, either through dedicating one special chapter to it –so do the Norvegian one[24], the Polish one[25], the Serbian one[26], the Swedish one[27], the Taiwanese one[28]- or through impartiality rules alongside other rules concerning officers capacitated to conduct an administrative procedure -so do the Austrian one[29], the Chilean one[30]-.

Freedom of Information

In some cases, the rules concerning access to administrative data are included in the GAPA: thus, in the Italian one –Chap. V, *"Access to administrative documents"*-. In others, they are located in distinct legislation: Denmark has a specific *"Data Protection Act"*, the United States have a *"Freedom of Information Act"*.

Administrative Liability

The Spanish Administrative Procedure Act is apparently the only one in which extensive rules on administrative liability can be found –articles 139–144-.

---

[21] Article 1.

[22] Article 4.

[23] Article 4.

[24] § 6 and sq.

[25] Articles 24 and sq.

[26] Articles 32 and sq.

[27] Sect. 11 and 12.

[28] Article 32 and sq.

[29] § 7.

[30] Article 12.

9.3.2   Combination with Other Sources

When analyzing the GAPAs, one must not forget that many of them are leaning on constitutions which contain some principles related with administrative procedure, either because they are explicitly aiming at it or because constitutional case-law drew from them implications concerning it: the rule of due process, famously, in the US Constitution but also, for example in the Constitution of Paraguay, also in the Brazilian one[31] and in the Taiwanese one, the principle of good administration, present for instance in the Finnish Constitution, the resembling principle of "buon andamento" in the Italian Constitution[32], or the various principles articulated in the article 103 of the Spanish Constitution: *"The Public Administration shall serve the general interest in a spirit of objectivity and shall act in accordance with the principles of efficiency, hierarchy, decentralization, deconcentration and coordination, and in full subordination to the law"*.

In the –rather frequent, as already mentioned- cases where the GAPA is complemented by one or several pieces of specific legislation, then the question arises of how they are connected together. Several solutions can be detected.

The first one can be phrased impermeability. The GAPA and the specific laws apply separately, each one being fully applicable in its proper scope of application: that is, for instance, the relation established between the Estonian GAPA and other statutes concerning procurement.

The second one relies on the predominance of the GAPA: one example of this is given by the Swedish Administrative Procedure Act, whose Sect. 6 reads: *"Where an Act or an ordinance contains a provision that is inconsistent with this Act, that provisions shall prevail"*.

In the third one, the relationship between the GAPA and specific statutes is based upon the subsidiary application of the former: the GAPA rules play the role of "default" rules, applicable to procedural issues which are not regulated in the specific statutes. The relationship between the German Administrative Procedure Acts and specific legislation is thus organized under a general principle, the GAPA being, following its article 1, applicable *"where no federal law or regulation contains similar or conflicting provisions"*. In other cases, the subsidiarity relationship applies to some particular fields: for example, the Spanish GAPA, normally, does not apply to administrative procedures in the field of taxes, but it recovers an auxiliary role where there is a gap in the tax legislation[33].

The fourth one is the one in which the GAPA and specific legislation apply complementarily: their provisions can apply jointly if this creates an added value. This is how it works as a general rule in the Chilean system[34], as well as in the Portuguese system or in the Swiss one. This is how the Finnish Administrative Procedure Act combines

---

[31] Article 5.

[32] Article 97.

[33] 11th additional provision.

[34] Article 1 of the GAPA.

with the Municipal Act, which, as it was mentioned, contains some provisions about procedural requirements applicable to local authorities.

In some laws, the relationship between the GAPA and specific legislation is variable. Thus, in Czech law, the application of specific statutes sometimes excludes the application of GAPA rules, but in general the GAPA plays a subsidiary role in relation to specific statutes. In Estonian law, the Administrative Procedure Act rules – in its § 112- that it is applicable in a field covered by a specific statute only where this statute so prescribes; however, courts have admitted that a direct reference to the GAPA is only necessary when the special act has the same level of specificity as the GAPA, while, if the special statute has a lower level of regulativeness, the GAPA is also applicable even without a direct reference.

Obviously, in some systems, specific legislation which must be coordinated with the GAPA is not only sector-specific, in the sense of concerning one particular fields of administrative action, but also agency-specific, in the sense of specifically applicable to one particular a gency or group of agencies. In the US system, for example, the Administrative Procedure Act is very much complemented by the organic statute proper to one particular agency.

An important question is whether the administrative authorities are entitled to complement by themselves, and even adjust, the GAPA rules. In the German system, agencies have sometimes a margin of manoeuvre for adapting the procedure to the more or less complex character of the case. In other laws, they have an apparently wider room for adjusting their procedures: in Estonia, agencies have an extensive freedom to arrange details, and the same situation seems to exist in Taïwan. In Portuguese law, many of the GAPA provisions are facultative and agencies can deviate from them where they deem them not adapted.

9.3.3 Concepts and Principles

GAPAs are More or Less Centred on the Administrative Act.

As already suggested above, the administrative act, or decision or order[35], etc. . . . plays in general an important role in GAPAs, the function of which is essentially to regulate the procedural ways through which administrative acts, decisions, etc. . . . are made. In Polish law, the national reporter informs us, "*the key constructions of the Code of Administrative Procedure are the notions of party and decision*". All GAPAs centred on the administrative act do not accept the same definition of it, that said: we have already underlined that.

Then, there are also GAPAs which do not refer to the concept of administrative act: this is the case of the US Administrative Procedure Act, whose basic concepts are, as already recalled, rulemaking and adjudication.

---

[35] The Dutch GAPA favours this concept: See national report p.

And there are also GAPAs that, while retaining the administrative act as a basic concept, are not entirely focused on it because they are based upon a vision of what administrative action or administrative procedure consists of which is wider. The purpose of the Finnish Administrative Procedure Act is to regulate the means by which public authorities deal with "administrative matters", and administrative decisions are just one of these means. As we will see later on, other GAPAs retain the idea that the outcome of an administrative procedure can be something else than a decision, and for example an agreement. Similarly, the Italian GAPA accepts that an administrative procedure can end in something else than a decision: Italian administrative law expresses this in two different concepts, "*procedimento*" and "*provedimento*".

GAPAs' Approach is More or Less Judicial-like

Some GAPAs handle the issue of regulating procedure in a quasi-judicial way. As we will see further on in more details, they design a kind of administrative (internal) lawsuit, regulate the way it starts, the way it runs, how it ends, and they raise nearly all the questions usually addressed in judicial procedural law: burden of proof, ways of proof, contradiction, hearings, and so on and so forth. They lay down rules about how the "case" will be circumscribed: how the issue will be submitted to the administration, who will be party, what the time-limits will be. Typical of this approach are the Croatian GAPA and the Serbian one, which regulate meticulously all these issues.

Many other GAPAs will not concern themselves with producing such precise regulation, and they will be less inspired by the judicial model. However, it is obvious that the contemporary trend towards nurturing the rights of the citizens in their relations with administrative authorities creates a general attraction of administrative procedural law towards this model, which the most recent GAPAs are more resembling than the oldest ones.

Differences Related to Principles Put Forward in the GAPAs

Some GAPAs place the rules they lay down under the heading of principles, and some do that extensively, while other GAPAs are not too much preoccupied by making explicit their underlying principles.

The Italian GAPA rules, in its article 1, that "*Administrative action shall pursue the objectives established by law and shall be founded on criteria of economy of action, effectiveness, impartiality, publicity and transparency, in accordance with the modalities provided for both by this Law and by the other provisions governing individual procedure,as well as by the principles underpinning the Community's legal order*". According to Sect. 7 of he Swedish Administrative Procedure Act, "*each matter to which a person is a party shall be handled as simply, rapidly and economically as is possible without jeopardizing legal security. In its handling of matters, the authority shall avail itself of the opportunity of obtaining information from and the views of other authorities, if there is a need to do so. The authority shall also by other means make matters easy for the people with whom it deals"*. As to the Taiwanese GAPA, its article 1 reads: *"this Act is enacted to ensure that all administrative acts are carried out in pursuance of a fair, open and democratic process based on the principle of administration by law so as to protect the rights and interest of the people, enhance administrative efficiency and further the people'reliance on administration"*.

The widest range of principles appealed to can probably be found in the Polish Code, which evidences eleven: *"(1) the principle of rule of law (legality), (2) the principle of objective truth, (3) the principle of taking into account the social public and the right interest of the party, (4) the principle of protection of legitimate expectations, (5) the principle of providing information, (6) the principle of hearing the parties, (7) the principle of explaining the legitimacy of reasons for action (persuading), (8) the principle of speed and simplicity of procedure, (9) the principle of amicable solutions for cases where there are parties with contradictory interests, (10) the principle of writing (11) the principle of two instance procedure, (12) the principle of stability of final decisions, (13) the principle of court control of the decision in reference to the conformity with the law"*. The Croatian Administrative Procedure Act only refers to nine: lawfulness, proportionality in protection of rights of parties and public interest, assistance to a party, establishment of material truth, independence and discretion in the evaluation of evidence, efficiency and cost efficiency, access to data and data protection, right to a legal remedy, and protection of acquired rights[36].

Some administrative laws on procedure retain a principle under which procedural requirements have to be established at a level which balances public and private interests: this is the case of the German one, of the Swiss one, of the US one. This proportionality-type principle inspires for example the beginning of the Croatian GAPA's article 1: *"The right of a party may be limited by the action of an administrative body only where so anticipated by law and if such action is necessary for achieving the purpose determined by law and proportionate with the aim that is to be achieved"*.

One Procedural Pattern or Several?

Some GAPAs design one all-use procedural pattern, leaving room for specific legislation to complement it by specific rules: this is the case, for example, of the Swedish Administrative Procedure Act.

Other GAPAs provide for several kinds of proceedings, or allow for different proceedings in some cases.

---

[36] Articles 5 and sq. See national report p.

The US Administrative Procedure Act lays down different rules for rulemaking and adjudication, and, in both cases, it also differentiates formal and informal procedures. The German Administrative Procedure Act contains specific procedures for planning[37], and so does the Taiwanese one[38]. The Spanish GAPA has special provisions concerning the issuing of decisions which have the nature of sanctions[39]. As a result, this type of GAPAs tend to have a scale of procedural requirements, depending on the more or less sensitive character of the matter–: sanctions call for stricter ones.

Some GAPAs contain differentiations which rather correspond to an adaptation to certain contextual situations. Thus, the Chilean one envisages specifically the situations of emergency[40], and the Norwegian one the situations in which the country is "at war or under the threat of war"[41].

Room for Participation of Lay Citizens

The GAPAs are more or less influenced by the development of participatory democracy, and make the procedure more or less open to the direct participation of citizens.

The issue takes its real meaning when related to the issuing of regulatory decisions, but it is not quite absent from the regulation of procedures leading to individual acts. Indeed, in some GAPAs, rules can be observed that allow the people who are not parties to a –non regulatory- procedure to take part to it: thus, in the Finnish Administrative Procedure Act, whose Sect. 41 reads: "*if the decision of a matter may have a significant effect on the living or working conditions of others than the parties, the authority shall reserve such persons the opportunity to receive information on the bases and objectives of the consideration of the matter and to express their opinion thereon*".

It is in the field of rulemaking that participation of the citizens becomes of the greatest significance: as a way of associating them to the production of norms which, contrary to parliamentary law, are not adopted by people they have elected. Some GAPAs have allowed a large room for citizens participation in that respect: it is famously the case of the US Administrative Procedure Act, in particular with the "*notice and comment*" procedure[42]. Similar kinds of proceedings can be found in various other GAPAs[43], like the Brazilian one or the Portuguese one.

---

[37] Articles 72 and sq.

[38] Articles 163 and sq.

[39] Article 127 and sq.

[40] Article 63.

[41] § 5.

[42] Administrative Procedure Act., § 553.

[43] In some systems, they will rather be imposed by specific legislation: this is the case in Estonia.

In countries where referenda can be made on administrative matters—in general, at the local level-, apparently this is not addressed by the GAPA, but rather in specific legislation: it is what the Finnish national reporter signals, for example.

9.4 The Content of GAPAs: Concrete Arrangements

Let us notice at first that most of the GAPAs—at least the ones which were made since the 80s- offer provisions on electronic procedures and the consequences of IT on the relations between citizens and administrative authorities: by exception, the Greek one does not. The Chilean GAPA admits as a principle that administrative procedures may be conducted by electronic means[44]. The Austrian one makes clear that submissions by citizens may be filed by e-mail[45]. The Croatian one rules that "administrative bodies, parties and other persons participating in the procedure may also communicate in electronic form", and contains provisions on the electronic signature, the date when a submission made by e-mail is regarded to be filed, and so on[46].

9.4.1 Proceedings

Jurisdictional Issues

Some GAPAs provide answers to the question "who will be in charge of the procedure?". In fact, this coin has two sides, that some GAPAs neatly distinguish.

The first one is determining which administrative organization has jurisdiction for driving the procedure. Some GAPAs devote an entire chapter to this problem: the Croatian one[47], the Polish one[48], the Serbian one[49], the Taiwanese one[50]. One issue they especially address is the one of territorial jurisdiction, the determination of which administrative entity is competent according to the place where the submission is made, or the location of the issue it raises, or whatever other territorial criterion they put forward. Some GAPAs will inclusively address the issue of conflicts on jurisdiction: this is the case of the Croatian one, for example.

The second one, which is also considered by some GAPAs, is, provided that one particular administrative segment has jurisdiction, which officer, within this segment,

---

[44] Article 10.

[45] § 13.

[46] Article 75.

[47] Article 15 and sq.

[48] Article 19 and sq.

[49] Article 17 and sq.

[50] Article 11 and sq.

will be in charge of the procedure[51]. The Croatian GAPA dedicates one entire chapter to this issue[52], and so does the Italian one[53].

Starting up of the Procedure

The main question, here, is "who can initiate the procedure?".

In Croatian law, an administrative procedure, the national reporter writes, is always initiated by an administrative authority: but it can initiate it further to an application of the party or "in the line of duty" –ex officio-. According to article 22 of the German Administrative Procedure Act, "*the authority shall decide after due consideration whether and when it is to instigate administrative proceedings*".

The Spanish GAPA[54] rules that administrative procedures can be started either ex officio or under the solicitation of a citizen. Similarly, article 61 of the Polish GAPA provides that "*administrative shall be commenced ex officio or at the instigation of the parties to the proceedings*": however, article 182 of the same text also gives the "*public prosecutor*" the right to "*require the proper public administration body to begin proceedings for the purpose of correcting a state of affairs that is not in accordance with the law*".

Parties

Where GAPAs come close to a "quasi-judicial" vision of administrative procedure, they naturally concern themselves with determining who is "party" to the procedure and what the rights of the parties are. Obviously, the issue arises in procedures concerning individual situations and not in rulemaking, where what is at stake is the different issue of participation of lay citizens: we have already come across it. Some intermediary situations can be considered by GAPAs, though: for example, pursuant to § 44 of the Austrian one –which as we mentioned, does not cover rulemaking-, "*if more than 100 persons are likely to be involved in an administrative matter or in joint administrative matters, the authority may publicly announce the submission or the submissions by edict*", and several specific provisions will apply, among them one which allows the authority to conduct a public debate.

Who is party? Several GAPAs give a clear definition of it. According to article 1 of the Austrian one, "*Persons who make use of the services performed by an authority or who are affected by the activity of such authority, are persons involved, and, to the extent they are involved in the matter on the grounds of a legal title or a legal interest, they are parties*". Under article 3 of the Norwegian GAPA, a party

---

[51] Sometimes, corresponding provisions will include the rules about impartiality of administrative organs, and conflicts of interest: thus, in the Croatian GAPA.

[52] Article 23 and sq.

[53] Sect. 4 and sq.

[54] Articles 68 and sq.

is simply *"a person to whom a decision is directed or whom the case otherwise directly concerns"*. In the Serbian one, article 28 rules that *"a party to proceedings ("a party") is any person whose legal interests or responsibilities are the object of the proceedings or who requires the intervention of a body in respect of their legal interests or responsibilities"*. In an effort to be more precise, the Taiwanese GAPA provides, in its article 20, that *"The term "party" used in this Act denotes the following persons: 1. An applicant and the adverse party to an application. 2. A person subject to the administrative disposition rendered by an administrative authority. 3. The opposite party to an administrative contract signed with an administrative authority. 4. A person for whom administrative guidance is employed. 5. A person filing a petition with an administrative authority; and 6. Any other person intervening into administrative procedures under this Act"*.

Some GAPAs envisage the case of persons who are not initially parties to the procedure, but turn out to be affected by it. In that spirit, for example, article 23 of the Taiwanese one provides that" *when the conduct of a procedure will affect the right or legal interest of a third person, the administrative authority may ex officio or upon application give such person a notice of intervention into the procedure as a party thereto"*.

Some GAPAs devote a range of detailed provisions to the rights of parties: three chapters in the Danish one[55], one chapter in the Croatian one[56]. Among the rights usually granted to them, two are of a prominent importance. The first one is the right to be informed on all relevant elements of the case: as the Swedish GAPA rules in its Sect. 16, *"An applicant, appellant or other party is entitled to have access to the material that has been brought into the matter, provided that the matter concerns the exercise of public power in relation to someone"*. The second one is the right to be heard and to contradiction: this prerogative was, for example, added in 1991 to the Portuguese GAPA, which did not contain it previously.

Evidence

An essential issue, especially in GAPAs which have adopted a "quasi-judicial" stance, is about the establishment of the facts, the burden of proof, the modes of proof, and so on.

Actually, most of the GAPAs adopt an inquisitorial viewpoint and place the burden of proof on the administrative authority: this is the case of the German one—article 24: *"The authority shall determine the facts of the case ex officio. It shall determine the type and scope of investigation and shall not be bound by the participants' submissions and motions to admit evidence"*-, of the Polish one –article 7: *"Public administration bodies . . . shall take all necessary steps to clarify the facts of a case . . ."*-, of the Portuguese one

[55] Chap. 3–5.
[56] Articles 30 and sq.

Some GAPAs contain precise rule about various concrete issues related to the establishment of facts, notably about the participation of witnesses –Croatian GAPA, articles 62 and sq.,—and experts –for example, Austrian GAPA, § 53-, about oral hearings—for example Croatian GAPA, article 54- but also about the probatory effect of public and private deeds –Austrian GAPA, § 47-, or inspections –Austrian GAPA, § 54, Polish one, article 85, Norwegian one, § 15-.

Other Issues

In the most detailed GAPAs, one can find provisions about a lot of concrete issues, of which we will give only a list of examples:

- Time-limits in which authorities in charge of a procedure must decide: Italian GAPA, Sect. 2 (90 days), Serbian GAPA, article 208 (30 days if there is no need to conduct a separate investigation, 90 Days otherwise), Spanish GAPA, article 42 (3 months, unless specific regulation rules otherwise);
- Language of the procedure: German GAPA, article 23 (special rules on applications not made in German), Spanish GAPA, article 36 (applications to statal authorities normally in castellan, but some room for applications made in the official languages of some autonomous communities), Swedish one, Sect. 8 (resort to an interpretor when the applicant does not have a command of the Swedish language);
- Representation of the parties: Austrian GAPA, § 10, Norwegian one article § 12– "*A party has the right to call on the assistance of an advocate or other agent at all stages of the proceedings*"-, Polish one article 32, Spanish one, article 32;
- Service of documents by the administration: Polish GAPA, article 39, Serbian one, article 71 and sq., Taiwanese one, article 67 and sq.;
- Minutes: Croatian GAPA, article 76 ("Minutes shall be kept about oral hearings or other important actions in the procedure, as well as about important verbal statements of parties or third parties in the procedure"), Norwegian one article § 11d, Polish one –"The public administration body shall make concise minutes of each act in the proceedings that is of relevance for a decision in the case, unless such act has been recorded in writing by some other means");
- Fees payable to experts –Austrian GAPA, § 52,witnesses –Austrian GAPA, § 51, and determination of who bears the costs of the procedure –Croatian APA, article 161: "*The administrative body bears the regular expenses of the procedure, expect for the expenses of administrative fees or other expenses which are borne by the parties under special regulations*", Norwegian one, § 36, Polish one article 261: "*The party shall be liable for any costs of proceedings that: (1)were caused by its own fault, (2)were conducted in the interest or at the instigation of the party, and which are unrelated to any statutory duty of the body conducting the proceedings*", Serbian one, articles 103 and sq., Taiwanese one, articles 52 and sq.-;
- Etc. . . .

9.4.2   *Outcome*

Kinds of Possible Outcomes

A most interesting comparative observation is that, if normally the GAPAs expect a decision to be taken at the end of the procedure, some consider other possible outputs. Apart from the fact that they sometimes lay rules about various incidents which put a natural end to the procedure, like renunciation from the applicant, or objective impossibility of concluding –for example, in the Spanish GAPA, article 87-, the most striking is that some GAPAs accept that an administrative procedure can end up in an agreement rather than in a unilateral decision: this is the case of the German Administrative Procedure Act, whose article 54 rules that "*the authority may, instead of issuing an administrative act, conclude an agreement under public law with the person to whom it would otherwise direct the administrative act*", along with, for example, the Spanish one[57]. Interestingly enough, some GAPAs make possible that the procedure would lead to an agreement between the parties, or some of them: thus, the Croatian one –Article 57-, the Polish one –Article 13: "*Cases which involve parties with conflicting interests may be settled by means of a settlement drawn up before the public administration body (administrative settlement)* and article 114*"-*, the Serbian one –Article 124-.

In cases where the conclusion of the procedure must be a decision – which means in all cases for some GAPAs, in all but some for others-, the latter is in general required to be a written one –see Chilean GAPA, article 5, Polish GAPA, article 109, Serbian GAPA article 196-. Still, some GAPAs envisage decisions taken orally- Norwegian GAPA, § 23: "*An individual decision shall be in writing except where, for practical reason, this would be particularly burdensome for the administrative agency*", Spanish one article 55- or just by making a "note on the file –Croatian GAPA-.

Some other aspects of the decisions taken at the conclusion of administrative procedures are also often addressed. Their motivation is frequently required: it is made obligatory, for example, by the German GAPA –article 39-, the Norwegian one -§ 24-, the Polish one –article 107: "*A decision should contain . . . a factual and legal justification*"-, the Serbian one –article 199-, the Spanish one –article 54-, the Swedish one –Sect. 20, which allows a range of exceptions-, the Taiwanese one –articles 96 and 97-. Another issue the GAPAs often deal with is the publicity decisions reached at the end of a procedure must receive: thus, for example, in the Greek GAPA—articles 18 and 19-, the German one –article 41-, the Norwegian one -§ 27-, the Spanish one –article 52-.

---

[57] Article 88.

Obligation to Issue an Outcome and Consequences of Inertia

Some GAPAs establish an explicit obligation for the administrative authority to lead the procedure to a conclusion –which will in general be a decision-: article 2 of the Greek GAPA edicts a principle of "ex officio action", which is interpreted as meaning that public authorities have both the right and the obligation to act, a similar principle is laid down in the Chilean GAPA –articles 8 and 14- and in the federal Swiss one. As we have already noticed, some GAPAs even prescribe time-limits for an outcome to be issued.

Then, what about situations in which the administration remains silent, or becomes silent at a certain stage of the procedure, and does not lead the procedure to an output? Comparative administrative law teaches us that this problem has three main possible solutions: the first one is to give the applicants a recourse before another authority –other than the one who is in charge of the procedure-, the second one is to assign legal consequences to the administrative silence, the third one is to make possible for the citizens to ask a judge that he instructs the administration to decide.

An example of the first species is given by the Serbian GAPA, whose article 208 rules: "*If the authority whose decisions are subject to appeal fails to adopt a decision and serve it on the party within the specified time period, the party shall be entitled to file an appeal as if his/her requested were rejected. In case an appeal may not be filed, the party may directly initiate an administrative dispute proceedings before the court of competent jurisdiction in accordance with the law regulating administrative disputes*".

The second solution, which is adopted by several GAPAs, is known to create frequent problems in its application. It consists of deciding that when the administrative authority has not produced an output to the procedure at a certain time –which can be the end of time-limits for deciding if there exist some, or special ones-, it has the legal value of a positive or a negative decision. In German law, the former solution normally prevails: "*Upon expiry of a specified decision-making period, an approval that has been applied for shall be deemed granted (fictitious approval) if this is stipulated by law and if the application is sufficiently clearly defined in content*" –GAPA, art. 42 a-. A principle of "*Silence-equals-assent*" is also laid down by the Spanish GAPA –article 43- and by the Italian one –Sect. 20-: in the latter case, it has famously raised many problems in practice, so that the corresponding provisions have been modified several times. In Chilean law, the administrative silence normally equates to an acceptance of the application, but it has the sense of a refusal in some fields – GAPA, articles 64 and 65-.

The third method is represented by the judicial action in issuance of an administrative act which exists in German law—but is not regulated by the GAPA, since it is organized by the Code of Administrative Court Procedure, article 42: "*The rescission of an administrative act (rescissory action), as well as sentencing to issue a rejected or omitted administrative act (enforcement action) can be requested by means of an action.*"- and has some echo in article 25 a of the Swiss federal GAPA.

Consequences of Procedural Irregularities on the Outcome of Procedures

GAPAs impose procedural requirements on the administrative authorities, and some of them do so extensively. They correspondingly create a contentious risk, all the rules they lay down being potential arguments for challenging the decisions taken without their having been respected in details. Some GAPAs try to reduce this contentious risk by restricting the consequences of procedural irregularities on final decisions[58]. Under the Estonian one -§ 58-, the annulment of an administrative act cannot be demanded solely for the reason that procedural requirements were not met if this violation did not affect the resolution of the matter. The German one similarly reads in its article 46: *"Application for annulment of an administrative act. ... cannot be made solely on the ground that the act came into being through the infringement of regulations governing procedure, form or local competence, where it is evident that the infringement has not influenced the decision on the matter"*. In slightly different terms, the Italian GAPA –Sect. 21 octies- rules that *"a measure that is adopted in breach of rules governing procedure or the form of instruments shall not be voidable if, by virtue of the fettered nature of the measure, it is evident that the provisions it contains could not have been other than those actually adopted"*.

Appeals

Many GAPAs concern themselves with arranging appeals which can be filed to another administrative body instead of, or before, acting in court, where the outcome of the procedure is found not satisfactory.

In several GAPAs, appeal corresponds to a right, which is only ruled out in certain situations: it is so, for example, in the Croatian one –article 105-, in the Polish one – article 15: *"Administrative proceedings will be two-tier, with provision for appeal"*-, in the Serbian one –article 213-. The Norwegian GAPA and the Spanish one –article 107- exclude the possibility of administrative appeals against regulatory decisions. Conversely, some GAPAs make the exercise of an appeal an obligatory step before going to courts: this is the case of the Dutch one.

Then, GAPAs which design appeal procedures in details encounter a large scope of issues, among which:

- who the appeal must be submitted to: it may be the authority who made the contested decision like in Swedish law –GAPA, Sect. 23- and Croatian law, or a superior one like in Norwegian law –GAPA, § 28- and Polish law –GAPA, article 127-. In some cases, appellate bodies will be independent ones like in Austrian law –GAPA, § 67- and in the US system of "administrative law judges";
- time-limits for appealing: which may be two weeks –Austrian GAPA, § 63- or 15 days –Croatian GAPA, article 109, Serbian GAPA, article 220-, three weeks

---

[58] In some jurisdictions, the same kind of restrictions is admitted rather in case-law: thus, in Denmark.

–Norwegian GAPA, § 29, Swedish GAPA, Sect. 23-one month –Spanish GAPA, article 115-;

- suspensive effect of the appeal: admitted (Austrian GAPA, § 64), or not (Spanish GAPA, article 111), or left for the appellate entity to decide (Swedish GAPA, Sect. 29: *"An authority that has to consider an appeal may decide that the decision appealed against shall be suspended until otherwise ordered."*)
- whether the outcome of the appeal may be less favourable to the appellant than the initial one: such a result is excluded in principle in Norwegian law (GAPA, § 34: *"The administrative decision may not be altered to the detriment of the appellat unless it is considered that his interests must yield out of consideration for other private individuals or the public interest."*) and the Polish one (GAPA, article 139: *"An appeal body may not issue a decision which would be disadvantageous for the party bringing the appeal, unless the challenged decision fragrantly breaches the law or is flagrantly against the public interest."*);
- etc. . . .

Modification and Revocation of Decisions

One important point that some GAPAs regulate is the extent to which and the ways by which an administrative decision –reached through an administrative procedure- can be modified or annulled by the administrative authority –possibly an appellate body-.

As everyone knows, modification and revocation of administrative acts are one of the trickiest issues in administrative law, and each domestic system copes with it in its own manner, with a mixture of case-law –predominant in general- and written provisions. This means that even the most detailed GAPAs will reflect only part of the principles under which the matter is dealt with.

That said, GAPA provisions on the matter will for example be related to the possibility of revoking a decision which has produced beneficial effects to its addressee. A time-limit of five years is established in Brazilian law. In the law of Paraguay, a decision which has granted acquired rights can never be declared null and void: if the administrative authority wants such a decision to be declared null and void, it must exercise a certain type of judicial action.

Rules concerning modification and revocation of administrative acts also vary upon the fact that the act is lawful or unlawful: this divide is the basis of the provisions contained in the German GAPA –articles 48 and sq.-, and is also present in the Italian one –Sect. 21 quinquies and sq, beginning with a rather uncommon provision: *"For subsequently arising reasons of public interest or in cases where concrete situations change or the original public interest is re-assessed, administrative measures having continuing effect may be revoked by the organ that issued them or by another organ so empowered by law ... If the revocation adversely affects the parties directly concerned, the authority shall have the duty to compensate them."*-.

Rather predictably, GAPAs will often allow a larger possibility of modification or revocation of acts when the addressees who may have vested rights consent: so does the Polish one –article 154-, the Serbian one –article 255-.

Close to these rules concerning revocation and modification are the ones that can be found in some GAPA s about the reopening of a procedure, for example when the ruling has been fraudulently obtained –Austrian GAPA, § 69-, if new facts are discovered –Croatian GAPA, Article 123-, if evidence by which the essential factual circumstances of the fact were established is discovered to be false—Polish GAPA, article 145-, if the decision was adopted by an officer who was not authorized for its adoption –Polish GAPA, article 239- or simply because the decisions was manifestly wrong –Swedish GAPA, Sect. 27-.

9.5   The Evolution of GAPAs

A survey of the history of the various GAPAs shows that they are subject to evolutions which can be characterized as internal and external: internal in the sense that their content can vary in time, external in the sense that their interrelations with other sources of administrative procedural rules can evolve.

Some GAPAs have experienced dramatic changes in their very content because of strong political transformations: this occurred in some communist countries like the Czech Republic after 1989. Others are subject to an ongoing process of limited modification, like the Croatian one. Sweden has recently embarked in a total redrafting of its GAPA.

In fact, it seems that all GAPAs are subject to frequent discussion, and suggestions of reform. In 2006, an empirical survey on the implementation of the Finnish one highlighted a range of drawbacks. The US Administrative Procedure Act has recurrently been subject to strong criticisms, either from people who believe that it tends to restrain the production of regulations by "*ossification*", or by people who, on the contrary, think that it does not sufficiently limit the production of norms.

In other jurisdictions, rather than the content of it, it is the respective weigh of the GAPA and of competing sources which has varied: thus, in some countries – like Denmark which tries to limit this phenomenon-, one witnesses a trend towards "*decodification*" by proliferation of specific statutes deviating from the GAPA.

9.6   Living Without a GAPA

In its substance, the law on administrative procedure which one can find in jurisdictions without a GAPA may not be very different from the one which applies on the ground of a GAPA. This is because the addition of non codified written sources—the Constitution and parliamentary law mainly- and of case-law can results in a regulation of administrative procedure which will often be similar to the one provided in a GAPA. In the absence of codification, the law of Israel carries most of the basic principles one can find in a GAPA. France, which does not have a GAPA, possesses a rather sophisticated law on administrative procedure, which was historically built and is still in large part produced by jurisprudence.

In some countries, the absence of a GAPA is compensated by partial codifications: in Australia, general rules on appeals, on judicial review, on ombudsman, on freedom of information, are laid down in statutes. In China, local codifications have started to appear.

In European countries, any assessment of national laws on administrative procedures, whether codified or not, must take into account the fact that many important rules in this matter derive from the European convention on human rights. Regarding member States of the European Union, a less and less negligible input of rules concerning administrative procedure comes from European Union Law, and in particular from the Charter of Fundamental Rights: these rules being applicable to domestic administrative authorities when they are implementing EU Law, but producing sometimes spillover effects in pure domestic law.

Some countries without a GAPA are subject to a pressure –from various social sectors, which can be the business, the lawyers, etc. . . . - in favour of a codification: this is the case of China. In France, the resistance to codification of administrative procedure –which emanated from some administrations, willing to keep their procedural peculiarities, and from administrative judges, willing to retain the kind of supervision they still have on procedural administrative law- is in the process of giving in: the *"Commission Supérieure de Codification"*, governmental body in charge of making codes has recently started to work on the drafting of a GAPA.

Even if it does not concern any more a domestic system, it is worth mentioning that the European Union has also recently engaged in a reflection on a codification of its procedural law in a general text which would take the form of a Regulation –the main kind of text the European authorities can issue below the basic treaties-.

The Australian national reporter raises a quite intriguing issue: are not GAPAs outdated at the age of legal databases? One can incline to answer yes because IT make less relevant the fact that rules concerning administrative procedure are well orderly in one particular place or not, since, anyway, they make possible to find them. Nevertheless, the IT argument is not quite convincing because what GAPAs require is more than simply having things well tidied up in the same instrument. It is also, and it is mainly about reflecting previously about the logics which make, or could possible better make, the coherence of the system of administrative procedure that one particular legal system accommodates.

Part V
Criminal Law Codification Beyond the Nation State

Chapter 10
The Model Penal Code and the Dilemma of Criminal Law Codification in the United States

The History of Attempts to Codify the Criminal Law in the US: The Antecedents of the Model Penal Code

Stephen C. Thaman

10.1 The Livingston Codes and the Influence of Jeremy Bentham

Edward Livingston was a New York lawyer, who represented New York in the federal Congress, and then moved to Louisiana after the Louisiana Purchase in 1804, where he became one of the greatest codifiers of his time. His four Penal Codes, consisting of Codes of Crimes and Punishments, Procedure, Evidence, and Reform and Prison Discipline were considered to be a monument of Benthamite utilitarian principles which melded the common law with the civil law traditions inherited from Spain and France, which had previously governed Louisiana. Following the French tradition, Livingston wanted the codes to be compehensive and to contain all the law needed to decide cases. Common law crimes would disappear. He distrusted judges: they were to be "mouths of the law" and not lawmakers in the common law tradition.[1] His four criminal codes, completed in 1821, influenced European criminal law reformers in Europe, among them Carl Joseph Mittermaier in Germany, with whom Livingston corresponded.

Livingston even went beyond Bentham, by eliminating capital punishment from his Criminal Code.[2] On the other hand, Livingston introduced at least ten different maximum and ten different minimum punishment gradations, with numerous fractional increments for aggravating circumstances, along with a detailed specification of aggravating and mitigating circumstances, which could be seen as a precursor to the 1984 US Sentencing Guidelines. The judge was also required to pronounce the reasons for his final judgment in criminal cases, and criticism, something virtually unknown to the common law.[3]

---

[1] (Kadish, 1100–01).
[2] Kadish (1978, 1102–03).
[3] Ibid, 1104.

S. C. Thaman (✉)
School of Law, Saint Louis University, 100 N.Tucker, St. Louis Mo 63101, USA
e-mail: thamansc@slu.edu

W.-Y. Wang (ed.), *Codification in International Perspective*, Ius Comparatum – Global Studies in Comparative Law, DOI 10.1007/978-3-319-03455-3_10,
© Springer International Publishing Switzerland 2014

Livingston's radicalism was too much for the slave-holding society of Louisiana at the time and his criminal codes were never enacted into law. His Civil and Commercial Codes did, however, become law. Sir Henry Maine called Livingston, "the first legal genius of modern times."[4]

10.2   The Field Codes: The First Successful Attempt at Criminal Law Codification

Daved Dudley Field, who drafted the first comprehensive New York codes, was also a New York lawyer and Benthamite.[5] Field created not only a Penal Code, but also a civil code, political code and codes of civil and criminal procedure. He was not a radical reformer, like Livingston, but a pragmatist who attempted to manage, in his words, "the lawless science of our law," to "reduce its bulk, clear out the refuse, condense and arrange the residuum, so that the people, and the lawyer and judge as well, may know what they have to practice and obey."[6]

Submitted to the New York legislature in 1865, the Field penal code was not enacted until 1881. It had a remarkable influence on American law, taking root, in Dakota in 1865, California in 1872, and at least six other Western states thereafter.[7]

10.3   The American Law Institute's Model Penal Code

10.3.1   State of Criminal Codes Before the MPC

In the mid-twentieth century, American criminal law consisted, in some jurisdictions, in a collection of unrelated statutes, adopted sporadically over nearly 200 years. The Field codes, where adopted, were augmented by randomly enacted legislation until the new laws made the old codified structure unrecognizable. The resulting stew included archaic and outdated laws, inconsistent treatment of similar acts, wildly disparate penalties, and incomprehensible and unjust prohibitions. The field was objectively ripe for reform.[8]

10.3.2   The Genesis of the Model Penal Code of 1962

The American Law Institute's (ALI) Model Penal Code (MPC) of 1962 was one of the great intellectual accomplishments of American legal scholarship. Unlike the ALI's

---

[4] Ibid, 1106.

[5] Ibid, 1132.

[6] Ibid, 1134.

[7] Ibid, 1137–38.

[8] Lynch (2003, 225).

traditional "restatements" of the common law, its authors felt that the substantive penal law in the US was unworthy of being "restated," as Field did in his codes, but required a model statute, which could be adopted, in whole or in part, by the States and the federal Congress.[9]

Another New York lawyer, Herbert Wechsler, a Columbia law professor and veteran of the Nuremberg trials, was its guiding force. To draft the code, he assembled a distinguished and remarkably diverse advisory committee of law professors, judges, lawyers, and prison officials, as well as experts from the fields of psychiatry, criminology, and even English literature.[10]

The MPC combined Livingston's systematic ambition and integrated utilitarian approach with Field's pragmatism and legislative success. Like Livingston's code, the MPC was specifically designed to wrest the criminal law out of the hands of the judiciary which, after centuries of common-law making, had left the criminal law an unprincipled mess.[11]

The MPC authors provided an extensive commentary to its thirteen tentative drafts which filled six-volumes. The body of the work revitalized criminal law scholarship, provided a new starting point for writing in the field and profoundly influenced the direction of criminal law study in American law schools.[12]

10.3.3   MPC as Catalyst for a Wave of Codification

The MPC and its tentative drafts contributed in the next 20 years to major new codifications in 34 states.[13] It also had great influence on the case law in the federal system and in States which enacted none of its provisions. Despite the later turn of modern American penal law towards retribution and severe sentences, and away from the largely liberal positions of the MPC authors, the MPC approach to any given issue is still likely to be persuasive authority, or a starting point for analysis, even where that position is not ultimately adopted.[14]

The best-organized codes all were heavily influence by the MPC. The general organizational scheme is easy to recognize: a distinct "general part," containing principles of liability, justifications, responsibility, and inchoate crimes, followed by a "special part" grouping offenses into categories: crimes against the person, against property, against the family, against public administration, public order and decency, all laid out in decreasing order of seriousness.[15] This can be compared with the federal criminal laws, which, in 1948 were organized alphabetically into Title 18 of the U.S. Code, with no concern for the interests protected by the respective offenses.

---

[9] Ibid, 220.

[10] Robinson, Dubber (2007, 323).

[11] Ibid, 332.

[12] Kadish (1978, 1140).

[13] Robinson, Dubber (2007, 326).

[14] Lynch (1998, 299).

[15] Robinson et al (2000, 35–36).

10.4 The General Part of the MPC and Its Influence in the Reform of American Criminal Law

10.4.1 Element Analysis and the Limitation of Strict Liability

Prior to the MPC, statutory and case law used a confusing array of terms to describe guilty *mens rea,* some moralistic, such as "wilful," "malicious," "wantonly," "corruptly," and other overly flexible concepts like specific and general intent. The MPC reduced the possible guilty mental states to four—purpose, knowledge, recklessness, and negligence (MPC § 2.02)[16]—and also differentiated the act component of criminal offenses into three objective elements: the nature of the conduct, the attendant circumstances, and the result of the conduct (MPC § 1.13(10)). The innovation of the MPC was to recognize, that different mental states could accompany the different objective act elements, and that each act element had to be accompanied by a guilty *mens rea.* Seven factors thus replaced the common law's simple understanding of *actus reus* and undifferentiated intent or *mens rea.*[17] Another innovation of the MPC, was that where the grade of the offense depends on the mental state with which it was committed—such as homicide—then the level is determined according to the lowest level of mental state accompanying any material element of the crime (MPC § 2.02(10)). This factor is of great importance in relation to how justifications and excuses affect liability under the MPC, discussed in Sect. 2.4.3.3, below.

The MPC's "element analysis" is considered by some to be the most important contribution of the MPC to criminal law theory.[18] If a statute were silent as to the mental state required, then the MPC would require either purpose or recklessness to prove that element (MPC § 2.02(3)). This approach, which tends to restrict criminal liability, was followed by eleven states. Six States, however, including New York, make negligence the default *mens rea.*[19]

If a statute fixes a mental state such as "knowingly" for conviction, but clearly contains more than one objective element (i.e. an act and an attendant circumstance), then the MPC presumes this mental state will apply to each objective element of the offense, unless a "contrary purpose plainly appears." (MPC § 2.02(4)). This comes close to a rejection of "strict liability" public welfare offenses, otherwise accepted in the US common law,[20] unless they constitute "violations" punishable by no more than a fine (MPC 2.05(1)(a)). Although a voluntary act or omission is a *sine qua non* for a crime (MPC § 2.01), the MPC will allow for strict liability as to an "attendant circumstance" only rarely, such as with sexual acts performed against a child under 10 years of age (MPC § 213.1(d)).

---

[16] All cites from the MPC taken from Dubber (2002).

[17] Dubber (2002, 50–51).

[18] Robinson, Dubber (2007, 335).

[19] Simons (2003, 188); Dubber (2002, 58–59).

[20] See Morissette v. United States, 342 U.S. 246 (1952).

The rejection of strict liability is also reflected in the fact that, if mistakes of fact or law lead to the negation of the mental state required in relation to an act, attendant circumstance or result, the person is not guilty (MPC § 2.04(1)(a)). The only exception here is for voluntary intoxication, which only can negate the mental states of purpose or knowledge, but will be no defense if a crime may be committed with a reckless or negligent mental state (MPC § 2.08(1,2)).

The four mental states of the MPC clearly reflect diminishing levels of guilt, with inadvertent risk-creation (negligence) being treated as less culpable than knowing risk creation (recklessness). This has been criticized as ignoring an important third possible category—namely, where an actor realizes that she is creating some risk, but concludes (either reasonably or unreasonably) that the risk is insignificant (like the German concept of *Fahrlässigkeit*). Although this is "knowing" risk creation, German theory treat this as being comparable to negligence and therefore meriting a lesser punishment.[21] When an actor gives no thought to a risk, because he erroneously believes his conduct is not punishable, then such ignorance of law might mean that the actor only had a negligent mental state, whereas actors who are diligent enough to ascertain the legal requirements that govern their actions are more likely to be perceived as reckless under the MPC test.[22]

On the whole, the 34 States which reformed their criminal codes under the influence of the MPC, adopted the four MPC mental states and the basics of element analysis. But some of these States either failed to eliminate the old common law terminology, or included it in post-MPC legislation. Thus, while the General Part of the Illinois code follows the MPC approach, numerous provisions in the Special Part employ other generally undefined terms like: "specific intent," "having reason to know," "willfully," "maliciously," "fraudulently," "designedly," or a combination therof.[23]

The situation is even worse in the federal system, where, over the last two centuries, Congress has used at least 78 different terms in Title 18 of the U.S. Code, which is dedicated to criminal law and procedure, to describe the *mens rea* of the various offenses. The confusion is enhanced by the courts who have variously interpreted the most commonly used of the statutory terms–"willfully"-in different contexts to mean "voluntarily," "intentionally," "stubbornly," "with bad purpose," and, in at least one instance, "with studied ignorance."[24]

10.4.2   The MPC Subjectivist Approach Replaces the Objectivist Approach of the Common Law

The general part of the MPC, by eliminating strict liability and insisting on the subjective assessment of guilt, is not radically different from the German theorizing

---

[21] Simons (2003, 191).

[22] Ibid, 194.

[23] Robinson, Cahill (2005, 640–41).

[24] Gainer (1998, 70–71).

of *Schuld*.[25] Had the authors of the MPC introduced a substantive offense such as the German "complete intoxication"[26] (*Vollrausch*, § 323a StGB), to cover actors who due to voluntary intoxication have obliterated their mental responsibility for the underlying crime, instead of undermining its edifice of "element analysis" with a presumption of reckless guilt of the charged crime when committed in an inebriated state, the consistency of the subjective emphasis on *mens rea* in the General Part would have been nearly complete.

The MPC thus replaced the common law's objectivist approach, which was geared primarily to grading criminal offenses based on the gravity of their harmful results and employed strict liability to assess liability independent of fault. For example, the MPC abolishes strict liability felony murder by introducing a rebuttable presumption of recklessness if a suspect kills while in the course of a serious felony, such as rape, robbery, burglary, arson, kidnapping or escape (MPC § 210.2(1)(b)). It also punishes inchoate crimes—such as attempt or solicitation—based solely on intent, rather than proximity to dangerous results. The MPC also limits the scope of accomplice and conspiratorial liability by requiring that the defendant share the guilty mental state of the person who actually carries out the *actus reus* of the crime (MPC §§ 5.03(1); 2.06(2)(a)), thus rejecting objectivist doctrines which would find a conspirator or accomplice guilty of any crime committed by an accomplice which was "reasonably foreseeable" even though the person did not share that criminal intent.[27]

10.5   The MPC Approach to Justifications and Excuses in Light of Common Law Practice

10.5.1   The MPC Approach

The MPC clearly distinguishes between justifications and excuses. Although there is no chapter discussing "excuses," several standard excuses are listed in Chap. 2, including duress (MPC § 2.09), military orders (MPC § 2.10) and entrapment (MPC § 2.13), and the entirety of Chap. 4 deals with the excuse of insanity (MPC § 4.01) and the procedure for establishing it and treating a person acquitted due to insanity. On the other hand, Chap. 3 of the MPC is dedicated to "principles of justification" and includes detailed explanations of several justifications, the most important of which are "choice of evils" (MPC § 3.02); execution of public duty (MPC § 3.03); self-defense (MPC § 3.04); use of force for the protection of others (MPC § 3.05); use of force for the protection of property (MPC § 3.06); and use of force in law enforcement (MPC § 3.07).

---

[25] Lynch (2003, 222)

[26] *Vollrausch*, § 323a Strafgesetzbuch, which punishes those who

[27] Cf. Pinkerton v. United States, 328 U.S. 640 (1946).

The MPC also recognizes, as do European codes, that an excuse is peculiar to the actor and does not render an act non-criminal, as will a justification. Accomplices of an excused offense may therefore be found guilty thereof if they are not also personally excused.

10.5.2 The Confusion in the Codes

In Paul Robinson's ranking of State codes, the lowest-ranked States have no general justification provisions. In fact, North Carolina is the only state among those with the five worst codes to include any justification defense at all–a provision justifying "use of deadly physical force against an intruder." In contrast, the five highest-ranked codes all contain comprehensive general justification sections similar to those in the MPC.[28]

North Carolina, Michigan, Massachusetts, West Virginia, Rhode Island, Mississippi, and Maryland are among the states that fail to define any excuses or nonexculpatory defenses in their penal codes. Numerous other codes include only a fraction of the commonly recognized excuses and nonexculpatory defenses.[29]

Title 18 of the U.S. Code has no general provisions on jurisdiction, voluntariness, actus reus, mens rea, causation, mistake, entrapment, duress, infancy, justification, self-defense, or inchoate offenses. The only exception is that of the insanity defense, which Congress swiftly enacted after John Hinckley was found not guilty by reason of insanity of the attempted assassination of President Reagan in 1981.[30]

10.5.3 MPC Justifications and Their Reception

When the act is committed in order to avoid a lesser evil (MPC § 3.02(1)) or in self-defense (MPC § 3.04(1)), the MPC differs from the conventional common law approach by placing the focus on the actor's subjective perception of risk and not its reasonableness. As Paul Robinson has said: "By defining 'justified' conduct as conduct that the actor 'believes' is justified, the Code has contaminated its concept of justification, packing both objectively justified conduct and mistaken justification into the single term."[31]

The MPC's innovation, here, is that if the actor is negligent (that is, unreasonable) or reckless in his belief that committing a lesser-evil crime or the use of deadly force is necessary, he will be guilty of a negligent or reckless offense (such as manslaughter) but not an intentional or knowing offense (like murder) (MPC §§ 3.02(2), 3.09(2)).

---

[28] Robinson et al (2000, 26–27).

[29] Ibid, 40.

[30] Dubber (1999, 80–81).

[31] Robinson (1998, 40–41).

Even those codes which were influenced by the MPC have not, by and large, followed this purely subjective approach to justifications.[32] For instance, New York's Penal Law (§ 35.15) requires that a person be "reasonable" in her belief that she is under attack, in order to resort to self-defense and requires that the actor "actually" choose the lesser evil to be able to plead "choice of evils" (N.Y. Penal Law § 35.05). In Illinois, the belief the act is necessary to avoid a greater evil must be reasonable (Ill. Rev. Stat. 1971, ch. 38, §§ 7–13).

10.5.4   MPC Excuses and Their Reception

The MPC excuse of duress employs a "reasonableness" approach, rather than a strictly subjective one, in relation to the person's ability to withstand the coercion alleged to have induced the commission of the crime. It speaks in terms of force or threat of force which a "person of reasonable firmness in his situation would have been unable to resist." (MPC § 2.09(1)). This formulation was adopted by a large number of the states which were influenced by the MPC in their recodifications. The MPC would also allow a person to plead the excuse of duress in homicide cases, a departure from the common law only followed by a few States.[33]

The MPC's greatest influence, however, came in the modernization of the insanity defense. In 1954, 3 years after work began on the MPC, the federal appellate court for the District of Columbia, in the famous *Durham* case,[34] replaced the common law test[35] with a test designed to reflect advances in the field of psychiatry. Whereas *M'Naghten* focussed exclusively on the defendant's cognitive inability to understand the wrongfulness of his conduct, the MPC provided for the defense when, "as a result of mental disease or defect [the defendant] lacks substantial capacity either to appreciate the criminality (wrongfulness) of his conduct or to conform his conduct to the requirements of the law." (MPC § 4.01(1).

The MPC insanity provisions were adopted in over half of the States and in all but one of the federal circuit courts of appeal. But after the Hinckley acquittal, many States, California included, and the federal system returned to a version of the purely cognitive *M'Naghten* approach. Today, around 30 States now adhere to some form of *M'Naghten* and only 15 still follow the two-pronged MPC approach.[36]

10.5.5   The MPC's Inadequate Treatment of Mistake of Law

According to the MPC, "Neither knowledge nor recklessness or negligence as to whether conduct constitutes an offense or as to the existence, meaning or application of the law determining the elements of an offense is an element of such offense,

---

[32] For an exception, see Shannon v. Commonwealth, 767 S.W.2d 548, 550 (Ky. 1988).

[33] Kadish et al (2012, 940).

[34] Durham v. United States, 214 F.2d 862 (D.C.Cir. 1954).

[35] Based on M'Naghten's Case, 10 Cl & F. 200, 8 Eng. Rep. 718 (1843).

[36] Kadish et al (2012, 991).

unless the definition of the offense or the Code so provides."(MPC § 2.02(2)(9)). This is a restatement of the ancient maxim *ignorantia legis non excusat* and no longer makes sense today for three reasons: (1) the increasing complexity of the criminal law and the proliferation of *mala prohibita* offenses related to protection of public health and safety and the smooth functioning of administrative regulatory schemes; (2) the continued existence in the U.S. of unnecessary, duplicative and sometimes antiquated, or even absurd criminal prohibitions; and (3) the persistence of "common law" crimes, either expressly recognized, as in Rhode Island, or where the definition is only to be found in case law.

Although the MPC allows for a few exceptions to the maxim that "ignorance of the law is no excuse," namely, for laws that have not been published, or in cases where a public official or organ misleads a citizen to believe his or her conduct is permitted (MPC § 2.04(3)), these exceptions rarely apply.

The increasing criminalization of conduct formerly governed only by private law and civil regulation has made it increasingly unfair to presume that all persons are aware of the criminal law. Therefore some critics believe that it is perhaps time to seriously consider providing a more general excuse to all defendants who are faultlessly ignorant or mistaken with respect to the criminal law. New Jersey has taken this step.[37] Whereas the doctrine of "mistake of law" has become increasingly sophisticated and crucial to German dogma, the US has stuck with its dogmatic approach, virtually excluding it from ever mitigating or eliminating guilt.[38]

10.5.6   MPC Approach to Inchoate Crimes

In relation to the inchoate crimes of solicitation, attempt and conspiracy, the MPC departs from the common law by providing for the same punishment for inchoate, as for completed crime, except when the target crime is homicide (MPC § 5.05(1)). This was one of the least successful innovations of the code.[39] In tune with the MPC's subjectivist approach, the intent to commit the target crime suffices for attempt liability, if the actor has taken a "substantial step" towards its commission (MPC § 5.01(1)(c)). Under the common law's objectivist approach, attemptors must come in close proximity to achieving the desired result. Under the MPC, a guilty mind would suffice, even if, due to mistake of fact, the actor actually committed a harmless act which could never have resulted in the cosummation of the intended crime (MPC § 5.01(1)(a)).

The Code's authors felt that the primary purpose of punishing attempts was to neutralize dangerous individuals, rather than to deter dangerous acts.[40] The "substantial step" test for attempt is now the prevalent view among the states and the

---

[37] Simons (2003, 203–04).

[38] Fletcher (1978, 737–44).

[39] Robinson, Dubber (2007, 336).

[40] Dubber (2000, 67–68).

federal courts (through its case law), though some state courts, like Illinois, interpret the "substantial step" to be almost equivalent to the common law "close proximity" test.[41]

George Fletcher asserts, that without a general theory of interests protected by the criminal law, such as one finds in German law, it is impossible to decide whether an act is a completed crime or an inchoate crime.[42] He distinguishes between the objective approach to attempt, which identifies which acts will constitute attempt, and the subjective, where the nature of the acts is relatively unimportant.[43] In German theory, for instance, it is only objectively dangerous acts which threaten to injure legally protected interests that and can suffice for attempt liability.[44]

Three major reforms of conspiracy laws introduced by the MPC have achieved widespread adoption. They are: (1) the limitation of the objectives of a criminal agreement to statutorily defined crimes; (2) the treatment of conspiracy as a unilateral offense, which can be committed with a police informant who only feigns agreement; and (3) the requirement of specific intent to promote or facilitate the commission of the target crime.[45]

10.5.7 Appraisal of the General Part

The General Part of the MPC has been praised for its comprehensive articulation and systematization of a general theory of criminal law, and most critics do not think it requires thoroughgoing reform.[46] Yet some critics feel the General Part is too comprehensive, and dispute whether a code should attempt to precisely define the mental elements of crime or the principles of excuses or justifications (like "choice of evils").[47]

Fletcher also criticizes the MPC for attempting to make rules for causation and for attempting to define what a "voluntary act" is.[48] He feels the MPC authors showed not only "contempt for European thinking about criminal law," but also for historical common law doctrine.[49]

10.5.8 MPC Sentencing Philosophy

The MPC adopted the indeterminate sentencing model based on a rehabilitationist philosophy. Felonies are broken down into three categories, the first of which is

---

[41] Robinson, Cahill (2005, 648).
[42] Fletcher (1978, 133).
[43] Ibid, 138.
[44] Ibid, 141.
[45] Buscemi (1975, 1188).
[46] Lynch (1998, 349).
[47] Dubber (2000, 75–76); Fletcher (1998, 6).
[48] Ibid, 5–6.
[49] Ibid, 10.

punishable by up to life imprisonment, with the lesser categories carrying a max-imum of 10 years and 5 years, respectively (MPC § 6.06)). The sentencing rules of the MPC have fallen out of fashion with the current U.S. emphasis on retribu-tive and incapacitative sentences, rigid sentencing guidelines and long mandatory minimum sentences, which many States adopted after originally following the MPC rehabilitationist model.[50]

Many of the drafters of the MPC opposed capital punishment, but they feared that if it was not included in the code, it would not be taken seriously. So the MPC offered an option of abolition, but included an alternative death penalty sentencing procedure based on structured jury discretion (MPC § 210.6). After the death penalty was revived by the USSC,[51] however, the MPC approach was adopted in most States which continued to use the death penalty.[52]

10.6   The Special Part of the MPC and Its Relative Lack of Influence

10.6.1   Approach to Homicide

The MPC eliminated the two aggravating factors which triggered the possibility of capital punishment in the 1794 Pennsylvania statute, premeditation and felony murder, and settled for a single level of murder, which could be committed either purposely, or recklessly with manifest disregard for human life (MPC § 210.2(1)). In doing so it restated the two types of second degree common law murder—those committed with direct and implied malice aforethought. The MPC authors were convinced that premeditation was not always a sign of aggravation, and that sudden, rash killings could be more aggravated than, say, a premeditated mercy killing. A sizeable number of States, many, like New York and Illinois influenced by the MPC, have only one level of murder, however, most of the States still break murder into two degrees.[53] Ironically, the MPC elimination of first degree murder transformed the equivalent of second degree murder into the predicate for capital punishment in the dozen or so death penalty states with one level of murder.[54]

Another MPC innovation is the reform of the definition of voluntary manslaughter. Under the common law, an intentional killing could be partially excused and charac-terized as voluntary manslaughter, if committed under the influence of a sudden heat

---

[50] Lynch (2003, 228–29).

[51] Gregg v. Georgia, 428 U.S. 153 (1976).

[52] Lynch (2003, 232).

[53] According to my research in 2008 of the 36 jurisdictions which then allowed capital punishment, 23 States and the federal system split murder into two degrees, and 13 only had one degree. Barnes et al (2009, 360–61).

[54] The finding of one of a list of aggravating circumstances would then trigger a possible death penalty. See MPC § 210.6.

of passion caused by witnessing a provocative act. The defense was strictly limited. Mere words conveying a provocative act were as a matter of law insufficient and the types of provocation, which often reflected old-fashioned male-oriented values, were more or less limited to an assault on the actor or a close relative or the discovery of one's spouse engaged in adultery.

MPC § 210.3(1)(b) provided for manslaughter liability in the case of a killing, which would otherwise be murder (i.e. committed purposely), which was committed "under the influence of extreme mental or emotional disturbance for which there is a reasonable explanation or excuse." This broadened the types of factors which could excuse an intentional killing far beyond what was allowed under the common law. This MPC innovation was adopted *en toto* by five states, and in part by another dozen states or so.[55]

As was mentioned above (Sect. 2.4.2), the MPC also eliminated strict-liability felony-murder, but this reform was rejected by nearly all the States.

10.6.2   The MPC's Outmoded Approach to Rape

Nearly all commentators agree, that the MPC's treatment of rape is outmoded and must be changed. The MPC was published before feminism triggered a profound transformation of the law of rape in the U.S. Although the MPC authors took a scientific approach and relied on the famous Kinsey Report in articulating its provisions,[56] they basically re-codified the old Common Law of rape which required that the perpetrator, in addition to having non-consensual intercourse with a woman, not his wife, either threaten the victim with death or great bodily injury, or actually use physical force beyond that needed to consummate the act of sexual intercourse (MPC § 213.1(1)).

In its endeavor to focus on the "objective manifestations of aggression by the actor," and not the actions of the victim, the MPC did eliminate the old common law requirement that the victim "resist to the utmost." The code's authors, however, also wanted to protect the defendant against unfair prosecution. This was a time when rape was still a capital offense in some states, and where the ultimate penalty was virtually reserved for African-American men charged with raping white women.[57]

The MPC rape provisions only applied to male on female violence, but today, nearly all rape statutes in the US are gender neutral.[58] The marital immunity rule, still included in the MPC, has also been narrowed or abolished in nearly all states.[59]

The common law rule mandating that no person be convicted of rape upon the uncorroborated testimony of the alleged victim, was also included in MPC § 213.6(5).

[55] Kadish et al (2012, 456).

[56] Denno (2003, 208).

[57] Ibid, 209.

[58] Ibid, 211.

[59] Ibid, 213.

This was heavily criticized and followed by only a few states. The MPC also made the dubious choice of barring prosecution if a complaint was not made promptly (MPC § 213.6(4)).

10.6.3   The Inadequacy of the Special Part of the MPC

While some think the broadly comprehensive General Part of the MPC looks more like a criminal law textbook than a penal code, its special part fails to cover a wide range of penal norms codified in modern American penal codes. For example, the MPC does not deal with drug offenses, to the prosecution of which American prosecutors, especially in the federal system, dedicate the lion's share of their resources.[60]

A revised Special Part of the MPC would likely contain some of the new crimes introduced into federal law which deal with organized crime, such as the racketeer influenced and corrupt organizations law (RICO), the law punishing large-scale illicit drug rings as "continuing criminal enterprise," and laws punishing money laundering and "continuing financial crimes."[61] The war on terrorism also let to the promulgation of new substantive crimes, one of the most commonly used being that of providing material support to terrorist organizations.[62]

10.6.4   The Sprawling Mess of Modern Codes and the Need for Special Part Reform

The failure of the MPC's Special Part is one reason why U.S. criminal codes are still in such a horrendous state 50 years after its enactment. Many U.S. codes are still characterized by the following grave flaws: (1) the criminalization of harmless conduct; (2) the massive criminalization of violations of administrative regulations; and (3) a plethora of redundant criminal offenses punishing the same conduct.

10.6.5   Criminalization of Harmless Conduct

The worst U.S. codes often criminalize harmless conduct. Some limit punishment of harmless acts only in part of the State. A typical example is Maryland's law against fortune-telling: "in Caroline County, Carroll County, and in Talbot County."[63]

---

[60] Dubber (1999, 79).

[61] Brickey (1998–1999, 162–63).

[62] Lynch (2003, 236).

[63] Robinson et al (2000, 44–45).

Michigan devotes an entire chapter of its penal code to prohibiting performance of the national anthem with "embellishments of national or other melodies," or "as a part or selection of a medley of any kind."[64]

Florida prohibits unmarried women from parachuting on Sundays, and farting on Thursdays after 6 p.m. It also prohibits married men from kissing their wives' breasts and all men from having sex with porcupines. Alabama prohibits men from spitting in the presence of women and having sexual intercourse with their wives other than in the missionary position. In Tampa Bay, Florida, eating cottage cheese after 6 p.m. on Sundays is prohibited. In Norfolk, Virginia, one cannot spit on seagulls and in the same State in Stafford one cannot beat one's wife on the courthouse steps until 8 p.m. Alaska prohibits pushing elk out of airplanes when in flight. In Baltimore, Maryland, one may not throw hay balls from the first floor of a building or take lions into a theater. In Minnesota, sleeping naked is *verboten*, as is crossing the border with a duck on one's head. And finally, when in Oklahoma, don't grimace at dogs, or fish for whale.[65] Cal. Penal Code § 598 punishes "destroying any bird's nest, except a swallow's nest" in a "public cemetery or burial ground."

10.6.6 Criminal Punishment for Violations of Administrative Regulations

Many important federal criminal offenses are not to be found in Title 18 of the U.S. Code, but are buried within administrative regulatory provisions of other titles. Aircraft highjacking is located among provisions dealing with interstate transportation. Major espionage offenses are locate in regulations of atomic energy. Federal narcotics offenses are found in regulatory provisions of titles involving food, drugs and shipping, and in California they are in the Health and Welfare Code. Today, when a congressional committee adopts new administrative regulations, regardless of whether they relate to health and safety, it routinely provides that any deviation from the norms constitutes a federal crime.[66]

Taking into account the numerous, discrete rules and regulations enforceable under such regulatory statutes, there are more than 10,000 federal regulatory requirements or proscriptions carrying criminal sanctions.[67] Criminal offenses in the States are also spread out over penal codes, non-penal codes, administrative rules and regulations, and county, town, and village codes. (Dubber, 1999, 78).[68]

---

[64] Ibid, 46.

[65] von Rimscha (1999).

[66] Gainer (1998, 72–73).

[67] Ibid, 74.

[68] Dubber (1999, 78).

10.6.7   Redundant Offenses and Code Sprawl

Many U.S. criminal codes are not cohesive, well-structured, and self-contained statutory schemes, as a "code" should be. Even in States which adopted the structure of the MPC, subsequent ad hoc legislation has made them dramatically less systematic and internally consistent. Code deterioration is sometimes the result of legislators' ignorance of the code's structure, but more likely stems from the practice of politicians who enact so-called "crimes de jour" in response to a particularly news-grabbing crime.[69] The "crimes de jour" are often duplicative or or inconsistent with the laws that preceded them, and contribute to re-establishing the same hodge-podge which led to work on the MPC in the first place.[70]

Since the Pennsylvania Crimes Code was enacted in 1972, it has been amended at least 797 times, and at least 1,532 new crimes were added to other non-criminal codes and statutes.[71] In the words of Paul Robinson, there has been a "serious and growing degradation of most criminal codes."[72]

The proliferation of potentially redundant offenses make it more difficult for the average citizen to understand what the criminal code commands.[73] The same conduct may be punished by one offense as a felony, and by another as a misdemeanor or higher grade felony.[74] Pennsylvania punishes stealing a rare book valued at \$3,000 by up to 7 years if stolen from an individual, but by at most 1 year if stolen from a library. In addition, stealing from an individual is punished with much longer prison terms than stealing the same item from a store.[75]

Title 18 of the U.S. Code contains roughly 5,000 sections, produced over 200 years by different draftsmen, with different conceptions of law, the English language, and common sense, extending from common law offenses such as murder and arson to the transportation of alligator grass across a state line, using the slogan "Give a hoot, don't pollute" without authorization, or pretending to be a 4-H Club member with intent to defraud.[76] A prime illustration of the reality of duplicative and overlapping provisions is the fact that one could, at one time, find 232 separate federal statutes pertaining to theft and fraud, 99 pertaining to forgery and counterfeiting, 215 pertaining to false statements, and 96 pertaining to property destruction.[77]

---

[69] Robinson et al (2000, 2).

[70] Lynch (2003, 224).

[71] Robinson et al (2010, 737)

[72] Robinson, Cahill (2005, 634).

[73] Ibid, 638.

[74] Robinson et al (2010, 711–12).

[75] Ibid, 726–27.

[76] Gainer (1998, 58, 66–67).

[77] Green (2000, 335).

10.6.8 *"Method in the Madness": Prosecutorial Benefits in "Degraded" Federal Criminal Law and the U.S. Sentencing Guidelines*

A complex code with countless overlapping provisions is a boon to prosecutors in inducing plea bargains. Cases can be overcharged with duplicative offenses and deals achieved by an offer to dismiss redundant charges carrying higher potential punishments.[78] Robinson believes that such a state of affairs undermines the rule of law by shifting *de facto* sentencing authority from the courts to the prosecutor.[79]

The shift to prosecutorial sentencing has also been facilitated by the U.S. Sentencing Guidelines, enacted in 1984, which are administered by an independent body, not the courts, and apply to the unsystematic mish-mash of criminal offenses. They have now trumped Title 18 of the U.S. Code and are the most important penal rules in the federal system.[80]

The Sentencing Guidelines replaced the legislatively defined and alphabetized penal norms of Title 18, and other codes with eighteen offense categories, consisting in certain groups of basic offense conduct. The Guidelines also contain provisions on mens rea, complicity, duress, intoxication, mistake, consent, necessity, and inchoate crimes, all subjects scarcely mentioned in Title 18. They have become a "shadow code" of federal criminal law upon which court practice is now solidly based.[81]

This has resulted in a paradigm shift from the guilt phase of a criminal proceeding to the sentencing phase. Even in the handful of federal cases that still are decided by juries, the decisive findings of fact often occur not at trial, but at sentencing, where the judge may consider evidence which was inadmissible at trial, and decides based on a mere preponderance of evidence, rather than "proof beyond a reasonable doubt," to which jurors are held. Although the judge's power at sentencing has been reduced in the last decade or so by a line of cases that has expanded the jury's right to *establish* sentence-determining factors[82] over 95 % of cases are resolved without a jury through plea bargaining or co-operation agreements. In these cases, the prosecutor controls the parameters of sentencing through his charging policy, and has exclusive power under the Sentencing Guidelines to agree to a sentence below a mandatory minimum.[83]

---

[78] Robinson, Cahill (2005, 645–46).

[79] Robinson et al (2010, 712).

[80] Dubber (1999, 80).

[81] Ibid, 81–83.

[82] Among the most important being Apprendi v. New Jersey, 530 U.S. 466 (2000) and United States v. Booker, 543 U.S. 220 (2005).

[83] 18 U.S.C. § 3553(e); U.S. Sentencing Guideline 5K1.1.

10.7   The Way Out of the Morass

10.7.1   A New Model Penal Code?

Paul Robinson believes that the A.L.I. should produce a revised MPC, as he doubts the capacity of State legislators to actually create a modern code.[84] Lynch believes the structure of the MPC, and the bulk of the General Part could be maintained, but the Special Part should be augmented with model statutes in areas in need of concrete reform, such as sexual assault, narcotics, money laundering, organized crime offenses, etc. The indetermininate sentencing provisions based on rehabilitationism should also be scuttled in favor of more modern approaches.[85]

10.7.2   Robinson's Idea of Separate Codes of Conduct and Adjudication

The penal code, as Meir Dan-Cohen has pointed out,[86] is addressed to at least two different audiences. It issues "conduct rules" to the population at large (don't do x), and "decision rules" to judges, lawyers, jurors (if someone does x, punish her with consequence y).[87] Paul Robinson and co-authors have followed this idea and produced separate codes containing these different types of rules. In the code of conduct, language relating to liability and grading is eliminated. The prohibited conduct, however, is succintly and clearly described for all to understand. His draft code of conduct is one-fifteenth the length of the MPC and covers the same material.[88] For example, the crime "injury to a person" provides: "You may not cause bodily injury or death to another person." This substitutes not only for assault offenses but also for murder, manslaughter, negligent homicide, and reckless endangerment. The concepts of complicity or conspiracy would be replaced by the simple prohibition: "You may not agree with, ask, assist, or encourage another to commit a crime." The code of conduct would also eliminate all excuses and nonexculpatory defenses, and include only the objective requirements of justifications.[89] Robbery would not be included, for it would be covered by the separate prohibitions for assault and theft. Other "combined" offenses, such as burglary (trespass and theft) could also be eliminated.[90]

---

[84] Robinson (1998, 42–43)

[85] Lynch (2003, 229–38).

[86] Meir Dan-Cohen (1984).

[87] Lynch (1998, 326).

[88] Robinson et al (1996, 306).

[89] Ibid, 307.

[90] Ibid, 309–10.

The adjudication code would have the adjudicator (whether judge or jury) answer three questions: (1) Has the defendant violated the rules of conduct?; (2) If so, is the violation sufficiently blameworthy that criminal liability ought to attach? (3) If so, how much liability should be imposed?[91] A verdict of "not guilty" under such a system would be able to distinguish cases where: (1) the actor's conduct *did* not violate the rules of conduct, and (2) those, where the actor's conduct *did* violate the rules of conduct but was excused.[92]

Robinson's radical idea for a bifurcated code has not been warmly received in the literature. Green rejects, for instance, the idea that traditional common law categories such as robbery and burglary should be abandoned, believing they have a value that transcends the sum of their parts, largely as a result of the moral, linguistic, and social meanings that have become attached to such labels.[93]

10.7.3 Concentration of All Criminal Offenses in a Comprehensive Penal Code?

According to Dubber, a modern penal code can no longer define every crime, but he believes the great majority of regulatory offenses in other codes or Titles should be decriminalized, or perhaps included in a Code of Administrative Violations such as exists in Germany and Russia.[94] Gainer believes that serious regulatory offenses should be included in the penal code, and the others either decriminalized or covered in the code by a generic regulatory offense.[95] Such a generic regulatory offense was included in the 1971 Draft Federal Criminal Code, which died in Congress. Green supports this idea,[96] and the Russian Criminal Code of 1996 took a similar approach.[97]

Herbert Wechsler felt that environmental and other regulatory crimes should be contained in administrative codes dealing with the particular subject matter as is done in Germany, for these prohibitions are usually addressed to a relatively narrow group of potential defendants and are often enforced by specialized agencies.[98]

---

[91] Ibid, 318.

[92] Ibid, 327.

[93] Green (2000, 305).

[94] Dubber (2000, 86–89).

[95] Gainer (1998, 80).

[96] Green (2000, 334).

[97] Thaman (2010, 416–17).

[98] Green (2000, 333).

References

Barnes, K., Sloss, D., Thaman, S. 2009. Place Matters Most: An Empirical Study of Prosecutorial Decision-Making in Death-Eligible Case. *Arizona Law Revew* 51: 305–79 (2009).

Brickey, K.F. 1998–1999. Federal Criminal Code Reform: Hidden Costs, Illusory Benefits, 2 *Buffalo Criminal Law Review* 2: 161–89.

Buscemi, P. 1975. Note: Conspiracy: Statutory Reform Since the Model Penal Code, *Columbia Law Review* 75: 1122–88.

Dan-Cohen, M. 1984. Decision Rules and Conduct Rules: On Acoustic Separation in Criminal Law. *Harvard Law Review* 97: 625–77.

Denno, D.W. 2003. Why the Model Penal Code's Sexual Offense Provisions Should Be Pulled and Replaced. *Ohio State Journal of Criminal Law* 1: 207–18.

Dubber, M.D. 1999. Reforming American Penal Law. *Journal of Criminal Law and Criminology* 90: 49–108.

Dubber, M.D. 2000. Penal Panopticon: the Idea of a Modern Model Penal Code. Buffalo Criminal Law Review 4: 53–100.

Dubber, M.D. 2002. *Criminal Law: Model Penal Code*. New York: Foundation Press.

Fletcher, G. P. 1978. *Rethinking the Criminal Law*. Boston: Little Brown.

Fletcher, G.P. 1998. Dogmas of the Model Penal Code. *Buffalo Criminal Law Review* 2: 3–24.

Gainer, R.L. 1998. Federal Criminal Code Reform: Past and Future. *Buffalo Criminal Law Review* 2: 45–159.

Green, S.P. 2000. Prototype Theory and the Classification of Offenses in a Revised Model Penal Code: A General Approach to the Special Part. *Buffalo Criminal Law Review* 4: 301–4 Buff. Crim. L. Rev. 301–39.

Kadish, S.H. 1978. Codifiers of the Criminal Law. *Columbia Law Review* 78: 1098–144.

Kadish, S.H., Schulhofer, S.J., Steiker, C.S., Barkow, R.E. 2012. *Criminal Law and Its Processes*. 9th ed. New York: Wolters Kluwer.

Lynch, G.E. 1998. Towards a Model Penal Code, Second (Federal?): The Challenge of the Special Part, *Buffalo Criminal Law Review* 2: 2 Buff. Crim. L. Rev. 297–349.

Lynch, G.E. 2003. Revising the Model Penal Code: Keeping It Real, *Ohio State Journal of Criminal Law* 4: 219–39.

Robinson, P.H. 1998. In Defense of the Model Penal Code: A Reply to Professor Fletcher, *Buffalo Criminal Law Review* 2: 25–43.

Robinson, P.H., Cahill, M.T. 2005. The Accelerating Degradation of American Criminal Codes. *Hastings Law Journal* 56: 633–55.

Robinson, P.H., Dubber, M.D. 2007. The American Model Penal Code: A Brief Overview, 10 *New Criminal Law Review* 10: 319–41.

Robinson, P.H., Greene, P.D., Goldstein, N.R. 1996. Making Criminal Codes Functional: A Code of Conduct and a Code of Adjudication, *Journal of Criminal Law and Criminology* 86:304–65.

Robinson, P.H., Cahill, M.T., Mohammad, U. 2000. The Five Worst (and Five Best) American Criminal Codes, *Northwestern University Law Review* 95: 1–84.

Robinson, P.H., Gaeta, T., Majarian, M., Schultz, M., Weck, D.M. 2010. The Modern Irrationalities of American Criminal Codes: An Empirical Study of Offense Grading, *Journal of Criminal Law and Criminology* 100: 709–45.

Simons, K.W. 2003. Should the Model Penal Code's Mens Rea Provisions Be Amended?, *Ohio State Journal of Criminal Law* 1: 179–205.

Thaman, S.C. 2010. Russia, in *The Handbook of Comparative Criminal Law*, ed. K.J. Heller, M.D. Dubber, 414–54. Stanford: Stanford University Press.

von Rimscha, R. 1999. Möwen bespucken verboten, *Der Tagesspiegel*, 27 June 1999, 32.

Part VI
Codification of Human Rights

Chapter 11
The Codification of Human Rights at National and International Levels

General Report

Giuseppe Franco Ferrari

11.1 Introduction

Rights have definitely been the strongest idea in the evolution of public law in the twentieth century, at least after World War II, and are going to be just as important in the new millennium. They have been the real engine of the transformation both of constitutional and international law. They are the ground on which constitutional law and international law interplay and have been the main actor in the creation of so called "multilevel constitutionalism", a term which is generally assumed to describe the contemporary structure of public law, not only in Europe[1].

Yet the culture of rights is furrowed by debates, heterogeneous viewpoints, tensions, inconsistencies, but also simplifications, trivializations and conscious (or even unaware) misunderstandings that tend to mislead public opinion, which is supposed to be able to play an important role in the definition of the balance of values and principles that are the basis of the co-existence of different rights and types of rights.

From a philosophical point of view rights, freedom and liberty/ies are "essentially contested concepts"[2]: their meaning is controversial and needs to be either systematically pointed out before a discussion between scholars, even of the same field, or integrated through the use of adjectives in order to be understood, or again postulated through the stipulation of a prior agreement as to their meaning.

---

[1] Other definitions mention a European common constitutional space (P. Häberle, *Gemeineuropäisches Verfassungsrecht*, in *EuGRZ*, 1991, 261 ff.) or European inter-constitutional law (A. Ruggeri, *Sovranità dello Stato e sovranità sovranazionale, attraverso i diritti umani, e prospettive di un diritto europeo "intercostituzionale"*, in *DPCE*, 2001, 544).

[2] In W.B. Gallie, *Essentially Contested Concepts*, in *Proceeding of the Aristototelic society*, 1955/56, 167 ff.

G. F. Ferrari (✉)
Bocconi University, via Roentgen, 1-20136 Milano, Italy
e-mail: ferrari.giuseppe@unibocconi.it, giuseppe.ferrari@unibocconi.it

W.-Y. Wang (ed.), *Codification in International Perspective,* Ius Comparatum – Global Studies in Comparative Law, DOI 10.1007/978-3-319-03455-3_11,
© Springer International Publishing Switzerland 2014

Such concepts have undergone deep transformations over the years and the centuries. According to Wittgenstein[3] such a concept is, *a posteriori*, the result of several conceptualizations over the ages. The concept is logically a priori, and therefore needs to be stipulated, but its meaning can be drawn only *a posteriori* on the basis of different conceptualizations based on different periods of thought. Such concepts necessarily need to be situated in different epochs through which they have been generated, hence the need to apply a diachronic method.

As early as 1913 the American theorist, W.N. Hohfeld[4] rendered explicit the variety of meanings which lawyers and other scholars often attempt to convey through the use of the single word 'right'. According to Hohfeld we must be very careful with the terminology of rights. For instance, he proposes that 'right' should be used only with regard to a claim right, which corresponds to a duty placed on others. On the other hand privilege is one of the faculties belonging to a right, but it does not have a correlated duty imposed on others, such as the possibility of entering one's land. With this parameter, most freedoms would be Hohfeldian privileges, not involving correlative duties; yet an individual has the right not to be interfered with, while others, first and foremost the State, have a duty not to breach that right by assaults, prohibitions and so on.

The growth of human rights during the second half of the twentieth century and the beginning of the twenty-first century has transformed human rights into a *Leitmotiv* of contemporary culture and not only of legal culture. In a way human rights have been turned into a kind of secular religion. Again, however, the terms need to be conceptualized, given that they have different meanings for different authors and because it is almost impossible to find scholars who are not inclined to praise liberties and fundamental rights. Criticizing the new religion is almost like cursing the name of God. Human rights and the market are probably the two most widespread and respected ideas in the contemporary world. However, while there is a widespread economic, sociological and political literature criticizing the market ideology and the so-called Washington consensus such as Serge Latouche in France, Ulrich Beck in Germany and even authors in the US, there are virtually no critics of the human rights philosophy.

The only author who has dared to criticize the philosophy of human rights is an almost unknown Slovenian and openly Marxist professor of psychology at Lubiana, Slavoj Žižek, whose main book[5] was published by the New Left publisher, once known for its books by Lord Anthony Wedgwood Benn (better known simply as Tony Benn). Žižek defines himself as a scholar of hard thought.

In brief, Žižek's theory is the following: the religion of human rights is a kind of Western fundamentalism imposed by US and European modernization. Ethnic conflicts are due to the need to please the eye and conscience of the Western world. The most significant genocide that took place before World War II was the massacre

---

[3] *Philosophical Investigations*, Oxford, Blackwell, 1953.

[4] See *Some fundamental legal conceptions as applied in judicial reasoning*, in 23 *Yale L.J.*, 16 (1913).

[5] S. Žižek, *Against human rights*, in *New Left Review*, 34, 2005.

of the Armenians, which was perpetrated not by the old Islamic Ottomans, but by the modernized new Turks. Religious-ethnic conflicts arc the form of struggle best fitting globalized capitalism and provide a justification for humanitarian interventions under the name of the new God, human rights. The most important right of our time is the right to privacy conceived as the right to be left alone; yet at international level a militarist humanitarianism is emerging, where permanent emergency and even torture are included in human rights philosophy. This is the totalitarian drift of enlightenment. Violence is justified, absorbed and transformed into a temporary condition of a Hegelian process which leads the whole of humanity to reason harmony. Politics is deprived of content due to the human rights ideology: humanitarianism, says Michael Ignatieff, aims at preventing or curing human sufferings and distress, but it does not allow one to draw up plans for political transformation. In other words, being a subject of human rights might diminish the importance of enjoying the status of citizen and of the rights of citizenship. The rights of men, if depoliticized, deprive citizenship and civil rights of their importance and leave men naked, in the condition of *homo sacer*[6]. They conceal the real nature of Western imperialism, military intervention and neo-colonialism.

This point of view may appear whimsical, odd and radical, but it represents an exception to the rather dull contemporary cultural landscape and therefore it deserves to be mentioned because of its originality.

To the contrary, the contemporary conceptualization of liberties and rights rests upon the idea that they represent the instrument to straighten up the "crooked timber of humanity", in the words of Immanuel Kant.

The progressive rise of the rights doctrine is perceived as the "ability to see more and more differences among people as morally irrelevant[7].". It could appear as the moral consequence of globalization[8] and, along with the efficiency of the markets, represents the *secular religion* of contemporary (global) culture.

Contemporary conceptions of liberty present a number of different meanings, ranging from its negative meaning, to that of equality, freedom, or even enjoyment of community life. Defining the idea of liberty by referring to its history (the history of the *concept* of liberty as history of the *meanings* this term has been supposed to describe) has precisely the aim to limit the diversity of possible interpretations. On one hand the history of concepts helps reduce the polysemy of ethical concepts; on the other, it prevents from identifying an ethical concept as liberty with a universal and immutable category.

It is necessary to look for the historic reasons why specific individual claims have shifted from a merely factual status to a legal one, thus creating correspondent legal provisions for ethical issues, and therefore a true legal sub-system[9].

---

[6] H. Arendt, *The Origins of Totalitarianism*, New York, Harcourt, 1951; G. Agamben, *Homo Sacer*, Torino, Einaudi, 1995.

[7] R. Rorty, *Truth and Progress*, Cambridge, Cambridge University Press, 1998, 167.

[8] M. Ignatieff, *Human Rights as Politics and Idolatry*, Princeton, Princeton University Press, 2001.

[9] G. Peces-Barba Martinez, *Teoría de los derechos fundamentales*, Madrid, Eudema, 1991.

11.1.1   The National Dimension

The domestic level of rights goes back to the ancient world, though in the face-to-face society[10] of the old republics they used to be conceived and enjoyed only in their social dimension, not in an individualistic fashion, as Benjamin Constant had been the first to incisively summarize albeit not to fully understand[11]. With regard to the modern version of rights, the national level develops its model in the context of British history from the Magna Charta to the Bill of rights and finds its natural environment in modern European States after the Treaty of Westphalia. It is however only with the American and French revolutions that rights achieve general positivization and develop into different generations of claims. World War II demonstrates that the national shield is no longer able to guarantee a full protection from abuses to the individual rights. Liberal-democratic constitutionalism in Western Europe and beyond is the answer to the gaps and lapses of the recent past. Indeed, the constitutionalization of values and principles, with the dignity of man on top, systematically balanced by constitutional or supreme courts in strict dialectic correspondence with public opinion, is the contemporary solution that after the fall of the Soviet empire and the disintegration of the communist bloc spreads Eastward and becomes one of the symbols of Western civilization, regardless of the U.S. model.

11.1.2   The International Dimension

The international dimension of human rights is probably just as old, if one looks back at Sophocles' Antigone, the *ius gentium* of the Roman tradition, the Christian medieval doctrine of human dignity expressed by Saint Thomas, the natural rights theory of William of Ockham and the Italian legal and humanistic scholarship of the Renaissance, the Spanish theology concerning the condition of the American Indians, John Milton's vindication of the right of man to self-determination[12]. However, the true "invention" of human rights[13] can be dated back to the age of Grotius (who proposed a list of natural rights applicable to the whole of humanity beyond State borders and domestic legal traditions) and Pufendorf (with the idea of an ethically free man, equal in dignity to all others) up to the Enlightenment and the two Declarations of 1776 and

[10] In the words of M.I. Finney, *Democracy Ancient and Modern*, London, Rutgers University Press, 1995.

[11] *De la liberté des anciens comparée à celle des modernes*, Paris, 1819.

[12] There is an extremely vast literature on this topic: J.N. Figgis, *Political Thought from Gerson to Grotius: 1414–1625*, New York, Harper, 1960; R. Tuck, *Natural Rights Theories: Their Origin and Development*, Cambridge, Cambridge University Press, 1979; B. Tierney, *The Idea of Natural Rights: Studies on Natural Rights, Natural Law and Church Law 1159–1625*, Atlanta, Scholar Press of Emory University, 1997.

[13] See L. Hunt, *Inventing Human Rights: A History*, New York, W. W. Norton & Company, 2007, and also G. Oestreich, *Geschichte der Menschenrechte und Grundfreiheiten im Umriss*, Berlin, Duncker & Humblot, 1978; A. Dershowitz, *Rights from Wrongs. A Secular Theory of the Origins of Rights*, New York, Basic Books, 2004; M. Flores, *Storia dei diritti umani*, Bologna, il Mulino, 2008.

1789. An excellent synthesis of the new concept is Tom Paine's The Rights of Man[14], which, on one hand, was described as the most brilliant and powerful political rocket ever launched in English political history and, on the other, was considered an attack on monarchy, religion, and the recognized forms of government[15]. Yet, the idea is almost obliterated in the age of romanticism and positivism due to the emerging of imperialism and the strengthening of the States as exclusive holders of sovereignty. However, the signing of the two Geneva conventions of 1864 and 1906 and the two Hague conventions of 1899 and 1907 marks the birth of humanitarian international law and somehow tempers the role of the State or at least creates the premises for an international order, reinforced by the foundation of the Society of Nations and the International Labor Office in the aftermath of World War I. Finally, the positivization of human rights begins with the creation of the United Nations in June 1945 and the approval of the Universal Declaration of Human Rights on December 10, 1948[16].

11.1.3   The Coexistence of the Two Dimensions

The positivization of human rights and the co-existence of two kinds of rights at two different levels as well as the availability of two different sets of guarantees have greatly enriched the human condition in the contemporary age but at the same time have raised enormous problems, still unsolved, in terms of relocating or even redefining sovereignty, of coordinating domestic constitutional law in the revised post World War II fashion with international law whose evolution is under way as well, of defining a new statute for non-citizens in the age of mass migrations, of elaborating regional systems for the protection of rights that combine traditional domestic guarantees with supra-national institutions, of reconciling political and economic constitutionalism.

11.2   Fundamental Rights in the Domestic Dimension

One of the most controversial issues regarding the codification of human rights, both on national and international level, concerns the qualification of rights as fundamental. The concept of fundamental rights or fundamental liberties implies a hierarchy of rights: some deserve the qualification of essential, intangible or preferred. The qualification is made in positive terms, that is to say that "basicness" is not a metaphysical category. It is considerably one of the possible classifications of rights.

---

[14] 1791.

[15] The summary description exposed in the text is not contradicted neither by the use of the expression "human rights" by William Blackstone, *Commentaries on the Laws of England*, Oxford, Clarendon Press, 1765–1769, I, 121, nor by Jean-Jacques Burlamaqui, *Principes du droit naturel*, Genève, Barillot et fils, 1747, I, VII, 4.

[16] L. Henkin, *The Age of Rights*, New York, Columbia University Press, 1990; T. Boergenthal, *The Normative and Institutional Evolution of International Human Rights*, in 19 *Human Rights Quarterly*, 1997, 703 ff.

11.2.1 Basicness or Fundamentality

This status sometimes depends on an express constitutional provision as interpreted by constitutional Courts, as in Germany[17] or in France, where the *Conseil Constitutionnel* has included in the category of fundamental guarantees, mentioned both by art. 34 and by the Preamble of the 1946 constitution[18], fundamental rights and liberties of constitutional value, pertaining to any persons living in the French territory, though non citizens, like freedom of marriage, right to normal family life or to move freely. In Spain constitutional interpretation on one hand connects the character of fundamentality to the essential structure of the legal system[19], assuming the radiating effect of fundamental rights; on the other it identified a general criterion to select those rights which should be conceived as fundamental[20]: they might be isolated or selected from a group of rights when, due to their stronger social value, they present a measure of prevalence on others, and accentuate their condition of subjective right through a direct justiciability in court.

Basicness may be also defined by judicial decisions[21], or by definition included in a statute[22]. Israel's case should be placed in the space between these two groups: before the early Nineties, the recognition of fundamental rights derived only from judicial decisions. Eventually, in 1992 two Basic Laws, marking the era of "constitutional revolution", were passed, affording protection to a specific set of constitutional rights, mainly through an express "Limitation Clause"[23].

Finally, the fundamental character of some rights may depend on decisions of administrative judges, at least in systems where a statute introduces specific procedures[24].

The Argentine case is sui generis, because the Supreme Court recognized social rights since 1922 and 1934[25], absent any formal provision of the 1853/1860 Constitution, while after the amendment of 1957, including in the constitutional text the

---

[17] See FRG, arts. 1–19 GG.

[18] See CC dec. 22.1.1990, 13.8.1993, and 22.4.1997.

[19] See art. 10.2 and Title I Spanish Const. and TC dec.14.7.1981, stating that fundamental rights have the double nature of guarantee of legal status and of essential elements of the legal system.

[20] TC dec. 25/1981; 64/1988; 53/1995.

[21] Italy, Court of cassation 22.6.1985, n. 3769; US Supreme Court *inter alia* Gitlow v. New York, 268 U.S. 652 (1925); Engblom v. Carey, 357 U.S 449 (1958); McDonald v. Chicago, 561 U.S. 3025 (2010); France: freedom of association, CE, 11.07.1956; dignity of human being, 2.7.1993; right of property, Civil Cassation 4.1.1995; *droit au logement*, Civil Cassation 10.3.1993.

[22] France: l.22.6.1982 e 6.7.1989 on slum clearance and house sanitation and hygiene; l. 21.1.1995 on public security.

[23] See National Report at 6–7.

[24] France, l.30.6.2000, creating the procedure called *référé-liberté*, aiming at giving the administrative judge powers on an equal footing with the civil judge, including "all measures necessary and proper to safeguarding a fundamental liberty menaced or damaged by a public body or a private body encharged with public functions or services": see L. Favoreu, *La notion de liberté fondamentale devant le juge administratif des référés*, Paris, Dalloz, 2001, Chronique, 1739.

[25] *Ercolano* and *Avico* decisions, described in par.3 of the Country Report.

new art. 14bis containing the protection of labor and social security, it has kept on elaborating both on the qualification of such claims as fundamental rights and on the introduction of the guarantee of the *acción de amparo* in support of them[26].

In some areas, like Europe, the transformation of a constitutional right into a fundamental one may be determined even by an international treaty, like the ECHR, art. 15, prohibiting the sacrifice or diminution of a right in the cases listed in art. 15. The same effect derives from the Maastricht Treaty of 1992 (art, F.2), the Amsterdam Treaty of 1997 (art. 6, § 1), or the Nice Treaty of 2000, proclaiming the Charter of fundamental rights of the EU.

11.2.2   Status of Fundamental Rights in Constitutional Law

A number of consequences derive from the status of fundamental rights. In the German case, it includes the protection of art. 19: limitations by ordinary statutes must have general character and must not be addressed to single cases, mention the specific right they aim at limiting, and must not invade the essential content (*le noyeau dur*; *das Wesensgehalt*). Furthermore, in case of prejudice to a fundamental right by a public authority it must be always possible to sue in a court of law.

The German model is widely followed in Europe. The Greek Constitution of 1975, in less specific terms, at art. 25 only admits limitations through statute[27] and, after the amendment of 2001 to art. 17, imposes the requirement of proportionality.

In the US case the main effect of the classification of a right as fundamental is to afford federal judges the right to protect it against any public actions, mainly by States; therefore, in the presence of a fundamental right, the nature of federalism changes, switching from the dual version to the cooperative one. If the individual, the American citizen, feels menaced or damaged by his own State, the federal power offers his help in order to prevent the State from invasion of the individual's sphere of liberty, guaranteeing the equal treatment of all citizens inside the Union. With this instrument, the protection of individual rights is strengthened at the same time that the Federation increases its prerogative towards the States. This is precisely the reason why the Federalist resisted the introduction of a federal bill of rights in the 1787 Constitution, lest rights could mean powers to protect them, in a phase of the constitutional history of America when it was hard to persuade the public opinion to follow those who ask for a strengthening of the links between central federal power and territorial instances of government[28]. Many of the liberties have been incorporated following this method, and were included in the "honor roll of superior

---

[26] See, *infra*, par. 2.2.

[27] Though the case law is quite tolerant toward administrative limitations: see National Report, par.1.

[28] *The federalist* No. 84, by A. Hamilton.

rights", according to the words of J. B. Cardozo[29], or the "slot machine"[30] in the less reverent words of J. Felix Frankfurter. The Supreme Court has never accepted the theory of J. Hugo Black that would have promoted all the rights listed in the federal bill of rights, that is in the ten amendments dated 1789–1791 to the federal constitution, to the ranking of fundamental right[31].

In the French case after 1984 the special protection afforded to fundamental rights is construed by the CC along three main lines. First, no prior authorization (*autorisation préalable*) is possible. No "*régime préventif*" or "*de police*" is compatible with a right qualified by the constitutional judge as fundamental. Such is the status of freedom of association[32]. This does not exclude controls of a mere technical nature, like an exam (certificate of professional aptitude, driving license), nor the payment of a previous tax like a motorway fee or a fee to start a commercial activity. In France about 4.500 prior authorizations have been counted, and about 450 of them have something to do with the enjoyment of constitutional rights, some of them in the form of a declaration and tacit approval or silence by the public authority, though silence normally means denial, according to the statute dated 12.4.2000. The unavailability of previous controls means that rights classified as fundamental are compatible with "a posteriori" controls only. Second, in the presence of a fundamental right the legislative power can only make its protection wider, not narrower: for instance in 1984 the CC sustained the statute on the financial transparency of the press, arguing that financial openness improves and does not restrict, the freedom of the press. Yet, a statute can restrict a fundamental right in all cases when balancing is needed with another principle of constitutional value: for instance in decisions dated 25.1.1985 and 9.9.1986 the "*ordre public*" was considered a value susceptible of limiting the freedom of movement to and from New Caledonia and freedom of non-citizens to reside in France. Third, in presence of a fundamental right, the way it is protected must be alike all over France: for example, decision 18.1.1985, *Loi Chevènement*, states that contracts between the State and private schools cannot depend for their approval on the consent of single Communes, because that would undermine the equality of treatment of the founders and owners of private schools and consequently of the fundamental right of teaching (*liberté de l'enseignment*). The new (2003) text of art. 72–74 now seems to have generalized this principle from the standpoint of the possibility of modifying local statutes safeguarding the treatment of (both) fundamental and ordinary public liberties. At the moment, freedom of association, press, movement, teaching and asylum have been judicially defined fundamental. To the contrary, the right of property has been declared ordinary and non-fundamental several times, for instance in decisions of 27.11.1959, 16.1.1982, where various nationalizations were accepted by the CC without apparent difficulties. The freedom of audiovisual communication was also defined ordinary in decisions

---

[29] *Palko v. Connecticut*, 302 U.S 319 (1937).

[30] See H.J. Abraham, B.A. Perry, *Freedom and the Court. Civil Rights and Liberties in the United States*, New York, Oxford University Press, 1978.

[31] *Adamson v. California*, 332 U.S. 68 (1947).

[32] CC 16.7.1971.

27.7. and 16.1.1982, or at least recognized of constitutional value, but non-absolute and necessarily constrained in limits defined by a statute.

Most French authors appreciate the surplus of protection afforded to fundamental liberties, though they sometimes regret the weakening of the guarantee of ordinary freedoms that the parliamentary legislator feels authorized to limit.

In Italy, the term "fundamental rights" does not have the significance it has in Germany or Spain. On the one hand, the Italian Constitution uses the adjective "fundamental" to describe the social right to health, enshrined in art. 32[33]. On the other hand, the key article on human rights (art. 2) refers to the category of inviolable rights of the person, which are considered pre-existing the State as well as the final aims of its action, on the basis of a line of argument that is grounded on the circumstances that art. 2 is among the basic principles of the Constitution.

The analysis of case law confirms this interpretation. Indeed, up until 1990 the term 'fundamental right' appears less than thirty times in constitutional rulings. Moreover, in most cases, the adjective is assigned a "naïve" meaning, as a synonym for "of central importance" or "basic"; in other words, special consequences do not follow from the label of fundamental right. In its rulings the Constitutional Court called fundamental rights, for example: the freedom of correspondence (dec. 77/1972); the right to develop one's own personality (163/1983); the right to vote and to be voted (dec. 235/1988); personal freedom (469/90); the rights of defense (dec. 587/1990). Exception to this trend are: the right to health, in which the adjective is used to pay homage to the wording of the constitutional provision, as well as three decisions on housing rights (cfr. 217/88; 399/89; 419/91), which are defined as fundamental social rights. Those decisions however remained completely isolated in Italian Constitutional Court rulings. Even in more recent times, despite the increasing use by the Constitutional Court, the expression has not acquired an independent and significant meaning and the concept has remained essentially extraneous to Italian constitutional law.

In the Spanish Constitution the term "fundamental rights" is used to describe a variety of subjective legal positions: art. 10 states "Provisions relating to the fundamental rights and liberties recognized by the constitution shall be construed in conformity with the Universal Declaration of Human Rights and international treaties and agreements thereon ratified by Spain". It seems to indistinctly define as fundamental the whole of the catalogue of rights enshrined in the constitution.

In art. 25, the term refers only to those rights listed in Chap. 2 (Rights and freedoms), thus excluding the Principles governing Economic and Social Policy (Chap. 3), whereas in art. 94 it appears to apply to all the rights listed in Part 1 (Fundamental Rights and duties, including both Fundamental Rights and Public Freedoms of Chap. 2 and Principles governing Economic and Social Policy of Chap. 3). In other words, the Framers of the Spanish Constitution used *derechos* and *derechos fundamentales*, apparently without attaching a specific meaning to the latter expression.

---

[33] Art. 32 states: "The Republic safeguards health as a fundamental right of the individual and as a collective interest".

As a result, scholars have tried to identify which rights should be considered as fundamental, starting from a systematic interpretation of the articles of the constitution.

There are three different approaches scholars have developed to identify the fundamental rights of the Spanish constitution.

The first one, which now represents a minority position (even though it was sometimes shared by the *Tribunal Constitucional*) considers as *"fundamentales"* the rights listed in Chap. 2, Title 1, Sect. 1, (art. 14–29). The arguments that purport this doctrine are three: a. the special and reinforced procedure necessary to amend the constitutional provisions related to those articles; b. the organic law reserve (art. 81 CE) that is required in order to regulate those rights; c. the *amparo* remedy against any violation of rights listed in that Chapter[34].

Other scholars advance an alternative explanation: fundamental rights are those listed in the whole of Chap. II, Sect. 1 and 2 (art. 14–38 CE). According to this theory, the main distinction should be drawn between *derechos fundamentales*, which are both binding on public authorities (art. 53, c. 1) and enforceable, and *derechos prometidos*, which are neither binding, nor enforceable[35]. The rights listed in Chap. III, Title I fall in the latter category, as they represent merely "Guiding Principles of Economic and Social Policy" (*principios rectores*).

Some scholars justify this conclusion differently. They argue that those rights enshrined in arts. 14–38 are *derechos fundamentales* as they pre-exist the constitution. The argument is based on art. 53, which states that any limitation of rights protected under Title 1 must respect the "essential content". The essential content is supposed to be broader with regards to the rights declared in arts. 14–38 as they imply a stronger limitation on the public authorities' actions. As a consequence, those rights should be deemed as fundamental rights.

A third approach extends the range of fundamental rights, arguing that all the rights guaranteed in the Constitution are fundamental[36]. However, they have a different "co-efficient of fundamentality", which depends on the remedy provided for each right. From this point of view, there are three categories of fundamental rights: *derechos fundamentales básicos* (art. 14–29, Chap. II, sec. I); *derechos fundamentales complementarios* (art. 30–38, Chap. II, sec. II); *derechos fundamentales informadores* (art. 39–52, Chap. III).

The first and the second categories are "effective" subjective legal positions, while the third category identifies subjective legal positions that require the legislation to render them effective[37].

---

[34] M.S. Massó Garrote, *I diritti fondamentali e le libertà pubbliche nella costituzione del 1978 e nella giurisprudenza costituzionale*, in L. Pegoraro, A. Rinella, R. Scarciglia (Eds), *I venti anni della Costituzione spagnola nella giurisprudenza del Tribunale costituzionale*, Padova, CEDAM, 2000, 43 ff.

[35] J. Jiménez Campo, *Derechos fundamentales. Concepto y garantías*, Madrid, Editorial Trotta, 1999.

[36] L.M. Díez-Picazo, *Los sistemas de derechos fundamentales*, Madrid, Civitas, 2005.

[37] J. de Esteban, *Tratado de derecho constitucional español*, Madrid, Servicio de Publicaciones de la Facultad de Derecho, UCM, 2001, 298 ss.

Recently, the *Tribunal Constitucional* identified fundamental rights with "those rights that, ensuring liberty and equality, limit the exercise of power of the Cortes generales as well as of the legislative assemblies of Comunidades Autonomas, without any exception"[38]. The *Tribunal Constitucional* assumes that fundamental rights have a radiating effect (dec. 25/1981, 64/1988, 53/1995), their expansive strength being susceptible to different modulations by public powers in various branches of the legal system, and that they are capable of direct defense through judicial protection, the core of which is the individual *amparo* in the decision 34/1994 states that fundamental rights bind all public powers, according to the explicit text of art. 53.1 CE, are immediate source of rights and obligations, being no mere guideline, and this principle of immediate application suffers no exception that is not explicitly imposed by the constitution or clearly deriving form the nature of the rights themselves.

In the Portuguese system the fundamental nature of some rights is formally recognized in art. 2, which connects the democratic nature of the State with "the respect and guarantee of the effective implementation of fundamental rights and freedoms"[39]. The formal effects of the fundamental character of a right are as follows: a. constitutional and legislative provisions concerning fundamental rights need to be interpreted and if needed integrated in conformity with the Universal Declaration of HR (art. 16); b. the normative discipline of fundamental rights shall be applied analogically to other rights of a similar nature (art. 17); c. rights and freedoms are one of the limits to the amendment of the Constitution (art. 288, d and e). Furthermore, art. 18, always included in Title I, General Principles, also states that constitutional precepts concerning rights and their guarantees are directly applicable to and binding for public authorities, and that statutes restricting rights, freedoms and their guarantees shall have general character, cannot be retroactive, nor can they diminish the extension and width of the essential content (*conteúdo esencial*) of the pertaining constitutional provision, but this provision does not mention the character of fundamentality and apparently concerns all rights independently of their fundamentality. Yet, many authors (for instance Miranda and Gomez Canotilho, two of the foremost constitutional scholars of Portugal) believe that the Constitution also includes other fundamental rights (*direitos fundamentais dispersos, fora de catálogo*) mentioned in other constitutional articles, and even rights of a similar nature, analogically construed, having a statutory foundation but not expressly mentioned in Constitution (*direitos só formalmente constitucionais*), though having access to constitutional status through the "open clauses" of arts. 2 and 16. Though there are different opinions as far as a full equalization of social, economic and cultural rights to civil and political rights is possible[40], apparently the inflation of fundamentality in the Portuguese system draws on the conclusion that the Portuguese fundamentality is mainly rhetoric.

---

[38] Thus requiring recognition through a "constitutional imprimatur": using this argument, TC rejected the claim of *Comunidades Autónomas* for an independent catalogue of fundamental rights, see STC, dec. 31/2010, see also *infra* par. 5.

[39] On this issue, see the national report.

[40] For instance J. Miranda denies it (*Manual de direito constitucional*, Vol. IV, Coimbra, Editora Tema, 2008), while J.J. Gomes Canotilho admits it (*Tomemos a sério os direitos económicos, sociais e culturais*, in *Estudos sobre direitos fundamentais*, Coimbra, Editora Tema, 2004).

The English case is, as always, absolutely unique. The British system as such does not recognize any kind of fundamental right, at least in the case law based upon domestic sources. This is a natural consequence of the prevalence of parliamentary sovereignty and representative democracy over the idea of fundamental rights. Parliament has repeatedly introduced or restored conditions of full enjoyment of civil rights: in 1828, 1829 and 1866 this was done by removing disqualifications excluding people of faith other than that of the Church of England from participation in public life; in 1832 and 1867 by widening the electorate; in 1968 by outlawing discrimination on grounds of race, in 1975 of sex and in 1995 of disability. Yet, there has never been an attempt to codify human liberties or rights or to identify some of them as fundamental. Albert Venn Dicey, at the end of the nineteenth century and early in the twentieth, mentioned two characteristic features of the British constitution: its foundation on people's liberty protected by the common law and the power of Parliament to amend or abrogate any statute, regardless of its impact on liberty. The underlying assumption was that political, rather than judicial, controls were sufficient to prevent excessive interference by statute with people's liberty. After the growing influence of human rights in the aftermath of World War II, in the 70s the United Kingdom came into the orbit of the European Economic Community and later of the EC and of the EU, perceiving the trickling down of fundamental rights assumed to be forming the general principles of European law and deriving from the common constitutional traditions of the Member States. In the end, the human rights standards recognized by the Luxembourg Court of Justice were codified in art. 6 (2) of the Treaty on the EU, formerly art. F2 of the Maastricht Treaty. The UK did not subscribe the Social Chapter, which was then accepted by the Labour majority after 1997. Then the Nice Treaty, initially used as an aid to interpretation to EC law by the Luxembourg Court, and lately incorporated in the Treaty in art. 6 (2).

Several scholars and some judges began to argue about the existence of fundamental rights embedded in the common law[41], such as equality before the laws, access to courts, right to fair procedures, right to dignity and bodily integrity. Other authors[42] assume that British courts a. interpreted domestic law presuming that Parliament had intended to legislate in conformity with UK's obligations under international law; b. tried to make sure the international obligations were fulfilled as effectively as possible; c. developed the common law as far as possible in conformity with human rights; d. scrutinized administrative acts under a stricter standard of scrutiny. Through these and other routes fundamental rights found in the common constitutional traditions of Member States found their way into domestic adjudication, being British courts bound to apply Community law.

Finally, the adoption of the Human Rights Act of 1998 incorporates into domestic law the idea itself of fundamental rights, since Sect. 1(1) defines the Convention rights as the rights and fundamental freedoms set out in various articles of the ECHR

---

[41] J. Laws, *Is the High Court of Justice the Guardian of Fundamental Constitutional Rights?*, in *Pub. L.*, 1993, 59 ff.; T.R.S. Allan, *Law, Liberty and Justice*, Oxford, Clarendon Press, 1993.

[42] A. Burrows, D. Feldman (Eds.), *English Public Law*, Oxford, Oxford University Press, 2009.

specified in Sect. 1 of the Act. The concept of fundamentality now is part of British law through the ECHR[43].

In Belgium, up to 1980 the case law mentioned only *libertés publiques* in the French way, but then in that year a *Cour d'Arbitrage* was created, initially only to umpire conflicts between central State and local authorities. In the following years the *Cour* quickly changed its role exercising a full review of constitutionality control thanks to the delegation of functions by the State to local entities in the field of school organization and teaching: in that case the Court started to apply articles 10 and 11 of the Constitution, concerning the principles of equality and non-discrimination, not directly pertaining to the issues of regionalism and/or federalism. Parliament in the subsequent years applied clause 142 widening the functions of the *Cour* through ordinary legislation. At the end of this process the *Cour* had switched completely from an arbitrary Court to a fully-fledged constitutional court, also thanks to the special statute dated 9 March 2003, which formally authorizes all the rights included in Title II and in articles 170, 172, 191 of the Constitution to be used as a parameter for constitutional review. After 1989 the *Cour* openly speaks of fundamental rights, starting from the right to vote as "fundamental political right of representative democracy"; in 1992 the right to be elected is defined "fundamental right in a democratic society", with the consequence that it "cannot be object of specific limitations which, though indirect, need to be justified with precise exigencies strictly correlated to peculiar functions". The above-mentioned decision 32/92, concerning education, declares that fundamental rights are not only those enunciated in Title II, but also those depending on international treaties including obligations for Belgium that entered in the domestic legal order. Such fundamental rights also have compulsory effects on the national legislator and local authorities[44]. Art. 23, guaranteeing the right to a life consistent with human dignity, is widely utilized in order to promote to the dignity of fundamentality the economic, social and cultural rights mentioned in that article in a non-exhaustive list, opened by the word "notamment". By transforming the *libertés publiques* into *droits fondamentaux*, the *Cour* substitutes the political protection of the legislator with the judicial protection offered by itself. Belgian authors[45], emphasize the importance, in this process of judicial creation of fundamental rights of the ECHR, due to the fact that ordinary judges, presided over by the *Cour de Cassation*, have consistently preferred, in case of conflict, obligations deriving from international treaties to domestic norms. Through this channel they suggest that the recently created *Cour* has integrated its parameter with the provisions of international treaties on human rights and above all of the ECHR. Finally, the statute of 12 July 2009 has added a proposition to art. 26 of the special statute of 1989 compelling judges to ask the *Cour* whenever a fundamental right guaranteed in Title II of the constitution or in a similar form in a European or international disposition is at stake.

---

[43] The UK has obtained an "opt-out" clause as far as the social chapter of the Lisbon Treaty is concerned.

[44] Dec. 107/1998 and 124/1999.

[45] N. Uyttendaele, *Précis de droit constitutionnel belge*, Bruxelles, Bruylant, 2006; F. Delpérée, *Ledroit constitutionnelde laBelgique*, Bruxelles, Bruylant, 2003. See also N. Bonbled, M. Verdussen, *Le droits constitutionnels en Belgique*, Vol. I, Bruxelles, Bruylant, 2011.

In the Netherlands, as has been clearly pointed out in the national report, the human rights recognized under Dutch constitutional law are commonly referred to as fundamental rights. Thus, both classical civil liberties and social rights are conceived as fundamental. However this kind of classification does not bear consequences in itself in terms of efficacy, levels or means of protection, possibility and extension of limitations. In other words, the character of fundamentality is not the result of an implicit or explicit hierarchy of rights.

Similarly, the Greek Constitution of 1975 does not mention fundamentality, but both the Court of Cassation and the Council of State treat all constitutional rights, including social and economic rights, as fundamental, applying important consequences to all of them[46].

11.2.3   Fundamental Rights and Horizontal Efficacy

One of the possible consequences of a right being qualified as fundamental is, according to specific clauses of the respective constitutions or decisions of constitutional or supreme courts, the eventual applicability of its protection beyond the sphere of public power, against which they are originally conceived of, to the relationship between private subjects or inside private associations. This extension of efficacy is well known to constitutional lawyers, having been conceptualized by German scholars under the name of *Drittwirkung* and borrowed by Spanish and Italian authors as "horizontal efficacy". In Spain this problem has been directly addressed because the LOTC apparently excluded the availability of the *amparo* remedy in situations where only private relations were at stake: the TC has gotten round this difficulty opening the way to it even in some cases of merely private relevance, like labor cases or controversies concerning the internal organization of associations[47].

In the US context the presence of fundamental rights has been interpreted as authorizing the intervention of federal judges in order to protect the enjoyment of the guarantees of the bill of rights and of the XIV and XV Amendments if and only if there has been some measure of State action[48], with the exclusion of individual invasion of individual rights, not covered by the Amendments. The majority of the Court has always refused to assume that governmental inaction or failure to redress private discrimination or violation of a fundamental right amounts to state action[49]. The state action requirement reflects a concern for values of pluralism and personal freedom[50]. However government cannot be allowed to use private agents to promote discrimination or violate fundamental rights, escaping constitutional restraints: therefore

---

[46] See *infra*, par. 2.2.

[47] TC 18/1984, 47/1985, 1709/1987, 177/1988.

[48] *Civil rights cases*, 109 U.S. 3 (1883).

[49] *Bell v. Maryland*, 378 U.S. 226 (1964); *DeShaney v. Winnebago County Dpt. of Social Services*, 489 U.S. 189 (1989).

[50] N. Vieira, *Constitutional civil rights in a nutshell*, St. Paul, West Publishing, 1998.

private subjects dealing with public functions, or receiving significant public aid or somehow involved in the performance public activities are included in the state action requirement: thus, Amtrak cannot discriminate on base of race; neither can primary elections though open to electors enrolled in the political party only, on the assumption[51] that the management of the electoral processes is an inalienable governmental function[52]; a private company owning a shopping center cannot prevent labor union affiliates from picketing and distributing literature against the owner's union policy[53]; State courts cannot enforce private racially restricted covenants[54]; a state constitutional amendment though supported by a referendum vote cannot protect the right of individuals to sell or lease residential property or to refuse to do so in absolute discretion[55]; nor can a State lend textbooks to students in private segregated schools or provide them other services without committing state action[56]. But Moose Lodge[57] states that the regulations of private clubs holding a liquor license amount to violation of the XIV Amendment. The involvement concept, in other words, tends now to be flexible and weighed in consideration of factual circumstances. In this perspective, yet, civil rights can be enforced in contexts where the requisite of state action is not clearly present through congressional intervention: the enforcement clauses of the Civil War Amendments authorize appropriate legislation to implement the substantive sections of the amendments; furthermore Congress does have the commerce clause to protect the rights of national citizenship against private as well official interference[58]. Legislative activity in the field of civil rights has been particularly intense first in the Reconstruction period and later after Brown v. Board of Education. Discrimination, as a result, is now regulated not only when imposed under color of law (de jure), but also in many private contexts if involving racially motivated interference with business. Comprehensive civil rights laws enacted by Congress are for instance the Civil Rights Act of 1964[59], the Voting Rights Act of 1965[60], the Civil Rights Act of 1968[61], prohibiting, among other things, purposeful discrimination in private employment, governing the burden of proof in litigation about such discrimination, and even prohibiting facially neutral practices having discriminatory impact[62]. Another congressional intervention in the field of private party's violation of fundamental rights is the provision of 42 USCA § 1983, enacted

---

[51] H. Wechsler, *Toward Neutral Principles of Constitutional Law*, in 73 *Harv.L. Rev.,* 1, 31 (1959).

[52] *Smith v. Allright*, 1944; *Terry v. Adams*, 1953.

[53] *Amalgamated Food Employees Union v. Logan Valley Plaza*, 1968; later limited and almost overruled in *Hudgens v. NLRB*, 1976.

[54] *Shelley v. Kramer*, 1948.

[55] *Reitman v. Mulkey*, 387 U.S. 369 (1967).

[56] *Norwood v. Harrison*, 413 U.S. 455 (1973).

[57] *No. 107 v. Irvis* (1972).

[58] *U.S. v. Classic*, 313 U.S. 299 (1941).

[59] 42 USCA § 2000.

[60] 42 USCA § 1973.

[61] 42 USCA § 3601.

[62] *Griggs v. Duke Power Co.*, 1971.

as part of the Ku Klux Klan Act of 1871, which introduces the damage liability of "every person who under color of any statute, ordinance, regulation, custom or usage of any state or territory subject any other person to the deprivation of any rights, privileges or immunities secured by the constitution". This provision allows public officers, federal, state o municipal, to be held liable beyond any immunity.

According to U.S. case law, one of the most important consequences of qualifying a right as fundamental is that federal judges will apply strict forms of review ("strict scrutiny") under the equal protection and due process clauses of the XIV Am. The value of such rights is so essential to individual liberty that judges are authorized to a very demanding control of any suspect law. Several scholars believe that this kind of scrutiny is no more than the recognition of the natural law concepts[63] first exposed by Justice Chase in Calder v. Bull[64].

In the Argentine system, it has been the Supreme Court in 1957, in the silence of the constitution, to introduce the *amparo* remedy as a summary proceeding to obtain from any judge the review of a governmental action allegedly in violation of fundamental rights whenever ordinary instruments would prove useless, and shortly after to extend it to violations of constitutional rights by private parties. All opposition by

---

[63] In the history of the US Supreme Court, there are plenty of examples of different opinions of judges as to the use of a natural law approach or alternatively the use of specific provisions of the Bill of rights. For instance, J. Hugo Black accused Frankfurter (see *Rochin v. California*, 342 U.S. 165 (1952)). of assuming too great an authority by adoption of a natural law approach. The natural law approach has been massively used in the years 1880–1937 to protect property, contract and economic rights from fed and State regulations in favour of workers, women, child labourers, and so on (substantive due process) After 1937 the Court decided to stop this approach and in 1938 the famous footnote 4 appended to the text of U.S. v. Carolene Products declared the intention of protecting civil and political rights in a special manner: "There may be narrower scope for operation of the presumption of constitutionality when legislation appears on its face to be within a specific prohibition of the constitution, such as those of the first ten amendments, which are deemed equally specific when held to be embraced within the Fourteenth. It is unnecessary to consider now whether legislation which restricts those political processes which can ordinarily be expected to bring about repeal of undesirable legislation is to be subjected to more exacting judicial scrutiny under the general prohibitions of the Fourteenth Amendment than are most other types of legislation. [. . .] Nor need we enquire whether similar considerations enter into the review of statutes directed at particular religious, Pierce v. Society of Sisters, 268 U. S. 510, or national, Meyer v. Nebraska, 262 U. S. 390; Bartels v. Iowa, 262 U. S. 404; Farrington v. Tokushige, 273 U.S. 284, or racial minorities, Nixon v. Herndon, supra: whether prejudice against discrete and insular minorities may be a special condition, which tends seriously to curtail the operation of those political processes ordinarily to be relied upon to protect minorities, and which may call for a correspondingly more searching judicial inquiry" (*U.S. v. Carolene Products Co*, 304 U.S. 144 (1938), ft. 4). Balancing gives structure to a mobile hierarchy of values, a flexible, soft order *(weiche Ordnung)*. Even the principle of precaution, so important in EU law above all in the environmental sector, is drawn from the balancing process. Measuring the standard of acceptable risk to public health and hygiene, it derives from a balance of values. After 1938, the US SC has consistently enough followed the program described in Carolene Products, at least with the Warren Court (1953–1969) and the Burger Court (1969–1986). In 1961 the younger J. Harlan first advocated the protection of a right not formally included in the BoR, the right to privacy in the form of the right of married persons to use contraceptive devices (*Poe. v. Ullman*, 1962).

[64] 3 U.S. 386 (1798).

Parliament, in order to limit the availability of such remedy when the constitution-ality of a statute is at stake, has been resisted by courts and finally the constitution has been amended in 1994 to give the *amparo* express constitutional status through new art. 43[65].

In Greece, though there is no mention of fundamentality in the Constitution of 1975, art. 25 is interpreted by the Council of State as establishing the horizontal applicability of constitutional rights[66].

11.3   Some Alternative Classifications

Several other classifications parallel the most utilized distinction between fundamen-tal and non-fundamental rights at the domestic level. Some of them are of scholarly elaboration but some have been positivized in constitutional texts.

A conceptual couple very frequent in French culture is the one concerning individ-ual v. collective liberties[67]. Individual liberties can be enjoyed by single individuals without joining other people (freedom of disposition of one's body, physical in-tegrity and safety, privacy, movement, opinion); collective liberties can be enjoyed only collectively (meeting, association, press, audiovisual communication, teaching, union rights). According to this division, some liberties are non classifiable (religion, communication). Not even property can be enjoyed in solitude without a relation-ship with others. From a historical point of view, French authors emphasize that the original Declaration recognized only individual liberties, except for the press, while the collective ones were introduced only after 1791.

Another distinction, used by several French authors, is the one between physical v. intellectual liberties, probably founded on the Christian distinction between body and soul[68]. Physical liberties help man to realize himself fully from the physical point of view: they are classified in five groups: a. right to disposal of one's body (i.e. the right to sexual relations, to procreation, and the right to die); b. right to physical integrity (to prevent torture and cruel or unusual punishments, to avoid medical or scientific treatment without consent, not to be reduced into slavery or involuntary servitude); c. right to safety (not to be arbitrarily imprisoned); d. right to movement (to come and go, to stay in a place of one's choice); e. right to one's private life (domicile, secret, correspondence, normal familiar life, protection of personal information). Intellectual liberties help man to realize himself as a spiritual creature; opinion and

---

[65] See National Report, par.3.

[66] National Report, par.1.

[67] See Y. Madiot, *Droits de l'homme et libertés publiques*, Paris, Masson, 1976; L. Richer, *Les droits de l'homme et du citoyen*, Paris, Economica, 1982; J. Morange, *Droits de l'homme et libertés publiques*, Paris, Robert Laffont, 1985; J.-J. Israel, *Droit des libertés fondamentales*, Pars, LGDJ, 1998; J. Duffar, J. Robert, *Droits de l'homme et libertés fondamentales*, Paris, Montchrestien, 2009.

[68] See G. Burdeau, *Les libertés publiques*, Paris, LGDJ, 1972; C.-A. Colliard, *Libertés publiques*, Paris, Dalloz, 1989; J. Rivero, *Les libertés publiques*, Paris, PUF, 1996; D. Turpin, *Libertés Publiques et Droits Fondamentaux*, Paris, Ed. du Seuil, 2004.

expression, religion, teaching, press, audiovisual communication. However safety and private life not only fit in the physical dimension. The right to safety is also a condition for the enjoyment of other liberties.

Other liberties, like assembly, association, union rights, property and entrepreneurial rights hardly fit the main division, and are classified as others (for instance as of collective expression[69], or as economic and social rights[70]).

Much debate has been aroused and in part still is open on the dichotomy between absolute v. relative rights, which is probably devoid of real content. Some authors[71], the closest to the original conceptualization of iusnaturalism, underline that provisions like art. XII of the Virginia declaration of 1776 and art. 4 of the French Declaration of 1789 presuppose the Lockian assumption that any limitations of human rights are *contra naturam*: in the historic phase of the overturn of the absolute powers of monarchies, such a conclusion could amount to a special emphasis on the new religion of rights.

In contemporary legal literature the opinion that no right, not even fundamental, originated in the domestic system or in international law, can be unlimited (*Schrankelose*, irrestringibile) is overwhelmingly prevalent. Most constitutional and supreme courts of Western countries expressly stick to the same line.

Proportionality and equality are likely to be the most important logical instruments in modern (contemporary) constitutional law. Equality implies a horizontal relationship between things or persons. Proportionality implies a vertical relationship between elements inside the some sphere, like ends/means in a legislative process. Peter Lerche[72] says that Robinson Crusoe could not be treated by an imaginary State power on equal or unequal terms, but he could be treated in a disproportionate way.

The Italian Constitutional Court in its first decision (no. 1/56), for instance, stated that the concept of limit is naturally rooted inside the idea itself of right; the Spanish TC as well stated in decision 11/1981 (right to strike) and later in decision 98/2000 (*derecho a la intimidad*) that no constitutional right is unlimited. The Swiss ST[73], in revising the decision of a local court with regard to the right of property declared "inviolable" in the constitution of a Canton, concluded that such a proclamation does not mean that the legislative power cannot restrict it for reasons of public interest under the common value of public order. The German CT shares the opinion that some external limitations on fundamental rights are guaranteed without reservations[74]. The Strasbourg Court, which dedicates all its work to the maximization of the Convention rights, has constantly believed that "some measure of conciliation between the imperative safeguard of individual rights and the imperative of the

---

[69] J. Rivero, *supra* note 68; J. Robert, *supra* note 67.

[70] See *supra* note 68.

[71] See B. de Castro Cid, A. Fernández- Galiano, *Lecciones de Teoría del Derecho y Derecho Natural*, Madrid, Editorial Universitas, 1993, *passim*.

[72] *Übermass und Verfassungsrecht*, Köln, Heymann, 1961.

[73] M. Bolz, *Das Verhaltnis von Schutzobjekt und Schranken der Grundrechte*, Zürich, Schulthess, 1991.

[74] BVerGE 32, 98, 107.

defense of democratic society is inherent to the Convention system"[75]. One of the most distinguished commentators of the ECHR[76] remarks that requiring rights to be absolute means undermining the same rights the Convention intends to protect. For different reasons, linked to the originally economic leaning of the EC, the Luxembourg Court has stated that "rights, far from looking like absolute expectations, are to be considered in the light of the social function of goods and activities that they protect"[77]. The application of such principles to specific rights further demonstrates this assumption.

As far as the right to life is concerned the following confirms that limitations are possible or even necessary, for example, the death penalty (in the States where it is still possible within limits) legitimate defense, state of necessity, intentionally procured abortion, euthanasia (where admitted), risk to life while carrying out public service, even police rules like the so called "salvation final shooting" rule, according to which in several German Länder the police are authorized to shoot the author of a crime under the proportionality principle.

As far as the right not to be submitted to torture is concerned, this right is actually recognized in several international instruments, but it can more properly be defined as a part of the right to physical and moral integrity, which can be limited in presence of public interest needs, but its limitations cannot overcome the limit (limit of limits, counter-limit) of torture; therefore, the meaning of torture as inhuman or intolerably degrading treatment or punishment necessarily implies the exercise of some discretion in evaluating the concrete circumstances of the mental or physical suffering that can be imposed on a detainee. In German literature, where torture represents a sort of dogmatic taboo, some authors[78] try to define the conditions under which torture could be justified: a clear (1) and present (2) danger (3) to the life and physical integrity of innocent person(s) (4), caused by an identifiable subject (5), being the only one who could prevent the concretization of the risk (6) and is legally obliged to do it (7), therefore being physical force the only way to obtain the information necessary to prevent the concretization of the risk (8). The right to personal integrity can thus be limited for reasons of legitimate defense, application of force by police officers in order to preserve public order or to capture or detain criminals or to prevent crime commission, corrective means by parents and teachers in several systems (in loco parentis doctrine), corrective means in criminal trial or in detention, compulsory sanitary treatment, compulsory alcoholemic tests, paternity tests, X-ray sessions in a penitentiary or during airport controls, compulsory hair and beard trimming in penitentiaries or military plants, clinical experiments or sterilization of incompetent subjects under certain conditions in some legal systems.

In the same way, the prohibition of hard labor in art. 12 GG or in the ECHR, or the prohibition of slavery, like the one of torture, rather than an autonomous right is

---

[75] 6.9.1978, *Klass v. Germany*; 21.2.1986, *James*.

[76] R. Beddard, *Human Rights and Europe*, Cambridge, Grotius Publications, 1993.

[77] *Nold*, 14.5.1974.

[78] W. Brugger, *Das andere Auge*, in *Frankfurter Allgemeine Zeitung*, Mar. 10, 2003; W. Hecker, *Relativierung des Folterverbots in der BRD?*, in *Kritische Justiz*, 2003, 210–218.

a barrier to limitations on physical freedom or right to work: these require a case-by case proportionality exam in order to understand whether the specific treatment amounts to compulsory hard labor or not. So it can be better qualified as a barrier to barriers.

The ban on discrimination is also not an absolute right; it can better be interpreted as an expectation concerning different vital ambits protected by other fundamental rights: therefore it does not impose absolute equality in any sector of life, but simply forbids unreasonably different or disproportionate treatments, independently of the kind of scrutiny or judicial test applied in the different systems in order to verify the rationality of legislative choice from the point of view of various classifications.

Similarly, the right to a due process in courts[79] is not an absolute right. The Strasbourg Court[80], summing up former decisions, states that such a right can suffer limitations in time and space and the State enjoys wide discretion within reasonable application of the proportionality principle in formulating their regulations.

The so called fundamental right not to declare one's ideology, religious faith or personal ideas is another example of limit on limits: freedom of conscience in all its forms can be limited under certain circumstances, like the conscientious objector having to declare the reason of the objection to avoid conscription or the taxpayer obliged to declare his/her religious faith in order to assign a percentage of his income tax to a church through an allowance in the tax return.

According to the case law of the German BVG, even human dignity, as a (fundamental) right or a "superprinciple" founding other rights, according to different theories, declared intangible in art. 1 GG, may be violated if a subjective element, an *animus malus*, the intention of deliberate contempt toward a person[81] is lacking. For instance in the case of a prisoner on an airplane carried handcuffed in order to prevent assault or damages to passengers and crew. A famous decision by the German BVG stated that the application of perpetual chain on prisoners[82] may not conflict with their dignity in case of permanent danger and need to protect the community, at least in concrete situations.

The most celebrated dictum concerning the limits to an otherwise fundamental right is suggestion by Justice O.W. Holmes in Schenck v. U.S.[83] that freedom of expression does not protect a man that shouts "fire" in a crowded theatre.

Generally speaking, we could say that unlimited rights do not exist because the whole balancing process which implies never-ending confrontation, often conflicts, continuous conciliation between rights does not afford the full affirmation of one and the complete sacrifice of the other. The prevailing logic is either or (et et), and not the alternative (aut aut) logic. Or in the language of Robert Alexi, the German constitutional law scholar who has elaborated these concepts in most depth, fundamental rights are principles, not rules: rules are made to be fully implemented or

---

[79] Art. 111 Italian Con.; art. 24 Spanish Con.; art. 6 ECHR; Amendments V and XIV US Con.

[80] *Lithgow*, 8.8.1986.

[81] BVerG 20, 1, 26.

[82] BVerG 45, 187, 242.

[83] 249 U.S. 47 (1919).

not observed at all according to factual conditions, while principles, as optimization mandates, aim at the best possible implementation after balancing to other principles and rules, and can therefore be implemented to different degrees.

The distinction between rights needing implementation through legislation v. directly applicable rights (*Schutzbereiche der Grundrechte mit Rechts- und Normprägung/ohne Rechts- und Norm-Prägung; derechos fundamentales con acuñamiento jurídico o normativo/sin acuñamiento*) is often repeated in constitutional law textbook, but is not compatible with the most common construction of the role and working of rights. Most rights, or even all of them, to achieve real efficiency, need the interposition of the legislator whose intervention aims at introducing the legal conformation of the relationships and ambits that they have to protect. Sometimes Parliaments implement express constitutional mandates, when the constitutional provision needs to be applied with a statute that defines the details of the discipline. In other cases, in the absence of an explicit constitutional precept, the obligation can be presumed or deduced from the constitutional text. For instance, the equality between man and woman, the freedom of the press, the legal status of marriage and family, property safeguards can only be guaranteed through statutory provisions. As Peter Häberle has emphasized, if rights are not to be reduced to a condition of insignificance in terms of efficacy, they need the legislator's interposition; rights become effective only in the sphere of positive law, not as natural rights, and the legislator from this viewpoint is no enemy to freedoms; to the contrary he is their necessary tutor. This same construction applies to those rights which can apparently be enjoyed naturally, out of human nature without statutory support, like life, physical integrity, freedom of movement, freedom to assemble or to express opinions. In this case, a costly apparatus is often required on the part of public powers, such as the organization of a police force or the predisposition of measures in favor of the press and audiovisual media. Some German authors, like Konrad Hesse (1995) or Roman Herzog (1985) distinguish between the activities of conforming and concretizing rights, though they might overlap or partially coincide. In both cases, the activity of the legislator is bound to the constitutional parameters, and its loyalty to the constitutional prescriptions is scrutinized by judges, where constitutionality adjudication is decentralized, and to constitutional courts where it is centralized, as is the case everywhere in Europe, with the obvious exceptions of Great Britain, Holland and the Scandinavian countries.

The possible class of inviolable rights is expressly made use of by some Constitutions in Europe. The Italian Constitution resorts to it in art. 2, referring to the inviolable rights of man recognized in the same instrument, and in several articles of Title I of Part I, defining and regulating specific civil rights, like personal freedom (art. 13), domicile (art. 14), the free and secret character of correspondence (art. 15), while other rights are put in the name of citizens only (like freedom of assembly and association (art. 16 and 17)). Most authors[84] assume that the difference means that inviolable rights are enjoyed by citizens, aliens and stateless persons alike, while

---

[84] See A. Pace, *Problematica delle libertà costituzionali. Parte generale*, Padova, CEDAM, 1992, 10 ff. and P. Barile, *Diritti dell'uomo e libertà fondamentali*, Bologna, il Mulino, 1984, 31 ff.

other rights belong to citizens only as constitutional rights, the legislator having only a faculty, but no duty to extend its enjoyment to non-citizens.

Following the examples of the Italian and German constitution, the Spanish constitution also precedents, mentions the inviolable rights, in art. 10.1, connecting them with human dignity, "to which they are inherent". As it overlaps with the class of fundamental rights, this class has not been specifically elaborated.

Is it possible to conceive of unenumerated (basic) rights? Where rights and the form of government are regulated in detail, together, in modern constitutions after WWII, with constitutional values, that conform the constitution as a perpetual process, is there room for unenumerated rights? And, in the affirmative, where do non-listed rights come from? Once recognized that natural rights, whatever their foundation in terms of social consensus, ius natural, religious feelings, become positive rights through formal constitutionalization or constitutional revision, can we admit that further rights can come to existence beyond the catalogue? And which procedure can eventually give way to the recognition of new (fundamental) right[85]? The answer to these questions is positive and depends on the specific constitutional systems.

During the '60s, in the most celebrated years of the U.S. Supreme Court led by Earl Warren, federal judges started to elaborate new ideas as to this problem. For instance, in Griswold v. Connecticut, where the Court struck down a statute prohibiting the use of contraceptives by married persons, the majority opinion, written by Justice W.O. Douglas, could find a fundamental right to privacy in the "penumbras" of several guarantees of the Bill of Rights, like those protecting personal freedom, domicile, and so on. Justice Goldberg, who concurred in the decision, being unable to formulate criteria to look through the shadows in order to discover new rights, preferred not to rely on specific guarantees of the Bill of Rights, but on the IX Amendment. In his opinion, the IX Amendment gives textual recognition to values not mentioned explicitly in the first eight amendments. In other words, the Amendment does not directly create new rights, but authorizes the Court to identify them and protect them against the other branches of government, or even, if they are fundamental, the States. His ideas about the identification of such values was that the Court should rely on "the traditions and conscience of the nation" in order to determine which values deserve protection. Justice Harlan looked for another way, both in *Griswold* and earlier in Poe v. Ullman[86] natural law is the place where values having a historical and philosophical standing sufficient to be proclaimed fundamental can be picked up and enforced by the judiciary even against the will of the political majority. Justice Hugo Black objected to this natural law approach, finding no clear basis for this right in the text of the Bill of rights.

In a later case, Richmond Newspapers, Inc. v. Virginia[87], concerning the right of the public to attend criminal trials, Chief Justice Burger led a majority to find a

---

[85] 381 U.S. 479 (1965).

[86] 367 U.S. 497 (1961).

[87] 448 U.S. 555 (1980).

fundamental right, stating that "Madison's efforts, culminating in the IX Amendment, served to allay the fears of those who were concerned that expressing certain guarantees could be read as excluding others".

The concept of fundamental values not having a clear constitutional foundation, and of fundamental rights construed through this procedure remains vague today, both in the case-law and in scholarly theories.

One theory, the most conservative one (lead by Raoul Berger and Louis Lusky) would like to stick only to the original meaning of the constitutional clauses (Originalism).

Another one (Alexander Bickel, Learned Hand, Herbert Wechsler, Kent Greenawalt) would have the Court apply only obvious principles, plainly acceptable to a generality of the population, because they are plainly stated in the constitution or because almost universally shared; the Court should not, however, manufacture principles: this position is often called Scholarly tradition.

Other scholars, more inclined to promote the social good through courts, require all branches, including the judiciary, to comply with the principles of moral and political philosophy which they believed to be evidenced by the history and provisions of the constitution and approved by societal consensus. These theories are called value oriented and followed by scholars like Michael Perry, Lawrence Tribe, Bruce Ackerman.

In the case law, the Court has recognized at least six types of fundamental rights without textual foundation: 1. Freedom of association as implied by I Amendment guarantees (NAACP v. Alabama ex rel. Patterson[88]; 2. Right to vote and to participate in the electoral process (Harper v. Virginia State Board of Elections[89]); 3. Right to interstate travel as a right to personal mobility (Shapiro v. Thompson[90]); 4. Right to fairness in the criminal process (Douglas v. California[91]: right to counsel in first appeal); Mayer v. Chicago[92]: right to transcript in misdemeanor appeals); Bounds v. Smith[93]: right to legal materials and access to courts); 5. Right to fairness in procedures concerning individual claims against governmental deprivation of life, liberty and property: revoking or reducing social benefits, salaries, retirement benefits, firing public employees; 6. Fundamental right to privacy including various forms of freedom of choice in matters relating to the individual's personal life.

In Italy, the scholarly discussion arose around the interpretation of art. 2. Is it an open or closed clause? Or, to state it more clearly, does art. 2 simply summarize the catalogue of civil liberties listed in Part I, so closing the catalogue, or does it open the way to the recognition, by way of case-law, of new rights, as a channel of communication with some form of natural law? In the first case, art. 2 would simply have the meaning of a shorthand summary and a mere synthesis value; in the second

---

[88] 357 U.S. 449 (1958).

[89] 383 U.S. 663 (1966).

[90] 394 U.S. 618 (1969).

[91] 372 U.S. 353 (1963).

[92] 404 U.S. 189 (1971).

[93] 430 U.S. 817 (1977).

case, it would have constitutive value, giving access into the constitution to some natural laws, at least when cited by the constitution itself, like in art. 29.

The analysis of the rulings of the Italian Constitutional Court is not conclusive. Traditionally it has denied that art. 2 can be construed as an open clause. On the contrary, the Court has stated that it refers to those liberties listed in constitution, Part. I[94]. However, since 1987 the Constitutional Court has changed its mind. It started to ascribe some liberties directly to art. 2: for instance, sexual freedom[95], the right to expatriate[96] or the right to cultural education[97]. However, according to some scholars, it is necessary to point out that these rights could be also ascribed to liberties expressly guaranteed by constitution, Part. I.

Spanish scholars tend to consider the rights enshrined in the constitution as a close and complete catalogue.

As a result, there is virtually no debate on the possibility to afford protection to un-enumerated rights. Nevertheless, some scholars underline that article 10, Sect. 1 and 2 can be interpreted as a source of rights not expressly mentioned in the constitution, even though potentially protected in other constitutional rights.

Art. 10, Sect. 1 stating the principle of human dignity, is construed as an instrument for the implementation or specification of the rights already listed in the constitution. The combined interpretation of art. 10, Sect. 1 and any another article of Chap. 2 can result in the protection of a right which is not expressly listed in the constitution, but somehow implied in the scope of the other constitutional right subjected to interpretation. From this point of view, the principle of human dignity justifies the expansion of the personal sphere of individual, which should be held free from interference of public authorities.

For instance, the *Tribunal constitucional* recognized the prohibition of salary seizure[98], grounding its decision on art. 10, Sect. 1 and on other constitutional provisions, such as art. 39.1 (protection of family rights), art. 43 (right to health), and art. 47 (right to enjoy decent and adequate housing).

Generally speaking, Spanish scholarship does not construe art. 10, Sect. 2 as an open clause either. Section 2 states that provisions relating to fundamental rights and liberties recognized by the constitution shall be interpreted in conformity with the Universal Declaration of Human Rights and international treaties ratified by Spain. The common understanding of art. 10, Sect. 2 clause is that constitutional right must be construed in a manner consistent with the judicial interpretation of that right at the international level. As a consequence, international law as well as international judicial interpretation enrich the meaning of constitutional rights, rather than create "new" rights.

---

[94] See dec. 29/1962. See also: 37/1969; 102/1975; 238/1975; 98/1979.

[95] Dec. 561/1987.

[96] Dec. 287/1992.

[97] Dec. 383/1998.

[98] STC, 158/1993.

11.4   Group or Collective Rights

A certain number of rights are assigned not to persons as individuals, but to groups or communities, either concentrated in the same territory and generating a local majority[99] or randomly distributed inside a wider national State. The reference here is to indigenous peoples only, living in a territorial space before colonizers, ordinarily coming from Europe[100], the so called First Nations; we leave aside the rights of minorities in general, which would deserve separate consideration[101].

In domestic constitutional law, the rights of aboriginal or indigenous peoples are normally classified as third generation rights, due to their capacity of being enjoyed collectively. However, the most important forms of protection are guaranteed by international instruments. First of all, Convention no. 169 of 1989[102], proposed by the International Labor Organization, listing a long catalogue of rights of indigenous peoples and including the self-determination principle, of great symbolic importance but strongly opposed by several States, if extending beyond simple inner self-government inside national borders. More recently, the UN declaration on the rights of indigenous peoples has been adopted by the General Assembly in the New York Session of September 13, 2007: presently non-binding, it simply requests the approval of the measures most convenient to safeguard and promote both individual and collective rights of indigenous persons[103].

Convention no. 169 has not been ratified by the most of the States hosting aboriginal peoples in their territory, possibly due to the fear of vindication of outer self-determination, leading to some form of political independence: in fact, only Denmark in 2009 revised the statute of autonomy of 1978, expressly contemplating a referendum on the independence of Greenland, to be held after 2020[104]. All common law countries, including the United States, Canada, Australia and New Zealand, have not ratified the Convention, causing severe criticism from NGOs, like Survival International and the International Work Group for Indigenous Affairs. To the contrary, several Latin-American countries, like Argentina, Bolivia, Brazil, Chile, Colombia, Costa Rica, Ecuador, Guatemala, Honduras, Mexico, Nicaragua, Paraguay, Peru, Venezuela did ratify the Convention, but the level of implementation

---

[99] Such as in Greenland with the Inuit or Eskimo people, or in the Nunavut Territory, created in Canada in 1999, or in Bolivia, where according to the 2001 census indigenous peoples amount to 49.95 % of the whole population.

[100] But not necessarily, like in the case of the Islamic colonization in Ottoman North Africa.

[101] For an exhaustive classification of the different models see F. Palermo, J. Woelk, *Diritto costituzionale comparato dei gruppi e delle minoranze*, Padova, CEDAM, 2011 and also S. Choudry, *Constitutional Designs for Divided Society: Integration or Accommodation?*, Oxford, Oxford University Press, 2008.

[102] A comment in L. Swepton, *A New Step in the International Law on Indigenous and Tribal Peoples: ILOConvention No.169 of 1989*, in 15 *Okla. C. Un. L. Rev.*, 677 (1990).

[103] See S. Allen, A. Xanthaki (Eds.), *Reflections on the UN Declaration on the Rights of Indigenous Peoples*, Oxford, Hart Publishing, 2011.

[104] See F. Duranti, *Sulla via dell'indipendenza: il nuovo statuto di autonomia per la Groenlandia*, in *DPCE*, 2010, 957.

of its provisions seems to be quite limited[105]. In Northern Europe, where the Lapps or Saamis live[106], Norway and Denmark have ratified the Convention, while Sweden, Finland, and Russia did not: their condition varies, therefore, from full protection in the Danish case to marginalization or even discrimination in the Russian context. Even more complicated is the African situation, where indigenous peoples are not distinguished from the remaining non-European inhabitants: some groups would deserve special treatment, like Tuaregs in Morocco, Pygmies in Congo, and Bushmen in Austral Africa[107].

The area of collective rights is highly controversial not only from a constitutional viewpoint, representing for sociologists and political scientists the preferred ground of debate between communitarians, like Michael Walzer[108], Paul Selznick[109] and Amidai Etzioni[110] and liberals like John Rawls[111]. One of the most fortunate compromising solutions between the two extremes is the proposal by Will Kymlika[112] of construing a "difference-friendly" liberalism on the premise of a cultural membership not aimed at the inter-temporal preservation of a group, but object of individual choices, enriched and diversified by the existence of local contexts. His solution fits the Canadian case quite well, but can hardly be applied to other national contexts, where State disintegration, trends toward devolution, vindications of national or regional autonomy, and other struggles for recognition[113] have taken place in the decade following the formulation of his theory.

11.5   Infra-State Rights

In the last few decades, some State systems, not necessarily of the federal kind, often under the shelter of supranational rules, have opened the way to formalizing catalogues of rights at the infra-State level.

For instance, the *Estatutos de Autonomía de las Comunidades Autónomas*, passed between 2006 and 2007, contained bills of rights and opened a discussion about the possibility to enrich the catalogue of constitutional rights with those rights recognized (only) by an *estatuto de Autonomía*.

---

[105] See S. Lanni (Ed.), *I diritti dei popoli indigeni in America Latina*, Napoli, ESI, 2011.

[106] S. Pierré-Caps, J. Poumareède, N. Rouland, *Droit des minorités et des peuples autochtones*, Paris, PUF, 1996.

[107] Commission Africaine des Droits de l'Homme et des Peuples, *Peuples autochtones d'Afrique: les peuples oubliés?* Banjul, CADHP, 2006.

[108] *Spheres of Justice, A Defense of Pluralism and Equality*, New York, Basic Books, 1983.

[109] *The Moral Commonwealth. Social Theory and the Promise of Community*, Los Angeles, University of California Press, 1992.

[110] *Rights and the Common Good: The Communitarian Perspective*, New York, St. Martin's Press, 1995.

[111] *The Law of Peoples*, Cambridge, Harvard University Press, 1999.

[112] *Liberalism, Community and Culture*, Oxford, Clarendon Press, 1991, and *Multicultural Citizenship: A Liberal Theory of Minority Rights*, Oxford, Oxford University Press, 1995.

[113] A. Honneth, *Kampf an Anerkennung. Zur moralishen Grammatik der sozialer Kämpfe*, Frankfurt a. Main, Suhrkamp, 1992.

Spanish scholarship is basically divided between two different orientations. On one hand, there are scholars who argue that the *estatuto de Autonomía* lacks competence to include a bill of rights as art. 147, Sect. 2, CE does not embrace this subject matter within its scope[114]. Among those scholars, Díez Picazo underlines that, even accepting an extensive interpretation of art. 147, Sect. 2, there is still an obstacle to "regional" bills of rights: the principle of equality. By allowing *Comunidades Autónomas* to include autonomous bills of rights within their *estatutos*, Spain allows to unreasonably differentiate the enjoinment of rights between Spanish citizens.

On the other hand, there are authors who contend that the power to regulate the rights of *Comunidades Autónomas* citizens is inherent in the principle of regional autonomy (or self-government)[115]. The TC has finally settled the matter, declaring that Statute of Autonomy is not a qualified source of law as far as the recognition of rights is concerned[116]. As a consequence, Statutes of Autonomy can effectively include rights only if their provisions merely duplicate constitutional guarantees.

The French *Conseil Constitutionnel* had already confronted the same type of problems since 1991, when it reviewed the Statute of Autonomy of Corsica. Decision 290/1991 and later decision 454/2001 stated that the Corsican people do not exist as a separate entity from the French people, whose indivisibility is intimately connected to the refusal of any discrimination between citizens. Linguistic rights of the Corsican population can be recognized, including the teaching of the Corsican language in the public schools, but they cannot imply limitations or discriminations concerning the use of the French language. Thus, complementary courses of native language can be activated putting its financial burden on the local administration of the Corsica Region[117].

The Italian Constitutional Court too confronted with the issue of infra-State rights. Decision 106/2002 reviewed the choice of Liguria Region to define Parliament its elective council, concluding that the national Parliament and regional assemblies are representative bodies both charged with legislative powers but having a different position within the constitutional architecture

Even some federal States, like Canada, have experienced the introduction of territorial bills of rights only recently. The three *Lois sur le droits de la personne* have been adopted in Yukon in 1987, in the North Western Territory in 2002, in Nunavut in 2003[118], therefore long after the 1982 federal codification.

---

[114] See L.M. Díez Picazo, *¿Pueden los estatutos de Autonomía declarar derechos, deberes y principios?*, in *Revista española de derecho constitucional*, 2006, 63; J.V. Martín Oviedo, *Artículo 147, Estatutos de Autonomía, su contenido y reforma*, in O. Alzaga Villaamil (Eds.), *Comentarios a la Constitución española de 1978*, Madrid, Edersa, 1978, 127.

[115] See F. Caamaño, *Sí, pueden. (Declaraciones de derecho y Estatutos de Autonomía)*, in *Revista española de derecho constitucional*, 2007, 33; M. Carrillo, *Los derechos, un contenido constitucional de los Estatutos de Autonomía*, in *Revista española de derecho constitucional*, 2007, 49.

[116] See STC, dec. 31/2010.

[117] See M. Mazza, *Decentramento e riforma delle autonomie territoriali in Francia*, Torino, Giappichelli, 2004.

[118] See National Report, par. 2.1.2.

11.6   Human Rights in the International Perspective

The flourishing of the human rights culture after World War II is not necessarily attributable to the clash of civilizations[119] and to the possible prevalence of Western values in the latter part of the twentieth century: there are in fact authoritative theories asserting oriental origins of such an ideology[120].

With the advent of globalization[121], the progressive incorporation of human rights in international conventions of global or continental scope has increased its pace towards a completion of the entire process. A growing number of human rights have been positivized[122]; their recognition has become wider; their scope has been first enlarged and then some of them have been re-particularized, as was previously the case with civil liberties in the domestic sphere; their protection has been made more efficient, even if several problems remain to be solved; the role of international organizations in their protection has been strengthened through new means, such as peace keeping or peace restoring missions[123], the creation of international tribunals for the judgment of crimes against humanity and more generally the transformation of international law from a set of rules governing relations between States to a system of norms applicable to and actionable by individuals[124]. This evolution is sometimes described as the constitutionalization of international law[125] and is co-responsible (together with the opening of national constitutional law systems to sources or systems of sources of international or supra-national law) of the creation of a two-tier system of constitutional law, which in some regions, where continental conventions for the protection of rights exist, tends to become a multi-level system.

Obviously the concrete efficacy of such complex sets of instruments, most incisively operating on the area of individual rights, depends on factors that fall outside the perimeter of normative prescriptions and belongs to the factual dimension[126]: the relevance of such circumstances depends on socio-economic contexts, most of all in

---

[119] To use the words of S. Huntington, *The Clash of Civilizations and the Remaking of World Order*, New York, Simon & Schuster, 1996.

[120] See e.g. D. Little, J.Kelsay, A.A.Sachedina (Eds.), *Human Rights and the Conflict of Cultures: Western and Islamic Perspectives on Religious Liberty*, Columbia, University of South Carolina Press, 1988; A. Sen, *Freedom as Development*, Oxford, Oxford University Press, 1999; S. Bessis, *L'Occident et les autres. Histoire d'une suprématie*, Paris, La Découverte, 2002. A shorthand of Chinese, Muslim and Hindu theories was already in Unesco, *Human Rights. Comments and Interpretations. A Symposium*, London, A. Wingate, 1949.

[121] See e.g. D. Held, A. McGrew, *Globalization/Anti-Globalization*, Cambridge, Polity Press, 2002.

[122] According to the terminology of G. Peces-Barba Martínez, *Teoría de los derechos fundamentales*, *supra* note 9 and N. Bobbio, *L'età dei diritti*, Torino, Einaudi, 1997.

[123] S.C. Breau, *Humanitarian Intervention: the United Nations and Collective Responsibility*, London, Cameron May, 2005.

[124] See M. Sterio, *The Evolution of International Law*, in 31 *B.C. Int'l & Comp. L. Rev.*, 213 (2008).

[125] See J. Habermas, *The Constitutionalization of International Law and the Legitimation Problems of a constitution for World Society*, in 15 *Constellations,* 444 (2008); J. Klabbers, A. Peters, G. Ulfstein, *The Constitutionalization of International Law*, Oxford, Oxford University Press, 2009.

[126] See J. Habermas, *Faktizität und Geltung*, Frankfurt a. Main, Suhrkamp, 1992.

countries that have only recently done away with authoritarian regimes. Therefore, when the level of protection guaranteed to rights is measured according to conventional parameters, which are sensitive to factual conditions, this does not necessarily mean that the quality of the formal structure of legal sources corresponds to the rating of a country in terms of efficiency of the protection afforded. However, public law scholars need to limit themselves to the strictly legal evaluation of normative systems: as a consequence, both papers concerning the national systems and this general report generally leave aside considerations based on the sheer output of results and their classification.

11.6.1 Some Techniques for the Measurement of the Protection of Human Rights at the Domestic Level

Some questions should be initially posed in order to select the areas of interest that help to measure the recognition and protection of human rights at domestic level.

First, the rate of integration between domestic constitutional law and international law: does a constitution simply impose on national judges and the constitutional court an obligation to conform to the case law of international courts? Or does it contain precepts concerning the position of international law in the internal system of legal sources, and, in the affirmative, is this position comparable to that of ordinary statutes or of constitutional law? Furthermore, are international customary law and bi- or multilateral conventions put on an equal footing or does the constitution or the case law of the supreme or constitutional court distinguish between the two and/or isolate a *jus cogens* as the only binding part of international law? In such a case, do human rights conventions enjoy a special status in comparison with other international treaties?

Second, does the level of integration between constitutional and international law, measured on the basis of the above parameters, have concrete consequences inside the domestic legal sources system? In the case of a difference in content, or even discordance or clash between norms concerning rights and belonging to different systems, how is the conflict resolved? Is a preference for the international standard prescribed and how is the possible prevalence established? Is the domestic source declared void or simply deprived of effects? Finally, is the prevalence of international law provided by any judge (i.e. on the basis of a diffused/decentralized system) or by a constitutional or supreme court (i.e. on the basis of a concentrated/centralized model)?

Third, in the areas where two systems of international or supranational agreements coexist, and each contains principles and rules concerning the protection of individual rights, are they both afforded the same treatment in domestic constitutional law or are they given different status, with varying effects? For example, this problem is of particular importance in Europe, where the ECHR and EU (formerly EC) law overlap, two regional courts operate at the same time covering much the same space, though elaborating different sets of values. The treatment that each Member State affords to the Convention and to EU law is a conditioning factor of the protection of rights, and the two-party dialogue between domestic judges and an upper level court becomes a three-party network: the Strasbourg court works within an axiological framework where the protection of rights is the only aim to be achieved, while the Luxembourg court, which only "discovered" rights at the beginning of the '70s[127] as a response to the resistance of some constitutional courts to the supremacy of EC law, carves values and principles out of the *acquis* of Strasbourg and the common constitutional traditions of the Member States, using a wide discretion instead of adopting a truly comparative method. Moreover, its axiological guide is represented not only by the values now incorporated in art. 6 of the Treaty but also by the economic principles underlying the free circulation of goods, services and workers. The situation is further complicated when the attribute of fundamentality is introduced to the list of rights recognized and protected by regional systems: in that case there may not only be a difference in the degree of the legal definition of a claim, but even a difference in fundamentality, with concrete downfalls in terms of protection.

Fourth, the domestic treatment of international law for the purpose of protecting human rights can be compared with the use, or at least some of the possible uses, of foreign law aiming at an analogous end. This practice, which in the last decade or so has come under the focus of public law scholars all over the world[128], is only exceptionally imposed or authorized in written constitutions or anyway formalized in legal sources, while in the average depends on more or less explicit choices of ordinary or constitutional judges. The recourse to foreign law, in terms of court precedents, scholarship, or even statutes, is ideologically neutral, because it does not imply any value choices, but is practically most suitable for the aim of a more efficient protection of claims neglected or understated in the domestic context. It also offers rich and interesting material for comparatists. It has been noted[129] that, when a Supreme Court recalls the practice of civilized nations[130] or the standards of decency in a civilized society[131] or the notion of justice of English-speaking peoples[132], echoing the decent respect of the opinions of mankind mentioned in par. 1 of the American Declaration of independence, though the argument is twofold[133], it

---

[127] Starting with *Nold* (C-4/73) and *Stauder* (C-29/69).

[128] See in particular B. Markesinis, *Comparative Law in Courtroom and Classroom, The Story of the Last Thirty-five Years*, Oxford-Portland, Hart Publishing, 2003; M. Andenas, G. Canivet, D. Fairgrieve (Eds.), *Comparative Law before the Courts*, London, BIICL, 2004; B. Markesinis, J. Fedtke, *Judicial Recourse to Foreign Law, A New Source of Inspiration?*, London, Routledge-Cavendish, 2006; G.F. Ferrari, A. Gambaro (Eds.), *Corti nazionali e comparazione giuridica*, Napoli, ESI, 2006.

[129] G.F. Ferrari, *La comparazione giuridica nella giurisprudenza della Corte suprema degli Stati Uniti d'America*, in G.F. Ferrari, A. Gambaro, *Corti nazionali*, *supra* note 128, 307 ff.

[130] Like the U.S. Supreme Court in *Twining v. New Jersey*, 211 U.S. 78, 113 (1908).

[131] Like Justice Felix Frankfurter in *Adamson v. California*, 332 U.S. 46 (1947) or in *Stein v. New York*, 346 U.S. 156, 199 (1953).

[132] Like again Justice Frankfurter in *Rochin v. California*, 342 U.S. 165, 169 (1952).

[133] As suggested by V. Jackson, *Narratives of Federalism: Of Continuities and Comparative Constitutional Experience*, in 51 *Duke L. J.*, 223 (2001), 247 ff.

makes no real difference between the recourse to foreign law and to international law for the better protection of a given claim: this is what happens, for instance, in U.S. case law in order to distinguish claims afforded ordinary guarantees and preferred or fundamental freedoms, worth being included in the "honor roll" of incorporated rights and destined to be protected in case of violation by the federal judge even toward or against State authorities.

11.6.2   The Gradual Conversion of Domestic into Human Rights: Some Other Problems

These are just a sample of the numerous problems arising from the overlapping of systems of protection of rights or, in other words, from the gradual conversion of domestic rights into human rights. Several others stem out of the same matrix, but belong to a second level, even if they are no less important in the practice of new constitutionalism.

Within this category, one has to mention the question of the so-called standards of protection. Every claim that has been positivized as a right first at the national and later at the international level (or sometimes in the opposite order) has a given content and certain limits, either coessential to it or deriving from the balancing process with other rights or principles, depending on the acceptance of either one of the theories that German, Italian and Spanish constitutional scholarship calls the absolute and relative theories of the core of rights. Each supreme or constitutional court reaches (albeit slightly) different conclusions, often at the end of long chains of precedents: such variations may depend on historical conditions or on the normative density of the specific constitutional provision or on the different formulation of constitutional principles. It is hard to say which solution comparatively corresponds to a better standard, both because such a choice presupposes a value statement and because the preference for either solution depends on the combination with other rights. In any case the search for the better standard or even for the best standard[134] is one of the favorite arguments of constitutional and international law scholars since the dawn of multilevel governance. The openness of a domestic constitutional system to international (or foreign) law is coextensive with the practicability of converting a national into a human right, whenever the protection standard of the outer system is apparently better than the domestic one. All constitutional systems, even when founded on homogeneous cultural premises, are confronted with this problem in different ways. The degree of openness towards international law depends on the epoch to which a constitution belongs, because since World War II it has continuously increased with each constitutional cycle, like in '70s with the Portuguese, the Spanish and the Greek constitutions and at the beginning of the '90s with the wave of post-Soviet bloc constitutions. Furthermore, every constitutional system is naturally jealous of its prerogatives, including its principles and related safeguards, and tends

---

[134] See *infra*, par. 6.6.

to resist the penetration of rules from outside, lest it might jeopardize the democratic structure of the State itself. The reaction of the German *Verfassungsgerichthof* to the supremacy of European law[135] is the most representative example of this reaction, but the French *Conseil constitutionnel*'s confrontation with the European Court of justice is much the same[136].

A second very important area of rapid transformation of public law, the conclusion of which is not yet foreseeable, is the treatment of non-citizens. The universalization of human rights throws a shadow on the traditional prerogatives of citizenship, at a moment when unprecedented mass migrations seem to render national borders less important than ever. Yet considering thousands and sometimes millions of immigrants fully entitled to political and social rights under the shelter of the protection of human rights means first of all setting at risk the survival of welfare states built up over at least a century and secondly endangering the structure of democracy, since the treaty of Westphalia founded on citizenship[137]. Submerging domestic rights in human rights in the name of a still not completely defined global identity is something close to a fascinating reductionism very similar to utopia, at least until a worldwide democratic State seriously looms on the horizon. On the contrary, celebrating the ethnic or religious belonging to micro-units, either by exalting the naturality of a unique affiliation or rediscovering communitarian identities, is a different form of reductionism, that Amartya Sen defines as plural monoculturalism[138]. Democratic constitutionalism, already put to a severe test by the radical changes in economics, like financial deregulation, liberalization and privatization[139], is still looking for a new formula, while awaiting the realization of so called societal constitutionalism[140]. When citizenship becomes flexible[141] and fragmented, between disarticulation of State sovereignty[142], growing supranational systems evolving in the direction of federalism and international agreements for the protection of human rights, democratic constitutionalism suffers from tensions between the global and cosmopolitan potentiality of rights and the exigencies of State unities politically legitimated by their

---

[135] BVerfGE 37, 271 *Solange-I-Beschluss* (1974); BVerfGE 73, 339, *Solange-II-Beschluss* (1986); BVerfGE 89, 155 *Maastricht-Beschluss* (1993); BVerfGE Az 2 BvL 1/97, *Bananenmarkt-Entscheidung* (2000); BVerfGE 123, 267, *Lissabon-Urteil* (2009).

[136] Cons. Const., dec. 2004-496 DC; 2004-505 DC; 2006-540 DC.

[137] In the meaning made famous by T.H. Marshall, *Sociology at the Crossroad*, London, Heinemann, 1950.

[138] *Identity and Violence, The Illusion of Destiny*, New York, W. W. Norton & Company, 2006.

[139] A synthesis in R.B. Reich, *Supercapitalism. The Transformation of Business, Democracy, and Everyday Life*, New York, Alfred A. Knopf, 2007.

[140] G. Teubner, *Societal Constitutionalism, Alternative to State-Centered Constitutional Theory?*, in C. Joerges, I.J. Sand, G. Teubner (Eds.), *Transnational Governance and Constitutionalism*, Oxford-Portland, Hart Publishing, 2003.

[141] As suggested by A. Ong, *Flexible Citizenship: The Cultural Logic of Transnationality*, Durham, Duke University Press, 1999.

[142] See e.g. J.H. Jackson, *Sovereignty-Modern: A New Approach to an Outdated Concept*, in 92 *Am.J.Int'l L.*, 782–802; S. Tierney, *Reframing Sovereignty? Sub-State National Societies and Contemporary Challenges to the Nation-State*, in 54 *Int. & Comp. Legal Q.*, 161–83 (2008).

demos and bound to define its distinctive line. There is apparently no immediate solution to this kind of problem. The only possible approach is to conceive of the demos not as a closed entity self-imposing in a constituent procedure once and for all, as was the case in old-fashion constitutionalism, but self-regenerating and self-defining gradually through progressive reciprocal adjustments of demos and ethnos: democratic processes, which necessarily keep on being internal to the State community, both deliberate admission and naturalization policies and at the same time open themselves to international and supranational dialogue, being increasingly available to the penetration of superior systems of norms[143].

Singling out some areas of interest in the field of codification of human rights is unfortunately only the beginning of the task, which is much more demanding. Most of the comparative work still has to be done. The ways codification is carried out are numerous, and, as one has seen, imply different relationships between the national and international levels.

11.6.3   Rights of Citizens and of Human Being

In the domestic sphere, it is initially important to check whether the internal legal sources, and first of all the written constitution, recognize rights or at least some categories of rights to each person or human being or to the contrary confine them only in the ambit of citizenship. The first choice is definitely rare, and it is normally to be found in imposed constitutional charters, adopted in special circumstances, such as after the end of an international conflict or of a civil war. This is e.g. the case of Japan, where art. 11, and possibly arts.13 and 97 Const., apparently do not distinguish between man and citizen: the national report illustrates the prevailing scholarly position favoring the wide interpretation of the pertinent provisions and the case law suggesting the limitation to Japanese nationals only of claims by nature hard to be enjoyed by non-citizens, including most political rights, but not social rights. The same choice is made by the Bosnia-Herzegovina Constitution, which refers to *Human Rights and Fundamental Freedoms*, without distinctions. Coherently, art. II, Sect. 1 guarantees the "highest level of internationally recognized human rights", within domestic legal order. The catalogue of rights reflects this approach and contains a simple list of liberties, unsupplied with a specific constitutional discipline and thus virtually without prescriptive value. It indistinctly refers to "All persons within the territory of Bosnia and Herzegovina". Anyway, it is worth pointing out that the subjective rights enshrined in the Constitution cover only first generation rights, with the sole exception of right to education[144].

---

[143] This is a shorthand summary of the persuading theory of S. Benhabib, *The Claims of Culture: Equality and Diversity in the Global Era*, Princeton, Princeton University Press, 2002, and *The Rights of Other. Aliens, Residents and Citizens*, Cambridge, Cambridge University Press, 2004. The idea of democratic iteration is also in J. Derrida, *Signature, événement, contexte*, in *Marges de la philosophie*, Paris, Les Éditions de Minuit, 1972.

[144] See art. (II, Sect. 3 1).

In Argentina, after the end of the military dictatorship in 1983, courts began to consider human rights treaties prevailing on domestic legal sources and to qualify formerly domestic rights, including welfare rights, as fundamental human rights, thus paving the way to the constitutional revision of 1994.

Other charters, belonging to different historical contexts or drafted by constituent assemblies more worried about the preservation of national character, systematically reserve some rights to citizens, while extend others to all. This is for instance the case of the Italian constitution, where some essential civil rights, like personal freedom, domicile and correspondence belong to all, while rights to peacefully assemble and to associate, being presupposed by political activities, are reserved to citizens[145]: however, the constitutional language does not prevent the legislator from extending some rights not constitutionally guaranteed to other categories of subjects.

In the Irish context, several rights that elsewhere belong to persons or human beings or that are declared inviolable in order to be attributed to every person subject to the jurisdiction of the State where they physically are in the Irish context belong to citizens (art. 40): then property, life, person, good name (art. 40.3.2), dwelling (art. 40.4.5), expression (art. 40.4.6), peaceful assembly are claims all together defined personal rights. On the contrary, some rights elsewhere no longer qualified as human or simply reduced in their core and submitted to stricter limitations than before, like property, are declared human rights. This choice could depend on the epoch of adoption of the present constitution, which precedes the post-World War II constitutional phase and its renewed sensibility toward international law and the internationalization of rights, as well as on the need to emphasize the legal condition of citizens after the recent achievement of independence from the United Kingdom through the experience of the Irish Free State.

11.7   The Treatment of Non-citizens

The incomplete constitutional transformation of domestic into human rights brings with it the problem of the treatment of aliens and stateless persons. The responses to it vary widely. The United States solution consists in leaving full discretion with Congress, with special reference to conditions of naturalization (art. I, § 8, cl. 4), to immigration policy, implicitly grounded on sovereignty[146], and to conditions of expulsion, though previous application of the due process and equal protection tests to different concrete conditions[147]. The German case law is based on the distinction between human rights globally recognized and rights reserved to German citizens, among which those guaranteed by art. 116 GG; there is, however, a trend toward

---

[145] Besides the National Report, see A. Pace, *La garanzia dei diritti fondamentali nell'ordinamento costituzionale italiano: il ruolo del legislatore e dei giudici "comuni"*, in *RTDPC*, 1989, 685 ff.; Id., *Dai diritti del cittadino ai diritti fondamentali dell'uomo*, in www.rivistaic.it, 2010.

[146] *Chinese Exclusion Case*, 130 U.S. 581 (1889).

[147] See e.g. *Graham v. Richardson*, 403 U.S. 365 (1971), *Toll. V. Moreno*, 458 U.S. 1 (1982), *Bernal v. Fainter*, 467 U.S. 216 (1984).

balancing dignity, equality, freedom to develop one's personality and intangible core of the rights, in order to make more rights available to non-citizens[148]. The Spanish constitutional Tribunal applies the principle of equality of art. 14 only to Spaniards[149] and extends to foreigners the public liberties discretionally recognized by the Cortes or by international treaties according to art. 13.1[150]; yet personal dignity provided for in art. 10.1 can be used in order to enlarge the statute of foreigners with rights concerning the person[151]. Art. 15 of the Portuguese constitution excludes resident aliens from political rights, with the possible exceptions of residing Portuguese speakers from other countries, nationals of Union States, other foreigners under conditions of reciprocity.

The condition of aliens and stateless persons is even more important in the field of social services where, as recalled earlier, the conservation of the welfare State in its traditional shape is at stake. There are significant differences in the treatment of immigrants even in regional areas supposedly governed by uniform principles, like Europe. Portugal, for instance, implements art. 15 Const. by recognizing vocational education, social insurance and assistance, health services and access to housing facilities to all regular immigrants; France guarantees even irregular immigrants urgent health services (*Aide médicale d'État*, AME), education of minors, coverage of work accidents; Great Britain requires fees for the access to national health services by immigrants, excluding urgent assistance and sexually transmissible diseases but a communication to the Immigration and Naturalization Department (IND) in case of fruition of social benefits has been introduced. In Germany the *Asylbewerberleistungsgesetz* contemplates health assistance for illness, pregnancy and childbirth, though not free of costs, with compulsory communication of irregular situations to the *Ausländerbehörde*. Rumania and Greece put regular immigrants on equal footing as citizens, while in Bulgaria art. 51 Const. imposes a reservation of social services to citizens only. Luxembourg excludes foreigners from social rights while Holland denies them to irregular immigrants. Outside Europe, Argentina is very generous toward immigrants in terms of social services, traditionally favoring immigration.

Israel until 2006 recognized foreign workers only limited rights. The two Supreme Court decisions, described in the national report, dated 2006 and 2007 respectively, have significantly improved the condition of foreigner workers, though the extension of the protection only concerns the rights listed in the Basic Law: Human Dignity and Liberty, of 1992. The same apparently applies to the other Basic Law: Freedom of Occupation, also of 1992.

---

[148] Besides the National Report, see L. Michael, M. Morlok, *Grundrechte*, Berlin, Duncker & Humblot, 2009, 226.

[149] Sent. 23-11-1984, n. 107.

[150] Sent. 30-9-1985, n. 99 and 7-11-2007, n. 48.

[151] Sent. 11-9-1995, m. 130. A complete review of several legal systems in G.F. Ferrari, *Relazione conclusiva*, in *Lo statuto costituzionale del non cittadino*, Atti del XXIV Convegno annuale, Cagliari, 16–17 ottobre 2009, Associazione italiana dei costituzionalisti, Padova, CEDAM, 2010, 516 ff.

In the Taiwan context some very special circumstances apply both to the naturalization of persons originally from China and to the eventual enjoyment of political rights[152].

11.7.1 International Law in the Constitutional Law Sources

A typically critical point of junction between constitutional law and international law is the ranking of international legal sources in the Constitutions, with possible distinctions between customary law and treaties, with the possible addition of a core of *jus cogens*, and a possible special status afforded to conventions and agreements concerning human rights. The degree of openness of a domestic system of legal sources runs in parallel to its availability to fully incorporate human rights trickling down from an upper system, whether truly international or supranational.

At one extreme of the spectrum of formulas is the Dutch model, traditionally most open to any kind of international law: arts. 93 and 94 Const. declare treaties and resolutions by international institutions binding in the domestic context, under the only condition of having been published, and prevailing over statutory regulations. Such provisions, therefore, prescribe the direct efficacy of conventional international law in the Dutch legal system, putting it on top of the legal system of sources, but they ignore customary law, even *jus cogens*, and decisions of international tribunals, which are devoid of such force, though some statutory provisions refer to international law in general and can be interpreted as to indirectly authorize the precedence over domestic law of international self-executing provisions other than those mentioned in arts. 93 and 94[153]. The Dutch system is described as moderately monist by domestic scholars, but in fact it is the first in Europe in terms of openness toward external sources, also because courts deem obvious that when a basic right is enshrined both in the Constitution and in treaty law, the prevailing provision is the most conducive to the better protection of the right.

At the other extreme is the U.S. model, where Congress very seldom ratifies human rights instruments and when they do whenever Presidents impose reservations, understandings and declarations (the so called RUDs) in order to make treaties hardly enforceable in US courts or in international courts, like the Inter-American Court of Human Rights of San José de Costarica. As far as the federal case law is concerned, the Supreme Court has been eager to consider international treaties prevailing over State law, due to obvious reasons of supremacy[154], but much less disposed to consider human rights treaties binding on federal authorities, in the absence of express executing legislation by Congress[155]. Such an approach, possibly strengthened after 9/11

---

[152] National Report, par. 2.

[153] Besides the National Report, see P.P.T. Bovend'Eert, C.A.J.M. Kortmann, *Dutch Constitutional Law*, The Hague, Kluwer Law International, 2000.

[154] Since the *Paquete Habana case*, 175 U.S. 677 (1900).

[155] *Sosa v. Alvarez-Machain*, 542 U.S. 692 (2004) and *Medellin v. Texas*, 552 U.S. 491 (2008).

and the Patriot Act, is often defined exceptionalist[156]: the triumph of the American political model in 1989, which was soon after presented as the end of history[157], has paved the way to a bi- directional circulation of values and patterns, while up until recently legal scholars and public opinion were accustomed to a one-way export of ideas and doctrines typical of the American identity. As a consequence, much debate has been aroused, in the U.S. within public law scholarship and inside the Supreme Court with regard to the forms and limits of the recourse to foreign law, most of all in the field of human rights; around the world, about the difficulty of reaching a new definition of sovereignty in the age of globalization through international law, due to the American position. Canadian constitutional law somehow resembles the U.S. formula, at least from a practical viewpoint, though the theory is quite different. No guiding principles are present at the constitutional level on the ranking of international law, either customary or conventional: therefore it is usually treated as a material source, i.e. a mix of unwritten principles, helping the judge and the interpreter to fill gaps in domestic law or to integrate its construction. It is interesting to note that, being the authoritativeness of international sources left with the federal Supreme Court, a non-ratified treaty is compared to foreign law[158].

In Europe there are the most different solutions. In Austria, treaty law modifying or integrating constitutions is virtually equalized to constitutional provisions, thus requiring the amending procedure[159]. In Greece, both customary and conventional law prevail over statutes, but not over constitutional provisions, while the ECHR, after some controversy, has been equated to other international sources, exactly as EU law after the amendment of 2001 to art. 28: furthermore, the Supreme Court has construed this last clause as imposing an interpretation of the Constitution itself as consistent as possible with EU law[160].

Many other national systems, in an in-between position, treat customary law and conventions or treaties differently. As far as Britain is concerned, there is a clear dichotomy between international customary law and treaties from the viewpoint of their position in the hierarchy of legal sources. Treaties traditionally remain within the royal prerogative, but since the Crown cannot change the law of the land, treaties are no direct source in the United Kingdom, unless legislation is expressly passed in order to give effect to their terms[161]. Customary law, on the contrary, is assimilated to the common law, as a matter of usage and judicial decisions: up until the beginning of the

---

[156] S.M. Lipset, *American Exceptionalism: A Double-Edged Sword*, New York, N.Y., 1996; M. Ignatieff, *Introduction: American Exceptionalism and Human Rights*, in Id. (Ed.), *American Exceptionalism and Human Rights*, Princeton, Princeton University Press, 2003.

[157] In the words of Francis Fukuyama, *The End of History and the Last Man*, New York, Free Press, 1992.

[158] See the National Report and in details G. Van Ert, *Using International Law in Canadian Courts*, Toronto, Irwin Law, 2nd ed., 2008.

[159] See art. 50 Const.

[160] See National Report, par. 4.

[161] See e.g. E. Ellis, *Sources of Law and the Hierarchy of Norms*, in A. Burrows, D. Feldman (Eds.), *English Public Law*, *supra* note 42, 63 ff.

nineteenth century it was considered automatically incorporated into English law[162]; later on, courts became more reluctant to admit such consequence and preferred to require formal transformation[163] until Lord Denning MR in 1977 persuaded a majority of the Court of appeal to follow him on the conclusion that, since the rules of international law change over time, they need to be considered part of English law, to prevent the introduction in the legal system of outdated rules[164].

The same distinction exists also under the Portuguese Constitution, whose art. 8 is interpreted as involving a full reception of general international law directly by the constitution, while both scholarship and constitutional case law qualify conventional law as infra-constitutional but supra-legal, and violations of conventional law by statutes are within the competence of the *Tribunal constitucional*. Similarly, under art. 10.2 of the Spanish Constitution, international law is fully incorporated into the legal system, though it does not have constitutional status, being qualified as guidance in the interpretation of the law as well as, according to some scholars, even as possible mean of integration of the constitutional parameter[165].

Indeed, both the Portuguese[166] and the Spanish[167] Constitutions include a provision imposing or requesting ordinary and/or constitutional judges to conform to the indications of international law or to the judicial *acquis* of international courts in interpreting domestic provisions. In these cases, a sort of presumption is operating in the judicial review of statutes, requiring that between two or more possible meanings preference be given to the one concordant with international law principles or provisions. The existence of such a clause, however, is not conclusive, since it can be coupled with other dispositions about the ranking of international law in the system of domestic legal sources, thus determining very different results.

A similar clause is now included in the British Human Rights Act 1998 (s. 3(1)), which is read in the sense that all legal rules must be construed on a rights-based interpretation. The approach is therefore similar to those imposed with reference to EU law. The main difference, however, is that whenever it proves impossible to read domestic law to make it comply with Convention rights, courts can strike down only secondary norms, while statutes are made object of a "declaration of incompatibility", which gives Parliament the opportunity to have the last word on the problem.

The Rumanian Constitution (art. 20) imposes the conformity of the interpretation of domestic law with the Universal Declaration and other human rights treaties, with prevalence of conventional rules in case of conflict with domestic provisions.

The Israeli position is peculiar, since the "presumption of concordant meaning" doctrine is not grounded on the Basic Laws and, absent a written constitution, is

---

[162] *De Wutz v Hendricks* (1824) 2 Bing 314.

[163] *R v. Secretary of State for the Home Department, ex p Thakrar* [1974QB 684.]

[164] *Trendtex Trading v Bank of Nigeria* [1977] 1 QB 529.

[165] A. Saiz Arnaiz, *La apertura al derecho internacional y europeo de los derechos humanos. El artículo 10.2 de la Constitución*, Madrid, Consejo General del Poder Judicial, 1999.

[166] Art. 16, assuming as parameter only the *Universal Declaration*.

[167] Art. 10.

simply adopted by courts, under the only condition that the original intention of the legislator is not entirely distorted[168].

Sometimes the supra-legal status of treaties and conventions expressly derives from Constitution, like in France[169]: judicial interpretation plays the most significant role, guaranteeing the supremacy of Constitution in case of possible conflict between international law and national law implementing constitutional provisions[170]. The French example has possibly been followed by several East-European Constitutions, like those of Slovakia (art. 11), Czechia (art. 10), Moldova (art. 4), Russia (art. 15.4), Rumania (art. 20), Bosnia (art. A 6 and Annex 6), Slovenia (art. 8), expressly declaring conventional international law prevailing over domestic law. The Constitution of Albania at art. 122 leaves with the Constitutional Court the decision of the compatibility of international agreements with the Constitution, thus recognizing treaties a sub-constitutional status, but ECHR is mentioned separately in order to prevent limitations to rights and freedoms protected by the Constitution from overriding the restrictions provided by the ECHR[171], conferring a special constitutional status to the Convention. In approximately the same way the Azerbaijan Constitution of 1995 at art. 151 provides for the prevalence of international agreements on domestic statutes in case of conflict, while a constitutional law regulates restrictions on freedoms on freedoms, forbidding not only disproportionate measures, but also limitations inconsistent with the ECHR[172]. In Croatia art. 141 of the Constitution makes international agreements part of the national legal order in a position lower the Constitution itself, while the Constitutional Court seems to use the ECHR as a source of constitutional ranking in abstract constitutional review[173]. In Estonia[174] Sect. 123 of the Constitution states the prevalence of ratified international treaties on domestic sources, but no special status is reserved to the ECHR. The same conclusions is followed by art. 6, par. 2 of the Constitution of Georgia[175]. Latvia[176], Lithuania[177], Moldova[178], Poland, though isolating the domestic system from outer standards[179], and Ukraine[180] follow the same approach.

---

[168] HCJ 11437/05 *Kav Laoved v. Interior Ministry* (2011).

[169] See art. 55 Const.

[170] See S. Carmeli, *La difficile* cohabitation *tra diritto interno e diritto internazionale: la Corte di cassazione si allea al Consiglio di Stato per difendere la sovranità nazionale*, in *DPCE*, 2000, 1978.

[171] See E. Alimehmeti, E. Met-Hasani Çani, *Albania*, in F. Emmert, L.Hammer, *The European Convention on Human Rights in Central and Eastern Europe*, The Hague, Eleven International Publishing, 2012, 39 ff.

[172] J. Gavirov, *Azerbaijan*, in F. Emmert, L.Hammer, *The ECHR in Central and Eastern Europe*, *supra* note 171, 75 ff.

[173] S. Rodin, *Croatia,* in *ibidem*, 138 ff.

[174] C. Ginter, R. Värk, *Estonia*, in *ibidem*, 183 ff.

[175] E. Lomtatidze, B. Pataraia, *Georgia*, in *ibidem*, 197 ff.

[176] A. Repšs, L. Rugāte, I. Stankevičs, *Latvia*, in *ibidem*, 279 ff.

[177] R. Beržanskiené, *Lithuania*, in *ibidem*, 293 ff.

[178] M. Chicu, V. Gribincea, N. Hriptievschi, *Moldova*, in *ibidem*, 311 ff.

[179] See P. Korzec, *Poland*, in *ibidem*, 356 ff.

[180] A. Khvorostyankina, A. Meleshevich, *Ukraine*, in *ibidem*, 560 ff.

Those countries in which a dualistic approach prevails follow the opposite solution. In Germany, conventions and treaties should be incorporated by statute enabling international provisions to have the same force as ordinary law. The Italian case, though somehow close to the German formula as far as treaty law is concerned, is characterized by the recognition of a special status to ECHR, which is conceived as *interposed* parameter (*parametro interposto*) in case of constitutional adjudication of ordinary law. In other words, those laws conflicting with ECHR provisions as construed by the Strasbourg Court[181] are considered as indirectly violating the Constitution itself, which assigns special force to international sources binding Italy.

Outside Europe, the Israeli system of sources distinguishes international customary law and treaties, as effect of case law, absent a written constitution: the first one is automatically part of domestic law, but provided that it does not conflict which existing internal legislation, while treaties need to be expressly adopted.

The Japanese report explains how, due to the absence of clear provisions in the Constitution as well as in Asian regional conventions, scholarship and government policies have been able to locate international law at a level higher than statutes and to single out established law of nations, treaties defining the territory and conditions of surrender as *jus cogens*. The Taiwan report[182] illustrates how in that system treaties, if ratified, are on equal foot with statutes, but they prevail even on successive domestic statutes as *leges speciales*. Recent efforts to incorporate human rights treaties, after the rejection of their ratification by the UN, through domestic legislation, and subsequently to transform covenant principles into *cogens* customary law have not yet completely reached the desired result.

In the Constitution of Argentina as revised in 1994, not only are political rights recognized in art. 37 and some third generation rights, like the rights to a healthy environment and to the protection of the cultural heritage in art. 41 and consumers' rights in art. 42, also receive recognition, but above all a long list of international human rights conventions and treaties are constitutionalized and included in the so called "*bloque de constitucionalidad*". The result is that all of them, as a consequence of the insufficient protection of domestic rights through the ordinary instruments of traditional constitutionalism in the age of military *golpes*, now enjoy constitutional ranking on an equal footing with the constitution, and can loose such status only with a two-thirds vote of each House of Parliament. Since customary law is not mentioned, it has been the Supreme Court case law to recognize analogous condition to it, at least in the part that can be qualified as *jus cogens*, thanks to decisions of the Inter-American Commission and of the Inter-American Court on Human Rights[183].

---

[181] See CC dec. 348 and 349/2007. On these issues see A. Ruggeri, *La CEDU nelle sentenze 348 e 349 della Corte costituzionale*, in *DPCE*, 2008, 171 ss.

[182] Par. 4 and 5.

[183] See the National Report.

11.7.2   Standards in the Protection of Rights

The problem of the search for the most favorable standard in the protection of rights is not ordinarily addressed by Constitutions in direct terms, apart from the clauses concerning the treatment of international law in the hierarchy of domestic legal sources and their interpretation. Only imposed Constitutions, like the one of Bosnia (art. A 2), ensure the best international standard in the interpretation of norms concerning rights. Other recent Constitutions, defining the admissible limitations on rights, include those afforded by the ECHRs and its judicial interpretation: such are the cases of Albania (art. 17) and Moldova (art. 54.2).

European public law scholars, on the contrary, have been stimulated by a lively debate concerning the standards of protection by the intersection of the so-called multi-tier constitutionalism. Some authors have emphasized the different techniques applied by the Luxembourg and Strasbourg courts and the national constitutional and supreme courts[184]: it is obvious that once the *acquis* of Strasbourg is filtered and selectively transposed into the Luxembourg case law together with the constitutional traditions of Member States, the construction of individual claims and the definition of their content and limits are brought about in very different manners, also due to the diversity in axiological frameworks and balancing techniques. Therefore, signaling collisions and tensions[185] gives evidence to the pluralistic context, but does not solve any problems[186]. At the other extreme, authors like Besselink[187] strongly recommend that the European Court of Justice, through an accurate analysis of every concrete case, stick to the criterium of the comparison of the theoretically available doctrines and of the choice of the most protective one (universalized maximum standard). The main objection to this theory is that the difference between doctrines is not merely quantitative and their effect is not always measurable in quantitative terms. The reason why the value-balancing process gives different results in the various contexts is in most cases attributable to the axiological framework whence it stems out. A general political system with national traditions, a supranational system with originally limited competences in transition towards the political community dimension in the federal perspective, an international mono-functional treaty-based system are naturally different. Their courts necessarily operate on different value premises.

The respective fundamental charters do contain provisions potentially able to soften the impact of collisions and crashes between different systems of protection.

---

[184] Like J.H.H. Weiler, *Eurocracy and Distrust*, in 61 *Wash. L. Rev.* (1986), 1103, re-elaborated in *Fundamental rights and fundamental boundaries: on standards and values in the protection of human rights*, in N.A. Neuwahl, A. Rosas, *The European Union and Human Rights*, The Hague, Martinus Nijhoff, 1995, 51 ff.

[185] Like R. Lawson, *Confusion and conflict? Diverging interpretation of the European Convention on Human Rights Law among Europe's regional courts*, in M. De Blois, R. Lawson (Eds.), *The Dynamics of the Protection of Human Rights in Europe*, The Hague, Martinus Nijhoff, 1994, 253 ff.

[186] L.F.M. Besselink, *Entrapped by the maximum standard: on fundamental rights, pluralism and subsidiarity in the European Union*, in 35 C. *Mkt.L.Rev.*, 629 (1998).

[187] In L.F.M. Besselink, *Entrapped by the maximum standard*, *supra* note 186.

In the ECHR art. 53 precludes interpretations capable of jeopardizing or damaging rights guaranteed by constitutional or other domestic provisions: therefore the Convention qualifies itself as a subsidiary instrument and at the same time defines its protection as the minimum standard. On the side of EU law, art. 307 (formerly art. 234) of the Treaty declares untouched the rights, and for the States the obligations, deriving from conventions subscribed before 1958: it is well known that all Western European States ratified the ECHR before that date, with the exception of France. The ECHR, however, though imposing a minimum standard, in art. 55 (formerly 62) tries to introduce a safeguard to it by preventing Member States from transferring through further treaties the power to decide controversies concerning their own object: thus, decisions of other judges, different from the national one, applying lower standards in overlapping spaces are precluded. Such a provision means that the ECHR protects itself through a rigidity, which cannot be by-passed downwards. In other words, in multi-tier constitutionalism contexts, each legal system coexisting with others in the same territory deploys some arrangements in order to protect itself and at the same time to prevent frequent conflicts with others. Nevertheless conflicts are possible and even frequent. They are most likely to take place in the field of rights but very hard to systematize. Their forms and types depend on the concrete and evolving balancing of values and rules and on the consequent standard of protection applied to a specific right. Furthermore, in Europe, in every domestic constitutional scenario the ranking of EU law on one hand and of international law on the other take into account sources with different strength.

Despite a continuous and sometimes exhausting debate, a really complete classification of the possible situations has never been worked out. Would it be tried, it should be founded on the rate of monism/dualism of every national context, keeping into account that the level of openness on the communitarian and conventional sides is often different.

For instance, the U.K., though a late comer to the Union, is the most open towards EU law, at least after the *Factortame* decision, while its incorporation of the ECHR in 1998 did not imply the automatic prevalence of conventional provisions on domestic norms, but only the declaration of incompatibility by the national judge, besides possible Government interventions: therefore, the EU standard apparently prevails over the conventional standard. The Swedish legal system, having adjusted itself to the EU through a timely constitutional revision, can now rely on art. 5 of Chap. 10, which authorizes transfers of sovereignty to the Union only in presence of guarantees of protection of rights equivalent to those included in the *Regeringsformen* itself or in the ECHR: therefore, apparently ordinary judges should be dispensed from the application of ultra vires EU law and be kept of the application of the better standard. The situation of Greece should be more or less the same, because art. 28.3 only admits restrictions on sovereignty that are imposed by overwhelming national interests, do not jeopardize human rights and the foundations of the democratic regime and are fulfilled respecting the equality principle, while art. 28.1 recognizes ratified international treaties ranking higher than statutes.

The Italian and German Constitutional Courts have been interpreting Charters that, though most open with respect to their generation, did not contain any "Europe clauses". Consequently they defended the national right protection standard, first by alleging the absolute absence of a bill of rights in the communitarian system, and then questioning the lack of fundamental democratic attributes in the institutions to which growing parts of the national sovereignty were being delegated and the possible disregard of the fundamental principles of the domestic constitutional order, at least up to the ad hoc German constitutional revision. At the same time, they have used the ECHR at most as an interpretive help in the constitutional interpretation of their own catalogue.

Finally, art. 52.3 of the Nice Charter prescribes for rights recognized by the EU in correspondence with the ECHR the same content and width prescribed by the Convention. Hence, the national interpreter is bound, according to the strength of the EU source in his system, to apply the Strasbourg level of protection as common minimum standard.

In regional contexts of multi-tier constitutionalism conflicts and collisions cannot be avoided, nor can the search for a better standard. In other words, the introduction of human rights at a supranational level, far from imposing dull uniformity into traditionally variegated national systems, apparently improves their rate of variety.

11.8   Concluding Remarks

If a *fil rouge* can be traced in such a wide and congested space, it is the search for points of intersection between domestic constitutional law and public international law.

From the point of view of constitutional law scholarship, the first junction point is likely to be the qualification of a right as fundamental. It ordinarily comes from the domestic system of legal sources as a positive definition, but it is more and more evident that it often derives either from some natural law justification or from its relation to some international or supra-national sources, which in the last decades have also started to use this category to qualify rights or groups of rights. Therefore the dichotomy fundamental versus non-fundamental rights has lately become more important and prevails on several other classifications, often used above all by French scholarship: such classification is much more useful in the codification perspective just because it is situated in a central position between domestic constitutional law and international law.

A second important point of intersection is the recognition of rights to groups, which stems almost always from international conventional sources, though among difficulties and hurdles of various nature.

A third point of intersection, even if declining, is the codification of rights at the infra-State level. Above all in the European Union regional infra-State units are very relevant in terms of measures of political economy. Therefore the European institutions have at least involuntarily contributed to a feeling of regional self-consciousness, sometimes even tending to evolve into the perception of a stronger national identity.

A fourth point of intersection is represented by the treatment of international law and its different sources in the domestic legal systems: this is no single problem, but a cluster of problematic phenomena, such as the ranking of international customary and conventional law in internal constitutional law, including the possible special status of human rights conventions; the tension between national constitutional or supreme courts and international or supranational courts, with the consequent search for the better or best standard of protection of rights; the condition of non-citizens in the epoch of unprecedented mass migrations. The rate of openness or friendliness to international law is simply a synthetic formula to concentrate the whole of the dynamic evolution lines of contemporary public law.

It is quite clear that in an era of continuous and rapid transformation of most of the consolidated concepts of public law a full codification of human rights implies a high rate of monism in terms of openness towards international law. Yet, a complete conversion of domestic liberties, though fundamental, into human rights, implies the imposition of uniform rules, which brings about several inconveniences: not only the reduction of the natural variety of claims and standards of protection, but also the decline in the role of national democratic States without the emergence of alternative models of political institutions. For at least some decades ahead, such a final output is unthinkable: the most reasonable solution is careful balancing between traditional instruments of codification of rights and the uniform globalization of individual claims.

References

Books and Chapters

Abraham, H.J. & B.A. Perry (1978) *Freedom and the Court. Civil Rights and Liberties in the United States*. New York, Oxford University Press.
Agamben, G. (1995) *Homo Sacer*. Torino, Einaudi.
Allan, T.R.S. (1993) *Law, Liberty and Justice*. Oxford, Clarendon Press.
Allen, S. & A. Xanthaki (eds.). (2011) Reflections on the UN Declaration on the Rights of Indigenous Peoples. Oxford, Hart Publishing.
Andenas, M., G. Canivet & D. Fairgrieve (eds.). (2004) *Comparative Law before the Courts*. London, BIICL.
Arendt, H. (1951) *The origins of totalitarianism*. New York, Harcourt.
Arnaiz, A. Saiz (1999) La apertura al derecho internacional y europeo de los derechos humanos. El artículo 10.2 de la Constitución. Madrid, Consejo General del Poder Judicial.
Barile, P. (1984) *Diritti dell'uomo e libertà fondamentali*. Bologna, il Mulino, 31 ff.
Beddard, R. (1993) *Human Rights and Europe*. Cambridge, Grotius Publications.
Benhabib, S. (2002) *The Claims of Culture: Equality and Diversity in the Global Era*. Princeton, Princeton University Press.
Benhabib, S. (2004) *The Rights of Other. Aliens, Residents and Citizens*. Cambridge, Cambridge University Press.
Bessis, S. (2002) *L'Occident et les autres. Histoire d'une suprématie*. Paris, La Découverte.
Blackstone, W. (1765–1769) *Commentaries on the Laws of England*. Oxford, Clarendon Press, I, 121.

Bobbio, N. (1997) *L'età dei diritti*, (1997) Torino, Einaudi.
Bolz, M. (1991) Das Verhaltnis von Schutzobjekt und Schranken der Grundrechte Zürich, Schulthess.
Bonbled, N. & M. Verdussen (2011) *Le droits constitutionnels en Belgique. Vol. I.* Bruxelles, Bruylant.
Bovend'Eert, P.P.T. & C.A.J.M. Kortmann (2000) *Dutch Constitutional Law*. The Hague, Kluwer Law International.
Breau, S.C. (2005) Humanitarian Intervention: the United Nations and Collective Responsibility. London, Cameron May.
Burdea, G. (1972) *Les libertés publiques*. Paris, LGDJ.
Burlamaqui, Jean-Jacques (1747) *Principes du droit naturel*. Genève, Barillot et fils, I, VII, 4.
Burrows, A. (2009) D. Feldman (ed.). *English Public Law*. Oxford, Oxford University Press.
Caamaño, F. (2007) Sí, pueden. (Declaraciones de derecho y Estatutos de Autonomía). In Revista española de derecho constitucional, 33.
Campo, J. Jiménez (1999) *Derechos fundamentales. Concepto y garantías*. Madrid, Editorial Trotta.
Carrillo, M. (2007) Los derechos, un contenido constitucional de los Estatutos de Autonomía. In: Revista española de derecho constitucional 49.
Choudry, S. (2008) Constitutional Designs for Divided Society: Integration or Accommodation? Oxford, Oxford University Press.
Colliard, C.-A. (1989) *Libertés publiques*. Paris, Dalloz.
Commission Africaine des Droits de l'Homme et des Peuples (2006) *Peuples autochtones d'Afrique: les peuples oubliés?* Banjul, CADHP.
Constant, B. (1819) De la liberté des anciens comparée à celle des modernes. Paris.
de Castro Cid, B. & A. Fernández-Galiano (1993) *Lecciones de Teoría del Derecho y Derecho Natural*. Madrid, Editorial Universitas, *passim*.
de Esteban, J. (2001) *Tratado de derecho constitucional espanol*. Madrid, Servicio de Publicaciones de la Facultad de Derecho, UCM, 298 ss.
Delpérée, F. (2003) Le droit constitutionnel de la Belgique. Bruxelles, Bruylant.
Derrida, J. (1972) *Signature, événement, contexte*, in *Marges de la philosophie*. Paris, Les Éditions de Minuit.
Dershowitz, A. (2004) Rights from Wrongs. A Secular Theory of the Origins of Rights. New York, Basic Books.
Díez-Picazo, L.M. (2005) *Los sistemas de derechos fundamentales*. Madrid, Civitas.
Díez-Picazo, L.M. (2006) ¿Pueden los estatutos de Autonomía declarar derechos, deberes y principios?, Revista española de derecho constitucional 63.
Duffar, J. & J. Robert (2009) *Droits de l'homme et libertés fondamentales*. Paris, Montchrestien.
Emmert, F. & L. Hammer (2012) *The European Convention on Human Rights in Central and Eastern Europe*. The Hague, Eleven International Publishing, 39 ff.
Etzioni, Amidai (1995) *Rights and the Common Good: The Communitarian Perspective*. New York, St. Martin's Press.
Favoreu, L. (2001) La notion de liberté fondamentale devant le juge administratif des référés. Paris, Dalloz.
Ferrari, G.F. (2010) *Relazione conclusiva. Lo statuto costituzionale del non cittadino*. Atti del XXIV Convegno annuale, Cagliari, 16–17 ottobre 2009, Associazione italiana dei costituzionalisti, Padova, CEDAM 516 ff.
Ferrari, G.F. & A. Gambaro (eds.). (2006) *Corti nazionali e comparazione giuridica*, Napoli, ESI.
Figgis, J.N. (1960) Political Thought from Gerson to Grotius: 1414–1625. New York, Harper.
Finney, M.I. (1995) *Democracy Ancient and Modern*. London, Rutgers University Press.
Flores, M. (2008) *Storia dei diritti umani*. Bologna, il Mulino.
Fukuyama, F. (1992) *The End of History and the Last Man*. New York, Free Press.
Gallie, W.B. Essentially Contested Concepts. In Proceeding of the Aristototelic society, 1955/56 167 ff.

Gomes Canotilho, J.J. (2004) Tomemos a sério os direitos económicos, sociais e culturais, Estudos sobre direitos fundamentais. Coimbra, Editora Tema.

Häberle, P. (1991) Gemeineuropäisches Verfassungsrecht. In EuGRZ 261 ff.

Habermas, J. (1992) *Faktizität und Geltung*. Frankfurt a. Main, Suhrkamp.

Hamilton, A. *The federalist* No. 84.

Hecker, W. (2003) Relativierung des Folterverbots in der BRD?. In Kritische Justiz 210–218.

Held, D. & A. McGrew (2002) *Globalization/Anti-Globalization*. Cambridge, Polity Press.

Henkin, L. (1990) *The Age of Rights*. New York, Columbia University Press.

Honneth, A. (1992) Kampf an Anerkennung. Zur moralishen Grammatik der sozialer Kämpfe. Frankfurt a. Main, Suhrkamp.

Hunt, L. (2007) *Inventing Human Rights: A History*. New York, W. W. Norton & Company.

Huntington, S. (1996) *The Clash of Civilizations and the Remaking of World Order*. New York, Simon & Schuster.

Ignatieff, M. (2001) *Human Rights as Politics and Idolatry*. Princeton, Princeton University Press.

Ignatieff, M. (2003) Introduction: American Exceptionalism and Human Rights. In Id. (Ed.). American Exceptionalism and Human Rights. Princeton, Princeton University Press.

Israel, J.-J. (1998) *Droit des libertés fondamentales*. Pars, LGDJ.

Klabbers, J. & A. Peters, G. Ulfstein (2009) *The Constitutionalization of International Law*. Oxford, Oxford University Press.

Kymlika, W. (1991) *Liberalism, Community and Culture*. Oxford, Clarendon Press.

Kymlika, W. (1995) *Multicultural Citizenship: A Liberal Theory of Minority Rights*. Oxford, Oxford University Press.

Lanni, S. (2011) (ed.). *I diritti dei popoli indigeni in America Latina*. Napoli, ESI (2011).

Laws, J. (1993) Is the High Court of Justice the Guardian of Fundamental Constitutional Rights? Pub. L., 59 ff.

Lawson, R. (1994) Confusion and conflict? Diverging interpretation of the European Convention on Human Rights Law among Europe's regional courts. In M. De Blois, R. Lawson (eds.). The Dynamics of the Protection of Human Rights in Europe. The Hague, Martinus Nijhoff, 253 ff.

Lerche, Peter (1961) *Übermass und Verfassungsrecht*. Köln, Heymann.

Lipset, S.M. (1996) American Exceptionalism: A Double-Edged Sword. New York, N.Y.

Little, D., J. Kelsay & A.A. Sachedina (eds.). (1988) *Human Rights and the Conflict of Cultures: Western and Islamic Perspectives on Religious Liberty*. Columbia, University of South Carolina Press.

Madiot, Y. (1976) *Droits de l'homme et libertés publiques*. Paris, Masson.

Markesinis, B. (2003) Comparative Law in Courtroom and Classroom, The Story of the Last Thirty-five Years. Oxford-Portland, Hart Publishing.

Markesinis, B. & J. Fedtke (2006) *Judicial Recourse to Foreign Law, A New Source of Inspiration?* London, Routledge-Cavendish.

Marshall, T.H. (1950) *Sociology at the Crossroad*. London, Heinemann.

Martin Oviedo, J.V. (1978) Artículo 147, Estatutos de Autonomía, su contenido y reforma. In O. Alzaga Villaamil (ed.). Comentarios a la Constitución española de (1978) Madrid, Edersa, 127.

Peces-Barba Martinez, G. (1991) *Teoría de los derechos fundamentales*. Madrid, Eudema.

Massó Garrote, M.S. (2000) I diritti fondamentali e le libertà pubbliche nella costituzione del 1978 e nella giurisprudenza costituzionale. In L. Pegoraro, A. Rinella, R. Scarciglia (eds.). I venti anni della Costituzione spagnola nella giurisprudenza del Tribunale costituzionale. Padova, CEDAM 43 ff.

Mazza, M. (2004) Decentramento e riforma delle autonomie territoriali in Francia. Torino, Giappichelli.

Michael, L. & M. Morlok (2009) *Grundrechte*. Berlin, Duncker & Humblot, 226.

Miranda, J. (2008) *Manual de direito constitucional* Vol. IV. Coimbra, Editora Tema.

Morange, J. (1985) *Droits de l'homme et libertés publiques*. Paris, Robert Laffont.

Oestreich, G. (1978) Geschichte der Menschenrechte und Grundfreiheiten im Umriss. Berlin, Duncker & Humblot.

Ong, A. (1999) Flexible Citizenship: The Cultural Logic of Transnationality. Durham, Duke University Press.

Pace, A. (1992) Problematica delle libertà costituzionali. Parte generale. Padova, CEDAM, 10 ff.

Palermo, F. & J. Woelk (2011) Diritto costituzionale comparato dei gruppi e delle minoranze. Padova, CEDAM.

Pierré-Caps, S., J. Poumareède & N. Rouland (1996) *Droit des minorités et des peuples autochtones*. Paris, PUF.

Rawls, J. (1999) *The Law of Peoples*. Cambridge, Harvard University Press.

Reich, R.B. (2007) Supercapitalism. The Transformation of Business, Democracy, and Everyday Life. New York, Alfred A. Knopf.

Richer, L. (1982) *Les droits de l'homme et du citoyen*. Paris, Economica.

Rivero, J. (1996) *Les libertés publiques*. Paris, PUF.

Rorty, R. (1998) *Truth and progress*. Cambridge, Cambridge University Press, 167.

Rosas, A. (1995) *The European Union and Human Rights*. The Hague, Martinus Nijhoff, 51 ff.

Selznick, P. (1992) *The Moral Commonwealth. Social Theory and the Promise of Community*. Los Angeles, University of California Press.

Sen, A. (1999) *Freedom as Development*. Oxford, Oxford University Press.

Sen, A. (2006) *Identity and Violence, The Illusion of Destiny*. New York, W. W. Norton & Company.

Teubner, G. (2003) Societal Constitutionalism, Alternative to State-Centered Constitutional Theory? In C. Joerges, I.J. Sand, G. Teubner (eds.). Transnational Governance and Constitutionalism, Oxford-Portland, Hart Publishing.

Tierney, B. (1997) The Idea of Natural Rights: Studies on Natural Rights, Natural Law and Church Law (1159–1625). Atlanta, Scholar Press of Emory University.

Tuck, R. (1979) *Natural Rights Theories: Their Origin and Development*. Cambridge, Cambridge University Press.

Turpin, D. (2004) *Libertés Publiques et Droits Fondamentaux*. Paris, Ed. du Seuil.

Unesco (1949) Human Rights. Comments and Interpretations. A Symposium. London, A. Wingate.

Uyttendaele, N. (2006) Précis de droit constitutionnel belge. Bruxelles, Bruylant.

Van Ert, G. (2008) *Using International Law in Canadian Courts*. Toronto, Irwin Law, 2nd ed.

Vieira, N. (1998) *Constitutional civil rights in a nutshell*. St. Paul, West Publishing.

Walzer, M. (1983) Spheres of Justice, A Defense of Pluralism and Equality. New York, Basic Books.

Wittgenstein (1953) *Philosophical Investigations*. Oxford, Blackwell.

Cases

Cour d'Arbitrage, Dec. 107/1998 and 124/1999.

De Wutz v Hendricks (1824) 2 Bing 314.

R v. Secretary of State for the Home Department, ex p Thakrar [1974QB 684.].

Trendtex Trading v Bank of Nigeria [1977] 1 QB 529.

Conseil Constitutionnel.

CC dec. 22.1.1990.

CC dec. 13.8.1993.

CC dec. 22.4.1997.

French Constitutional Council 16.7.1971.

Cons. Const., dec. 2004-496 DC.

Cons. Const., dec. 2004-505 DC.

Cons. Const., dec. 2006-540 DC.

France, CE, 11.07.1956.

France, CE, 2.7.1993.

France, CE, Civil Cassation 4.1.1995.
Civil Cassation 10.3.1993.
France: l.22.6.1982 e 6.7.1989.
France: l. 21.1.1995.
France, l.30.6.2000.
German CT, BVerGE 32, 98, 107.
Strasbourg Court, CC dec. 348 and 349/2007.
Strasbourg Court*Lithgow*, 8.8.1986.
Strasbourg Court 6.9.1978, *Klass v. Germany*.
Strasbourg Court 21.2.1986, *James*.
BVerfGE 37, 271 *Solange-I-Beschluss* (1974).
BVerfGE 73, 339, *Solange-II-Beschluss* (1986).
BVerfGE 89, 155 *Maastricht-Beschluss* (1993).
BVerfGE Az 2 BvL 1/97, *Bananenmarkt-Entscheidung* (2000).
BVerfGE 123, 267, *Lissabon-Urteil* (2009).
German BVG, BVerG 20, 1, 26.
German BVG, BVerG 45, 187, 242.
Italian Constitutional CourtDec. 29/1962.
Italian Constitutional CourtDec. 561/1987.
Italian Constitutional CourtDec. 287/1992.
Italian Constitutional CourtDec. 383/1998.
Italian Constitutional Court 37/1969.
Italian Constitutional Court 102/1975.
Italian Constitutional Court 238/1975; 98/1979.
Italy, Court of cassation 22.6.1985, n. 3769.
HCJ 11437/05 Kav Laoved v. Interior Ministry (2011).
Nold, 14.5.1974.
Nold (C-4/73).
Stauder (C-29/69).
Spanish constitutional Tribunal
Sent. 23-11-1984, n.107.
Sent. 30-9-1985, n. 99 and 7-11-2007, n.48.
Sent. 11-9-1995, n- 130.
Spain, STC, dec. 31/2010.
TC dec.14.7.1981
TC dec. 25/1981; 64/1988; 53/1995.
Tribunal Constitucional STC, dec. 31/2010
Tribunal constitucional STC, 158/1993.
Adamson v. California, 332 U.S. 46 (1947).
Adamson v. California, 332 U.S. 46 (1947).
Amalgamated Food Employees Union v. Logan Valley Plaza, 1968.
Bartels v. Iowa, 262 U. S. 404.
Bell v. Maryland, 378 U.S. 226 (1964).
Bernal v. Fainter, 467 U.S. 216 (1984).
Calder v. Bull, 3 U.S. 386 (1798).
DeShaney v. Winnebago County Dpt. of Social Services, 489 U.S. 189 (1989).
Farrington v. Tokushige, 273 U.S. 284.
Graham v. Richardson, 403 U.S. 365 (1971).
Griggs v. Duke Power Co., 1971.
Hudgens v. NLRB, 1976.
Medellin v. Texas, 552 U.S. 491 (2008).
Meyer v. Nebraska, 262 U. S. 390.
Nixon v. Herndon

Norwood v. Harrison, 413 U.S. 455 (1973).
No. 107 v. Irvis (1972).
Palko v. Connecticut, 302 U.S 319 (1937).
Paquete Habana case, 175 U.S. 677 (1900).
Poe. V. Ullman, 1962
Pierce v. Society of Sisters, 268 U. S. 510.
Reitman v. Mulkey, 387 U.S. 369 (1967).
Rochin v. California, 342 U.S. 165 (1952)
Rochin v. California, 342 U.S. 165, 169 (1952).
Shelley v. Kramer, 1948.
Smith v. Allright, 1944; Terry v. Adams, 1953.
Sosa v. *Alvarez-Machain*, 542 U.S. 692 (2004).
Stein *v. New York*, 346 U.S. 156, 199 (1953).
Toll. *V. Moreno*, 458 U.S. 1 (1982).
U.S. v. Classic, 313 U.S. 299 (1941).
U.S. *v. Carolene Products Co*, 304 U.S. 144 (1938), ft. 4.
U.S. Supreme Court, *Twining v. New Jersey*, 211 U.S. 78, 113 (1908).
130 U.S. 581 (1889).
109 U.S. 3 (1883).

Journals and Articles

A. Ruggeri La CEDU nelle sentenze 348 e 349 della Corte costituzionale. DPCE, 2008, 171 ss.
Duranti, F. (2010) Sulla via dell'indipendenza: il nuovo statuto di autonomia per la Groenlandia. DPCE, 957.
H. Wechsler Toward Neutral Principles of Constitutional Law. 73 Harv. L. Rev., 19591, 31.
J.H.H. Weiler Eurocracy and Distrust. 61 Wash. L. Rev (1986), 1103.
J.H. Jackson Sovereignty-Modern: A New Approach to an Outdated Concept. 92 Am. J. Int'l L., 782–802.
J. Habermas The Constitutionalization of International Law and the Legitimation Problems of a constitution for World Society. 15 Constellations, 444 (2008).
L.F.M Besselink.Entrapped by the maximum standard: on fundamental rights, pluralism and subsidiarity in the European Union. 35 C. Mkt. L. Rev., 629 (1998).
L. Swepton A New Step in the International Law on Indigenous and Tribal Peoples: ILO Convention No.169 of 1989.15 Okla. C. Un. L. Rev., 677 (1990).
M. Sterio The Evolution of International Law. 31 B.C. Int'l & Comp. L. Rev., 213 (2008).
Pace, A. (1989) La garanzia dei diritti fondamentali nell'ordinamento costituzionale italiano: il ruolo del legislatore e dei giudici "comuni". In RTDPC (1989) 685 ff.
S. Carmeli La difficile cohabitation tra diritto interno e diritto internazionale: la Corte di cassazione si allea al Consiglio di Stato per difendere la sovranità nazionale. DPCE, 2000, 1978.
S. Tierney Reframing Sovereignty? Sub-State National Societies and Contemporary Challenges to the Nation-State. 54 Int. & Comp. Legal Q. 161–83 (2008).
S. Žižek Against human rights. New Left Review, 34, 2005.
T. Boergenthal The Normative and Institutional Evolution of International Human Rights. In 19 Human Rights Quarterly (1997), 703 ff.
V. Jackson Narratives of Federalism: Of Continuities and Comparative Constitutional Experience. 51 Duke L. J., 223 (2001), 247 ff.
W.N. Hohfeld Some fundamental legal conceptions as applied in judicial reasoning. 23 Yale L.J., 16 (1913).

Online Database

A. Pace. Dai diritti del cittadino ai diritti fondamentali dell'uomo. In www.rivistaic.it, 2010.

Paper Presented at a Conference

Akiko Ejima. A Possibility of Multi-layered Human Rights Implementation System of Underpinned by the Simultaneous Codification of the Constitution of Japan and the International Human Rights Treaty.
Argentine National Report.
Canada National Report.
Chien-liang Lee. Rule of Law in Taiwan: Transplantation and Codification.
Greek National Report.
Ida Lintel, Marthe Lot Vermeulen. Codification and Implementation of Human Rights in the Netherlands.
Italy National Report.
Leila Nadya Sadat, Henry H. Oberschelp. The United States and Human Rights: Paradoxes and Challenges.
Luísa Neto. Portuguese National Report on the The national and international codification of human rightspresented to the Thematic Congress of the International Academy of Comparative Law.
Tomer Broude, Yonatan Weisbrod. The Codification of Human Rights at the National and International Levels.

Press

W. Brugger, Das andere Auge. In Frankfurter Allgemeine Zeitung, Mar. 10, 2003.

Statutes

art. 50 Const.
Bosnia-Herzegovina Constitution art. II, (Sect. 31).
Art. 6 ECHR.
France
art. 55 Const.
FRG, arts. 1-19 GG.
Italy
Art. 111 Italian Con.
Portugal
Portuguese Constitution Art. 16
Spain
Art. 24 Spanish Con.
Spanish Constitution Art. 10.
Spanish Const. art. 10.2.
Spanish Const. Title I.
U.S.A.
Amendments V US Con.
Amendments XIV US Con.
42 USCA § 2000.

42 USCA § 1973.
42 USCA § 3601.
249 U.S. 47 (1919).
357 U.S. 449 (1958).
367 U.S. 497 (1961).
372 U.S. 353 (1963).
381 U.S. 479 (1965).
383 U.S. 663 (1966).
394 U.S. 618 (1969).
404 U.S. 189 (1971).
430 U.S. 817 (1977).
448 U.S. 555 (1980).

Chapter 12
International Academy of Comparative Law (IACL)

Intermediate Congress at Taiwan from 24 to 26 May 2012 Finnish Report HUMAN RIGHTS IN FINLAND

Hannu Kiuru

12.1 Preamble

Under Sect. 22 of the Constitution of Finland (731/1999) in force since 1 March 2000, the public authorities must guarantee the observance of fundamental rights and freedoms and human rights. The provision stresses that, in addition to ensuring adherence to procedural requirements in connection with fundamental rights, every effort must also be made to ensure that fundamental rights are put into practice in a substantial sense. Under the provision, the public authorities must ensure that both the fundamental rights laid down in the Constitution and the human rights enshrined in international conventions binding Finland are adhered to, and in this respect it is in accordance with the premises of human rights conventions and the manner in which they are interpreted by international monitoring bodies. The Constitution of Finland also endeavors to ensure fundamental and human rights by following the principle of direct application. International human rights obligations provide our judicial system with minimum standards for fundamental and human rights.

An overall reform of the basic rights and liberties took effect on 1 August 1995. Its main purpose was to create in Finland a basic rights system that is in full compliance with the international human rights obligations and thus reinforce the fulfillment of these obligations at national level. The Constitution of Finland guarantees the inviolability of human dignity and the freedoms and rights of the individual and promotes justice in society. One of the objectives of the basic rights reform carried out was to increase the direct applicability of basic rights and liberties by courts and other authorities.

In addition to the European Court of Human Rights (ECHR) and the European Committee of Social Rights, there are nine other international enforcement and investigating bodies (three coming under the Council of Europe and six coming under the United Nations).

H. Kiuru (✉)
Freesenkatu 5 A 10, FIN-00100 Helsinki, Finland
e-mail: hannu.kiuru@kotikontu.fi

W.-Y. Wang (ed.), *Codification in International Perspective*, Ius Comparatum – Global
Studies in Comparative Law, DOI 10.1007/978-3-319-03455-3_12,
© Springer International Publishing Switzerland 2014

The Finnish Government submits periodic reports on human rights conventions to six UN-supported and three COE-supported bodies monitoring the national implementation of the conventions. After examining the reports, the monitoring bodies in question submit their conclusions based on the report to the states in question. The bodies also monitor the national implementation of the conclusions. The UN monitoring bodies also invite government representatives to hearings in which the reports are examined orally.

12.2   Status of Asylum Seekers and Refugees/Basic Rights

The fundamental rights enshrined in the Constitution of Finland apply to asylum seekers, refugees and other immigrants in the same manner as to Finnish citizens. Thus these groups have the right to pre-primary education and basic education and to essential social welfare and health care service and social assistance. A person can only make full use of social welfare and health care service if he/she is a resident of a municipality and is permanently residing in Finland. Asylum seekers do not meet these requirements. An asylum seeker has an unrestricted right to work after remaining in Finland for an uninterrupted period of three months. The reception centre provides an asylum seeker with temporary accommodation for the duration of the asylum process.

12.3   Status of Immigrants

Finland, previously a country with a very homogeneous culture, is in the process of becoming a modern multicultural state. Finland is home to about 150,000 foreign-born people, and the figure is expected to reach 250,000 by the year 2015. The unemployment rate among immigrants is almost three times higher than among Finns. In this respect, the situation among immigrant women is worse than among immigrant men. There are, however, differences in the employment situation depending on nationality, and the length of the period spent in Finland is also a factor. Inadequate knowledge of Finnish is the biggest single reason for employment problems among immigrants. Thus, ensuring smooth integration of immigrants and particularly their children into Finland's day care and education systems and the labor market is a major challenge for the future. There is also room for improvement in the attitude of Finns, which is reflected in continuing discrimination against immigrants and minorities on the labor market.

12.4   Judgments of the ECHR and Their Implementation

In a number of the judgments of the ECHR concerning Finland the question of fair trial has been considered, including the right to trial within a reasonable time. In addition the ECHR has also considered the following issues: the right to oral proceedings, the opportunity of the accused to put questions and the duty of the prosecutor to provide the defense with all evidence.

The cases concerning the right to private life have covered such matters as images published on the Internet, illegal viewing of personal data and taking children into urgent care (urgent placement). Many of the judgments on freedom of expression have concerned decisions of Finnish courts that give priority to the right to privacy over freedom of expression.

The implementation of the judgments in which Finland has been found to be in violation of the Convention is monitored by the ministerial committee of the Council of Europe. Implementation of the judgments covers payment of any compensation within the period laid down in the judgment and other practical measures aimed at preventing the recurrence of similar violations.

In many cases the national legislation has already been changed before the ECHR has issued its judgement, eliminating the need for any specific implementation measures. An example of this is a certain section of the Criminal Investigation Act, which contains provisions on video recordings of the questioning of the injured party or the witness in cases where the persons being questioned cannot, on account of their young age, attend the trial in person. Even though the sections has already been incorporated in the Criminal Investigation Act in 2003, the ECHR has since then issued a number of judgments stating that the manner in which minors have been heard in connection with cases involving sexual exploitation of minors has not been in accordance with the law. The crimes in question had taken place before the Act was amended.

12.5   Strengthening the Fundamental Rights of the EU

Both the establishment of the EU Agency for fundamental Rights and the Charter of Fundamental Rights adopted 2000, the provisions of which are made binding by the Treaty of Lisbon, contribute to strengthening the Union's fundamental rights dimension. The decision to establish the EU agency for Fundamental Rights has been considered one of the most important achievements of the Finnish Presidency of the EU in 2006. Agreement on the matter was reached at the meeting of the Council of Justice and Home Affairs in December 2006.

The Agency for Fundamental Rights is an independent EU body that provides the Member States, EU institutions and other parties responsible for the implementation of European Union Law with expert advice on fundamental rights. To this end, it cooperates with the Council of Europe, the Organizations for Security and Co-operation in Europe (OSCE), the UN and other international organizations.

12.6 National Monitoring System

In Finland, there are a number of bodies responsible for monitoring the implementation of fundamental and human rights. In addition to the supreme supervisors of legality, *ombudsmen*, the courts and other authorities, civil society also plays a central role in the monitoring process.

12.7 Constitutional Law Committee of the Parliament

The task of the Parliamentary Constitutional Law Committee is to issue opinions on whether the matters under consideration in the Parliament are in compliance with the Finnish Constitution and international human rights conventions. The monitoring carried out by the Committee is pre-emptive and abstract in character, and therefore is not a significant number of issues covering a wide range of fundamental rights. The Committee also issues opinions on how the matters under consideration relate to human rights conventions, particularly to the European Convention on Human Rights. The effectiveness of pre-emptive constitutional monitoring is demonstrated by the fact that there have been very few situations concerning the interpretation of case law referred to in Sect. 106 of the Constitution of Finland.

12.8 Supreme Supervisors of Legality

The task of the supreme supervisors of legality, the Parliamentary Ombudsman and the Chancellor of Justice of the Government, is to monitor the implementation of fundamental and human rights. Both submit an annual report on their activities to the Parliament, which contains a separate section on the monitoring of fundamental and human rights. There has been a sharp increase in the number of complaints and other matters concerning the supervision of legality submitted to the Parliamentary Ombudsman during the past few years.

Chancellor of Justice is responsible for supervising the lawfulness of the official actions of the Government and the President of the Republic and the activities of authorities and other public bodies. Issues concerning fundamental and human rights arise both during supervision of legality of Government activities and during the overall supervision of the legality of authorities' activities. In the supervision of Government activities, questions of fundamental and human rights usually arise in connection with reviews of legislative proposals and in reviews of Government Bills brought before the Parliament and the decrees issued by the Government and the President of the Republic. The complaints submitted to the Chancellor of Justice are less numerous than those received by the Parliamentary Ombudsman.

12.9   Other Ombudsmen

In addition to the supreme supervisors their are even other supervisors. Ombuds-man for Minorities deals with complaints on ethnic discrimination and other types of inappropriate treatment and issues concerning the application of legislation on aliens. The tasks of the Ombudsman for Equality relate to monitoring of the bans on discrimination laid down by the Equality Act, they also include the promotion of equality. Most of the contacts concern employment. The Data Protection Ombuds-man guides and monitors the processing of personal data and issues advice on these issues. The work of the Ombudsman for Children focuses mainly on monitoring of the implementation of children's rights, influencing decision-making in society at large and promoting cooperation between different parties.

12.10   The Independence of the Judiciary

The Finnish Constitution guarantees everyone the right to have his case heard ap-propriately and without undue delay by a court or public authority. Everyone also has the right to have a decision affecting his rights and duties reviewed by a court or other judicial body.

In addition the Constitution contains the basic provision on fair trial and good governance. The main guarantees of these are the publicity of proceedings, the right to be heard, the right to receive a decision containing the grounds, and the right to appeal against the decision.

The independence of the judiciary is constitutionally guaranteed. The courts are under the sole obligation to apply the law in force.

The courts are also part of the system of monitoring the implementation of funda-mental and human rights, and in individual cases they can take a stand on the issue. Under Sect. 106 of the Constitution of Finland concerning the primacy of the Consti-tution, a court must give primacy to the Constitution if, in the case being considered by the court, the application of a legal provision would be in evident conflict with the Constitution. So far, there have been few cases involving an evident conflict with the Constitution. There have also been a small number of cases in which Sect. 106 of the Constitution has been considered but not applied. References to fundamental and human rights in court practice have substantially increased, particularly after the introduction of the fundamental rights reform. In general terms, courts play a central role in ensuring the legal protection of citizens, and the cases they consider are often a question of implementing a right protected by the Constitution and/or human rights conventions.

12.11   Civil Society

There are a number of advisory boards in different administrative branches that are connected with the work on fundamental and human rights and in which different actors of civil society are represented. These include the Advisory Board for Human Rights, the Advisory Board on Romani Affairs, the Advisory Board for Ethnic Relations, the Child Advisory Board, the Advisory Board for Minority Issues, the Council for Equality and the Advisory Board on Sami Affairs. The Advisory Board for Civil Society Policy was established as a result of the citizen participation policy programme with the aim of strengthening interaction between the public authorities and civil society. The possibility of representatives of the organizations to participate in the consideration of periodic reviews in the convention-monitoring bodies has proved a good practice: the Government has also been in close cooperation with NGOs when Human Rights Policy Reports to the Parliament have been under preparation.

12.12   Establishment of the National Human Rights Institution

The field of human rights actors in Finland can be considered somewhat fragmented and uncoordinated. The idea of establishing a national human rights institution has arisen from the fragmented nature of the present system and the need to coordinate the gathering, assessment and exchange of information, in particular for international cooperation. A national human rights institution must be independent as it is stated in the international recommendations laid down as the Paris Principles. It must promote and protect human rights. The new institution shall monitor and supervise the national human rights situation, issue recommendations and submit proposals for promoting human rights.

12.13   General Courts in Civil and Criminal Matters/Court Procedures

12.13.1   District Courts

Finland is divided into a number of judicial districts, each with a District Court. A District Court is made up of a Chief Judge and a number of other professional judges.

In civil cases the proceedings start with the pre-trial phase of the procedure, after which the case is ajourned to the main hearing. The case also can be resolved already in the course of the partly written and partly oral pre-trial procedure.

Also in criminal procedure the principles of orality, directness and concentration of the trial are stressed. The main hearing is divided into opening statements of the parties, the presentation of evidence and the conclusions.

The rights of the accused are respected as stated in the European Convention of Human Rights. In Finland the victim has the right to claim damages from the accused in connection with the criminal proceedings and it is the public prosecutor's duty in certain situations to present the claim for damages on behalf of the victim.

In criminal cases and in some cases concerning family law the court is composed of one presiding professional judge and three lay members (volunteers elected by the municipal councils). In ordinary civil cases the court can even consist of three professional judges. One single judge presides over the pre-trial procedure of a civil case. Minor cases are tried by one judge.

The greatest volume of cases dealt with the district courts concern petitionary matters. Such matters are normally decided in chambers without a hearing being held.

12.13.2 Courts of Appeal

The parties have a right to appeal to the Court of Appeal and to refer both questions of fact and questions of law. In the Courts of Appeal the cases are heard by three judges. The Court first carries out a screening procedure, where it is determined if the matter is to be taken up for further consideration. If the Court considers that the decision has been correct already in the district court, the appeal will not be entertained.

The appeal procedure is similar in both civil and criminal cases. After preliminary preparation the case can be solved either after hearing or in written procedure. The Courts of Appeal have to arrange an oral hearing if the evidence of the case has to be evaluated again or when a party so requests unless the appeal is e.g. clearly without merit.

12.13.3 The Supreme Court

The Supreme Court is the third and final instance. Its most important task is to establish precedents, thus giving guidelines to the lower courts on the application of the law. The Supreme Court hears both civil and criminal cases and may grant leave to appeal in cases in which a precedent is necessary for the correct application of the law, serious error has been committed in the proceedings before a lower court or another special reason exists in law.

Normally two members decide whether leave should be granted. If leave is granted, the case is decided in a composition of five members. If the matter is important in principle and has far-reaching consequences, it is decided in a pleanary session or in a reinforced composition of eleven members. Usually the cases are decided on the basis of written materials; the Supreme Court may, however, also conduct oral hearings and inspections.

12.13.4 Administrative Jurisdiction

A general right of administrative appeal exists in Finland. The right can only be restricted with a specific legislative provision to that effect. The administrative courts hear appeals of private individuals and corporate bodies against the acts of the authorities. In certain cases the State and municipal authorities also have the right of appeal.

An appeal is usually first heard by a regional Administrative Court. The administrative courts hear tax, municipal, construction, social welfare, health care and alien cases as well as other administrative cases. In certain of these the appeal must be preceded by a complaint to a separate lower appellate body.

The administrative court consists of three judges. The procedure is mainly written. The administrative courts also conduct oral hearings. They have to be held whenever it is necessary for the resolution of the case or when a party so requests.

The Supreme Administrative Court finally decides the legality of the acts of the authorities. The bulk of it case-load consists of appeals against the decisions of the Administrative Courts.

Usually no leave to appeal is required. The main exception to this rule is an appeal against a decision in a tax case, for which leave is required. The Supreme Administrative Court itself grants the leave. The cases are heard by five judges. The Supreme Administrative Court may conduct also inspections or oral hearings.

In addition to its purely judicial tasks, the Supreme Administrative Court supervises the lower judicial authorities in the field of administrative law.

12.13.5 Enforcement of Judgments

In Finland the enforcement of civil judgments is the duty of the District Bailiffs, who are administratively within the ambit of the Ministry of Justice.

The bailiffs have general jurisdiction to ensure compliance with obligations laid down in court judgements. In practice these most often take the form of judgment debts, If the judgment is not heeded voluntarily, it is carried out compulsorily, by way of enforcement. Due taxes and public fees, as well as certain compatible civil debts, are executable without need for a judgment.

Also criminal sanctions of a monetary nature, such as fines, are collected by way of enforcement. In addition, the enforcement authorities are charged with the carrying out evictions, court-ordered asset seizures and court orders on child custody and right of access. The decisions of bailiffs are subject to appeal in a District Court.

12.13.6   System of Sanctions

In Finland, the punishment imposed on a convicted criminal takes the form of imprisonment, fine, fixed-sum fine or community service. Community service can be imposed instead of unconditional imprisonment for at most eight months.

A special juvenile punishment can be imposed on a young person, if a fine is considered insufficient and unconditional imprisonment too severe. Juvenile punishment consists of supervision and work and an educational program.

Successful mediation may result in a decision not to prosecute or less severe sentencing by a court.

Notwithstanding mediation, serious offences are likely to be considered by a court of law.

A sentence if imprisonment is passed either for a fixed period or for life. The minimum fixed period is fourteen days and the maximum 12 years. There is an opportunity for parole when a given proportion of the sentence has been served. Even an offender serving an imprisonment for life can be paroled after having served at least 12 years of the sentence, if Helsinki Court of Appeal so decides.

The Prison Service enforces prison sentences and fine conversion sentences passed by the courts and takes care of the enforcement of remand imprisonment. The Probation Service carries out the enforcement of community service and juvenile punishment. The Probation Service also sees to the supervision of conditionally sentenced young offenders and prisoners out on parole.

12.13.7   Supervision of the Administration of Justice

In addition to the senior overseers of legality the Chancellor of Justice of the Council of State and the Parliamentary Ombudsman, there are certain specialized authorities who have similar duties in more limited fields: the Consumer Ombudsman, the Ombudsman for Equality, the Data Protection Ombudsman, the Ombudsman for Minorities and the Bankruptcy Ombudsman (see ahead page 3).

Chapter 13
The Codification of Human Rights at the National and International Levels in Germany

Uwe Kischel

At first sight, national human rights in Germany are widely codified in a complex system (13.1.1). Nevertheless, the limits of codification are clearly visible. Thus, some important basic rights have been developed by the courts without any direct reflection in the text of the German constitution, the Grundgesetz (Basic Law) (13.1.2). Moreover, the content and limits of all basic rights as applied in practice are, to a large extent, the result of court decisions and not directly prescribed by the wording of the constitution (13.1.3). Codification of human rights in Germany is not a singular historical incident, but an ongoing process. The Grundgesetz can and will be changed to accommodate new developments, although there are certain aspects that no majority of the German legislature is allowed to touch (13.1.4). Basic rights are thoroughly protected, in Germany, by a comprehensive system of judicial review as well as by the general awareness of their content and importance among jurists and citizens alike (13.1.5). The interactions of German law with international law (13.2.1.) and, in particular, of German basic rights with the European Convention on Human Rights (13.2.2) as well as with fundamental rights of the European Union (13.2.3) form a highly complex system that is constantly evolving.

13.1 National Human Rights

13.1.1 Terminology and Categorization

True to their general approach to law, German jurists have developed a specific terminology in the field of human rights. This terminology includes a host of

Prof. Dr. Uwe Kischel, LL.M. (Yale), attorney-at-law (New York), Mercator Professor of Public Law, European Law and Comparative Law (North-Eastern Europe), Ernst-Moritz-Arndt-University, Greifswald, Germany

U. Kischel (✉)
University of Greifswald, Faculty of Law and Economics,
Domstr. 20a, 17489 Greifswald, Germany
e-mail: kischel@uni-greifswald.de

W.-Y. Wang (ed.), *Codification in International Perspective,* Ius Comparatum – Global Studies in Comparative Law, DOI 10.1007/978-3-319-03455-3_13,
© Springer International Publishing Switzerland 2014

categorizations—only a few of which will be mentioned here—taken for granted in any German statement on human rights and without which much of the content of German discourse on human rights might remain somewhat obscure.

Two Misleading Notions: "Human Rights" and "Codification"

The notion of "human rights" (*Menschenrechte*) is not normally used in Germany to describe constitutionally guaranteed individual rights against the State. The usual and traditional notion is "basic rights" (*Grundrechte*). In contrast, "human rights" is generally understood to refer exclusively to international human rights. This also holds true for the art. 1 para. 2 of the Grundgesetz (GG), the only article in which "human rights" are explicitly mentioned in the Grundgesetz.[1]

Using the notion of "codification" in the context of basic rights would be a rare occurrence in a purely national German context. "Codification" implies the existence of rights prior to their being embedded in a unified text, the code. Although the age-old debate between natural law and positivism exists in Germany as it does in many other countries,[2] the basic rights enshrined in the Grundgesetz are, for all practical purposes and in spite of their partly long constitutional history,[3] considered to be the result of the deliberations by the mothers and fathers of the Grundgesetz in 1948/1949, not the accumulation of rights already existing before and independent of the text of the Grundgesetz. Neither does Germany have a tradition of multiple constitutional texts[4] which might, at a certain moment, have been converted and, thus, codified into one single document. Like its predecessor, the Weimar Constitution, the Grundgesetz is the only and comprehensive constitutional enactment in Germany.

Categories of Rights

Basic rights can be categorized in different ways. None of these categories, however, imply a hierarchical difference or refer to different levels of fundamentality

---

[1] Cf. e.g. BVerfGE 111, 307 (329); for the position that art. 1 para. 2 GG refers to natural law positions cf. e.g. Hillgruber, Christian, in: Epping, Volker; Hillgruber, Christian: Grundgesetz, Kommentar, 2009, art. 1 marginal notes 53 ff.; Vöneky, Silja: Recht, Moral und Ethik, Grundlagen und Grenzen demokratischer Legitimation für Ethikgremien, 2010, 111.

[2] Cf. only Rüthers, Bernd: Rechtstheorie—Begriff, Geltung und Anwendung, 4th ed. 2008, 175 ff.; Zippelius, Reinhold: Rechtsphilosophie, 6th ed. 2011, 72 ff.

[3] On the development of the German constitution until 1949 cf. the articles by Dieter Grimm, Rainer Wahl, Walter Pauly, Ernst Rudolf Huber, Hans Schneider and Rolf Grawert in: Isensee, Josef; Kirchhof, Paul: Handbuch des Staatsrechts der Bundesrepublik Deutschland, vol. 1, 3rd ed. 2003, 3–265.

[4] For such traditions for instance in Austria cf. Wiederin, Ewald: Grundlagen und Grundzüge des staatlichen Verfassungsrechts: Österreich, in: Bogdandy; Armin v.; Villalón, Pedro Cruz; Huber, Peter M. (eds.): Handbuch Ius Publicum Europaeum, vol. 1, 2007, § 7, 389 (408 f.); in Sweden cf. Carlson, Laura: The fundamentals of Swedish law, A guide for foreign lawyers and students, 2009, 40.

or basicness.[5] Hierarchical aspects only enter the picture where those parts of the constitution arc concerned that cannot be changed by any constitutional revision.[6]

Basic Rights and Equivalent Rights

One category is of very little practical value but can be very misleading: Certain basic rights—for instance those concerning judicial procedure—are not found in sect. 1 of the Grundgesetz (entitled "The basic rights") but in other sections. To ensure that a constitutional complaint procedure[7] can nevertheless be based on their violation, the relevant art. 93 para. 1 no. 4a GG enumerates them article for article, in addition to the generic term of "basic rights", which is read to refer to Sect. 1 of the Grundgesetz, exlusively. These additional rights are, therefore, called "rights equivalent to basic rights" (*grundrechtsgleiche Rechte*), and will, for all practical purposes, be treated exactly like any other basic rights, although some authors have tried—in vain—to give that category some original material content.[8]

Citizens' Rights and Rights for all Persons

Certain basic rights[9] are explicitly reserved for Germans[10] by the text of the Grundgesetz. This restriction as such is mostly accepted and has led to little debate,[11] mainly

---

[5] The short questionaire provided by the general rapporteur mentions fundamentality and basicness as a possible point of discussion. To elucidate certain structural aspects of this national report, it might be helpful to the reader to know the full content of this non-exhaustive questionaire: "- The written constitution and categories of rights considered or classified in it, with special reference to basicness or fundamentality and its treatment. - Possible distinction between rights belonging to the citizen in the domestic system and rights pertaining to men besides national borders and/or citizenship. - Instruments of protection in the domestic order and their efficacy as such (rating of each country from the point of view of effectiveness of individual rights). - Ranking of international law sources in the constitutional source system, with separate reference to customary law, treaties, ius cogens, mentioning the reasoning, in its historical evolution, of the constitutional/supreme court and its main cases. - Possible status, in the domestic system, of regional or continental conventions on human rights, and their influence on former treatment of rights. - Citizenship nowadays: its relationship with rights in a multi-level constitutionalism."

[6] Cf. infra 13.1.4, at "The Unchangeable Constitution"

[7] Cf. infra 13.1.5, at "Constitutional Complaint"

[8] Cf. for such endeavors Appel, Ivo: Grundrechtsgleiche Rechte, Prozeßgrundrechte oder Schranken-Schranken? Zur grundrechtsdogmatischen Einordnung von Art. 103 Abs. 2 und 3 GG, Juristische Ausbildung 2000, 571 (575 ff.).

[9] These are: freedom of assembly, art. 8 GG; freedom of association, art. 9 para. 1 GG; freedom of movement, art. 11 GG; occupational freedom, art. 12 para. 1 GG; protection against extradition, art. 16 GG; right of resistance, art. 20 para. 4 GG, equal citizenship, art. 33 para. 1 GG; equal eligibility for public office, art. 33 para. 2 GG; voting rights, art. 38 para. 1 s. 1 GG.

[10] Germans in this sense are not only those with German citizenship, but all Germans in the sense of art. 116 GG, which includes e.g. German refugees who form part of the German people, cf. e.g. von Mangoldt, Hans: Die deutsche Staatsangehörigkeit als Voraussetzung und Gegenstand der Grundrechte, in: Isensee, Josef; Kirchhof, Paul: Handbuch des Staatsrechts der Bundesrepublik Deutschland, vol. 5, 2nd ed. 2000, § 119, 617 (622 ff.).

[11] Some have tried to partly circumvent the restriction by using e.g. the concept of human dignity, art. 1 para. 1 GG, cf. e.g. Bleckmann, Albert: Staatsrecht II—Die Grundrechte, 4th ed. 1997,

due to the fact that practical problems are solved by other means: Firstly, all EU-citizens will be treated as if they were Germans due to art. 18 TFEU.[12] Secondly, all non-Germans are protected by the general liberty of action, art. 2 para. 1 GG, a catch-all right that constitutionally protects any action or non-action by anybody.[13] Thus, for instance, a Turkish butcher is not protected by the right to work, art. 12 para. 1 GG; nevertheless, his professional behavior is covered by art. 2 para. 1 GG.[14] It is an open, but rarely asked question whether and in how far this formal difference in applicable basic rights would and could lead to a difference in result.[15]

Rights to Freedom and Rights to Equality

German doctrine differentiates between freedom rights—a very broad category—and equality rights. The main difference between these two groups lies in their analytic structure: freedom rights are analyzed as having a certain area of protection (*Schutzbereich*) (e.g. all "assemblies"), of which there must be an infringement (*Eingriff*), which in turn might be justified because one of its limits (*Schranken*) applies. In other words, the area of protection answers the question *what* is protected, the infringement *against what* there is protection (for instance against the mere taking of photos of an assembly),[16] and limits answer the question which justification might exist for the infringement. Equality rights, on the other hand, are usually analyzed by asking, firstly, in how far several objects are (un)equal and have been treated (un)equally, and, secondly, whether there exists a justification, i.e. a substantial reason for the equal or unequal treatment in view of the differences and similarities.[17]

173; sometimes in conjunction with art. 1 para. 2 GG and art. 19 para. 2 GG cf. especially Dürig, Günter, in: Maunz, Theodor; Dürig, Günter: Grundgesetz, Kommentar, 1960, loose-leaf, art. 1 para. 2 marginal note 85, art. 2 para. 1 marginal note 66; for a comprehensive overview on this topic cf. Siehr, Angelika: Die Deutschenrechte des Grundgesetzes, Bürgerrechte im Spannungsfeld von Menschenrechtsidee und Staatsmitgliedschaft, 2001, 329 ff.

[12] This result is either achieved by a direct application of the rights restricted to Germans, cf. e.g. Wernsmann, Rainer: Die Deutschengrundrechte des Grundgesetzes im Lichte des Europarechts, Juristische Ausbildung 2000, 657 (658 ff.) or by a modified application of the general liberty of action, cf. e.g. Dreier, Horst, in: Dreier, Horst: Grundgesetz, Kommentar, vol. 1, 2nd ed., art. 2 para. 1 marginal note 17 f.

[13] Cf. also infra 13.1.2, at "A German Peculiarity (...)"

[14] Cf. e.g. BVerfGE 104, 337 (345 f.).

[15] Cf. e.g. Gundel, Jörg: Der grundrechtliche Status der Ausländer, in: Isensee, Josef; Kirchhof, Paul: Handbuch des Staatsrechts der Bundesrepublik Deutschland, vol. 9, 3rd ed. 2011, § 198, 843 (847) (noting less protection for non-Germans); practical example for lesser protection ibid. p. 890; for an in-depth analysis cf. Siehr, Angelika: Die Deutschengrundrechte des Grundgesetzes, Bürgerrechte im Spannungsfeld von Menschenrechtsidee und Staatsmitgliedschaft, 2001, 363 ff.

[16] Clear description in Manssen, Gerrit: Staatsrecht II, Grundrechte, 8th ed. 2011, 39 ff.

[17] On the highly debated structure of equality cf. e.g. Kischel, Uwe, in: Epping, Volker; Hillgruber, Christian: Beck'scher Online-Kommentar GG, 12th ed. 2011, art. 3 marginal note 14; Kischel, Uwe: Systembindung des Gesetzgebers und Gleichheitssatz, Archiv des öffentlichen Rechts 124 (1999), 174 (180 ff.) with further references.

Functions of Basic Rights

Basic rights are, according to a much cited description by the German Federal Constitutional Court (*Bundesverfassungsgericht*, BVerfG), "first of all, defensive rights of the citizen against the State".[18] Apart from this subjective function, there are several objective functions:[19] Basis rights may guarantee the very existence of legal institutions such as marriage, family, property, universities, civil service, or self-government of local communities, thus protecting these institutions against direct or indirect abolishment (e.g. through deprivation of meaningful legal content). Basic rights are also used as a means of interpreting other norms, and of informing all State powers in their activities.[20] Basic rights may also, under certain circumstances, oblige the State to protect the individual against infringements by *other* individuals (*Schutzpflichten*), and they may give the individual rights to demand benefits from the State (*Leistungspflichten*).[21] Finally, according to a theory that is still valid, but no longer a focus of attention, basic rights may also influence norms on organization and procedure.

Customary Constitutional Law and General Principles of Law

Customary law and general principles of law may, in any given legal order, form a body of non-codified constitutional law. In Germany, however, this is not the case. There is a very marginal debate about the possible existence of customary constitutional law;[22] the notion does not, however, play any role whatsoever in everyday constitutional debate or practice. General principles of law are not even considered to be a (formal) source of law in Germany.[23]

---

[18] BVerfGE 7, 198, 1st headnote: "in erster Linie Abwehrrechte des Bürger gegen den Staat".

[19] For an overview cf. e.g. Manssen, Gerrit: Staatsrecht II, Grundrechte, 8th ed. 2011, 14 ff.; for a closer analysis cf. e.g. Alexy, Robert: A theory of constitutional rights, 2002, 288 ff.; Alexy, Robert: Grundrechte als subjektive Rechte und als objektive Normen, Der Staat 29 (1990), 49 (passim).

[20] This later point is commonly described as basic rights building an objective order of values (objektive Wertordnung), cf. e.g. BVerfGE 7, 198 (205); a theory that is rejected by parts of the literature, cf. e.g. Goerlich, Helmut: Wertordnung und Grundgesetz- Kritik einer Argumentationsfigur des Bundesverfassungsgerichts, 1973, passim.

[21] International law has, much later, developed a similar scheme when distinguishing, in the area of human rights, the duties to respect, to protect, and to fulfill, cf. on these duties Klee, Kristina: Die progressive Verwirklichung wirtschaftlicher, sozialer und kultureller Menschenrechte, 2000, 101 ff. with further references.

[22] Cf. Tomuschat, Christian: Verfassungsgewohnheitsrecht?, Eine Untersuchung zum Staatsrecht der Bundesrepublik Deutschland, 1972, passim; Wolff, Heinrich Amadeus: Ungeschriebenes Verfassungsrecht unter dem Grundgesetz, 2000, 427 ff.

[23] On the difference between formal and material sources of law cf. e.g. Verdross, Alfred; Simma, Bruno: Universelles Völkerrecht, Theorie und Praxis, 3rd ed. 1984, 321.

The Catalogue of Basic Rights and Equivalent Rights

The codification technique used by the Grundgesetz is that of a catalogue in art. 1–19 GG. These articles contain, roughly, the following basic rights: human dignity (art. 1), general liberty of action, right to life, right to physical integrity, freedom of the person (art. 2), equality rights (art. 3), freedom of religion, freedom of conscience, conscientious objection (art. 4), freedom of opinion, freedom of information, freedom of the press, of film, and of broadcasting (art. 5 para. 1), freedom of arts, freedom of science (art. 5 para. 3), protection of marriage, family and children (art. 6), freedoms relating to school (art. 7), freedom of assembly (art. 8), freedom of association (art. 9), privacy of correspondence, mail and telecommunication (art. 10), freedom of movement (art. 11), freedom of occupation (art. 12), inviolability of the home (art. 13), guarantee of property and inheritance (art. 14), protection against expatriation and extradition (art. 16), right to asylum (art. 16a), right to petition (art. 17), right to legal remedies (art. 19 para. 4).

In addition, there are the rights equivalent to basic rights,[24] roughly: the right to resistance (art. 20 para. 4), equality with regard to citizenship and protection of traditional principles of civil service (art. 33), right to vote (art. 38), right to the judge provided by law (art. 101), right to a hearing, nulla poena sine lege, ne bis in idem (art. 103), rights concerning deprivation of liberty (incarceration) (art. 104).

A final category, that is easily overlooked, are special rights with regard to religion contained in art. 136–139, 141 of the Weimar Constitution of 1919, which are directly incorprated into the Grundgesetz by art. 140 GG. The codification technique used here is rather unique. It is due to the fact that the Parliamentary Council charged with drafting the Grundgesetz could not find a common ground when it came to regulating the relationship between church and State. Therefore, the deputies simply agreed to leave the question open and to refer to the former legal status under the Weimar Constitution. However, the Weimar articles where themselves the results of a compromise.[25] Maybe for that reason, and in spite of their sometimes clear wording, these articles have not attained any pronounced importance in the jurisprudence of the BVerfG. For instance, the court has ruled that the reservations to the freedom of religion contained in art. 136 of the Weimar Constitution are superimposed by the general provisions of art. 4 GG.[26]

13.1.2   The Limits of Codification (I): Non-codified Basic Rights

The Development of Unwritten Basic Rights

In spite of this rather long list of codified basic rights, the BVerfG and the German literature have developed some, if not many, additional basic rights. It should be

---

[24] Cf. supra 13.1.1, at "Basic Rights and Equivalent Rights"

[25] On the constitutional history of art. 140 GG cf. Morlok, Martin, in: Dreier, Horst: Grundgesetz, Kommentar, 2nd ed. 2008, vol. 3, art. 140 marginal notes 11 ff.

[26] Cf. BVerfGE 33, 23 (30 f.).

noted, however, that the exact delimitation between the extensive interpretation of an existing right[27] and the creation of a genuinely new right is often difficult and open to doubt.

The clearest example of an unwritten basic right is probably the so-called general personality right (*allgemeines Persönlichkeitsrecht*) which the BVerfG has developed through a joint reading of art. 1 para. 1 GG (human dignity) and art. 2 para. 1 GG (general liberty of action).[28] The court quite simply explained that to guarantee human dignity as the highest constituting principle, the narrow personal sphere of life and the basic conditions underlying it have to be secured. This, however, cannot be fully achieved by written basic rights alone. The necessity to go further, the Court continues, is especially evident with respect to modern developments and the new dangers for human personality that they entail.[29] The general personality right thus developed has been generally accepted by German jurists. This reveals a non-originalist approach to constitutional law in general,[30] which has sometimes been heavily criticized in small parts of the German literature.[31] When evaluating the non-originalist approach, two different situations should be distinguished: Firstly, if there is a change of facts, for instance the development of new technological possibilities to use or to endanger given freedoms, it must be considered the duty of the courts to apply existing law to the new circumstances which the legislature had not foreseen, thus creating new law.[32] If, however, there simply is a perceived change in general attitudes and values pertaining to certain freedoms, such change can only be considered to be clear and widespread enough to warrant judicial activity if it leads the relevant majority in the legislature to actually change text of the constitution. Otherwise, the democratic will of the people as expressed in the text of the constitution would be disregarded. This presupposes, of course, that—unlike in the United States—constitutional amendments are a viable political possibility and option, which clearly is the case in Germany.[33]

---

[27] Cf. infra 13.1.3

[28] Cf. the basic decision BVerfGE 54, 148 (153 f.); on this topic cf. e.g. Jarass, Hans D.: Die Entwicklung des allgemeinen Persönlichkeitsrechts in der Rechtsprechung des Bundesverfassungsgerichts, in: Erichsen, Hans-Uwe; Kollhosser, Helmut; Welp, Jürgen (eds.): Recht der Persönlichkeit, 1996, 89 (passim); Hufen, Friedhelm: Schutz der Persönlichkeit und Recht auf informationelle Selbstbestimmung, in Badura, Peter; Dreier, Horst (eds.): Festschrift 50 Jahre Bundesverfassungsgericht, vol. 2, 2001, 104 (108 ff.).

[29] BVerfGE 54, 148 (153).

[30] On originalism in the US cf. Chemerinsky, Erwin: Constitutional law, principles and policies, 4th ed. 2011, 17 ff.; against the assumption that originalism is an exclusively American phenomenon cf. Varol, Ozan O.: The origins and limits of originalism: A comparative study, Vanderbilt Journal of Transnational Law 44 (2011), 1239 (1242 ff.) referring to the Turkish example.

[31] Cf. notably Hillgruber, Christian: Ohne rechtes Maß? Eine Kritik der Rechtsprechung des Bundesverfassungsgerichts nach 60 Jahren, Juristenzeitung 2011, 861 (863 f.); cf. also Wolff, Heinrich Amadeus: Ungeschriebenes Verfassungsrecht unter dem Grundgesetz, 2000, 170 ff. (insisting that non-orginialst approches should label their results as unwritten constitutional law).

[32] Contra even in this situation Hillgruber, Christian: Ohne rechtes Maß? Eine Kritik der Rechtsprechung des Bundesverfassungsgerichts nach 60 Jahren, Juristenzeitung 2011, 861 (864).

[33] On constitutional amendments in Germany cf. infra 13.1.4, at "The Ongoing Codification"

A certain reluctant attitude towards unwritten basic rights can be discerned in the unusual structure of the general personality right: Unlike all other basic rights, it lacks a clearly defined area of protection. Instead, it is, in its very conception, an open right that can be and has been adapted to new technical or social developments. The application of the general personality right is casuistic, and there are different possibilities to systematically organize the existing jurisprudence.[34] This open character makes it superfluous to develop further unwritten basic rights in the general area of personality protection. Nevertheless, the disparity of the aspects covered by the general personality right is so great that certain of its aspects can and have been treated as unwritten basic rights of their own, for instance the right to informational self-determination (*informationelle Selbstbestimmung*),[35] or the right to confidentiality and integrity of systems of information technology (commonly called the computer basic right).[36]

A German Peculiarity: Necessity for Unwritten Basic Rights?

A major reason for the German reluctance to develop new basic rights can be found in the simple lack of a practical necessity to go to such lengths: art. 2 para. 1 GG works, in practice, as a catch-all basic right. Its area of protection is not restricted to specific circumstances but protects any action, any status, and any legal position of any person. In other words, art. 2 para. 1 GG is infringed whenever the State burdens any person with any disadvantage. In fact, the original proposal for the wording of this provision, changed later in the drafting process for purely esthetic reasons, read simply "Anybody can do or not do what he likes".[37] Thus, to the amazement of some foreign jurists, smoking drugs, getting drunk, having hetero- or homosexual sex, running naked, desecrating the flag, insulting others, or sitting in front of the TV all day long are all constitutionally protected acts so that any restrictions constitutionally require justification. This catch-all quality, however, is not all-encompassing, since not all situations that might require constitutional protection can be framed as a state infringement of a general liberty of action. For instance, the (mis-)representation of a person in public or the simple gathering of personal data neither forces a person to act nor does it inhibit him to do as he likes: it is here that the general personality right comes into play, this is the reason why it needed to be developed.

---

[34] Cf. e.g. Hufen, Friedhelm: Staatsrecht II, Grundrechte, 3rd ed. 2011, 176 ff. or Pieroth, Bodo; Schlink, Bernhard: Grundrechte, Staatsrecht II, 27th ed. 2011, 91 ff.

[35] This right allows anybody to determine himself when and inhowfar aspects of his personal life are to be revealed, inter alia in the area of data protection, cf. BVerfGE 65, 1 (42); for an (implicit) treatment as a basic right of its own cf. e.g. Hufen, Friedhelm: Staatsrecht II, Grundrechte, 3rd ed. 2011, 193 ff.

[36] Cf. BVerfGE 120, 274; for its (implicit) treatment as a basic right of its own cf. e.g. Bär, Wolfgang: Anmerkung zum Urteil des BVerfG v. 27.02.2008, 1 BvR 370/07, 1 BvR 595/07, Multimedia und Recht 2008, 325 (326).

[37] Cf. Mangoldt, Hermann v., in: Parlamentarischer Rat, Verhandlungen des Hauptausschusses, Bonn 1948/49, 42. Sitzung, 533;BVerfGE 6, 32 (36f.) ("Jeder kann tun und lassen was er will").

13.1.3   The Limits of Codification (II): Judicial Influence on Existing Basic Rights

Necessity and Development of Judicial Interpretation

Even in the vast and near-exhaustive sphere of codified basic rights, however, the importance of codification, i.e. of the written text of the constitution, is quite limited. Any written norm has only a limited capacity to predetermine the solution of legal issues. The all-important details of a norm's application are only determined through interpretation either by the literature or by the courts. In spite of the many debates in legal methodology, one point is beyond discussion today: law is not merely a logical process of applying norms to facts.[38] This is generally considered to be particularly true with respect to basic rights, due to their often very open and descriptive language.[39]

The actual meaning and content of basic rights is thus developed outside—although with some reference to—the written text of such rights. Any application requires interpretation. If art. 8 GG, for instance, protects the right of assembly, it is sufficiently clear that any ordinary political demonstration is protected. What, however, of a group of people simply gathering to stare at a traffic accident? What of a scientific congress or the once famous Love Parade in Berlin? The simple word "assembly" needs further interpretation to answer these questions.[40] The same holds true for any other basic right: Is gambling or drug-dealing an occupation in the sense of art. 12 GG, is Scientology a religion in the sense of art. 4 GG, are pension rights acquired within the public social security system property in the sense of art. 14 GG?—None of these questions can be solved by looking at the text of the constitution or the will of its founders alone.

The vast influence of literature and courts can be seen even more clearly with regard to the limits of basic rights. The few hints given, here, by the text of the Grundgesetz do not even scratch the surface of the entire body of law on this topic. Not only have limits been "found" even for those basic rights for which the Grundgesetz does not provide any limits. What is more, the entire structure of limits, and

---

[38] Cf. Alexy, Robert: Theorie der juristischen Argumentation, 1983, 17.

[39] Cf. Böckenförde, Ernst-Wolfgang: Grundrechtstheorie und Grundrechtsinterpretation, Neue Juristische Wochenschrift 1974, 1529, with an in-depth analysis of the major methodological schools in Germany, ibid. pp. 1530 ff. It should be noted, however, that the theoretical discussion on the interpretation of basic rights has always remained a rather sterile exercise with little direct influence on the works of other constitutional lawyers or courts. Cf. on this general peculiarity of German methodological discussions in law Esser, Josef: Vorverständnis und Methodenwahl in der Rechtsfindung, Rationalität der richterlichen Entscheidungspraxis, 1970, 7 ff., who remarked that legal practitioners tend to regards books on methodology with great respect, but to leave them in the bookshelves.

[40] On the answers cf. e.g. Schulze-Fielietz, Helmuth, in: Dreier, Horst: Grundgesetz, Kommentar, 2nd ed. 2004, art. 8 marginal notes 24 ff.; Hufen, Friedhelm: Staatsrecht II, Grundrechte, 3rd ed. 2011, 489.

in particular the ever-important principle of proportionality have been developed completely outside any codification.[41]

The judicial influence on existing basic rights discussed here cannot be clearly delimitated from the judicial creation of new basic rights discussed before. Both will always start with the text of one or more written basic rights, elaborating more or less new thoughts and aspects. Whether the result is called a new interpretation of an existing right or a new right based on the existing one, will often be a question of personal taste rather than a question of any legal relevance.

Judicial Interpretation Contra Constitutionem and Contra Legislatorem Constitutionis

Much of this may not be very surprising, since courts will out of necessity interpret norms, thus developing their contents and filling any possible normative gaps.[42] The German Constitutional Court has, however, gone well beyond a mere interpretation of norms and has, in certain cases, not hesitated to develop an interpretation contrary to the wording of the Grundgesetz and sometimes even contrary to the express will of its founders.

Examples of judicial interpretation contra constitutionem are not difficult to find. For instance, art. 12 para. 1 GG guarantees the freedom of occupation using the following words: "All Germans shall have the right freely to choose their occupation, their place of work and their place of training. The practice of an occupation or profession may be regulated by or pursuant to a statute." This seems rather clearly to indicate a difference between the right to choose and the right to practice; only the right to practice would be regulated "by or pursuant to a statute", and there would be no right to practice concerning the place of work and of training. None of this, however, is accepted by the BVerfG or by the majority of German writers. Quite on the contrary, freedom of occupation is considered to be a homogeneous right, comprising, without difference, the right to choose and the right to practice, both concerning occupation, place of work, and place of training, which are all subject to a uniform limit, i.e. that of "may be regulated by or pursuant to statute".[43] Similarly, art. 8 para. 1 GG guarantees the right "to assemble (. . .) without prior notification or permission". Nevertheless, the BVerfG has declared the general statutory duty to

---

[41] On limits to basic rights cf. e.g. Michael, Lothar; Morlok, Martin: Grundrechte, 2nd. ed. 2010, 267 ff.; Dreier, Horst, in: Dreier, Horst: Grundgesetz, Kommentar, vol. 1, 2nd. ed. 2004, Vorb. marginal notes 134 ff.

[42] For a very clear example of judicial activism in the field of basic rights and the possibility for the BVerfG to entirely change its own jurisprudence cf. BVerfGE 124, 300 (freedom of opinion for statements glorifying the Third Reich); on this decision Kischel, Uwe: La liberté d'opinion au défi du néonazisme—la culture juridique allemande évolue, Revue Française de Droit Constitutionnel (forthcoming).

[43] Cf. BVerfGE 7, 377 (401 ff.); in the literature cf. e.g. critically Wieland, Joachim, in: Dreier, Horst: Grundgesetz, Kommentar, vol. 1, 2nd ed. 2004, art. 12 marginal notes 62 ff.

notify the relevant authorities of the intent to assemble to be constitutional, requiring only slight exceptions for spontaneous assemblies.[44]

Occasionally, the BVerfG goes even further and introduces, through the back door, new contents to basic rights for which the 2/3-majority necessary for constitutional amendment could not be attained in the political process. For instance, it would decidedly be very difficult, on the political level, to insert a rule against discrimination based on sexual orientation into art. 3 para. 3 GG.[45] Nevertheless, the BVerfG has decided that a differentiation based on sexual orientation carries such weight that there must always be very strict judicial review of its possible justifications in any given case.[46] Nothing else would be achieved by actually inserting sexual orientation into art. 3 para. 3 GG;[47] the BVerfG has thus effected a change in constitutional law not only contra constitutionem but even contra legislatorem constitutionis.

13.1.4 The Ongoing Codification

Changing the Text of the Constitution

Requirements for and Frequency of Constitutional Amendments

Codification of constitutional law and of basic rights is not a singular historical incident, but rather an ongoing, if often slow process. A change in the text of the constitution is not even a rare or wholly unusual occurrence in Germany. The German constitution requires a 2/3-majority in parliament as well as a 2/3-majority in the Bundesrat, i.e. in the representation of the German Länder on the federal level, for any change of the constitution, art. 79 para. 2 GG. Politically, this prerequisite is fulfilled if the two major political parties in Germany, the Social Democrats and the Christian Democrats, agree. Out of the 58 laws amending the Grundgesetz that have been passed since 1949, seven have effected changes in the basic rights section of the GG.[48] An example of a major change has been the introduction of art. 16a GG, which regulates the right to asylum in a much stricter way than the former art. 16 GG. Art.

---

[44] Cf. BVerfGE 69, 315 (349 ff.); contra e.g. Höfling, Wolfram, in: Sachs, Michael, Grundgesetz, Kommentar, 5th ed. 2009, art. 8 marginal notes 57 f.

[45] On the unsuccessful attempt cf. Bundesrat-Drucksache 741/09, Bundesrat-Drucksache 741/1/09, Bundesrat-Drucksache 741/09(B)(neu).

[46] Cf. BVerfGE 24, 199 (219 f.).

[47] Cf. Hillgruber, Christan: Anmerkung zum Urteil des BVerfG v. 07.07.2009, 1BvR 1164/07, Juristenzeitung 2010, 41 (42 f.); Kischel, Uwe, in: Epping, Volker; Hillgruber, Christian:, Beck'scher Online-Kommentar, 12th ed. 2011, art. 3 marginal notes 42.2, 50a.1.

[48] Art. 1 Gesetz zur Ergänzung des Grundgesetzes of 19.03.1956 concerning art. 1, 12, 17a GG; art. 1 Siebzehntes Gesetz zur Änderung des Grundgesetzes of 24.06.1968 concerning art. 9, 10, 11, 12, 12a, 19 GG; art. 1 Gesetz zur Änderung des Grundgesetzes (Art. 16 und 18) of 28.06.1993 concerning art. 16, 16a, 18 GG; art. 1 Gesetz zur Änderung des Grundgesetzes (Art. 3, 20a, 28, 29, 72, 74, 75, 76, 77, 80, 87, 93, 118a und 125a) of 27.10.1994 concerning art. 3 GG; art. 1 Gesetz zur Änderung des Grundgesetzes (Art. 13) of 26.03.1998 concerning art. 13 GG; art. 1 Gesetz

16a GG is much longer and goes much more into detail than is usual for provisions in the basic rights section, mainly due to the fear of the legislature that the BVerfG might otherwise revert to its former jurisprudence and hold unconstitutional the changed provisions of the German law on asylum, which were passed simultaneously.[49]

Limiting Constitutional Amendment by Doctrinal Framework

Indeed, this fear was well-founded: In any area of law, a systematic approach to law—like the one that is typical for the German legal culture—limits the influence of the legislature. Over the years, legal doctrine forms an unwritten body of rules as well as a framework into which all written norms are inserted. The more detailed this doctrinal framework, the more difficult it becomes for the legislature to cause major changes. For the framework as such has been developed without the legislature and is, therefore, not likely to be changed—or changeable—by it. If, for instance, the legislature ever tried to abolish parts of the constitutional proportionality test, it would be very hard put to do so effectively. As a last resort, the courts might even insist that proportionality, as a central aspect of all basic rights and as a part of *Rechtsstaat* (rule of law), cannot be changed by any majority, due to the so-called eternity clause of art. 79 para. 3 GG.[50] A more probable example can be seen in art. 3 para. 2 sentence 2 GG which reads: "The State shall promote the actual implementation of equal rights for women and men, and take steps to eliminate disadvantages that now exist." This phrase, introduced in 1994, could easily be understood to enable the State to take positive action and, especially, to revert to quota based on sex in order to promote equality between men and women. Indeed, this was assuredly the intent of some of its supporters in parliament, although the legislative materials clearly point out that the legal discussion on this point was to be left open.[51] Nevertheless, the BVerfG read art. 3 para. 2 sentence 2 GG as merely clarifying a point that the BVerfG had already made earlier, i.e. that equality should be achieved in reality, that real equality should be achieved in the future.[52] Therefore, the new provision had practically no effect on the jurisprudence of German courts.

---

zur Änderung des Grundgesetzes (Art. 16) of 29.11.2000 concerning art. 16 GG; art. 1 Gesetz zur Änderung des Grundgesetzes (Art. 12a) of 19.12.2000 concerning art. 12a GG.

[49] On the history of art. 16a GG cf. e.g. Masing, Johannes, in: Dreier, Horst: Grundgesetz, Kommentar, vol. 1, 2nd ed. 2004, art. 16a marginal notes 9 ff.

[50] On this clause cf. infra 13.1.4, at "The Unchangeable Constitution"; on proportionality as part of the norms protected by this clause cf. Dreier, Horst, in: Dreier, Horst: Grundgesetz, Kommentar, vol. 2, 2nd ed. 2006, art. 79 para. 3 marginal note 53; Sachs, Michael, in: Sachs, Michael: Grundgesetz, Kommentar, 5th ed. 2009, art. 79 marginal note 78 with further references.

[51] Cf. Bundestag-Drucksache 12/6000, 49 f.

[52] Cf. BVerfGE 85, 191 (206 f.); cf. on this problem Kischel, Uwe, in: Epping, Volker; Hillgruber, Christian: Beck'scher Online-Kommentar, 12th ed. 2011, marginal notes 162 f., 175 ff.

The Unchangeable Constitution

The ongoing codification of basic rights finds its limits in art. 79 para. 3 GG: "Amendments to this Grundgesetz affecting (...) the principles laid down in articles 1 and 20 shall be inadmissible." Clearly, basic rights (mostly found *between* and not *in* art. 1 and 20 GG) are not generally and as such protected by this so-called eternity clause. Nevertheless, it is generally accepted that a core of basic rights is unchangeable, since this core is founded upon the principles of Rechtsstaat and democracy (art. 20 GG), and since art. 1 GG not only mentions human rights but in its para. 3 ("The following basic rights ...") presupposes the existence of at least some basic rights.[53]

13.1.5   Instruments of Protection

Judicial Protection

Judicial protection of basic rights in Germany is generally considered to be highly efficient. Indeed, there is no specific area in which this protection would be considered lacking or inadequate. Quite on the contrary, some writers regard the influence of the judiciary, and especially the BVerfG, on the legislative process and outcome as too great.[54]

The Federal Constitutional Court and its Procedures

A great variety of judicial procedures can be used in the BVerfG.[55] To give effect to basic rights, three procedures dominate: the abstract control of norms, the concrete control of norms, and, more than any other, the constitutional complaint.

Abstract Control of Norms

The abstract control of norms (art. 93 para. 1 no. 2 GG) allows the federal government, the government of a Land or 1/4 of the members of the Bundestag (the federal parliament) to challenge the constitutionality of any federal statute if they are convinced that the statute is unconstitutional and therefore null. This type of control is independent of any possible application of the norm (thus: abstract), although the statute must already have been promulgated. A preventive control of the constitutionality of norms, i.e. before promulgation, does not exist. The abstract control of

---

[53] Cf. Sachs, Michael, in: Sachs, Michael: Grundgesetz, Kommentar, 5th ed. 2009, art. 79 marginal note 57.

[54] Cf. e.g. Wieland, Joachim, in: Dreier, Horst: Grundgesetz, Kommentar, vol. 3, 2nd. ed. 2008, art. 93 marginal notes 32 f. with further references; on questions of a political nature cf. Schneider, Hans-Peter: Acht an der Macht! Das BVerfG als "Reparaturbetrieb" des Parlamentarismus?, Neue Juristische Wochenschrift 1999, 1303 (passim).

[55] Cf. the enumeration in § 13 of the Gesetz über das Bundesverfassungsgericht (BVerfGG).

norms is not used very frequently,[56] but once instituted it tends to be high-profile, ensuring, for instance, intensive coverage by the media.

Concrete Control of Norms

The concrete control of norms (art. 100 para. 1 GG) is a procedure that may be instituted by any German court before the BVerfG. The procedure is admissible if the lower court is convinced that a parliamentary statute which it needs to apply in order to decide the case is unconstitutional.

In other words, all German courts have the right and the duty to inquire whether any statute is unconstitutional, but they may not decide to disregard the statute or to declare it null; this is the exclusive province of the BVerfG.[57] The lower court will first determine whether the statute in question is absolutely necessary to decide the case. Only then will it proceed to a full legal inquiry into its constitutionality. If the lower court considers the statute constitutional or if it only has doubts about the constitutionality, this is the end of the matter and the statute will be applied. Only if the court is convinced of the unconstitutionality, it will stay its proceedings and, through an intermediate decision, bring the constitutional issue before the BVerfG. In this intermediate decision, the lower court is required to provide comprehensive reasons on two points: in how far the statute is necessary to decide the case; and why it is, in the opinion of the court, unconstitutional. Incomplete reasons on these two points are a typical case of inadmissibility.

It should be noted that this procedure is open to all courts; no court is required to receive the approval of any higher court before addressing the BVerfG. Statistically, the concrete control of norms is not rare. All judges are aware of this possibility, the total number of procedures being limited[58] mostly because judges, as trained jurists, will not easily come the conclusion that a statute is clearly unconstitutional and because, psychologically, the request for a decision by the BVerfG will usually stir a lot of attention among their brethren and thus tends to be handled with some restraint.

Constitutional Complaint

The constitutional complaint is by far the most common procedure before the BVerfG. In 2009, for instance, 6308 out of 6508 cases submitted to the BVerfG were constitutional complaints.[59] This procedure can be instituted by any person alleging that her

---

[56] E.g. in 2009 only two of the 6308 cases submitted to the BVerfG were abstract controls of norms; in 2010 among 6,422 cases there was no abstract control of norms, cf. <http://www.bundesverfassungsgericht.de/organisation/gb2010/A-II-2.html> (last accessed on Jan. 20, 2012).

[57] As an exception to this rule, statutes that have been passed before the Grundgesetz was promulgated may be declared void by any court, cf. BVerfGE 2, 124 (128); this exception, however, has been riddled with counter-exception, cf. BVerfGE 6, 55 (65), so that it plays hardly any role in practice; for a brief summery cf. BVerfGE 64, 217 (220 f.).

[58] In 2009, of the 6,508 cases submitted, 47 were concrete controls of norms; in 2010 among 6,422 cases were 19 concrete controls of norms, cf. <http://www.bundesverfassungsgericht.de/organisation/gb2010/A-II-2.html> (last accessed on Jan. 20, 2012).

[59] <http://www.bundesverfassungsgericht.de/organisation/gb2010/A-II-2.html> (last accessed on Jan. 20, 2012); in 2010, the respective figures were 6251 out of 6422, ibid.

basic rights or her rights equivalent to basic rights[60] have been violated by any act of public authority, i.c. by the legislative, executive or judicial branch of government.

The formal requirements are rather easy to fulfill. It is not necessary to use an attorney, and the complaint may be a simple written statement in any form (but no e-mail). Only if the complaint is directed against a court decision, it will, in practice, need to be accompanied by a copy of the decision to be admissible. The complaint must be made within four weeks after the act of public authority occurred; only for complaints against statutes, or if there is no legal action available against the act in other courts, the period is one year. The major filter to prevent a total overburdening of the BVerfG[61] are the requirements of exhaustion of legal remedies and of subsidiarity: Any legal remedies directly or indirectly available against the act of public power must be used and exhausted before a constitutional complaint is admissible.[62]

Additionally, a complaint directly against statutes is only admissible if the statute is self-executing, i.e. if there is, according to the wording of the statute or according to administrative usage, no further State action necessary for its application. This requirement relieves the burden of the BVerfG, but does not prevent any person from claiming her constitutional rights: If further action, e.g. an individual administrative decision, is necessary, the citizen is not legally burdened until this decision is actually taken. Once the decision is taken, however, the citizen can challenge it in the ordinary courts. If he wins, he is, again, not burdened. If he looses, he can, after exhausting all remedies, challenge the entire line of court decisions, the administrative decision, and the underlying statute by way of a constitutional complaint to the BVerfG. Indeed, this so-called indirect control of norms is the most common way of challenging statutes.

The Role of Other Courts

Interaction Between Constitutional Complaint and Concrete Control of Norms

From the point of view of the plaintiff, the constitutional complaint and the concrete control of norms are thus complementary: The usual course of action when a person believes her basic rights have been infringed by the government is to first institute procedures in the ordinary courts, since the constitutional complaint is inadmissible as long as not all national legal remedies have been exhausted. The ordinary court will not only look at the case on the statutory level, but will also consider any constitutional questions, including the constitutionality of any statute that must be

---

[60] On these equivalent rights cf. supra 13.1.1, at "Basic Rights and Equivalent Rights"

[61] On the problem of overburdening of the BVerfG in general cf. e.g. Kunze, Wolfgang, in: Umbach, Dieter C.; Clemens, Thomas; Dollinger, Franz-Wilhelm: Bundesverfassungsgerichtsgesetz, Mitarbeiterkommentar und Handbuch, 2nd. ed. 2005, vor para. 17 ff. marginal notes 32 ff.; Wahl, Rainer: Die Reformfrage, in: Badura, Peter; Dreier, Horst (eds.): Festschrift 50 Jahre Bundesverfassungsgericht, vol. 1, 2001, 475 ff.

[62] On these requirements and their exact delimitation cf. e.g. Hillgruber, Christian; Goos, Christoph: Verfassungsprozessrecht, 3rd 2011, 87 ff.

applied. If the court agrees with the plaintiff that the statute is unconstitutional, it will request a concrete control of norms by the BVerfG. In other words, the plaintiff will get the decision he wanted without having to exhaust all remedies. If the lower court does not agree with the plaintiff, he must challenge the final decision of this court, and will then have another chance to a concrete control of norms in the higher court, and so forth through all instances. If even the court of last instance does not request a concrete control of norms, the plaintiff can decide whether, in spite of the arguments of all court decisions, he still wishes to continue and raise a constitutional complaint, thus gaining his own direct access to the BVerfG.

Unconstitutionality of Non-Statutory Acts

It should be noted that statutes are by no means the only direct or indirect object of a constitutional complaint. Ordinances, individual administrative decisions or court decisions—to mention some important examples—may be unconstitutional and thus form the object of a constitutional complaint, although the statute on which they are based is clearly constitutional. In such cases, however, any court may and will declare the unconstitutionality of the non-statutory act; there is no exclusive right of the BVerfG to void an act for unconstitutionality if that act is not a statute.

Statutory Interpretation in Conformity with the Constitution

What is more, all courts have a duty to consider the constitution and its basic rights when interpreting any legal norm or when applying it to any given case. Often, this will already help the plaintiff to achieve the desired results. An important example of the influence of basic rights on the interpretation of norms is the so-called interpretation in conformity with the constitution (*verfassungskonforme Auslegung*): When a norm can be interpreted in several ways, some of which would be unconstitutional, the State and especially the courts are required to disregard any unconstitutional interpretation and apply the norm only in its constitutional reading. The practical effect of such interpretations may not only be very similar to that of a declaration of nullity. It may even go beyond it, since nullity might instigate the legislature to interfere, whereas interpretation may bring about results that the legislature, unlike the court, had not intended, but which gain immediate statutory power.[63] Moreover, this method of interpretation is by no means restricted to the BVerfG. On the contrary, all courts are constitutionally required to use it, and to thus avoid the result that a norm as such is unconstitutional. According to the BVerfG, a request for a concrete control of norms is not even admissible if the lower court has not considered, and with good

---

[63] On the criticism of this form of interpretation in the literature cf. Geis, Max-Emanuel: Die "Eilversammlung" als Bewährungsprobe verfassungskonformer Auslegung, Verfassungsrechtsprechung im Dilemma zwischen Auslegung und Rechtsschöpfung, Neue Zeitschrift für Verwaltungsrecht 1992, 1025 (1026 f.); Stern, Klaus, in: Stern, Klaus; Sachs, Michael: Das Staatsrecht der Bundesrepublik Deutschland, vol. III/2, 1994, § 90, 1147 ff.; Voßkuhle, Andreas: Theorie und Praxis der verfassungskonformen Auslegung von Gesetzen durch Fachgerichte, Kritische Bestandsaufnahme und Versuch einer Neubestimmung, Archiv des öffentlichen Rechts 125 (2000), 177.

reasons denied, the possibility of interpreting the relevant statute in conformity with the constitution.[64]

Overall Efficiency

The overall efficiency of the judicial protection of basic rights in Germany is generally considered to be excellent.[65] It would be a very rare occurrence, and would require some very special circumstances to find a situation where the State might reasonably be considered to have infringed basic rights, but where there is no action in ordinary courts or in the BVerfG available that might remedy the violation. One of the few examples that come to mind are inactivities of the legislature, where the plaintiff asks for a constitutional court decision requiring parliament to enact a statute protecting his rights in a certain situation.[66] The very reduced possibilities of such actions, however, are not so much due to procedural constraints, but rather to the limited scope of basic rights in this area: an omission of the legislature will, under most circumstances, not be considered to be a violation of a person's basic rights.[67]

The high efficiency of judicial protection is not, however, equivalent to a high rate of successful actions. In the important case of constitutional complaints, for instance, only 2.4 % of all complaints have turned out to be successful.[68] To German jurists, this low rate does not put the efficiency of constitutional complaints in doubt, but rather shows that the State does not, on a regular basis, violate basic rights, and that by no means all constitutional complaints are well-founded. In reality, a large part of constitutional complaints are clearly unfounded. The legislature has reacted to this by allowing the BVerfG to deal with complaints in smaller, so-called chambers of three justices, which may refuse a complaint without being required to give any reasons.[69] In fact, 65 % of all complaints are thus refused in a one-line decision,[70] a further 25 % do not contain any merits but include a few additional

---

[64] Cf. e.g. BVerfGE 85, 329 (333 f.).

[65] Cf. e.g. Bethge, Herbert, in: Maunz, Theodor; Schmidt-Bleibtreu, Bruno; Klein, Franz; Bethge, Herbert: Bundesverfassungsgerichtsgesetz, Kommentar, loose-leaf, vol. 2, § 90 marginal note 15.

[66] On this question cf. e.g. Gleixner, Werner: Die Normenerlaßklage, Der Anspruch auf Erlaß untergesetzlicher Normen und formeller Gesetze, 1993, 77 ff.; Schenke, Wolf-Rüdiger: Rechtsschutz gegen das Unterlassen von Rechtsnormen, Verwaltungs-Archiv 82 (1991), 307 (318 ff.).

[67] Cf. Hufen, Friedhelm: Staatsrecht II, Grundrechte, 3rd. ed. 2011, 53 ff.; Manssen, Gerrit: Staatsrecht II, Grundrechte, 8th ed. 2011, 15 ff.

[68] Average rate from 1951 to 2010, cf. Bundesverfassungsgericht—Aufgaben, Verfahren und Organisation, <http://www.bundesverfassungsgericht.de/organisation/gb2010/A-I-1.html> (last accessed on Jan. 20, 2012).

[69] On these chambers and their procedure cf. Graßhof, Karin, in: Maunz, Theodor; Schmidt-Bleibtreu, Bruno; Klein, Franz; Bethge, Herbert: Bundesverfassungsgerichtsgesetz, Kommentar, loose-leaf, vol. 2, § 93b marginal notes 1 ff., § 93d marginal notes 1 ff.

[70] Including temporary injunctions, cf. <http://www.bundesverfassungsgericht.de/organisation/gb-2010/A-III-2.html> (last accessed on Jan. 20, 2012).

words of explication inserted into the main sentence of the operative part of the decision (so-called *Tenorbegründung*).[71]

The Living Law: General Conscience of Basic Rights

The rather large number of constitutional complaint procedures instituted each year in the BVerfG already shows that there is no significant difference between law in the books and law in action in the area of German basic rights. Indeed, the figure is, statistically, an understatement, since by no means all "complaints" addressed by private persons to the BVerfG are officially registered as constitutional complaints. Rather, all such petitions to the court will first have to pass a little-known filter: If the paralegals employed at the court consider a petition to be clearly and without doubt inadmissible or unfounded, they will consider it to be simply an informal letter to the court. The petitioner will be informed of this assessment, along with a short explanation of the legal requirements for a constitutional complaint. This reply will also indicate that the petitioner may and should write back to the BVerfG if he nevertheless intends his original petition to be treated as a constitutional complaint.[72] Most petitioners do not insist. The amount of petitions that are never treated as a constitutional complaint easily equals that of formal complaints.

Germans thus tend to place great trust in their constitutional court as an effective means of protecting their basic rights. In October 2011, a survey revealed that 80 % of all Germans trusted the BVerfG, a rate that was only surpassed by trust in the police (89 %).[73] This also implies that the institution of the BVerfG and the effective existence of basic rights is very well known to ordinary German citizens. "Going to Karlsruhe" (the seat of the BVerfG) has become a standard phrase in the German language to describe that someone will fight for his rights up to the highest court. Lawyers are no less aware of basic rights and the procedures available to protect them. Unlike the situation in some other jurisdictions, it is perfectly normal for a German attorney to raise the protection of basic rights in an ordinary lawsuit when appropriate, and for a German judge, even at a lower court, to consider constitutional issues in his decisions. The German Grundgesetz has thus turned out to be a living and very lively legal instrument.

---

[71] Including temporary injunctions, cf. <http://www.bundesverfassungsgericht.de/organisation/gb-2010/A-III-2.html> (last accessed on Jan. 20, 2012); a Tenorbegründung will often simply refer to the reasons mentioned in the merits of the judgment that is challenged.

[72] On the procedure known as the general register (Allgemeines Register), cf. Benda, Ernst; Klein, Eckart: Verfassungsprozeßrecht, 2nd. ed. 2001, 72 f.

[73] Cf. GPRA Vertrauensindex, Oktober 2011, <http://prreport.de/home/gpra-vertrauensindex/oktober-2011/?L=0%25252F> (last accessed on Jan. 20, 2012); by comparison, only 43 % trusted the churches, only 16 % trusted political parties.

13.2   The Influence of International Human Rights

13.2.1   International Law in the German Hierarchy of Norms

The Formal Hierarchy

The rank of international law within the German legal order cannot be reduced to one of the well-known theories commonly associated with monism or dualism.[74] In practice, the Grundgesetz differentiates between treaties on the one hand, and customary law and general principles of law on the other hand. For treaties, art. 59 para. 2 GG requires ratification by a so-called statute of approval (*Zustimmungsgesetz*), which orders the treaty to be applied internally (*Rechtsanwendungsbefehl*). The rank of the treaty is the same as the rank of this order. In practice, therefore, nearly all treaties have the internal rank of an ordinary federal statute.[75] Art. 25 GG, on the other hand, stipulates that "general rules of public international law" rank above federal statutes. In spite of this unusual terminology and some debate, it is today widely accepted that this notion of "general rules" refers to customary international law as well as general principles of law.[76] When the German constitution ranks both above federal statutes, it does not, however, make any explicit statement as to their rank vis-à-vis the Grundgesetz. Constitutional history can even be viewed as pointing towards a rank above the constitution.[77] Nevertheless, the BVerfG has, early in its history and without any particular explanation, decided that the "general rules" rank below the constitution, thus opening up a new, intermediate level in the German hierarchy of norms.[78] The majority of the German literature has followed this result,[79] arguing

---

[74] For a short overview of the major trends within these theories cf. Kischel, Uwe: State Contracts, Völker-, schieds- und internationalprivatrechtliche Aspekte des anwendbaren Rechts, 1992, 295 ff.; for another theoretical approach, i.e. the Transformationslehre and the Vollzugslehre (which concern the question whether nationally applicable international law remains international law or is transformed into national law) cf. e.g. Becker, Florian: Völkerrechtliche Verträge und parlamentarische Gesetzgebungskompetenz, Neue Zeitschrift des Verwaltungsrecht 2005, 289 (289 ff.); Schweitzer, Michael: Staatsrecht III, Staatsrecht, Völkerrecht, Europarecht, 10th ed. 2010, 168 ff.

[75] On rare occasions, a treaty will not require a federal Zustimmungsgesetz either because its contents touch on subject matters that fall under the jurisdiction of the German Länder, or because they are considered to be mere administrative agreements. In such cases, the rule remains that their rank will be decided by the rank of the respective application order (Rechtsanwendungsbefehl), which could for instance be a Länder statute that ranks below all federal law. On these questions with very minor practical importance cf. Sauer, Heiko: Staatsrecht III, Auswärtige Gewalt, Bezüge des Grundgesetzes zu Völker- und Europarecht, 2011, 70 f.

[76] Cf. only BVerfGE 96, 68 (86).

[77] Cf. Koenig, Christian, in: Mangoldt, Hermann v.; Klein, Friedrich; Starck, Christian: Kommentar zum Grundgesetz, vol. 2, 6th ed. 2010, art. 25 marginal note 52.

[78] Cf. BVerfGE 6, 309 (363); 111, 307 (318).

[79] Cf. e.g. Heinegg, Wolff Heintschel v., in: Epping, Volker; Hillgruber, Christian: Beck'scher Online-Kommentar GG, 12th ed. 2011, art. 25, marginal note 27; Kunig, Philip: Völkerrecht und staatliches Recht, in: Graf Vitzthum, Wolfgang (ed.): Völkerrecht, 5th ed. 2010, 87 (134 f.); on the

for instance that the wording of art. 25 GG only mentions statutes ("*Gesetze*") which does not usually include the constitution, that a constitution cannot provide other norms with a rank higher than its own, or that the list of legal principles which cannot be altered even by constitutional amendment (art. 79 para. 3 GG) does not mention any international law. The intermediate rank of customary international law also applies to ius cogens—for which a core of human rights is often considered an example—although a smaller part of the literature would like to transfer the higher rank of ius cogens within the system of international law into German law, thus giving ius cogens the same rank as the constitution or even place it above.[80]

The "Friendliness" of the German Constitution Towards Public International Law

These details do not, however, fully grasp the relationship between the Grundgesetz and public international law. They are, today, often viewed as emanations of a principle underlying the entire German constitutional order, i.e. the principle of "friendliness" towards public international law (*Völkerrechtsfreundlichkeit*).[81] This principle expresses the openness of the Grundgesetz towards international cooperation and integration as evidenced not only in art. 25, 59 GG, but also in art. 23, 24 para. 1, 2 GG (allowing the transfer of sovereign rights to international organizations in general and to the European Union in particular), in art. 24 para. 3 GG (on the participation in systems for the peaceful settlement of international disputes), and in art. 26 GG (declaring activities against peace, especially a war of aggression, to be unconstitutional). On the other hand, the BVerfG points out that *Völkerrechtsfreundlichkeit* does not mean that Germany gives up control or surrenders the sovereign right to have the last word.[82] It is easy to imagine that the exact delimitation between these open and restrictive aspects gives rise to a great amount

---

doctrinal debates surrounding this question cf. Koenig, Christian, in: Mangoldt, Hermann v.; Klein, Friedrich; Starck, Christian: Kommentar zum Grundgesetz, 6th. ed. 2010, art. 25 marginal notes 50 ff.

[80] For a supraconstitutional rank e.g. Pernice, Ingolf, in: Dreier, Horst: Grundgesetz, Kommentar, vol. 2, 2nd ed. 2006, art. 25 marginal note 25; for a constitutional rank (of all general rules of public international law) Koenig, Christian, in: Mangolt, Hermann v.; Klein, Friedrich; Starck, Christian: Kommentar zum Grundgesetz, 6th ed. 2010, art. 25 marginal note 55; for a constitutional rank (only of ius cogens) Doehring, Karl: Das Friedensgebot des Grundgesetzes, in: Isensee, Josef; Kirchhof, Paul: Handbuch des Staatsrechts, vol. 7, 1992, § 178, 687 (699); contra e.g. Heinegg, Wolff Heintschel v., in: Epping, Volker; Hillgruber, Christian: Beck'scher Online-Kommentar, 12th ed. 2011, art. 25 marginal note 27; Kunig, Philip: Völkerrecht und staatliches Recht, in: Graf Vitzthum, Wolfgang: Völkerrecht, 5th ed. 2010, 87 (135).

[81] For a short description of the concept cf. BVerfGE 111, 307 (317 ff.).

[82] Critically on this last word Richter, Dagmar: Völkerrechtsfreundlichkeit in der Rechtsprechung des Bundesverfassungsgerichts—Die unfreundliche Erlaubnis zum Bruch völkerrechtlicher Verträge, in: Giegerich, Thomas (ed.): Der "offene Verfassungsstaat" des Grundgesetzes nach 60 Jahren, 2010, 159 (163 ff.).

of debate in Germany.[83] Thus, *Völkerrechtsfreundlichkeit* is not, in effect, a clearly defined legal principle with results that are, at least to some extent, determinable, but rather a label[84] that covers a wide range of debatable and debated issues.[85]

There is, however, one generally accepted legal requirement that will mostly be viewed as a direct result of *Völkerrechtsfreundlichkeit*: All German law is to be interpreted in a way that best ensures its compatibility with Germany's international law obligations.[86] This rule of interpretation, which applies to all international obligations and, therefore, also to treaties, clearly dampens the potential effect of a strict application of the hierarchy of norms. In other words, a later German statute will not simply override a prior treaty. Rather, judges and other jurists will be obliged to find a solution in conformity with the treaty by creatively interpreting the statute in the light of international law. In practice as well as in the literature, major problems[87] with this rule have only appeared in the context of the European Convention on Human Rights, which is also the context in which most of the decisions and debates on this principle of interpretation are placed.

---

[83] Cf. e.g. Fastenrath, Ulrich: Souveräne Gesetzesinterpretation—Zum Staatsbild des Bundesverfassungsgerichts (Zweiter Senat), in: Giegerich, Thomas (ed.): Der "offene Verfassungsstaat" des Grundgesetzes nach 60 Jahren, 2010, 295 (301 ff.); Schorkopf, Frank: Völkerrechtsfreundlichkeit und -skepsis in der Rechtsprechung des Bundesverfassungsgerichts, in: Giegerich, Thomas (ed.): Der "offene Verfassungsstaat" des Grundgesetzes nach 60 Jahren, 2010, 131 (142 ff.); Hillgruber, Christian: Der Nationalstaat in der überstaatlichen Verflechtung, in: Isensee, Josef; Kirchhof, Paul: Handbuch des Staatsrechts der Bundesrepublik Deutschland, vol. 2, 3rd ed. 2004, § 32, 929 (980 ff.); Gröpl, Christoph: Staatsrecht I, Staatsgrundlagen, Staatsorganisation, 3rd ed. 2011, 197 ff.; Sauer, Heiko: Die neue Schlagkraft der gemeineuropäischen Grundrechtsjudikatur, Zur Bindung deutscher Gerichte an die Entscheidung des Europäischen erichtshofs für Menschenrechte, Zeitschrift für ausländisches öffentliches Recht und Völkerrecht 65 (2005), 35 (46 ff.).

[84] On the debatable exact status of Völkerrechtsfreundlichkeit cf. e.g. Schorkopf, Frank: Völkerrechtsfreundlichkeit und -skepsis in der Rechtsprechung des Bundesverfassungsgerichts, in: Giegerich, Thomas (ed.): Der "offene Verfassungsstaat" des Grundgesetzes nach 60 Jahren, 2010, 131 (151 ff.); Payandeh, Mehrdad: Völkerrechtsfreundlichkeit als Verfassungsprinzip, Ein Beitrag des Grundgesetzes zur Einheit von Völkerrecht und nationalem Recht, Jahrbuch des öffentlichen Rechts der Gegenwart neue Folge 57 (2009), 465 (465 ff.).

[85] Cf. the detailed descriptions of the diverse problems through individual articles by Andreas Paulus, Felix Arndt, Susanne Wasum-Rainer, Frank Schorkopf, Dagmar Richter and Alexander Proelß in Giegerich, Thomas (ed.): Der "offene Verfassungsstaat" des Grundgesetzes nach 60 Jahren, 2010, 73–193.

[86] Cf. BVerfG, 1st Chamber of the Second Senate, 2. BvR 1526/04, Neue Zeitschrift für Verwaltungsrecht-Rechtsprechungs-Report 2007, 266 (267 f.); Schorkopf, Frank: Völkerrechtsfreundlichkeit und -skepsis in der Rechtsprechung des Bundesverfassungsgerichts, in: Giegerich, Thomas (ed.): Der "offene Verfassungsstaat" des Grundgesetzes nach 60 Jahren, 2010, 131 (150); Sauer, Heiko: Staatsrecht III, Auswärtige Gewalt, Bezüge des Grundgesetzes zu Völker- und Europarecht, 2011, 84.

[87] On the rare examples of German statutes that are not successfully interpreted in this way cf. the examples on international tax law given by Vogel, Klaus: Wortbruch im Verfassungsrecht, Mit einer Bemerkung zum Verhältnis zwischen Bundesverfassungsgericht und demokratischem Gesetzgeber, Juristenzeitung 1997, 161 (162).

13.2.2 The European Convention on Human Rights

The Convention in the Hierarchy of Norms

The European Convention on Human Rights (Convention) is a treaty and, therefore, enjoys the rank of a federal statute. Nevertheless, the principle of *Völkerrechts-freundlichkeit*[88] applies with special emphasis:[89]

The Basic Setting: Importance, but not Precedence of the Convention

Thus, *statutes* need to be interpreted in a way compatible with the Convention since it is to be assumed that the legislature intended to act in conformity with its international obligations.[90] The limits of this interpretation would be reached if parliament made it clear that it positively wanted to infringe the Convention. In practice, this has never happened and is generally considered to be highly unlikely.[91] Furthermore, even when interpreting and applying not statutes but basic rights of the German *constitution*, courts will take the Convention into consideration, based on art. 1 para. 2 GG which stipulates that the German people positively acknowledges human rights as the basis for any human community.[92] For purposes of interpreting the constitution (or statutes), the Convention will not be used in an abstract fashion, but rather in the interpretation that it has itself received by the European Court of Human Rights (ECHR).[93] Decisions of the ECHR, therefore, gain importance well beyond their legal force in the particular case that was decided. They are afforded, in the words of the BVerfG "at least factually, prejudicial effect".[94] In practice, this does not mean,

---

[88] Cf. supra 13.2.1, at "The "Friendliness" (...) Towards Public International Law"

[89] For a clear description of the following cf. Sauer, Heiko: Staatsrecht III, Auswärtige Gewalt, Bezüge des Grundgesetzes zu Völker- und Europarecht, 2011, 93 ff.; the most recent decision by the BVerfG, summing up the legal principles relevant here, is BVerfG, decision of May 4, 2011, 2 BvR 2365/09, marginal notes 86 ff., <http://www.bundesverfassungsgericht.de/entscheidungen/rs20110504_2bvr236509.html> (last accessd on Jan. 20, 2012); cf. also Giegerich, Thomas: Wirkung und Rang der EMRK in den Rechtsordnungen der Mitgliedstaaten, in: Grote, Rainer; Marauhn, Thilo: EMRK/GG, Konkordanzkommentar zum europäischen und deutschen Grundrechtsschutz, 2006, Chap. 2, 61 (81 ff.); Grabenwarter, Christoph: Nationale Grundrechte und Rechte der Europäischen Menschenrechtskonvention, in: Merten, Detlef; Papier, Hans-Jürgen: Handbuch der Grundrechte in Deutschland und Europa, vol. VI/2, 2009, § 169, 33 (39 ff.).

[90] Cf. BVerfGE 74, 358 (370).

[91] Cf. e.g. Giegerich, Thomas: Wirkung und Rang der EMRK in den Rechtsordnungen der Mitgliedstaaten, in: Grote, Rainer; Marauhn, Thilo: EMRK/GG, Konkordanzkommentar zum europäischen und deutschen Grundrechtsschutz, 2006, Chap. 2, 61 (84 f.).

[92] BVerfG, decision of May 4, 2011, 2 BvR 2365/09, marginal note 90, <http://www.bundesverfassungsgericht.de/entscheidungen/rs20110504_2bvr236509.html> (last accessed on Jan. 20, 2012).

[93] Cf. BVerfGE 74, 358 (370).

[94] BVerfG, decision of May 4, 2011, 2 BvR 2365/09, marginal note 89 ("zumindest faktischen Präzedenzwirkung"), <http://www.bundesverfassungsgericht.de/entscheidungen/rs-20110504_2bvr23-6509.html> (last accessed on Jan. 20, 2012).

however, that the BVerfG will on any regular basis check its own jurisprudence in the area of basic rights against the jurisprudence of the ECHR. Quite on the contrary, this remains a rare occurrence and happens only in cases where the relevance of ECHR decisions is evident and has been raised by a party.

The rule of interpretation in conformity with the Convention does not imply that the Convention simply takes precedence over German law.[95] On the contrary, there are several qualifications and limits: Firstly, the possibility to interpret basic rights as well as statutes in the light of the Convention cannot go beyond the sphere of what could be considered an acceptable interpretation in accordance with recognized methods.[96] Secondly, the BVerfG points out that taking the Convention into consideration does not imply a schematically parallel interpretation of equivalent provisions in the Grundgesetz, since the Convention is only interested in the final results being in conformity with its requirements, not in the exact way such results are reached. Rather, the different context needs to be considered so that the contents of the Convention have to be adapted to the German legal environment. This is especially true, the BVerfG continues, since the German context—either on the constitutional or on the statutory level—will regularly be characterized by a developed systematic approach with its own categories and terminology; courts will always need to try and take special care not to disrupt the relevant German system. For instance, instead of integrating or adopting typical legal notions used by the ECHR, the BVerfG might simply integrate the value judgments that lie behind such notions when applying the principle of proportionality that forms an integral part of basic rights.[97] Thirdly, the Convention must not lead to a weakening of the protection afforded by German basic rights. At first glance, this last limit poses little problems since art. 53 of the Convention itself excludes such an effect.[98] A second glance, however, reveals that only the very simple situation in which an individual defends his rights against the State can be solved this easily.

The Problem of Multipolar Relationships

In many other cases, the basic rights of two or more persons have to be weighed against each other. In such multipolar relationships, there is, by definition, no solution that better or worse protects individual rights; rather, any alternative solution will always burden one party more while burdening the other less.[99] A well known

---

[95] For German statutes cf. the unambiguous statement in BVerfGE 111, 307 (329).

[96] BVerfGE 111, 307 (329); BVerfG, decision of May 4, 2011, 2 BvR 2365/09, marginal note 93, <http://www.bundesverfassungsgericht.de/entscheidungen/rs20110504_2bvr236509.html> (last accessed on Jan. 20, 2012).

[97] On all this BVerfG, decision of May 4, 2011, 2 BvR 2365/09, marginal notes 91 f., 94, <http://www.bundesverfassungsgericht.de/entscheidungen/rs20110504_2bvr236509.html> (last accessed on Jan. 20, 2012).

[98] Cf. BVerfGE 74, 358 (370).

[99] BVerfG, decision of May 4, 2011, 2 BvR 2365/09, marginal note 93, <http://www. bundesverfassungsgericht.de/entscheidungen/rs20110504_2bvr236509.html> (last accessed on Jan. 20, 2012).

example is the case of the princess Caroline of Monaco who fought against the publication of photos taken of her private life by the German press.[100] The basic rights conflict was thus between the freedom of the press on the one hand, and the general personality rights of the princess on the other hand. Broadly speaking, German courts, with the final support of the BVerfG, decided in favor of the freedom of the press. Upon an application by the princess, however, the ECHR came to a different conclusion and decided in favor of her personality rights.[101] Here, art. 53 of the Convention does not help, since the European decision was strengthening the freedom of the press, but at the same time weakening the personality rights of the princess.

German courts, here, do not accept a simple subjugation of German constitutional law under the Convention and relevant European case law. The BVerfG even talks of a barrier to the reception of Convention rights.[102] This is probably due to the extreme importance placed by Germans on their national basic rights, which, to them, seem to be rather the cure than the illness, rather something to export abroad than to import from elsewhere. The basic rights guaranteed by the Grundgesetz are an integral part of their national identity, which Germans would be hard put to loose or to place under an outside authority. Moreover, basic rights are often formed and developed under very specific national conditions, which are not always shared by other European countries. Thus, a Justice at the German Constitutional Court recently pointed out that liberties like the freedom of religion, the right to conscientious objection, the very strong protection of the freedoms of opinion, of the press and of broadcasting, the freedom of assembly and the freedom to form labor associations are all the consequences of a very painful process of learning in Germany, the results of which should not be thrown overboard in a European euphoria simply because other States did not have problems in these areas or solved them in a different way.[103] The German legal literature is intensively debating possible alternative solutions to the problem of multipolar relationships. Solutions are broadly seen in an ongoing dialogue between the two courts[104] and more specifically in a wider margin of appreciation granted by the ECHR to the Member States when solving the conflict between different basic rights in a multipolar relationship, thus determining a mere corridor of acceptable solutions within which the national courts are at liberty to reach their own conclusions.[105]

---

[100] Cf. e.g. Sauer, Heiko: Staatsrecht III, Auswärtige Gewalt, Bezüge des Grundgesetzes zu Völker- und Europarecht, 2011, 98 ff.

[101] Cf. BVerfGE 101, 361; ECHR, Caroline von Monaco v. Germany (59320/00), decision of June 24, 2004.

[102] BVerfG, decision of May 4, 2011, 2 BvR 2365/09, marginal note 93, <http://www.bundesve­rfassungsgericht.de/entscheidungen/rs20110504_2bvr236509.html> (last accessed on Jan. 20, 2012).

[103] Kirchhof, Ferdinand: Grundrechtsschutz durch europäische und nationale Gerichte, Neue Juristische Wochenschrift 2011, 3681 (3682).

[104] Cf. Kirchhof, Ferdinand: Grundrechtsschutz durch europäische und nationale Gerichte, Neue Juristische Wochenschrift 2011, 3681 (3682 f.).

[105] Cf. e.g. Hoffmann-Riem, Wolfgang: Kontrolldichte und Kontrollfolgen beim nationalen und europäischen Schutz von Freiheitsrechten in mehrpoligen Rechtsverhältnissen—Aus der Sicht des

The Implementation of Specific ECHR Judgments

When it comes to the effects of a specific judgment of the ECHR, declaring the decision of a German Court to violate the Convention, on that very decision, one of the main problems used to be the legal finality (*Rechtskraft*) of German decisions of last instance: Such decisions could not be overturned, so that the payment of damages was the only possible solution, which, in turn, was not always feasible or sufficient. Germany solved this problem in 2006 by adding this situation to the very restrictive lists of possible grounds for re-opening a court procedure (cf. e.g. § 580 No. 8 ZPO, § 359 No. 6 StPO, § 153 para. 1 VwGO). For the BVerfG, the same result has been reached, in 2011, not by a legislative change in its rules of procedure but by a new decision of the court itself that allows complainants to question the constitutionality of a statute even though the BVerfG has already declared this very statute to be constitutional, on the condition that a new relevant decision of the European Court of Justice has been rendered.[106]

The German court that is called to re-decide the case on account of an intervening ruling of the ECHR will have to consider that ruling carefully, but will not automatically and without exception have to follow it. Rather, the rules on the general relationship between the Convention and German law, as described above, apply. This general rule, was laid down in the landmark decision Görgülü,[107] in which Mr. Görgülü, father of a child born out of wedlock and given up for adoption by the mother, had unsuccessfully sought custody and a right of access in German courts, including the BVerfG, than gained a judgment by the ECHR in his favor, but lost again in the court of second instance in Germany. The ensuing (second) decision of the BVerfG has been heavily criticized by many German authors for not giving unquestioning and full effect to those judgments of the ECHR that directly declare a German court decision to be contrary to the Convention.[108] Nevertheless, it should be noted that the BVerfG held that, in the case of Mr. Görgülü, the relevant German court of second instance had *not* sufficiently taken the decision of the ECHR into consideration.[109] Moreover, when the entire case was finally decided after the second

---

Bundesverfassungsgerichts, Europäische Grundrechte Zeitschrift 2006, 492 (496 f.); Sauer, Heiko: Staatsrecht III, Auswärtige Gewalt, Bezüge des Grundgesetzes zu Völker- und Europarecht, 2011, 99 f.

[106] BVerfG, decision of May 4, 2011, 2 BvR 2365/09, marginal notes 81 f., <http://www.bundesverfassungsgericht.de/entscheidungen/rs20110504_2bvr236509.html> (last accessed on Jan. 20, 2012).

[107] BVerfGE 111, 307 (331).

[108] Cf. e.g. Cremer, Hans-Joachim: Zur Bindungswirkung von EGMR-Urteilen—Anmerkung zum Görgülü-Beschluss des BVerfG vom 14.10.2004, EuGRZ 2004, 741, Europäische Grundrechte Zeitschrift 2004, 683 (693 ff.); Klein, Eckart: Anmerkung zum Urteil des BverfG v. 14.10.2004, 2 BvR 1481/04, Juristenzeitung 2004, 1176 (1177 f.); Bergmann, Jan: Diener dreier Herren?—Der Instanzrichter zwischen BVerfG, EuGH und EGMR, Europarecht 2006, 101 (107 f.); Breuer, Marten: Karlsruhe und die Gretchenfrage: Wie hast du's mit Straßburg?, Neue Zeitschrift für Verwaltungsrecht 2005, 412 (413 f.).

[109] Cf. BVerfGE 111, 307 (330 ff.).

decision of the BVerfG, the complainant Görgülü received what he had fought for and to what, according to the ECHR, he had a right.[110]

Procedurally, since the Convention does not have constitutional status in Germany, it is not possible to base a constitutional complaint to the BVerfG directly on an infringement of Convention rights. Nevertheless, the BVerfG has decided that a constitutional complaint must at least be possible if a German state institution, especially a court, has not taken a relevant decision of the ECHR into consideration.[111] The language of the court on this issue is, however, quite loose, so that the exact details and limits of this possibility remain to be seen.[112]

Criticism in the Literature

There is probably not a single aspect of the relationship between Convention and Grundgesetz that has not been extensively criticized in the German literature. While some authors support at least the general tendencies of the BVerfG, others demand a more open and receptive attitude towards the Convention and the decisions of the ECHR.[113] The entire issue is also intrinsically linked to the debate about the general role of international law within the German legal order, since the Convention—in spite of its very specific character—is frequently used as the main example to discuss the role of treaties in Germany. Often, it is difficult or even impossible to determine which statements, in the literature as well as in judicial decisions, apply to international law or treaties in general and which are specifically adapted to the situation of the Convention.

The most basic question, however, remains if the Convention really ranks no higher than a federal statute. Here, German authors have developed a whole range of alternative solutions:[114] the Convention as an international institution with sovereign rights in the sense of art. 24 para. 1 GG; Convention rights as general rules of public international law in the sense of art. 25 GG, as part of the principle of *Rechtsstaat* (rule of law), or as a minimum standard for any German basic rights; and the use of art. 1 para. 2 GG as a stronger argument for a special constitutional role of the Convention. None of these propositions have, however, managed to convince German courts.

---

[110] This is particularly pointed out by Schorkopf, Frank: Völkerrechtsfreundlichkeit und -skepsis in der Rechtsprechung des Bundesverfassungsgerichts, in: Giegerich, Thomas (ed.): Der "offene Verfassungsstaat" des Grundgesetzes nach 60 Jahren, 2010, 131 (144).

[111] BVerfGE 111, 307 (317, 329 f.).

[112] Cf. e.g. Heckötter, Ulrike: Die Bedeutung der Europäischen Menschenrechtskonvention und der Rechtsprechung des EGMR für die deutschen Gerichte, 2007, 272 ff.; Schlaich, Klaus; Korioth, Stefan: Das Bundesverfassungsgericht, Stellung, Verfahren, Entscheidungen, 8th ed. 2010, 237 ff.; Sauer, Heiko: Staatsrechts III, Auswärtige Gewalt, Bezüge des Grundgesetzes zu Völker- und Europarecht, 2011, 96 ff.

[113] Cf. e.g. the description in Grabenwarter, Christoph: Nationale Grundrechte und Rechte der Europäischen Menschenrechtskonvention, in: Handbuch der Grundrechte in Deutschland und Europa, vol. VI/2, 2009, § 169, 33 (passim); Ruffert, Matthias: Die Europäische Menschenrechtskonvention und innerstaatliches Recht, Europäische Grundrechte Zeitschrift 2007, 245 (passim).

[114] Cf. the detailed report by Giegerich, Thomas: Wirkung und Rang der EMRK in den Rechtsordnungen der Mitgliedstaaten, in: Grote, Rainer; Marauhn, Thilo: EMRK/GG, Konkordanzkommentar zum europäischen und deutschen Grundrechtsschutz, 2006, Chap. 2, 61 (84 ff.) with further references.

13.2.3 Fundamental Rights of the European Union: The Relationship Between EU Law and German Constitutional Law

The relationship between EU law and German constitutional law in the specific area[115] of basic rights is a long and often told story.[116] It has been the first, and remains one of the most important points of conflict between Germany and the BVerfG on one hand, and the EU and the ECJ on the other. In more recent years, the relevant discussions have somewhat quieted down, probably because of the ongoing, unofficial dialogue between the two courts, and because all participants have realized that there is, in practice, very little chance that the conflict will ever break out openly in a concrete case.

Development of the Case Law: From *So-long-as* to *Lisbon*

In the decision So-long-as I (*Solange I*), the BVerfG in 1974 decided that EU-law[117] was not to interfere with the basic rights part of the Grundgesetz. As long as the EU did not have a catalogue of basic rights equivalent to that of the Grundgesetz, the BVerfG would review the compatibility of EU-law with German basic rights.[118] In 1986, the decision So-long-as II (*Solange II*) reversed this situation: The BVerfG accepted that the EU and in particular the ECJ was generally granting an effective protection of basic rights, which was in essence equivalent to the protection afforded under the Grundgesetz. As long as this remains the case, the BVerfG would no longer review the conformity of secondary EU-law as applied by German authorities with German basic rights.[119] The two decisions thus have a different outcome, but are based on the same basic assumption: The EU has to guarantee a protection of basic rights that is in essence equivalent to that of the Grundgesetz; but in So-long-as II, unlike in So-long-as I, the BVerfG considered this requirement to be fulfilled. In

---

[115] On the other specific aspect of this relationship, i.e. of the EU overstepping the bounds of the Treaty (referred to as ausbrechender Rechtsakt or ultra vires), especially in the area of competences, cf. e.g. Mayer, Franz C.; Walter, Maja: Die Europarechtsfreundlichkeit des BVerfG, Juristische Ausbildung 2011, 532 (537 ff.); Pötters, Stephan; Traut, Johannes: Die ultra-vires.Kontrolle des BVerfG nach "Honeywell"—Neues zum Kooperationsverhältnis von BVerfG und EuGH?, Europarecht 2011, 580 (580 ff.).

[116] For a short overview up to the Maastricht decision cf. Kischel, Uwe: Der unabdingbare grundrechtliche Mindeststandard in der Europäischen Union—Zur Auslegung des Art. 23 Abs. 1 S. 1 GG, Der Staat 39 (2000), 523 (524 ff.) with further references; in English cf. Mayer, Franz C.: Multilevel constitutional jurisdiction, in: Bogdandy, Armin v.; Bast, Jürgen (eds.): Principles of European constitutional law, 2nd ed. 2011, 399 (410 ff.).

[117] For reasons of simplification, the modern designation "EU" and "Union" will be used in this report, even if, at the time, one had to speak of the European Economic Community, the European Community or the European Communities.

[118] BVerfGE 37, 271 (285).

[119] BVerfGE 73, 339 (387).

1992, the same idea was repeated in the Maastricht-decision.[120] At the same time, the German parliament amended art. 23 para.1 sentence 1 GG which now reads: "With a view to establishing a united Europe, the Federal Republic of Germany shall participate in the development of the European Union (. . .) that guarantees a level of protection of basic rights essentially comparable to that afforded by this Grundgesetz." This amendment was explicitly meant to adopt the formula used in So-long-as II into the very text of the Constitution.[121] The Lisbon decision in 2009 again supported the established case-law.[122] Loosely in this context, the BVerfG talked about its own "reserve competence",[123] and made clear that it had accepted the finality of ECJ decisions only in principle,[124] i.e. not necessarily in any case.

So-long-as as a Security Valve

In sum, the So-long-as formula of the BVerfG, which has been incorporated into the text of the Grundgesetz, today functions as a security valve. The BVerfG will accept an exclusive jurisdiction of the ECJ on the compatibility of EU-law with human rights, but guards a possibility to reclaim that part of its jurisdiction if, to put it loosely, the protection of fundamental rights on the EU level defaults. Many details here are still open to discussion: When exactly can fundamental rights of the EU be considered "comparable" and "essentially" comparable to German basic rights? What is the exact relation of this guarantee to the eternity clause[125] of art. 79 para. 3 GG? When does EU law "generally" guarantee the protection, and how does this "general" guarantee relate to the explicit guarantee of the essence (*Wesensgehalt*) of basic rights in Art. 19 para. 2 GG? All of these points are debated in the German literature.[126] Only one point should be quickly mentioned, here: The security valve of art. 23 para. 1 sentence 1 GG will not be triggered by single decisions of the ECJ which, in the opinion of the BVerfG, do not conform with or even go directly against what would be required by German basic rights. Rather, there would have to be several decisions which reveal that European institutions, especially the ECJ, are in general no longer willing or able to guarantee the necessary protection of basic rights. This restriction is inherent in the basic assumptions that underlie the decisions of the

---

[120] BVerfGE 89, 155 (174 f.); the decision also introduced the idea of a "cooperative relationship" between BVerfG and ECJ, in which the ECJ guarantees the protection of basic rights in each single case for the entire territory of the EU, while the BVerfG can thus restrain itself to a general guarantee of the inalienable standard of basic rights, BVerfGE 89, 155 (175), an idea that adequately describes the relationship, while the notion of "cooperative relationship" as such gave rise to extensive scholarly debate and criticism and was not repeated in the Lisbon decision, BVerfGE 123, 267.

[121] Cf. Bericht der Gemeinsamen Verfassungskommission, Bundestag-Drucksache 12/6000, 21.

[122] BVerfGE 123, 267 (399).

[123] BVerfGE 123, 267 (401).

[124] BVerfGE 123, 267 (399).

[125] On the eternity clause cf. supra 13.1.4, at "The Unchangeable Constitution"

[126] Cf. e.g. the detailed discussion in Kischel, Uwe: Der unabdingbare grundrechtliche Mindeststandard in der Europäischen Union—Zur Auslegung des Art. 23 Abs. 1 S. 1 GG, Der Staat 39 (2000), 523 (527 ff.) with further references.

BVerfG since So-long-as I,[127] and has been indirectly confirmed by the BVerfG in its Lisbon-decision, where the court pointed out that inacceptable decisions by the ECJ in singular cases could not trigger even the so-called ultra-vires control by the BVerfG.[128]

Similar to the area of international law, the label of "friendliness" has been used to describe the treatment of German (constitutional) law, including basic rights, in its relation to European Union law (*Europarechtsfreundlichkeit*). Since 2009, the BVerfG has adopted this notion, claiming it as a description of its own position.[129] Only a part of the literature follows this assessment,[130] while many share a less positive view, regarding the BVerfG at least in part as a European skeptic.[131] Again, the notion of *Europarechtsfreundlichkeit* is more a label, a quick value-judgment on given facts than a legal notion with determinable results.

While the debate on the So-long-as issue continues, European attitudes towards fundamental rights law have long found other ways to enter the German legal sphere. For instance, after the general exclusion of women from military service had been held to violate EU law,[132] the German constitution was amended without much political resistance to allow women in the military.[133] Another example is the lack of decisions by the BVerfG on the question of quota for women. Here, it is simply assumed, without resistance even from European skeptics, that the relevant ECJ decisions reflect (or: determine) the question in German constitutional law, as well.[134] In the field of sex equality, the BVerfG often even cites European Union law or ECJ decisions.[135] In the field of age discrimination, the BVerfG has accepted the relevant ECJ decisions although it has been claimed by German authors that the ECJ acted outside the competences of the EU.[136]

The protection of basic rights in Germany, with its multiple connections to the law of the European Union as well as the European Convention on Human Rights, can thus be seen as an excellent example of the practical possibilities, but also

---

[127] Cf. Kischel, Uwe: Der unabdingbare grundrechtliche Mindeststandard in der Europäischen Union—Zur Auslegung des Art. 23 Abs. 1 S. 1 GG, Der Staat 39 (2000), 523 (536 ff.) with further references.

[128] Cf. BVerfGE 126, 286 (307).

[129] Cf. BVerfGE 123, 267 (347); 126, 286 (327), 127, 293 (334).

[130] Cf. e.g. Kischel, Uwe: Europarechtsfreundlichkeit oder Europarechtsskepsis, Unterwerfung oder Integration?—Sprachliche Einkleidung und sachliche Probleme, in: Giegerich, Thomas (ed.): Der "offene Verfassungsstaat" des Grundgesetzes, 2010, 285 (passim) with further references.

[131] Cf. e.g. Mayer, Franz: Europarechtsfreundlichkeit und Europarechtsskepsis in der Rechtsprechung des Bundesverfassungsgerichts, in: Giegerich, Thomas (ed.): Der "offene Verfassungsstaat" des Grundgesetzes, 2010, 237 (passim) with further references.

[132] Cf. Case C-285/98, Kreil [2000] ECR I-00069, marginal note 31.

[133] Cf. Bundesgesetzblatt, part I, no. 56, 2000, 1755.

[134] Cf. e.g. Kischel, Uwe: Epping, Volker; Hillgruber, Christian: Beck'scher Online-Kommentar, 12th ed. 2011, art. 3 marginal notes 157, 179.

[135] Cf. e.g. BVerfGE 113, 1 (20 f.); BVerfGE 97, 35 (43); cf. also BVerfGK 13, 501 (502 ff.).

[136] Cf. BVerfGE 126, 286 (301 ff.); for the criticism cf. e.g. Gerken, Lüder; Rieble, Volker; Roth, Günter H.; Stein, Torsten; Streinz, Rudolf: "Mangold" als ausbrechender Rechtsakt, 2009, passim.

of the complications and problems that the idea of a multi-level constitutionalism (*Verfassungsverbund*)[137] without a clear-cut hierarchy of norms could offer today.

References

Books

Alexy, Robert: Theorie der juristischen Argumentation, 1983

Alexy, Robert: A theory of constitutional rights, 2002

Badura, Peter; Dreier, Horst (eds.): Festschrift 50 Jahre Bundesverfassungsgericht, vol. 1, 2001.

Benda, Ernst;Klein, Eckart: Verfassungsprozeßrecht, 2nd. ed. 2001

Bogdandy, Armin v.; Bast, Jürgen (eds.): Principles of European constitutional law, 2nd ed. 2011

Bogdandy; Armin v.; Villalón, Pedro Cruz; Huber, Peter M. (eds.): Handbuch Ius Publicum Europaeum, vol. 1, 2007

Bleckmann, Albert: Staatsrecht II—Die Grundrechte, 4th ed. 1997

Carlson, Laura: The fundamentals of Swedish law, A guide for foreign lawyers and students, 2009

Chemerinsky, Erwin: Constitutional law, principles and policies, 4th ed. 2011

Detlef Merten; Hans-Jürgen Papier;Handbuch der Grundrechte in Deutschland und Europa, vol. VI/2, 2009

Dreier, Horst (ed.): Festschrift 50 Jahre Bundesverfassungsgericht, vol. 2, 2001

Dreier, Horst: Grundgesetz, Kommentar, vol. 1, 2nd ed. 2004

Dreier, Horst: Grundgesetz, Kommentar, vol. 2, 2nd ed. 2006

Dreier, Horst: Grundgesetz, Kommentar, vol. 3, 2nd. ed. 2008

Epping, Volker; Hillgruber, Christian: Grundgesetz, Kommentar, 2009

Epping, Volker; Hillgruber, Christian: Beck'scher Online-Kommentar GG, 12th ed. 2011

Esser, Josef: Vorverständnis und Methodenwahl in der Rechtsfindung, Rationalität der richterlichen Entscheidungspraxis, 1970

Gerken, Lüder; Rieble, Volker;Roth, Günter H.; Stein, Torsten;Streinz, Rudolf: "Mangold" als ausbrechender Rechtsakt, 2009

Giegerich, Thomas (ed.): Der "offene Verfassungsstaat" des Grundgesetzes nach 60 Jahren, 2010

Gleixner, Werner: Die Normenerlaßklage, Der Anspruch auf Erlaß untergesetzlicher Normen und formeller Gesetze, 1993

Goerlich, Helmut: Wertordnung und Grundgesetz, Kritik einer Argumentationsfigur des Bundesverfassungsgerichts, 1973

Graf Vitzthum, Wolfgang: Völkerrecht, 5th ed. 2010

Grote, Rainer; Marauhn, Thilo: EMRK/GG, Konkordanzkommentar zum europäischen und deutschen Grundrechtsschutz, 2006

Gröpl, Christoph: Staatsrecht I, Staatsgrundlagen, Staatsorganisation, 3rd ed. 2011

Heckötter, Ulrike: Die Bedeutung der Europäischen Menschenrechtskonvention und der Rechtsprechung des EGMR für die deutschen Gerichte, 2007

Hillgruber, Christian; Goos, Christoph: Verfassungsprozessrecht, 3rd 2011

Hufen, Friedhelm: Staatsrecht II, Grundrechte, 3rd ed. 2011

Hufen, Friedhelm: Schutz der Persönlichkeit und Recht auf informationelle Selbstbestimmung, in Badura, Peter

Isensee, Josef; Kirchhof, Paul: Handbuch des Staatsrechts, vol. 7, 1992

Isensee, Josef; Kirchhof, Paul: Handbuch des Staatsrechts der Bundesrepublik Deutschland, vol. 5, 2nd ed. 2000

---

[137] On the development of this idea cf. the concise remarks and references in: Mayer, Franz C.: Multilevel constitutional jurisdiction, in: Bogdandy, Armin v.; Bast, Jürgen (eds.): Principles on European constitutional law, 2nd 2011, 399 (428 f.).

Isensee, Josef; Kirchhof, Paul: Handbuch des Staatsrechts der Bundesrepublik Deutschland, vol. 1, 3rd ed. 2003

Isensee, Josef; Kirchhof, Paul: Handbuch des Staatsrechts der Bundesrepublik Deutschland, vol. 2, 3rd ed. 2004

Isensee, Josef; Kirchhof, Paul: Handbuch des Staatsrechts der Bundesrepublik Deutschland, vol. 9, 3rd ed. 2011

Klee, Kristina: Die progressive Verwirklichung wirtschaftlicher, sozialer und kultureller Menschenrechte, 2000

Kunig, Philip: Völkerrecht und staatliches Recht, in: Graf Vitzthum, Wolfgang: Völkerrecht, 5th ed. 2010

Maunz, Theodor; Schmidt-Bleibtreu, Bruno; Klein, Franz; Bethg, e, Herbert: Bundesverfassungsgerichtsgesetz, Kommentar, loose-leaf, vol. 2

Mangoldt, Hermann v.; Klein, Friedrich; Starck, Christian: Kommentar zum Grundgesetz, vol. 2, 6th ed. 2010

Maunz, Theodor; Dürig, Günter: Grundgesetz, Kommentar, looseleaf

Manssen, Gerrit: Staatsrecht II, Grundrechte, 8th ed. 2011

Merten, Detlef; Papier, Hans-Jürgen: Handbuch der Grundrechte in Deutschland und Europa, vol. VI/2, 2009

Michael, Lothar;Morlok, Martin: Grundrechte, 2nd. ed. 2010

Parlamentarischer Rat, Verhandlungen des Hauptausschusses, Bonn 1948/49, 42. Sitzung

Pieroth, Bodo; Schlink, Bernhard: Grundrechte, Staatsrecht II, 27th ed. 2011

Rüthers, Bernd: Rechtstheorie—Begriff, Geltung und Anwendung, 4th ed. 2008

Sachs, Michael: Grundgesetz, Kommentar, 5th ed. 2009

Sauer, Heiko: Staatsrecht III, Auswärtige Gewalt, Bezüge des Grundgesetzes zu Völker- und Europarecht, 2011

Schlaich, Klaus; Korioth, Stefan: Das Bundesverfassungsgericht, Stellung, Verfahren, Entscheidungen, 8th ed. 2010

Schweitzer, Michael: Staatsrecht III, Staatsrecht, Völkerrecht, Europarecht, 10th ed. 2010

Siehr, Angelika: Die Deutschenrechte des Grundgesetzes, Bürgerrechte im Spannungsfeld von Menschenrechtsidee und Staatsmitgliedschaft, 2001

Stern, Klaus; Sachs, Michael: Das Staatsrecht der Bundesrepublik Deutschland, vol. III/2, 1994

Tomuschat, Christian: Verfassungsgewohnheitsrecht?, Eine Untersuchung zum Staatsrecht der Bundesrepublik Deutschland, 1972

Umbach, Dieter C.; Clemens, Thomas;Dollinger, Franz-Wilhelm: Bundesverfassungsgerichtsgesetz, Mitarbeiterkommentar und Handbuch, 2nd. ed. 2005

Verdross, Alfred; Simma, Bruno: Universelles Völkerrecht, Theorie und Praxis, 3rd ed. 1984

Vöneky, Silja: Recht, Moral und Ethik, Grundlagen und Grenzen demokratischer Legitimation für Ethikgremien, 2010

Welp, Jürgen (eds.): Recht der Persönlichkeit, 1996

Wolff, Heinrich Amadeus: Ungeschriebenes Verfassungsrecht unter dem Grundgesetz, 2000.

Zippelius, Reinhold: Rechtsphilosophie, 6th ed. 2011

Articles

Alexy, Robert: Grundrechte als subjektive Rechte und als objektive Normen, Der Staat 29 (1990), 49

Bär, Wolfgang: Anmerkung zum Urteil des BVerfG v. 27.02.2008, 1 BvR 370/07, 1 BvR 595/07, Multimedia und Recht 2008, 325

Becker, Florian: Völkerrechtliche Verträge und parlamentarische Gesetzgebungskompetenz, Neue Zeitschrift des Verwaltungsrecht 2005, 289

Bergmann, Jan: Diener dreier Herren?—Der Instanzrichter zwischen BVerfG, EuGH und EGMR, Europarecht 2006, 101

Böckenförde, Ernst-Wolfgang: Grundrechtstheorie und Grundrechtsinterpretation, Neue Juristische Wochenschrift 1974, 1529

Breuer, Marten: Karlsruhe und die Gretchenfrage: Wie hast du's mit Straßburg?, Neue Zeitschrift für Verwaltungsrecht 2005, 412

Cremer, Hans-Joachim: Zur Bindungswirkung von EGMR-Urteilen—Anmerkung zum Görgülü-Beschluss des BVerfG vom 14.10.2004, EuGRZ 2004, 741, Europäische Grundrechte Zeitschrift 2004, 741

Geis, Max-Emanuel: Die "Eilversammlung" als Bewährungsprobe verfassungskonformer Auslegung, Verfassungsrechtsprechung im Dilemma zwischen Auslegung und Rechtsschöpfung, Neue Zeitschrift für Verwaltungsrecht 1992, 1025

Hillgruber, Christan: Anmerkung zum Urteil des BVerfG v. 07.07.2009, 1BvR 1164/07, Juristenzeitung 2010, 41

Hillgruber, Christian: Ohne rechtes Maß? Eine Kritik der Rechtsprechung des Bundesverfassungsgerichts nach 60 Jahren, Juristenzeitung 2011, 861

Hoffmann-Riem, Wolfgang: Kontrolldichte und Kontrollfolgen beim nationalen und europäischen Schutz von Freiheitsrechten in mehrpoligen Rechtsverhältnissen—Aus der Sicht des Bundesverfassungsgerichts, Europäische Grundrechte Zeitschrift 2006, 492

Jarass, Hans D.: Die Entwicklung des allgemeinen Persönlichkeitsrechts in der Rechtsprechung des Bundesverfassungsgerichts, in: Erichsen, Hans-Uwe; Kollhosser, Helmut; Welp, Jürgen (eds.): Recht der Persönlichkeit, 1996, 89

Kirchhof, Ferdinand: Grundrechtsschutz durch europäische und nationale Gerichte, Neue Juristische Wochenschrift 2011, 3681

Kischel, Uwe: Systembindung des Gesetzgebers und Gleichheitssatz, Archiv des öffentlichen Rechts 124 (1999), 174

Kischel, Uwe: Der unabdingbare grundrechtliche Mindeststandard in der Europäischen Union—Zur Auslegung des Art. 23 Abs. 1 S. 1 GG, Der Staat 39 (2000), 523

Kischel, Uwe: Europarechtsfreundlichkeit oder Europarechtsskepsis, Unterwerfung oder Integration?—Sprachliche Einkleidung und sachliche Probleme, in: Giegerich, Thomas: Der "offene Verfassungsstaat" des Grundgesetzes, 2010, 285

Kischel, Uwe: La liberté d'opinion au défi du néonazisme—la culture juridique allemande évolue, Revue Française de Droit Constitutionnel (forthcoming)

Kischel, Uwe: State Contracts, Völker-, schieds- und internationalprivatrechtliche Aspekte des anwendbaren Rechts (1992)

Klein, Eckart: Anmerkung zum Urteil des BverfG v. 14.10.2004, 2 BvR 1481/04, Juristenzeitung 2004, 1176

Mayer, Franz: Europarechtsfreundlichkeit und Europarechtsskepsis in der Rechtsprechung des Bundesverfassungsgerichts, in: Giegerich, Thomas: Der "offene Verfassungsstaat" des Grundgesetzes, 2010, 237

Mayer, Franz C.; Walter, Maja: Die Europarechtsfreundlichkeit des BVerfG, Juristische Ausbildung 2011, 532

Payandeh, Mehrdad: Völkerrechtsfreundlichkeit als Verfassungsprinzip, Ein Beitrag des Grundgesetzes zur Einheit von Völkerrecht und nationalem Recht, Jahrbuch des öffentlichen Rechts der Gegenwart neue Folge 57 (2009), 465

Pötters, Stephan; Traut, Johannes: Die ultra-vires.Kontrolle des BVerfG nach "Honeywell"—Neues zum Kooperationsverhältnis von BVerfG und EuGH?, Europarecht 2011, 580

Ruffert, Matthias: Die Europäische Menschenrechtskonvention und innerstaatliches Recht, Europäische Grundrechte Zeitschrift 2007, 245

Sauer, Heiko: Die neue Schlagkraft der gemeineuropäischen Grundrechtsjudikatur, Zur Bindung deutscher Gerichte an die Entscheidung des Europäischen erichtshofs für Menschenrechte, Zeitschrift für ausländisches öffentliches Recht und Völkerrecht 65 (2005), 35

Schenke, Wolf-Rüdiger: Rechtsschutz gegen das Unterlassen von Rechtsnormen, Verwaltungs-Archiv 82 (1991), 307

Schneider, Hans-Peter: Acht an der Macht! Das BVerfG als "Reparaturbetrieb" des Parlamentarismus?, Neue Juristische Wochenschrift 1999, 1303

Varol, Ozan O.: The origins and limits of originalism: A comparative study, Vanderbilt Journal of Transnational Law 44 (2011), 1239

Vogel, Klaus: Wortbruch im Verfassungsrecht, Mit einer Bemerkung zum Verhältnis zwischen Bundesverfassungsgericht und demokratischem Gesetzgeber, Juristenzeitung 1997, 161

Voßkuhle, Andreas: Theorie und Praxis der verfassungskonformen Auslegung von Gesetzen durch Fachgerichte, Kritische Bestandsaufnahme und Versuch einer Neubestimmung, Archiv des öffentlichen Rechts 125 (2000), 177

Wernsmann, Rainer: Die Deutschengrundrechte des Grundgesetzes im Lichte des Europarechts, Juristische Ausbildung 2000, 657

Court Decisions

BVerfGE 2, 124
BVerfGE 6, 32
BVerfGE 6, 55
BVerfGE 6, 309
BVerfGE 7, 198
BVerfGE 7, 377
BVerfGE 24, 199
BVerfGE 33, 23
BVerfGE 37, 271
BVerfGE 54, 148
BVerfGE 64, 217
BVerfGE 65, 1
BVerfGE 69, 315
BVerfGE 73, 339
BVerfGE 74, 358
BVerfGE 85, 191
BVerfGE 85, 329
BVerfGE 89, 155
BVerfGE 96, 68
BVerfGE 97, 35
BVerfGE 101, 361
BVerfGE 104, 337
BVerfGE 111, 307
BVerfGE 113, 1
BVerfGE 120, 274
BVerfGE 123, 267
BVerfGE 124, 300
BVerfGE 126, 286
BVerfGE 127, 293
BVerfG, decision of May 4, 2011, 2 BvR 2365/09, <http://www.bundesverfassungsgericht.de/entscheidungen/rs20110504_2bvr236509.html>
BVerfG, 1st Chamber of the Second Senate, 2. BvR 1526/04, Neue Zeitschrift für Verwaltungsrecht-Rechtsprechungs-Report 2007, 266 (267 f.)
BVerfGK 13, 501
ECHR, Caroline von Monaco v. Germany (59320/00), decision of June 24, 2004

Internet

Bundesverfassungsgericht—Aufgaben, Verfahren, und Organisation, <http://www.bundesverfassungsgericht.de/organisation/gb2010/A-I-1.html>

Bundesverfassungsgericht—Gesamteingänge der letzten fünf Geschäftsjahre <http://www.bundes-verfassungsgericht.de/organisation/gb2010/A-II-2.html>

GPRA Vertrauensindex, Oktober 2011, <http://prreport.de/home/gpra-vertrauensindex/oktober-2011/?L=0%25252F>

Other

Bericht der Gemeinsamen Verfassungskommission, Bundestag-Drucksache 12/6000, 21

Chapter 14
Codification of Human Rights at National and International Levels General Perspectives

National Report—Israel

Tomer Broude and Yonatan Weisbrod

14.1 Introduction

Israeli human rights law is strongly linked to a variety of historical and political circumstances. Israel is considered to be a 'mixed jurisdiction', with common law roots incorporating aspects of civil law as well as deference to religious legal systems in some dimensions. This diversity is evident also in the constitutional protection of human rights. Israel lacks a comprehensive formal constitution, and yet some institutions and rights are enshrined in statutory instruments that enjoy a higher status in the legal hierarchy. Otherwise, much of the constitutional law is judge-made, primarily by the Israeli Supreme Court in its capacity as High Court of Justice. In 1992, the Israeli parliamentary assembly (the Knesset) adopted two substantive laws of a fundamentally constitutional character, significantly enhancing the scope of judicial review of legislation on some human rights bases. This development is widely known as Israel's 'constitutional revolution', as explained in more detail below.

On the level of international law, Israel is bound by most of the existing universal human rights treaties, and this has had some expression in Israeli jurisprudence; nevertheless, there is no explicit implementing legislation in the field, significantly weakening the impact of international human rights law in Israel. Moreover, Israel's legal system's incorporation of international human rights, including the application of human rights to non-nationals and beyond the territory of the state has to a large extent been defined by Israel's belligerent occupation of territories on the West Bank and the Gaza Strip since June, 1967.

In this report, we will provide a survey of Israel's constitutional protection of human rights according to the following headings. First, we will set out the existing system of basic laws, its genesis and the substantive rights protected therein, whether

T. Broude (✉) · Y. Weisbrod
Faculty of Law, Hebrew University of Jerusalem, Mt. Scopus, 91905 Jerusalem, Israel
e-mail: tomerbroude@gmail.com

Y. Weisbrod
e-mail: yoni.weisbrod@gmail.com

W.-Y. Wang (ed.), *Codification in International Perspective,* Ius Comparatum – Global Studies in Comparative Law, DOI 10.1007/978-3-319-03455-3_14,
© Springer International Publishing Switzerland 2014

explicitly or implicitly (Sect. 2). Then we will compare the constitutional protection before and after the 'constitutional revolution' (Sect. 3 and 4 respectively). Subsequently we will address the application of Israeli constitutional law to non-Citizens and to territories outside the municipal boundaries of the state of Israel, and the status of international human rights law in Israeli domestic law (Sect. 5 and 6 respectively).

14.2 Israel's Piecemeal Constitution: The Basic Laws and the Rights Protected

Israel's Declaration of Independence (the "Independence Document") charged the nation's constituent[1] or founding assembly—in essence, the first Knesset—with the task of formulating a constitution. However, agreeing on a constitution proved to be too formidable a task for the Knesset, with a range of objections posed by different Members of Knesset (MKs). The state was in a precarious situation, finding itself fighting for its survival from birth in the War of Independence, and many felt that it was simply not the right time to carry out the constitutional project. Then Prime Minister Ben-Gurion expressed the position that it would be impossible to protect civil rights to the extent required by any proper bill of rights during wartime. Furthermore, he posed the unique argument that the constitution of the Jewish state should not be formulated when so much of the Jewish people lived abroad. Religious groups initially opposed the formulation of a constitution, not wanting to declare allegiance to a secular document, and fearing that it would bring a change to the status quo with respect to the presence of religion in the State. However, once convinced that the majority supported a constitution, they played an active role in its formulation. Narrower partisan political considerations also prevented the adoption of a written constitution, and many of the above issues continue to pose a challenge to Israel's constitutional development today.[2]

In an attempt to deal with these objections while satisfying the State's commitment to formulating a constitution, the first Knesset adopted a resolution proposed by MK Yizhar Harari, subsequently known as the "Harari Decision" or the "Harari Compromise". The gist of the decision was that in lieu of adopting a full formal written constitution, the Knesset would engage in a gradual process of passing individual "Basic Laws", until a complete constitution was formulated. The Harari Decision failed to address many normative questions about the Basic Laws—what would be their normative status vis-à-vis regular laws? Would each basic law have constitutional status, or would they all possess such status only when the entire set was complete? What would be the issues addressed in substance in the Basic Laws?

---

[1] UN General Assembly Resolution 181 of November 29, 1947 (the "Partition Plan") called for the creation of separate states for Palestine's Jewish and Arab populations, requiring each state to elect a Constituent Assembly that would draft a constitution.

[2] For a discussion on the initial objections to a constitution, see Ruth Gavison (1985) The Controversy over Israel's Bill of Rights. 15 Isr. Y.B. On Hum. Rts. 113:148–49 (opposition of religious parties to constitution), and 137–38 (opposition on the basis of timing).

Ultimately, nine Basic Laws were passed from 1948 to 1986, mostly dealing with various state institutions, not with substantive rights. In 1992, two additional Basic Laws were passed that heralded a new era in Israeli constitutional law—the 'constitutional revolution' (this topic will be discussed in greater depth in Sect. 4). Israel's Basic Laws are as follows:

Basic Law: The Knesset (1958);
Basic Law: The Israeli Lands (1960);
Basic Law: The President of the State (1964);
Basic Law: The Government (1968, replaced in 1992 and in 2001);
Basic Law: The State Economy (1975);
Basic Law: The Army (1976);
Basic Law: Jerusalem, the Capital of Israel (1980);
Basic Law: The Judiciary (1984);
Basic Law: The State Comptroller (1986);
Basic Law: Freedom of Occupation (1992, replaced in 1994);
Basic Law: Human Dignity and Liberty (1992, amended in 1994).

A number of human rights are granted explicit protection under *Basic Law: Freedom of Occupation* and *Basic Law: Human Dignity and Liberty*. These include: the freedom of occupation; the sanctity of life, body, and dignity; the right to property; the right of every person to leave Israel, and the right of Israeli nationals to enter Israel;[3] and the right to privacy. These rights are not unlimited, as will be explained below.

There are several important rights that are not expressly protected, but have nevertheless been recognized in the framework of a 'judicial bill of rights' developed by the courts in the absence of protective constitutional legislation. These include: the right to equality; freedom of religion and conscience; freedom of expression; the right to due process; and the right to personal autonomy.[4]

Perhaps the most conspicuously absent among the explicitly enumerated rights is the right to equality, a right incorporated into the constitutions of most Western democracies. Nonetheless, the Supreme Court has ruled that equality is an integral part of the *Basic Law: Human Dignity and Liberty* as a necessary extension of the protection of human dignity,[5] albeit limiting this inclusion to only those aspects of equality that are 'closely related' to the principle of human dignity.[6] Like the right to equality, the Supreme Court has interpreted *Basic Law: Human Dignity and Liberty* to implicitly include other rights as well. In the 2006 *Shani Cohen* decision, the court

---

[3] Note that freedom of movement is not included, due to concerns by religious groups of legislation that would infringe on the status quo regarding transportation on the Sabbath (Suzie Navot (2007) The Constitutional Law of Israel. Kluwer, Netherlands).

[4] For examples of relevant case law, see Navot, 210.

[5] 'Today the principle of equality can be considered included in the Basic Law: Human Dignity and Liberty. This inclusion implies the elevation of the principle of equality to a constitutional, super-legislative normative status.' per Justice Or in HCJ 5394/92 *Hoppert v. 'Yad Vashem' Holocaust Martyrs and Heroes Memorial Authority*, P.D. 48(3) 353, 362 (1994).

[6] HCJ 7052/03 *Adalla v. Minister of Interior*, P.D. 61(2) 202 (2006), at paragraph 39.

emphasized that due process extended from the explicitly protected rights to human dignity and property,[7] and the 2005 *Hadar* decision provided the same treatment for Freedom of Contract.[8]

Israel's foundation is not only as a democratic state, but as a Jewish state as well.[9] Nevertheless, the freedom of religion is upheld, albeit subject to limitations. Most religious legislation is pluralistic, often allowing the various religious sects to set their own rules.[10] Some laws are uniquely associated with Judaism and with Jewishness—such as the prohibition on the importation of non-Kosher meat into Israel[11], and the Law of Return[12], which allows Jews to immigrate and receive automatic citizenship. On this backdrop, the courts have nevertheless exercised a measure of protection of freedom of religion, declaring it to be "among the fundamental human liberties," and invalidating secondary legislation as *ultra vires* if it violated the freedom of religion.[13]

14.3 Human Rights Protection Before the 'Constitutional Revolution'

As a result of the failure of the Harari Decision to address normative issues regarding the Basic Laws, the courts consistently held these laws to be of regular normative status. In fact, under the principle of the superiority of specific laws to general laws on a particular issue, provisions of the Basic Laws were even held to be normatively inferior to regular laws in some instances.[14] Amending a Basic Law did not require another Basic Law—it could be effected by way of regular legislation.[15]

---

[7] HCJ 2171/06 *Shani Cohen v. Knesset Speaker* (2011), at paragraph 19.

[8] SC 8163/05 *Hadar Insurance Co. v. Anon.* (2007), atparagraph 23.

[9] As determined in Israel's Independence Document, declaring the "establishment of a Jewish State in the land of Israel." For a broader discussion on religious freedom in Israel, see Natan Lerner (2007) Religious Liberty in the State of Israel. 21 Emory Int'l L. Rev. 239 (Hereinafter: '*Lerner*'); and Stephen Goldstein (1991–1992) Israel: A Secular or Religious State. 36 St Louis U. L. J. 143.

[10] For example, while Saturday is the official day of rest for Jews, members of other religions may choose to take their day of rest on Friday, Saturday, or Sunday pursuant to Art. 7 of the *Labor and Rest Hours Law,* 1951. Likewise, matters of marriage and divorce are under the jurisdiction of the religious courts of each individual religion in Israel, as a remnant of the Ottoman "*Millet*" system.

[11] *Meat and Meat Products Law*, 1994.

[12] *Law of Return*, 1950.

[13] In CR 3471/87 *State of Israel v. Kaplan*, P.D. 5748(2) 26 (1987) (Hereinafter: '*Kaplan*'), the Jerusalem Magistrate's Court invalidated a municipal regulation that prohibited the running of cinemas on Shabbat as a violation of freedom of religion.

[14] HCJ 98/69 *Bergman v. Finance Minister* 23(1) 693 (1969).

[15] "The only difference between basic laws and regular ones is semantic, and there is no basis to the claim that only a basic law can amend a basic law." HCJ 60/77 *Ressler v. Chairman of Elections Committee*, P.D. 31(2) 556, 560 (1977).

There were particular Basic Law provisions that did receive normative superiority, but these received a 'formal' entrenchment—an absolute majority of Knesset members was required in order to pass laws that violated these provisions. The Knesset could override Basic Law provisions with a majority vote, and therefore the Basic Laws did not yet serve as an instrument that could limit the Knesset's legislative authority.

Still, even before the 'Constitutional Revolution', the State had a long history of protecting basic human rights on a judicial basis. Citing the Independence Document as the ideological foundation of the State, the courts took a variety of measures in protecting those values that emerged from the Independence Document's description of Israel as a state founded on Jewish and Democratic values. The Independence Document did not have superior constitutional status,[16] so the courts could not strike down primary legislation that contravened its values. However, they could disqualify government actions or secondary legislation that infringed upon these values, deeming them *ultra vires*[17]; and when presented with multiple interpretations of legislation, they expressed a preference for interpretations that conformed with these values. Consequently a 'judicial bill of rights' developed out of the Supreme Court's case law, providing precedents for the protection of a number of human rights without a written bill of rights.

This 'judicial bill of rights' developed by the Supreme Court eventually included almost all basic human rights, including freedom of expression[18], personal liberty[19], certain aspects of the right to equality[20], the right to privacy[21], as well as procedural due process[22], and this bill of rights continues to be developed by the courts even after the existence of a formal, if piecemeal constitution has been recognized, since a number of basic rights were omitted from the *Basic Law: Human Dignity and Liberty*.

14.4 Human Rights Protection Following the 'Constitutional Revolution'

In 1992, the Knesset passed two important new Basic Laws which ushered in a 'Constitutional Revolution', the full significance of which became apparent in the landmark *Mizrahi* ruling in 1995[23]. The constitutional difference between these two

---

[16] Dalia Dorner (1991) Does Israel Have a Constitution? 43 St. Louis U. L.J. 1325 (Hereinafter: '*Dorner*').

[17] For instance, see *Kaplan*, ibid. Note 13.

[18] HCJ 73/53 *Kol Ha'am v. Interior Minister*, P.D. 7(2) 871 (1953).

[19] HCJ 7/48 *El-Karbotli v. Minister of Defense*, P.D. 2(5) (1949).

[20] HCJ 7052/03 *Adalah v. Interior Minister* (2006).

[21] HCJ 355/79 *Katlan v. Prison Services*, P.D. 34(3) 294 (1980).

[22] HCJ 3/58 *Berman v. Interior Minister*, P.D. 12(2) 1508 (1958).

[23] SC 6821/93 *Bank Mizrahi v. Migdal*, P.D. 49(4) 22 (1995) (Hereinafter: '*Mizrahi*').

most recent Basic Laws and the earlier nine is the inclusion of a 'Limitation Clause' (similar to the 'Reasonable Limits' clause found in the Canadian Constitution[24]). The Limitation Clause in Art. 8 of *Basic Law: Human Dignity and Liberty* reads as follows: "There shall be no violation of rights under this Basic Law except by a law befitting the values of the State of Israel, enacted for a proper purpose, and to an extent no greater than is required." The inclusion of the clause served a dual purpose: first, it limited the power of the Knesset to impair the rights constitutionally protected in the Basic Law, subjecting such impairment to certain substantive rather than formal conditions, establishing the supremacy of the Basic Law; and second, pursuant to the Supreme Court's ruling in the *Mizrahi* case, this shift from a formal entrenchment to a substantive entrenchment of constitutional rights effectively granted powers of judicial review to the courts.

This Limitation Clause is also found in *Basic Law: Freedom of Occupation*, although an additional 'Override Clause' (similar to the 'Notwithstanding Clause' of the Canadian Constitution[25]) was added in 1995 when the Knesset wished to pass legislation that would not have satisfied the limitation clause. The Override Clause allows for the legislation of laws that do not meet the Limitation Clause provided that the law expressly states that it shall be in effect notwithstanding the provisions of that Basic Law, and the law automatically expires after four years.[26] Note that the impact of the Override Clause was tempered in the 1994 *Meatrel* case[27] where the Supreme Court asserted that a law infringing upon *Basic Law: Freedom of Occupation* could concurrently be in violation of *Basic Law: Human Dignity and Liberty* as well, rendering the law subject to constitutional scrutiny on the basis of both basic laws. Since the latter does not contain an Override Clause, such a law would still be subject to judicial review.

The 1995 *Mizrahi* case was the first to deal with a wide array of constitutional issues following the 1992 legislation of the two basic laws, including the constitutional ramifications of the new Limitation Clause. The case scrutinized the 'Gal Law', a law that introduced measures to help the agricultural sector recover from a crippling economic crisis, including extending their dates of loan repayment to the various industrial banks. The banks argued that the Gal Law violated their constitutional right to property, under *Basic Law: Human Dignity and Liberty*. The Supreme Court found that the law violated the banks' property rights, and that it did have the authority to strike down the law—but that the violation was justified under the Limitation Clause.

---

[24] "The Canadian Charter of Rights and Freedoms guarantees the rights and freedoms set out in it subject only to such reasonable limits prescribed by law as can be demonstrably justified in a free and democratic society.", Sect. 1 of the *Canadian Charter of Rights and Freedoms*, Part I of the Constitution Act, 1982 being Schedule B to the Canada Act 1982 (U.K.), 1982, c. 11. (Hereinafter: '*Canadian Constitution*').

[25] Section 33 of the Canadian Constitution. See HCJ 4676/94 *Meatrel Ltd. v. Israel Knesset*, P.D. 50(5) 15 (1996) (Hereinafter: '*Meatrel*') at paragraph 13, where Barak asserts that the Canadian Notwithstanding Clause was adopted in Israel with certain changes, and only with respect to Freedom of Occupation. (paragraph 13).

[26] Article 8(a) of *Basic Law: Freedom of Occupation*.

[27] *Meatrel*, at p. 25.

The recognition of the authority of the court to strike down laws that violated the new Basic Laws, subject to the review of their compatibility with the substantive requirements of the Limitations Clause, can be compared to the United States' *Marbury v. Madison* decision, completely changing Israeli constitutional law by recognizing the normative supremacy of the Basic Laws, and by providing the courts with the authority to exercise judicial review. The newfound normative superiority attributed to the Basic Laws as a result of the *Mizrahi* case meant that amending Basic Laws could now only be done by way of a Basic Law, since a law can only be amended by means of a law of equal normative weight.[28] However, because most Basic Laws do not include any 'formal entrenchment' requiring a particular Knesset majority to make amendments, most Basic Law provisions can be amended by means of a simple voting majority.

The Limitation Clause included in the two most recent Basic Laws can be reduced to four requirements for the legitimate infringement of constitutional rights by the Knesset or the government: (1) that the infringement be authorized by law or by explicit consent, (2) that it be for a proper purpose, (3) that it befit the values of the State of Israel, and (4) that it be proportional. A 'proper purpose' is a public goal that could justify an infringement of a fundamental right in a democratic system. The term 'values of the State of Israel' refers to the application of Jewish and Democratic values in the State (and there are a number of opinions on the right way to synthesize these two value systems). The 'proportionality' requirement ensures that the degree of harm to the right be no greater than that which is necessary to attain the goal, and it is implemented by way of three balancing tests: (i) the suitability of the means to the objective; (ii) the adoption of a measure that infringes on a fundamental right only as a last resort, where no other reasonable means are sufficient; and (iii) the adoption of a measure that infringes on a fundamental right only where the objective is sufficiently important that the harm that would result from not pursuing such an objective justifies the harm to the fundamental right.[29]

Many questions about the scope and nature of judicial review remain unanswered in the jurisprudence to date. At the present time it is very broad, both in terms of which courts can exercise judicial review, and in terms of matters that are subject to the courts' scrutiny. The courts have raised the possibility of reviewing primary legislation in the following situations: if there were procedural flaws in enacting the law[30], if the law violates a basic principle of a democratic society,[31] or if the law fundamentally violates a protected human right[32]. In practice, the courts have exercised restraint in utilizing their authority to review primary legislation and only

[28] *Mizrahi*, at pp. 320–321.

[29] Dorner, p. 1331, paragraph 12.

[30] HCJ 4885/03 *Poultry Growers Association v. Government of Israel*, P.D. 59(2) 14 (2004). Note that the case was dismissed.

[31] Suggested in the minority opinion of Justice Chaim Cohen in HCJ 1/65 *Yardor v. Chairman of the Elections Committee*, P.D. 19(3) 365, 384 (1965), which has not found acceptance in later opinions.

[32] As charged in the *Mizrahi* case.

very few legal provisions that violated protected constitutional rights have been stricken by the courts as unconstitutional.

In a 2011 High Court of Justice petition against Israel's National Insurance Institute (NII), a provision of the *Income Support Law*[33] preventing those with regular access to a car from receiving income support was stricken. The NII proposed that a more limited system of judicial review be employed for matters governing social-economic rights as opposed to civil-political rights, since, it was argued, laws protecting social rights involve the expenditure of government resources and are based on policy questions that are the purview of the legislature, not the judiciary. The High Court of Justice ruled against the idea of employing different systems of judicial review, rejecting the validity of the dichotomy proposed by the NII.[34]

While direct concrete challenges to the constitutionality of laws or government actions are normally within the exclusive jurisdiction of the Supreme Court in its capacity as the High Court of Justice, any Israeli court may examine the constitutionality of a statutory provision within the indirect framework of a legal case or dispute.[35] Such cases are, however, extremely rare. As part of a criminal case, a 1996 amendment to the Income Tax Code which prohibited anyone not listed in the Registry of Tax Consultants from providing tax consultancy services was deemed to disproportionately limit freedom of occupation, and was struck down by the Tel Aviv Magistrate's court.[36] To date, this is the only case where a court of lower jurisdiction than the Supreme Court exercised such judicial review.

14.5 Human Rights Protection of Non-Citizens

The core human rights protected under *Basic Law: Human Dignity and Liberty* apply to all people in Israel, including non-Israeli citizens, with the exception of the right of entry, which expressly applies only to Israeli citizens present outside of Israel. The major precedents on the protection of human rights for non-citizens is a High Court of Justice decision from 2006, as well as another by the same petitioner in 2011— the petitioner being *Kav Laoved,* a non-governmental organization representing the rights of weaker segments of the working population. In 2006, the court ruled on the legality of an immigration law which stipulated that a foreign worker could only work for the particular employer that sponsored his visa, having the name of that employer stamped in his passport, and risking deportation if he stopped working for that employer. According to the court, this law led to a situation where workers were badly mistreated, effectively creating modern-day slavery for these workers.[37] In the 2011 decision, the Court ruled on the legality of a Ministry of Interior protocol that

---

[33] *Income Support Law*, 1980.

[34] HCJ 10662/04 *Salah Hassan v. National Insurance Institute* (2012), not yet published.

[35] Navot, p. 160.

[36] CR (T"A) 4696/01 *Israel v. Moshe Handelman* (2003).

[37] HCJ 4542/02 *Kav Laoved v. Government of Israel* (2006) (Hereinafter: '*Kav Laoved* (2006)').

forced foreign workers that became pregnant to leave the country.[38] In both cases, the Court ruled that the basic human rights protected under *Basic Law: Human Dignity and Liberty* apply to all persons in Israel—not only citizens. Since these measures violated the right to autonomy and the right to human dignity respectively, both were struck down by the High Court of Justice.

Note that the extension of human rights protection to all people in Israel has been enforced only with respect to the rights found in *Basic Law: Human Dignity and Liberty. Basic Law: Freedom of Occupation* protects "Israeli nationals and residents," and therefore it is not clear whether the courts will extend this protection to non-Israelis as well. Presently, the courts have abstained from ruling on this question; however, the Court did indicate that the position which holds that the Basic Law completely denies foreign workers protection from violations of freedom of occupation was untenable.[39]

14.6 Extra-Territorial Application of Human Rights Protections

After the 1967 Six Day War, Israel remained in control of Judea and Samaria (formerly under Jordanian rule) and the Gaza Strip (formerly under Egyptian rule), and after establishing military rule in accordance with international law, the areas were considered as under belligerent occupation and therefore subject to the provisions of the 1949 Fourth Geneva Convention Relative to the Protection of Civilian Persons in Times of War ("*Fourth Geneva Convention*") and the 1907 Regulations Annexed to the Hague Convention (IV) Respecting the Laws and Customs of War on Land ("*Hague Regulations*"). In the 1972 *Hilu* decision[40], the High Court of Justice established that challenges against the legislative and administrative orders of the military governor could be heard by the Court. Ruling that the Hague Regulations constituted customary international law while the Fourth Geneva Convention was conventional international law that had not been incorporated into domestic law, the court ruled that such cases would be decided based on the Hague Regulations and based on Israeli administrative law.[41] Consequently, this ruling opened the door to a large number of cases that dealt with the application of international law on Israeli actions, especially with respect to Israel's actions in the territories.

In 2005, the High Court of Justice ruled on the legality of the Israeli government's decision to remove Israeli residents from occupied territory in the Gaza Strip, as part of the disengagement plan. The court held that Israeli civilians living in the Gaza Strip were entitled to constitutional protection since they lived under effective

---

[38] HCJ 11437/05 *Kav Laoved v. Interior Ministry* (2011) (Hereinafter: '*Kav Laoved* (2011)').

[39] *Kav Laoved* (2006), paragraph 41 of the decision of J. Levy.

[40] HCJ 302/72, *Hilu* et al. *v. Government of Israel* et al., 27 (2) P.D. 169, 176 (1972).

[41] HCJ 606/78, *Ayub* et al. *v. Minister of Defence* et al., 33 (2) P.D. 113, 120–23, 125–29 (1979). It should be noted, however, that in subsequent jurisprudence the Government of Israel has stated that it applies the humanitarian provisions of the Fourth Geneva Convention in the occupied territories.

Israeli rule, and subsequently reviewed the government decision under the Limitation Clause. Thus the court provided a basis for the extra-territorial application of Israeli constitutional law, albeit one limited to Israeli citizens in areas under effective Israeli control. The court carefully abstained from ruling on the protection of non-Israelis living under Israeli rule in the Occupied Territories on the basis of the constitution, as well as the question of whether the constitution may be applied extra-territorially in general, focusing instead on the application of the constitution on a personal level to Israeli nationals[42].

14.7 International Human Rights Commitments and Their Status in Israeli Domestic Law

The status of international law in Israeli domestic law is not determined in any statute, and the courts have developed legal rules to fill this void.[43] Israel, like other common law countries, follows a dualistic system with respect to the distinction between international and domestic laws. Provisions of international treaties are only binding in domestic law if explicitly adopted by legislation.[44] The traditional rationale for requiring domestic implementing legislation is that insofar as the treaty-making power is the prerogative of the executive branch, automatic incorporation of treaties into domestic law would turn the executive into a de facto legislator. A secondary rationale expressed by the Supreme Court is that automatically incorporating international treaties would bind the Israeli public to laws that have not been formulated in accordance with Israeli needs and conditions, though this rationale seems to ignore the fact that customary law, which is also not necessarily attuned to the Israeli system, is automatically adopted into domestic law.[45]

The Knesset's adoption of international treaties in domestic law can take place in a number of ways, including the adoption of an entire treaty as an addendum to a law[46]; the adoption of provisions of the treaty in a domestic law; legislating that a minister has the authority to grant legal status to provisions of a treaty in the framework of a by-law; etc. Note that even without explicit domestic adoption, the courts tend to interpret domestic legislation in harmony with ratified international treaties, under the "presumption of concordant meaning" doctrine[47], provided this

---

[42] HCJ 1661/05 *Hof Azza Regional Municipality v. Israel Knesset*, 59(2) PD 481 (2005), at paragraph 80.

[43] Yaffa Zilbershats (1996) The Adoption of International Law into Israeli Law—The Real is Ideal. 25 Isr. Y.B. On Hum. Rts. 243 (Hereinafter: '*Zilbershats*').

[44] HCJ 785/87 *Affo* et al. *v. Commander of IDF Forces in the West Bank* et al., P.D. 42(2), 4, 37 (1988) (Hereinafter: '*Affo*').

[45] Zilbershats, p. 248.

[46] As is the case with the *Hague Convention (Return of Abducted Children) Law*, 5751–1991, stating that "The articles of the Convention, the language of which appears in the Schedule, shall have statutory effect, and shall apply notwithstanding any law."

[47] *Kav Laoved* (2006), at paragraph 37.

interpretation does not entirely distort the original intention of the law, in which case the domestic statute prevails[48].

In contrast, customary international law (including "declaratory" treaty provisions that codify existing custom) is automatically considered part of domestic law provided that it does not conflict with existing Israeli legislation[49], without requiring any internal legislation.[50] The automatic incorporation of customary law does not negate the separation of powers because customary international law binds states without any action on the part of the government.

Israel is committed to most universal human rights treaties. It has ratified the two major conventions on human rights of 1966—the International Covenant on Civil and Political Rights (ICCPR), and the International Covenant on Economic, Social and Cultural Rights (ICESCR), although entering a reservation on Art. 23 of the former, which deals with matters of marriage and family: Israel reserved the right to decide matters of personal status by way of religious law.[51]

Similarly, Israel has signed most of the other international conventions on human rights. Israel's ratification of the 1948 Convention Against Torture and Other Cruel, Inhuman or Degrading Treatment or Punishment notably included two reservations: firstly, Israel did not recognize the competence of the Committee set up by the convention for the investigation of allegations of torture; and secondly, Israel did not authorize the International Court of Justice in the Hague to adjudicate disputes that arose out of the convention. Among the main treaties that Israel has signed and ratified are the 1948 Convention on the Prevention and Punishment of the Crime of Genocide, the 1965 International Convention on the Elimination of All Forms of Racial Discrimination, the 1979 Convention on the Elimination of all Forms of Discrimination Against Women, the 1989 Convention on the Rights of the Child, and the 2006 Convention on the Rights of Persons with Disabilities.

Israel has not signed the 1990 Convention on the Protection of the Rights of All Migrant Workers and Members of their Families and the 2006 Convention for the Protection of All Persons from Enforced Disappearance.

Aside from these conventions, Israel is not a party to any of the regional conventions, the most notable of which is the 1950 European Convention for the Protection of Human Rights and Fundamental Freedoms, which established the European Court of Human Rights. As a non-European state, Israel cannot formally be a party to this treaty. Nonetheless, Israeli courts have frequently cited judicial decisions from the European Court of Human Rights, since it is considered authoritative on matters of human rights that also relate to the interpretation of the universal human rights treaties.[52]

---

[48] See Tomer Broude (2009) The Status of International Law in Domestic Law. In: Robbie Sabel (ed) International Law § 3 (in Hebrew), at Note 15.

[49] CR 5/51 *Steinberg v. Attorney General*, 5 P.D. 1061.

[50] See the Affo decision, at p. 35, where the court held that customary international law was automatically part of Israeli law, so long as it does not conflict with existing legislation.

[51] Sabel, pp. 211–212.

[52] See, for instance, 2160/99 *L. v. L.* (Jerusalem Family Court, 2005), where the court cited two cases of the European Court of Human Rights dealing with cases of degrading treatment of children by their parents, holding that these violated various human rights conventions.

14.8 Conclusion

Israel's founding document describes a state built on the protection of equality, freedom, and other human rights for all of its inhabitants. Absent a formal constitution, however, the courts could only protect human rights through the development of a 'judicial bill of rights' that they employed to disqualify secondary legislation and government actions. With the legislation of two additional 'basic laws', laws that were meant to eventually form a constitution, and the inclusion of a Limitation Clause, the court began scrutinizing primary legislation (albeit infrequently) against the enumerated rights, as well as rights that, for reasons outlined above, were not included in the basic laws, but were included in the judicial bill of rights. The courts play an important role in Israeli society, with a willingness to examine a broad range of government actions and legislation.

Israel has signed and ratified most major international treaties on human rights, and is consistent with other common law countries regarding the adoption of international law, requiring explicit internal legislation for incorporating treaties, and deferring to international law when it believes that it has customary status (such as the 1907 Hague Regulations). To date, the extent of the application of Israeli constitutional law on an extra-territorial basis has not been completely settled. The courts have applied it on a personal basis to Israelis living in Israeli-controlled territories, but many questions remain.

References

Books and chapters

Ruth Gavison (1985) The Controversy over Israel's Bill of Rights. 15 Isr. Y.B. On Hum. Rts. 113:148–49 and 137–38.
Suzie Navot (2007) The Constitutional Law of Israel. Kluwer, Netherlands.
Yaffa Zilbershats (1996) The Adoption of International Law into Israeli Law—The Real is Ideal. 25 Isr. Y.B. On Hum. Rts. 243.
Tomer Broude (2009) The Status of International Law in Domestic Law. In: Robbie Sabel (ed.) International Law § 3 (in Hebrew), at Note 15.

Cases

CR 5/51 *Steinberg v. Attorney General*, 5 P.D. 1061.
CR 3471/87 *State of Israel v. Kaplan*, P.D. 5748(2) 26 (1987).
CR (T"A) 4696/01 *Israel v. Moshe Handelman* (2003).
HCJ 1/65 *Yardor v. Chairman of the Elections Committee*, P.D. 19(3) 365, 384 (1965).
HCJ 3/58 *Berman v. Interior Minister*, P.D. 12(2) 1508 (1958).
HCJ 7/48 *El-Karbotli v. Minister of Defense*, P.D. 2(5) (1949).
HCJ 60/77 *Ressler v. Chairman of Elections Committee*, P.D. 31(2) 556, 560 (1977).
HCJ 73/53 *Kol Ha'am v. Interior Minister*, P.D. 7(2) 871 (1953).

HCJ 98/69 *Bergman v. Finance Minister* 23(1) 693 (1969).

HCJ 302/72, *Hilu* et al. *v. Government of Israel* et al., 27 (2) P.D. 169, 176 (1972).

HCJ 355/79 *Katlan v. Prison Services*, P.D. 34(3) 294 (1980).

HCJ 606/78, *Ayub* et al. *v. Minister of Defence* et al., 33 (2) P.D. 113, 120–23, 125–29 (1979).

HCJ 785/87 *Affo* et al. *v. Commander of IDF Forces in the West Bank* et al., P.D. 42(2), 4, 37 (1988).

HCJ 1661/05 *Hof Azza Regional Municipality v. Israel Knesset*, 59(2) PD 481 (2005).

HCJ 2171/06 *Shani Cohen v. Knesset Speaker* (2011), at paragraph 19.

HCJ 4542/02 *Kav Laoved v. Government of Israel* (2006).

HCJ 4676/94 *Meatrel Ltd. v. Israel Knesset*, P.D. 50(5) 15 (1996).

HCJ 4885/03 *Poultry Growers Association v. Government of Israel*, P.D. 59(2) 14 (2004)

HCJ 5394/92 *Hoppert v. 'Yad Vashem' Holocaust Martyrs and Heroes Memorial Authority*, P.D. 48(3) 353, 362 (1994).

HCJ 7052/03 *Adalla v. Minister of Interior*, P.D. 61(2) 202 (2006), at paragraph 39.

HCJ 10662/04 *Salah Hassan v. National Insurance Institute* (2012).

HCJ 11437/05 *Kav Laoved v. Interior Ministry* (2011).

SC 6821/93 *Bank Mizrahi v. Migdal*, P.D. 49(4) 22 (1995) (2004).

SC 8163/05 *Hadar Insurance Co. v. Anon.* (2007), at paragraph 23.

2160/99 *L. v. L.* (Jerusalem Family Court, 2005).

Journals and articles

Natan Lerner (2007) Religious Liberty in the State of Israel. 21 Emory Int'l L. Rev. 239.

Dalia Dorner (1991) Does Israel Have a Constitution?. 43 St. Louis U. L.J. 1325

Stephen Goldstein (1991–1992) Israel: A Secular or Religious State. 36 St Louis U. L.J. 143.

Statutes

Labor and Rest Hours Law, 1951.

Basic Law: Freedom of Occupation.

Hague Convention (Return of Abducted Children) Law, 5751–1991.

Income Support Law, 1980.

Law of Return, 1950.

Meat and Meat Products Law, 1994.

Constitution Act, 1982, Canada Act 1982 (U.K.), 1982, c. 11.

UN General Assembly Resolution 181 of November 29, 1947.

Chapter 15
A Possibility of the Multi-layered Human Rights Implementation System Underpinned by the Simultaneous Codification of the Constitution of Japan and the International Human Rights Treaty

Akiko EJIMA

15.1 Introduction

The paper examines the present situation of the national and international codification of human rights. Before starting an analysis on the basis of his questions, I would like to emphasise several characteristics of the Japanese situation to facilitate an understanding of my analysis.

First, Japan's legal history has a history of transplants of legal systems from other countries.[1] In particular, two major transplants of western legal systems at the end of the nineteenth century and after World War II should be noted. First, Japan transplanted a western legal system to modernise the country and catch up with the international standard at that time. The Japanese Meiji Government[2] chose the Prussian constitutional system as a model for the Japanese system after a debate on which country was suitable for Japan to follow as a model. The reason for this choice was the similarity of the conditions in Japan and Prussia, as the latter had also gone through modernisation and industrialisation to catch up with more developed countries at that time. The French model was rejected as too radical for Japan, which wanted to keep the sovereignty of the emperor.

The second transplant took place during the US-Allied Powers occupation (1945–1952), the purpose of which was to make Japan democratic and liberal. The initial draft of the Constitution of Japan was prepared by personnel of the US occupation army, including lawyers and experts on Japanese studies, because the initial draft prepared by the Japanese government was not compatible with the standard expected

---

[1] It should be added that a by-product of the history of consecutive transplants was a flourish of comparative legal studies in Japan.

[2] The Edo Government (1603–1867), ruled by Tokugawa Shogun, failed to achieve modernisation and gave up the ruling power to the Meiji Government (1868–1912) ruled by Meiji Emperor.

A. EJIMA (✉)
Law School, Meiji University, 1-1 Kanda-Surugadai, Chiyodaku, 1018301 Tokyo, Japan
e-mail: ejima@kisc.meiji.ac.jp

W.-Y. Wang (ed.), *Codification in International Perspective,* Ius Comparatum – Global Studies in Comparative Law, DOI 10.1007/978-3-319-03455-3_15,
© Springer International Publishing Switzerland 2014

by the US. Unfortunately, the international political situation (the beginning of the Cold War) did not allow General MacArthur, Supreme Commander for Allied Forces, to be patient enough to take a gentler measure, such as guidance and consultation. Basic resources for drafting Japan's constitution were apparently so lacking that one of the American drafting members visited public and university libraries to collect constitutions of the world, including the Declaration of Independence, the US Constitution, the Magna Carta, the Constitution of France, the Weimar Constitution, Constitutions of Scandinavian countries and Constitutions of the Soviet Union (Gordon (1995):149). A drafting member confessed that she was attracted by the richness of the social rights clauses in the Weimar Constitution and Soviet constitutions, but felt the American Bill of Rights was rather ungenerous regarding women's rights as it contained only one clause of female suffrage (Gordon (1995):151–153).

The draft itself is a hybrid of the world constitutions at that time. It adopts US-style judicial review; the ordinary courts have power to strike down statutes. It maintains a bicameral system of the legislature and a Cabinet system based on the UK model, although the House of Lords was replaced by the House of Councillors as an elected House. The draft Constitution included a complete bill of rights of the people, which is richer in content than that of the US, as it includes social rights and equality between men and women. Moreover, the bill of rights was entrenched by the aforementioned judicial review. The new democratically elected House of Representatives deliberated the draft, made amendments to it and passed it by a vote of 429 to 8.[3]

Second, the current Constitution of Japan was drafted when the nascent idea of international human rights protection was incorporated into a document such as the Universal Declaration of Human Rights (UDHR). In other words, the birth and development of the Constitution of Japan coincided with the development of international human rights law. The Constitution of Japan was promulgated on 3 November 1946 and came into effect on 3 May 1947. On the other hand, UDHR was adopted by the General Assembly of the United Nations on 10 December 1948. There was no direct connection or exact similarities in text, unlike those between Eastern European constitutions and the European Convention on Human Rights (ECHR). However, there was a subtle but important correlation highlighted by two examples. First, the Constitution of Japan and the UDHR (and the Charter of the United Nations) stand on the same ideal that the majority of American drafters also shared. The Preamble of the Constitution of Japan provides that

> We believe that no nation is responsible to itself alone, but **the laws of political morality are universal**; and that obedience to such laws is incumbent upon all nations who would sustain their own sovereignty and justify their sovereign relationship with other nations.[4]

---

[3] For the first time, Japanese women over twenty years of age participated in the election.

[4] Emphasis is added by the author. The text of the Constitution of Japan (English) I use in my paper can be seen on a government website: http://www.kantei.go.jp/foreign/constitution_and_government_of_japan/constitution_e.html (visited 31/01/2012). The translation is based on American spellings.

This sentence is the compromised outcome of a debate between Commander Hussey and Colonel Kades. Hussey had initially proposed to insert a sentence into the Preamble as follows:

> We acknowledge that no people is responsible to itself alone, but that laws of political morality are universal and it is by these laws that we obtain sovereignity [sic]. (Takayanagi et al. (1972a): 248)

Kades immediately opposed this proposal and argued 'The promulgation of a universal law of morality, based upon ideology rather than pragmatics, is unhappily reminiscent of the divine right of kings (Takayanagi et al. (1972a): 248)'. His idea was strongly contradicted by Hussey, who argued that 'the establishment of the United Nations Organization makes reasoning of this kind both archaic and foolish (Takayanagi et al. (1972a): 250)'. The idea that 'No nation has the right to exercise sovereignity [sic] if its exercise violates universal morality' coincides with the change in international law. Human rights are not domestic matters but international concerns. The idealism that the UN plays a great role in maintaining peace, and therefore a state has to cooperate with the UN was prevailing in the early years of the Constitution whose preamble itself declares that 'we have determined to preserve our security and existence, trusting in the justice and faith of the peace-loving peoples of the world. We desire to occupy an honoured place in an international society striving for the preservation of peace, and the banishment of tyranny and slavery, oppression and intolerance for all time from the earth. We recognize that all peoples of the world have the right to live in peace, free from fear and want'.

Another noteworthy example is Article 25, concerning social rights, which was added by the proposal of a socialist member of the lower house. Since neither the US constitution nor the previous Japanese constitution, the Meiji Constitution, has a clause on social rights, the idea had to come from somewhere else. It is not so exaggerated to say that a Japanese Member of Parliament's (MP's) proposal did not appear groundless or unrealistic to his colleagues in the lower house, because of international recognition of social rights (although with strong controversy) and the suffering of the Japanese people under the severe poverty and starvation during the war and even afterwards.

Third and last, the substantial influences of international human rights treaties upon the Japanese legal system is still limited despite the similarities of the origin, background and even content (to some degree) of the national codified document, such as the Constitution of Japan and the international codified document, which includes the International Covenant of Civil and Political Rights (ICCPR) and the International Covenant of Social, Economic and Cultural Rights (ICSECR). A hypothesis may be that a country such as Japan, which went through the democratization and liberalisation as a part of a package of modernisation and industrialisation (nowadays globalisation), is ready or even eager to accept the minimum requirement as an adoption of the international standard. However, it is more challenging for such a country to implement the standard into practice and establish new machinery for its implementation when the existing machinery is not appropriate or satisfactory.

Japan has not ratified any of the Optional Protocols of human rights treaties[5] that enable an individual to communicate a violation of human rights to one of the UN institutions. Moreover, Japan has not succeeded in establishing a national human rights institution.

15.2 Rights Clauses in the 1946 Constitution of Japan as a Written Constitution

15.2.1 General Character of the Rights; Inherent, Inviolate and Universal

Chapter 3 (Articles 10–40) of the Constitution was devoted to rights and duties of the people of Japan. Article 11 prescribes:

> **Article 11.** The people shall not be prevented from enjoying any of the fundamental human rights. These fundamental human rights guaranteed to the people by this Constitution shall be conferred upon the people of this and future generations as eternal and inviolate rights.

Therefore, fundamental human rights guaranteed by the Constitution of Japan are considered inviolate and universal rights inherent in every human being (Miyazawa (1971): 77,78; Ashibe (2011): 80–82; Sato (2011): 110). The origin of the idea seems to come from the US Declaration of Independence (Ashibe (2011): 80, 81):

> We hold these Truths to be self-evident, that all Men are created equal, that they are endowed by their Creator with certain unalienable Rights, that among these are Life, Liberty and the pursuit of Happiness.[6]

The latter part of this sentence reappears in Article 13 of the Constitution of Japan:[7]

> **Article 13.** All of the people shall be respected as individuals. Their right to **life, liberty and the pursuit of happiness** shall, to the extent that it does not interfere with the public welfare, be the supreme consideration in legislation and in other governmental affairs.[8]

Article 97 fortifies the above general character of the rights by prescribing them again in Chap. X on the Supremacy of the Constitution. Article 97 explains the primary reason why the Constitution is supreme; it is because the Constitution protects fundamental human rights (Sato (2011): 25, 26).

> **Article 97.** The fundamental human rights by this Constitution guaranteed to the people of Japan are fruits of the age-old struggle of man to be free; they have survived the many exacting tests for durability and are conferred upon this and future generations in trust, to be held for all time inviolate.

---

[5] The Optional Protocols of the ICCPR, ICSECR, CEDAW, CAT, CRPD and CRC.

[6] http://www.archives.gov/exhibits/charters/declaration_transcript.html (visited 31/01/2012).

[7] Rights in the Constitution may be restricted when they interfere with the public welfare as provided by Article 13.

[8] Emphasises are added by the author.

15.2.2 Classification of Rights: Rights to Freedom, Social Rights and Procedural/Political Rights

Although the Constitution itself does not classify rights, academic scholars have been trying to do so by referring to the origin and history of rights and freedoms and consulting comparative legal studies. The most common classification in the textbooks is the right to freedom, social rights and others (procedural rights/political rights) (Cf., Ashibe (2011): 83, 84; Matsui (2011): 157, 158). This classification is based on the historical development of human rights. Initially, the idea of human rights flourished at the end of the eighteenth century when the inherent, inviolate and universal rights and freedoms were proclaimed against the despot. Therefore, the right to freedom (as well as negative rights/freedoms) were fundamental at that time.

The right to freedom is sub-classified as 'mental' freedoms (freedom of mental activities), economic freedoms and personal freedoms.[9] Mental freedoms contain freedom of thought and conscience (Article 19), religious freedom (Article 20), freedom of expression (Article 21) and academic freedom (Article 23). Economic freedoms include freedom to choose one's occupation (Article 22), freedom to choose and change one's residence (Article 22) and the right to property (Article 29). Personal freedoms (including criminal procedural rights) are prescribed in detail in Articles 31–40 because of the misuse and abuse of the police power against the suspects and inmates during the Meiji Constitution era.

Social rights are often captioned as the rights of the twentieth century, emphasising that the freedom from the state established in the nineteen century is not appropriate to improve a life of the people who by themselves cannot 'maintain the minimum standards of wholesome and cultured living' in severe structural poverty. Article 25 of the Constitution stipulates 'All people shall have the right to maintain the minimum standards of wholesome and cultured living. In all spheres of life, the State shall use its endeavours for the promotion and extension of social welfare and security, and of public health'. Moreover, the Constitution guarantees the right to receive education (Article 26), the right to work (Article 27) and rights of workers (Article 28).

The third and last group of rights are named in various ways according to the standpoints of scholars. The most prominent rights in this group are the right to vote (Article 15), the procedural rights including the right to seek redress (Article 17) and the right of access to the court (Article 32).

Article 13 (individual dignity and the right to life, liberty and the pursuit of happiness) is considered a comprehensive clause for rights in general. Therefore, when it is necessary to create a new right, Article 13 may be used as a basis. Article 14 guarantees equality under the law.

---

[9] They are the equivalent of prohibition of torture and cruel treatment (ICCPR Article 7), the freedom from slavery (ICCPR Article 8) and the right to liberty and security (ICCPR Article 9).

15.3 Rights of the Citizen and Rights of Men

The title of Chap. III is 'Rights and Duties of the People'. **Article 10** provides that 'The conditions necessary for being a Japanese national shall be determined by law'. It is understood that the people who are Japanese nationals (citizens) are entitled to have the protection of rights under the Constitution. The law that determines who are Japanese nationals is the Nationality Act. The general rule of the Nationality Act is that a person either of whose parents is a Japanese national becomes a Japanese national.

The question is whether a foreigner/non-citizen is entitled to enjoy the protection under the Constitution of Japan. In other words, does the Constitution protect every person who exists in the territory of Japan? In the text of the Constitution, there is no distinction between the citizen and the man (the natural person). The subjects of the right/freedom clauses vary. In Articles 11–15, 26, 27 and 30, the subjects are 'the people'. In Articles 16–20, 22, 31–35 and 38–40, the subjects are 'every person' or 'all'. In Articles 19, 21, 23 and 28, the subjects of the clauses are freedoms or rights.[10] It appears that the differences of subjects (the people or every person) are not relevant to the differences of the characters of rights.[11] If a narrow technical interpretation is adopted, it is clear that rights in the Constitution are only for Japanese nationals as the title of Chap. III of the Constitution itself is 'the Rights and Duties of the People'. However, it is a widely accepted academic view (Ashibe (2011): 92; Sato (2011): 142) that a foreigner should be entitled to be protected under the Constitution since rights prescribed in the Constitution had existed before a state was established, and one of the general principles of the Constitution is international cooperation. In the *McLean* Case, the Supreme Court of Japan also held that 'the guarantee of fundamental rights included in Chapter Three of the Constitution extends also to foreign nationals staying in Japan except for those rights, which by their nature, are understood to address Japanese nationals only'.[12]

What are the rights that by their nature address Japanese nationals only? The first are political rights, such as the right to vote, the right to stand for an election and the right to become public officials (as a political right in a broader sense). Article 15 of the Constitution provides that 'The people have the inalienable right to choose their public officials and to dismiss them'. Then, the Public Offices Election Act is restricted to Japanese nationals only. The Supreme Court held that by the nature of the right to vote, Article 15 addresses Japanese nationals only and not foreigners.[13]

---

[10] Article 28 is clearly for workers.

[11] There was an unsuccessful attempt to distinguish rights guaranteed for non-citizens and those not guaranteed for them by relying on textual differences.

[12] Supreme Court, Grand Bench, 4 October 1978, 32 *Saikou Saibansho Minji Hanreishu* (hereinafter *Minshu*) 1223. The Court, however, turned down McLean's claim and held that 'Guarantee of fundamental rights to foreign nationals by the Constitution should be understood to be granted only within the scope of such a system of the sojourn of foreign nationals and does not extend so far as to bind the exercise of discretionary power of the state, i.e. does not include guarantee that acts which are guaranteed as fundamental human rights under the Constitution during the sojourn should not be considered as negative circumstances in renewing the term of sojourn'.

[13] Supreme Court, 3rd Petty Bench, 28 February 1995, 49 *Minshu* 639.

On the other hand, interestingly, the Court stated that to allow foreigners to vote in the local election is not prohibitcd in thc Constitution, mentioning Sect. 2 of Article 93 (local government) and suggesting a close relationship between foreign residents and local governance.[14]

As far as the right to become public officials is concerned, there is no law restricting that right to Japanese nationals only, but in reality opportunities for foreigners to become public officials have been severely restricted by the policy of central and local governments. Once the Supreme Court decided that 'considering that the Japanese people shall, as the sovereign of the nation under the principle of sovereignty of the people, have final responsibility for governance by the national government and ordinary local public bodies (See Article 1 and 15, Para. 1 of the Constitution), it is contemplated that, in principle, Japanese nationals shall take office as local government employees with public authority, and it is not contemplated under the Japanese legal framework that foreign nationals who belong to a nation other than Japan and have rights and obligations as the people of the nation, may take office as local government employees with public authority in Japan'.[15]

Second, social rights were once considered rights whose protection should be realised by a state to which a person belongs as a national. However, it is now accepted that foreigners who live in Japan should be treated as equal to Japanese nationals as to social rights protection because it is more human and reasonable to immediately help a person in need, and this way of thinking is more in line with the concept of human rights. Besides, there is no fundamental and theoretical obstacle such as the sovereignty of the people, which has been the principal reason to oppose voting rights for foreign residents. Japan abolished the nationality clauses in its social security legislation after Japan ratified ICSECR and the Convention relating to the Status of Refugees, the latter of which guarantees refugees the same treatment as nationals for social services. The Supreme Court also upheld the protection of social rights to foreigners in Japan, but held that it is acceptable that Japanese nationals would be more favourably treated than foreign residents under a limited budget.[16]

Third and last, it has been considered that foreigners are not entitled to the right to enter and depart from Japan since a sovereign state has discretion to decide who are allowed to enter a country according to the customary international law.[17] It is an open question whether a foreigner's right to re-enter Japan should be guaranteed under the Constitution (Ashibe (2011): 95; Sato (2011): 143).[18]

---

[14] Id.

[15] Supreme Court, Grand Bench, 1 January 2005, 59 *Minshu* 128.

[16] Supreme Court, 1st Petty Bench, 2 March 1988, 35–9 *Sosho Geppou* 1754.

[17] Supreme Court, Grand Bench, 19 June 1957, 11 *Saikou Saibansho Keiji Hanreishu* (hereinafter *Keishu*) 1663.

[18] Supreme Court, 1st Petty Bench, 16 November 1992, 166 *Saikou Saibansho Minji Saibanshu* (hereinafter *Shumin*) 575.

15.4   Instruments of Protection of Human Rights in Domestic Order and their Efficacy

The essential principle of government in the Constitution of Japan, which guarantees protection of rights, is the principle of separation of powers. The constitutional design adopted by the Constitution is a rather classic model: how to bind the power of each institution. The executive cannot work without authorization of the legislation. The activities of the executive are under the scrutiny of the legislature. The judiciary invalidates the legislation via judicial review if it is unconstitutional. The judiciary is under the democratic control of the legislature and its nomination is done by the executive. The independence of the judiciary is strictly guaranteed by the Constitution.

Judicial review was initially expected to work as a guardian of rights. In the 1960s and 1970s various controversial political and social issues were brought to the courts. The biggest one was the constitutionality of the Self-Defence Forces (a plaintiff argued that SDF violated the rights to peaceful existence). There were, however, only eight cases in which the Supreme Court recognised the violation of the Constitution of the legislation since the Court was established in 1947. Its deferential attitude towards the Diet has been criticised by academics.

The Lower House, the Upper House or The Diet as a whole has no selected or special committee on human rights. Therefore, whether human rights concerns are raised in the legislature depends on an individual or collective initiative from members of the Houses when they have a specific cause. A good example is the hardship of patients infected with the Hepatitis-C virus through tainted blood products due to the negligence of the government to supervise the pharmaceutical companies. After the long-lasting huge-scale legal battle against the government and companies coupled with few MPs' support, the situation has slowly improved, culminating in the enacting of the Basic Act on Hepatitis Measures in 2010. The more shocking plight of the former Hansen's disease patients is an eloquent example of the lack of human rights protection by the Diet. The Leprosy Prevention Act (1907) and the 1953 Act (which replaced the 1907 Act) forced patients to enter a sanatorium. The Act was kept in force even after it became scientifically clear that the virus was very weak and medication was established. The Kumamoto District Court admitted that the negligence of the executive and legislature was so grievous that former patients were entitled to receive compensation. The 1953 Act was finally abolished in 1996. Moreover, the Diet passed the Act on Payment of Compensation to Inmates of Hansen's Disease Sanatorium (2001) and the Act on Promotion of Resolution of Issues Related to Hansen's Disease (2008). Those examples show the Diet's disadvantage in that it is not designed to tackle human rights issues systemically and thoroughly. On the other hand, they illustrate that once the Diet becomes aware of the existence of human rights violations and is determined to cope with them, it can offer a more complete and thorough solution as legislation that the executive can implement.

The Ministry of Justice has a human rights bureau and related agencies.[19] It also appoints private citizens as human rights volunteers (about 14,000 people). However, there is no effective independent national human rights institution compatible with the Paris Principles.[20] In 2002, the government tried to pass the Human Rights Protection Bill to cope with human rights complaints. The Bill intended to establish a human rights commission as a national human rights institution. However, the Bill was severely criticised by the media and academics. It was scrapped in 2003 after the dissolution of the lower house. The media argued that the bill would impede the free activities of journalists as watchdogs. Academics doubted the independence of the commission, since the Bill intended to establish a commission as an external agency of the Ministry of Justice. In December 2011, the government announced that it was going to prepare a bill to establish a national human rights institution.[21]

15.5 Ranking of International Law Sources in the Constitution

The Constitution of Japan does not specify the status of international law in the Japanese domestic legal hierarchy.[22] Once it was a controversial question. The most important clause to answer the question is Article 98. Section 1 of Article 98 prescribes that 'This Constitution shall be the supreme law of the nation and no law, ordinance, imperial rescript or other act of government, or part thereof, contrary to the provisions hereof, shall have legal force or validity'. This declares that the Constitution of Japan is superior to 'any law' that does not include a treaty. On the other hand, Sect. 2 of Article 98 provides that 'The treaties concluded by Japan and established laws of nations shall be faithfully observed'.[23]

Some scholars argue that a treaty should be superior to the Constitution because one of its fundamental principles is international cooperation, and Sect. 2 of Article 98 prescribed the faithful observation of the treaties. If the Constitution is superior to treaties, the faithful observation of the treaty is impossible. Moreover, they pointed out that Article 81 excludes a treaty as an object of judicial review (Miyazawa (1978): 816–818).

---

[19] http://www.moj.go.jp/ENGLISH/HB/hb–01.html; http://www.moj.go.jp/ENGLISH/HB/hb-04 .html (visited 31/01/2012).

[20] Principles relating to the Status of National Institutions were adopted by the General Assembly Resolution 48/134 in 2003.

[21] http://www.moj.go.jp/JINKEN/jinken03_00062.html(visited 31/01/2012).

[22] In Japanese law a treaty is considered to obtain an internal effect (domestic legal effect) after it is promulgated (Ashibe (1992): 89). The reason is as follows: the Constitution of Japan adopts the principle of international cooperation (Article 98); the conclusion of a treaty has to be accompanied by the approval of the Diet (Article 73). Since the international customary law is considered as 'established laws of nations' (Article 98 of the Constitution), it also has an internal effect.

[23] The original draft of this section was proposed by the Ministry of Foreign Affairs, which believed it was important to sweep away the past impression of Japan that it did not observe treaties (Takayanagi et al. (1972b): 281, 282).

Other scholars oppose the above view, relying on the following reasons (Kiyomiya (1979): 450; Ashibe (1992):92, 93). First, the principle of international cooperation is too broad and ambiguous to deduce a concrete conclusion. Second, authority to conclude a treaty comes from the Constitution. Therefore, it is impossible to say that a treaty can change the Constitution from which the legitimacy of the treaty is derived. Third, Sect. 2 of Article 98 does not require the government to respect a treaty, which is contrary to the Constitution. Fourth, the reason why Sect. 1 of Article 98 does not include a treaty is that it is a clause to declare the superiority of the Constitution in the domestic legal system. Moreover, the reason why Article 81 does not include treaties is that it takes into account a possibility that a treaty is not appropriate to be an object of judicial review since it is a consensus between states. Fifth and last, the procedure to conclude a treaty is simpler than the constitutional reform procedure, which requires the special majority (two-thirds or more of all the members of each House) and a majority of the peoples' referendum (Article 96).

The view that a treaty is superior to the Constitution was popular when the Constitution was in a nascent stage because of the remorse about World War II and the idealistic expectation toward the UN. However, the Cold War started, and Japan changed its defence policy to conclude the Security Treaty between the US and Japan in 1951 (which took into effect in 1952 and was replaced by the Treaty of Mutual Co-operation and Security between the US and Japan in 1960). The constitutionality of the treaty was strongly questioned in the late 1950s and onwards. Therefore, the view that the Constitution is superior to a treaty prevailed in order to argue that the treaty was unconstitutional. In the *Sunagawa* case, the Supreme Court indirectly admitted the superiority of the Constitution by suggesting a possibility that even a highly important political treaty might be reviewed if it was clearly unconstitutional.[24]

On the other hand, another approach to the question became popular. It distinguished 'established laws of nations' and treaties concerning demarcation of territory and conditions of surrender, among other things (Higuchi (2004): 349; Takahashi (2010): 17; Hasebe (2011): 444). The government maintains a similar position (Asano (2003): 517). The question must be revisited by taking into account the current development of international human rights law.

A treaty is superior to a statute or an Act. International customary law is considered to have the same status as a treaty (Kodera (2010): 125). The Japanese government accepts the existence of *jus cogens* (the answer of the head of the International Legal Affairs Bureau, Ministry of Foreign Affairs at the Standing Committee on Foreign Affairs and Defence, 2 June 2009).

---

[24] Supreme Court, Grand Bench, 12 December 1959, 13 *Keishu* 3225 (*Sunagawa* case).

15.6   Status and Influence of Human Rights Treaties in the Domestic Constitutional System

Japan ratified major international human rights treaties, but it should be emphasised that Japan has not ratified any Optional Protocols, which enable individuals to communicate human rights violations to the UN bodies. As to the status of human rights treaties, they are superior to statues but inferior to the Constitution. In Asia a regional human rights treaty has not been established yet. The influences of human rights treaties can be observed at two levels: the domestic and international implementation.

15.6.1   Domestic Implementation of Human Rights Treaties

The domestic implementation may be classified into five spheres. First, the influences upon the legislature have been modest. The most influential moment is when the government ratifies a human rights treaty, since the government has to get approval from the Diet. A good example is the ratification of the Convention on the Elimination of All Forms of Discrimination against Women in 1985. To ratify the Convention, the Diet passed the Act on Securing Equal Opportunity and Treatment between Men and Women in Employment in 1985. Moreover, the Nationality Act was amended to make it possible that a child of a Japanese female national who married a foreign man becomes a Japanese national. On the other hand, when the government ratified the Convention on the Rights of the Child, no legislative action was taken, presupposing that the condition of children in Japan is compatible with the standards the Convention requires. In general, awareness of international human rights treaties is not high in the Diet except for a few MPs who maintain special causes such as the abolition of the death penalty.

The second sphere is the government (the executive), which has the principal role of examining whether there is any discrepancy between the domestic legislation and practice and the treaty, which the government will ratify. After ratification the government is responsible for implementing the international standards. A good example is again the establishment of the Council for Gender Equality and the Gender Equality Bureau at the Cabinet Office of the government in 2001. The Gender Equality Bureau is mandated with the formulation and overall coordination of plans for matters related to promoting the formation of a gender-equal society, as well as promoting the Basic Plan for Gender Equality and formulating and implementing plans for matters not falling under the jurisdiction of any particular ministry.[25] However, it must be noted that the outcome is not yet satisfactory. Japan is ranked as 57th among 109 countries in terms of the gender empowerment measure (The 2009 UN Development Report). Moreover, women have been poorly represented in

---

[25] http://www.gender.go.jp/english_contents/category/sorcial2_e.html (visited 31/01/2012.)

the policy decision-making process. The government set the goal of a 20 % participation rate in 1996, but it failed in every field such as the legislature, the judiciary and the executive, except for the members of the inquiry/consultation commission, which is just a consultative body without any substantial decision-making authority and whose members the government can freely nominate. At present, the government has set another ambitious goal of 30 % participation by 2020, although it is likely to fail unless the government adopts some radical measures and strong positive actions (Tsujimura and Yano (2007)). As far as other international human rights treaties are concerned, there is no governmental body that specifically works on the implementation of the treaties.

The third sphere is the judiciary. In general, the judiciary has been very slow to use or even refer to international human rights treaties. Lawyers often refer to human rights treaties when they discover a clearer and more detailed clause in the treaty that would support her or his argument. However, until now, the courts have been reluctant to accept such citation of treaties. First, if the Constitution protects the same human rights that the international treaty protects, it is not necessary for courts to look at international ones. Second, domestic judges find it difficult to use international text due to lack of understanding in specific cases as well as the limited cases available in the UN body (In the European system, domestic judges can consult the rich case law of the European Court of Human Rights). Third, when the legislature is not enthusiastic to utilise the treaty, it is rather dangerous for judges to admit that a statute is incompatible with a treaty since they might be criticised that they are not legislators. Fourth and last, a violation of a treaty is not considered a successful reason to appeal to the Supreme Court. Therefore, the frequent use of international human rights treaties in the courts has been deadlocked.

The Supreme Court, particularly, has consistently denied the existence of violations of human rights treaties without much explanation. A good example is a case about the right of access to the court (Article 32 of the Constitution). The plaintiff, a prisoner who sued a prison warden because of maltreatment by the prison officers, claimed that his right of access to the court was denied because the head of the prison curtailed the meeting time with his lawyer, and all the meetings were supervised by prison officers. The local district court and the high court interestingly admitted the plaintiff's argument partially on the basis of the ICCPR and even the ECHR case law (particularly the *Golder* case and the *Silver* case) and awarded the plaintiff compensation. Conversely, the Supreme Court denied the violations of the ICCPR without explanation.[26]

However, there is a new indication that the Supreme Court would take into account the human rights treaties as well as the comparative law (Ejima (2009)). In a case where in the constitutionality of the Nationality Act was questioned (the Act denied to grant Japanese nationality to a child born between a Japanese father and a non-Japanese mother, who were not legally married), the Supreme Court referred to the ICCPR and CRC as well as legislative trends in other countries.

---

[26] Supreme Court, 1st Petty Bench, 7 September 2000, 199 *Shumin* 283.

In addition, it seems that other states are moving towards scrapping discriminatory treatment by law against children born out of wedlock, and in fact, **the International Covenant on Civil and Political Rights** and **the Convention on the Rights of the Child**, which Japan has ratified, also contain such provisions to the effect that children shall not be subject to discrimination of any kind because of birth. Furthermore, after the provision of Article 3, para.1 of the Nationality Act was established, many states that had previously required legitimation for granting nationality to children born out of wedlock to fathers who are their citizens have revised their laws in order to grant nationality if, and without any other requirement, it is found that the father-child relationship with their citizens is established as a result of acknowledgement.[27]

The fourth sphere is the activities of human rights Non-Governmantal Organizations (NGOs), which have been very strong. There are general and specific NGOs that work for awareness campaigns and offer voluntary help to the individuals who have specific problems such as poverty, domestic violence and discrimination. Moreover, NGOs play an important role when they submit a counter-report to the UN monitoring bodies. The fifth and last sphere is the private sector. Companies become more aware of the human rights value and some of them joined the Global Compact with the UN but they are still in a nascent stage and how they would develop remains to be seen.

15.6.2 International Implementation of Human Rights Treaties

The core of the international implementation of human rights treaties for Japan is the periodic State Party reports to the UN bodies, as Japan has not adopted individual communication measures. The Japanese government submits periodic reports under the obligation of six international human rights treaties: ICCPR; ICSECR; Convention on the Elimination of All Forms of Discrimination Against Women; International Convention on the Elimination of All Forms of Racial Discrimination; the Convention on the Rights of the Child; and the Convention against Torture and Other Cruel, Inhuman or Degrading Treatment or Punishment. Moreover, it is now subject to the Universal Periodic Review by the Human Rights Council of the UN.[28] Concluding observations given by the monitoring bodies of treaties are sometimes reported by the Japanese media, although the impact is limited.

Because of strong and effective participation of the human rights NGOs that submit counter-reports to UN bodies to challenge Japanese government report, a cordial custom gradually has been established in which the Japanese government offers an opportunity to receive opinions of the NGOs about a government report before the government submits it to a UN body. Taking into account the detailed content and regularity of the report, there is an undeveloped potential to utilise a process and the result of the monitoring system of the government report to accelerate the domestic implementation (Ejima (2011)).

---

[27] Supreme Court, Grand Bench, 4 June 2008, 62 *Minshu* 1367. Emphasises are added by the author.

[28] Report of the Working Group on the Universal Periodic Review: Japan. A/HRC/8/44, 30 May 2008.

15.7   Citizenship

The Nationality Act provides that a child shall be a Japanese citizen in the following cases: (1) If the father or mother is a Japanese citizen at the time of birth; (2) If the father died before the child's birth and was a Japanese citizen at the time of death; or (3) If born in Japan and both of the parents are unknown or are without nationality. Therefore, a person cannot become a Japanese citizen even if s/he is born in Japan and lives for a lifetime unless s/he acquires Japanese nationality through naturalization.

The most challenged issue has been the status of Korean residents in Japan whose ancestors lived in Japan before World War II as Japanese citizens but continue to do so as foreign nationals. Their Japanese nationality was stripped by the government on the basis of the Peace Treaty (signed in 1951 and effective in 1952). Because of the Nationality Act, Korean residents are considered foreigners despite having settled in Japan for many years and most of them using Japanese as their principal language (even the younger generation do not speak Korean). Certain issues, such as the obligatory finger print registration system and permission of re-entry to Japan, were politically resolved but the issue of voting rights have remained controversial.[29]

15.8   Conclusion

It is time for Japan to re-examine the traditional constitutional design on the basis of the classic separation of powers to develop a multi-layered implementation system between a domestic constitutional system and the international system of human rights treaties. It is possible to establish one taking into account many connections between the national and international codified bills of rights.

What is the starting point? First, the legislature, the executive and the judiciary as traditional constitutional institutions can explore the merit of referring to and even relying on international human rights treaties and their outcome such as views, observations, decisions and judgements of monitoring bodies (quasi-judicial institutions), as well as resolutions and recommendations of political or quasi-legislative institutions, such as General Assembly and the treaty-based organisations concerning human rights. Second, it is time for new additional bridges. The most plausible and effective candidates for Japan nowadays are national human rights institutions and individual communication to the UN institutions. Third and last, taking into account that the international machinery is still subsidiary to the national machinery, it is extremely important that the national machinery takes an initiative to protect and promote human rights, strengthened by the simultaneous codification of human rights nationally and internationally. It should be kept in mind that the effectiveness of a multi-layered system depends not on the strength of international measures but in the consensus of countries that share similar human rights as codified texts and similar effective machinery to realise them.

---

[29] Several private members' bills have been proposed to the Diet in vain.

References

Asano, Ichiro et al (2003), *Kenpou Toubenshu*, Shinzansha (Publisher).

Ashibe, Nobuyoshi (1992), *Kenpougaku I*, Yuhikaku (Publisher).

Ashibe, Nobuyoshi (2011), *Kenpou*, 5th Edn (Supplanted By Takahashi, Kazuyuki), Iwanamishoten (Publisher).

Ejima, Akiko (2009), Enigmatic Attitude of The Supreme Court of Japan towards Foreign Precedents—Refusal at Front Door and Admission at Back Door, 16 *Meiji Law Journal* (Meiji University) 19.

Ejima, Akiko (2011), Kenpou no Miraizou ni okeru Kokusai Jinken Joyaku no Position, In Tsujimura, Miyoko, And Hasebe, Yasuo (Eds), *Kenpou Riron no Saisouzou*, Nihon Hyoronsha (Publisher).

General Assembly Resolution 48/134 in 2003.

Gordon, Beate Shirota (1995), *1945 Nen no Kurisumasu*, Kashiwa Shobo (Publisher).

Hasebe, Yasuo (2011), *Kenpou*, 5th Edn, Shinseisha (Publisher).

Higuchi, Yoichi (2001), *Five Decades of Constitutionalism in Japanese Society*, University of Tokyo Press.

Higuchi Yoichi et al (2004), *Chukai Houritsugaku Zenshu Nihonkoku Kenpou IV*, Seirin Shoin (Publisher).

Inoue, Kyoko (1991), *Macarthur's Japanese Constitution: A Linguistic and Cultural Study of Its Making*, University of Chicago Press.

Kiyomiya, Shirou (1979), *Kenpou I*, Yuhikaku (Publisher).

Kodera, Akira et al (2010), *Kogi Kokusaihou*, Yuhikaku (Publisher).

Luney, Percy R. Jr. and Takahashi, Kazuyuki (Eds.) (1993), *Japanese Constitutional Law*, University of Tokyo Press.

Matsui, Shigenori (2011), *The Constitution of Japan*, Hart Publishing.

Miyazawa, Toshiyoshi (1971), *Kenpou II*, Yuhikaku (Publisher).

Miyazawa, Toshiyoshi (1978), *Zentei Nihonkoku Kenpou* (Supplanted by Ashibe, Nobuyoshi), Nihon Hyoronsha (Publisher).

Sato, Koji (2011), *Nihonkoku Kenpou*, Seibundo (Publisher).

Supreme Court, Grand Bench, 19 June 1957, 11 *Saikou Saibansho Keiji Hanreishu* (hereinafter *Keishu*) 1663.

Supreme Court, Grand Bench, 12 December 1959, 13 *Keishu* 3225 (*Sunagawa* case).

Supreme Court, Grand Bench, 4 October 1978, 32 (*Saikou Saibansho Minji Hanreishu*, hereinafter *Minshu*) 1223.

Supreme Court, 1st Petty Bench, 16 November 1992, 166 *Saikou Saibansho Minji Saibanshu* (hereinafter *Shumin*) 575.

Supreme Court, 3rd Petty Bench, 28 February 1995, 49 *Minshu* 639.

Supreme Court, 1st Petty Bench, 7 September 2000, 199 *Shumin* 283.

Supreme Court, Grand Bench, 1 January 2005, 59 *Minshu* 128.

Supreme Court, Grand Bench, 4 June 2008, 62 *Minshu* 1367.

Takahashi, Kazuyuki (2002), Why Do We Study Constitutional Laws of Foreign Countries, and How?, In Vicki Jackson And Mark Tushnet (Eds.), *Defining the Field of Comparative Constitutional Law*, Prager.

Takahashi, Kazuyuki (2010), *Rikkenshugi to Nihonkoku Kenpou*, Yuhikaku (Publisher).

Takayanagi, Kenzo et al (1972a), *Nihonkoku Kenpou Seitei no Katei I*, Yuhikaku (Publisher).

Takayanagi, Kenzo et al (1972b), *Nihonkoku Kenpou Seitei no Katei II*, Yuhikaku (Publisher).

Tsujimura, Miyoko, and Yano, Emi (Eds.) (2007), *Gender & Law in Japan*, Tohoku University Press.

Universal Periodic Review: Japan. A/HRC/8/44, 30 May 2008.

Yakushiji, Kimio et al (2006), *Kokusai Jinken Hou*, Nihon Hyoronsha (Publisher).

http://www.kantei.go.jp/foreign/constitution_and_government_of_japan/constitution_e.html (visited 31/01/2012)

http://www.archives.gov/exhibits/charters/declaration_transcript.html (visited 31/01/2012)
http://www.moj.go.jp/ENGLISH/HB/hb-01.html (visited 31/01/2012)
http://www.moj.go.jp/ENGLISH/HB/hb-04.html (visited 31/01/2012)
http://www.moj.go.jp/JINKEN/jinken03_00062.html (visited 31/01/2012)
http://www.gender.go.jp/english_contents/category/sorcial2_e.html (visited 31/01/2012)

Chapter 16
Codification and Implementation of Human Rights in the Netherlands

Ida Lintel and Marthe Lot Vermeulen

16.1 Human Rights Codified in Dutch Law

16.1.1 Fundamental Rights Codified in the Constitution of the Netherlands

1. Introduction

The human rights enshrined in Dutch constitutional law are commonly referred to as fundamental rights. Chap. 1 of the Dutch Constitution contains 23 articles which make up the bill of rights. Some articles that can be classified as enshrining fundamental rights can be found elsewhere in the Constitution, for example, in Article 114 which prohibits the death penalty.

2. Specific Fundamental Rights

The right to equality and non-discrimination is placed in the Dutch Constitution at the top of the human rights catalogue, namely in Article 1. Article 2 states that legislation regulates who qualifies as a Dutch national. Moreover, the article addresses the admission and expulsion of aliens. Article 3 guarantees that all Dutch nationals are equally eligible for appointment to public office. It should be noted that this does not prevent demands being made with regard to the suitability of appointment. For

Ida Lintel, LL.M. is currently studying Dutch Law at Utrecht University and Dr. Marthe Lot Vermeulen, is a trainee judge at the Amsterdam District Court. This contribution is written in their personal capacity.

I. Lintel (✉)
Former intern at the Netherlands Institute of Human Rights,
Achter Sint Pieter 200, 3512 HT Utrecht, The Netherlands
e-mail: idalintel89@gmail.com, i.m.a.lintel@uu.nl

M. L. Vermeulen
Former staff member of the Netherlands Institute of Human Rights,
Achter Sint Pieter 200, 3512 HT Utrecht, The Netherlands
e-mail: marthelot@gmail.com

W.-Y. Wang (ed.), *Codification in International Perspective,* Ius Comparatum – Global Studies in Comparative Law, DOI 10.1007/978-3-319-03455-3_16,
© Springer International Publishing Switzerland 2014

example, a person's political persuasion or convictions about life may play a role in the selection procedure.[1] Also, since this article concerns the appointment to public office, nothing prevents non-nationals for the appointment to many public posts. Article 3 can be said to be *lex specialis* to the prohibition of discrimination. For all Dutch nationals, the right to directly elect members of the general representative bodies and to be elected as a member of such bodies is enshrined in Article 4 of the Constitution. Article 5 contains an age-old right; the right of petition. This right is applicable to everyone without exception.

The guarantee to freedom of religion is laid down in Article 6. This right covers explicitly also the freedom of (non-religious) belief. Article 7 articulates the freedom of expression. This article distinguishes between different forms of freedom of expression. Freedom of the press enjoys the widest protection.[2] Paragraph two covers radio and television and paragraph three relates to the expression of opinions by other means than the press, radio and television. Commercial advertising is excluded from formal constitutional protection. Article 8 provides for the freedom of association, applying to legal persons and other groups of persons. The freedom to hold meetings and demonstrations is laid down in Article 9. The right to hold demonstrations was newly included in the 1983 Constitution.

Articles 10–13 cover the protection of rights in the sphere of privacy. Article 10 states that restrictions to privacy may only be imposed by, or pursuant to, an Act of Parliament. This is a classical fundamental right. Paragraphs 2 and 3, however, are classified as social rights. Paragraph 2 obliges the legislator to adopt rules to protect privacy in relation to the recording and dissemination of personal data. Pursuant to paragraph 3, the legislator should lay down rules related to the right of individuals to have access to information recorded on them. At the instance of the Chamber of Deputies, the right of all to the inviolability of the physical person was included as a separate right in 1983.[3] This right is laid down in Article 11 of the Constitution. Both Article 10(1) and 11 can in certain circumstances be applied horizontally.[4] Article 12 protects privacy within the home against governmental interference. This right was already codified in 1798. Article 13 deals with the protection of correspondence, telephone and telegraph communication from government interception. Of the three means of communication, the privacy of correspondence enjoys the strongest protection.

The issue of expropriation is dealt with in Article 14. Expropriation is only allowed when it serves a general interest and under prior guarantee of compensation, in accordance with rules laid down by or pursuant to an Act of Parliament.

Article 15, known as the *habeas corpus* provision, protects citizens against arbitrary deprivation of life and guarantees a detainee certain rights. Article 16 contains the *nullum crimen, nulla poene sine praevia lege poenali* principle; this principle is

---

[1] Kortmann CAJM, Bovend'Eert PPT (1993) Dutch Constitutional Law. Kluwer Law International, The Hague, p. 136.

[2] Kortmann & Bovend'Eert (2000), p. 153.

[3] Annex to *Handelingen* II 1975/76, 13 872, no. 3, p. 38.

[4] Kortmann & Bovend'Eert (2000), p. 155.

part of the legality principle that prohibits the retrospective penalization of a specific act. This article applies to substantive criminal law; constitutional law does not specifically rule out the retrospective effect of new legislation in other fields of law. Nevertheless, as a general rule, laws that are onerous for individuals should not have retrospective force.[5] Article 17 states that no-one can be deprived of his right to appeal to a judicial body to which he is entitled under the law.

The aforementioned provisions are all classical rights, which entails *inter alia* that they can be invoked in court. In contrast, Articles 18–23, which predominantly include social and economic rights, provide instructions to the government and are not invocable in court. There are, however, some exceptions to this rule. For the purpose of this report it is useful to briefly address the content of the social and economic rights that are invocable in court. Article 18(1) reads that everyone, in judicial as well as administrative proceedings, is entitled to legal representation. The right to a free choice of employment is guaranteed in Article 19(3), though limited by or pursuant to an Act of Parliament. In practice, naturally, many limitations exist on the basis of requirements on, amongst others, qualification. According to Article 20(3), all Dutch nationals who are residing in the country have a right to financial assistance from the government as regulated by an Act of Parliament if they are unable to provide for themselves. Article 23(2) guarantees the freedom to provide education, subject to the supervision by the government as regulated by the law. Furthermore, the government is allowed to set standards of competence and moral integrity for teachers for forms of education designated by an Act of Parliament.

3. Limitations

Fundamental rights primarily govern the relationship between the government and the people. The government is allowed to limit the exercise of certain classical fundamental rights.[6] For example, the government can limit the exercise of freedom of religion outside buildings and enclosed places in order to protect, *inter alia,* public health, as outlined in Article 6(2) of the Constitution. The question of limitations does not affect social fundamental rights.

Only a few rights are so fundamental that they cannot be restricted, namely the principle of equality and the prohibition against discrimination, the right of petition, the ban on censorship and the prohibition on the death penalty.[7] Formally, the government may only restrict an individual's exercise of fundamental rights as long as the limitation can be traced back to a constitutional limitation clause. In practice, however, a limitation is allowed when it constitutes a reasonable interpretation of the scope of a right and in the application of fundamental rights and their limitation clauses.[8]

---

[5] Kortmann & Bovend'Eert (2000), p. 156.

[6] Bunschoten DE (2009) Tekst en Commentaar Grondwet, commentaar op hoofdstuk 1 Gw. Kluwer Navigator.

[7] See Articles 1, 5, 7(1) and 114 of the Dutch Constitution, respectively.

[8] Besselink LFM (2004) Constitutional law of the Netherlands: an introduction with texts, cases and materials. Ars Aequi Libri, Nijmegen, p. 156. See also case law in which limitations were

4. Vertical and Horizontal Effect of the Fundamental Rights

Constitutionally, fundamental rights can be invoked by individuals against the government regardless of the capacity in which the government acts. This means that the vertical effect does not only apply when the government fulfils typical governmental tasks, but also when the government carries out activities which could have been fulfilled by an individual.[9]

Overall, it can be stated that fundamental rights were not created to apply to relationships between individuals. Fundamental rights have only occasionally been invoked between citizens *inter se*,[10] and the " Hoge Raad" (hereinafter: the Supreme Court) held in relation to certain articles that parties could indeed rely on fundamental rights. In order to come to a decision in such cases, a concession on the right of one of the opposing parties had to be accepted.[11] When confronted with a case in which fundamental rights are invoked in relations between citizens, the judge decides the case by weighing the interests of both parties. Also important to note is that social fundamental rights are especially unfit to operate horizontally. Since a citizen is not required to bear responsibility for sufficient employment, facilities for public health, or improvement of the living environment.

5. Subjects of Fundamental Rights

In principle, classical fundamental rights can be invoked by anybody against the government, regardless of age, nationality or place of residence. Thus, fundamental rights also apply to persons who are in a special legal position in relation to the government, like military personnel, civil servants, and prisoners (though prisoners can be limited in the exercise of their fundamental rights).[12] Some fundamental rights, however, are only guaranteed for individuals having the Dutch nationality. This concerns Articles 3, 4, 19(3) and 20(3). Apart from individuals, legal entities and groups of persons may also be the subjects of fundamental rights, depending on the nature of the right.[13]

6. Absence of a Hierarchy

The Dutch Constitution does not establish a hierarchy between fundamental rights. That is why, when tension or conflict between fundamental rights arises, not only the judge but also the legislator has in certain circumstances the task to decide, within the framework of the constitutional possibilities, the meaning of the right in relation to other rights.[14] Regarding the judiciary, the Supreme Court has decided that, when

---

allowed in the absence of a constitutional limitation clause: HR, 11 February 1986, *NJ 1986, 673*, (*Drukkerij*); Vzngr ARRvS 16 February 1989, *AB 1990, 9* (*Evangeliegemeente De Deur*).

[9] Kortmann & Bovend'Eert (2000), p. 147.

[10] See *e.g.* HR 2 February 1990, nr. 13 727 (interim injunction proceedings) (*Goeree and Van Manschot v. Van Zijl*).

[11] HR, 18 June 1993, RvdW 1993, 136.

[12] Explanatory memorandum, *Kamerstukken* II 1975/76, 13 872, no. 3, pp. 11 and 12.

[13] *Ibid.*, p. 11.

[14] *Handelingen* II 1985/86 (6 februari 1986), p. 3163.

a conflict of fundamental rights occurs, a cautious weighing of interests is needed, in which all the factors of the specific situation are taken into consideration, to decide which fundamental right prevails.[15]

16.1.2 Human Rights Transformed in Dutch Law Other than the Constitution

1. Human Rights Codified as a Crime in Criminal Law

Apart from the codification of human rights in the Constitution, the definition of human rights has permeated in Acts of Parliament. A number of international human rights are codified and defined in criminal law, notably torture and, recently, enforced disappearance. In 2003 the International Crimes Act was adopted in accordance with the Rome Statute. This Act defines *inter alia* torture and enforced disappearance as a crime against humanity. Additionally, this Act brought Dutch criminal law in line with the obligation arising from Article 4 of the Convention against Torture (CAT) by means of the criminalization of a single act of torture. In anticipation of the ratification of the International Convention for the Protection of all Persons from Enforced Disappearance (ICPPED), which the Netherlands has now ratified, the International Crimes Act was amended in 2010 to make a single crime of enforced disappearance punishable by law.[16]

2. The Equal Treatment Act

A second Act of Parliament that deserves mentioning is the Equal Treatment Act, which elaborates in more detail the scope and content of Article 1 of the Constitution. Also, it mentions explicitly additional grounds on the basis of which discrimination is prohibited, namely the grounds of nationality, heterosexual or homosexual orientation or civil status.[17]

16.2 The Applicability of International Human Rights Law in the Netherlands

16.2.1 The Status of International Law in the Dutch Legal Order

Articles 93 and 94 of the Constitution govern the relationship between Dutch law and international law. The text of these articles reads as follows:

---

[15] HR, 4 maart 1988, para. 3.5, NJ 1989, 361 (*Borbon Parma*) m.nt. C.J.H. Brunner.

[16] Article 8(a) of the International Crimes Act; Dutch Enforced Disappearance Convention Implementation Act (2010). See similarly, Dutch Torture Convention Implementation Act (1989).

[17] Equal Treatment Act (AWGB) (2 March 1994).

Article 93 Provisions of treaties and of resolutions by international institutions which may be binding on all persons by virtue of their contents shall become binding after they have been published.

Article 94 Statutory regulations in force within the Kingdom shall not be applicable if such application is in conflict with provisions of treaties that are binding on all persons or of resolutions by international institutions.[18]

The Constitution provides for a 'moderate monist system',[19] which implies that international law forms part of the Dutch legal order. Articles 93 and 94 of the Constitution set the conditions for the internal effect of international law.[20] The moderate nature lies in the fact that only provisions of international treaties and of resolutions by international institutions take precedence over statutory regulations as long as they are 'binding on all persons by virtue of their contents' and after they have been published.[21]

The importance of Articles 93 and 94 is emphasized by the limitation of constitutional review laid down in Article 120 of the Constitution. Article 120 of the Constitution precludes the Dutch courts from reviewing the constitutionality of Acts of Parliament and treaties.[22] This limitation firstly means that, while the task of the judge is to decide upon the binding nature of provisions of international law, Dutch courts are not entitled to question the validity of treaties. The assessment of the validity of treaties is the task of the Parliament.[23] Hence, when a treaty is approved by Parliament it is binding on the Netherlands. Secondly, Dutch courts may not assess the compatibility of Acts of Parliament with the Constitution.[24] This limited possibility of review underscores the importance of the internal effect of international law. Dutch courts, after all, may assess the compliance of Parliamentary Acts with binding provisions of treaties.[25] At the same time, it follows from Article 120 that courts may review the compliance of delegated statutory law with the Constitution,

---

[18] Translation found in Alkema EA (2010) International Law in Domestic Systems. EJCL 14–3:1–22, at p. 2.

[19] *Kamerstukken* II (2007–2008), 29 861, no. 19, p. 3 and footnote 1 (noting that the distinction between 'monist' systems and 'dualist' systems, which is a distinction that originates in academic debate, touches upon the extent to which international law has to be transformed into national law before it has legal effect).

[20] Alkema (2010), p. 1.

[21] The way in which treaties and resolutions by international organizations have to be published is laid down by Act of Parliament in accordance with Article 95 of the Constitution. The *Tractatenblad* is the official place for publication in the Netherlands.

[22] The text of Article 120 of the Constitution reads: 'The constitutionality of Acts of Parliament and treaties shall not be reviewed by the courts'.

[23] Van Empel M, De Jong M (2002) Constitution, International Treaties, Contracts and Torts. EJCL 6–4: 283–305.

[24] HR, 14 April 1989, AB 1989, 207. See also HR, 6 March 1959, NJ 1962, 2 (*Nyugat zaak*).

[25] HR, 4 June 1982, NJ 1983, 32; HR, 1 July 1983, NJ 1984, 161 and CRvB, 14 May 1987, AB 1987, 543.

general principles of law and binding provisions of treaties and decisions of international institutions.[26] A recent discussion in the Netherlands focuses on the pending legislation that proposes to amend Article 120 of the Constitution to include a second paragraph listing a number of fundamental rights that are exempted from the scope of the review prohibition.[27]

16.2.2 Enforceability of Human Rights in the Dutch Legal Order

The Netherlands has ratified all international and European human rights treaties and their protocols, apart from the Convention on Migrant Workers and the Convention on Persons with Disabilities (CRPD) and its Optional Protocol. While not ratified, the Netherlands had signed the CRPD. Generally speaking, there are two types of internal effects of international law in the Dutch legal order that can be distinguished, namely direct effect and indirect effect. These two forms will be discussed in the subsections below.

1. Direct Effect (Self-Executing Treaty Provisions)

As stated above, individuals can only rely directly on international norms before the Dutch courts if those norms (treaty provisions or resolutions by international institutions) are considered to be 'binding on all persons by virtue of their contents' according to Article 94 of the Constitution. Dutch courts have the task to further interpret this clause. Based on the text of this article, the Supreme Court mainly considers the content of the provision to be decisive, not the intentions of the States Parties to a treaty.[28] Scholars have furthermore discerned from the case-law additional criteria that have been taken into account. For example, the provision must be sufficiently concrete and clear in granting rights to or imposing obligations on individuals.[29] Courts have also taken into account whether the provisions only bind the state in its relations to other states. Additionally, provisions classified as self-executing do not require further elaboration by the legislature or administration before a court is

---

[26] HR, 16 May 1986, NJ 1987, 251 (*Sproeivliegtuigen*); *Rapport Staatscommissie Grondrechten* (2010), available at available at www.staatscommissiegrondwet.nl, p. 43.

[27] *Voorstel van wet van het lid Halsema tot verandering in de Grondwet, strekkende tot invoering van de bevoegdheid tot toetsing van wetten aan een aantal bepalingen van de Grondwet door de rechter, Kamerstuk* 34332 (2010).

[28] HR, 7 May 1986 (*NS/FNV*), NJ 1986, 688, para. 3.2.

[29] Direct effect may result in two different situations in the relationship between the state and the individual. On the one hand there are cases in which provisions providing rights for individuals or groups of individuals are invoked before the national courts, see e.g. HR, 21 March 1986, NJ 1986, 585. On the other hand there are cases concerning treaties imposing obligations on individuals (e.g. international crimes) or on states, see e.g. RvS, 30 December 1993, AB 1995, no. 24 (Zwiers v. Provincial Executive of Gelderland). For a discussion on this distinction, see Van Empel & De Jong (2002), p. 296.

able to apply them in concrete cases.[30] Finally, courts have considered whether the provision provides for a positive obligation or for gradual implementation,[31] which implies a non-self-executing character. Scholars have noted that Dutch courts generally avoid an open confrontation with the parliamentary legislature, when the law is potentially not in compliance with international law. In such cases, courts tend to 'abstain' from applying the international norm on the basis that it would fall outside their scope of competence. For instance, such approach has been taken if the court found that the decision to be made was beyond their judicial task and more suitable for political consideration.[32]

2. Economic, Social and Cultural Rights

The majority of the social rights cannot be invoked in court. In general, such rights are considered to be instructions addressed to the public authorities rather than self-executing rights of individuals. This nature means that public authorities have considerable leeway in how to interpret and implement such rights in their national system. There are four landmark cases in which the nature of economic, social and cultural rights was at stake. In 1986, the Supreme Court ruled that Article 6(4) of the European Social Charter (ESC) was a self-executing provision. This article entails, 'the right of workers and employers to collective action in cases of conflicts of interest, including the right to strike, subject to obligations that might arise out of collective agreements previously entered into.'[33] A second landmark case was handed down in 1990, when the Supreme Court ruled that Article 7(a)(i) International Covenant on Economic, Social and Culture Rights (ICESCR) (the right to the enjoyment of just and favourable conditions of work) does not have direct effect in the Dutch legal order. In this case, the Supreme Court held that the content was worded in general terms, which needed further clarification in national law. In addition, the Supreme Court examined the travaux préparatoires of the Dutch implementation law of this treaty, which states that Article 7 portrays a goal that has to be achieved. Lastly, the Court concluded that such interpretation is in line with Article 2 ICESCR, which obliges states to achieve the goals set in the provisions progressively.[34] The third landmark case was handed down by the Central Appeals Tribunal, in 1996.[35] This case challenged the Dutch legislation that obliged individuals to bear a portion of the costs for care by qualified midwives during labor given in hospital on medical indication. The complainants alleged that this legislation was in violation of inter alia

---

[30] Alkema (2010), pp. 7 and 8; *Rapport Staatscommissie Grondrechten* (2010), p. 131; Van Empel & De Jong (2002), p. 295.

[31] Alkema (2010), pp. 7 and 8.

[32] Alkema (2010), p. 8.

[33] HR, 30 mei 1986, NJ 1986, 688 (*Collectieve acties Spoorwegen*).

[34] HR, 20 April 1990, NJ 1992, 636 (*Hoogenraad/ZWO*).

[35] The Central Appeals Tribunal is the highest judicial authority mainly active in legal areas pertaining to social security and the civil service.

Article 10 of the International Labor Organization (ILO) Convention 102 on social security. This article establishes in paragraph (1)(b) that the benefit shall include 'in case of pregnancy and confinement and their consequences

i. pre-natal, confinement and post-natal care either by medical practitioners or by qualified midwives; and
ii. hospitalisation where necessary.'

The Central Appeals Tribunal decided that this article is self-executing taking into account its clear content, imperative formulation and minimum character as well as its interpretation as self-executing by the Committee of Experts of the ILO.[36]

In 2004, the same Tribunal decided that Article 9 ICESCR, which entails a right of everyone to social security, including social insurance, is not a self-executing provision.[37] As mentioned before, articles that are not self-executing may be used for interpreting self-executing provisions as, for instance, laid down in the European Convention on Human Rights (ECHR).

3. Decisions of International Institutions

As regards decisions of international institutions, the judgments of the ECtHR, both judgments against the Netherlands and against other states, have been considered as authoritative interpretation of the ECHR and enjoy as such the same binding force as the ECHR itself.[38] The views of the Human Rights Committee have obtained the same status in respect of the International Convention on Civil and Political Rights (ICCPR).

4. Indirect Effect

Non-self-executing provisions of international treaties are not per se excluded from being applicable in Dutch courts. As stated above, in applying such international law, the judiciary has the power to review delegated statutory law but not Acts of Parliament.[39] It must be noted that the legislature and the administration, however, are bound by the obligations emanating from all treaty law, whether self-executing or not.[40] Additionally, if those norms are transformed by means of national implementation legislation they are incorporated in Dutch law and as such individuals can rely directly on them. In such cases, the role of the international treaties is minimized to the use of the *travaux préparatoires* and other relevant sources to interpret and apply the domestic norm.[41] Finally, international law has also been used as a means to interpret national law in general.

---

[36] CRvB, 29 mei 1996, RVS 1997/9 (*Eigen bijdrage kraamzorg*).

[37] CRvB, 18 June 2004, JB 2004, 303.

[38] Alkema (2010), pp. 11 and 12.

[39] Alkema (2010), p. 3.

[40] *Kamerstukken* II (2007–2008), 29 861, no. 19, p. 5.

[41] Alkema (2010), p. 7.

16.3 Mechanisms to Enforce or Monitor Human Rights

16.3.1 Method and Scope of Review

1. Judicial Mechanisms

There is no Constitutional Court or any other specific constitutional mechanism for enforcing the fundamental rights in the Netherlands.[42] The highest court in the Netherlands in civil, criminal and tax matters is the Supreme Court. In administrative cases, the Administrative Jurisdiction Division of the Council of State is the highest court of appeal while the Central Appeals Court is the highest court mainly in legal areas pertaining to social security and civil service. There is a third special court, namely the Trade and Industry Appeals Tribunal, which is a specialized administrative court with the jurisdiction to rule on matters of social-economic administrative law.[43]

The method of review exercised by the highest courts can be either abstract or concrete. Abstract review means the 'review of the compatibility of a legal rule (not being an Act of Parliament) as such with a higher rule'. Such higher rule is often a constitutional norm.[44] In contrast, concrete review is concerned with the question whether the applicability of a legal norm in a specific case was compatible with the higher norm.[45] According to Article 53 ECHR, a Dutch judge needs to assess the compliance with both the Constitution as well as treaty law when both sources of law provide protection.

When the ECtHR finds a violation with respect to the Netherlands, it is likely to lead to a change in domestic law or a shift in the case law. In addition, there are a number of options available to redress the wrong done. In civil law cases, individuals may hold the state liable for a wrongful act on the basis of Article 6:162 of the Civil Code. In administrative law, Article 4:6 of the General Administrative Law Act provides the possibility to submit a new complaint, if the judgment of the ECtHR can be marked as a new fact. Lastly, in criminal law the conviction of a person that was ruled to be incompatible with the ECHR can be reviewed on the basis of Article 457(1)(3) of the Code of Criminal Procedure (CCP). This review may only take place when it is favorable to the convicted person.[46]

2. Non-Judicial Mechanism

Apart from the possibility for individuals to have their case reviewed by a court of appeal or the highest courts, there are two bodies concerned with the monitoring and implementation of human rights: the National Institute of Human Rights and the National Ombudsman.

---

[42] Van Empel & De Jong (2002), p. 294.

[43] www.rechtspraak.nl/English/Judicial-System.

[44] Van Empel & De Jong (2002), p. 300.

[45] *Ibid.*

[46] Klip A, Van der Wilt H (2002) Netherlands' report for the International Association of Penal Law on Ne bis in idem. Revue Internationale de Droit Pénal 73: 1091–1137.

The Netherlands Institute for Human Rights[47] protects human rights in the Netherlands. The Institute, among others things, monitors the national implementation of human rights norms, provides advice on human rights legislation, and supports human rights initiatives.

The National Ombudsman was established in the Netherlands pursuant to Chap. 4, Article 78a of the Dutch Constitution. Upon request from any person, the National Ombudsman (who is independent and impartial) may investigate the way in which an administrative authority has acted towards a natural person or legal entity in a particular matter.[48] The National Ombudsman is also allowed to launch investigations on his own initiative.[49] Based on the findings from the investigation, the Ombudsman determines whether the administrative authority acted properly in the matter concerned.[50] Upon closure of an investigation, the Ombudsman writes a (non-legally binding) report containing his findings and his decision, including any measures which he considers should be taken.[51] The Ombudsman may not examine government policy or the content of laws, rather he can only deal with actions of administrative authorities. It should be noted that the National Ombudsman functions as a 'fall-back' option; he can only address complaints from persons who have tried and failed to settle the matter with the administrative authority concerned.[52]

16.4 Examples of the Influence of International Law on the Treatments of Basic Rights in the Netherlands in the Past Three Years

16.4.1 United Nations Reports and National Follow-Up

The human rights situation in the Netherlands has been reviewed by most UN treaty bodies in the past years. In this section a brief overview is provided of the responses by the Netherlands to the latest UN reports. A selection of recommendations will be used to illustrate the national implementation efforts.

The Human Rights Committee evaluated the implementation of the ICCPR in July 2009. The Committee raised its continuing concern at the extent of euthanasia and assisted suicides in the Netherlands.[53] The fact that a physician can terminate a patient's life without independent review by a judge was alarming to the Committee

---

[47] The Institute was established by an Act of Parliament of 24 November 2011 (Wet College voor de rechten van de mens).

[48] National Ombudsman Act, Article 12.

[49] *Ibid.*, Article 15.

[50] *Ibid.*, Article 26.

[51] *Ibid.*, Article 27.

[52] http://www.nationaleombudsman.nl.

[53] Human Rights Committee, UN Doc. CCPR/C/NLD/CO/4 (30 July 2009), para. 7.

and therefore it recommended that the euthanasia legislation be reviewed in the light of the Covenant's recognition of the right to life.[54] A preliminary response was written by the Dutch Minister of Justice. The executive body of the Dutch government asserted that the practice of euthanasia is well regulated. The duty of caution regarding the consultation of a second independent physician guarantees a well-supervised procedure. Moreover, regional commissions evaluate whether the duty of caution has been fulfilled. In the evaluation of the Euthanasia-law it was concluded that the law functions according to its objectives. Consequently, the Netherlands does not intend to change its legislation.[55]

On 19 November 2010 the Committee on Economic, Social and Cultural Rights adopted its concluding observations on the Netherlands. The Committee recommended, inter alia, that the legislation in the Netherlands guarantees that asylum-seekers are detained only when it is absolutely necessary and for a time that is limited to a strict minimum.[56] With regard to the detention of asylum-seekers, it was remarked that detention can only be used as a last remedy. Moreover, since the 'Europese Terugkeerrichtlijn' is in force, the maximum time of detention is limited to six months.[57]

The Committee on the Rights of the Child has made recommendations to the Dutch government on 27 March 2009. The Committee started by noting that some previous recommendations were not sufficiently implemented. For example, it was stated that still no ombudsman for children existed.[58] Taking up this recommendation from the Committee, the Netherlands amended the Law National ombudsman (Wet Nationale ombudsman); a new provision establishing the children's ombudsman is in effect since 1 April 2011.[59]

The Committee on the Elimination of Racial Discrimination reviewed the implementation of its Convention in the Netherlands in March 2010. The Committee expressed its concern at the incidence of racist and xenophobic speech emanating from a few extremist political parties and it urged the state to take more effective measures to prevent and suppress manifestations of racism, xenophobia, and intolerance and to encourage a positive climate of political dialogue.[60] While not explicitly mentioned, it is clear that this was an indirect reference to statements made by Geert Wilders, the political leader of the Party for Freedom. The Netherlands has been

---

[54] *Ibid.*

[55] Ministry of Justice, Reactie op the aanbevelingen van het VN comité inzake burgerlijke en politieke rechten, 15 October 2009.

[56] Committee on Economic, Social and Cultural Rights, UN Doc. E/C.12/NLD/CO/4-5 (19 November 2010), paras. 21(a) and 25(a), respectively.

[57] Ministry of Social Affairs and Employment (2011) Kabinetsreactie op de conclusies van het verdragscomité van het VN verdrag inzake economische, sociale en culturele rechten, 1 June 2011, IZ/IA/2011/8390.

[58] Committee on the Rights of the Child, UN Doc. CRC/C/NLD/CO/3 (27 March 2009), para. 8.

[59] National Ombudsman Act, chap. IIa, Articles 11 (a)–(e).

[60] Committee on the Elimination of Racial Discrimination, UN Doc. CERD/C/NLD/CO/17-18, para. 8.

reluctant to blindly follow the recommendation, fearing that it would limit freedom of expression. The Dutch Minister of Foreign Affairs stressed that the Dutch society is characterized by diversity; this pluralism is only possible in a state that allows, in principle, a place for all opinions. Open public debate is of essential importance to a democratic state, but of course it can only be exercised within the limits of the law.[61] While not directly a result of the recommendation made by the Committee, it is interesting to note that criminal proceedings were initiated against Geert Wilders, who allegedly incited hatred and discrimination with his statements on Muslims and their religion. On 23 of June 2011, Wilders was acquitted of all charges.

The Committee on the Elimination of Discrimination against Women adopted its concluding observations on the Netherlands on 5 February 2010. The Committee made many recommendations, and a quite extensive parliamentary reaction was written in response. The Committee called upon the Dutch government to, inter alia, accelerate efforts to achieve equal representation in elected bodies.[62] The Dutch Parliament is of the opinion that the 'Charter Talent to the Top' is a good instrument to realize fundamental equality between men and women in decision-making positions. The Charter is a code with clear commitments to realize diversity at the top. To date, the Charter has been signed by 210 private and public organizations. The relative participation of women at the top has subsequently increased.

16.4.2   Regional Case Law and National Follow-Up

Dutch legislation in all fields of law is greatly influenced by the ECHR and the case law of the ECtHR. In fact, this regional instrument and its case law play a crucial role in the drafting of new legislation. It is beyond the scope of this paper to discuss the influence of the Strasbourg case law on Dutch domestic law in its entirety. Rather, this section concentrates on two examples that have recently led to proposals for a change in the law. One example is that of the widely discussed Salduz judgment. In this case against Turkey, the ECtHR interpreted Article 6(3) ECHR as entailing a right of an arrested person to access to a lawyer as from the first moment of interrogation by the police. This right is not absolute since compelling reasons may justify a restriction of this right. However, such restrictions may never unduly prejudice the rights of the accused.[63] This judgment has caused much discussion in the Netherlands, and the domestic courts at all levels have been confronted to a great extent with the interpretation of the exact scope of this right as well as of the accompanying right to

---

[61] Minister Rosenthal (2011) Beantwoording vragen van het lid Timmermans. 3 October 2011, DMH-MR/499/11.

[62] Committee on the Elimination of Discrimination against Women, UN Doc. CEDAW/C/NLD/CO/5 (5 February 2010), para. 33.

[63] ECtHR [GC], *Salduz v. Turkey* 27 November 2008 (Appl. no. 36391/02), para. 55.

waive such consultation.[64] For instance, there remains considerable ambiguity as to the exact moment from which access to a lawyer must be granted.[65] The Supreme Court has interpreted this right as a right to consultation of a lawyer before police interrogation, but has not extended its interpretation to including the presence of a lawyer during the interrogation. Such presence is a right afforded to suspects who are minors. The exceptions that allow restrictions of this right is when (1) the suspect has waived his or her right explicitly or silently but unequivocally or (2) there are 'compelling reasons', within the meaning given to this term by the ECtHR, to do so.[66]

Not only the courts but also the legislature has responded to the outcome of the Salduz Case. On 15 April 2011, draft legislation on legal assistance and police interrogation was presented.[67] This proposal incorporates the right of suspects of crimes, which are punishable by six or more years imprisonment, to have access to a lawyer during police interrogation. This right may be restricted, but in such cases the authorities must make a recording of the interrogation.

Another recent judgment of the ECtHR, this time against the Netherlands itself, ruled that the Dutch legislation on the protection of journalistic sources is not in conformity with the ECHR. In the case Sanoma Uitgevers B.V. v. the Netherlands, the Grand Chamber considered the lack of any statutory provision in Dutch law for prior judicial review by an independent body before the police or public prosecutors are allowed to seize or order disclosure of journalistic sources. In this Grand Chamber judgment, in contrast to the Chamber ruling, the Court decided that there was a violation of Article 10 ECHR due to this gap in the legislation.[68] Reacting to this case on 15 September 2010, the Minister of Justice stressed the importance of a legislative proposal as a result of the earlier Voskuil judgment on this issue.[69] This proposed legislation should amend the law on the criticized point.[70] This proposal has not been presented before the Parliament's Second Chamber yet but the Council of State has given its advice already.

A last remark on legislation and the ECHR is that currently draft legislation is pending that prohibits wearing of burka's and other face-covering attributes in public places (Wetsvoorstel verbod op het dragen van gelaatsbedekkende kleding). This draft legislation has been publicized on 6 February 2012.[71] The Council of State, which is inter alia the Crown's and Parliament's supreme advisory body, has voiced

---

[64] For an overview see Van de Laar T (2012) Het consultatierecht en afstand van recht. Een bespreking van de rechtspraak van het EHRM en diverse wetgevingsinitiatieven. NJ (3): 178–184.

[65] Loof JP, Van Emmerik M et al (2011) Mensenrechten-actualiteiten.nl. NJCM-Bulletin 36(1): 93.

[66] HR, 30 juni 2009, NJ 2009, 349, para. 2.5. See also HR, 10 januari 2012, RvdW 2012, 128.

[67] This draft proposal is available at www.internetconsultatie.nl/rechtsbijstandpolitieverhoor.

[68] ECtHR [GC], *Sanoma Uitgevers B.V. v. the Netherlands* 14 September 2010 (Appl. no. 38224/03), paras. 96–100.

[69] ECtHR, *Voskuil v. the Netherlands* 22 November 2007 (Appl no. 64752/01).

[70] www.rijksoverheid.nl/documenten-en-publicaties/persberichten/2010/09/15/reactie-op-uitspraak-in-de-zaak-sanoma.html.

[71] www.rijksoverheid.nl/documenten-en-publicaties/kamerstukken/2012/02/06/wetsvoorstel-algemeen-verbod-op-gelaatsbedekkende-kleding.html.

strong criticism on this proposal because of the lack of objective reasons to adopt such a general prohibition. It remains to be seen whether this proposal will pass Parliament and if so, what the European reaction will be once it enters into force.

16.5 Special Focus on the Relationship Between Basic Rights and Citizenship in Light of the Developments in International Law

1. Rights of Non-Citizens

In international human rights law there appears to be a trend toward achieving universality and indivisibility of human rights for non-citizens.[72] The foundation of human rights law is that all people, by virtue of their humanity, enjoy fundamental rights. Generally, therefore, human rights instruments require the equal treatment of citizens and non-citizens.[73] On the other hand, national law primarily addresses the rights of citizens.

It has already been addressed in Sect. 1 of the current report that while many fundamental rights enshrined in the Dutch Constitution apply to all individuals on Dutch territory, some rights are restricted to Dutch citizens. Non-citizens are not equally eligible for appointment to public office, nor do they have the right to vote or the free choice of work in the Netherlands.[74] Also, only Dutch nationals, who are incapable to sustain themselves, have a right to welfare assistance from the government.[75]

On the international level, the Netherlands is a State Party to all major human rights instruments. Accordingly, non-citizens residing in the Netherlands enjoy the rights accorded to them under these instruments. A human rights instrument which was not signed by the Netherlands and which is specifically related to the rights of a group of non-citizens is the Convention on Migrant Workers. However, the Netherlands is a State Party to most other international treaties related to rights of non-citizens.[76]

---

[72] Weissbrodt D, Meili S (2010) Human Rights and Protection of Non-Citizens: Whither Universality and Indivisibility of Rights? Refugee Survey Quarterly 28(4): p. 34.

[73] *Ibid.*, p. 37.

[74] See Articles 3, 4, 19(3) of the Dutch Constitution, respectively.

[75] Article 20(3) of the Dutch Constitution.

[76] Convention relating to the Status Refugees; Protocol relating to the Status of Refugees; Convention on the Reduction of Statelessness; Convention relating to the Status of Stateless Persons; UN Convention against Transnational Organized Crime; Protocol to Prevent, Suppress and Punish Trafficking in Persons, Especially Women and Children, supplementing the UN Convention against Transnational Organized Crime; Protocol against the smuggling of Migrants by Land, Sea and Air, supplementing the UN Convention against Transnational Organized Crime; Vienna Convention on Consular Relations.

Several UN human rights treaty bodies have in the recent past expressed concern about the treatment of a specific group of non-citizens in the Netherlands, namely the treatment of asylum seekers. The Human Right Committee has noted that under the "accelerated procedure" for the review of asylum applications, claims are evaluated within 48 working hours, and that there is a proposal for an eight-day procedure. The Committee recommended the Netherlands to 'ensure that the procedure for processing asylum applications enables a thorough and adequate assessment by allowing a period of time adequate for the presentation of evidence. The state must, in all cases, ensure respect for the principle of non-refoulement.'[77] Subsequently, the asylum procedure was amended; an improved procedure was included in the Dutch Aliens Act 2000 and became effective on 1 July 2010. Under the new situation, asylum seekers are informed sooner about the outcome of the procedure, and the procedure is taking place more meticulously. The procedure is preceded by a rest and preparation period for the asylum seeker of at least six days. Subsequently, the procedure in the application centres takes eight days instead of 48 h, to facilitate for addition time for legal aid to the refugee.[78]

The Committee on the Rights of the Child was concerned about the detention of refugee children. The Committee made a recommendation to reduce the use of aliens' detention for unaccompanied children and for families with children.[79] On 10 March 2011, the Dutch Minister for Immigration and Asylum announced that 'unaccompanied migrant children will no longer be placed in immigration detention.'[80] Instead, the central asylum authority will provide temporary housing for the minors. There are a few exceptions to this policy which relate to children with a criminal history; when removal is planned within two weeks; when minors leave the asylum premises without authorization; and when their age cannot be determined.

Lastly, it must be noted that, in deciding whether asylum seekers may be expelled, decisions of the Dutch Courts are closely scrutinized by the ECtHR and Dutch courts carefully take into account case-law on the *non-refoulement* principle.[81]

16.5.1 Changing Perspectives on the Rights of Non-Citizens

The relationship between rights and citizenship has been a topic of debate in the Netherlands.[82] One recent development in the interpretation of the law demonstrates a shift towards a more inclusive approach to rights that historically only belong to

---

[77] Human Rights Committee, UN Doc. CCPR/C/NLD/CO/4 (30 July 2009), para. 9.

[78] http://english.justitie.nl/currenttopics/pressreleases/archives-2010/100518new-asylum-procedure-in-force-on-1-july.aspx?cp=35&cs=1578.

[79] Committee on the Rights of the Child, UN Doc. CRC/C/NLD/CO/3 (27 March 2009), para. 68.

[80] http://www.detention-in-europe.org/index.php?option=com_content&view=article&id=295: netherlands-no-children-in-detention&catid=3:newsflash.

[81] ECtHR, *A v. Netherlands* 20 July 2010 (Appl. no. 4900/06); ECtHR, *Mawaka v. The Netherlands* 1 June 2010 (Appl. no. 29031/04).

[82] See e.g., *Burgerrechten*, inaugural speech by Prof. E.M.H. Hirsch Ballin, University of Amsterdam 2011, available at http://www.oratiereeks.nl/upload/pdf/PDF-3821Oratie_Hirsch_Ballin.pdf.

citizens. Lately, the application of a well-established principle that excludes illegal aliens from national provisions has been to a certain extent revisited in a number of administrative law cases. The Central Appeals Tribunal issued two important decisions in the summer of 2011. The first case concerned the granting of child allowance to a child of parents staying illegally in the Netherlands.[83] This Tribunal ruled that the exclusion of child allowance was disproportionate in this case on the basis of Articles 8 and 14 ECHR. The exception to the principle was based on the fact that the parents had for a longer period of time, of which a certain period was legal, stayed in the Netherlands. Furthermore, their stay was known to the Dutch authorities. As a result, the family felt closely connected to the Netherlands and should be considered Dutch residents ('ingezetenen'), according to this Tribunal. The Tribunal took its decision taking into account earlier case law of the Supreme Court.[84] This principle of exclusion was neither applied in a case of a handicapped child whose application for allowances on the basis of the Exceptional Medical Expenses Act ('AWBZ') had been rejected. The reason for the rejection was that the child and his mother were staying illegally in the Netherlands as their application for a permanent residence permit had been rejected earlier on. The Tribunal considered that at the time of his application for health insurance, the child and his mother were staying legally in the Netherlands. In conclusion, the Tribunal ruled that there was a positive obligation on the health insurer to provide the necessary care, given the special protection required for such vulnerable persons by Article 8 ECHR and the Convention on the Rights of the Child.[85]

16.6 Conclusion

The foregoing has demonstrated the importance attached to human rights in the Dutch legal order. A number of important fundamental rights, both civil and political as well as economic and social rights, have been codified in the Dutch Constitution. At the same time, several rights, such as the right to life, are absent from the Constitution. This absence together with the constitutional prohibition to assess the compliance of Acts of Parliament with the Constitution emphasizes the important place that the many international and regional human rights instruments have in the Dutch legal order. There is an important distinction to make with respect to the effect of such rights therein. Civil and political rights have been regarded as being self-executing while economic, social and cultural rights generally do not enjoy this status. The non-self-executing rights have mostly been used to interpret the scope or content of rights laid down in the Constitution.

This report has discussed some prominent developments that have taken place in the last few years that further strengthened the position of human rights. These

---

[83] CRvB, 15 juli 2011, JB 2011/202.

[84] *Ibid.*, paras. 4.13 and 4.14.

[85] CRvB, 4 August 2011, RSV 2011/341, paras. 4.2 and 4.4.

include, but are not limited to, the establishment of a national Children's Ombudsman, the establishment of the National Institute of Human Rights, and the fact that
unaccompanied migrant children will no longer be placed in detention centres. Furthermore, while no full account of the case law of the ECtHR has been provided in
this report, the influence of the Court should not be understated, which for instance
recently resulted in the proposal for legislation in criminal procedural matters.

The position of non-citizens in the Netherlands has been greatly influenced by
international and regional human rights and decisions of their monitoring bodies.
The way in which their integration should be promoted and the legal approach to
such integration remains a topic of debate. There seems to be an upcoming voice in
society to adopt an inclusive approach towards aliens that have been participating in
Dutch society as if they were citizens. In the words of the former Minister of Justice
and now law professor, Hirsh Ballin, '[p]ermanent denial of the full range of civil
rights to people that do participate in the society, but still considered to be aliens, is
detrimental to the quality of a democratic state.'[86]

References

Literature

Alkema EA (2010) International Law in Domestic Systems. EJCL 14-3:1–22, p. 1–3, 131, pp. 7
    and 8,11 and 12
Besselink LFM (2004) Constitutional law of the Netherlands: an introduction with texts, cases and
    materials. Ars Aequi Libri, Nijmegen, p. 156
Bunschoten DE (2009) Tekst en Commentaar Grondwet, commentaar op hoofdstuk 1 Gw. Kluwer
    Navigator
Hirsch Ballin EMH (2011), 'Burgerrechten', inaugural speech, University of Amsterdam, available
    at http://www.oratiereeks.nl/upload/pdf/PDF-3821Oratie_Hirsch_Ballin.pdf.
Klip A, Van der Wilt H (2002) Netherlands' report for the International Association of Penal Law
    on Ne bis in idem. Revue Internationale de Droit Pénal 73: 1091–1137
Kortmann CAJM, Bovend'Eert PPT (1993) Dutch Constitutional Law. Kluwer Law International,
    The Hague, p. 136
Kortmann CAJM, Bovend'Eert PPT (2000), Dutch Constitutional Law, Kluwer Law International,
    The Hague, p. 147, 153, 155–156
Loof JP, Van Emmerik M et al (2011) Mensenrechten-actualiteiten.nl. NJCM-Bulletin 36(1): 93
Van Empel M, De Jong M (2002) Constitution, International Treaties, Contracts and Torts. EJCL
    6–4: p. 283–305
Van de Laar T (2012) Het consultatierecht en afstand van recht. Een bespreking van de rechtspraak
    van het EHRM en diverse wetgevingsinitiatieven. NJ (3): 178–184
Weissbrodt D, Meili S (2010) Human Rights and Protection of Non-Citizens: Whither Universality
    and Indivisibility of Rights?. Refugee Survey Quarterly 28(4): p. 34, 37

[86] Hirsch Ballin (2011), p. 26 [translation by the authors].

National Policy Documents

Handelingen II 1975/76, 13 872, no. 3, p. 38
Handelingen II 1985/86 (6 februari 1986), p. 3163
Kamerstukken II 1975/76, 13 872, no. 3, pp. 11 and 12
Kamerstukken II (2007–2008), 29 861, no. 19, pp. 3 and 5
Ministry of Justice, *Reactie op the aanbevelingen van het VN comité inzake burgerlijke en politieke rechten*, 15 October 2009
Ministry of Social Affairs and Employment (2011) Kabinetsreactie op de conclusies van het verdragscomité van het VN verdrag inzake economische, sociale en culturele rechten. 1 June 2011, IZ/IA/2011/8390
Minister Rosenthal (2011) Beantwoording vragen van het lid Timmermans. 3 October 2011, DMH-MR/499/11
Voorstel van wet van het lid Halsema tot verandering in de Grondwet, strekkende tot invoering van de bevoegdheid tot toetsing van wetten aan een aantal bepalingen van de Grondwet door de rechter, Kamerstuk 34332 (2010)
Rapport Staatscommissie Grondrechten (2010), available at www.staatscommissiegrondwet.nl, p. 43

National and International Case Law

CRvB, 14 May 1987, AB 1987, 543
CRvB, 29 mei 1996, RVS 1997/9 (*Eigen bijdrage kraamzorg*)
CRvB, 18 June 2004, JB 2004, 303
CRvB, 15 juli 2011, JB 2011/202, paras. 4.13 and 4.14
CRvB, 4 August 2011, RSV 2011/341, paras. 4.2 and 4.4
ECtHR, *Voskuil v. the Netherlands* 22 November 2007 (Appl no. 64752/01)
ECtHR [GC], *Salduz v. Turkey* 27 November 2008 (Appl. no. 36391/02), para. 55
ECtHR, *Mawaka v. The Netherlands* 1 June 2010 (Appl. no. 29031/04)
ECtHR, *A v. Netherlands* 20 July 2010 (Appl. no. 4900/06)
ECtHR [GC], *Sanoma Uitgevers B.V. v. the Netherlands* 14 September 2010 (Appl. no. 38224/03), paras. 96–100
HR, 6 March 1959, NJ 1962, 2 (*Nyugat zaak*)
HR, 4 June 1982, NJ 1983, 32
HR, 1 July 1983, NJ 1984, 161
HR, 11 February 1986, NJ 1986, 673, (*Drukkerij*);
HR, 21 March 1986, NJ 1986, 585
HR, 7 May 1986 (*NS/FNV*), NJ 1986, 688, para. 3.2
HR, 16 May 1986, NJ 1987, 251 (*Sproeivliegtuigen*);
HR, 30 mei 1986, NJ 1986, 688 (*Collectieve acties Spoorwegen*)
HR, 4 maart 1988, para. 3.5, NJ 1989, 361 (*Borbon Parma*) m.nt. C.J.H. Brunner
HR, 14 April 1989, AB 1989, 207.
HR 2 February 1990, nr. 13 727 (interim injunction proceedings) (*Goeree and Van Manschot v. Van Zijl*)
HR, 20 April 1990, NJ 1992, 636 (*Hoogenraad/ZWO*)
HR, 18 June 1993, RvdW 1993, 136
HR, 30 juni 2009, NJ 2009, 349, para. 2.5.
HR, 10 januari 2012, RvdW 2012, 128
KB 20 April 1989, AB 1989, 304, (*Bestemmingsplan Driebergen*)
Vzngr ARRvS 16 February 1989, AB 1990, 9 (*Evangeliegemeente De Deur*)
RvS, 30 December 1993, AB 1995, no. 24 (*Zwiers v. Provincial Executive of Gelderland*)

National legislation

Equal Treatment Act (AWGB) (2 March 1994)
Articles 1, 3–5, 7(1), 19(3), 20(3), 114 of the Dutch Constitution
Article 8(a) of the International Crimes Act
Dutch Enforced Disappearance Convention Implementation Act (2010)
Dutch Torture Convention Implementation Act (1989)
National Ombudsman Act, Articles 12, 15, 16 and 27

International documents

Committee on Economic, Social and Cultural Rights, UN Doc. E/C.12/NLD/CO/4-5 (19 November
    2010), paras. 21(a) and 25(a)
Committee on the Elimination of Racial Discrimination, UN Doc. CERD/C/NLD/CO/17-18, para. 8
Committee on the Elimination of Discrimination against Women, UN Doc. CEDAW/C/NLD/CO/5
    (5 February 2010), para. 33
Committee on the Rights of the Child, UN Doc. CRC/C/NLD/CO/3 (27 March 2009), para. 8, 68
Human Rights Committee, UN Doc. CCPR/C/NLD/CO/4 (30 July 2009), para. 7, 9
Convention relating to the Status Refugees
Protocol relating to the Status of Refugees
Convention on the Reduction of Statelessness
Convention relating to the Status of Stateless Persons
UN Convention against Transnational Organized Crime
Protocol to Prevent, Suppress and Punish Trafficking in Persons, Especially Women and Children,
supplementing the UN Convention against Transnational Organized Crime
Protocol against the smuggling of Migrants by Land, Sea and Air, supplementing the UN
    Convention against Transnational Organized Crime; Vienna Convention on Consular Relations

Websites

www.rechtspraak.nl/English/Judicial-System
http://www.nationaleombudsman.nl
www.internetconsultatie.nl/rechtsbijstandpolitieverhoor
www.rijksoverheid.nl/documenten-en-publicaties/persberichten/2010/09/15/reactie-op-uitspraak-
    in-de-zaak-sanoma.html
www.rijksoverheid.nl/documenten-en-publicaties/kamerstukken/2012/02/06/wetsvoorstel-algem-
    een-verbod-op-gelaatsbedekkende-kleding.html
http://english.justitie.nl/currenttopics/pressreleases/archives-2010/100518new-asylum-procedure-
    in-force-on-1-july.aspx?cp=35&cs=1578
http://www.detention-in-europe.org/index.php?option=com_content&view=article&id=295:
    netherlands-no-children-in-detention&catid=3:newsflash

Chapter 17
Portuguese National Report on the *National and International Codification of Human Rights* Presented to the Thematic Congress of the International Academy of Comparative Law (Taiwan, 2012)

Luísa Neto

17.1 The System of Fundamental Rights of the Constitution of Portuguese Republic[1]

It is obvious that Constitutional Law is definitively not the only branch of law concerned with protecting the fundamental rights of human beings. Such was the case in Portugal with the first Civil Code of 1867, following the 1822' liberal Constitution and setting a pattern that was again followed by the current Civil Code of 1966.[2]

Nevertheless, the national human rights codification in Portugal has it clear main *focus* on the Constitution of Portuguese Republic (CPR) adopted on 2 April 1976 in the sequence of the 1974 revolution, which came into force on 25 April 1976. "The evolution of Portuguese constitutional law partly reflects this chronology, with the first four constitutional texts—dating from 1822, 1826, 1838 and 1911—evidencing a predominantly liberal view on fundamental rights. The Constitution of 1933, on the other hand, although drafted in the context of an authoritarian State, already enshrined some social rights. It was, however, only under the Constitution of 1976 that fundamental rights found their fullest expression, in a global concept that covered all the various generations of rights and freedoms emerged in the course of the evolution of the contemporary state".[3]

---

[1] For the preparation of this work, we chose to follow through some updated foreign-language sources available on the national Portuguese system of protection of rights, in order to ease the research of foreign experts. Also please note that english and french versions of the Constitution of the Portuguese Republic (CPR) may be found at the site of the Portuguese Parliament, Assembly of the Republic (www.parlamento.pt).

[2] Bacelar Gouveia, J, "Fundamental Rights", in Ferreira de Almeida, Assunção Cristas, Nuno Piçarra (Ed.), Portuguese Law, an overview, Almedina, Coimbra, 2007, p. 89–97, p. 90–91.

[3] Bacelar Gouveia, J, "Fundamental Rights", *op.cit.*, p. 90.

L. Neto (✉)
Faculty of Law, University of Porto, Rua dos Bragas 223, 4050-123 Porto, Portugal
e-mail: lneto@direito.up.pt

W.-Y. Wang (ed.), *Codification in International Perspective*, Ius Comparatum – Global Studies in Comparative Law, DOI 10.1007/978-3-319-03455-3_17,
© Springer International Publishing Switzerland 2014

The original text of the Portuguese Constitution was therefore the result of intense negotiation and compromise between different political forces, namely liberals and socialists. One of the consequences of this compromise is the establishment of a long catalogue of fundamental rights, combining classical freedoms with economic and social rights. This Constitution has been altered seven times since then, but the *core* of the fundamental rights' list has remained unchanged.[4]

The CPR text currently contains 295 articles distributed over 4 parts, some of which include chapters. It is preceded by an introduction and brought to a conclusion by a final part.

- General principles (Articles 1–11);
- Part I—Fundamental rights and duties (Articles 12–79);
- Part II—Economic organization (Articles 80–107);
- Part III—Organization of political power (Articles 108–276);
- Part IV—Revision of the constitution (Articles 277–289);
- Final and transitional provisions (Articles 290–295).

Furthermore, in the chapter of Fundamental Principles, Article 1 of the constitutional text states that "Portugal is a sovereign Republic, based on the dignity of the human person and the will of the people and committed to building a free, just and solidary society." This reference to the dignity of the human person, together with the will of the people sets the fundamental value upon which the Portuguese State, as a sovereign republic, is based and provides the unifying foundation of all fundamental rights enshrined in the Constitution, including economic and social rights.

The Part I that we referred to, has three Sections: Sect. I, "General Principles" (Articles 12–23) and divides fundamental rights into two other sections: Sect. II, "Rights, Freedoms and Guarantees" and Sect. III, "Economic, Social and Cultural Rights and Duties".

a. Those rights considered by articles 24–57 (Sect. II, **"Rights, freedoms and guaranties"**) roughly correspond to those that arose in the nineteenth century, closely linked to liberal political thought[5] and they divide themselves into three even more specific sets of rights, namely:
   I Personal rights and freedoms;
   II Rights and freedoms of political participation;
   III Workers' rights and freedoms.
b. Rights considered by articles 58–79 (**Sect. III, "Economic, social and cultural rights and duties"**) refer to the "second generation of fundamental social rights and may, in turn, be divided into three more specific sets of rights:
   I Economic rights and duties;
   II Social rights and duties;
   III Cultural rights and duties.

---

[4] This context is also made clear by Silveira, Alessandra, Pedro Madeira Froufe and Mariana Canotilho, FIDE 2012, Questionnaire General, Protection of Fundamental Rights post-Lisbon: The Interaction between the EU Charter of Fundamental Rights, the European Convention on Human Rights (ECHR) and National Constitutions, available at http://www.cedu.direito.uminho.pt/uploads/FIDE%202012_final.pdf, Questionnaire General Topic 1.

[5] Bacelar Gouveia, J, "Fundamental rights", idem, *op.cit.*, p. 90.

c. Moreover, Portuguese Constitution also reflects those rights that since the 1960's, emerged as a **third and fourth generation of fundamental rights.** These latter rights are not linked by a single guiding thread but rather give vent to new concerns related to multiple issues, such as the environment (Article 66), the protection of the individual against its misuse, the protection of man against genetic manipulation (Article 26 §§ 2 e 3), or the right of peoples and nations to safeguard their cultural autonomy (Article 7).[6]

d. Nevertheless, this does not mean that the constitutional sources of fundamental rights are uniquely concentrated in the above-mentioned sections of the Constitution. It is possible to identify **other sets of fundamental rights, for instance the non-enumerated fundamental rights,** set out in: Sect. I of Part I of the CPR, under "General Principles" of the "Fundamental rights and duties"; Sect. I of Part II of the CPR, under "General Principles" of the "Economic organization"; Sect. IX of Part III of the CPR, under "Civil service", which is part of the general topic of the "Organization of political power"[7].

Besides these general rules, "the rights included in the category *rights, liberties and guaranties* have a stricter legal regime that includes, among other rules, direct applicability (they may be enforced by a judge, no matter whether or not there is a law regarding that specific right), horizontal effect and a harder set of requisites in case of restriction. However, national doctrine has always emphasized that there is no hierarchy of fundamental rights under the Portuguese constitutional order. The legal value of both civic and political freedoms and economic, social and cultural rights is the same".[8] Moreover, nowadays, doctrine tends to propose a unified regime for both categories.

"Economic, social and cultural rights complete the global vision of fundamental rights enshrined in the CPR"[9] but they "certainly offer much less protection than the regime applicable to rights and freedoms. For instance, economic, social and cultural rights are not immediately enforceable and their fulfilment depends on the availability of favourable social and economic conditions. Moreover economic, social and cultural rights are not generically enforceable, as they are essentially addressed to public authorities, binding them to the realization of the existing constitutional programme on economic and social matters".[10]

However, it is important to stress the applicableness of the constitutional rules expressly related to "rights, liberties and guarantees" to fundamental rights of a similar kind, as foreseen in Article 17. According to this article the rules that apply to human rights contained in Sect. II of Part I can be extended to those constitutional rights that may be considered analogous to them. Rights considered as of a "similar kind" include: access to law and effective judicial protection (Article 20); the right

---

[6] BACELAR GOUVEIA, J, *idem, op. cit.*, p. 90.

[7] BACELAR GOUVEIA, J, *ibidem, op. cit,* p. 91/92.

[8] SILVEIRA, ALESSANDRA ET AL, FIDE 2012, *op. cit.,* Questionnaire General Topics 1 and 2, p. 2.

[9] BACELAR GOUVEIA, J, "Fundamental Rights", *op. cit.*, pp. 96/97.

[10] BACELAR GOUVEIA, J, *idem,* p. 97.

to resist (Article 21); the right to present complaints to the Ombudsman (Article 23); the right of workers to remuneration for their work, to a limit on the length of the working day, to a weekly rest day and regular holidays with pay, to assistance in case of involuntarily unemployment (Article 59); the right to private enterprise, co-operatives and worker-management (Article 61); the right to private property (Article 62); the right to a social minimum (Articles 1, 2 and 63); the right of women to an adequate period of leave from work without loss of remuneration and other privileges (Article 68); the right to free basic education [Article 74, § 2 *a)*]; the right of owners of estates that are compulsory acquired to appropriate compensation and to retain an area that is sufficiently large to enable the land to be utilized in a rational and viable way (Article 94, § 1); the right to registration of electors (Article 113, § 2); the right to present nominations (Articles 124); the rights and guarantees of citizens towards the Public Service (Article 268); the right of public officials to be heard and to present a defense in disciplinary proceedings (Article 269, § 3)[11].

Even if the Portuguese catalogue of fundamental rights is very long and complete, the Constitution itself foresees the reception and incorporation of fundamental rights recognized in other normative sources, both national and international. In fact, the catalogue of rights is not closed and the text of the Constitution itself explicitly opens the door to rights with no formal constitutional place—for instance, those residing in the Universal Declaration of Human Rights, a text which is promoted as a general hermeneutic criterion of the Constitution[12] in § 1 of article 16.

17.2 Possible Distinction Between Rights Belonging to the Citizen in the Domestic System and Rights Pertaining to Men Besides National Borders and/or Citizenship

Regarding the titular of fundamental rights, Article 14 of Portuguese Constitution states that "*Portuguese citizens who find themselves or who reside abroad enjoy the state's protection in the exercise of the rights and are subject to the duties that are not incompatible with their absence from the country.*"

On the other hand, Article 15 (on *Foreigners, stateless persons, European citizens*) states that

1. *Foreigners and stateless persons who find themselves or who reside in Portugal enjoy the same rights and are subject to the same duties as Portuguese citizens.*
2. *Political rights, the exercise of public functions that are not predominantly technical in nature, and the rights and duties that the Constitution and the law reserve exclusively to Portuguese citizens are excepted from the provisions of the previous paragraph.*

---

[11] This list is for instance settled at CONSTITUTIONAL COURT OF PORTUGAL, The portuguese human rights constitutional law, The human rights law (Presentation at the World Conference on Constitutional Justice—Cape Town South Africa, 23–24 January 2009) available at http://www.venice.coe.int/WCCJ/Papers/POR_Moura_Ramos_E.pdf, p. 3.

[12] FERREIRA DA CUNHA, P, Human and Fundamental Rights and duties in the Portuguese constitution. Some reflections, available ar http://works.bepress.com/pfc/5., p. 6.

3. *Save for access to appointment to the offices of President of the Republic, President of the Assembly of the Republic, Prime Minister and President of any of the supreme courts, and for service in the armed forces and the diplomatic corps, rights that are not otherwise granted to foreigners are accorded, as laid down by law and under reciprocal terms, to the citizens of Portuguese-speaking states who reside permanently in Portugal.*
4. *Under reciprocal terms, the law may accord foreigners who reside in Portugal the eligibility to vote for and stand for election as officeholders of local authority organs.*
5. *Under reciprocal terms, the law may also accord citizens of European Union Member States who reside in Portugal the eligibility to vote for and stand for election as Members of the European Parliament.*

Furthermore, it is necessary to stress that Portugal is party to most major human rights treaties existing universal and regional levels. Here are some examples[13]:

17.2.1 United Nations

International Covenant on Economic, Social and Cultural
  International Covenant on Civil and Political Rights (and Optional Protocols)
  International Convention on the Elimination of All Forms of Racial Discrimination
  Convention on the Elimination of All Forms of Discrimination against Women
Convention on the Rights of the Child (also Optional Protocols)
  Convention against Torture and Other Cruel, Inhuman or Degrading
  Convention on the Rights of Persons with Disabilities (also Optional Protocol to
the Convention on the Rights of Persons with Disabilities)

i) International Labour Organization (ILO)

Convention No. 29 of the ILO on forced or compulsory labor; Convention No. 87 ILO Freedom of Association and Protection of the Right; Convention No. 97 of the ILO concerning Migrant Workers; Convention No. 98 of the ILO concerning the Application of Principles of the Right to Organise and Collective Bargaining; Convention No. 100 ILO concerning Equal Remuneration for the hand-labor-Hand Men and Women in labor Work of Equal Value; Convention No. 105 ILO Abolition of Forced Labour; Convention No. 111 of the ILO concerning Discrimination in Respect of Employment and Occupation; Convention No. 122 ILO on Employment Policy; Convention No. 135 concerning the protection and facilities to provide workers' representatives in the company; Convention No. 138 ILO, Minimum Age for Admission to Employment; Convention No. 143 of the ILO concerning Migrations

---

[13] This list is not intended to be exhaustive. For more complete information, please see http://direitoshumanos.gddc.pt/DireitosHumanos/4/IVPAG4_1.htm#

in Abusive Conditions and the Promotion of Equality of Opportunity and Treatment of Migrant Workers; Convention No. 151 ILO on the Protection of the Right to Organise and Procedures for Establishment of working conditions in the Civil Service; Convention No. 156 ILO on the Equal Opportunity and Treatment for Workers of Both Sexes: Workers with Family Responsibilities; Convention No. 182 on the Worst Forms of Child Labour and Immediate Action for the Elimination

ii) United Nations Education, Science and Culture Organization

Convention on the Fight Against Discrimination in Education

17.2.2 European Union

Charter of Fundamental Rights of the European Union

17.2.3 Council of Europe

Convention for the Protection of Human Rights and Fundamental Freedoms (also Additional Protocols)
  Revised European Social Charter
  Framework Convention for the Protection of National Minorities
  European Convention for the Prevention of Torture and Inhuman or Degrading Treatment or Punishment
  European Convention on the Legal Status of Migrant Workers
  Council of Europe Convention on Action against Trafficking in Human Beings European Convention on Nationality
  Convention on Human Rights and Biomedicine (also Additional Protocol)
  If one compares the catalogue and shaping of fundamental rights in the Portuguese Constitution with the European Convention or with the Charter of Fundamental Rights of the European Union one must conclude that the first is generally more extensive and more detailed than the two last ones. On the other hand, as was mentioned, the "open clause" of Article 16, § 1, acknowledges rights conferred to the individual by international law.
  In fact, "[m]any of the *newest* rights protected by the Charter were already stated in the national constitution, such as the right to genetic identity (Article 26 of the Portuguese Constitution), the prohibition of discrimination on the grounds of sexual orientation (Article 13, § 2, of the Portuguese Constitution), the right to a healthy and ecologically balanced environment (Article 66 of the Portuguese Constitution) and consumers' rights (Article 60 of the Portuguese Constitution)".[14]

---

[14] Silveira, Alessandra et al, FIDE 2012, *op. cit.*, Questionnaire General, Topic 1, p. 2. On this topic, please follow trough See the intervention of Jorge Miranda, in "Reunião Conjunta das

17.3 Instruments of Protection in the Domestic Order and Their Efficacy as Such

As we have previously seen, Article 18 of the Constitution states that rights are binding to public and private entities. "This recognition of horizontal effect naturally leads to the emergence of conflicts of rights"[15], but the "limitation is only justifiable in terms of constitutional law if it is necessary in order to safeguard other rights or interests protected by the Constitution. This necessity is evaluated in terms of the principle of proportionality"[16] that derives from the principle of rule of law stated in Article 2 and set by Article 18:

1. *This Constitution's provisions with regard to rights, freedoms and guarantees shall be directly applicable to and binding on public and private persons and bodies.*
2. *The law may only restrict rights, freedoms and guarantees in cases expressly provided for in this Constitution, and such restrictions shall be limited to those needed to safeguard other rights and interests protected by this Constitution.*
3. *Laws that restrict rights, freedoms and guarantees shall possess an abstract and general nature and shall not possess a retroactive effect or reduce the extent or scope of the essential content of the provisions of this Constitution.*

As already mentioned, effective protection of fundamental rights in its non-jurisdictional form, drives from the expanding role of the ombudsman[17] (*Provedor de Justiça*), while in its jurisdictional form protection is provided by the courts, which can invalidate unconstitutional legal provisions, as well as apply mechanisms of civil and criminal responsibility against the infringement of fundamental rights[18]. Jointly with the officeholders of their entities and organs and their staff and agents, the state and other public entities are civilly liable for actions or omissions that are committed in or because of the exercise of their functions and result in a breach of rights, freedoms or guarantees or in a loss to others.

As specified by Article 202 of Portuguese Constitution

1. *The courts are the organs with supreme authority that have the power to administer justice in the name of the people.*

Comissões de Assuntos Europeus e de Assuntos Constitucionais, Direitos, Liberdades e Garantias sobre a Carta dos Direitos Fundamentais da União Europeia" (Joint Meeting of the European Affairs and Constitutional Matters Parliamentary Commissions), 14th April 2000, in *A Carta dos Direitos Fundamentais da União Europeia—A Participação da Assembleia da República*, Assembleia da República, Comissão de Assuntos Europeus, Lisboa, 2001.

[15] Silveira, ALESSANDRA ET AL, FIDE 2012, *op. cit.,* questions 3, 4, 5 and 6, pp. 4/5.

[16] CONSTITUTIONAL COURT OF PORTUGAL, The portuguese human rights constitutional law, *op. cit.,* p. 7.

[17] Article 23.

[18] Article 22.

2. *In administering justice, the courts are under a duty to safeguard the rights and interests of citizens that are legally protected, to punish breaches of democratic legality and to resolve public and private disputes.*
3. *In performing their functions, the courts are entitled to the assistance of other authorities.*
4. *The law may provide for alternative methods of dispute resolution that do not involve the courts.*

The most important aspect of enforcing fundamental rights in Portuguese system is the fact that, according to Article 204 of Portuguese Constitution, "*in matters brought before them for decision, the courts shall not apply any rules that contravene the provisions of this Constitution or the principles contained there*".

Every court (judicial, administrative and fiscal) is vested with jurisdiction to review complaints involving violation of human rights. Moreover, every single judge is, in itself, a sort of "constitutional court", since he must control the constitutionality of the rules that are applicable to the matters that are brought before him. If he thinks that those rules contravene the provisions of the Constitution he must refuse to apply them. However, the decisions in constitutional issues of other courts are not definitive, since there is always the possibility to appeal to the Constitutional Court.

Nevertheless, the Constitutional Court created in 1982 is the only authority vested with ultimate jurisdiction to review of constitutionality, so that Article 221 of Portuguese Constitution states "The Constitutional Court is the court that has the specific power to administer justice in matters involving questions of legal and constitutional nature."[19]

"In Portugal concrete control of constitutionality is one of the basic mechanisms available to individuals for the protection of their fundamental rights. It is exercised by *all Courts* since they all have a duty not to apply legal provisions which are in breach of the Constitution. The *Constitutional Court* is the final instance of concrete constitutional control."[20] "And it must be said that there is a very high level of general compliance to the Constitutional Court decisions by the other courts. It is very difficult to measure this level of compliance, but some empirical studies have shown that it's very high."[21]

---

[19] Constitutional COURT OF PORTUGAL, The portuguese human rights constitutional law, *op. cit.*, p. 6.

[20] CORTÊS, ANTÓNIO AND TERESA VIOLANTE, Concrete Control of Constitutionality in Portugal: A Means Towards Effective Protection of Fundamental Rights, Spring, 2011, 29 Penn St. Int'l L. Rev. 759, Report drafted for Co.Co.A. (Comparing Constitutional Adjudication), Third Edition, 2008 organized by the Faculty of Law (Department of Legal Sciences) of the University of Trento, available at http://www.tribunalconstitucional.pt/tc/content/files/relatorios/relatorio_001.pdf, pp. 1.

[21] CONSTITUTIONAL COURT OF PORTUGAL, The portuguese human rights constitutional law, *op. cit.*, p. 11.

17.3.1 Constitutionality Review

In what regards the Constitutional Court, it reviews the constitutionality of legal rules in three different ways, which correspond to three more forms of procedure:

a) Prior Review[22]

The first involves prior review—i.e. before a legal text is published and comes into force. This control is provided for by Article 278 of the Constitution, but is only applicable to the more important rules in the legal order. The request can be presented by the President of the Republic, by the appropriate Representative of the Republic—in the case of rules contained in regional legislative decrees, and by the Prime Minister, or one fifth of all the Members of the parliament in full exercise of their office in the case of rules set out in decrees of the parliament that are sent to the President of the Republic for enactment as organizational laws.

This form of controlling constitutionality by prior review is exclusively directed at rules that are specifically mentioned in the request, and whoever issues the request must also specify the rules or constitutional principles that are being breached [Article 51(§ 1) of the Law of Constitutional Court[23]]. Under the principle governing such requests, the Court can only declare the unconstitutionality of rules in relation to which a review has been requested of it, but it can do so on the grounds of constitutional rules or principles other than those whose breach was alleged [Article 51 (§ 5) of the Law of Constitutional Court].

According to Article 279, § 1, if the Constitutional Court rules that a provision of a decree or international agreement is unconstitutional, the instrument must be vetoed by the President of the Republic or the Minister for the Republic, as the case may be, and shall be returned to the organ that approved it. The decree may not be signed or promulgated unless the organ that approved it deletes the provision ruled to be unconstitutional or, as appropriate, confirms it by a majority of two-thirds of the Deputies present, provided that the majority exceeds an absolute majority of the Deputies entitled to vote [Article 279(§ 3) of the Constitution].

In the event that the Constitutional Court pronounces the unconstitutionality of rules set out in international treaties, the President of the Republic must restrict himself to informing the Assembly of the Republic that he cannot ratify it. The Assembly of the Republic can then approve the treaty by a two-thirds majority, whereupon the President of the Republic is able to ratify it [Article 279(§ 4) of the Constitution].

---

[22] We follow through the description of the Constitutional Court itself in Tribunal Constitucional, *The guarantee of the Constitution and the Constitutional Court,* available at http://www.tribunalconstitucional.pt/tc/en/jurisdiction.html#guarantee. See also *Jurisdiction and Procedure, idem, passim.*

[23] The Law of the Constitutional Court is Law n.° 28/82, of 15 November (modified by Law n.°. 143/85, of 26 November, Law n.°. 85/89, of 7 September, Law n.°. 88/95, of 1 September and by Law n.°. 13-A/98, of 26 February) and sets the rules for the Organization, Functioning and Procedure in the Constitutional Court.

When the Court does not pronounce the text unconstitutional, the President of the Republic or the Representative of the Republic, as appropriate, must enact or sign it, unless he opts to exercise his right to impose a political veto, the deadline for which runs from the publication of the Constitutional Court's decision [Articles 136(§ 1) and (§ 4) and 233(§ 2) of the Constitution].

b) Successive Review[24]

i) Successive Abstract Review

Every rule in the Portuguese legal system is subject to this type of review, from those contained in laws to those set out in simple local authority regulations.

This form of review can be requested by the President of the Republic, the President of the Assembly of the Republic, the Prime Minister, the Ombudsman, the Attorney General, one tenth of the Members of the Assembly of the Republic, and also, when a breach of the autonomous regions' rights is at stake, the Representatives of the Republic, the Legislative Assemblies of the autonomous regions, their Presidents or one tenth of their members, and the Presidents of the Regional Governments [Article 281(2) of the Constitution]. Constitutional Court Justices and the Public Prosecutors' Office's representatives to the Court are also entitled to initiate this kind of review in relation to rules that have been deemed unconstitutional in three concrete review cases [Article 281(§ 3) of the Constitution and Article 82 of the Law of Constitutional Court]. This is thus not a procedure that is available to citizens in general, whose only option is to ask one of the aforementioned persons or bodies to exercise his/its right to request it.

In the event that the Constitutional Court concludes that one or more rules which it has been asked to review are unconstitutional, its decision possesses generally binding force. This means that the rule is eliminated from the legal system and can no longer be applied, be it by the courts, the public administration, or private individuals. Some of the specific problems raised by this system are addressed and resolved by Article 282 of the Constitution.

ii) Concrete Review

From a statistic point of view, the concrete control is, far large, the main instrument of control of the constitutionality of legal limits to human rights. Currently, concrete control of constitutionality represents more than 90 % of the cases submitted to the Constitutional Court. Thus, "[T] he control of constitutionality by the Constitutional Court in judicial cases takes place in a proceeding designated *constitutionality appeal.*

---

[24] We continue to follow through Tribunal Constitucional, *The guarantee of the Constitution and the Constitutional Court, op.cit.* See also *Jurisdiction and Procedure, idem, passim.*

It is *not a procedural incident* and, accordingly, there is no staying of proceedings; it is a *proper appeal* and, as such, *presupposes a previous judicial decision* on the subject."[25]

The Constitutional Court has jurisdiction to hear appeals against any of the following court decisions[26]:

a. Decisions refusing to apply a legal rule on the ground of unconstitutionality;
b. Decisions applying a legal rule, the constitutionality of which was challenged during the proceedings.

The responsibility for conducting a concrete review belongs first of all to the court before which the case is pending, inasmuch as under Article 204 of the Constitution all Portuguese courts are empowered to review whether or not the rules they have to apply comply with the Constitution (. . .) It is this form of appeal that grants citizens in general the possibility of gaining access to the Constitutional Court. The appeal can be made directly to the Constitutional Court when it concerns a judicial decision which applies a rule that either the Constitutional Court itself or the Constitutional Commission has already judged unconstitutional, or which refuses to apply a rule on the grounds of its unconstitutionality. However, in the event of a decision that applies a rule whose unconstitutionality has unsuccessfully been raised during the case itself, an appeal to the Constitutional Court is only admissible once all the available ordinary appeals have been exhausted [Article 70(§ 2) and (§ 5) of the Law of Constitutional Court].

In the event that the appeal is (totally or partially)successful, the case file returns to the court *a quo* so that it can reformulate the decision or order its reformulation in accordance with the Constitutional Court's ruling on the question of unconstitutionality [Article 80(§ 2) of the Law of Constitutional Court].

In either of the possible situations—an appeal against a decision that did not apply a rule because it was deemed unconstitutional, or an appeal against a decision that did not accept a challenge to the constitutionality of a rule and applied it—the Constitutional Court's decision does not possess generally binding force; in other words, it only applies in the specific case in which it is handed down [Article 80(§ 1) of the Law of Constitutional Court][27].

---

[25] CORTÊS, António ET AL, Concrete Control of Constitutionality, *op.cit.,* p. 1.

[26] We continue to follow through TRIBUNAL CONSTITUCIONAL, *The guarantee of the Constitution and the Constitutional Court, op.cit.* See also *Jurisdiction and Procedure, idem, passim.*

[27] The restricted effects of these judgments may however be expanded by the Constitutional Court in one situation. Indeed, if a norm has been judged unconstitutional in three concrete cases the Public Prosecutor or any of the Justices may promote a proceeding of successive abstract control of that norm—[Article 281(§ 3) of the Constitution and Article 82 of the Law of Constitutional Court]. Under these circumstances a decision that declares the rule in question unconstitutional does possess generally binding force.

c) Review of Unconstitutionality by Omission[28]

The Constitution—going beyond that which is customary in analogous documents—also gives the Court the power to examine cases involving unconstitutionality by omission; in other words, to "review and verify any failure to comply with this Constitution by means of the omission of legislative measures needed to make constitutional rules executable" (Article 283 of the Constitution).

The procedure that is followed in such cases is similar to that of the successive abstract review of constitutionality. However, given the great sensitivity surrounding both the problem of 'legislative omissions' and the Constitutional Court's fulfillment of this important responsibility, this process can only be initiated by the President of the Republic or the Ombudsman, or, in cases in which the rights of an autonomous region are at stake, the President of the Legislative Assembly in question.

If the Constitutional Court concludes that an omission does exist, the Court must restrict itself to 'verifying' that a case of unconstitutionality by omission exists, and to 'informing' the legislative body thereof.

d) Procedures Concerning the Review of Legality[29]

The procedure for reviewing the legality of rules—due to a breach of a law which possesses superior force, of an autonomous region's statute (by rules contained in regional decrees), or of those of an autonomous region's rights that are enshrined in its statute (by rules contained in a decree that emanated from a body that exercises sovereign power)—is identical to that used to abstract and concrete review of constitutionality (as per Articles 280 and 281 of the Constitution), with the exception of the prior review, which is not permitted in this case, and the control of unconstitutionality by omission, which would not make sense.

17.4   Ranking of International Law Sources in the Constitutional Source System and Reasoning, in its Historical Evolution, of the Constitutional/Supreme Court and Its Main Cases

The openness of the Portuguese Constitutional Court[30] to international law is, for instance, clear in the Constitutional Court Sentence 121/2010. As we have already referred, Article 16 provides the setting for determining the scope and interpretation of fundamental rights *vis à vis* international order as it states that "*the fundamental*

---

[28] We follow again The guarantee of the Constitution and the Constitutional Court, op.cit.

[29] *Idem, ibidem.*

[30] For decisions of Portuguese Constitutional Court please see http://www.tribunalconstitucional.pt.

rights enshrined in the Constitution shall not exclude any others set out in applicable international laws and legal rules" and that "*the constitutional precepts concerning fundamental rights must be interpreted and completed in harmony with the Universal Declaration of Human Rights*".

Furthermore, the Portuguese Constitution includes an Article 8 that specifically states on ranking of international law sources[31] in the constitutional source system:

1. *The norms and principles of general or common international law form an integral part of Portuguese law.*
2. *The norms contained in duly ratified or approved international conventions come into force in Portuguese internal law once they have been officially published, and remain so for as long as they are internationally binding on the Portuguese state.*
3. *The norms issued by the competent organs of international organizations to which Portugal belongs come directly into force in Portuguese internal law, on condition that this is laid down in the respective constituent treaties.*
4. *The provisions of the treaties that govern the European Union and the norms issued by its institutions in the exercise of their respective competences are applicable in Portuguese internal law in accordance with Union law and with respect for the fundamental principles of a democratic state based on the rule of law.*

In what regards this last paragraph, let us also finally point out that the Constitutional revision of 2005 added Article 295, stating clearly that "*the provisions of Article 115(§ 3) do not prejudice the possibility of calling and holding referenda on the approval of treaties concerning the construction and deepening of the European Union*".

Ranking of international law sources in the constitutional source system has not been a relevant question to the Portuguese Constitutional Court because of the specific constitutional clause of Article 8 and the almost unanimous doctrine of the full reception of general international law by the Portuguese Constitution. This full reception has been stated in several decisions of the Portuguese Constitutional Court such as 47/84, 5/85, 24/85, 118/85, 66/91, 100/92.

In what regards conventional law, most Portuguese doctrine, as well as the Portuguese Constitutional Court sustain that they are infraconstitutional but supralegal. This is the main reasoning in decisions 62/84, 24/85, 118/85, 158/85, 66/91.

The only cause of dispute between two sections of the Constitutional Court was to decide whether the violation of a conventional international law by an internal law should be considered as a case of unconstitutionality because of the breach of § 2 of Article 8 above mentioned (Decisions 24/85, 118/85, 158/85, 66/91) or if it should be not considered a case of unconstitutionality as it refers to two infraconstitutional rules (Decisions 47/84, 88/84, 107/84, 118/84, 8/85, 154/90, 281/90, 185/92). The dispute was settled, assuming the competence of Constitutional Court, as ruled in Decisions 321/92 and 603/92.

---

[31] Please consider the list provided in Chap. II of this Report

17.5   Possible Status, in the Domestic System, of Regional or Continental Conventions on Human Rights

"Portugal is recognized by various activities in the area of international human rights; for its work in promoting the Rights of Youth, Children's Rights and the Right to Education—as a regular prosecutor of United Nations resolutions on these Rights; for its efforts to eliminate the Death Penalty where Portugal holds special authority as the first country to abolish capital punishment; in the area of Economic, Social and Cultural Rights, where Portugal is responsible and one of the main drivers of the Working Group in charge of drafting the Optional Protocol to the International Covenant on Economic, Social and Cultural Rights, establishing a system of individual complaints; with regard to refugees, including the full support of the activities of United Nations High Commissioner for Refugees António Guterres; the development and recognition of the Right to Water and Sanitation, where a Portuguese national currently holds the post of UN Special Rapporteur for these rights."[32]

At the national level, it is important to stress the creation in 2010 of the National Commission for Human Rights, that has developed a strategic plan for the commitment of the Portuguese Government.

As we have already stressed out in Chap. 4 of this Report, "it is important to note that at least the Portuguese Constitutional Court (although not all the ordinary courts) is reasonably aware of European law and jurisprudence, both from the European Court of Justice and—especially—from the European Court on Human Rights"[33].

Indeed, "the Portuguese members of the judiciary became used to cite the European Charter of Fundamental Rights only to confirm a right already protected by the Portuguese Constitution or the European Convention on Human Rights—it was merely a confirmation of what other more familiar normative elements already stated, but it did not really make any difference that they were declared in a European Charter of Fundamental Rights."[34]

In what regards the impact of the jurisprudence of the European Court of Human Rights "there is quite a considerable impact of the jurisprudence of international and supranational courts, namely of the European Court on Human Rights, on Portuguese constitutional case-law. However, European Convention on Human Rights decisions' are usually followed only in specific matters, such as guarantees of defense during criminal procedure and limitations on fundamental rights (especially on the right to freedom, right to privacy and to respect for family life).

The right to face an independent and impartial court, established by law, is one of the guaranties attached to the right to due process, as the European Court on Human Rights has ruled in many cases. The Portuguese Constitutional Court has also

---

[32] Portugal's Communiqué on the International Human Rights Day 63rd Anniversary, available at http://www.isria.com/RESTRICTED/D/2011/DECEMBER_16/13_December_2011_75.php.

[33] Silveira, ALESSANDRA ET AL, FIDE 2012, *op. cit.*, p. 3.

[34] SILVEIRA, ALESSANDRA ET AL, FIDE 2012, *op. cit.*, questions 7 and 8, pp. 7/9 and p.16. For further developments on multi-level protection see Chap. VI of this Report.

adopted this position, underlining the importance given to the increased sensitivity of the public to the fair administration of justice, following the decisions in European Court on Human Rights' cases. Moreover, both jurisprudences (Portuguese and European) share the understanding that the concept of impartial court implies the existence of both an objective and a subjective dimension, as it has been stated in European Court on Human Rights's cases Golder *v.* United Kingdom (1975) and Saraiva de Carvalho *v.* Portugal (1994). (. . .) Other than the guaranties of defense during criminal procedure, and as we have said before, the Portuguese Constitutional Court has closely followed the European Court on Human Rights' jurisprudence on limitations on fundamental rights. A good example of this is our national case-law on the restrictions on the right to family life due to the expulsion of foreigners. On this matter, the Constitutional Court has frequently invoked Article 8 of the European Convention of Human Rights to limit the application of the Portuguese legislation on the expulsion of foreigners. Following European Court on Human Rights' decisions in cases Moustaquim *v.* Belgium (1991) and Beldjoudi *v.* France (1992)—among many others—it has been stated that the expulsion of foreigners cannot cause, either in a direct or indirect manner, the separation of parents and children or the subsequent expulsion of the children (minors and at the parents' charge), in order to follow the expelled parent.

Another matter in which the impact of the European Court on Human Rights' jurisprudence on Portuguese case-law is quite remarkable is the right to privacy. In fact, the Constitutional Court has imposed several demands in order to consider legal the interception of telephone calls during a criminal investigation, namely authorization and following by a judicial authority. To justify his position, the Court mentioned, among other arguments, the European Court on Human Rights' decisions in cases Valenzuela Contreras *v.* Spain (1998), Klass and others *v.* Germany (1978), Malone *v.* United Kingdom (1984), PG and JH *v.* United Kingdom (2001), Prado Bugallo *v.* Spain (2003), Kruslin *v.* France (1990) and Huvig *v.* France (1990).

Regarding the right to liberty, the Constitutional Court has closely followed the European Court on Human Rights' jurisprudence to establish a distinction between deprivation of liberty, within the meaning of Article 5 of the European Convention, and restrictions on liberty of movement and freedom to choose one's residence. It has been said that there is a difference of intensity between the two, to be evaluated having in mind all the factors of a concrete case, taken cumulatively.

The Portuguese Constitutional Court has also invoked the European Court on Human Rights' jurisprudence on forced or compulsory labour. Resorting to the European Court's decisions in the case Van der Mussele *v.* Belgium (1983), our national case-law has underlined the fact that one has to regard to all the circumstances of a case in order to determine whether a service required of an individual falls within the prohibition of compulsory labour. Furthermore, it is important to bear in mind that the person's prior consent is not, in itself, sufficient to consider that the required work is not compulsory, because it can have been determined by the menace of a penalty or comparable risks. Therefore, and as it has been stated, a broader evaluation has to be done."[35]

---

[35] Constitutional COURT OF PORTUGAL, The portuguese human rights constitutional law, *op. cit.,* pp. 9/11.

17.6   Citizenship and Multi-Level Constitutionalism

Nowadays, "there are three dimensions by which citizenship can be seen today: the political dimension, the social dimension and another dimension that I call civil. (...) As for social citizenship, (...) it refers to a set of relationships established between people, wherever they are, and refer to a certain economic welfare and social, health education, through consumer protection and the protection of an environment sound, to the desire to share a special standard of living by the standards prevailing in society, understood even at a global level, planetarium".[36]

But even from a legal point of view we have to consider a multi-level legal order, hence, of citizenship. "The civic citizenship based on respect of person, which formed the basis of Article 6 of the Universal Declaration of Human Rights and the substantive test then used: the automatic recognition of each individual as a legal entity. (...) Wherever you are, anyone can claim their legal personality, aware that you are guaranteed the status of subject of rights and duties and therefore the status of citizen".[37]

We have already mentioned Article 15 of Portuguese Constitution stating that foreigners and stateless persons residing in Portugal may not, by rule, exercise political rights, which are reserved to Portuguese citizens. But the Constitution provides for exceptions, related to three specific situations. A first situation covers the citizens of the Portuguese speaking countries with permanent residence in Portugal, since it is provided the basis of reciprocity (Article 15, § 3). A second situation of nationals of Member States of the Union residing in Portugal, since it also is provision for a reciprocal basis, but in this case is concerned only when the right to elect and be elected to Parliament (Article 15, § 5). The third situation is addressed largely to foreigners resident in Portuguese territory, whatever its provenance, creasing the need to be provided for the system of reciprocity. The Constitution gives them the active and passive electoral capacity for the election of local bodies (Article 15, § 4).

We must also remember that European citizenship was introduced in the Treaty on European Union in 1992. Article 17 of this Treaty is clear: *"There shall be a citizenship of the Union."* And among the three defined rights to European citizens, that is, next to the right of movement and residence and the right to diplomatic and consular protection in third countries, the Treaty included the right to elect and be elected in elections to the European Parliament and for municipal elections in the country where you live.

"Of course, not supra-national citizenship, European, or the sub-national, regional or municipal, to replace state citizenship. On the contrary, Complement it. Moreover, to dispel any doubt, the Treaty of Amsterdam in 1997, stipulated that "the citizenship of the Union shall complement national citizenship and does not replace", which allows us to draw two corollaries: first, you must have the citizenship of a Member

---

[36] We follow through GARCIA, M G, A tripla cidadania: a Nação, a Europa e o Mundo, Instituto de Estudos Académicos para Seniores, Academia das Ciências de Lisboa, 19/10/2011, available at http://s1.acad-ciencias.pt/, pp. 6/7.

[37] GARCIA, M G, *idem*, ibidem.

State to benefit from the citizenship of the Union and, secondly, European citizenship rights to benefit from complementary and additional to national citizenship. It is also within this context of deepening of participatory democracy that should be read in the new rights guaranteed in the Treaty of Lisbon."[38]

Furthermore, with the *Zambrano* decision, the European Court of Justice confronted "the urgent need for densification of the scope of application of fundamental rights in the European Union and the consequent access by citizens to the European standard of protection, in order to avoid an inadmissible difference in the treatment of the so-called dynamic citizens (who exercise their classic European rights/economic freedoms and therefore benefit from the European standard of fundamental rights) on one hand, and of static citizens (who do not exercise economic freedoms, and for that reason do not benefit from the European standard) on the other."[39]

Thus, "[I]f we have to identify what the *Zambrano* sentence adds to the so-called *citizenship acquis*, it is possible to say that, in between the lines of the decision one may read the following conclusions: (1) European citizenship is not subordinated to the previous exercise of an economic freedom and (2) through European citizenship one may accede to the European standard of fundamental rights' protection. It seems little, but it is not so. In spite of apparently being one more sentence on the protection of third country nationals related to European citizens."[40]

Multi citizenship equalizes European citizens' legal protection, through the prosecution of the highest level of protection under the European Convention for the Protection of Human Rights and Fundamental Freedoms and the European Charter of Fundamental Rights[41]. This is the real consequence of "transconstitutionalism", expression adopted by Marcelo Neves[42] to define the schema of "power sharing" once presented by Pernice as "divided sovereignty" or "shared" multi-level constitutionalism[43]. Among Portuguese doctrine, J.J. Gomes Canotilho uses the expression "multilevel approach"[44] or interconstitutionality[45], corresponding to the reflexive interaction of norms from several sources that co-exist in the same political space—and

---

[38] GARCIA, M G, *ibidem*, pp. 12/13.

[39] SILVEIR A, ALESSANDRA ET AL, FIDE 2012, *op. cit.*, The future of fundamental rights' protection (questions 11, 12, 13 and 14), pp. 18/19.

[40] SILVEIRA, ALESSANDRA ET AL, *idem*, p. 19.

[41] These are the so called "spill-over effects": GOMES CANOTILHO, J.J. AND SUZANA TAVARES DA SILVA, Método multinível: "Spill-over effects" e interpretação conforme o direito da União Europeia, Revista de Legislação e de Jurisprudência, Ano 138, n. 3955 (2009), p. 182–199.

[42] NEVES, MARCELO, Transconstitucionalismo, WMF, New York, 2009, pp. 152 ff.

[43] PERNICE, INGOLF, Multilevel constitutionalism in the European Union, in European Law Review, 27, 2002.

[44] "Brancosos" e Interconstitucionalidade: itinerários dos discursos sobre historicidade constitucional, Coimbra, Almedina, Coimbra, 2006, p. 186.

[45] GOMES CANOTILHO, J. J., *Estado de direito e internormatividade*, in Alessandra Silveira (ed.), Direito da União Europeia e transnacionalidade, Quid juris, Lisboa, 2010. This is also an expression of PAULO RANGEL, in *Uma teoria da "interconstitucionalidade": pluralismo e Constituição no pensamento de Francisco Lucas Pires*, in O estado do Estado. Ensaios de política constitucional sobre justiça e democracia, Dom Quixote, Alfragide, 2009.

demands a networked performance to solve common problems. But the expression
"transconstitutionalism" is perhaps more impressive than the original expression of
multi-level constitutionalism and is able to embrace the overflowing of the territorial
constitution—that must be interconnected and complemented with top level rules of
law -, and the densification of a national cultural matrix[46]. And this is, indeed, a new
framework for state citizenship.

References

AAVV, A Carta dos Direitos Fundamentais da União Europeia—A Participação da Assembleia da
    República, Assembleia da República, Comissão de Assuntos Europeus, Lisboa, 2001
ALMEIDA, CARLOS FERREIRA DE/CRISTAS, MARIA ASSUNÇÃO/PIÇARRA, NUNO (Ed.), Portuguese
    Law, an overview, Almedina, Coimbra, 2007
BACELAR GOUVEIA, JORGE, "Constitutional Law", in FERREIRA DE ALMEIDA, ASSUNÇÃO CRISTAS,
    NUNO PIÇARRA (Ed.), Portuguese Law, an overview, Almedina, Coimbra, 2007, pp. 75–87
BACELAR GOUVEIA, JORGE,"Fundamental Rights", in FERREIRA DE ALMEIDA, ASSUNÇÃO CRISTAS,
    NUNO PIÇARRA (Ed.), Portuguese Law, an overview, Almedina, Coimbra, 2007, pp. 89–97
CONSTITUTIONAL COURT OF PORTUGAL, The portuguese human rights constitutional law, The
    human rights law (Presentation at the World Conference on Constitutional Justice—Cape
    Town South Africa, 23–24 January 2009) available at http://www.venice.coe.int/WCCJ/Papers/
    POR_Moura_Ramos_E.pdf
CORTÊS, ANTÓNIO AND TERESA VIOLANTE, Concrete Control of Constitutionality in Portugal: A
    Means Towards Effective Protection of Fundamental Rights, Spring, 2011, 29 Penn St. Int'l L.
    Rev. 759, Report drafted for Co.Co.A. (Comparing Constitutional Adjudication), Third Edition,
    2008 organized by the Faculty of Law (Department of Legal Sciences) of the University
    of Trento, available at http://www.tribunalconstitucional.pt/tc/content/files/relatorios_001.pdf
CUNHA, PAULO FERREIRA DA, Human and Fundamental Rights and duties in the Portuguese
    constitution. Some reflections, available at http://works.bepress.com/pfc/5
FERREIRA DE ALMEIDA, ASSUNÇÃO CRISTAS, NUNO PIÇARRA (Ed.), Portuguese Law, an overview,
    Almedina, Coimbra, 2007, p. 89–97, p. 90 -91.
For decisions of Portuguese Constitutional Court please see http://www.tribunalconstitucional.pt
For the list of conventions in which Portugal takes part, please see http://direitoshumanos.gddc.pt/
    DireitosHumanos/4/IVPAG4_1.htm#
GARCIA, M G, A tripla cidadania: a Nação, a Europa e o Mundo, Instituto de Estudos Académicos
    para Seniores, Academia das Ciências de Lisboa, 19/10/2011, available at http://s1.acad-
    ciencias.pt/
GOMES CANOTILHO, J. J., "Brancosos" e Interconstitucionalidade: itinerários dos discursos sobre
    historicidade constitucional, Coimbra, Almedina, Coimbra, 2006
GOMES CANOTILHO, J. J., Estado de direito e internormatividade, in Alessandra Silveira (ed.),
    Direito da União Europeia e transnacionalidade, Quid juris, Lisboa, 2010
GOMES CANOTILHO, J.J. AND SUZANA TAVARES DA SILVA, Método multinível: "Spill-over
    effects" e interpretação conforme o direito da União Europeia, Revista de Legislação e de
    Jurisprudência, Ano 138, n. 3955 (2009), p. 182–199

[46] These are the aspects brought forward by TAVARES DA SILVA, S. (2011), Os direitos fundamentais
na arena global, Imprensa da Universidade de Coimbra, Coimbra. On the concepts of constitutionalism, neoconstitutionalism, and multilevel constitutionalism, p. 9. On the principles and method
of fundamental rights and judicial dialogue, p. 23. On the difficulties of the multi-level governance,
p. 144.

MIRANDA, JORGE in "Reunião Conjunta das Comissões de Assuntos Europeus e de Assuntos Constitucionais, Direitos, Liberdades e Garantias sobre a Carta dos Direitos Fundamentais da União Europeia" (Joint Meeting of the European Affairs and Constitutional Matters Parliamentary Commissions), 14th April 2000, in A Carta dos Direitos Fundamentais da União Europeia—A Participação da Assembleia da República, Assembleia da República, Comissão de Assuntos Europeus, Lisboa, 2001

NEVES, MARCELO, Transconstitucionalismo, WMF, New York, 2009, pp. 152 ff.

RANGEL, PAULO, Uma teoria da "interconstitucionalidade": pluralismo e Constituição no pensamento de Francisco Lucas Pires, in O estado do Estado. Ensaios de política constitucional sobre justiça e democracia, Dom Quixote, Alfragide, 2009

PERNICE, INGOLF, Multilevel constitutionalism in the European Union, in European Law Review, 27, 2002

PORTUGAL's Communiqué on the International Human Rights Day 63rd Anniversary, available at http://www.isria.com/RESTRICTED/D/2011/DECEMBER_16/13_December_2011_75.php

SILVEIRA, ALESSANDRA, PEDRO MADEIRA FROUFE AND MARIANA CANOTILHO, FIDE 2012, Questionnaire General, Protection of Fundamental Rights post-Lisbon: The Interaction between the EU Charter of Fundamental Rights, the European Convention on Human Rights (ECHR) and National Constitutions, available at http://www.cedu.direito.uminho.pt/uploads/FIDE%-202012_final.pdf

TAVARES DA SILVA, S., Os direitos fundamentais na arena global, Imprensa da Universidade de Coimbra, Coimbra, 2011

TRIBUNAL CONSTITUCIONAL, Jurisdiction and Procedure, available at http://www.tribunalconstitucional.pt/en/jurisdiction.html#guarantee

TRIBUNAL CONSTITUCIONAL, The guarantee of the Constitution and the Constitutional Court, available at http://www.tribunalconstitucional.pt/tc/en/jurisdiction.html#guarantee

Chapter 18
Codification in the Field of Human Rights

Irina Moroianu Zlătescu

PhD, Professor, National School of Political and Administrative Studies, Ecological University of Bucharest, Director of the Romanian Institute for Human Rights, Member of the International Academy of Comparative Law.

Codification, according to one of its accepted meanings, is a legislative technique consisting in a methodical presentation of the juridical rules that are already in effect, without substantial alterations and without changing their nature. According to another accepted meaning, it is an original operation by which the previous rules are transformed in an attempt to regulate its subject matter in a new way.[1]

At present, the doctrine has reached the conclusion that codification is part of the juridical terminology in effect in many systems of law.[2] In the framework of numerous scientific reunions, international conferences and congresses held in late twentieth century and early twenty-first century, the participants analyzed the place held by codification in the evolution of the sources of law[3].

Some authors are doubtful about the chances codification has to develop in the next years for it is a creation of modern law[4], while others believe it will have its place

---

[1] *See* H. El Onfir, La codification du droit marocain, in Revue juridique et politique—Independence et coopération, no 3–4/1986, p. 391 et seq, as well as V. D. Zlătescu, Introducere în legistica formală, Ed. Romprint, 1995, p. 138 et seq.

[2] Id.

[3] For the sake of illustration, let us mention the Congress held by the International Academy of Comparative Law in Caracas, 1982, the Congress of the International Institute of Law of French Expression and Inspiration of Louisiana, 1985, the Colloquium at the University of Laval, Quebec 2004, etc. On occasion of one edition of the International University of Human Rights, organized by the Romanian Institute for Human Rights, it was pointed out that the first Code, a token of acknowledgement of the fundamental human rights, was the small clay cylinder inscribed with the edict of Cyrus the Great (534 B.C.); see Irina Moroianu Zlătescu, R. C. Demetrescu, Din istoria drepturilor omului, Ed. IRDO, 2001, p. 7 et seq.

[4] See B. Oppetit, L'avenir de la codification, in Droits, issue 24/1998, p. 73 et seq.

I. M. Zlătescu (✉)
Romanian Institute for Human Rights, 42 Alexandru Constantinescu,
sector 1, 011474 Bucharest, Romania
e-mail: irina.zlatescu@irdo.ro

W.-Y. Wang (ed.), *Codification in International Perspective*, Ius Comparatum – Global Studies in Comparative Law, DOI 10.1007/978-3-319-03455-3_18,
© Springer International Publishing Switzerland 2014

in the post-modern era for universalism gives it a vocation to make its contribution to the development of the world legal order[5].

It has been noticed that the term "code" tended to be mistaken for "codification", whereas "code" is "a vague and also prestigious word"[6], which covers more than five thousand years of juridical history. The term has a technical side for it aims at better knowledge of the law, and a social and political side for quite often social and political antagonisms have to be taken into account in the elaboration of a code, while it should contribute to the attenuation of these antagonisms, serving the glory of the leader who attaches his name to it—for instance the Code of Ur-Nammu, the Code of Lipit-Istar, the code of Hammurabi, the Code of Theodosian, the Code of Justinian, the Code of Euric, or the Code of Napoleon, etc.—or asserting the independence of a new state.

According to the doctrine, codification is a common, yet not necessarily universal tradition. It is situated in a certain social environment, responding to certain legal exigencies and related to the political concerns. There is therefore a social group it is devoted to, there are technicians who elaborate it, and there is a power that demands and often sanctions it. Three aspects have to be taken into account in relation to codification: the social aspect, the technical aspect and the political aspect[7], which is to be further referred to.

Thus, considering the social aspect, one can see that it is often circumscribed to a crisis of the society which, by means of codified law, attempts to reduce antagonisms or settle the new rules of the game, this way responding to a new situation. It settles new life rules of the social game and responds to the need for security.[8]

As far as the technical aspect is concerned, it can be seen that, according to the doctrine, codification corresponds to certain technical exigencies.[9] Since it provides the framework of the social life, law requires accuracy and certainty. It has to be known by its users. Hence the need to put together in coherent ensembles rules that have different origins and come from different times, which is one form of codification. More recent customs have to give way to a uniform law, which often can be within the state's political frontiers, while they sometimes may go beyond these frontiers. It is often the technical exigency that determines a certain codification.

Nevertheless, considering the political aspects as well, one may notice that codification reflects a country's political structure. Hence its complexity as a juridical phenomenon. Codification is viewed as a general phenomenon in most societies and at all times. Professor Gaudemet shows that we should ask ourselves what is the reason

---

[5] See F. Zenati-Castaing, L'avenir de la codification, in Revue internationale de droit comparé, issue no. 2, 2011, p. 355 et seq.

[6] See P. Decheix, Raport susţinut la Universitatea Internaţională a Drepturilor Omului, Mangalia, 2000; see also, P. Decheix, Le Congrès de Louisiane, in Revue juridique et politique . . . , loc. cit., p. 207 et seq.

[7] See J. Gaudemet, La codification, ses formes et ses fins, in Revue juridique et politique . . . , loc. cit., p. 239 et seq.

[8] Id.

[9] Id.

for being of this generality and above all how much diversity is hidden behind the word 'code'.[10]

Obviously, promulgation of a text including numerous articles is not enough to entail codification, meaning that beside putting together several dispersed laws it is necessary for a set of rules to be put in order so as to obtain a certain value in relation to other rules, with which they form a system based on the general principles, stated or implied.

Codification is a systemization, an implementation of this philosophy, for it advances a common law of humanity. It is a special process using the codes in the field of law. The corpus of law resulting from this process goes beyond the classical codes—a phenomenon as old as legislation—which quite often used to be mere compilations of laws. As the eminent jurist, member of the French Academy, Alain Plantay would explain many years ago, codification is an ancestral social phenomenon, widespread in the world, for it is an epic and fundamental approach to the norm issue in all its constitutional, criminal, civil, administrative, and later, in our time, international variants.[11]

Let us remind, for instance, that attempts of systemization, therefore not just unifications of the norms, were made as far back as the incipient phase of the formation of the Roman-Germanic system of law[12]. Such attempts were made in the fifth–sixth centuries, then later in the Middle Ages. In Eastern Europe, such attempts were made starting in the ninth century, while in Western Europe in the eleventh century. Of major importance, particularly for the evolution of the system of law in the western states, was the systemization of norms in the Canonic law in the sixteenth century[13]. Also, in the Romanian Principalities, there were Eustatie's Code of Laws (1562), the Code of Putna (1581) and the Code of Laws of Bistriţa Moldovenească (1618).

Under such circumstances, in fifteenth–eighteenth centuries France, Germany and Austria important codifications of private and public law were made, the most significant ones in civil and criminal law. Everything starts with a wording of the customs, which often gets the form of a codification.[14]

At about the same time, important codes that also included provisions related to human rights emerged in the Romanian Principalities. For example, in the seventeenth century, Vasile Lupu's *Romanian Book of Learning* was adopted in Moldova (1646), while Matei Basarab's *Great Code of Laws* (or *Reformation of the Law*) was adopted in Wallachia in 1652.[15]

The eighteenth century saw the publication of highly scientific works where the tradition of the science of law and the mere interpretation of the latter had been given

---

[10] Id.

[11] See A. Plantay, Discours, in Revue juridique et politique . . . , loc. cit., p. 231 et seq.

[12] See V. D. Zlătescu, Mari sisteme de drept contemporan, Editura Pro Universitaria, Bucureşti, 2012, pp. 15–24.

[13] Id.

[14] See Jean Gaudemet, op. cit.

[15] See V. D. Zlătescu, Irina Moroianu Zlătescu, Le droit roumain dans le système juridique romano-germanique, in Revue internationale de droit comparé, No. 2/1992.

up in favour of a corpus of law that paralleled the Roman law to the local law and the spirit of nature[16].

As a matter of fact, the notion of codification came forth in the seventeenth and the eighteenth centuries and was owed to the great jurists of the time who actually codified the law[17]. "In non-western countries, codification was an instrument of modernization. It was achieved in most countries that were not under the influence of *common law* in the nineteenth and the twentieth centuries and, to be sure, in the Arab world"[18]. Thus, in Europe and in Latin America, the phenomenon of codification gained impetus in the nineteenth century and the first decades of the twentieth century, while in Africa it started in the 1960s.[19]

As far as the Romanian Principalities are concerned, the following were elaborated: Drafts of Codes of general law, by Mihai Fotino, in the period 1765–1777, the Compilation of Laws of 1780, and the Caragea Code of 1818. At the same time, the French Commercial Code was adopted as a national law in Wallachia in 1830, the Organic Regulations were adopted in Wallachia in 1831 and in Moldova in 1832. In 1832, the Romanian Principalities introduced Napoleon's French Criminal Code, with the amendments operated by the Italian Civil Code, as well as the Calimachi Code, of Romanistic inspiration, in Moldova in 1865, which codified a few human rights norms.[20]

As known, codification refers to a corpus that reinstituted law while redefining plurality of sources. It is above all the outcome of the movement transforming the sources of law that took place under the action of modern states by shifting the focus from the customary law to the written law. This was a novelty. Its effect was unification of the customary law by means of the Roman law and as a result of its modernization in contact with the natural law[21]. Undoubtedly, it should not be reduced to an art or a mere technique serving the practicing of law and justice, as traditionally used to be the codes before it, but rather be seen as animated by the philosophy of the school promoting the modern natural law, according to which the positive law is an attempt to reveal the natural law, a common law for all humans, while such revelation can be made through a mere exercise of reason[22].

---

[16] See V. R. Zimmermann, Roman law, contemporary law, European law, the civilian tradition today, Oxford University Press, 2004.

[17] See F. Zenati-Castaing, loc. cit., p. 358.

[18] See D. Deronssin, F.Garnier, Passé et présent du droit, no. 6, Compilations et codifications juridiques, t. 3; V. S. Jahel, Code civil et codification dans les pays du monde arabe, 1804–2004, Le code civil, un passé, un présent, un avenir, Dalloz, 2004, p. 831 et seq. apud F. Zenati-Castaing, loc. cit., p. 359, as well as Irina Moroianu Zlătescu, Address upon receiving the title of Doctor Honoris Causa of Ovidius University, Constanţa, 11 octombrie 2011.

[19] See P. Armenjon, B. Nolde, M. Wolff, Traité de droit comparé, tomme I, LGDJ Paris, 1950, p. 71. et seq; R. David, Les grands systèmes du droit contemporain, Dalloz, Paris, 1964; J. Constantinesco, Traite de droit comparé, tomme II, LGDJ Paris, 1972, p. 50 et seq.

[20] See V. D. Zlătescu, Panorama marilor sisteme contemporane de drept, Ed. Continent XXI, Bucureşti, 1994, p. 118 et seq.

[21] See P. Decheix, loc. cit.

[22] See F. Zenati-Castaing, loc.cit., p. 360.

As was shown before, it is obvious that in order to be successful codification needs to meet the traditions and the expectations of the population it is addressed to. The political discourse cannot be a source for the interpretation of the codes as long as it is not materialized in a text of law. At the level of international law, attempts have been made to reach international uniformity of the solutions by means of conventions, which may lead to many difficulties in practice. States codify their domestic rules pushing them towards the international custom and sometimes commit "the sin of excessive nationalism"[23].

A codification of human rights in international law can be reckoned to have occurred only after the establishment of the League of Nations. However, unfortunately, as is known, though founded with the purpose to keep peace, a consensus agreement included in the Peace Treaty signed at Versailles in 1919, human rights issues were not consistently dealt with. This was done by an organization established at the same time, the International Labour Organization, which codified the right to work and a series of connected rights, which has proved its usefulness up to the present day.[24]

Before that, one could rather speak about the codification of the domestic law of human rights. Thus, mention should be made of those Constitutions that included codifications of human rights, such as the English Constitution of 1215, the American Constitution of 1776 with its subsequent amendments, or the French Constitution of the Revolution, considered to be the most advanced Constitution of the moment as it codified a large number of human rights. Later on, the Russian Constitution of 1918, the Mexican Constitution of 1917, the Constitution of Weimar of 1919, the Constitution of Romania of 1923, etc., proclaimed a new dimension of human rights. However, it wasn't these rights that law-makers were concerned about; it was the formal inclusion of economic, social and cultural rights that they were most interested in. This was the moment when these rights were also included in the international system alongside with the civil and political rights.[25]

In the Romanian Principalities, the above-mentioned Organic Regulations, acts of a constitutional nature, were followed by the First Constitutional Act of the United Principalities of 1858, which also includes human rights norms, followed in turn by the Constitution of 1866, the first Constitution proper of an independent state that also included the codification of some human rights.[26]

Public international law has two sources of codification, namely, the international custom, which doesn't consist of so many rules, and the institutional treaties as well, which always include provisions of the treaty-law kind. In fact the United Nations Charter itself is an example of institutional treaty. Of course, it provides for the development of the international law, but at the same time it has imposed

---

[23] See P. Decheix, Le Congrés de Louisiane, La codification et l'évolution du droit, in Revue juridique et Politique Indépendance et Coopération, 1985, p. 210.

[24] See Irina Moroianu Zlătescu, Drepturile omului—un sistem în evoluție, Ed. IRDO, București, 2008, p. 16 et seq.

[25] See Irina Moroianu Zlătescu, R. C. Demetrescu, op. cit., p. 3 et seq.

[26] Irina Moroianu Zlătescu, International Encyclopaedia of Laws : Constitutional Law in Romania, Kluwer Law International, the Netherlands, 2012. p. 5 et seq.

general conduct rules on the Member States. They were prohibited, for instance, to make use of force except for cases of legitimate defence, of course. As can be noticed, at international level *customary law is reflected faithfully, which points out the importance of the custom,* while States may use the treaty-law method to enter completely new rules. In terms of international law, codification means the written, coherent, systemized wording of the rules in international law as a whole, or it may refer to a specified subject matter.

Codification in international law is related to the essence of law, transforming, developing and completing it on consent by the States adopting it. The United Nations International Law Commission provides, as a whole, coverage of the great forms of civilization and the main legal systems of the world.

Referring again to the United Nations Charter, it can be seen that it provides for the development of the international law, while codification is hampered by more and more obstacles because of the difficulties consisting in meeting a consensus in relation to the norms of law that refer to new fields that are undergoing a transformation process. This is the reason why making the difference between the international custom and the codified convention can often be a difficult task. The idea, considered by some authors[27] "a little bit strange not to say aberrant", has also been advanced that acceptance of a conventional provision by a certain number of states would give birth to an "instantaneous custom"[28], whereas by its very essence a custom involves a behaviour repeated for a certain period of time. In fact, this period of time could be pretty short, as for example in the case of the United Nations work to codify human rights.

Obviously, there are several techniques to achieve codification. A good result could be obtained if the task of codification is assigned to one single author, for it has been noticed that, when a commission is established, the effect is much lesser even though we may be enthusiastic for the period of time needed for the codification is shorter[29].

In the last decades of the twentieth century, computer science has opened new horizons for codification; nevertheless, the major difficulty often consists in the use of the specific terms in different languages for it often happens that the computer fails to assign a word its correct legal meaning.

It has also been noticed that codification attempts are paralleled by a counterpart movement of decodification, which is owed to the emergence of new branches of law; likewise, there is a risk that codification could be ruined by the excessive powers given to the judge, particularly in the *common law* system.[30]

---

[27] See Georges Perrin, "La codification et le développement progressif du droit international public", Revue juridique et politique . . . , loc. cit., p. 861 et seq.

[28] Id.

[29] Id.

[30] Part of the ideas promoted in this study were the basis of a report prepared for the scientific lectures session on "Science and codification in Romania (1864–2009)", organized by the Institute for Legal Research "Acad. Andrei Rădulescu", on 30 March 2012.

If we refer to the codification of the fundamental human rights, it should be mentioned that the international law of human rights emerged in the late nineteenth century and the early twentieth century, following the adoption of the Geneva Conventions, also known as the Red Cross Conventions, and the Hague Conventions, which were meant to humanize wars. In the previous centuries, as was mentioned before, human rights were to be found in the domestic law in the framework of the constitutional law.

When it comes to the codification of the fundamental human rights, it should be clarified that the international law of human rights was born as late as the beginning of the twentieth century. In the previous centuries, human rights were to be found in the domestic law, in the framework of the constitutional law.

The period following the creation of the United Nations Organization, the elaboration of the UN Charter and the adoption of the Universal Declaration of Human Rights, is considered to be the contemporary era of human rights, characterized by the emergence of numerous regulations in the field and codification of the fundamental rights. Thus, the United Nations Charter is a codification of a special type. The Charter includes the Universal Declaration of Human Rights, the International Covenant on Civil and Political Rights, the International Covenant on Economic, Social and Cultural Rights, and the Additional Protocols to the two Covenants.[31]

At domestic level, most United Nations Member States codified the fundamental human rights in their constitutions. To illustrate, let us mention the USA or even Canada, which adopted in 1960, at federal level, in both Chambers of Parliament, the Canadian Declaration of Human Rights. Then one after another, the Canadian provinces adopted "Human Rights Codes", where the fundamental rights are codified. Part I of the Constitutional Law of 1982 includes the Constitutional Charter where the fundamental rights are laid down. The Canadian Charter joins together the 10 provinces and Quebec, though in 1975, Quebec had adopted an exhaustive Charter of the Rights of Persons[32].

---

[31] The United Nations Commission on Human Rights, which ended its activity based on Resolution 60/251 of 15 March 2006, when it was replaced with the United Nations Human Rights Council, provided the international community with a universal framework of human rights, including the Universal Declaration of Human Rights, the International Covenants on Civil and Political Rights and on Economic, Social and Cultural Rights, respectively, their Protocols, as well as other fundamental human rights treaties.The 65 years since the proclamation of the Universal Declaration of Human Rights by the United Nations General Assembly, more precisely on 10 December 1948, has hardly diminished the power of the message conveyed by this document of exceptional importance, meant to consecrate a common ideal for all nations, the foundation on which the construct of human rights has been edified. It is appreciated nowadays that the Declaration is the genuine interpretation of the United Nations Charter as it explains in detail the meaning of the terms "human rights and fundamental freedoms", which the United Nations Member States committed themselves to respect when they became a party to the Charter (See Sohn L., The New International Law: Protection of the rights of individuals rather than States, American University Law Review, 1982, vol. 32, p. 16 et seq.

[32] See G. Beaudoin, La codification des droits fondamentaux au Canada: un commentaire, in Revue juridique et politique . . . , loc. cit., p. 491 et seq.

At European level, the Council of Europe Member States as a matter of fact revised their Constitutions or adopted new ones with the assistance of the European Commission for Democracy through Law (the Venice Commission) to include the fundamental rights laid down in the Universal Declaration of Human Rights, thus giving the latter binding powers by means of the Constitutions. If we were to take Romania as an example, it is arts. 11 and 20 in the Constitution and the entire chapter devoted to human rights that initiated the process of domestic codification of human rights.[33] Thus the codification of human rights at international level reaches the national level. At the same time, at the level of the European Union, one may speak of the Charter of Fundamental Rights of the European Union, which has the force of a European Treaty. As part of the European legal order, it is binding and preeminent, taking precedence over the domestic laws and being consonant with the international legal order. At the same time, the Member States of the European Union are also Member States of the Council of Europe, which adopted the European Convention on Human Rights with its Additional Protocols, the European Social Charter with its Additional Protocols and the European Social Charter revised.

National jurisdictions apply the jurisprudence of the European Court of Justice but, since these countries are also members of the Council of Europe, they also apply the jurisprudence of the European Court of Human Rights in the terms of the treaty.

Also, as far as Romania is regarded, during this period it adopted the Civil Code and the Criminal Code, as well as the Civil Procedure Code and the Criminal Procedure Code. These play an important role in the modernization of the legislation in consonance with the tendency of universalization of law.[34]

Hence the obvious conclusion that the human rights codification process in terms of the international, regional and national law belongs to the present day[35].

References

Armenjon, P., Nolde, B., Wolff, M., Traité de droit comparé, tomme I, LGDJ Paris, 1950, p. 71
Beaudoin, G., La codification des droits fondamentaux au Canada: un commentaire, in Revue juridique et politique . . . , loc. cit., p. 491
Constantinesco, J., Traité de droit comparé, tomme II, LGDJ Paris, 1972, p. 50
David, R., Les grands systèmes de droit contemporain, Dalloz, Paris, 1964
Decheix, P., Le Congrés de Louisiane, La codification et l'évolution du droit, in Revue juridique et politique Indépendance et Coopération, 1985, p. 210
Decheix, P., Le Congrès de Louisiane, in Revue juridique et politique . . . , loc. cit., p. 207
Decheix, P., Raport susţinut la Universitatea Internaţională a Drepturilor Omului, Mangalia, 2000

---

[33] See Irina Moroianu Zlătescu, Constitutional Law in Romania . . . , p. 121 et seq.

[34] See Irina Moroianu Zlătescu, Monna Lisa Magdo Belu, La culture juridique et l'acculturation du droit: rapport national roumain in "Legal culture and legal transplants—la culture juridique et l'acculturation du droit", XVIII Congress of the International Academy of Comparative Law, ISAIDAT Law Review, vol. 1, issue 2, 2011, p. 260 et seq.

[35] Id.

Deronssin, D., Garnier, F. Passé et présent du droit, no. 6, Compilations et codifications juridiques, t. 3

Gaudemet, J., La codification, ses formes et ses fins, in Revue juridique et politique . . . , *loc. cit.*, p. 239

Jahel, V. S., Code civil et codification dans les pays du monde arabe, 1804–2004, Le code civil, un passé, un présent, un avenir, Dalloz, 2004, p. 831 et seq. apud Zenati-Castaing, F., *loc. cit.*, p. 359

Oppetit, B., *L'avenir de la codification*, in Droits, issue 24/1998, p. 73

Oufir, Hassan El, La codification du droit marocain, in Revue juridique et politique—Independence et coopération, no 3–4/1986, p. 391

Perrin, Georges, "La codification et le développement progressif du droit international public", Revue juridique et politique . . . , *loc. cit.*, p. 861

Plantay, A., Discours, in Revue juridique et politique . . . , *loc. cit.*, p. 231

Sohn, L., The New International Law: Protection of the rights of individuals rather than States, American University Law Review, 1982, vol. 32, p. 16

Zenati-Castaing, F., *L'avenir de la codification*, in Revue internationale de droit comparé, issue no. 2, 2011, p. 355, 358

Zimmermann, V. R., Roman law, contemporary law, European law, the civilian tradition today, Oxford University Press, 2004

Zlătescu, V. D., Panorama marilor sisteme comntemporane de drept, Ed. Continent XXI, Bucureşti, 1994, p. 118

Zlătescu, V. D., Introducere în legistica formală, Ed. Romprint, 1995, p. 138

Zlătescu, Irina Moroianu, Demetrescu, R. C., *Din istoria drepturilor omului*, Ed. IRDO, 2001, p. 7

Zlătescu, Irina Moroianu, Drepturile omului – un sistem în evoluţie, Ed. IRDO, Bucureşti, 2008, p. 16

Zlătescu, Irina Moroianu, International Encyclopaedia of Laws: Constitutional Law in Romania, Kluwer Law International, the Netherlands, 2012. p. 5, 121

Zlătescu, V. D., *Mari sisteme de drept contemporan*, Editura Pro Universitaria, Bucureşti, 2012, pp. 15–24

Zlătescu, V. D., Zlătescu, Irina Moroianu, Le droit roumain dans le système juridique romano-germanique, in Revue internationale de droit comparé, No. 2/1992

Chapter 19
The United States and Human Rights: Paradoxes and Challenges

Leila Nadya Sadat

19.1 The United States Constitution and Human Rights

During the eighteenth century, even prior to the elaboration of the U.S. Declaration of Independence and the Revolutionary War, America's Founders and other intellectuals clearly thought about liberty in "human rights" terms, referring often to the "rights of man," "rights of mankind," and "human rights."[1] The well-known language of the Declaration of Independence provides:

> We hold these truths to be self-evident: that all men are created equal; that they are endowed, by their Creator, with certain unalienable Rights; that among these are life, liberty, and the pursuit of happiness.

These words undoubtedly inspired the authors of the French *Déclaration des droits de l'homme et du citoyen* as well. Subsequently, however, as references to the divine origin of human rights faded from legal and political discourse, the French and American Revolutions took "natural rights" and made them "secular, rational, universal, individual, democratic and radical."[2] The American rights tradition drew heavily on the writing of John Locke and other English antecedents, and emphasized civil and political rights. Moreover, although we now think of the Federal Constitution as being of central importance in the protection of individual human rights, at the founding of the Republic it was primarily the states, not the federal government, which were the guarantors of the individual rights found in their charters and constitutions. The "Constitution, as conceived, was not essentially a charter of rights and liberties, but a blueprint of government."[3] Thus, a fundamental reason for the adoption of the

---

[1] Paust, Jordan J. 1996. International Law as Law of the United States, 169. Durham: Carolina Academic Press.

[2] Henkin, Louis. 1978. The Rights of Man Today, 3–13. Boulder: Westview Press.

[3] *Id.*

L. N. Sadat (✉)
School of Law, Washington University, One Brookings Drive,
Campus Box 1120, St. Louis, Missouri 63130-4899, USA
e-mail: sadat@wulaw.wustl.edu

W.-Y. Wang (ed.), *Codification in International Perspective,* Ius Comparatum – Global Studies in Comparative Law, DOI 10.1007/978-3-319-03455-3_19,
© Springer International Publishing Switzerland 2014

federal Bill of Rights, which was ratified in 1791,[4] was worry about federal intrusion into state affairs and into the lives of America's citizens.

The federal Bill of Rights includes many human rights found in modern international conventions, including fair trial rights (5th, 6th and 7th Amendments); rights of due process (5th Amendment); a right to religious freedom and the separation of church and state (1st Amendment); a right to free speech, freedom of assembly and to petition the government and to a free press (1st Amendment); a right to be free from cruel and unusual punishment (8th Amendment); property rights (5th and 8th Amendments), and a right to privacy (to be free from unreasonable searches and seizures, 4th Amendment). Through the practice of judicial review, many of these rights have been expanded and elaborated upon; and they have been applied not only to federal government action, which is specific in the text ("Congress shall make no law respecting . . ."), but to the states as well, through their selective incorporation into the fourteenth Amendment.[5]

The modern observer will quickly note an absence of economic, social and cultural rights in this list of U.S. "human" (constitutional) rights. In addition, certain rights enumerated in the Bill of Rights are peculiar to the United States, such as the Second Amendment's "Right to Bear Arms," which, according to a recent study, has been copied by only two percent of Constitutions worldwide.[6] Additionally, the words of the Declaration of Independence notwithstanding, at the time of the Constitution's adoption and the ratification of the Bill of Rights, slavery was legal in many U.S. states, and only property-owning white men (not women) could vote and fully exercise their political and civil rights. Following the Civil War (1861–1865), the federal Constitution was amended by a "second Bill of Rights," which added the 13th, 14th and 15th Amendments outlawing slavery, guaranteeing the equal protection of the laws, and assuring the right to vote to members of racial minorities.[7] Women did not receive the vote until the twentieth century with the adoption of the 19th Amendment, and youth (age 18 and over) received it in 1970 with the adoption of the 25th Amendment.

The United States is a federal system. The federal government and all fifty states have their own Constitutions and rights provisions. State courts hear cases involving state law—including questions of rights under state constitutions—while federal courts hear cases involving questions of federal law, including allegations of unconstitutional actions by state government officials, questions of international law

---

[4] Farnsworth, E. Allen. 2010. An Introduction to the Legal System of the United States, ed. Steve Sheppard, 4th edition, 7. New York: Oxford University Press.

[5] Initially, the Supreme Court took the position that the first ten Amendments to the U.S. Constitution were not applicable to the states, but subsequently held, following the adoption of the Fourteenth Amendment, that selective provisions of the Bill of Rights were incorporated into the Fourteenth Amendment and thus made applicable to the states. See Nowak, John E. & Rotunda, Ronald D. 1995. Constitutional Law, 340–41 (5th edition). Eagan: West Publishing.

[6] Law, David S. & Veerstig, Mila. 2012. The Declining Influence of the U.S. Constitution, New York University Law Review 87:3.

[7] Neuborne, Burt. 1996. An Overview of the Bill of Rights. In Fundamentals of American Law, ed. Alan B. Morrison, 83. New York: Oxford University Press.

(although this a somewhat complex issue as outlined below), and questions of state law arising between citizens of different states. For simplicity's sake, this National Report will focus largely upon federal law and the jurisprudence of federal courts, but it should be noted that particularly as regards criminal procedure, most prosecutions take place in state courts, and state constitutional rights are very important. Another area driven more by state than federal action relates to the question of same-sex marriage, with state supreme courts sometimes interpreting state constitutions to prohibit discrimination against individuals based upon sexual orientation. For areas governed more by state than federal law, the federal constitution imposes a floor or minimum protective standard below which state constitutional protections cannot fall. Additionally, recent scholarship has noted the critical importance of state and local government in human rights implementation, either through direct implementation of treaty norms, or through the activity of local human rights commissions.[8]

19.2 International Law as Part of U.S. Law and U.S. Participation in and Leadership of International Human Rights Regimes

19.2.1 International Law as U.S. Law

In the United States, the rules governing the intersection between U.S. and international law appertain to a branch of law somewhat idiosyncratically termed "foreign affairs law." For many decades, foreign affairs law was not a particularly vibrant area of specialization for U.S. lawyers, but in recent decades, it has emerged as one of the most difficult and contested areas of U.S. Constitutional law. The framers of the 1787 Constitution devoted some attention to the issue of international law and its relationship to U.S. law, but references to the law of nations (customary international law) and treaties are sparse in the text itself. Article I, Sect, 8 grants Congress the power to "define and punish... Offenses against the Law of Nations," and Article VI provides that "Treaties made, or which shall be made, under the Authority of the United States [are] the supreme law of the Land," binding upon state courts "any Thing in the Constitution or Laws of any State to the contrary notwithstanding."[9] The federal courts were granted jurisdiction over questions of treaty interpretation, cases involving ambassadors and other questions of international law, but the Constitution was mostly silent on the relationship between U.S. and international law. There is little doubt, however, that in the early days of the Republic, at a time when the United States was a small and relatively weak nation, international law was seen as generally helpful to the new nation both in establishing its *bona fides* as a new sovereign,

---

[8] *See e.g.*, Kaufman, Risa E. 2011. State and Local Commissions as Sites for Domestic Human Rights Implementation. In Human Rights in the United States: Beyond Exceptionalism, ed. Shareen Hertel & Kathyrn Libal. Cambridge: Cambridge University Press.

[9] Although the President "makes" treaties, they must be ratified by two-thirds of the Senate. "He shall have Power, by and with the Advice and Consent of the Senate, to make Treaties, provided two thirds of the Senators present concur;" U.S. Const. art. II, § 2, cl. 2.

and in terms of protecting its rights.[10] In the first part of the twentieth century, the supremacy of treaties as against conflicting state policies was upheld in important cases such as *Missouri v. Holland*,[11] and the Supreme Court famously articulated, in *The Paquete Habana* that "international law is part of our [U.S.] law" and justiciable in U.S. federal courts.[12] Subsequently, as one commentator has noted, the period between 1946 and 2000 seems "at times internationalist and at times nationalistic."[13]

Recent decisions of the U.S. Supreme Court have called into question the supremacy of international law and its direct applicability as federal law. While the short space of this Report does not permit a full treatment of this subject, recent decisions of the United States Supreme Court have surprised many observers by explicitly rejecting—or extensively constraining—prewar understandings about the relationship between international and U.S. law. For example, in *Sosa v. Alvarez-Machain*,[14] the United States Supreme Court addressed the question whether the federal courts could assess claims involving breaches of "the law of nations" (customary international law) in the context of U.S. Alien Tort Statute litigation. Although it responded in the affirmative, the decision suggests that within the U.S. legal system, customary international law must take on a decidedly positivist cast.[15] From a human rights perspective, *Sosa* is particularly disappointing, as it held that an individual unlawfully abducted from Mexico to stand trial in the United States had no claim in U.S. courts under international law norms prohibiting arbitrary arrest and detention.[16]

Similarly, in *Medellin v. Texas*,[17] the U.S. Supreme Court ruled that a decision of the International Court of Justice in the *Avena* case regarding individual rights granted by the Vienna Convention of Consular Relations had no binding effect in U.S. Courts. The rationale of the majority was that the UN Charter provision requiring U.S. compliance with *Avena* was non-self executing, meaning it could not be relied upon by individuals before the federal courts, but could only be enforced through Congressional legislation. The decision was surprising not only from a jurisprudential perspective, given its apparent reversal of two centuries of precedent,[18] but was contrary to a Presidential memorandum indicating that the United States

---

[10] Flaherty, Martin S. 2008. Global Power in an Age of Rights: Historical Commentary, 1946–2000. In International Law in the U.S. Supreme Court: Continuity and Change, ed. David L. Sloss, et al, 416 [hereinafter International Law in the U.S. Supreme Court]. Cambridge: Cambridge University Press.

[11] Missouri v. Holland, 252 U.S. 416 (1920).

[12] The Paquete Habana, 175 U.S. 677, 700 (1900).

[13] Flaherty, *supra* note 10, at 416.

[14] Sosa v. Alvarez-Machain, 542 U.S. 692 (2004).

[15] McGinnis, John O. 2008. Sosa and the Derivation of Customary International Law. In International Law in the U.S. Supreme Court, *supra* note 10, at 482.

[16] Alvarez-Machain was tried and acquitted of all charges.

[17] Medellin v. Texas, 552 U.S. 491 (2008).

[18] Damrosch, Lori F. 2008. *Medellin* and *Sanchez-Llamas:* Treaties from John Jay to John Roberts. In International Law in the U.S. Supreme Court: Continuity and Change, ed. David L. Sloss, et al, 452, 456. Cambridge: Cambridge University Press.

would comply with the ICJ's decision in *Avena*. As an aside, the *Medellin* case and the *Avena* decision involved litigation relating to one of the most contested U.S. practices in terms of human rights issues: the continued use of capital punishment, objected to by most U.S. allies and abolished in most western nations.

19.3   U.S. Participation in and Leadership of International Human Rights Regimes

In terms of adherence to Post-World War II international human rights instruments, although Eleanor Roosevelt was one of the four primary drafters of the *Universal Declaration of Human Rights*, U.S. participation in international human rights treaties and treaty systems and leadership in the area of international human rights has been sporadic and inconsistent. As a formal matter, the United States ratified the United Nations Charter, and voted in favor of the *Universal Declaration of Human Rights* when it was presented to the General Assembly in 1948. It is also a party to several major human rights treaties, including the International Covenant on Civil and Political Rights (ICCPR), the Genocide Convention and the Convention Against Torture. The United States has adopted legislation implementing the Genocide Convention and the Convention Against Torture.[19] At the same time, the United States is not a party to many major international human rights treaties including the International Covenant on Economic, Social and Cultural Rights, the Convention on the Rights of the Child, the Convention for the Elimination of Discrimination Against Women, the Rome Statute of the International Criminal Court, the Convention on Enforced Disappearance, the Convention on the Rights of Persons with Disabilities, and several weapons conventions banning cluster munitions and land mines.[20] Even when the United States Senate ratifies human rights conventions, it often attaches "RUDs"—reservations, understandings and declarations—that often limit the applicability of the treaty in question either generally or as to specific provisions. This is the case, for example, with respect to the ICCPR, to which the Senate attached a proviso that the treaty was "non-self executing," meaning unenforceable in U.S. courts. This pattern is repeated elsewhere, meaning that international human rights norms—as opposed to constitutional rights—typically have little or no salience to U.S. litigants. As Martin Flaherty has observed, "where international agreements and constitutional rights cross paths most famously, they do so as antagonists."[21]

In terms of international human rights regimes, although the United States is a party to the ICCPR, it has not ratified the Optional Protocol permitting individual complaints to be brought to the Human Rights Committee. Thus it files periodic reports with the Human Rights Committee, but does not respond to individual petitions. It also submits periodic reports to the Committee Against Torture as a party to

---

[19] *See* Genocide, 18 U.S.C. §§ 1091–93; Implementation of Torture Convention in Extradition Cases, 22 C.F.R. Part 95.

[20] *See* Human Rights Watch. 2009. U.S. Ratification of Human Rights Treaties. http://www.hrw.org/news/2009/07/24/united-states-ratification-international-human-rights-treaties.

[21] Flaherty, *supra* note 10, at 426.

that treaty, as well. The United States is a member of the Organization of American States (OAS) and has ratified the OAS Charter, but not the American Convention, which was signed by President Carter in 1977 but never ratified by the Senate. This means that it is subject to the (non-binding) supervision of the Inter-American Commission on Human Rights, but not the jurisdiction of the Inter-American Court of Human Rights. Some interesting cases have arisen involving the United States and human rights issues before the Commission, including challenges to the juvenile death penalty,[22] and to detention of prisoners captured following the 9/11 attacks at Guantanamo Bay.[23] Indeed, on March 31st, 2012, the Commission decided for the first time to hear a case involving the situation of an Algerian national held at Guantanamo, Djamel Ameziane, who has argued that his forcible repatriation to Algeria would subject him to persecution.[24]

In spite of its hesitancy to ratify international human rights treaties and participate in binding regional human rights adjudication, the United States Department of State prepares, each year, a report on the performance of other countries as regards human rights practices, and a second report on international religious freedom.[25] The State Department's official website notes that the reports will be used "as a resource for shaping policy, conducting diplomacy and making assistance, training and other resource allocations."[26] Internationally, the United States has been at the forefront of efforts to eliminate trafficking in persons, and many states have been active in this area as well.[27]

19.4   Human Rights and the "War on Terror": Treatment of Citizens and non-Citizens

Perhaps one of the most contested areas regarding the human rights practices of the United States in recent times has been the conduct of the U.S. "war on terror," which was launched in October 2001 in response to the attacks of September 11,

---

[22] The Miguel Domingues Case: Report of the Inter-American Commission on Human Rights, Report No. 62/02, Merits, Case 12.285 (Oct. 22, 2002).

[23] *See* Organization of American States, Resolution No. 2/11, *Regarding the Situation of the Detainees at Guantanamo Bay, United States*, MC 259-02 (July 22, 2011).

[24] 2012. International Human Rights Body Issues Landmark Admissibility Ruling. Center for Constitutional Rights. http://ccrjustice.org/newsroom/press-releases/international-human-rights-body-admits-first-guant%C3%A1namo-case%3A-rights-groups-urge-end-indefinite-dete.

[25] *See* Bureau of Democracy, Human Rights and Labor, 2010 Country Reports on Human Rights Practices.
http://www.state.gov/j/drl/rls/hrrpt/2010/frontmatter/154328.htm. Other countries have been critical of the U.S. practice of issuing reports on human rights practices abroad, given what they perceive to be a certain hypocrisy in the United States evaluating other countries, but refusing to ratify most international human rights instruments.

[26] *Id.*

[27] The United States established an office of monitor and combat trafficking in persons, and has adopted legislation to enforce prohibitions on trafficking and provide assistance to victims. *See* United States Dept. of State, Trafficking in Persons Report. www.state.gov.

2001. These terrorist attacks, in which four civilian aircraft were hijacked and used to target and destroy important U.S. buildings and locales, were identified as the work of the al Qaeda terrorist organization which was, at the time, operating from bases in Afghanistan. The attacks resulted in the deaths of more than 3500 individuals, and were horrific both in terms of human carnage and the extensive destruction of property. Additionally, they had an extraordinarily strong psychological effect on Americans, creating an atmosphere of fear as Americans anticipated the possibility of more attacks to come, as well as feeding calls for revenge against the ostensible authors of the attacks and their supporters.

Domestically, the attacks were followed in short order by the adoption of legislation known as "The Patriot Act," which permitted the government broad powers of investigation and surveillance hitherto forbidden.[28] As a matter of international law, the decision to treat the September 11th attacks as acts of war, rather than international crimes,[29] as well as the decision of the United States to wage that war without the constraining influence of the Geneva Conventions or the application of international human rights law, has led to the adoption of practices for which the United States has been heavily criticized: The establishment of a prison camp at Guantanamo Bay; the use of torture and cruel, inhuman and degrading treatment by U.S. investigators and prison guards; the use of extraordinary rendition as a technique to interrogate and subsequently eliminate terror suspects; and, more recently, the use of drone attacks and other military methods alleged to result in civilian deaths, sometimes arguably, other times certainly, in violation of international humanitarian or international human rights law. U.S. actions have been the subject of extensive criticism by the European Parliament, the Committee Against Torture and the UN Human Rights Committee, as well as UN Special Rapporteurs. Of particular relevance to this Report, the United States argued to both the Human Rights Committee and the Committee Against Torture (CAT) that the war time and extraterritorial nature of U.S. activities meant that neither the ICCPR nor CAT applied to U.S. action in the "war on terror," assertions rejected by both Committees.[30] The human rights problems in Guantanamo translated to U.S. detention facilities in Iraq after the invasion of 2003, in particular the prison camp at Abu Ghraib.[31]

Although President Barack Obama pledged to close the prison at Guantanamo Bay during the 2008 election,[32] strong resistance from Congressional and local

---

[28] The Patriot Act contained provisions enhancing the ability of U.S. officials to obtain wiretaps, and criminalized "material support" to groups designated as terrorists.

[29] Sadat, Leila Nadya. 2004. Terrorism and the Rule of Law. Washington University Global Studies Law Review 3:135.

[30] *See* Sadat, Leila. 2007. Extraordinary Rendition, Torture, and other Nightmares from the War on Terror. George Washington University Law Review 75:1200, 1216–26.

[31] Sadat, Leila. 2004. International Legal Issues Surrounding the Mistreatment of Iraqi Detainees by American Forces, ASIL Insight. www.asil.org/insights_2004.cfm.

[32] The President signed Executive orders to close the prison at Guantanamo Bay as well as banning the use of torture on January 22, 2009, soon after he took office. More recently, however, the administration announced that because Congress had blocked efforts to try several "most wanted" September 11th defendants in federal court, they would be tried by military commissions at

officials to trials in federal courts, as well as the difficulty of repatriating individuals held at Guantanamo, made this campaign pledge impossible to keep. Much to the consternation of human rights organizations, the Obama administration therefore decided to press ahead with the use of military commissions, constituted and held in Guantanamo Bay, for the trial of prisoners captured during military operations in Afghanistan and elsewhere, and has intimated that some prisoners may be indefinitely detained there, with no formal charges being brought.

While the brevity of this Report prevents a complete discussion of this issue, one question relevant to the themes under discussion is the nationality of the accused in this "war" or struggle against international terrorism.[33] President Bush made it clear in his November 13, 2001 order justifying the establishment of the prison at Guantanamo, that U.S. citizens could not be imprisoned there.[34] Subsequent counter-terrorism actions of the United States have, in general, targeted aliens and, in particular, many have targeted individuals of Arab or Muslim ethnicity or heritage. From a human rights perspective, this is problematic, and from a law enforcement perspective, many experts have argued that it has also been counterproductive, resulting in alienation of otherwise law abiding individuals.

Many observers believe that one reason so little outcry has resulted over the Abu Ghraib or Guantanamo Bay detention facilities and the widespread abuses there was the ethnic origin and/or religious affiliation of those imprisoned there. Recent debates in the United States governing the treatment of non-citizens more generally have been equally contested, and a vigorous debate has ensued between individuals promoting equality of treatment for non-U.S. citizens and those advocating for the expulsion and deportation of all individuals—including children—present in the United States without proper visas or a right to citizenship or permanent residence. In 2007–08, the UN Special Rapporteur on the Human Rights of Migrants concluded in his report on a mission to the United States of America that:

> The Special Rapporteur notes with dismay that xenophobia and racism towards migrants in the United States has worsened since 9/11. The current xenophobic climate adversely affects many sections of the migrant population, and has a particularly discriminatory and devastating impact on many of the most vulnerable groups in the migrant population, including children, unaccompanied minors, Haitian and other Afro-Caribbean migrants, and migrants who are, or are perceived to be, Muslim or of South Asian or Middle Eastern descent.[35]

Guantanamo Bay. *See* Greene, Brian William, *Khalid Sheikh Mohammed to be Tried in Military Court*, U.S. News and World Report, April 5, 2012. http://articles.chicagotribune.com/2012-04-05/news/sns-201204051128usnewsusnwr201204040404ksmapr05_1_mohammed-and-four-ali-abdul-aziz-ali-civilian-court.

[33] The administration of President Bush took the legal position that the United States was engaged in an armed conflict against al Qaeda and its allies, a position contested by the International Committee of the Red Cross, and ultimately abandoned as a formal matter by the Obama administration. At the same time, the Obama administration, while abandoning the "war on terror" designation as a formal matter, continues to assert that the United States is engaged in armed conflict against members of al Qaeda and their allies, which gives the United States a right to use military strikes against al Qaeda members whether or not located in Afghanistan.

[34] *Detention, Treatment, and Trial of Certain Non-Citizens in the War Against Terrorism*, Military Order of November 13, 2001, 66 Fed. Reg. 57831 (Nov. 16, 2001).

[35] Report of the Special Rapporteur on the human rights of migrants, Jorge Bustamante, Addendum, Mission to the United States of America, UN Doc. A/HRC/7/12/Add.2 (Mar. 5, 2008), at p. 2.

Although President Obama (who himself has been the object of untrue attacks on national and religious grounds on many occasions both during the Presidential elections and subsequently) has committed himself to immigration reform,[36] recently there have been efforts by states to "crack down" on undocumented immigrants by giving law enforcement officials sweeping powers and criminalizing illegal immigration status at the state level. The state of Arizona, for example, adopted a particularly harsh law.[37] The federal government has contested these laws on many grounds, including their intrusion into the lawmaking authority of the federal government, but public opinion polls suggest that at least a significant percentage of the U.S. population supports these measures, no matter the pernicious effect they many have on the human rights of non-U.S. citizens (or any individuals believed to fall into that category by law enforcement officials).

19.5   Conclusion: Human Rights and the Obama Administration

With a strong constitutional framework and commitment to democratic values, the United States of America generally has a positive human rights record.[38] Particularly as regards property rights, religious freedom and freedom of expression, the U.S. rights tradition remains strong. At the same time, as this Report has noted, there is room for improvement. Capital punishment, high rates of incarceration for members of racial minorities, economic and social rights and treatment of non-citizens, particularly in the area of U.S. counterterrorism policy, are a few examples. The Obama administration took office promising to rectify what many Americans believed to have been the human-rights-unfriendly policies of his predecessor. Certainly, he has engaged on the world stage in a much more multilateral manner by supporting U.S. election to the Human Rights Council, participating in meetings of the International Criminal Court's governing body, attending other major international conferences including conferences on climate change and sustainability, entering into a nuclear weapons reduction treaty with Russia (and obtaining Senate ratification of the treaty),

---

[36] On June 15, 2012, President Obama announced a new policy of declining to prosecute undocumented immigrants that entered the country under the age of sixteen, are not yet thirty, have completed high school or served in the armed forces, and are not considered to pose "a threat to national security or public safety." *See* Napolitano, Janet. Memo on Exercising Prosecutorial Discretion with Respect to Individuals Who Came to the United States as Children, June 15, 2012. http://www.dhs.gov/xlibrary/assets/s1-exercising-prosecutorial-discretion-individuals-who-came-to-us-as-children.pdf.

[37] In 2010, Arizona adopted an anti-illegal immigration measure that was the broadest and most restrictive in recent U.S. history. The federal government obtained an injunction blocking the law's most controversial provisions as impinging upon federal prerogatives, a decision that was upheld on appeal. The United States Supreme Court invalidated much of the law on June 25, 2012, but upheld the provision requiring law enforcement officers to verify individuals' immigration status during the course of a stop, detention, or arrest if the officer suspected the individual was in the country unlawfully. Arizona v. United States, 132 S.Ct. 2492 (2012).

[38] The United States receives a rating of "free" and top scores on political rights and civil liberties in the annual report published by the human rights NGO *Freedom House*, for example. *See* Freedom House. *Freedom in the World 2012.* http://www. freedomhouse.org.

and pledging to push for ratification of important treaties such as Committee on the Elimination of Discrimination Against Women (CEDAW).[39] He has also pledged not to use torture, to close the prison at Guantanamo Bay, and to address economic, social and cultural rights, including a right to health care. He also has committed himself to immigration reform, and his appointees to the Supreme Court included two women and the Court's first Hispanic member.

Yet a reluctant Congress and a conservative Supreme Court have made it difficult to fully achieve these objectives. President Obama has not been able to close the prison at Guantanamo Bay, and continues to use military commissions to try those accused there, commissions that many experts believe do not comply with international standards. He has also increased the use of drone attacks against individuals living in Afghanistan, Pakistan and even Yemen,[40] and has deployed missiles not only against foreign individuals but, in one case, a U.S. citizen, actions that have been criticized by the United Nations, many other democracies and human rights group in the United States.[41] The absence of effective and binding international human rights law norms on U.S. actions as well as the imperviousness of the U.S. Constitution to the incorporation of international norms means that there is little external control or moderating influence that these norms can exercise directly upon U.S. action. For the most part, national and local politics drive U.S. human rights practices and policies, not international legal norms.

References

Articles

Law, David S. &, Mila. 2012. The Declining Influence of the U.S. Constitution, New York University Law Review 87:3.

Michael Posner, U.S. Assistant Secretary for Democracy, Rights and Labor, The Four Freedoms Turn 70, American Society of International Law, March 24, 2011.

Organization of American States, Resolution No. 2/11, *Regarding the Situation of the Detainees at Guantanamo Bay, United States*, MC 259-02 (July 22, 2011).

Sadat, Leila Nadya. 2004. Terrorism and the Rule of Law. Washington University Global Studies Law Review 3.

Sadat, Leila. 2007. Extraordinary Rendition, Torture, and other Nightmares from the War on Terror. George Washington University Law Review 75.

---

[39] Remarks of Michael Posner, U.S. Assistant Secretary for Democracy, Rights and Labor, *The Four Freedoms Turn 70*, American Society of International Law, March 24, 2011.

[40] *See, e.g.*, Bergen, Peter L., *Warrior in Chief*, N.Y. Times at SR1 (April 29, 2012), *available at* http://www.nytimes.com/2012/04/29/opinion/sunday/president-obama-warrior-in-chief.html?pagewanted=all.

[41] *See, e.g.*, Heyns, Christof. *Report of the Special Rapporteur on extrajudicial, summary or arbitrary executions, Follow-up to country recommendations: United States of America*, U.N. Doc. A/HRC/20/22/Add.3 (March 30, 2012).

Books

Farnsworth, E. Allen. 2010. An Introduction to the Legal System of the United States, ed. Steve
   Sheppard, 4th edition, 7. New York: Oxford University Press.
Henkin, Louis. 1978. The Rights of Man Today, 3–13. Boulder: Westview Press.
Human Rights in the United States: Beyond Exceptionalism, ed. Shareen Hertel & Kathyrn Libal.
   Cambridge: Cambridge University Press.
International Law in the U.S. Supreme Court: Continuity and Change, ed. David L. Sloss, et al,
   Cambridge: Cambridge University Press.
Neuborne, Burt. 1996. An Overview of the Bill of Rights. In Fundamentals of American Law, ed.
   Alan B. Morrison, 83. New York: Oxford University Press.
Nowak, John E. &, Rotunda, Ronald D. 1995. Constitutional Law, 340–41 (5th edition). Eagan:
   West Publishing.
Paust, Jordan J. 1996. International Law as Law of the United States, 169. Durham: Carolina
   Academic Press.

Cases

Medellin v. Texas, 552 U.S. 491 (2008).
Sosa v. Alvarez-Machain, 542 U.S. 692 (2004).
Arizona v. United States, 132 S.Ct. 2492 (2012).
Missouri v. Holland, 252 U.S. 416 (1920).
The Paquete Habana, 175 U.S. 677, 700 (1900).

Statute

Detention, Treatment, and Trial of Certain Non-Citizens in the War Against Terrorism, Military
   Order of November 13, 2001, 66 Fed. Reg. 57831 (Nov. 16, 2001).
Genocide, 18 U.S.C. §§ 1091-93; Implementation of Torture Convention in Extradition Cases, 22
   C.F.R. Part 95.

U.N. Documents

Heyns, Christof. *Report of the Special Rapporteur on extrajudicial, summary or arbitrary ex-
   ecutions, Follow-up to country recommendatio*ns: United States of America, U.N. Doc.
   A/HRC/20/22/Add.3 (March 30, 2012).
Report of the Special Rapporteur on the human rights of migrants, Jorge Bustamante, Addendum,
   Mission to the United States of America, UN Doc. A/HRC/7/12/Add.2 (Mar. 5, 2008), at p. 2.

Internet and Other Sources

Bergen, Peter L., *Warrior in Chief*, N.Y. TIMES at SR1, *available at* http://www.nytimes.com/2012/
   04/29/opinion/sunday/president-obama-warrior-in-chief.html?pagewanted=all.
Bureau of Democracy, Human Rights and Labor, 2010 Country Reports on Human Rights Practices.
   http://www.state.gov/j/drl/rls/hrrpt/2010/frontmatter/154328.htm.
Freedom House. *Freedom in the World 2012*, available at http://www.freedomhouse.org.

Greene, Brian William, *Khalid Sheikh Mohammed to be Tried in Military Court*, U.S. NEWS AND WORLD REPORT, April 5, 2012. http://articles.chicagotribune.com/2012-04-05/news/sns-201204051128usnewsusnwr201204040404ksmapr05_1_mohammed-and-four-ali-abdul-aziz-ali-civilian-court.

Human Rights Watch. 2009. U.S. Ratification of Human Rights Treaties. http://www.hrw.org/news/2009/07/24/united-states-ratification-international-human-rights-treaties.

International Human Rights Body Issues Landmark Admissibility Ruling. Center for Constitutional Rights. http://ccrjustice.org/newsroom/press-releases/international-human-rights-body-admits-first-guant%C3 %A1namo-case%3A-rights-groups-urge-end-indefinite-dete.

Napolitano, Janet. Memo on Exercising Prosecutorial Discretion with Respect to Individuals Who Came to the United States as Children, available at http://www.dhs.gov/xlibrary/assets/s1-exercising-prosecutorial-discretion-individuals-who-came-to-us-as-children.pdf.

Sadat, Leila. 2004. International Legal Issues Surrounding the Mistreatment of Iraqi Detainees by American Forces, ASIL Insight. www.asil.org/insights_2004.cfm.

The Miguel Domingues Case: Report of the Inter-American Commission on Human Rights, Report No. 62/02, Merits, Case 12.285 (Oct. 22, 2002).

United States Dept. of State, Trafficking in Persons Report. www.state.gov.

Printed by Publishers' Graphics LLC